BY JAY A. BROWN
AND THE EDITORS OF
CONSUMER GUIDE®

RATING THE
MOVIES

BEEKMAN HOUSE
New York

Louis Weber, President
Publications International, Ltd.
3841 West Oakton Street
Skokie, Illinois 60076

Library of Congress Cataloging in Publication Data
Main entry under title:

Rating the movies.

  1. Moving-pictures—Plots, themes, etc. I. Consumer
guide.
PN1997.8.R37   791.43'75   82-413
ISBN 0-517-35983-9   AACR2

This edition published by:
Beekman House
Distributed by Crown Publishers, Inc.
One Park Avenue
New York, New York 10016

Film Research: Don Casciato, Calvin Green, Rose
McArdle, and Phyllis Brown.
Acknowledgment: The Editors of Consumer Guide® wish
to thank the Motion Picture Association of America for
supplying MPAA ratings information.

Cover Design: Frank E. Peiler

CONTENTS

An Introduction to Rating the Movies
Page 4

Alphabetical Movie Listings

Star Profiles

AN INTRODUCTION TO RATING THE MOVIES

A bowl of popcorn, a drink, an easy chair, and you're just about ready to dim the lights and watch *Kramer vs. Kramer*, *The Godfather*, *Patton*, *Singin' in the Rain*, *Casablanca*, or some other movie classic or recent release that's being broadcast by network, cable, or pay television.

Each week scores of motion pictures are being shown on television, and thousands on videocassettes or videodiscs are available for sale or rent. You're probably familiar with a number of these films—you saw them in the theater, friends may have recommended some highly, you've read a critic's comments in your daily newspaper. But there are literally thousands of other movies that you know little or nothing about, especially many foreign films. How do you decide whether you're likely to enjoy one of them? How do you determine whether they're worth getting for your videocassette or videodisc library? How can you avoid wasting time and money?

RATING THE MOVIES is the answer; you'll find it's a convenient guide to help you increase your enjoyment of motion pictures now being shown on network, cable, or pay TV, or available on tape or disc. It will give you more information than most movie listings. This book is filled with concise reviews of motion pictures from the 1930s to the 1980s—memorable movies, prizewinning productions, run-of-the-mill features, and even some turkeys. And some terrific early classics aren't ignored, but the emphasis is on more recent movies—the ones that are most likely to appear on network or cable TV.

The Movie Reviews

The following explanatory notes will help you interpret our reviews of motion pictures:

Title—This is the name of the film. Most movies have only one title, but a few may have an alternate title. Sometimes a title is changed when a movie is released in another country. Alternate titles are listed alphabetically and will refer you to the title with the film's review.

Year—Generally, the year appearing immediately after a film's title is the one in which the movie was initially released to the public. Occasionally, you may find that another source lists another year for a film. There may be a number of reasons for this. For example, after completion, a movie may be kept off the market for a year or more, and a foreign film may be released in the United States several years after its release in its country of origin.

Star Rating—This is the CONSUMER GUIDE® rating system for movies. It ranges from **no stars** to a maximum of four. Because critics don't always agree, it's certain that you won't agree with every evaluation in the book, but we're confident that you'll find our ratings and comments on target most of the time. ★★★★, the top rating, indicates that a film is exceptionally well produced, acted, and directed; it's an enjoyable and engrossing movie and, in most cases, has something important to say. ★★★ indicates a good film; it's entertaining and has sufficient quality in most areas. It may, however, have a few flaws preventing it from receiving the highest rating. ★★ indicates a fair film; it's worth some interest, but probably has noticeable drawbacks, such as mediocre acting or direction, or a thin plot. ★ indicates a boring movie; you may find yourself dozing off or becoming restless well before it ends. **No stars** indicates a poor film, a cinema bomb, or a movie that's in extremely poor taste. In short, it's definitely not worth watching.

Review—After the list of a film's starring actors, there's a concise description of the plot, additional actors, and a comment about the movie, the acting, the direction or the film's production values.

Director—The director (or directors) is listed because this individual has vital overall responsibility for the production of the film. Good direction is crucial to a movie's success.

Foreign-Language Film—For movies with dialogue in a language other than English, an indication of the language and the fact that the film has English subtitles will be mentioned; for example, "In French with English titles."

MPAA Rating—The MPAA is the Motion Picture Association of America, and the ratings "G," "PG," "R," and "X" comprise its classification system. "G" indicates "General Audiences; all ages admitted." "PG" indicates "Parental Guidance Suggested; some material may not be suitable for children." "R" indicates

"Restricted; a person under 17 requires accompanying parent or adult guardian." "X" indicates "No one under 17 admitted (age limit may vary in certain areas)."

This system began in the latter half of 1968, so most films released before this time don't have such ratings. However, some older films, which have been re-released to theaters, may have MPAA ratings. Other movies, including many foreign films, may not have been submitted to the MPAA for a rating. Also, some films may have been released in more than one version. For example, *Saturday Night Fever*, originally an "R" film, was later released in a "PG" version to capture a younger audience.

Academy Awards—In most cases, Academy Awards or nominations for these awards received by a movie or individuals can be a meaningful indicator of a film's merits. The awards and nominations for major Academy Award categories have been included because this may influence your decision on whether you should see a film. Note that some descriptions of Oscar categories, such as cinematography and writing, have changed slightly over the years.

Running Time—At the end of each review, we list the film's running time for the initial theatrical release. Keep in mind that most films are edited to fit time slots for network television.

Finally, because most recent movies are in color, this fact is not noted after the running time; however, black-and-white movies are designated "b&w" immediately after the running time, and those few films that contain a few scenes in black and white or color are designated "b&w/color."

Star Profiles

Throughout RATING THE MOVIES you will find profiles of some of Hollywood's most popular stars. For example, you'll find interesting facts about such early film figures as Humphrey Bogart and Clark Gable, as well as relative newcomers such as Sissy Spacek and Robert De Niro. An alphabetical list of the stars profiled appears on the Contents page.

A
- Aaron Loves Angela
- Abbott and Costello Meet Captain Kidd
- Abbott and Costello Meet Frankenstein
- Abduction
- The Abominable Snowman
- Above and Beyond
- Absence of Malice
- The Absent-Minded Professor
- Ace in the Hole

A

AARON LOVES ANGELA (1976)
★★

Kevin Hooks
Irene Cara

A black Romeo falls in love with a Puerto Rican Juliet amid the rubble of Harlem. Or is it *West Side Story* again, this time with the music of José Feliciano? The film certainly is familiar stuff, although there are some original, touching, and tender moments. Hooks and Cara turn in mediocre performances as the leads. Moses Gunn, as the boy's father, does well. **Director**—Gordon Parks, Jr. (R) *98 minutes*

ABBOTT AND COSTELLO MEET CAPTAIN KIDD (1952)
★★

Bud Abbott
Lou Costello

Routine Abbott and Costello farce with the boys competing with the venerable pirate for buried treasure. Abbott and Costello are really not up to par here. Charles Laughton as Captain Kidd is on board having a high time in a role beneath his stature. **Director**—Charles Lamont. *70 minutes*

ABBOTT AND COSTELLO MEET FRANKENSTEIN (1948)
★★★

Bud Abbott
Lou Costello

Abbott and Costello are at their funniest in this knockabout spoof of hor-

In Abbott and Costello Meet Frankenstein, the comics run into the monster and the Wolf Man.

ror films. Costello's brain is slated for the monster. Dracula and the Wolf Man get in a few licks, too. It's a nice blend of laughs and scares, with Bela Lugosi and Lon Chaney lending their talents to the merriment. **Director**—Charles T. Barton. *92 minutes b&w*

ABDUCTION (1975)
(no stars)

Judith-Marie Bergan
Leif Erickson
Dorothy Malone

The humdrum exploitation film of the Patty Hearst story concerns the kidnapping of a girl, Patty Prescott, from a college campus by left-wing radicals. Her sexual activities with her captors are recorded, and the videotape is sent to her father. It's merely a dreary softcore porno film based on yesterday's headlines. **Director**—Joseph Zito. (R) *100 minutes*

THE ABOMINABLE SNOWMAN (1957)
★★★

Peter Cushing
Forrest Tucker

Tucker and Cushing lead an expedition to high altitudes in this horror outing about the elusive and mysterious monster of the Himalayas. Effective scripting and acting help flesh out the characters. The suspense, however, lags somewhat. Maureen Connell and Richard Wattis co-star. **Director**—Val Guest. *85 minutes b&w*

ABOVE AND BEYOND (1952)
★★★

Robert Taylor
Eleanor Parker

Semibiography of Col. Paul Tibbetts, the pilot of the *Enola Gay*, the B-29 that dropped the atomic bomb on Hiroshima. There is some overblown sentimentality involved, especially when the film deals with domestic problems, but the issue of conscience is handled with sensitivity. The cast performs admirably. Taylor is Tibbetts. Parker plays his wife. Cast

includes Jim Backus and James Whitmore. **Directors**—Melvin Frank, Norman Panama. **Academy Award**—Beirne Lay, Jr., writing (motion picture story). *122 minutes b&w*

ABSENCE OF MALICE (1981)
★★★★

Sally Field
Paul Newman

A brisk, intelligent drama that takes a penetrating look at the ethics of journalism in view of the quest for truth and justice. Field stars as an eager-beaver newspaper reporter, who is duped into writing misleading and damaging stories about an investigation of a mobster's son, played by Newman. His only crime is being related to unsavory people. Newman is magnificent as the outraged innocent victim, and he extracts revenge in a clever climax. Sydney Pollack's direction is crisp and to the point. Superb supporting performances enhance the production. (PG) *116 minutes*

THE ABSENT-MINDED PROFESSOR (1961)
★★★

Fred MacMurray
Tommy Kirk
Keenan Wynn

Better-than-average Disney comedy about a scientist who invents flubber, a rubbery substance that overcomes gravity. First-rate special effects enhance the fun. MacMurray, in the title role, is at top form piloting his flubber-powered Model T through the skies. The story involves the pursuit of spies, led by Keenan Wynn, who want to steal the amazing material. Cast includes Nancy Olson and Ed Wynn. **Director**—Robert Stevenson. (G) *97 minutes b&w*

ACE IN THE HOLE (1951)
★★★★

Kirk Douglas
Jan Sterling

Powerful drama about a reporter, played by Douglas, who tries to promote his career by delaying the rescue of a man trapped in a cave. Splendid performances by Douglas and Sterling. Masterful direction adds to the hard-hitting impact. The film is unrelenting in its portrayal of cruelty and grim irony. **Director**—Billy Wilder. **Alternate Title**—*The Big Carnival.*

112 minutes b&w

ACROSS THE GREAT DIVIDE (1976)
★★★

Heather Rattray
Mark Hall

Two charming and spunky preteen orphans fight wild animals and encounter other hardships en route to the lush Oregon land they inherited. Rattray and Hall are the two attractive kids who are exceptionally good in their acting debuts. There's spectacular photography of the Utah and British Columbia landscapes where the film was shot. It's a delightful lollypop for the youngsters and some adults, too. Written and directed by Stewart Raffill who did the same for *The Adventures of the Wilderness Family.* (G)

89 minutes

ACROSS THE PACIFIC (1942)
★★★

Humphrey Bogart
Mary Astor
Sydney Greenstreet

Bogart, Greenstreet, and Astor are re-teamed for this sleek World War II spy caper. Bogey tracks down enemy agents in Panama, keeps a menacing Greenstreet at bay, and falls in love with Astor. The trio is as effective as they were in *The Maltese Falcon.* Cast includes Keye Luke and Richard Loo. **Director**—John Huston.

97 minutes b&w

ACROSS THE WIDE MISSOURI (1951)
★★

Clark Gable
Ricardo Montalban

Despite proficient acting by Gable and Montalban, this period western

doesn't catch hold. Gable plays a stalwart fur trapper who marries an Indian girl. His talents are not fully realized. Cast includes John Hodiak, J. Carrol Naish, and Adolphe Menjou. **Director**—William Wellman.

78 minutes

ACT OF AGGRESSION (1975)
(no stars)

Jean-Louis Trintignant
Catherine Deneuve

This is the story of a mild-mannered man who seeks revenge against a motorcycle gang that brutally murdered his wife and daughter. It's a dreary production that would make an old Hollywood B-movie look good by comparison. The film is heavy on noise and car-chasing and light on plot and character development. Also with Claude Brasseur and Philippe Brigand. Poor direction by Gerard Pires. In French with English titles. (R)

94 minutes

ADAM'S RIB (1950)
★★★★

Spencer Tracy
Katharine Hepburn
Judy Holliday

A perfect teaming of Tracy and Hepburn who play husband and wife—and attorneys on opposite sides of a

murder trial. The rib-tickling comedy is expertly written and directed to bring out the special chemistry between the incomparable duo. Tom Ewell and David Wayne contribute their fine acting talents as well. **Director**—George Cukor. **Academy Award Nomination**—Ruth Gordon and Garson Kanin, writing (story and screenplay).

101 minutes b&w

THE ADVENTURES OF CAPTAIN FABIAN (1951)
★

Errol Flynn
Micheline Presle

Waterlogged costume sea drama about a ship captain from New Orleans who defends a servant girl accused of murder. Even swashbuckling Flynn, in the title role, can't keep this film, shot in France, afloat. Cast includes Vincent Price and Agnes Moorehead. **Director**—William Marshall.

100 minutes b&w

THE ADVENTURES OF DON JUAN (1948)
★★

Errol Flynn
Viveca Lindfors

Dashing Flynn romances Lindfors, who plays the Queen, and a number

(Continued)

Spencer Tracy and Katharine Hepburn are husband and wife in the comedy Adam's Rib.

A
- The Adventures of Mark Twain
- Adventures of the Wilderness Family
- Advise and Consent
- Affair in Trinidad
- An Affair To Remember
- The African Queen
- After the Fox
- Against All Flags

(Continued)

of maidens in this good-looking, tongue-in-cheek swashbuckler. This was the last of Flynn's lavish adventure films, and some self-mockery is evident. Cast includes Raymond Burr, Alan Hale, and Ann Rutherford. **Director**—Vincent Sherman.

110 minutes

THE ADVENTURES OF MARK TWAIN (1944)
★★★

**Fredric March
Alexis Smith**

This is a straightforward biography of the renowned writer-humorist. March turns in a memorable performance in the title role. Smith plays Twain's wife. The film follows Twain's life from steamboat pilot to acclaimed literary figure. The effort, however, doesn't match such great film biographies as *Pasteur* or *Zola*. Cast includes John Carradine, Donald Crisp, and C. Aubrey Smith. **Director**—Irving Rapper. *130 minutes b&w*

ADVENTURES OF THE WILDERNESS FAMILY (1975)
★★★

**Robert Logan
Susan Shaw**

Children should enjoy this adventure of a latter-day Swiss Family Robinson who, fed up with the din and smog of Los Angeles, hightail it to the mountain wilderness and set up housekeeping. They build a log cabin, befriend orphaned bear cubs, and face a menacing grizzly and wolves. Lots of striking mountain scenery. **Director**—Stewart Raffill. (G) *101 minutes*

ADVISE AND CONSENT (1962)
★★★

**Don Murray
Charles Laughton
Henry Fonda
Walter Pidgeon**

Fascinating screen adaptation of Allen Drury's novel of political maneuvering in Washington. Fine acting by a champagne cast heightens the drama surrounding the President's appointment of a controversial secretary of state. This was Laughton's last film. Other cast members include Gene Tierney, Franchot Tone, Lew Ayres, Burgess Meredith, and Peter Lawford. **Director**—Otto Preminger.

139 minutes b&w

AFFAIR IN TRINIDAD (1952)
★★

**Rita Hayworth
Glenn Ford**

Hayworth stands out in this sleek but routine tale of murder, espionage, and romance in the tropics. Hayworth, as a nightclub performer, seeks the murderer of her husband with the help of Ford, who plays her brother-in-law. Hayworth also does some notable dancing. Film is somewhat of a sequel to *Gilda*, which also starred Hayworth and Ford. **Director**—Vincent Sherman. *98 minutes b&w*

AN AFFAIR TO REMEMBER (1957)
★★★

**Cary Grant
Deborah Kerr**

Grant and Kerr star in this syrupy remake of *Love Affair*, which featured Charles Boyer and Irene Dunne. Grant, a debonair bachelor, romances former cafe singer Kerr aboard an ocean liner. The film begins as a comedy, turns into a tearjerker, and—of course—ends happily. Also includes Cathleen Nesbitt, Richard Denning, and Neva Patterson. **Director**—Leo McCarey. *119 minutes*

THE AFRICAN QUEEN (1951)
★★★★

**Humphrey Bogart
Katharine Hepburn**

Hepburn is a prim missionary and Bogart is a booze-soaked boat skipper. The odd couple find romance and danger on the Congo River during World War I. A triumph of acting and direction leads to a surprising achievement of wry comedy and adventure. Cast includes Theodore Bikel, Peter Bull,

In The African Queen, *Katharine Hepburn and Humphrey Bogart find romance.*

and Robert Morley. **Director**—John Huston. **Academy Award**—Bogart, best actor. **Nominations**—Huston, best director; Hepburn, best actress; James Agee and Huston, writing (screenplay). *106 minutes*

AFTER THE FOX (1966)
★★

**Peter Sellers
Victor Mature
Britt Ekland**

A rather forgettable Sellers comedy about an ingenious criminal who becomes a movie director as a front to pull off a gold heist. Mature, however, steals some scenes as a pompous has-been actor. The movie never gets off the ground despite Neil Simon's satirical script. Cast includes Lilia Brazzi, Akim Tamiroff, and Martin Balsam. **Director**—Vittorio De Sica.

103 minutes

AGAINST ALL FLAGS (1952)
★★

**Errol Flynn
Maureen O'Hara
Anthony Quinn**

Routine Flynn swashbuckler with Flynn as a dashing British officer challenging Caribbean pirate Quinn and romancing O'Hara. This is one of the last of Flynn's escapades, and he appears to wilt somewhat. With Mil-

- Agatha
- The Agony and the Ecstasy
- Ain't Misbehavin'
- Air Force
- Airplane
- Airport

A

dred Natwick. **Director**—George Sherman. *84 minutes*

AGATHA (1979)
★★

Dustin Hoffman
Vanessa Redgrave

Mystery writer Agatha Christie disappeared for 11 days in 1926. This pointless film imagines what happened during her absense. Redgrave turns in a crisp portrayal of the famous author. Hoffman provides a measure of humor in his role as an American journalist who traces Mrs. Christie to a health spa. But there's nothing to arouse much interest in the affair. Perhaps the real Agatha Christie would have come up with an exciting story. **Director**—Michael Apted. (PG) *98 minutes*

In Agatha, Dustin Hoffman is a journalist, and Vanessa Redgrave plays Agatha Christie.

THE AGONY AND THE ECSTASY (1965)
★★

Charlton Heston
Rex Harrison

Handsome but plodding story of Michelangelo's troubles while painting the Sistine Chapel at the urging of Pope Julius II. There are also some tiresome biographical references to the great artist's life and career, loosely based on Irving Stone's best-selling novel. Unfortunately, there's more agony than ecstacy. Heston plays Michelangelo. Harrison plays the pontiff. With Diane Cilento and Harry Andrews. **Director**—Carol Reed. *140 minutes*

AIN'T MISBEHAVIN' (1955)
★★

Rory Calhoun
Piper Laurie

Calhoun and Laurie star in this lightweight musical comedy with sly references to *Pygmalion*. Calhoun is a suave millionaire who marries cabaret singer Laurie, who then must learn the manners of the wealthy, as well as improve her education. Not a bad deal for Laurie. Cast includes Jack Carson, Reginald Gardiner, and Mamie Van Doren. **Director**—Edward Buzzell. *82 minutes*

AIR FORCE (1943)
★★★

John Garfield
Gig Young
Arthur Kennedy

Effective and often exciting World War II bomber crew saga despite propaganda and flag-waving. Garfield, Young, and Kennedy are among the flyboys who fight the Japanese from Manila to the Coral Sea. Characterizations of the flyers are colorfully portrayed. Also stars Faye Emerson, Harry Carey, and Charles Drake. **Director**—Howard Hawks. *124 minutes b&w*

AIRPLANE (1980)
★★★★

Robert Hays
Julie Hagerty
Peter Graves
Lloyd Bridges

Mel Brooks and Woody Allen have stiff competition from Jim Abrahams,

In Airplane, Julie Hagerty and Robert Hays parody From Here to Eternity.

David Zucker, and Jerry Zucker who wrote and directed this laugh-a-minute broadside spoof of airplane dramas. Their initial try was the unpolished comedy, *The Kentucky Fried Movie*. But this time they unleashed a torrent of effective gags with style and finesse. So fasten your seat belts, observe the "no smoking" sign, and settle back for hilarity galore. (PG) *88 minutes*

AIRPORT (1970)
★★★★

Burt Lancaster
Dean Martin
Jean Seberg
Helen Hayes
Van Heflin

Dean Martin and passengers face a life-threatening crisis in Airport.

Slick, gripping melodrama based on Arthur Hailey's popular novel about a busy Midwest airport on a snowy night. Lancaster is the unflappable airport manager who keeps things in order during efforts to land a damaged plane safely. Hayes stands out as an habitual and unlikely stowaway. There are also entertaining performances from George Kennedy and Martin. The cast also includes Jacqueline Bisset, Maureen Stapleton, Lloyd Nolan, and Barry Nelson. **Director**—George Seaton. (G) **Academy Award**—Hayes, best supporting actress. **Nominations**—best picture; cinematography; best screenplay (based on material from another medium). *137 minutes*

A
- Airport '77
- The Alamo
- Al Capone
- Alex and the Gypsy
- Alfie
- Alias Jesse James

AIRPORT '77 (1977)
★★

**Jack Lemmon
Lee Grant
Brenda Vaccaro
George Kennedy
James Stewart**

The *Airport* theme is thoroughly exhausted as demonstrated by this third and mediocre all-star disaster film inspired by the Arthur Hailey novel. This time it's a private 747 jumbo jet, outfitted like a flying Holiday Inn, that crashes somewhere in the Atlantic Ocean and sinks in 100 feet of water. All sorts of standard harrowing episodes take place among the passengers and crew while waiting for the inevitable rescue by the U.S. Navy. Lemmon is out of place as the pilot. Darin McGavin, Olivia de Havilland, and Joseph Cotten also star. **Director**—Jerry Jameson. (PG)
113 minutes

THE ALAMO (1960)
★★

**John Wayne
Richard Widmark
Laurence Harvey
Richard Boone**

John Wayne as Col. Davy Crockett leads the futile defense of the famous fort against the onslaught of the Mexican army. The drawn-out film is often sidetracked with cliché-strewn subplots, and it seems to take forever to reach the spectacular final attack, which is the only exciting part of the film. With Frankie Avalon, Patrick Wayne, and Linda Cristal. **Director**—John Wayne.
190 minutes

AL CAPONE (1959)
★★★

**Rod Steiger
Fay Spain
Martin Balsam**

Steiger is ideally cast as the ruthless gangster chieftain in this better-than-average biography. Steiger's excellent, energetic performance is enhanced by fine support from Spain and Balsam. The documentary account follows Capone's Prohibition days in Chicago up to his imprisonment for income tax evasion. Also with Murvyn Vye, Nehemiah Persoff, and James Gregory. **Director**—Richard Wilson.
105 minutes b&w

ALEX AND THE GYPSY (1976)
★

**Jack Lemmon
Geneviève Bujold**

Lemmon looks tired and unappealing in this cynical and grubby film about the torturous relationship between a bailbondsman and a gypsy woman. Bujold, as the gypsy, isn't much help either. They scream a lot, fight a lot, and roam about the countryside. It's all a rather numbing experience. Also with James Woods. **Director**—John Korty. (R)
99 minutes

ALFIE (1966)
★★★

**Michael Caine
Vivien Merchant
Shelley Winters**

Michael Caine is a womanizing Cockney with a fancy-free life-style in Alfie.

Caine's career got a big boost for his superb performance as a carefree womanizing Cockney. The film, based on Bill Naughton's play, also is noted for its frank treatment of sex. Winters and Merchant heighten the interest with no-nonsense performances as the objects of Alfie's affections. Alas, Alfie is shaken from his fancy-free life-style by a near-crisis. Also with Millicent Martin, Shirley Anne Field, and Denholm Elliot. **Director**—Lewis Gilbert.
114 minutes

ALIAS JESSE JAMES (1959)
★★★

**Bob Hope
Rhonda Fleming**

Only Hope could sell an insurance policy to the notorious outlaw, and he claims a lot of laughs in the process. It's a funny vehicle for Hope as a lot of

John Wayne as Davy Crockett helps defend the fort against the Mexican army in The Alamo.

⭐ STAR PROFILE

A

- Alias Nick Beal
- Alice Doesn't Live Here Any More
- Alice's Restaurant
- Alien
- Ali the Man: Ali the Fighter

gags hit the mark. Fleming plays a pretty lass who does a singing number with Hope. There's an uproarious ending with cameos by many Hollywood cowboys. **Director**—Norman McLeod. *92 minutes*

ALIAS NICK BEAL (1949)
★★★

Ray Milland
Thomas Mitchell

An upstanding politician almost sells his soul to the devil in this on-target, latter-day version of Faust. Satisfying performances from sinister Milland as the devil's disciple promising money and power, and Mitchell as the vulnerable district attorney who nearly accepts the deal. Efficient direction helps to bring the fantasy into sharp focus. Other good performances by Audrey Trotter and George Macready. **Director**—John Farrow. *93 minutes b&w*

ALICE DOESN'T LIVE HERE ANY MORE (1974)
★★★★

Ellen Burstyn
Alfred Lutter
Kris Kristofferson

Burstyn won an Oscar for her warm, funny, and energetic portrayal of a poor widow who learns to survive by her wits. She's broke, she has to care for her young son, and she wants to be a singer. Kristofferson also performs well as the new man in her life. The slice-of-life theme is somewhat of a cliché, but director Martin Scorsese adds vivid dimensions with a poignant reflection of contemporary America. With Jodie Foster. (PG) **Academy Award**—Burstyn, best actress. **Nominations**—Diane Ladd, best supporting actress; Robert Getchell, best original screenplay.
113 minutes

ALICE'S RESTAURANT (1969)
★★★

Arlo Guthrie
Pat Quinn

Folksinger Guthrie's popular song inspired this satirical melodrama about the freewheeling life-style of the 1960s. The theme is rather flimsy, but director Arthur Penn succeeds in wringing charm, energy, and comedy from the material. Guthrie, who does quite well in his film debut, is especially funny in a scene where he is briefly inducted into the U.S. Army. With James Broderick and Michael McClanathan. (PG) *111 minutes*

ALIEN (1979)
★★★

Tom Skerritt
Sigourney Weaver
John Hurt

The crew of a cargo-carrying spaceship, on a return voyage to earth, encounters a terrible monster. It's an effective horror film with impressive

Tom Skerritt, Sigourney Weaver, and Ian Holm discuss a distress signal in Alien.

and scary special effects that should send you away with your knees knocking. But it's also familiar stuff, with elements of *Star Wars, The Exorcist,* and *Jaws* blended into the script, which dangles many loose ends. The small cast does a good job, especially Weaver, who performs much in the style of Jane Fonda. Also with Ian Holm, Harry Dean Stanton, and Yaphet Kotto. **Director**—Ridley Scott. (R) *124 minutes*

ALI THE MAN: ALI THE FIGHTER (1975)
★★

This is a two-part documentary about prizefighter Muhammad Ali. The better part, *Ali the Fighter*, details the first Ali-Frazier fight. The other, *Ali the Man*, is a rather shallow summation of the champ's career and philosophy. Film clips of earlier fights are used. **Directors**—Rick Baxter and William Greaves. (PG) *142 minutes*

AL PACINO

Al Pacino was born in New York City in 1940. When his father, a mason, left the family, he was reared by his mother and grandparents. Pacino attended Manhattan's High School of Performing Arts and supported himself for several years with menial jobs. Finally, he was accepted in Herbert Berghof's acting school and later attended Lee Strasberg's Actors' Studio.

Pacino's training led to an impressive performance in The Indian Wants the Bronx, *an off-Broadway play for which he won an Obie Award. His first screen role was a small part in* Me Natalie *(1968), and then he gave a strong performance as a dope addict in* Panic in Needle Park *(1971).*

After only these two movies, he was selected to play the key role of Michael Corleone in Francis Ford Coppola's The Godfather *(1972), for which he was nominated for an Oscar as best supporting actor.*

In 1977, Pacino returned to the Broadway stage and won a Tony for the lead role in The Basic Training of Pavlo Hummel.

Pacino also starred in such films as Serpico *(1974),* The Godfather—Part II *(1974),* Dog Day Afternoon *(1975), . . . And Justice for All *(1979), and* Cruising *(1981).*

A
- All About Eve
- All Fall Down
- Alligator
- All My Sons
- All Night Long
- All Screwed Up
- All That Heaven Allows
- All That Jazz

ALL ABOUT EVE (1950)
★★★★

Bette Davis
George Sanders
Anne Baxter

This biting backstage comedy-drama about a fading actress, played by Davis, brims generously with entertainment values: a witty screenplay, top performances by a marvelous cast, and no-nonsense direction. Davis gives a memorable bitchy performance as the aging Broadway star who is menaced by an overreaching younger actress played by Baxter. One of the best films ever made about the legitimate theater. **Director**—Joseph L. Mankiewicz. **Academy Awards**—best picture; Mankiewicz, best director and writing (screenplay); Sanders, best supporting actor. **Nominations**—Baxter, Davis, best actress; Celeste Holm, Thelma Ritter, best supporting actress.   *138 minutes b&w*

ALL FALL DOWN (1962)
★★

Warren Beatty
Brandon de Wilde
Angela Lansbury

A generally well-acted drama about a spirited young man, played by Beatty, who falls in love with an older woman—Eva Marie Saint—and then causes her death. Unfortunately, the screenplay is rather farfetched and isn't redeemed by several good performances. The cast includes Karl Malden. **Director**—John Frankenheimer.   *110 minutes b&w*

ALLIGATOR (1980)
★★★

Robert Forster
Robin Riker

A baby pet alligator is flushed into a city sewer system and emerges 12 years later to devour some local citizens. At the outset, the film smacks of just another absurd horror picture, but director Lewis Teague quickly lays on the style and excitement. There are polished special effects, a serviceable script, and capable performances from Forster and Riker. This reptile isn't a match for the shark in *Jaws*, but it does have plenty of bite. Also with Henry Silva, Jack Carter, and Dean Jagger in cameo roles. (R)   *94 minutes*

ALL MY SONS (1948)
★★★

Edward G. Robinson
Burt Lancaster

This film version of Arthur Miller's play about family conflicts is generally compelling although it occasionally lacks conviction. A young man is shaken when he discovers that his wealthy father sold defective equipment to the military during World War II. Fine performances from Robinson, Lancaster, and Howard Duff. **Director**—Irving Reis.   *94 minutes b&w*

ALL NIGHT LONG (1981)
★

Barbra Streisand
Gene Hackman

A futile attempt at contemporary comedy that awkwardly deals with the numbing side effects of corporate life. Superstar Streisand, as a seductive housewife, takes second billing. She is sadly miscast without a song or the verve to carry off a zany portrayal. Only Hackman, who plays a deflated chain store executive, breathes some life into this shallow and silly story. **Director**—Jean-Claude Tramont. (R)   *100 minutes*

ALL SCREWED UP (1976)
★★★

Luigi Diberti
Isa Danieli
Lina Polito

Lina Wertmuller, the talented Italian director, presents a wry, witty, and energetic comedy about rural Sicilians caught up in materialistic life of Northern Italy. She again pursues her social-political-sexual theme with familiar style in this film. The story, written by Wertmuller, is rich in character and stark contrasts. Also with Nino Bignamini and Sara Rapisarda. In Italian with English titles. (PG)   *105 minutes*

ALL THAT HEAVEN ALLOWS (1955)
★★

Jane Wyman
Rock Hudson

Wyman and Hudson star in this slack and predictable soap opera about a widow who marries a younger man and is ostracized by her friends. Although the film reunites the stars of *Magnificent Obsession* and has a similar style, it doesn't work as well as the earlier film. Agnes Moorehead, Virginia Grey, and Conrad Nagel co-star. Heaven should allow more than this. **Director**—Douglas Sirk.   *89 minutes*

ALL THAT JAZZ (1979)
★★★

Roy Scheider
Jessica Lange
Ann Reinking

Director Bob Fosse's autobiographical movie is the ultimate backstage musical drama—a masterpiece of dance, ego, and soul. It's the story of a self-destructive Broadway director/choreographer—played by Scheider—his loves, obsessive work, and ultimate disintegration. Despite the adolescent shallowness of the central character, the overall production is completely

Ben Vereen and Roy Scheider perform in one of the final scenes in All That Jazz.

● All the Brothers Were Valiant ● All the King's Men ● . . . All the Marbles ● All the President's Men ● All the Young Men ● All Things Bright and Beautiful

A

absorbing. Fosse's breathtaking dance numbers are brilliantly staged, and Scheider's performance is outstanding. Leland Palmer, Cliff Gorman, and Ben Vereen co-star. (R) **Academy Award Nominations**—best picture; Fosse, best director; Scheider, best actor; Robert Alan Arthur and Fosse, best screenplay (written directly for the screen). *123 minutes*

ALL THE BROTHERS WERE VALIANT (1953)
★★

Stewart Granger
Robert Taylor

Granger and Taylor star in this soggy adventure, which is based on Ben Ames Williams's novel, of sibling rivalry between two stubborn whaling sailors. Trouble ensues when one brother decides to shun blubber and hunt for treasure. There's lots of action, but the acting is below par. Ann Blyth co-stars as the wife of one brother, and she adds to the tension on board ship. **Director**—Richard Thorpe. *101 minutes*

ALL THE KING'S MEN (1949)
★★★★

Broderick Crawford
John Ireland
Mercedes McCambridge
Joanne Dru

A gripping, high-powered drama about political corruption in Louisiana, based on the career of Huey Long. The film is fleshed out

In All the King's Men, Broderick Crawford gives an Oscar-winning performance as a politician.

with colorful detail and background. Most notable is the electrifying portrayal by Crawford as the honest small-town politician who is elected governor and is eventually overwhelmed by power. Commanding support from McCambridge, Ireland, and Dru. **Director**—Robert Rossen. **Academy Awards**—best picture; Crawford, best actor; McCambridge, best supporting actress. **Nominations**—Rossen, best director; Ireland, best supporting actor; Rossen, writing (screenplay). *109 minutes b&w*

. . . ALL THE MARBLES (1981)
★★★

Peter Falk

Director Robert Aldrich serves up pure and delectable Hollywood schmaltz with this rousing action-comedy about female wrestlers. Falk is excellent as the hustling manager of "The California Dolls," two young combatants, played by Vicki Frederick and Laurene Landon, who progress from tank-town matches to a championship bout in Reno's MGM Grand Hotel. The film offers good comic dialogue, appealing characterizations, a thrilling finale, and the "Dolls"—two gorgeous ladies who can act as well as wrestle. (R) *112 minutes*

ALL THE PRESIDENT'S MEN (1976)
★★★★

Robert Redford
Dustin Hoffman
Jason Robards, Jr.

The Watergate scandal comes into sharp focus and takes on a new dimension in this spellbinding film adaptation of Carl Bernstein's and Bob Woodward's best-selling book. It's a thriller from beginning to end and breathlessly entertaining. The exciting day-by-day account of how the two young Washington *Post* reporters conducted their investigation is portrayed in fast-paced semidocumentary style through the screenplay of William Goldman. Acting by the entire cast is spectacular. Redford as Woodward and Hoffman as Bernstein perform with perfection. Robards gives what may be his finest performance as *Post*

Robert Redford and Dustin Hoffman, in All the President's Men, portray reporters.

editor Ben Bradlee. Cast includes Hal Holbrook, Jack Warden, and Martin Balsam. Brilliantly directed by Alan J. Pakula. (PG) **Academy Awards**—Robards, best supporting actor; Goldman, best screenplay adaptation. **Nominations**—best picture; Pakula, best director; Jane Alexander, best supporting actress. *138 minutes*

ALL THE YOUNG MEN (1960)
★★

Alan Ladd
Sidney Poitier

Standard war yarn about a Marine unit in Korea that has to deal with internal tension as well as the enemy. Among the stereotypical situations is the problem of a black who is challenged because of his race when he takes command. Other clichés and platitudes abound. Also with Glenn Corbett, Ingemar Johansson, James Darren, and Mort Sahl. **Director**—Hall Bartlett. *87 minutes b&w*

ALL THINGS BRIGHT AND BEAUTIFUL (1979)
★★★

John Alderton
Lisa Harrow
Colin Blakely

A gentle, mildly amusing family film based on the best-selling memoirs of Dr. James Herriot, the Yorkshire veterinarian. Alderton plays the young vet with likable charm; Harrow plays his wife. Alderton tends to a variety of animal illnesses and the anxieties of the animal owners. The story isn't very dramatic, except for a
(Continued)

⭐ STAR PROFILE

A
- ● All This and Heaven Too
- ● All This and World War II
- ● All Through the Night
- ● An Almost Perfect Affair
- ● Along the Great Divide

GENE HACKMAN

Gene Hackman, a character actor who became a star in the early '70s, was born in San Bernardino, California, in 1931. The son of a pressman who moved his family east to Danville, Illinois, Hackman joined the Marines at 16, and in four years served in China, Japan, Hawaii, and Okinawa. After his discharge, he enrolled at the University of Illinois and then attended the School of Radio Technique in New York. Returning to California, he decided to pursue an acting career and joined the Pasadena Playhouse.

Hackman began his professional career off-Broadway. He made his Broadway debut in Irwin Shaw's Children at Their Games, *for which he won a Clarence Derwent Award. His first Broadway hit was* Any Wednesday *in 1964, the year he made his film debut in Robert Rossen's* Lilith.

He was nominated for an Academy Award for his performance in Arthur Penn's Bonnie and Clyde *(1967), and again for Gilbert Cate's* I Never Sang for My Father *(1969). He won an Oscar as best actor for his work in William Friedkin's* The French Connection *(1971), and also appeared in John Frankenheimer's sequel,* The French Connection II *(1975).*

Hackman's many other films include Jerry Schatzberg's Scarecrow *(1973), Francis Ford Coppola's* The Conversation *(1973), Mel Brooks's* Young Frankenstein *(1974), Arthur Penn's* Night Moves *(1975), Richard Brooks's* Bite the Bullet *(1975), Richard Donner's and Richard Lester's* Superman *(1978) and* Superman II *(1981), Jean-Claude Tramont's* All Night Long *(1981), and Warren Beatty's* Reds *(1981).*

(Continued)
short graphic scene of the birth of a calf; but it should appeal to most. Blakely is fine as a cantankerous older veterinarian who takes Herriot as a partner. **Director**—Eric Till. (G)

94 minutes

ALL THIS AND HEAVEN TOO
(1940)
★★★

Charles Boyer
Bette Davis

Boyer and Davis star in this somewhat stretched but well-made period melodrama, based on the Rachel Field novel, about a French nobleman who murders his wife after he falls in love with his governess. The elaborate story, set in the 19th century, is rather on the weepy side, but the acting has style and class. Barbara O'Neil, Virginia Weidler, and Jeffrey Lynn co-star. **Director**—Anatole Litvak.

143 minutes b&w

ALL THIS AND
WORLD WAR II (1977)
★

Documentary and fiction footage of World War II scenes are set to Beatles music. Putting scenes of death and destruction to such music appears to be bad taste. Most of the production is merely confusing. It ends with the atom bomb exploding. The film is a bomb too. **Director**—Susan Winslow. (PG)

88 minutes

ALL THROUGH THE NIGHT
(1942)
★★★

Humphrey Bogart
Peter Lorre

Bogart and Lorre team up in this entertaining spy caper set in New York City during World War II. Bogey's underworld gang helps the Feds nail some enemy agents. There are shades of wartime propaganda, but good fun nevertheless with just the right touch of comedy. There's a young Jackie Gleason and Phil Silvers among the cast. **Director**—Vincent Sherman.

107 minutes b&w

AN ALMOST PERFECT AFFAIR
(1979)
★★

Keith Carradine
Monica Vitti

The Cannes Film Festival is the backdrop to this satirical romance between a young American filmmaker, played by Carradine, and the wife of an Italian movie mogul, played by Vitti. Director Michael Ritchie handles the hoopla of the film festival with style and imagination, but the love story is essentially farfetched and rather uninteresting. There are some spirited performances, though, by the entire cast, which also includes Raf Vallone and Dick Anthony Williams. (PG)

93 minutes

Keith Carradine, who plays a young filmmaker, arrives in Cannes in An Almost Perfect Affair.

ALONG THE GREAT DIVIDE
(1951)
★★

Kirk Douglas
Virginia Mayo

Lawman Douglas saves an innocent man from the noose and nabs the real criminal despite a desert storm in this so-so western drama. The film has some spectacular scenery. John Agar, Ray Teal, and Walter Brennan round out the cast. **Director**—Raoul Walsh.

88 minutes b&w

- Alpha Beta
- Altered States
- Always Leave Them Laughing
- Ambush
- America at the Movies
- The American Friend
- The American Game
- American Gigolo
- American Graffiti

A

ALPHA BETA (1976)
★★★

**Albert Finney
Rachel Roberts**

Moving and searing performances by Finney and Roberts in this filmed play about a failed English working-class marriage. The entire cast is from the original London stage company. The film is divided into three acts to dramatically emphasize the stages of the breakup and the accumulation of the agony. The experience may be too morose and exhausting for some, but an experience it is indeed. **Director**—Anthony Page. (No MPAA rating)
67 minutes

ALTERED STATES (1981)
★★

**William Hurt
Blair Brown**

Director Ken Russell's mind-blowing psychedelic monster movie begins with mystery and exhilaration and ends as mere preposterous mumbo jumbo. Hurt is cast as a young psychophysiologist who alters his consciousness to the point of changing himself temporarily into an apelike creature. Russell lays on dazzling visual displays to create an outrageous hallucinogenic effect. Then the film falls apart when it urges viewers to accept as reality what can only be taken as visionary. Also with Charles Haid. (R) *102 minutes*

ALWAYS LEAVE THEM LAUGHING (1949)
★★

**Milton Berle
Bert Lahr**

Berle plays himself as a stand-up comedian on the rocky road to success. Berle, along with Lahr, hams it up delightfully for a few yocks, but the film falters somewhat when it dwells on sentimental stuff. At times, Lahr upstages the cocky Berle. You'll laugh—but not always. Virginia Mayo, Ruth Roman, and Alan Hale co-star. **Director**—Roy Del Ruth.
116 minutes b&w

AMBUSH (1949)
★★

**Robert Taylor
John Hodiak
Arlene Dahl**

A routine western with the U.S. Cavalry led by an army scout looking for an Apache chief who has kidnapped a white woman. There's some rousing action, helped along by the talents of Taylor, Hodiak, and Dahl. **Director**—Sam Wood. *89 minutes b&w*

AMERICA AT THE MOVIES (1976)
★★★

Apparently it's now easy to go to the film library and produce an entertaining feature composed of the best of our old movies. This coffee-table documentary is made up of scenes from 83 films divided into five sections: the land, the cities, the families, the wars, and the spirit of the American people. It's handsome, warm, and assembled with care. Produced by the American Film Institute. **Director**—Jack Masey. (PG) *116 minutes*

THE AMERICAN FRIEND (1977)
★★★

**Dennis Hopper
Bruno Ganz
Lisa Kreuzer**

This stylish psychological thriller by German director Wim Wenders packs tension that's typical of an Alfred Hitchcock film. Hopper, in the title role, plays a rogue who persuades a man, who is convinced he's dying from a rare disease, to become a paid killer. There is high-level acting by a colorful cast. Also with Nicholas Ray. Action was filmed in Hamburg, Paris, and New York City. (No MPAA rating). *127 minutes*

THE AMERICAN GAME (1979)
★★

A mildly interesting documentary that describes the fortunes of two high-school basketball stars from contrasting backgrounds. One comes from Indiana, the other from a Brooklyn ghetto. The film captures the pressures put on the young athletes by family, coaches, and community. The structure, however, is rather loose and vague; interest flags about midway. Written and directed by Jay Freund and David Wolf. (PG) *85 minutes*

AMERICAN GIGOLO (1980)
★★

**Richard Gere
Lauren Hutton**

This melodrama about a high-class male prostitute is a film dressed up in fancy duds for a trip to the corner drugstore. The atmosphere is sleek and plush, but the story needs some zip. Gere in the title role is impressive as a hustler who takes a cynical, businesslike attitude toward the older women he services. However, we never know what really makes him tick. Director Paul Schrader, who wrote and directed *Hard Core*, continues to pursue his obsession of exposing moral degradation in this film. (R) *117 minutes*

Richard Gere (center) stars as a hustler who preys on older women in American Gigolo.

AMERICAN GRAFFITI (1973)
★★★★

**Richard Dreyfuss
Ronny Howard
Paul Le Mat**

A right-on portrait of American youth culture shown through the experi-
(Continued)

In American Graffiti, *a portrait of youth in the '60s, Cindy Williams dances with Ronny Howard.*

(Continued)

ences of some high school seniors on the threshold of leaving for college or military service in the early 1960s. There's very little plot, but this landmark film sparkles with nostalgic atmosphere and hilarious dialogue. The story involves a memorable night of chasing girls, racing cars, harassing the cops, and hanging out at the local drive-in restaurant. The production enhanced the career of director George Lucas. Cast also includes Cindy Williams, Charles Martin Smith, and Candy Clark. You also should spot Harrison Ford and Suzanne Somers. (PG) **Academy Award Nominations**—best picture; Lucas, best director; Clark, best supporting actress; Lucas, Gloria Katz, and Willard Huyck, best story and screenplay (based on factual material or material not previously published). *110 minutes*

AMERICAN HOT WAX (1978)
★★

Tim McIntire
Fran Drescher

Rock 'n' roll music of the 1950s pours forth at full volume in this nostalgic film that depicts the rise and fall of disc jockey Alan Freed. But the plot comes on at a whisper with no point of view and little insight into that period of youthful defiance. Fans of Chuck Berry, Jerry Lee Lewis, et al, may find this film of interest. Otherwise, it is an earache. Also with Jay Leno, Laraine

Newman, and John Lehne. **Director**—Floyd Mutrux. (PG) *91 minutes*

AN AMERICAN IN PARIS (1951)
★★★★

Gene Kelly
Oscar Levant
Nina Foch

A vivacious, glittering musical blessed with the amazing choreography of Kelly and based on the music of George and Ira Gershwin. There's a simple romantic plot about an ex-GI, played by Kelly, who settles in Paris to be an artist and falls for a gamine, played by Leslie Caron. But it's really the show-stopping dance and music sequences that make the film a fabulous hit. It's one of the best musicals of this golden era. **Director**—Vincente Minnelli. **Academy Awards**—best picture; Alan Jay Lerner, writing (story and screenplay). **Nomination**—Minnelli, best director. *113 minutes*

Gene Kelly dances with Leslie Caron in An American in Paris, *an Academy Award-winning musical.*

AMERICAN POP (1981)
★★

Director-animator Ralph Bakshi (*Fritz the Cat; Heavy Traffic*) takes us down popular music's memory lane, from early burlesque to punk rock. This innovative cartoon feature is embellished with newsreel footage, still photographs, and rousing music spanning

more than 80 years. Although Bakshi's style is fresh and vigorous, he tries to pack in too much historical detail, and his problem leads to awkwardness and confusion. The overall effect isn't too satisfying. (R) *95 minutes*

THE AMERICANIZATION OF EMILY (1964)
★★★

Julie Andrews
James Garner

Garner and Andrews star in this unusual black comedy about an American naval officer who procures luxuries for the top brass. Paddy Chayefsky's poignant screenplay, based on William Bradford Huie's novel, is effective in its antiwar point of view. Andrews is excellent as a British war widow who perceives the officer's cowardice but falls in love with him just the same. Includes Melvyn Douglas, James Coburn, and Joyce Grenfell. **Director**—Arthur Hiller. *117 minutes b&w*

AN AMERICAN WEREWOLF IN LONDON (1981)
★★

David Naughton

John Landis, who directed *Animal House*, applies his brand of humor to the werewolf legend, and the result is a toothless mixture of comedy and horror. Two American students touring England are attacked by a mysterious beast, and the survivor, Naughton, turns into a marauding werewolf at full moon. Special effects

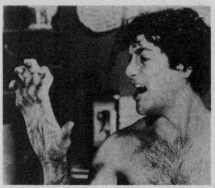

In An American Werewolf in London, *David Naughton watches in terror as his hands elongate.*

MARLON BRANDO

Marlon Brando was born in 1924 in Omaha, Nebraska. His father was a salesman, and his mother was a local actress. He attended Shattuck Military Academy of Minnesota and was expelled. He then went on to the Dramatic Workshop in New York and made his debut in I Remember Mama on Broadway in 1944.

In 1947, Brando earned recognition as an actor with his astounding portrayal of the brutish Stanley Kowalsky in A Streetcar Named Desire. His unique mumbling delivery ushered in the Method style of acting. Brando was also one of the first participants in Lee Strasberg's Actors' Studio.

In 1950, Brando made his screen debut as a paraplegic in The Men, and his film career soared in the early '50s with starring roles in the screen version of A Streetcar Named Desire (1951), Viva Zapata! (1952), and The Wild One (1953); he also played the young ex-fighter in On the Waterfront (1954), a part for which he won an Oscar.

Brando became known for his rebellious personality off the screen as well as in films. In the '60s, despite his charismatic appeal, his career faltered because of his involvement in many unappealing films. His astounding talent was resurrected with his magnificent portrayal of Don Corleone in The Godfather (1972), which earned him another Oscar, and again soon after with a portrait of middle-aged sexuality in Last Tango in Paris (1973).

Brando was married to actresses Anna Kashfi and Movita. Other Brando movies include Guys and Dolls (1955), Mutiny on the Bounty (1962), The Chase (1966), The Missouri Breaks (1976), Superman (1978), and Apocalypse Now (1979).

---

are impressive, but the comic angles don't gel. And the horror aspects seem absurd set in brightly lit London. Nothing to howl about. (R) 97 minutes

---

AMERICATHON (1979)
★

Harvey Korman
John Ritter

It's 1998 and the United States is broke. Gasoline is so scarce that most people use bicycles to get around. The President is a clown who presides from the California White House. There's enough here for a minor sit-com, but the comedy never really builds momentum. Korman stars as the host of a ridiculous telethon to raise money to save the country. With Fred Willard and Nancy Morgan. **Director**—Neil Israel. (PG) 90 minutes

---

THE AMITYVILLE HORROR
(1979)
★★★

James Brolin
Margot Kidder

This film would be just another haunted-house story were it not for plenty of effective hair-raising moments. Toilets ooze black goo, the front door is mysteriously ripped from its hinges, a rocking chair rocks with no one in it. Brolin and Kidder give adequate performances as the newly-wed couple who finally flee this strange Long Island home where the previous family had been murdered. The screenplay is based on Jay Anson's supposedly factual book. Cast includes Rod Steiger and Don Stroud. **Director**—Stuart Rosenberg. (R)   117 minutes

---

THE AMOROUS ADVENTURES OF MOLL FLANDERS (1965)
★★

Kim Novak
Richard Johnson
Angela Lansbury
George Sanders

This ambitious attempt to make a female version of Tom Jones doesn't quite make it. Novak, who fits awkwardly in the title role, is part of the problem. She plays a servant girl who cavorts with rich men. There are some bawdy romps among bedrooms in 18th-century England, but nothing too exciting. Costumes and period settings are nice. The film is based on Daniel Defoe's novel. Cast includes Lilli Palmer, Leo McKern, and Vittorio De Sica. **Director**—Terence Young.
126 minutes

THE AMSTERDAM KILL (1978)
★★

Robert Mitchum
Bradford Dillman
Richard Egan

Droopy-eyed Mitchum plays a narcotics agent who smashes an international drug-smuggling ring that operates in Hong Kong, Amsterdam, and London. Mitchum's performance is effective, but at times he seems too old to be slugging it out as the straight heavy. Robert Clouse directs this caper with a knack for fast-paced action. However, he overdoes the gunplay, and the body count climbs with each passing scene. Also with Leslie Nielsen and Keye Luke. (R)
90 minutes

AMY (1981)
★★★

Jenny Agutter
Barry Newman
Nanette Fabray

A sentimental, feel-good movie from the Disney studios about a woman who leaves her stuffy lawyer-husband to teach deaf children to speak. The title role is winningly portrayed by
(Continued)

A
- Anastasia
- Anatomy of a Murder
- Anchors Aweigh
- The Anderson Tapes
- . . . And Justice for All
- And Now for Something Completely Different

(Continued)

Agutter. There's stalwart support from Newman and Fabray. But the film is most convincing because of the impressive performances of students from the California School for the Deaf. The format is rather old-fashioned, but it's executed with ample warmth and appeal. **Director—** Vincent McEveety. (G)   *100 minutes*

ANASTASIA (1956)
★★★★

**Ingrid Bergman
Yul Brynner
Helen Hayes**

A charming drama set in Paris in 1928, about an amnesiac young woman, played by Bergman, who is recruited by exiled Russians to impersonate the daughter of the late czar. Bergman's gracious, award-winning performance heightens the entertainment to grand style. Hayes, as the grand duchess, also makes a magnificent acting contribution as she strives to determine Bergman's credentials. Also with Akim Tamiroff and Martita Hunt. **Director—**Anatole Litvak. **Academy Award—**Bergman, best actress.
105 minutes

Ingrid Bergman is recruited to impersonate the late Russian czar's daughter in Anastasia.

ANATOMY OF A MURDER
(1959)
★★★★

**James Stewart
Ben Gazzara
Lee Remick**

A long but engrossing courtroom drama, adapted from Robert Traver's best-selling novel, about a small-town lawyer in Michigan who defends an Army officer accused of murdering a bartender. Stewart is superb as the crafty defense attorney, and George C. Scott makes his mark as the prosecutor. The explicit dialogue caused a stir when the film was released. Also stars Eve Arden and Arthur O'Connell. Duke Ellington wrote the musical score. **Director—**Otto Preminger. **Academy Award Nominations—**best picture; Stewart, best actor; O'Connell, Scott, best supporting actor; Wendell Mayes, best screenplay (based on material from another medium).
160 minutes b&w

ANCHORS AWEIGH (1945)
★★★

**Frank Sinatra
Gene Kelly
Kathryn Grayson**

A light and lively musical about two sailors on liberty in Los Angeles who befriend a small boy yearning to join the Navy. The cast, led by Kelly, Sinatra, and Grayson, perform energetically. The film is notable for Kelly's dance sequence with a cartoon mouse, and the song, "I Fall in Love Too Easily." There's support from José Iturbi, Dean Stockwell, and Pamela Britton. **Director—**George Sidney.
140 minutes

THE ANDERSON TAPES (1972)
★★★

**Sean Connery
Martin Balsam
Dyan Cannon**

Stylish and lively crime drama about an ex-con's plan to stage a robbery at an apartment building, but the cops are onto the heist because of electronic surveillance. Connery is convincing as the thief, and the unusual climax is rather thrilling. However, a few plot holes mar the script. Also stars Alan King and Ralph Meeker. **Director—**Sidney Lumet. (PG)   *98 minutes*

. . . AND JUSTICE FOR ALL
(1979)
★★★★

**Al Pacino
Jack Warden
John Forsythe**

Pacino stars as a scruffy, idealistic lawyer who tangles with a tyrannical judge played by Forsythe. The film smartly indicts the legal profession much in the same spirit that *Hospital* took on medicine. This is a fascinating and compelling movie, featuring unforgettable performances and Norman Jewison's well-paced direction. Pacino generates so much power and feeling in this role, that he must be regarded as more than just a good actor. He's a superstar. Cast includes Lee Strasberg. (R) **Academy Award Nominations—**Pacino, best actor; Valerie Curtin and Barry Levinson, best screenplay (written directly for the screen).   *120 minutes*

Al Pacino as lawyer Arthur Kirkland is cited for contempt in . . . And Justice for All.

AND NOW FOR SOMETHING COMPLETELY DIFFERENT
(1972)
★★★

**John Cleese
Graham Chapman
Terry Gilliam
Eric Idle
Michael Palin
Terry Jones**

The zany stars of "Monty Python's Flying Circus" television show, Britain's latter-day version of the Marx

- Androcles and the Lion
- The Andromeda Strain
- And Then There Were None
- Andy Warhol's Bad
- Angel on My Shoulder
- Angels With Dirty Faces
- Animal Farm
- Animal House, National Lampoon's

A

Brothers, present a series of rip-roaring, rib-tickling sketches including blackouts and animated segments. The production is somewhat uneven, but there's loads of side-splitting comedy throughout. **Director**—Ian McNaughton. (PG)　*89 minutes*

ANDROCLES AND THE LION (1952)
★★

Alan Young
Jean Simmons
Robert Newton
Victor Mature

George Bernard Shaw's satiric fable set in the time of ancient Rome is mitigated by a lackluster production although some good performances perk things up at times. The story concerns a Christian who removes a thorn from the paw of a lion. When the two meet later in the arena, the lion remembers the kindness and refuses to eat the man. Young plays the Christian. Cast includes Reginald Gardiner, Alan Mowbray, Maurice Evans, and Elsa Lanchester. **Director**—Chester Erskine.　*98 minutes b&w*

THE ANDROMEDA STRAIN (1971)
★★★

Arthur Hill
David Wayne

Scientists race the clock to decontaminate a remote village infected by a deadly virus from a downed satellite. The film, based on Michael Crichton's novel, is somewhat drawn out, but it packs plenty of suspense just the same. Also, there's some reference to man's injustice to man. Also with James Olson, Kate Reid, and Paula Kelly. **Director**—Robert Wise. (G)　*137 minutes*

AND THEN THERE WERE NONE (1945)
★★★★

Walter Huston
Barry Fitzgerald
Louis Hayward

A superb, taut Agatha Christie mystery about ten people invited to a remote island where they begin being murdered one by one. Skillful direction and scripting bring out a stylish blend of black comedy and suspense. The superb cast also includes June Duprez, C. Aubrey Smith, Judith Anderson, Roland Young, and Richard Haydn. **Director**—René Clair.　*98 minutes b&w*

ANDY WARHOL'S BAD (1977)
(no stars)

Carroll Baker
Perry King
Susan Tyrrell

This is the revolting story of a suburban housewife who operates a small-scale murder-and-mayhem contracting business staffed by strange girls. There are numerous outrageous scenes of blood and gore, which probably will make you surrender your dinner. Much of the dialogue is boring. Some of the acting is fair; the rest is awful. "Bad" it certainly is. **Director**—Jed Johnson. (X)　*105 minutes*

ANGEL ON MY SHOULDER (1946)
★★★

Paul Muni
Claude Rains
Anne Baxter

A light comedy-drama about a dead criminal who makes a deal with the Devil for a new lease on life. He returns to Earth as a high-minded judge and turns the tables on Satan. The plot imitates *Here Comes Mr. Jordan*, but the film still maintains a lively entertainment level. Muni, Rains, and Baxter are excellent in starring roles. With Erskine Sanford and Hardie Albright. **Director**—Archie Mayo.　*101 minutes b&w*

ANGELS WITH DIRTY FACES (1938)
★★★

James Cagney
Pat O'Brien
Humphrey Bogart

A top cast graces this effective drama about a New York hood, played by Cagney, who develops a conscience

In Angels With Dirty Faces, *James Cagney gets the drop on Humphrey Bogart.*

when he is idolized by slum kids. O'Brien is effective as the gangster's brother who happens to be a priest. Bogart is notable as an unredeemed criminal. The Dead End Kids are effective as the impressionable youths. The film is a clever combination of brutality and moral judgment. Also with Ann Sheridan and George Bancroft. **Director**—Michael Curtiz.　*97 minutes b&w*

ANIMAL FARM (1955)
★★★

On-target animated cartoon faithfully based on George Orwell's political satire. The oppressed animals free themselves from their human masters and take over management of the farm only to find themselves governed by harsh restrictions. Some of the cartoon characters are pigs, but not the "Porky Pig" kind. **Director**—John Halas.　*75 minutes*

ANIMAL HOUSE, NATIONAL LAMPOON'S (1978)
★★

John Belushi
Tim Matheson
John Vernon
Verna Bloom

A raunchy, uneven comedy of frat-house silliness set in a small college in 1962. The film follows the bawdy style of the famed humor magazine, but the parody is soft-pedaled. Too many gags fall flat. The youthful players, led by Belushi, make an earnest effort, but they are thwarted by the unpolished material. However, there are enough glimpses of potential talent in all aspects of the film. Cast includes
(Continued)

A
- Anna and the King of Siam
- Anne of the Thousand Days
- Annie Get Your Gun
- Annie Hall

- The Anniversary
- Another Man, Another Chance
- Another Man's Poison

Thomas Hulce, Cesare Danova, and Donald Sutherland. **Director**—John Landis. (R)   *109 minutes*

ANNA AND THE KING OF SIAM (1946)
★★★

Irene Dunne
Rex Harrison

Impressive period drama about an English governess who takes a job in the palace in Bangkok teaching the king's many children and wins the respect of the tyrannical king. Gracefully produced with heartwarming touches. Harrison and Dunne are impressive in the key roles. The story, however, is better known in the musical version, *The King and I*. Cast includes Linda Darnell, Gale Sondergaard, and Lee J. Cobb. **Director**—John Cromwell.   *128 minutes b&w*

ANNE OF THE THOUSAND DAYS (1969)
★★★

Richard Burton
Geneviève Bujold

Burton gives one of his most impressive performances as Henry VIII in

Woody Allen and Diane Keaton attempt to solidify their relationship in Annie Hall.

this somewhat inaccurate historical drama involving the king's controversial romance with Anne Boleyn, played by Bujold. It's a compelling account of a famous love affair that involved adultery. The film is based on the 1948 play by Maxwell Anderson. Lavish costumes and scenery enhance the production. With John Colicos, Irene Papas, and Anthony Quayle. **Director**—Charles Jarrott. (PG) **Academy Award Nominations**—best picture; Burton, best actor; Bujold, best actress; Quayle, best supporting actor; Richard Sokolove, best screenplay (based on material from another medium).   *145 minutes*

ANNIE GET YOUR GUN (1950)
★★★

Betty Hutton
Howard Keel

Flashy film version of the Broadway hit musical about Annie Oakley, the celebrated female sharpshooter who toured with Wild West shows. Hutton and Keel belt out the lively Irving Berlin music with gusto. The direction is somewhat stilted, but the production is lavish. Edward Arnold, Keenan Wynn, Louis Calhern, and J. Carrol Naish lend support. Memorable songs include "Anything You Can Do" and "Doin' What Comes Naturally." **Director**—George Sidney. *107 minutes*

ANNIE HALL (1977)
★★★★

Woody Allen
Diane Keaton

Allen and Keaton glitter and shine in this hilarious and moving autobiographical film about their on-again, off-again romance. It's Allen's most personal film and one of his best. The familiar parade of Allen one-liners are there, but the film also is rich with emotion and introspection. He leans somewhat to Ingmar Bergman here, and this story could appropriately be named "Scenes From a Neurotic Love Affair." Cast includes Tony Roberts, Paul Simon, Shelley Duvall, Carol Kane, and Colleen Dewhurst. **Director**—Allen. (PG) **Academy Awards**—best picture; Allen, best director;

Keaton, best actress; Allen and Marshall Brickman, best original screenplay. **Nomination**—Allen, best actor.
94 minutes

THE ANNIVERSARY (1968)
★★

Bette Davis
Jack Hedley
James Cossins

Davis, bitchy as ever and wearing an eye patch, stars as an overbearing mother who dominates her grown sons. She gathers her clan together on the anniversary of her husband's death. This black comedy-horror outing, based on the Bill MacIlwraith play, affords an opportunity to see Davis ham it up to the hilt. Otherwise, the film is routine. Also with Sheila Hancock and Elaine Taylor. **Director**—Roy Ward Baker.   *95 minutes*

ANOTHER MAN, ANOTHER CHANCE (1977)
★★

James Caan
Geneviève Bujold

French director Claude Lelouch (*A Man and a Woman*) gives us his version of America's frontier days that looks like a western soap opera with a French accent. The complex plot concerns a veterinarian widower, played by Caan, who falls in love with a widowed photographer, played by Bujold, while both reside in a dusty frontier town. This film certainly isn't your typical western, but it cries out for some typical drama, action, and some dimensional characters. (PG)
128 minutes

ANOTHER MAN'S POISON (1952)
★★

Bette Davis
Anthony Steel
Gary Merrill

A murky melodrama about a woman writer who poisons her husband and is subsequently blackmailed. Davis isn't up to par as the hysterical authoress in this low-budget film. The

- Another Time, Another Place
- Any Number Can Play
- Any Wednesday
- Any Which Way You Can
- Anzio
- Apache
- The Apartment

A

material is mediocre as well. Emlyn Williams, Barbara Murray, and Reginald Beckwith co-star. **Director**—Irving Rapper. *89 minutes b&w*

ANOTHER TIME, ANOTHER PLACE (1958)
★

Lana Turner
Barry Sullivan

Tearful soap-opera movie with Turner as an American newspaper woman during World War II who is involved in an affair with a British war correspondent. Turner goes to pieces when her love is killed. This film introduced Sean Connery as an actor worth watching. Also with Glynis Johns and Sidney James. **Director**—Lewis Allen. *98 minutes b&w*

ANY NUMBER CAN PLAY (1949)
★★★

Clark Gable
Alexis Smith
Mary Astor

Skillful acting by Gable, Smith, and Astor perk up this otherwise routine drama about a gambler beset with numerous problems. Gable, who plays a casino operator, is estranged from his family, but the situation turns around when health problems prompt his retirement. Also with Wendell Corey, Audrey Totter, Marjorie Rambeau, and Lewis Stone. **Director**—Mervyn Le Roy. *112 minutes b&w*

ANY WEDNESDAY (1966)
★★★

Jane Fonda
Dean Jones
Jason Robards, Jr.

A business executive, played by Robards, visits his mistress once a week, but tension develops when a company subordinate discovers the affair. This somewhat stretched out sex farce is based on the Broadway comedy. Fonda's spritely performance as the kept girl, however, helps maintain interest. Cast includes Rosemary Murphy and Ann Prentiss. **Director**—Robert Miller. *109 minutes*

ANY WHICH WAY YOU CAN (1980)
★★★

Clint Eastwood
Sondra Locke

In Any Which Way You Can, *Clint Eastwood has a romance with Sondra Locke.*

This funny, rollicking sequel to *Every Which Way But Loose* is better than the original. Eastwood once again teams up with Clyde the orangutan for more nonstop monkeyshines and two-fisted farcical mayhem. It's an undisguised comic-action vehicle for Eastwood, who has the good sense not to take himself too seriously. Locke again is pleasant as Eastwood's romantic interest. **Director**—Buddy Van Horn. (PG) *115 minutes*

ANZIO (1968)
★

Robert Mitchum
Peter Falk
Arthur Kennedy

Trumped-up World War II drama about preparation for the 1944 invasion of the Italian peninsula. The flimsy film wastes the good cast seen struggling with their roles. Mitchum plays a war correspondent in on the action. Earl Holliman, Anthony Steel, and Robert Ryan also star. **Director**—Edward Dmytryk. *117 minutes*

APACHE (1954)
★★

Burt Lancaster
Jean Peters

Lancaster stars as an angry Indian warrior who boldly crusades for jus-tice for his tribe and then settles down. There are some good action scenes, but the unlikely story languishes in spots. Peters fills in the background as Lancaster's supportive squaw. John McIntire and Charles Bronson appear in supporting roles. **Director**—Robert Aldrich. *91 minutes*

THE APARTMENT (1960)
★★★★

Jack Lemmon
Shirley MacLaine

Witty, bittersweet comedy-drama about a lonely, vulnerable young office worker, played by Lemmon, who lends his apartment to his superiors for their extramarital affairs. Lemmon and MacLaine turn in classic performances that are unforgettable. Billy Wilder's direction is on target with just the right blend of cynicism, pathos, and laughs. Fred MacMurray is superb as Lemmon's philandering boss. **Academy Awards**—best picture; Wilder, best director; Wilder and I.A.L. Diamond, best story and screenplay (written directly for the screen). **Nominations**—Lemmon, best actor; MacLaine, best actress; Jack Kruschen, best supporting actor. *125 minutes b&w*

Shirley MacLaine takes Jack Lemmon for a ride in the comedy-drama The Apartment.

A
- Apocalypse Now
- The Apple Dumpling Gang Rides Again

- The Apprenticeship of Duddy Kravitz
- The April Fools
- April in Paris

- Arabesque
- Arabian Adventure
- Arch of Triumph

In Apocalypse Now, *Martin Sheen, in camouflage, cuts an eerie figure in the Vietnam jungle.*

APOCALYPSE NOW (1979)
★★★★

Marlon Brando
Martin Sheen
Robert Duvall

Francis Coppola's unforgettable masterpiece about the Vietnam War throbs with energy, horror, irony, and grandeur. It's a cinematic work of art; an involving adventure yarn, based on Joseph Conrad's *Heart of Darkness*. All the acting is first class, but Duvall stands out as a gung ho, pompous air-cavalry colonel who stages a brutal helicopter raid on a Viet Cong village. Top-billed Brando is finally seen in the last quarter of the film. He plays the shadowy Colonel Kurtz who has gone mad in the jungle and is slated for execution by an intelligence officer, played by Sheen. Also with Frederic Forrest, Albert Hall, and Sam Bottoms. (R) **Academy Award Nominations**—best picture; Coppola, best director; Duvall, best supporting actor; Coppola and John Milius, best screenplay (adapted from another medium). *139 minutes*

THE APPLE DUMPLING GANG RIDES AGAIN (1979)
★★

Tim Conway
Don Knotts

A lukewarm sequel to Disney's successful *Apple Dumpling* comedy, with Conway and Knotts again playing bumbling outlaws. They fare well with their slapstick routines, but the story gets knocked out of kilter by an irritating romantic subplot. Adults and kids may find it all rather tiresome after awhile. Also with Tim Matheson, Jack Elam, and Kenneth Mars. **Director**—Vincent McEveety. (G) *88 minutes*

THE APPRENTICESHIP OF DUDDY KRAVITZ (1974)
★★★

Richard Dreyfuss
Micheline Lanctot
Jack Warden

Poignant and amusing comedy-drama about a young Jewish man from Montreal trying to make it big in the world. Excellent scenes are brought to life from Mordecai Richler's bright screenplay adapted from his novel. Dreyfuss is superb as the ambitious teenager. Also with Randy Quaid, Denholm Elliott, and Joseph Wiseman. **Director**—Ted Kotcheff. (PG) **Academy Award Nomination**—Richler and Lionel Chetwynd, best screenplay (adapted from other material). *121 minutes*

THE APRIL FOOLS (1969)
★★

Jack Lemmon
Catherine Deneuve

Strained comedy-drama made as a star vehicle for Jack Lemmon, but it doesn't work too well. Lemmon is a restless business executive who runs off to Paris with the wife of his boss. All sorts of complications ensue, but everything is straightened out for the happy ending. Myrna Loy, Sally Kellerman, Charles Boyer, Jack Weston, Harvey Korman, and Peter Lawford are in supporting roles. **Director**—Stuart Rosenberg. (PG) *95 minutes*

APRIL IN PARIS (1952)
★★

Doris Day
Ray Bolger

Lackluster, silly musical with a flimsy plot about a chorus girl, played by Day, who is mistakenly sent to Paris where she charms an awkward state department official. Songs and dances for Day and Bolger are all pretty much forgettable. The cast includes Claude Dauphin, Eve Miller, and George Givot. **Director**—David Butler. *100 minutes*

ARABESQUE (1966)
★★

Gregory Peck
Sophia Loren

Peck and Loren star in this handsome spy thriller with a disappointing, empty plot. Peck plays a language professor who finds himself involved with espionage while on assignment for some Arabian oil men. Some amusing moments are lost amid the lavish settings. With Alan Badel, Kieron Moore, and Carl Duering. **Director**—Stanley Donen. *118 minutes*

ARABIAN ADVENTURE (1979)
★★★

Christopher Lee
Milo O'Shea
Oliver Tobias
Puneet Sira

Flying magic carpets, genies, assorted villains, and a clever orphan boy will keep the kiddies amused for an hour and a half. This colorful Ali Baba-like adventure offers continuous action and intriguing special effects. Lee plays an evil ruler, Tobias is a handsome prince, and Mickey Rooney is the custodian of a secret cave. **Director**—Kevin Connor. (G) *98 minutes*

ARCH OF TRIUMPH (1948)
★★

Ingrid Bergman
Charles Boyer
Charles Laughton

An ambitious melodrama with a first-class cast—Bergman, Boyer, Laughton—fails to catch hold despite expensive commitment from its producers. Boyer plays a refugee in Paris who has a tragic love affair with a troubled girl, played by Bergman. A depressing set of circumstances, indeed, and hardly a triumph. Louis Calhern is also in the cast. **Director**—Lewis Milestone. *120 minutes b&w*

- The Aristocats
- Around the World in Eighty Days
- The Arrangement
- Arsenic and Old Lace
- Arthur
- Artists and Models
- The Asphalt Jungle

A

THE ARISTOCATS (1970)
★★★

An inventive cartoon feature by the Walt Disney studios about a cat and her kittens who are abandoned in the country and then rescued by the other animals there. Fine characterizations enhanced by the voices of Eva Gabor, Phil Harris, and Sterling Holloway. The deft influence of Walt Disney is noticeably missing, yet it's still a nice lollypop for the kids. **Director—** Wolfgang Reitherman. (G) *78 minutes*

AROUND THE WORLD IN EIGHTY DAYS (1956)
★★★

**David Niven
Cantinflas
Shirley MacLaine
Robert Newton**

A splendid, charming film version of Jules Verne's magnificent travelogue with spectacular sketches from various parts of the world and scores of cameos from an all-star cast. Niven plays the British gentleman who, in 1872, honored a bet that he could circle the globe within 80 days. The lavish production works best on the large screen and unfortunately loses impact on television. **Director—**Michael An-

Shirley MacLaine and David Niven have a brief encounter in Around the World in Eighty Days.

derson. **Academy Awards**—best picture; James Poe, John Farrow, S. J. Perelman, writing (best screenplay—adapted). **Nomination**—Anderson, best director. *170 minutes*

THE ARRANGEMENT (1969)
★

**Kirk Douglas
Faye Dunaway
Deborah Kerr**

An unfocused melodrama about an advertising executive who becomes fed up with his job, bungles a suicide attempt, and then analyzes the meaning of his life. Elia Kazan, who directed from his own novel, provides rich detail about the stress of contemporary life, but the characters involved are colorless. Douglas, Dunaway, and Kerr are wasted. Also with Richard Boone and Hume Cronyn. (R) *127 minutes*

ARSENIC AND OLD LACE (1942)
★★★

**Cary Grant
Josephine Hull
Jean Adair**

Amusing and charming film adaptation of the Broadway play about two old ladies who poison gentlemen visitors to their Brooklyn home and then bury them in the cellar. It's a lot of fun despite the concentration on corpses. Director Frank Capra pulls out all stops to induce energy and hilarity from the excellent cast, which also includes Raymond Massey, Peter Lorre, Edward Everett Horton, and James Gleason. *118 minutes b&w*

ARTHUR (1981)
★★★

**Dudley Moore
Liza Minnelli
Sir John Gielgud**

Impish Moore is in the title role as an often-inebriated, poor little rich man who falls in love with a waitress, played by Minnelli. This spritely, screwball comedy is peppered with zingy, clever one-liners that Moore tosses off with hilarious aplomb. But

Dudley Moore is a drunk millionaire, and Liza Minnelli is an aspiring actress in Arthur.

it's Sir John Gielgud as Arthur's snobbish valet and Jiminy Cricket conscience who provides the real comic chemistry. He steals scenes with obvious relish. Minnelli is charming, but her part is rather thin. **Director**—Steve Gordon. (PG) *100 minutes*

ARTISTS AND MODELS (1955)
★★

**Dean Martin
Jerry Lewis**

Martin and Lewis are up to their usual comic routines. Lewis has nightmares that inspire the grist for comic strips drawn by Martin. The film features gorgeous women, some musical numbers, and cornball gags. It tires after a while. Also with Shirley MacLaine, Dorothy Malone, Eddie Mayehoff, and Eva Gabor. **Director**—Frank Tashlin. *109 minutes b&w*

THE ASPHALT JUNGLE (1950)
★★★★

**Sterling Hayden
Sam Jaffe
Louis Calhern**

Compelling crime drama astutely directed by John Huston, about a gang of criminals who try to commit the perfect crime. The film evolves as more of a character study than a mystery. Excellent, gritty performances by Hayden, Jaffe, and James Whitmore. Marilyn Monroe has a small part that she handles well. **Academy Award Nominations**—John Huston, best director; Ben Maddow and Huston, writing (screenplay). *112 minutes b&w*

A

- Assault on a Queen
- Atlantic City
- Attack
- At the Earth's Core
- At War With the Army
- Audrey Rose
- Auntie Mame

ASSAULT ON A QUEEN (1966)
★

Frank Sinatra
Virna Lisi

Some gangsters get their hands on a German submarine and set out to pirate a luxury liner. A rather unlikely crime caper that fails at many levels: Acting is stilted, special effects are unconvincing, and Rod Serling's screenplay falters. Also with Tony Franciosa, Richard Conte, and Alf Kjellin. **Director**—Jack Donohue.

106 minutes

ATLANTIC CITY (1981)
★★★

Burt Lancaster
Susan Sarandon
Kate Reid

French director Louis Malle has constructed a romantic, offbeat melodrama that is brimming with interesting and colorful people who act out their fantasies against the backdrop of this transforming resort city. The most engaging character is Lou, played by Lancaster, an elderly, petty criminal who at last realizes a delightful moment of glory and self-respect. Lancaster's gentle and touching portrayal is carried off with superb finesse. There are also polished performances from Sarandon and Reid. (R) *104 minutes*

ATTACK (1956)
★★★

Jack Palance
Eddie Albert
Lee Marvin

Gripping and intelligent drama about American soldiers involved in the Battle of the Bulge and led by a cowardly commander. The slick production is far above the routine war movie thanks to good acting, a finely tuned script, and impressive direction by Robert Aldrich. The theme touches on an antiwar element. Excellent performances from Palance, Albert, and Marvin. Also with Buddy Ebsen, Robert Strauss, and Richard Jaeckel.

107 minutes b&w

AT THE EARTH'S CORE (1976)
★

Doug McClure
Peter Cushing
Caroline Munro

An Edgar Rice Burroughs fantasy about two scientist-adventurers who build a burrowing machine and bore their way to the center of the Earth where they battle huge underground monsters. The acting, the script, the direction, and the special effects are hopelessly hokey. Perhaps young children will be impressed, but those who have graduated from the comic book phase will undoubtedly be bored to the core. **Director**—Kevin Connor. (PG) *90 minutes*

AT WAR WITH THE ARMY (1950)
★★

Dean Martin
Jerry Lewis

Martin and Lewis demonstrate their comic chemistry together in this routine service comedy based loosely on a play by James Allardice. There are a few clever gags, but it's not all that funny. Martin and Lewis are song-and-dance men with girl trouble. Polly Bergen and Jimmie Dundee co-star. **Director**—Hal Walker.

93 minutes b&w

AUDREY ROSE (1977)
★★

Marsha Mason
John Beck
Anthony Hopkins

Take a slice of *The Exorcist*, a measure of *The Omen*, a dash of *Rosemary's Baby*, and add plenty of water. The result is this tepid tale of an 11-year-old girl who is the reincarnation of another girl killed in a crash. The padded script contains a lot of mumbo jumbo about Indian mysticism and transmigration of souls. Mason, Beck, and Hopkins act their parts as if they have difficulty keeping a straight face. Also with Susan Swift, Norman Lloyd, and John Hillerman. **Director**—Robert Wise. (PG) *113 minutes*

AUNTIE MAME (1958)
★★★

Rosalind Russell
Forrest Tucker

Russell's tour-de-force portrayal of the eccentric aunt who takes a teenage boy under her wing graces this entertaining film rendition of Patrick Dennis's novel. Some priceless moments spark hilarity galore as Roz plays the colorful character to the hilt. Mame believes life is a bouquet, and she proves it. Peggy Cass is memorable for her "Miss Gooch" characterization. Coral Browne and Fred Clark also star.

Burt Lancaster and Susan Sarandon star in director Louis Malle's melodrama Atlantic City.

In Auntie Mame, Rosalind Russell plays an eccentric who takes a teenage boy under her wing.

Director—Morton DaCosta. **Academy Award Nominations**—best picture; Russell, best actress; Cass, best supporting actress.   *114 minutes*

AUTUMN SONATA (1978)
★★★

**Ingrid Bergman
Liv Ullmann**

Ingmar Bergman directs Ingrid Bergman for the first time in this film about a mother and daughter love-hate relationship. Ingrid Bergman is a successful concert pianist, and Ullmann is her middle-aged daughter. They turn in dynamic and inspired performances. Ingmar is on familiar territory relentlessly exposing complex human relationships and emotions. Strictly for Bergman fans. In Swedish with English titles. (No MPAA rating). **Academy Award Nominations**— Ingrid Bergman, best actress; Ingmar Bergman, best original screenplay.
97 minutes

AVALANCHE (1978)
★★

**Rock Hudson
Mia Farrow**

Hudson and Farrow star in this assembly-line disaster number that has Mother Nature on the rampage. Hudson builds a ski lodge next to a precariously snowy mountainside that eventually comes tumbling down on a crowd of skiers and sledders. In the end, he learns it's not nice to fool Mother Nature—or the audience, which may not appreciate such a snow job. **Director**—Corey Allen. (PG)
91 minutes

AVALANCHE EXPRESS (1979)
★

**Lee Marvin
Robert Shaw
Linda Evans**

Shaw, Marvin, Joe Namath, and a few other familiar players fumble through this languid melodrama about Soviet and American agents aboard a train traveling through Europe. The action stumbles along with much banal dialo-
(Continued)

PETER SELLERS

From his early British comedies like The Lady Killers *(1955)*, I'm All Right, Jack *(1959)*, and The Mouse That Roared *(1959)* to such American films as The Pink Panther series, Peter Sellers has provided the cinema with a gallery of hilarious characters. One count showed that he had taken 61 roles in 52 films, often playing multiple characters within a film, as he did in Dr. Strangelove *(1963)*, and, more recently, The Prisoner of Zenda *(1979)*.

Sellers, who was born in Southsea, England, in 1925, was first carried onto a stage at the age of two weeks. His parents, grandmother, and eight uncles were all in show business, but he became aware of his remarkable talent for mimicry while serving in the Royal Air Force in India. On his return to civilian life, he began working as a stand-up comic, and got his start at the BBC with what has become his trademark—he telephoned a producer there and recommended himself with the "borrowed" voices of two already established performers!

Sellers' work in radio led to the famous Goon Show with Spike Milligan, Harry Secombe, and Michael Bentine. The series, which revived radio humor, ran for nine years and made Sellers a household name throughout Great Britain, and was a great favorite of the Royal Family. Success in the theater, at the London Palladium, and at Royal Command Variety Performances followed rapidly. In 1950, he made his film debut and appeared in several films over the next few years. It was his work in The Lady Killers, with Alec Guinness, that brought him attention and led to movie roles that made him an international star. He received the British "Oscar" in 1959 for I'm All Right, Jack and was nominated for an American Academy Award for Dr. Strangelove.

Some of his other films include Lolita *(1962)*, Waltz of the Toreadors *(1962)*, The World of Henry Orient *(1964)*, A Shot in the Dark *(1964)*, After the Fox *(1966)*, I Love You Alice B. Toklas *(1968)*, The Return of the Pink Panther *(1975)*, Murder by Death *(1976)*, and Being There *(1979)*, which was one of his last films before his death in 1980.

A·B

- Avanti
- The Awakening
- Away All Boats
- The Babe Ruth Story
- Baby Blue Marine
- Baby Doll
- Baby Face Nelson

(Continued)

gue and clumsy direction. About midway, an avalanche is set off in an attempt to eliminate a defected Russian, played by Shaw. From then on, the film continues to slide downhill. **Director**—Mark Robson. (PG)

88 minutes

AVANTI (1972)
★★★

Jack Lemmon
Juliet Mills

Lemmon stars in this black comedy about a wealthy young man who falls in love with the daughter of his father's mistress. The film is drawn out, yet plenty of wit and style in the script and classy acting by a good cast sustain interest. Director Billy Wilder isn't at his top form, but his execution is satisfactory. Also with Clive Revill and Edward Andrews. (R)

144 minutes

THE AWAKENING (1980)
★★

Charlton Heston
Stephanie Zimbalist

Heston plays an archaeologist who invades the secret tomb of Egypt's Queen Kara and unleashes her nasty spirit on the world. The film, based on Bram Stoker's novel, starts off with intrigue and suspense as Heston uncovers the ancient crypt with its splendors. But with the mummy's curse on the loose, the atmosphere deteriorates to hokey horror fare with accentuated violence. Zimbalist does a

Stephanie Zimbalist and Charlton Heston discuss an ancient mummy in The Awakening.

fair job as Heston's daughter who is possessed by Kara's cruel spirit. **Director**—Mike Newell. (R)   *105 minutes*

AWAY ALL BOATS (1956)
★★

Jeff Chandler
George Nader
Julie Adams

Routine World War II action adventure with overwrought heroic displays dominating the film. Story revolves around a transport ship involved in the Pacific campaign. Chandler leads the troops into battle. There are supporting roles by Nader, Adams, Lex Barker, and Richard Boone. **Director**—Joseph Pevney.   *114 minutes*

B

THE BABE RUTH STORY (1948)
★★

William Bendix
Claire Trevor

Bendix is convincing as the "Sultan of Swat," but an unpolished script hamstrings this film biography. Events are presented in an overly sentimental fashion. However, the Babe's image remains intact. Charles Bickford and William Frawley play supporting roles. **Director**—Roy Del Ruth.

107 minutes b&w

BABY BLUE MARINE (1976)
★★

Jan-Michael Vincent
Glynnis O'Connor

Vincent plays a World War II bootcamp washout who pretends to be a Marine Ranger and is hailed as a hero in a small Colorado community. It's an overly sentimental story lacking significant impact to carry it through. There are warm and touching moments here and there, but the overall complexion is akin to a TV soap opera. Vincent and O'Connor, the girl who falls in love with him, are appealing and make the most of their parts. **Director**—John Hancock. (PG)   *90 minutes*

BABY DOLL (1956)
★★★

Karl Malden
Eli Wallach
Carroll Baker

An engrossing screen adaptation of Tennessee Williams's moody comedy of depravity among poor people in the Deep South. Typical Williams plot is enhanced by incisive direction of Elia Kazan. Baker is impressive as the child-bride who is seduced by her husband's acquaintance. Wallach and Malden perform well in striking roles. Also with Mildred Dunnock and Rip Torn. **Academy Award Nominations**—Baker, best actress; Dunnock, best supporting actress; Williams, writing (best screenplay—adapted).

116 minutes b&w

BABY FACE NELSON (1957)
★★★

Mickey Rooney
Cedric Hardwicke
Carolyn Jones

Mickey Rooney and Leo Gordon in Baby Face Nelson, *a film about the notorious gangster.*

Rooney's energetic and colorful performance in the title role graces this otherwise low-budget film about the notorious gangster of the Depression era. Lots of action involving bank heists, prison breaks, and shootings. Production looks good despite the skimpy budget. Also with Jack Elam, Chris Dark, Ted de Corsia, and Leo Gordon. **Director**—Don Siegel.

85 minutes b&w

- Baby, the Rain Must Fall
- The Bachelor and the Bobbysoxer
- Bachelor in Paradise
- The Bachelor Party
- Background to Danger
- Back Roads
- Back to Bataan
- The Bad and the Beautiful

B

BABY, THE RAIN MUST FALL (1964)
★★

Steve McQueen
Lee Remick

An ex-con returns home to his wife and daughter, tries to mend his ways but reverts to violence. His behavior leads to re-separation. McQueen and Remick give it a good shot but can't rescue the sentimental and pretentious material, which smacks of Tennessee Williams fare. The film is adapted from Horton Foote's play, *The Traveling Lady*. Cast includes Don Murray, Paul Fix, Josephine Hutchinson, and Ruth White. **Director—**Robert Mulligan. *100 minutes b&w*

THE BACHELOR AND THE BOBBYSOXER (1947)
★★★

Cary Grant
Myrna Loy
Shirley Temple

Ideal comedy vehicle for Grant, who plays a dashing playboy pursued by an impressionable teenager, played by Temple. Uncomplicated script paves the way for Grant's buoyant and breezy performance. It's a pleasant entertainment from every angle despite the triteness of the material. Also with Rudy Vallee, Ray Collins, and Harry Davenport. **Director—**Irving Reis. *95 minutes b&w*

BACHELOR IN PARADISE (1961)
★★

Bob Hope
Lana Turner
Janis Paige

Hope stars in this lightweight comedy about an unmarried columnist who settles in an upper-class community of married couples to write about its inhabitants. The film works only part of the time as romantic interludes interrupt the comic flow. But there are sufficient moments to exploit Hope's talents. Turner is effective in a typical glamorous role. The supporting cast includes Agnes Moorehead, Paula

Prentiss, and Jim Hutton. **Director—**Jack Arnold. *109 minutes*

THE BACHELOR PARTY (1957)
★★★

Don Murray
E. G. Marshall
Jack Warden

Paddy Chayefsky's TV play is expanded for the screen, and the result is an on-target social commentary graced by fine performances. A group of New York bookkeepers throw a party for a colleague prior to his wedding. The event emphasizes the emotional problems of the guests. The superb cast includes Carolyn Jones, Philip Abbott, and Patricia Smith. **Director—**Delbert Mann. **Academy Award Nomination—**Jones, best supporting actress. *93 minutes*

BACKGROUND TO DANGER (1943)
★★★

George Raft
Brenda Marshall
Sydney Greenstreet
Peter Lorre

A thrilling World War II spy story with Raft in Turkey pursuing Nazi agents. Based on Eric Ambler's novel, *Uncommon Danger*, the film provides lots of intrigue and fast-moving action, including a hair-raising car chase. Greenstreet and Lorre stand out in supporting roles as two menacing characters. Also with Turhan Bey and Osa Massen. **Director—**Raoul Walsh. *80 minutes b&w*

BACK ROADS (1981)
★★

Sally Field
Tommy Lee Jones

Field stars as a likable hooker who falls in love with a drifter-boxer, played by Jones, as they hitchhike from Alabama to California. Both portray cheerful, gritty characters, but the pedestrian screenplay quickly runs out of energy, and the film winds up on a dead-end street. It's difficult to perceive perky Field as a washed-up streetwalker. In one scene, she falls off a train smack

into a mud puddle. (R) **Director—**Martin Ritt. *94 minutes*

BACK TO BATAAN (1945)
★★★

John Wayne
Anthony Quinn

Wayne plays a Marine colonel who leads guerrilla troops on the road to victory in the Philippines against the Japanese. It's a rather routine war adventure, but there is substantial action and excitement, especially for fans of the Duke. Wayne is at his macho best and is helped out nicely by Beulah Bondi, Richard Loo, and Leonard Strong. **Director—**Edward Dmytryk. *97 minutes b&w*

John Wayne and Beulah Bondi react to the horror of war in Back To Bataan.

THE BAD AND THE BEAUTIFUL (1952)
★★★★

Kirk Douglas
Walter Pidgeon
Lana Turner
Dick Powell

A clever, slam-bang drama about ambitious Hollywood types, related as an inside story. Douglas is superb as a ruthless and ambitious producer who influences the lives and careers of people within his grasp. Other memorable performances from Gloria Grahame, who plays (a Southern belle), and Tur-
(Continued)

B

- Bad Day at Black Rock
- Bad for Each Other
- Badlands

- Bad News Bears
- The Bad News Bears Go to Japan

- The Bad News Bears in Breaking Training

(Continued)

ner, who plays an actress. There's electrifying entertainment throughout. Also with Barry Sullivan, Gilbert Roland, and Leo G. Carroll. **Director**—Vincente Minnelli. **Academy Awards**—Grahame, best supporting actress; Charles Schnee, writing (screenplay). **Nomination**—Douglas, best actor. *118 minutes b&w*

BAD DAY AT BLACK ROCK (1955)
★★★★

**Spencer Tracy
Robert Ryan
Dean Jagger**

A crackling suspense drama about a one-arm stranger, played by Tracy, who encounters hostility in a small Western town, and then discovers the community has something to hide. Director John Sturges expertly builds tension to a smashing climax. There are fine performances from the cast, which also includes Walter Brennan, Ernest Borgnine, and Lee Marvin. **Academy Award Nominations**—Sturges, best director; Tracy, best actor; Millard Kaufman, writing (screenplay). *81 minutes*

In Bad Day at Black Rock, *Spencer Tracy is confronted by a hostile community.*

BAD FOR EACH OTHER (1954)
★

**Charlton Heston
Lizabeth Scott**

Heston plays a high-minded doctor who serves poor coal miners in a Pennsylvania town after a wealthy woman tries to persuade him to cater to the social set. It's mostly dreary soap-opera stuff with the players in awkward situations. The film borrows some from *The Citadel*. Dianne Foster and Marjorie Rambeau also star. **Director**—Irving Rapper.

83 minutes b&w

BADLANDS (1973)
★★★

**Martin Sheen
Sissy Spacek**

A dim-witted teenage girl and her somewhat older boyfriend cross the country murdering people along the way. This skillfully perceived drama, which eventually became a cult film, is based on the actual killing spree of Charles Starkweather and Carol Fugate in the 1950s. Sheen and Spacek are impressive in the lead roles. And it's a successful debut for director Terrence Malick, who also wrote the script. Warren Oates and Ramon Bieri are in supporting roles. (PG)

94 minutes

BAD NEWS BEARS (1976)
★★★

**Walter Matthau
Tatum O'Neal**

A rather carefree and touching comedy about a down-in-the-mouth Little League baseball team—The Bears—which is rescued by a cigar-chomping, beer-guzzling coach, played by Matthau. O'Neal, in her first film since *Paper Moon*, is the ace pitcher who helps save the day. Director Michael Ritchie (*Smile; The Candidate*) continues to dwell on his favorite social theme of competition and concocts the right mixture of warmth and emotion. Matthau is at his best, and the child actors are appealing. Although this film is about kids, it is aimed primarily at adults. *Bad News* is good news. Also with Vic Morrow and Joyce Van Patten. (PG) *102 minutes*

THE BAD NEWS BEARS GO TO JAPAN (1978)
★

**Tony Curtis
Jackie Earle Haley**

What was originally an appealing story has finally worn thin in this third round of Little League baseball high jinks. This time the bumbling junior sluggers fly off to Japan for a ball game with the Asian Little League champs. Michael Ritchie—director of the original film—injects some pep as producer, but the familiar characters and theme fail to sustain interest. The "Bears" are yesterday's news. **Director**—John Berry. (PG) *91 minutes*

THE BAD NEWS BEARS IN BREAKING TRAINING (1977)
★★

**William Devane
Jackie Earle Haley**

This sequel about the hapless Little League team is loaded with sentimentality and only comes alive in the last quarter. The direction of Michael Ritchie and the acting talents of Walter Matthau and Tatum O'Neal, which contributed so much to the successful original, are sorely missed here. The

William Devane with Little Leaguers in The Bad News Bears in Breaking Training.

● The Bad Seed
● Bad Timing/A Sensual Obsession
● The Balcony
● The Baltimore Bullet
● Bambi
● Bananas
● The Band Wagon
● Bang the Drum Slowly

B

humor is forced, and the whole project has a made-for-TV image. Also with Jimmy Baio and Chris Barnes. Clumsily directed by Michael Pressman. (PG)   *100 minutes*

THE BAD SEED (1956)
★★★

Nancy Kelly
Patty McCormack

An intriguing story about an innocent-looking eight-year-old girl who maliciously murders various people, including some of her playmates. The film version faithfully recalls the stage play with Kelly repeating her role as the distraught mother. McCormack is convincing in the title role as the child who inherited evilness. Henry Jones and Eileen Heckart are in supporting roles. **Director**—Mervyn Le Roy. **Academy Award Nominations**—Kelly, best actress; Heckart, best supporting actress; McCormack, best supporting actress.   *129 minutes b&w*

BAD TIMING/A SENSUAL OBSESSION (1980)
★★

Art Garfunkel
Theresa Russell
Harvey Keitel

Nicolas Roeg (*Don't Look Now*) directs this ponderous drama with a lush style and mystery. But this story of two Americans—played by Garfunkel and Russell—in Vienna who become sexually obsessed with one another is strangely distant and uninvolving. Garfunkel and Russell act as if they learned their lines only minutes before the beginning of each scene. Keitel is miscast as a police inspector. Also with Daniel Massey and Denholm Elliott. (No MPAA rating)
123 minutes

THE BALCONY (1963)
★★★

Shelley Winters
Peter Falk
Lee Grant

Intriguing low-budget screen adaptation of Jean Genet's complex play about a Paris brothel that offers a variety of services for its customers. A lot of vivid symbolism is brought to bear in this film, which deals with sex in an unusual fashion. Winters is nicely cast as the accommodating madam, Grant displays her fine talents as the madam's lesbian friend, and Falk fares well as the police chief. Also with Peter Brocco, Ruby Dee, and Leonard Nimoy. **Director**—Joseph Strick.
86 minutes

THE BALTIMORE BULLET (1980)
★

James Coburn

Silly tale about pool hustlers and their world of gambling and high living. Coburn mugs his way along as an aging pool shark who is still the greatest. The story is accented by much free-for-all brawling and macho ogling of women. While there are some interesting scenes of sharp pool shooting, the film is a far cry from Robert Rossen's stylish classic *The Hustler*, which starred Paul Newman. (PG)
102 minutes

BAMBI (1942)
★★★★

This is one of Walt Disney's best cartoon features. It is the story of a fawn that grows to be a magnificent stag. The film, based on the book by Felix Salton, is sometimes overly sentimental, yet the forest animal characters are heartwarming and memorable. Thumper the rabbit is unforgettable. It's a remarkable achievement from a most skillful animator.   *72 minutes*

Bambi, one of Disney's best cartoons, is about a fawn that grows into a magnificent stag.

BANANAS (1971)
★★★

Woody Allen
Louise Lasser

Allen plays a meek factory worker who runs off to South America where he leads a revolution and becomes a hero. It's a typical offering of Allen's humor and unusual comic ideas, with a generous dose of sight gags. Many jokes are hilarious, but a few miss the mark. Carlos Montalban and Howard Cosell have supporting parts, and Sylvester Stallone has a minor part as a gangster. **Director**—Allen. (PG)
82 minutes

THE BAND WAGON (1953)
★★★★

Fred Astaire
Cyd Charisse
Jack Buchanan

Toe-tapping musical with the incomparable Astaire in splendid form. The standard simple plot, pegged on problems of producing a Broadway show, makes way for numerous delightful song-and-dance numbers, including "Shine on My Shoes," "Dancing in the Dark," "I Guess I'll Have to Change My Plan," and "Louisiana Hayride." Oscar Levant and Nanette Fabray are also in the cast. **Director**—Vincente Minnelli.   *112 minutes*

BANG THE DRUM SLOWLY (1973)
★★★

Michael Moriarty
Robert De Niro

De Niro and Moriarty stand out in this film version of Mark Harris's novel about a baseball player stricken with leukemia who wants to play another season before he dies. The story is somewhat cliché-strewn, but doesn't become overly sentimental. A few comic moments are handled nicely. Also with Vincent Gardenia and Phil Foster. **Director**—John Hancock. (PG) **Academy Award Nomination**—Gardenia, best supporting actor.
98 minutes

B
- The Bank Dick
- Bank Shot
- Barbarella
- The Barefoot Contessa
- Barefoot in the Park
- The Barkleys of Broadway
- Barry Lyndon

THE BANK DICK (1940)
★★★★

W. C. Fields

W. C. Fields, as Egbert Souse, foils a bank robbery in the classic film, The Bank Dick.

Yes indeed. The great Fields is at his funniest. As Egbert Souse, a sort of nonentity, Fields foils a bank heist. As a reward he's hired as a bank guard. All sorts of hilarious high jinks take place. It's classic humor in the Fields tradition. And there's fine support from Franklin Pangborn, Shemp Howard, and Jack Norton. **Director**—Eddie Cline. *73 minutes*

BANK SHOT (1974)
★★

George C. Scott
Joanna Cassidy

Unusual comedy about a gang of thieves who pull off a bank robbery by actually stealing the whole building using house-moving gear. There are some funny moments, but the film doesn't deliver enough laughs. Scott stars as the gang leader, and he doesn't quite make it in this role that demands comedy. Sorrell Booke, Clifton James, and Robert Balaban co-star. **Director**—Gower Champion. (PG) *83 minutes*

BARBARELLA (1967)
★★

Jane Fonda
John Phillip Law

Fonda stars as an attractive 41st-century astronaut in this French-Italian sci-fi based on comic strip fare. Razzle-dazzle special effects perk things up here and there, but the script is nonsense. There are supporting roles by Marcel Marceau, Anita Pallenberg, David Hemmings, and Ugo Tognazzi. **Director**—Roger Vadim. *98 minutes*

THE BAREFOOT CONTESSA (1954)
★★★

Humphrey Bogart
Ava Gardner
Edmond O'Brien

Bogart, Gardner, and O'Brien star in this handsome tale about the rise and fall of an actress. The film holds ample fascination, yet it is somewhat long-winded. The actors fare well with some clever dialogue. O'Brien stands out as a brassy press agent. **Director**—Joseph L. Mankiewicz. **Academy Award**—O'Brien, best supporting actor. **Nomination**—Mankiewicz, writing (story and screenplay). *128 minutes*

BAREFOOT IN THE PARK (1967)
★★★

Robert Redford
Jane Fonda

Neil Simon's Broadway comedy about some newlyweds coping with life in New York City holds up nicely on the screen with plenty of one-liners intact. Redford and Fonda are the charming couple who reside in a fourth-floor walkup apartment. Mildred Natwick plays the bride's mother-in-law. Charles Boyer and Herb Edelmann are also in the cast. **Director**—Gene Saks. **Academy Award Nomination**—Natwick, best supporting actress. *109 minutes*

THE BARKLEYS OF BROADWAY (1949)
★★★

Fred Astaire
Ginger Rogers

Astaire and Rogers star as a bickering song-and-dance couple who split and then make up. She wants to be a serious actress. Their dancing is delightful and some of the songs are memorable. Songs include "They Can't Take That Away From Me" and "You'd Be Hard to Replace." The script, however, is rather flat. Oscar Levant, Billie Burke,

The team of Ginger Rogers and Fred Astaire dance in The Barkleys of Broadway.

and Jacques François play supporting roles. **Director**—Charles Walters. *109 minutes*

BARRY LYNDON (1975)
★★

Ryan O'Neal
Marissa Berenson
Patrick Magee

Master director Stanley Kubrick turns to the 18th-century W. M. Thackeray novel for this ponderous costume drama about an Irish rogue who climbs to the top of English aristocratic society. It's an $11-million production—technically well made and beautifully photographed. But the energy is slowed to a creep, and emotion is sorely lacking. It's more like taking a stroll through a wax museum than watching a movie. Most moviegoers would probably walk out of this three-hour ordeal more dazed than entertained. O'Neal plays Lyndon, and Berenson plays the beautiful, sad, and wealthy countess he marries. Also with Hardy Kruger, Steven Berkoff, and Gay Hamilton. The production is set against the music of Bach, Handel, Schubert, Mozart, and Vivaldi. (PG) **Academy Award Nominations**—best picture; Kubrick, best director; Kubrick, best screenplay (adapted from another medium). *185 minutes*

BATAAN (1943)
★★★

Robert Taylor
George Murphy
Lloyd Nolan

A rousing World War II drama about American soldiers who defend a bridge on a Pacific island against the Japanese. The film smacks somewhat of propaganda with cardboard characters, but combat action and suspense are handled nicely. Plot is reminiscent of *The Lost Patrol*. The excellent cast includes Desi Arnaz, Robert Walker, Thomas Mitchell, Lee Bowman, and Barry Nelson. **Director**—Tay Garnett. *114 minutes b&w*

BATHING BEAUTY (1944)
★★

Esther Williams
Red Skelton

A foolish MGM musical comedy built around the aquatic talents of Williams, who plays a swimming instructor. Williams, however, is supported by an attractive cast that makes the most of some gags. Skelton, Basil Rathbone, Keenan Wynn, and Xavier Cugat lend their skills. **Director**—George Sidney. *101 minutes*

BATTLE BEYOND THE STARS (1980)
★

Richard Thomas
Robert Vaughn

Thomas and Vaughn star in this flimsy comic-book, sci-fi adventure that is inspired by *Seven Samurai* and tries to look like *Star Wars*. A peaceful planet is threatened by invasion, so mercenaries are recruited to repel the bad guys. The spacecraft combat looks like it was lifted from coin amusement machines. But the film has a sense of humor of sorts—primarily in the form of colorful odd characters, including five clones wrapped in a beach towel. Also with George Peppard, John Saxon, and Darleanne Fluegel. **Director**—Jimmy T. Murakami. (PG) *104 minutes*

BATTLE CIRCUS (1952)
★

Humphrey Bogart
June Allyson

Bogart is miscast as a doctor at an Army field hospital in Korea. A flimsy soap opera script is slim inspiration for the cast. Allyson, who plays a nurse, is the love interest, but there's virtually no chemistry between her and Bogey. Keenan Wynn, Robert Keith, and William Campbell co-star. **Director**—Richard Brooks. *90 minutes b&w*

SHIRLEY MacLAINE

Shirley MacLaine, an actress who attained her greatest popularity in the '50s and '60s, was born in 1934 in Richmond, Virginia, to Ira O. Beaty, a high-school principal, and his wife Kathlyn MacLean Beaty, a drama teacher and community theater actress. Shirley is the older sister of actor-director Warren Beatty. She began her professional career as a dancer and was in the chorus lines of Kiss Me, Kate *and* Me and Juliet *and was understudying Carol Haney in* The Pajama Game *on Broadway when the star injured her ankle. In the best 42nd Street tradition, MacLaine took over, was spotted by Hollywood producer Hal B. Wallis, and she has been performing out front ever since.*

In 1955, MacLaine made her motion picture debut in Alfred Hitchcock's The Trouble With Harry, *and for the next 15 years averaged two pictures a year, among them* Around the World in 80 Days *(1956),* Hot Spell *(1957),* The Matchmaker *(1958),* Some Came Running *(1958),* The Sheepman

BATTLE CRY (1954)
★★★

Van Heflin
Aldo Ray
Tab Hunter
Mona Freeman

Some good performances enhance this screen treatment of Leon Uris's World War II adventure of Marines on their way to war in the Pacific. Romantic subplots are woven in with some action scenes. Dorothy Malone is
(Continued)

(1958), Ask Any Girl *(1959),* Career *(1959),* Can-Can *(1959),* The Apartment *(1959),* My Geisha *(1962),* The Children's Hour *(1962),* Two For the Seesaw *(1963),* Irma La Douce *(1963),* What a Way To Go *(1964),* Gambit *(1966),* Sweet Charity *(1968), and* Desperate Characters *(1971).*

In the late '60s, MacLaine was actively involved in protests against U.S. involvement in Vietnam, and campaigned vigorously for George McGovern's presidential candidacy. At the 1968 and 1972 Democratic conventions, she was an outspoken delegate.

Beginning in 1972, MacLaine was off the screen for five years, but during that period she was hardly inactive. She joined the first women's delegation to China and produced and co-directed a documentary of her visit, The Other Half of the Sky, *which was nominated for an Academy Award and was telecast by the Public Broadcasting System. She also wrote two best-selling reminiscences,* Don't Fall Off the Mountain *and* You Can Get There From Here.

Her years away from the screen also saw the emergence of MacLaine as the singing-and-dancing star of a one-woman show, touring nightclubs and theaters around the world.

In 1977, MacLaine returned to film acting with an acclaimed performance in The Turning Point. *Subsequently, she has starred with Peter Sellers in* Being There *(1979) and with James Coburn, Susan Sarandon, and Stephen Collins in* Loving Couples *(1980) and in* A Change of Seasons *(1980).*

B
- Battleground
- Battle of the Bulge
- Battlestar Galactica
- Battle Stripes
- The Bawdy Adventures of Tom Jones
- Beatlemania

(Continued)

memorable as an older woman who falls for one of the young warriors. The cast also includes Raymond Massey, Nancy Olson, and James Whitmore. **Director**—Raoul Walsh.

148 minutes

BATTLEGROUND (1949)
★★★★

Van Johnson
John Hodiak
Ricardo Montalban

This drama about a group of American infantrymen involved in the Battle of the Bulge is a cut above the routine World War II action film. Excellent characterizations, inspired acting, and a compelling script complement the exciting and suspenseful action sequences. Johnson, Hodiak, Montalban, and James Whitmore are fine in memorable roles. William Wellman's efficient direction hits the mark. **Academy Award**—Robert Pirosh, writing (story and screenplay). **Nomination**—Wellman, best director.

118 minutes b&w

BATTLE OF THE BULGE (1965)
★★

Henry Fonda
Robert Shaw
Robert Ryan
Dana Andrews
George Montgomery

An overblown World War II action drama concerning the bloody and anx-

Jane Seymour and son flee from an outer-space gambling den in Battlestar Galactica.

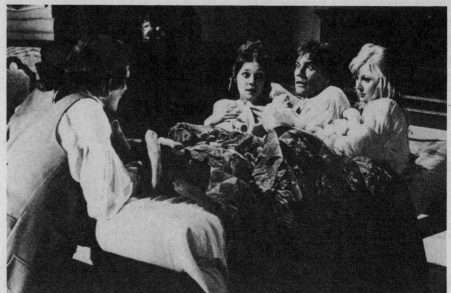
Nicky Henson is discovered with two servant girls in The Bawdy Adventures of Tom Jones.

ious confrontation with Nazi Panzers in the Ardennes, with Allied troops narrowly escaping defeat. Emphasis is on the action and the booming battle scenes. Script, acting, and character development take a back seat. The cast also includes Pier Angeli, Telly Savalas, Ty Hardin, Charles Bronson, and James MacArthur. **Director**—Ken Annakin.

167 minutes

BATTLESTAR GALACTICA
(1979)
★★

Richard Hatch
Dirk Benedict
Lorne Greene

This feature film is based on the short-lived TV sci-fi series that wasn't so hot to begin with. There's really not much improvement in this venture. Survivors of interplanetary warfare embark on a space journey to Earth to establish a new life there. Lavish special effects are notable, but the ragged story holds scant interest. The *Star Wars* format is mimicked right and left, but not its imagination and mysticism. Also with Ray Milland, Lew Ayres, Jane Seymour, and Laurette Spang. **Director**—Richard A. Colla. (PG)

125 minutes

BATTLE STRIPES
See The Men

THE BAWDY ADVENTURES OF
TOM JONES (1976)
★★★

Nicky Henson
Trevor Howard
Terry-Thomas

A British costume musical loosely based on Henry Fielding's novel. It's far removed in quality from the memorable *Tom Jones* film in 1963. Yet this current version is an inoffensive and pleasant romp. The standard "bawdy" antics are portrayed: low necklines, hiked skirts, leaps in and out of occupied beds. Cast also includes Arthur Lowe, Georgia Brown, and Joan Collins. Director Cliff Owen keeps the action going at a fast clip. (R)

94 minutes

BEATLEMANIA (1981)
★★

Since the Beatles disbanded, four look-and-sound-alikes have been performing Beatles songs in live stage performances. And now, this production is on film along with news clips of protest marches, personalities, and trends of the 1960s. The imitators play the famous rock music with professionalism, but it's still far afield from the magic of the originals. Perhaps it

- Beau Brummell
- The Beautiful Blonde From Bashful Bend
- Because You're Mine
- Becket
- The Bedford Incident
- Bedknobs and Broomsticks
- Bedlam
- Bedtime for Bonzo

B

would be more entertaining to recall film segments of the real Paul, John, George, and Ringo at the peak of their careers. (PG) **Director**—Joseph Manduke. *86 minutes*

BEAU BRUMMELL (1954)
★★

Stewart Granger
Elizabeth Taylor
Peter Ustinov
Robert Morley

Granger plays a foppish and colorful Englishman who befriends the Prince of Wales, played by Ustinov. This historical production is lavish and exquisitely photographed, but the stilted story is hard to believe. Regardless, the cast—including Taylor, at the height of her beauty—does an admirable job in the costume epic. Morley plays George III. **Director**—Curtis Bernhardt. *111 minutes*

THE BEAUTIFUL BLONDE FROM BASHFUL BEND (1949)
★★

Betty Grable
Cesar Romero

Preston Sturges made this tongue-in-cheek western about a tough saloon singer, played by Grable, who becomes a schoolteacher in a small town after she mistakenly shoots a sheriff. Nothing bashful about Grable, who seems right for the role, but Sturges doesn't execute the direction with a firm hand, and the film turns out to be rather silly. Hugh Herbert is funny as a doctor with eye problems. Rudy Vallee and Sterling Holloway are also in the cast. *77 minutes*

BECAUSE YOU'RE MINE (1952)
★

Mario Lanza

If you happen to like Lanza's singing, there's some entertainment value here. Otherwise, it's just a lackluster film with Lanza as an opera singer in the Army who courts his sergeant's sister. Mario sings a few numbers with gusto, but between the songs, there's just a lot of dead air. Doretta Morrow, James Whitmore, and Spring Byington

are in supporting roles. **Director**—Alexander Hall. *103 minutes*

BECKET (1964)
★★★

Richard Burton
Peter O'Toole
John Gielgud

Richard Burton, as Thomas à Becket, and Peter O'Toole, as King Henry II, star in Becket.

Sumptuous medieval spectacle that's rich with historical drama about the Archbishop of Canterbury Thomas à Becket and his relationship with King Henry II. Burton and O'Toole are superb in the key roles and seem to thoroughly enjoy their acting assignments. Some of the energy, however, is drained away by a too-long and, at times, tedious script. The film is based rather faithfully on Jean Anouilh's stage play. Fine supporting performances are given by Gielgud, Donald Wolfit, and Pamela Brown. **Director**—Peter Glenville. **Academy Award**—Edward Anhalt, best screenplay (based on material from another medium); **Nominations**—best picture; Glenville, best director; Burton, best actor; O'Toole; best actor; Gielgud, best supporting actor. *149 minutes*

THE BEDFORD INCIDENT (1965)
★★★

Richard Widmark
Sidney Poitier

A suspenseful Cold War drama about a gung ho skipper of an American destroyer, played by Widmark, who accidentally fires an atomic weapon while stalking a Soviet submarine in the North Atlantic. Widmark's portrayal of the obsessed naval officer is

superb. There's excellent acting, too, from Poitier, who plays a reporter on board; James MacArthur; and Martin Balsam. Tension swirls on board ship in the manner of *The Caine Mutiny*. There's some reference to *Dr. Strangelove*. **Director**—James B. Harris. *102 minutes b&w*

BEDKNOBS AND BROOMSTICKS (1971)
★★

Angela Lansbury

Below-par Walt Disney musical about a good-natured witch, played by Lansbury, and some children who help the British war effort in the early 1940s. The film seems disorganized, despite the elaborate production. It's rather pale compared with the popular *Mary Poppins*, which it tries to imitate. Special effects and some of the cartoon sequences are handled well. It also stars David Tomlinson, Sam Jaffe, and Roddy McDowall. **Director**—Robert Stevenson. (G) **Academy Award**—Special visual effects. *117 minutes*

BEDLAM (1946)
★★★

Boris Karloff

Excellent atmospheric effects enhance this chilling Val Lewton horror story about the infamous London insane asylum that flourished in the 18th century. Anna Lee plays a sane woman who is confined in an effort to expose the miserable conditions. The venerable Karloff is the head of the institution. Also with Billy House, Richard Fraser, and Ian Wolfe. **Director**—Mark Robson. *79 minutes b&w*

BEDTIME FOR BONZO (1951)
★★

Ronald Reagan

Nonsensical comedy with Ronald Reagan as a professor rearing a chimpanzee to prove that environment affects personality. The silly monkeyshines seem to have an appeal for grownups as well as kids. The film did well enough to spawn the sequel, *Bonzo Goes to College*. It should have

(Continued)

B
- The Beguiled
- Behold a Pale Horse
- Being There
- Bell, Book and Candle

(Continued)

some added interest since Reagan became President. Diana Lynn and Walter Slezak co-star. **Director—** Fredrick de Cordova.

83 minutes b&w

Ronald Reagan hugs the chimp in Bedtime for Bonzo; *his other co-star is Diana Lynn.*

THE BEGUILED (1971)
★★

**Clint Eastwood
Geraldine Page
Elizabeth Hartman**

Eastwood stars in this odd Civil War drama about a wounded Union soldier who is brought to a Confederate girls' school where he's to receive nursing care. Eastwood's presence sparks trouble among the sexually starved women. A strong finish with some brutal scenes along the way. Jo Ann Harris and Darleen Carr co-star. **Director—**Don Siegel. (R)

109 minutes

BEHOLD A PALE HORSE (1964)
★

**Gregory Peck
Omar Sharif
Anthony Quinn**

Peck stars in this slow-paced drama about a Spanish renegade who goes into hiding and then returns to trap and kill a sadistic police chief. The film seems to have some class about it, but it eventually loses its way in a web of talky dialogue. Peck and others try their best but can't save the film. Behold a pale movie. **Director—**Fred Zinnemann. *121 minutes b&w*

BEING THERE (1979)
★★★

**Peter Sellers
Shirley MacLaine
Melvyn Douglas**

A droll comic fable about an innocent simpleton, played by Sellers, who is suddenly thrust into the world of wealth and power politics. Sellers sets aside his familiar slapstick style, plays it rather straight-faced, and achieves a remarkably inspired funny performance. It's an insightful and intelligent adaptation of Jerzy Kosinski's novel. Hal Ashby's direction is to the point.

Peter Sellers and Shirley MacLaine star in Being There, *based on Jerzy Kosinski's novel.*

But the film is far too long, and it finally overworks its wisdom-of-innocence theme. (PG) **Academy Award—**Douglas, best supporting actor. **Nomination—**Sellers, best actor. *130 minutes*

BELL, BOOK AND CANDLE
(1958)
★★

**James Stewart
Kim Novak
Jack Lemmon**

Screen version of John Van Druten's play ends up as a routine comedy with Novak miscast as a witch who falls in love with a book publisher, played by Stewart. However, the top cast manages to squeeze some engaging moments from the sentimental mate-

---

DAVID NIVEN

David Niven, who was born in Kirriemuir, Scotland, in 1910, once planned on a career as a professional soldier. He attended the military academy at Sandhurst and served for several years in the Highland Light Infantry in Scotland, but eventually decided that a military career wasn't for him.

Niven then spent a number of years in the United States and Canada, as a lumberjack, a construction worker, a journalist, and finally as a movie extra in Hollywood, where he began his long film career that has spanned nearly five decades.

In 1935, Niven appeared in Barbary Coast. *Some other films he made in these early years include* Thank You, Jeeves *(1936),* Dodsworth *(1936),* The Prisoner of Zenda *(1937),* Bachelor Mother *(1939), and* Raffles *(1940).*

In 1940, Niven returned to Britain and enlisted. During World War II, he served as a second lieutenant with the Rifle Brigade, rose to the rank of major in the Commandos, and became a colonel assigned to special duty with the British Liberation Army, eventually taking part in the invasion of Normandy.

After the war, Niven resumed his movie career. Some of the other films he starred in include The Way Ahead *(1944),* Carrington V.C. *(1955),* Around the World in Eighty Days *(1956),* Separate Tables *(1958),* The Pink Panther *(1964),* The Brain *(1969),* King Queen Knave *(1972),* Murder By Death *(1976),* No Deposit, No Return *(1976), and* Candleshoe *(1977).*

In 1958, he received an Oscar as best actor for his performance in Separate Tables.

Niven has written two autobiographical books, The Moon's a Balloon *and* Bring On the Empty Horses, *and a novel,* Go Slowly, Come Back Quickly.

- The Bellboy
- A Bell for Adano
- The Bell Jar
- The Belle of New York
- Bells Are Ringing
- The Bells of St. Mary's
- Beloved Infidel

B

rial. Ernie Kovacs, Hermione Gingold, and Elsa Lanchester contribute their fine talents. **Director**—Richard Quine.
103 minutes

THE BELLBOY (1960)
★★

Jerry Lewis

Typical Lewis shenanigans with the comedian causing a ruckus at a swank Miami Beach hotel. There's no plot to speak of; just a series of blackout sketches with the usual line of gags. Worthwhile for those who appreciate Lewis; otherwise, it's so much silliness. There are cameos from Milton Berle and Walter Winchell. Alex Gerry and Bob Clayton co-star. **Director**—Lewis.
72 minutes b&w

A BELL FOR ADANO (1945)
★★★

John Hodiak
Gene Tierney

Charming and moving film, based on the John Hersey novel, about American occupation soldiers who earn the respect of citizens in a small Italian town by replacing the local bell. Director Henry King creates a pleasant mood and presents warm characterizations. Hodiak is fine as the American officer in charge of the town. Tierney plays the local female attraction. William Bendix, Richard Conte, and Henry Morgan also star.
103 minutes b&w

THE BELL JAR (1979)
★★

Marilyn Hassett
Julie Harris

The film is based on the haunting novel by Sylvia Plath, the extraordinary poet who committed suicide at 30. The screenplay faithfully follows the events of the book, but the movie fails to explore the mystery and the stress that led to the heroine's nervous breakdown. Drama and clarity are badly needed in place of the stifling flatness of Larry Peerce's direction. Anne Jackson, Barbara Barrie, and Robert Klein also star. (R)
107 minutes

In a scene from The Bell Jar, *Sylvia Plath (Marilyn Hassett) visits her father's gravesite.*

THE BELLE OF NEW YORK
(1952)
★★

Fred Astaire
Vera-Ellen

Astaire dances on the ceiling, and that seems to be the high point in this so-so musical set in New York City during the Gay Nineties. The middling plot has Fred as a playboy who flips for a Salvation Army girl, played by Vera-Ellen. There are some comic moments along with the dancing. "Let a Little Love Come In" is included among the songs. Marjorie Main, Keenan Wynn, and Alice Pearce are also in the cast. **Director**—Charles Walters.
82 minutes

BELLS ARE RINGING (1960)
★★★

Judy Holliday
Dean Martin

Holliday is at her best in this adaptation of the Broadway musical. She plays an answering service operator who listens in on conversations and can't help getting emotionally involved with clients' problems. Martin portrays an anxious playwright who becomes the object of Holliday's affections. Songs by Jule Styne include "Just in Time" and "The Party's Over." Cast includes Fred Clark, Eddie Foy, Jr., and Jean Stapleton. This was Holliday's last film. **Director**—Vincente Minnelli. *126 minutes*

THE BELLS OF ST. MARY'S
(1945)
★★★

Bing Crosby
Ingrid Bergman

Crosby and Bergman star in this worthy follow-up to *Going My Way*. Bing is a priest at a Catholic school, and Ingrid is a nun there. The two launch a clever strategy to raise money for a school addition. It's highly entertaining in a sentimental way, with the leads in top form. There's support from Henry Travers, William Gargan, and Ruth Donnelly. **Director**—Leo McCarey. **Academy Award Nominations**—best picture; McCarey, best director; Crosby, best actor; Bergman, best actress. *126 minutes b&w*

BELOVED INFIDEL (1959)
★★

Gregory Peck
Deborah Kerr

In Beloved Infidel, *Gregory Peck and Deborah Kerr portray F. Scott Fitzgerald and Sheilah Graham.*

True story of F. Scott Fitzgerald's turbulent romance with Hollywood columnist Sheilah Graham lapses into soap opera sentimentality. Peck is miscast as the famous novelist. Kerr fares better as Graham, who tries to cure Fitzgerald of alcoholism. The film mainly covers Fitzgerald's days in Hollywood in the late 1930s. It may satisfy someone looking for a good cry. Also with Eddie Albert and Philip Ober. **Director**—Henry King.
123 minutes

B • Beneath the Twelve Mile Reef
• Beneath the Valley of the Ultravixens
• Ben Hur
• Benji
• The Benny Goodman Story
• Best Boy
• The Best Man
• The Best Things in Life Are Free

BENEATH THE TWELVE MILE REEF (1953)
★★

Robert Wagner
Terry Moore

Wagner and Moore are involved with sponge divers off the Florida coast. The melodramatic plot offers a Romeo-and-Juliet romance and rivalries among the Greek businessmen who abide by their own set of rules. Spectacular scenery and breathtaking underwater photography upstage the acting; a menacing octopus harasses the divers. Gilbert Roland, Peter Graves, J. Carrol Naish, and Richard Boone co-star. **Director**—Robert D. Webb. *102 minutes*

BENEATH THE VALLEY OF THE ULTRAVIXENS (1979)
★★

Francesca Natividad
Ann Marie
Ken Kerr

Director Russ Meyer comes on strong once more with his particular brand of satirical soft-core pornography. As with many of his other film ventures, the story is meager and the women are of mammoth proportions. This frantic farce involves sexual escapades in a small town. Meyer fans won't be let down. (No MPAA rating) *93 minutes*

BEN HUR (1959)
★★★

Charlton Heston
Haya Harareet
Jack Hawkins

A spectacular and lavish rendition of Lew Wallace's historical novel about an aristocratic Jew, played by Heston, who is persecuted by the Romans and eventually follows Christ. Heston as Ben Hur is superb in the title role, and the film offers spectacular action sequences and magnificent cinematography. The tone, however, reverts to that of a good guy-bad guy western at times. A high point is the chariot race, with Ben Hur competing against a villain, played convincingly by Stephen Boyd. The outcome is predictable. Other cast members include Hugh Griffith, Martha Scott, and Sam Jaffe. **Directors**—William Wyler and Andrew Marton. **Academy Awards**—best picture; Wyler, best director; Heston, best actor; Griffith, best supporting actor; cinematography (color). **Academy Award Nomination**—Karl Tunberg, best screenplay (based on material from another medium).
217 minutes

BENJI (1974)
★★★

Higgins (the dog)
Peter Breck
Edgar Buchanan

Young children should enjoy this film about a dog who saves two children from kidnappers and winds up as a member of their family. An improbable story, but lovable animal characterization. Also with Terry Carter and Christopher Connelly. **Director**—Joe Camp. (G) *89 minutes*

THE BENNY GOODMAN STORY (1955)
★★

Steve Allen
Donna Reed

Allen portrays the famous clarinetist in this sentimental biography that's typical of Hollywood productions. The story traces Goodman's life from his upbringing in Chicago to celebrity status in the world of swing music. Allen is fairly convincing in the title role. And the film is enhanced significantly by the clarinet playing of the real Goodman and guest appearances by big band luminaries Gene Krupa and Harry James. Sammy Davis, Sr., and Martha Tilton lend support. **Director**—Valentine Davies.
117 minutes

BEST BOY (1980)
★★★★

This is a documentary film about Philly Wohl, a 52-year-old mentally retarded man who progresses toward self-reliance. But don't be put off by the subject. It's a thrilling, uplifting, intelligent story about love, devotion, and the texture of family life. The style of director Ira Wohl—Philly's cousin—is direct and unembellished without being sentimental. Undoubtedly, this is one of the most extraordinary documentaries ever made. (No MPAA rating) **Academy Award**—Ira Wohl, feature documentary. *110 minutes*

THE BEST MAN (1964)
★★★★

Henry Fonda
Cliff Robertson
Lee Tracy

High drama on the campaign trail as two presidential aspirants vie for nomination and seek the blessing of the dying ex-president. Rivals Fonda and Robertson are in top form in this engrossing film version of Gore Vidal's topical play, which gives a perceptive view of the political process. Tracy stands out as the dying former chief executive. Margaret Leighton, Edie Adams, Shelley Berman, Ann Sothern, Richard Arlen, and Mahalia Jackson are in supporting roles. **Director**—Franklin Schaffner. **Academy Award Nomination**—Tracy, best supporting actor. *102 minutes b&w*

THE BEST THINGS IN LIFE ARE FREE (1956)
★★

Ernest Borgnine
Gordon MacRae
Dan Dailey
Sheree North

The careers of songwriters DeSylva, Brown, and Henderson, who flourished in the 1920s, are the basis for this routine Hollywood musical. MacRae, Dailey, and Borgnine portray the Tin Pan Alley trio responsible for such hits as "Good News," "Sonny Boy," and "Birth of the Blues." As to be expected, there's not much plot but the music is enjoyable. Norman Brooks and Murvyn Vye are also in the cast. **Director**—Michael Curtiz.
103 minutes

● The Best Way
● The Best Years of Our Lives
● Betrayed

● The Betsy
● Between the Lines
● Beyond and Back
● Beyond the Forest

B

Myrna Loy, Fredric March, and Teresa Wright in The Best Years of Our Lives.

THE BEST WAY (1978)
★★★

Patrick Dewaere
Patrick Bouchitey

Claude Miller, frequently an assistant to François Truffaut, makes his directorial debut with this small, earnest French film. The drama, which concerns the conflicts between two counselors in a boy's summer camp, is seen as a microcosm of contemporary society. There are skillful performances by Bouchitey and Dewaere, and Miller handles this subject with conviction. In French with English titles. (No MPAA rating)   *85 minutes*

THE BEST YEARS OF OUR LIVES (1946)
★★★★

Fredric March
Myrna Loy
Teresa Wright
Dana Andrews

A powerful, provocative film about three GIs who return from World War II to a small American town and face difficulties adjusting to civilian life. Filmmaking quality prevails throughout with superior acting, no-nonsense direction, and perfect pacing. There are many touching moments—some amusing, some sad—that capture the mood of post-World War II America. Harold Russell, Virginia Mayo, Cathy O'Donnell, Hoagy Carmichael, Gladys George, and Ray Collins also star. **Director**—William Wyler. **Academy Awards**—best picture; Wyler, best director; March, best actor; Russell, best supporting actor; Robert E. Sherwood, writing (screenplay).
172 minutes b&w

BETRAYED (1954)
★★

Clark Gable
Victor Mature
Lana Turner

Plodding and trumped-up spy yarn about a Dutch intelligence man who discovers that a trusted underground fighter is a turncoat. However, a top-notch cast occasionally spices up the melodramatics. Gable and Mature supply the macho images while Turner provides the glamour. Also with Louis Calhern, Wilfrid Hyde White, and Ian Carmichael. **Director**—Gottfried Reinhardt.   *108 minutes*

THE BETSY (1978)
★★

Laurence Olivier
Robert Duvall
Katharine Ross
Tommy Lee Jones

This melodramatic saga of intrigue, sex, and power among the upper crust of the auto industry is like a '60 Cadillac—plush, but too much flash and too hard to handle. The classy cast, which also includes Jane Alexander and Lesley-Anne Down, turns out some neat performances. The unwieldy story line, based on the Harold Robbins novel, is a problem with too many twists and a lot of frivolous gloss. The dialogue is loaded with howlers. **Director**—Daniel Petrie. (R)
125 minutes

BETWEEN THE LINES (1977)
★

John Heard
Jill Eikenberry

Joan Micklin Silver, who did rather well directing *Hester Street*, disappoints with this shallow film about a successful underground Boston newspaper soon to be taken over by an establishment publisher. The story idea is interesting and inspired, but the loose script rambles with scant impact, and the characters seem lifeless. It's hard to believe these de-radicalized youths were once energetic and maverick journalists. Hopefully the earnest, fresh-faced young actors here may be destined for more important assignments and stardom. Also with Lewis Stadlen and Jeff Goldblum. (R)   *101 minutes*

BEYOND AND BACK (1978)
(no stars)

This is more hocus-pocus from the same producers who brought us *In Search of Noah's Ark*. This time it's a pseudo-scientific examination of life after death. There's even a glimpse of what a soul should look like! The acting, script, and direction are second-rate. The film seems mostly concerned with trying to prove that P. T. Barnum was right. Brad Crandall narrates. **Director**—James L. Conway. (G)
93 minutes

BEYOND THE FOREST (1949)
★

Bette Davis
Joseph Cotten

An absurd, hysterical murder mystery with Davis overacting and adding to the muddle of the screenplay. Davis, who plays the wife of a small-town doctor, has an affair with her wealthy neighbor, bungles a suicide attempt after murdering a witness, and then dies of a disease. The rest of the cast
(Continued)

B
● Beyond the Poseidon
Adventure
● Beyond the Reef

● Beyond the Valley of the
Dolls
● Bhowani Junction

● The Big Brawl
● The Big Bus
● The Big Carnival

(Continued)
also is regrettably lost in the woods. Cotten plays the doctor; David Brian is the neighbor. Ruth Roman, Minor Watson, and Dona Drake also star. **Director**—King Vidor. *96 minutes b&w*

BEYOND THE POSEIDON ADVENTURE (1979)
★

Michael Caine
Sally Field
Telly Savalas
Peter Boyle

Irwin Allen takes us back to the overturned S.S. *Poseidon* for Chapter II of this disaster story. Here we find an all-star cast rummaging around the dark upside-down innards of the stricken ocean liner looking for loot, dodging bullets, and mumbling idiotic dialogue. Caine, Field, Savalas, and other familiar performers have their acting reputations soaked to the skin. The audience may want to escape long before the players make it to the surface. Also with Jack Warden, Shirley Knight, Slim Pickens, Shirley Jones, and Karl Malden; what will they do? **Director**—Allen. (PG) *122 minutes*

BEYOND THE REEF (1981)
★★

Dayton Ká ne
Maren Jensen

Raffaella DeLaurentiis (Dino's daughter) produced this innocent boy-and-

his-shark movie using some of the scenic locations involved with *Hurricane*. Ká ne, the male star of *Hurricane*, plays a native lad who woos a beautiful native girl, played by Jensen, and raises a 16-foot tiger shark who knows enough to attack only the bad guys. The acting and script are limited, but the underwater photography is dazzling. **Director**—Frank C. Clark. (PG)   *91 minutes*

BEYOND THE VALLEY OF THE DOLLS (1970)
★

Dolly Read
Cynthia Myers
Marcia McBroom

Russ Meyer, the majordomo of soft-core pornography, serves up some exploitation fare with a bevy of young girls chosen more for their dimensions than their acting talents. The plot concerns an all-girl rock band trying to make it big in Hollywood. But this is merely incidental to the parade of bodies. You may find a laugh or two amid the frenzy. The film has no connection with Jacqueline Susann's novel. Also with Edy Williams. **Director**—Meyer. (X)   *109 minutes*

BHOWANI JUNCTION (1955)
★★★

Ava Gardner
Stewart Granger

A fairly faithful rendering of John Masters's novel about a beautiful Anglo-Indian girl involved in romance and intrigue during the waning days of British rule in India. Gardner is convincing as the half-caste beauty who is torn between her love for an Englishman, played by Granger, and loyalty to her family. Impressive photography of the Pakistani locations enhance the drama. Bill Travers and Francis Matthews also star. **Director**—George Cukor.   *110 minutes*

THE BIG BRAWL (1980)
★★★

Jackie Chan

This martial-arts film is a step above the usual; it has a blend of humor, a decent script, and well-executed kung fu action. Chan, in his first American movie, plays the son of a Chicago restaurateur who subdues some local gangster bullies and then wins a free-for-all in Texas. The spunky and charming Chan trains hard for the big contest and finally wins the day in a flurry of kicks and chops against men three times his size. It's sort of the *Rocky* of chop-socky. **Director**—Robert Clouse. (R)   *95 minutes*

THE BIG BUS (1976)
★

Joseph Bologna
Stockard Channing

This film is about a nuclear-powered bus that is a cross between a 747 jetliner and the *Queen Elizabeth* II. It's also a put-on of Hollywood disaster movies overstuffed with nonstop corny gags. A lot of frantic-looking passengers and crew members act silly as the bus makes its maiden express trip from New York to Denver. Most of the audience may want to get off somewhere east of the Mississippi. Also with John Beck, Ned Beatty, José Ferrer, Larry Hagman, Sally Kellerman, Richard Mulligan, and Lynn Redgrave. **Director**—James Frawley. (PG)   *85 minutes*

THE BIG CARNIVAL
See Ace in the Hole

Stewart Granger—with clipboard—meets Ava Gardner in Bhowani Junction.

- The Big Clock
- The Big Country
- The Big Fix
- The Big Land
- Big Red
- The Big Red One
- The Big Shot

B

THE BIG CLOCK (1947)
★★★

**Ray Milland
Charles Laughton**

A ruthless pulp magazine publisher, played by Laughton, murders his mistress, and his top crime reporter, Milland, is assigned to solve the case. It's a suspenseful drama with ace talent. Laughton isn't quite up to par, while Milland is convincing as the writer with a sticky task on hand. Maureen O'Sullivan, Rita Johnson, and Elsa Lanchester round out the cast. **Director**—John Farrow.   *95 minutes b&w*

THE BIG COUNTRY (1958)
★★★

**Gregory Peck
Jean Simmons
Charlton Heston**

Director William Wyler's overblown but entertaining spectacle western features a lively cast at top form. Peck plays a sailor who returns to settle down on the land and winds up in the middle of a bitter feud over water rights. Heston stands out as a mean-spirited cattle foreman, and Burl Ives is impeccably cast as a gruff patriarch of one of the feuding families. There are subtle references to the Cold War. Carroll Baker, Charles Bickford, and Chuck Connors have supporting roles. **Academy Award**—Ives, best supporting actor.   *166 minutes*

THE BIG FIX (1978)
★★★

**Richard Dreyfuss
Susan Anspach**

Dreyfuss is perfectly cast as a small-time, contemporary gumshoe with a background in 1960s radical politics in this engaging comedy-thriller. The film takes an interesting and intelligent look at the tumultuous decade. The plot, unfortunately, is so complex you may need the services of a detective to figure it out. Dreyfuss's performance is more subdued than usual, and his unorthodox private-eye character is memorable. There's fine support from Anspach, Bonnie Bedelia, John Lithgow, and F. Murray Abraham. **Director**—Jeremy Paul Kagan. (PG)   *108 minutes*

THE BIG LAND (1957)
★★

**Alan Ladd
Virginia Mayo
Edmond O'Brien**

Cattlemen and wheat farmers join to promote the building of a rail link to Texas. It's a somewhat ho-hum western with a few good production values. The cast, headed by Ladd, Mayo, and O'Brien, performs well enough despite the hackneyed material. The film is based on the novel *Buffalo Grass* by Frank Gruber. **Director**—Gordon Douglas.   *92 minutes*

Edmond O'Brien and Alan Ladd in The Big Land, *about building a rail link to Texas.*

BIG RED (1962)
★★

**Walter Pidgeon
Gilles Payant**

Run-of-the-mill boy-and-dog story from the Disney studios that borrows somewhat from the "Lassie, Come Home" episodes. Payant is the lad who becomes attached to an Irish setter owned by a wealthy man, played by Pidgeon. The dog eventually saves the boy from an attacking mountain lion. Nice diversion for the kids; nothing special for adults. The film was photographed in the magnificent outdoors of Quebec. **Director**—Norman Tokar.   *89 minutes*

THE BIG RED ONE (1980)
★★

**Lee Marvin
Mark Hamill**

In The Big Red One, *Lee Marvin plays a sergeant who leads an infantry squad.*

Samuel Fuller's intimate story of soldiers who fought with the First Infantry Division in World War II comes off as a glossed-over tour of famous battlefields. Marvin leads an infantry squad, which includes Hamill and Robert Carradine, from the North African deserts to Czechoslovakia. Part of the problem is the casting of Marvin, who looks like the oldest sergeant in the Army and hardly the type to lead young soldiers into battle. If you are expecting something on the order of *Battleground* or *Sands of Iwo Jima*, forget it. **Director**—Fuller. (PG)   *113 minutes*

THE BIG SHOT (1942)
★★

**Humphrey Bogart
Irene Manning**

Bogart plays his familiar role as a hardened criminal who is framed for a robbery and then breaks out of the big house. Bogey's tough-guy character comes over well, but the routine plot is B-movie fare. Also with Susan Peters, Richard Travis, Donald Crisp, Arthur Kennedy, and Howard da Silva in supporting roles. **Director**—Lewis Seiler.   *82 minutes b&w*

B
- The Big Sky
- The Big Sleep (1946)
- The Big Sleep (1978)
- Big Wednesday
- Billy Budd
- Billy Jack
- The Bingo Long Traveling All-Stars and Motor Kings

THE BIG SKY (1952)
★★★

Kirk Douglas
Arthur Hunnicutt
Elizabeth Threatt

Douglas is a Kentucky fur trapper who leads an expedition to establish a trading post on the Missouri River in 1830. All sorts of trouble ensues along the way as the party encounters Indians. The cast performs well, but the overloaded melodrama lapses after a while. The film is faithfully adapted from an historical novel by A. B. Guthrie, Jr. Dewey Martin and Buddy Baer also star. **Director**—Howard Hawks.
122 minutes b&w

THE BIG SLEEP (1946)
★★★

Humphrey Bogart
Lauren Bacall

Bogart and Bacall make the sparks fly in this saucy private-eye drama based on Raymond Chandler's novel. The plot is complex, but Bogey and Baby make things click with crisp acting, spicy dialogue, and generous doses of suspense and excitement. Bogart is gumshoe Philip Marlowe, who's hired to keep tabs on the freewheeling daughter of a wealthy man. Before long, he's confronted with several mysterious murders. Lots of smoky

Humphrey Bogart and Lauren Bacall in The Big Sleep, *based on Raymond Chandler's novel.*

atmosphere along the way. Also with Dorothy Malone, Martha Vickers, Regis Toomey, and Elisha Cook, Jr. **Director**—Howard Hawks.
114 minutes b&w

THE BIG SLEEP (1978)
★★

Robert Mitchum
Sarah Miles

This lukewarm remake of Raymond Chandler's classic gumshoe adventure, which originally starred Bogart and Bacall, is transplanted to contemporary London, where it loses its effective smoky atmosphere of Los Angeles in the '40s. This time Mitchum is private-eye Philip Marlowe, but he's no match for Bogart. Miles, who co-stars, is no Lauren Bacall either. The Bogey version of this caper remains the undisputed legend. Also stars Candy Clark, Richard Boone, James Stewart, John Mills, and Joan Collins. **Director**—Michael Winner. (R)
100 minutes

BIG WEDNESDAY (1978)
★

Jan-Michael Vincent
William Katt
Gary Busey

John Milius's ambitious tribute to surfing turned out all wet. The limp script follows the lives of three California surfing pals from 1962 to 1974. Vincent, Katt, and Busey—all capable performers—play the beach buddy roles with unusual stiffness. The tone throughout is one of muddled and uneventful seriousness. Also with Lee Purcell, Patti D'Arbanville, and Barbara Hale. **Director**—Milius. (PG)
120 minutes

BILLY BUDD (1962)
★★★

Peter Ustinov
Robert Ryan
Terence Stamp
Melvyn Douglas

Ustinov directed and stars in this handsome film version of the Herman Melville classic allegory of good and evil, set in the 18th century. Young

Billy goes to sea aboard a British man-of-war, where he kills a cruel officer and then faces execution for the deed. Ustinov stands out as a sympathetic captain, and Ryan is excellent as the evil master at arms. The screenplay, however, is somewhat dull. Also with Paul Rogers, David McCallum, and John Neville. **Academy Award Nomination**—Stamp, best supporting actor.
125 minutes b&w

BILLY JACK (1971)
★★★

Tom Laughlin
Delores Taylor

Laughlin plays the title role in this stylish and uplifting drama, which glorifies the counterculture of the '60s and '70s. He's effective as the half-breed Indian who fought in Vietnam and has returned to Arizona as a free-spirit champion of wildlife. Conflicts develop when local bigots interfere with his causes. Taylor, Laughlin's real-life wife, is excellent as principal of a "freedom school." Also with Bert Freed, Clark Howat, and Julie Webb. Laughlin directed under the pseudonym T. C. Frank. (PG)
113 minutes

Tom Laughlin plays the title role in Billy Jack, *a champion of wildlife and the underdog.*

THE BINGO LONG TRAVELING ALL-STARS AND MOTOR KINGS (1976)
★★★★

Billy Dee Williams
James Earl Jones
Richard Pryor

A high-spirited and highly entertaining comedy about a renegade black baseball team that barnstorms through

● Birch Interval
● Birdman of Alcatraz
● Bird of Paradise
● The Birds
● The Birth of the Blues
● Bite the Bullet

B

mid-America in 1939, when black ballplayers were barred from the white-controlled leagues. The film also has its dramatic and touching moments. The almost-all-black cast is superb. It's headed by Williams and Jones, who play a pair of razzle-dazzle ballplayers. However, character development is weak in some cases. There is a clear portrayal of how the All-Stars must resort to clowning as a means of survival in those pre-Jackie Robinson days. **Director**—John Badham. (PG)
110 minutes

BIRCH INTERVAL (1976)
★

Eddie Albert
Rip Torn
Ann Wedgeworth
Susan McClung

Pennsylvania's Amish country in 1947 is the backdrop of this fragile and understated story of troubled family life. The story focuses on a young girl sent to stay with her mother's family, who observes the painful disintegration of their relationships. The low-key and thin plot soon becomes monotonous. **Director**—Delbert Mann. (PG)
104 minutes

BIRDMAN OF ALCATRAZ (1962)
★★★★

Burt Lancaster
Karl Malden
Thelma Ritter
Edmond O'Brien

Lancaster is at his best in the title role of this engrossing biography of Robert Stroud, the celebrated convict who became a world authority on birds. Lancaster's measured delivery and John Frankenheimer's efficient direction perfectly illuminate Stroud's perplexing personality. The film also expertly explores the harshness and monotony of prison life. Malden stands out as the warden. Also with Telly Savalas, Betty Field, Neville Brand, and Hugh Marlowe. **Academy Award Nominations**—Lancaster, best actor; Savalas, best supporting actor; Ritter, best supporting actress; Burnett Guffey, cinematography (black and white).
148 minutes b&w

BIRD OF PARADISE (1951)
★★

Louis Jourdan
Jeff Chandler
Debra Paget

A standard South Sea Island tale about a European man who marries a beautiful native girl. The wedding angers the gods, so a virgin (what else?) is sacrificed to quiet an exploding volcano. The film, a remake of a 1932 version, is a bit pompous in tone, yet the exotic and romantic atmosphere remains intact. Jourdan, Chandler, and Paget do an adequate job in the key roles. Also with Maurice Schwartz, Everett Sloane, and Jack Elam. **Director**—Delmar Daves.
100 minutes

THE BIRDS (1963)
★★★

Rod Taylor
Tippi Hedren
Suzanne Pleshette
Jessica Tandy

Director Alfred Hitchcock, the wizard of suspense, digs into his bag of tricks for this gripping thriller about a small California coastal town that comes under attack by thousands of birds. Taylor, Hedren, and Pleshette are adequate in the principal roles, but they fade into the background when upstaged by the onslaught of special effects and offbeat shock tactics de-vised by the master. The incidental plot is merely a vehicle. *119 minutes*

THE BIRTH OF THE BLUES (1941)
★★★

Bing Crosby
Brian Donlevy

Crosby stars as a trumpet player who establishes a jazz band in New Orleans. The rather trivial plot is upheld by plenty of good jazz music, which makes the film worthwhile. Some of the classic tunes include "St. Louis Blues," "St. James Infirmary," and "Melancholy Baby." Bing gets support from Donlevy, Carolyn Lee, Eddie (Rochester) Anderson, Mary Martin, and jazz great Jack Teagarden. **Director**—Victor Schertzinger.
85 minutes b&w

BITE THE BULLET (1975)
★★

Gene Hackman
Candice Bergen
James Coburn

Who will win the 700-mile horse race through desert and other treacherous terrain of the Southwest? There's plenty of breathtaking scenery, but the story is loaded with platitudes and clichés. Also with Ben Johnson, Ian Bannen, Jan-Michael Vincent, and Paul Stewart. **Director**—Richard Brooks. (PG)
131 minutes

Rod Taylor and Tippi Hedren are among those who come under aerial attack in The Birds.

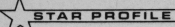
B
- Bittersweet Love
- Black and White in Color
- Blackbeard's Ghost
- Blackbeard the Pirate
- The Black Bird

CLARK GABLE

Clark Gable was affectionately known by his fans and in Hollywood as "The King," primarily because of his popularity as a rugged and attractive leading man for nearly 30 years.

He was born William Clark Gable in Cadiz, Ohio, in 1901, the son of an oil field worker. Gable left school at 14 and held a number of jobs, including tire factory worker and lumberjack, but his first love was acting.

Friend Lionel Barrymore arranged a screen test for Gable at MGM, which he failed. However, after Gable made an impressive film debut in The Painted Desert (1930), the studio changed its mind and signed him to a contract.

A series of successful films followed; in fact, he made eight movies in 1931 alone, but it was in 1934, when on loan to Columbia, that he scored a great triumph in Frank Capra's It Happened One Night, for which he received the Oscar as best actor.

Gable separated from his second wife, socialite Rhea Langham, in 1935 and married actress Carole Lombard in 1939, while he was in the midst of playing Rhett Butler in Gone with the Wind. In 1942, Lombard was killed in a plane crash, and shortly thereafter Gable joined the U.S. Army Air Force and flew several bombing missions over Germany during World War II.

After the war, Gable returned to Hollywood and made more films. Finally, in the '50s, age caught up with Gable and his popularity began to wane. In 1960, Gable died of a heart attack shortly after completing The Misfits, which also starred Marilyn Monroe.

Some of Gable's other films include Red Dust (1932), Mutiny on the Bounty (1935), San Francisco (1936), The Hucksters (1947), Command Descision (1948), Mogambo (1953), The Tall Men (1955), Soldier of Fortune (1955), Teacher's Pet (1958), Run Silent, Run Deep (1958), and It Started in Naples (1959).

BITTERSWEET LOVE (1977)
★★

Lana Turner
Robert Lansing
Celeste Holm
Robert Alda

An elegant-looking soapy tale of woe about a boy and girl who marry and later find out they're related. Scene after scene drips with emotion in dealing with the incestuous relationship, but the characters are too shallow to carry any dramatic charge. Turner, splendidly coiffed and dressed, is the girl's mother. Also stars Meredith Baxter Birney and Scott Hylands as the young anguished couple. **Director**—David Miller. (PG)   92 minutes

BLACK AND WHITE IN COLOR (1977)
★★★★

Jean Carmet
Jacques Dufilho
Catherine Rouvel

A witty, intelligent satire attacking the arrogant human condition that leads to war. Droll and subtle performances by an excellent cast complement a moving screenplay about a bored group of Frenchmen in colonial West Africa, who fight a mini-war against a neighboring German garrison. The film was shot entirely in the Ivory Coast. In French with English titles. **Director**—Jean-Jacques Annaud. (PG) **Academy Award**—best foreign-language film (1976).   90 minutes

BLACKBEARD'S GHOST (1967)
★★

Peter Ustinov
Dean Jones
Suzanne Pleshette

Ustinov stars in this slapstick Walt Disney comedy, as the ghost of the infamous pirate who returns to prevent a hotel from being converted into a gambling casino. The film is rather overbearing, but the cast works hard to bring forth a few engaging moments. Elsa Lanchester and Richard Deacon co-star. **Director**—Robert Stevenson.   107 minutes

BLACKBEARD THE PIRATE (1952)
★★★

Robert Newton
Linda Darnell

Newton growls, scowls, and hams it up with glee as the 17th-century buccaneer out for more blood and treasure. Clichés abound, yet it's good fun all the way, with the spirited cast giving their all. Beautiful Darnell is aboard, all decked out in a satin gown, playing the captive of the rascally pirate. Keith Andes, William Bendix, Irene Ryan, and Richard Egan have supporting roles. **Director**—Raoul Walsh.   99 minutes

THE BLACK BIRD (1975)
★

George Segal
Stephane Audran
Lee Patrick
Elisha Cook, Jr.

The Bogart classic of some 40 years ago, The Maltese Falcon, is back as a supposedly comic sequel. Segal plays Sam Spade, Jr., who's stuck with his father's private-eye business and involved in another struggle over the mysterious falcon statuette he finds stashed away in a file drawer. There are a few bright moments at the beginning, but the wobbly and narrow plot fails to develop. Characters are left milling about and aimlessly bumping into one another. Bogie, where are you? Also stars Lionel Stander, John Abbott, and Signe Hasso; includes Patrick and Cook, who were in the original film. **Director**—David Giler. (PG)   98 minutes

- The Blackboard Jungle
- Black Christmas
- The Black Hole
- The Black Marble
- Black Narcissus
- The Black Rose
- The Black Shield of Falworth
- The Black Stallion

B

THE BLACKBOARD JUNGLE
(1955)
★★★★

Glenn Ford
Anne Francis
Louis Calhern

Ford gives a credible and engaging performance as a young teacher who gets through to some tough kids in a New York City high school. The poignant film, adapted from Evan Hunter's novel, is an honest and straightforward portrayal of urban education. Sidney Poitier is outstanding as a rebellious student with repressed talent and sensitivity. Bill Haley and the Comets fill in the background with "Rock Around the Clock." The film is biting, penetrating entertainment, with top acting and direction. Also with Richard Kiley and Vic Morrow. **Director**—Richard Brooks. **Academy Award Nominations**—Brooks, writing (screenplay); Russell Harlan, cinematography (black and white).

101 minutes b&w

BLACK CHRISTMAS (1975)
(no stars)

Olivia Hussey
John Saxon
Keir Dullea

Two sorority sisters and a housemother are mysteriously killed on a campus during Christmas vacation. A dull script, poor direction, and lackluster performances make this Canadian-produced movie a loser. Also with Margot Kidder and Douglas McGrath. **Director**—Bob Clark. (R)

100 minutes

THE BLACK HOLE (1979)
★★

Maximilian Schell
Anthony Perkins
Robert Forster
Joseph Bottoms

The Disney studios joined Hollywood's space race with this $20-million job, which unashamedly rips off *Star Wars* and other sci-fi adventures. The comic-book plot has Schell as a mad scientist who commands a renegade spaceship on the edge of a

In The Black Hole, *Maximilian Schell commands a renegade spaceship.*

mysterious black hole—the doorway to eternity. Two friendly robots, which resemble floating fireplugs, have the best lines and upstage the human characters. There's so little imagination here that it's hard to believe this is a Disney project. Also with Yvette Mimieux and Ernest Borgnine. **Director**—Gary Nelson. (PG)   *97 minutes*

THE BLACK MARBLE (1980)
★

Robert Foxworth
Paula Prentiss

Joseph Wambaugh (*The Onion Field*) is on his favorite subject again with this screenplay about police and crime, written from his own novel. It's a crude comic romance about two cops, played by Foxworth and Prentiss, who pursue a dognapper. There are some grisly details of animal mutilation and some offbeat humor that never goes over. A few moments of wit emerge, but it's a crime the way director Harold Becker finally drives the film into the ground. (PG)   *113 minutes*

BLACK NARCISSUS (1946)
★★★★

Deborah Kerr
Flora Robson
Kathleen Byron

Kerr shines as a nun who deals with the tormenting problems of isolation and harsh climate in an effort to maintain a mission in the Himalayas. The film, based on Rumer Godden's novel, is exquisitely appointed and packs an emotional wallop. Sabu and Jean Simmons are excellent in supporting roles. **Directors**—Michael Powell and Emeric Pressburger. **Academy Award**—Jack Cardiff, cinematography (color).

100 minutes

THE BLACK ROSE (1950)
★★

Tyrone Power
Cecile Aubry

Opulent but ponderous costume adventure, set in the 13th century, about an Englishman—played by Power—who travels to the Orient and triumphs over tyrannical rulers. Nothing new here, but there is some interesting action en route. Aubry, the French actress, co-stars in her first Hollywood film, which became her last when she failed the popularity test with American audiences. Orson Welles, Jack Hawkins, Michael Rennie, Herbert Lom, and Laurence Harvey have supporting roles. **Director**—Henry Hathaway.   *120 minutes*

THE BLACK SHIELD OF FALWORTH (1954)
★★

Tony Curtis
Janet Leigh

Curtis and Leigh star in this medieval costume drama, which alternates from seriousness to adolescent humor. Curtis plays an English nobleman striving to achieve knighthood. He fends off numerous enemies with swashbuckling swordsmanship; wait for him to say, "Yondah lies the castle of my fodda." Leigh, all decked out in sumptuous costumes, cheers from the sidelines. Elaborate period settings are impressive. Supporting cast includes David Farrar, Barbara Rush, and Herbert Marshall. **Director**—Rudolph Maté.   *99 minutes*

THE BLACK STALLION (1979)
★★★

Kelly Reno
Mickey Rooney

Boy meets horse, tames him, and races him in this splendidly photographed
(Continued)

B
- Black Sunday
- The Black Swan
- Black Tuesday
- Blazing Saddles
- The Blob
- Blood Alley

(Continued)

adventure fantasy that will please all age groups. Reno turns in a strong performance as the boy who develops a spiritual relationship with the wild Arabian stallion that saves his life in a shipwreck. Rooney is excellent as the trainer. But it's Cass-ole, a magnificent animal, who practically steals the film. Also with Teri Garr, Clarence Muse, and Hoyt Axton. **Director**—Carroll Ballard. (G) **Academy Award Nomination**—Rooney, best supporting actor.
103 minutes

Kelly Reno and Mickey Rooney share a love for an Arabian horse in The Black Stallion.

BLACK SUNDAY (1977)
★★★

**Robert Shaw
Bruce Dern
Marthe Keller**

Meticulous direction and superb acting elevate an otherwise routine disaster film into a slick action adventure. Shaw, who skillfully plays a hardened Israeli government agent, races against time to thwart a Palestinian terrorist plot to drop a dart-spewing bomb from the Goodyear blimp onto 80,000 Super Bowl spectators. There's a powerful and extraordinary screen performance by Dern as the jangled and half-crazed blimp pilot who collaborates with the terrorists. Also with Fritz Weaver and Steven Keats. **Director**—John Frankenheimer. (R)
143 minutes

THE BLACK SWAN (1942)
★★★

**Tyrone Power
Maureen O'Hara**

Rootin'-tootin' swashbuckler, with Power as a dashing pirate chasing some scruffy buccaneers at a fast clip through the Caribbean. The adventure has just the right amount of hokey humor to enhance the entertainment value without spoiling its spirit. O'Hara is charming as a damsel in need of rescuing from some villains, played convincingly by Anthony Quinn and George Sanders. The screenplay is based on the novel by Rafael Sabatini. Laird Cregar and Thomas Mitchell also star. **Director**—Henry King. **Academy Award**—Leon Shamroy, cinematography (color).
85 minutes

BLACK TUESDAY (1954)
★★★

**Edward G. Robinson
Jean Parker
Peter Graves**

Robinson puts on his best scowl as a killer on the lam from the big house in this familiar but exciting gangster film. Graves is his accomplice. The duo try to elude the authorities by hiding out in an abandoned warehouse. Lots of tension and shoot-outs with the cops ensue. Parker is fine as a gun moll. Also with Milburn Stone, Warren Stevens, and Jack Kelly. **Director**—Hugo Fregonese.
80 minutes b&w

BLAZING SADDLES (1974)
★★★★

**Cleavon Little
Gene Wilder
Slim Pickens
Harvey Korman
Madeline Kahn**

Mel Brooks's howling comedy spoofs western movies and racial prejudice in a nonstop barrage of riotous skits and sight gags. Some of the comedy misfires, but there's still an onslaught of belly laughs, including a generous dose of scatological humor. Little is great as a black railroad worker who's

In the spoof Blazing Saddles, *Cleavon Little (left) is elected sheriff of a troubled town.*

elected sheriff of a western town. Brooks is hilarious in a brief role as a Yiddish-speaking Indian chief. Kahn is a riot in a Marlene Dietrich takeoff. Korman, Wilder, and Pickens also pitch in with the lunacy. **Director**—Brooks. (R) **Academy Award Nomination**—Kahn, best supporting actress.
93 minutes

THE BLOB (1958)
★★

**Steve McQueen
Aneta Corseaut**

Slimy goo from outer space invades a small town, and a young McQueen comes to the rescue. This puffed-up sci-fi nonsense is primarily aimed at adolescent audiences. There are, however, a few scary scenes scattered here and there, and McQueen makes the most of the situation. Also with Olin Howlin and Earl Rowe. The film spawned a sequel called *Beware! The Blob*, also known as *Son of Blob*. **Director**—Irwin S. Yeaworth, Jr.
83 minutes

BLOOD ALLEY (1955)
★★

**John Wayne
Lauren Bacall**

Wayne and Bacall flee down a river from China to Hong Kong, with Chinese Communists hot on their tails. A routine anti-Red adventure, with Wayne as a bigger-than-life hero taking on the enemy single-handedly. The name cast and the slick production can't seem to overcome the threadbare script. Anita Ekberg is involved as a burlap-clad refugee. Also with Paul Fix, Joy Kim, Barry Kroger, and Mike Mazurki. **Director—** William Wellman.   *115 minutes*

BLOOD BEACH (1981)
★★

David Huffman
Mariana Hill
Burt Young

A mysterious creature lurks beneath a Los Angeles beach, and drags victims through the sand to its underground lair. Despite the title, there's little blood and gore in this low-budget horror film. Director Jeffrey Bloom manages to come up with a bit of suspense, thanks to a competent cast and a tight script that's a cousin to *Jaws*. However, there's only sparse action and vague contact with the subterranean monster. (R)   *90 minutes*

BLOODBROTHERS (1978)
★★

Richard Gere
Paul Sorvino
Tony Lo Bianco

A high-pitched emotional story about an Italian-American family living in the Bronx. Gere plays a rebellious teenage son and nephew to construction-worker brothers who brawl, booze, and chase women. Good performances, but the characters are stereotypes, and the director goes overboard in exploiting emotions. **Director—**Robert Mulligan. (R)
116 minutes

BLOODLINE (1979)
★★

Audrey Hepburn
Ben Gazzara
James Mason

Hepburn stars as the head of an international pharmaceutical empire in this tepid murder mystery, based on Sidney Sheldon's popular novel. Gaz-

zara, Mason, Omar Sharif, and other well-known players appear as suspects in the murder of the company's patriarch. What little suspense there is quickly evaporates amid the complicated and ponderous plot. Hepburn looks rather weary much of the time, which seems to be in keeping with the pace of the film. Also with Michelle Phillips and Romy Schneider. **Director—**Terence Young. (R)
116 minutes

BLOW OUT (1981)
★★★

John Travolta

Director Brian De Palma fashions a stylish, electrifying drama about a movie sound man, played by Travolta, who stumbles upon a political assassination. The film bears some similarity to Antonioni's *Blow-Up*, and De Palma also cleverly weaves in subtle references to Chappaquiddick, Nelson Rockefeller's death, and Watergate plumbers. Travolta finally gets his teeth into an appealing, intelligent adult role, and sheds his hotshot teenage image. (R)   *108 minutes*

John Travolta stars as a sound technician caught in a web of intrigue in Blow Out.

BLOW-UP (1966)
★★★★

David Hemmings
Sarah Miles
Vanessa Redgrave

A fascinating and thought-provoking drama involving a London photog-

Redgrave and Hemmings in Blow-Up.

rapher who believes he has witnessed a murder. Hemmings is effective as the baffled young man, and there is a stylish performance from Redgrave. The film brims with psychological twists and complex symbolism; much is accomplished with scant plot and undeveloped characters, in the trendy twilight world of London's fashion business. Jill Kennington and Verushka are also featured. **Director—** Michelangelo Antonioni. **Academy Award Nominations**—Antonioni, best director; Antonioni, Tonino Guerra, and Edward Bond, best story and screenplay (written directly for the screen).   *110 minutes*

THE BLUE BIRD (1940)
★★

Shirley Temple
Spring Byington

Temple and Byington star in this classic fairy tale about two children who search for the bluebird of happiness, only to find true happiness at home. The film is based on Maurice Maeterlinck's fantasy, but the plot seems similar to *The Wizard of Oz*. The production is impressive, but it pales in contrast to the popular *Oz* film, which was released about the same time. Johnny Russell, Nigel Bruce, Gale Sondergaard, and Eddie Collins also star. **Director—**Walter Lang.
98 minutes

THE BLUE BIRD (1976)
★

Elizabeth Taylor
Jane Fonda
Ava Gardner

Détente comes to the movies, but the result is a disappointment. The first
(Continued)

B
- Blue Collar
- Blue Country
- The Blue Dahlia
- The Blue Lagoon (1949)
- The Blue Lagoon (1980)
- The Blue Max
- A Blueprint for Murder
- The Blues Brothers

(Continued)

major Soviet-American co-production, filmed in Leningrad, is the classic fable about two children who search for the bluebird of happiness; the audience will find the pigeon of boredom. Taylor, Fonda, Gardner, and Cicely Tyson appear briefly in cameo roles. The film is plagued with technical problems, dull dialogue, and lackluster sets. Also with Will Geer, Robert Morley, and Harry Andrews. Directed by George Cukor, who should have known better. (G)   *99 minutes*

BLUE COLLAR (1978)
★★★

**Richard Pryor
Harvey Keitel
Yaphet Kotto**

Paul Schrader, who wrote the script for *Taxi Driver*, is so-so as director of this powerful and gritty film about frustrated automobile factory workers who are pushed around by their union and management. This fast-paced comedy-drama is awkward at times. Even so, Schrader scores with his colorful profile of believable contemporary characters. Pryor, Keitel, and Kotto are the heroes of the assembly line; they play their parts to the hilt. Also with Ed Begley, Jr., and Harry Bellaver. (R)   *114 minutes*

Harvey Keitel, Richard Pryor, and Yaphet Kotto take a break from the assembly line in Blue Collar.

BLUE COUNTRY (1978)
★★

**Brigitte Fossey
Jacques Serres**

Writer-director Jean-Charles Tacchellas's gentle observations on French country life emit a warm glow, but don't evoke much interest. Tacchella provides hardly any plot, and he's far from achieving the level of his award-winning *Cousin, Cousine*. Fossey, however, is a delight to look at as the city girl tasting the pure country life. (PG)   *77 minutes*

THE BLUE DAHLIA (1946)
★★★

**Alan Ladd
Veronica Lake
William Bendix**

Ladd plays an ex-GI, home from the war, who discovers his wife has been unfaithful. After she's murdered, he becomes the prime suspect. The Raymond Chandler mystery packs excitement and suspense, with the cast turning in sharp performances. Also with Howard da Silva and Hugh Beaumont. **Director**—George Marshall. **Academy Award Nomination**—Chandler, writing (original screenplay).   *99 minutes b&w*

THE BLUE LAGOON (1949)
★★

**Jean Simmons
Donald Houston**

A syrupy romantic adventure about a boy and a girl, stranded on a tropical island, who mature, fall in love, and then try to return to civilization. The lush island setting can't redeem the listless material, based on the novel by H. de Vere Stacpoole. There is a bit of suspense when the couple is threatened by smugglers. Also with Noel Purcell, Cyril Cusack, and James Hayter. **Director**—Frank Launder.
103 minutes

THE BLUE LAGOON (1980)
★★

**Brooke Shields
Christopher Atkins**

Emmeline, played by Shields, and Richard, played by Atkins, are two shipwrecked children on a tropical island who grow up to be lovers. Everything is picture-postcard pretty, including Brooke and Christopher. But excitement and drama are nowhere to be found. The story some-

what unrealistically and awkwardly emphasizes innocent sexual awakening. The 1949 version with Jean Simmons worked better as a Hollywood-style fantasy. Also with Leo McKern, and William Daniels. **Director**—Randal Kleiser. (R)   *102 minutes*

THE BLUE MAX (1966)
★★

**George Peppard
James Mason
Ursula Andress**

Spectacular photography of World War I aerial dogfights is the only worthwhile virtue of this tepid drama involving German military pilots. Peppard plays an ambitious German flyer who woos the wife of his commander; Mason portrays a stereotyped German officer; and Andress is Peppard's love interest. Performances are fair but not too convincing. Also with Jeremy Kemp and Karl Michael Vogler. **Director**—John Guillermin.   *156 minutes*

A BLUEPRINT FOR MURDER (1953)
★★

**Jean Peters
Joseph Cotten**

Cotten plays a troubled man trying to prove that his sister-in-law, played by Peters, poisoned his brother and nephew. The rather familiar mystery plot twists and turns, with clues dangling left and right. Did Peters commit the perfect crime? If you're any good, you can figure it out before Cotten does. Gary Merrill, Catherine McLeod, and Jack Kruschen co-star. **Director**—Andrew Stone.
77 minutes b&w

THE BLUES BROTHERS (1980)
★★★

**John Belushi
Dan Aykroyd**

Belushi and Aykroyd star in this musical action comedy as improbable bandleaders who try to raise $5,000 for an orphanage and cause $50 million in property damage in the process. It's a rollicking smorgasbord of soul music, auto crashes, explosions, and crazy

- Blues in the Night
- Blue Skies
- Blume in Love
- Boardwalk
- Bob & Carol & Ted & Alice
- Bobby Deerfield
- Body and Soul (1947)

B

Dan Aykroyd and John Belushi, as Jake and Elwood Blues, perform in concert in The Blues Brothers.

fun. But it's really the spirited musical numbers that glue this madcap mess together. Delightful cameo performances by James Brown, Aretha Franklin, Ray Charles, and Cab Calloway add to the froth and frolic. **Director—**John Landis. (R)   *130 minutes*

BLUES IN THE NIGHT (1941)
★★★

**Priscilla Lane
Richard Whorf
Lloyd Nolan**

A pleasant score and a decent script go into this finely crafted musical drama about a jazz band that splits up, with the members suffering various problems. Music by Harold Arlen and Johnny Mercer includes "This Time the Dream's on Me." The earnest cast handles the smooth dialogue with conviction. Also with Jack Carson, Betty Field, and Elia Kazan. **Director—**Anatole Litvak.   *88 minutes b&w*

BLUE SKIES (1946)
★★★

**Fred Astaire
Bing Crosby
Joan Caulfield**

Crosby and Astaire star in this sunny musical loaded with Irving Berlin tunes. The threadbare, corny plot concerns a drawn-out rivalry for the attention of a girl. But that's incidental to the music and dancing. Bing sings the title song, and Fred dances to "Putting

On the Ritz." What more do you need? Caulfield, Billy de Wolfe, and Olga San Juan are fine in supporting roles. **Director—**Stuart Heisler.
104 minutes

BLUME IN LOVE (1973)
★★★

**George Segal
Susan Anspach
Kris Kristofferson**

Writer-director Paul Mazursky takes on middle-class marriage and divorce in this droll comedy-drama about a lawyer, played by Segal, who longs for his ex-wife, played by Anspach, and wants to win her back. Segal and Anspach are both affecting as sympathetic characters. And the film is blessed with sparkling supporting acting—Shelley Winters as an older woman whose husband left her for a stewardess, and Kristofferson as Anspach's bedmate of the moment. Also with Marsha Mason. (R)
116 minutes

BOARDWALK (1979)
★★

**Ruth Gordon
Lee Strasberg
Janet Leigh**

A rather depressing but sympathetic look at growing old in a deteriorating Brooklyn neighborhood. Surviving residents face chronic illness, attacks by youth gangs, and gnawing inflation, but all these troubles aren't presented clearly or convincingly. Gordon, Strasberg, and Leigh, however, turn in plausible performances. Also with Joe Silver, Eddie Barth, and Eli Mintz. **Director—**Stephen Verona. (No MPAA rating)   *98 minutes*

BOB & CAROL & TED & ALICE (1969)
★★★

**Natalie Wood
Robert Culp
Elliott Gould
Dyan Cannon**

An old-fashioned romantic comedy loaded with all sorts of trendy situations: wife-swapping, psychotherapy, pot smoking, and so on. A so-called

modern couple envy what seems to be their friends' ideal marriage, and they almost end up swapping partners. Gould and Cannon are exceptional as Ted and Alice—the nervous experimenters. Wood and Culp are the chic Carol and Bob. The wacky screenplay and smart dialogue keep the situations moving along, but the ending is somewhat absurd. **Director—**Paul Mazursky. (R) **Academy Award Nominations—**Gould, best supporting actor; Cannon, best supporting actress; Mazursky and Larry Tucker, best story and screenplay (based on material not previously published or produced); Charles B. Lang, cinematography.   *105 minutes*

BOBBY DEERFIELD (1977)
★

**Al Pacino
Marthe Keller**

Pacino, in his first romantic role, plays an emotionally drained race-car driver who falls in love with a dying European beauty, played by Keller. Both are miscast in this flat-footed European version of *Love Story*. Alvin Sargent's superficial script has the two leads blabbing endlessly without generating any pathos. The beautiful Anny Duperey stands out as Bobby's enduring mistress of convenience. Also with Walter McGinn and Romolo Valli. **Director—**Sydney Pollack. (PG)
124 minutes

BODY AND SOUL (1947)
★★★★

**John Garfield
Lilli Palmer**

Garfield stars as a young man from a poor family who becomes a top prizefighter by fair and foul means. It's a rough-and-tough drama that's perhaps a boxing film cliché. However, this study is compelling, exciting, and laced with impressive fight sequences. Garfield is perfection as the determined slugger, and Palmer stands out as the female lead. There's support from Hazel Brooks, William Conrad, Anne Revere, and Canada Lee. **Director—**Robert Rossen. **Academy Award Nominations—**Garfield, best actor; Abraham Polonsky, writing (original screenplay).   *104 minutes b&w*

B
- • Body and Soul (1981)
- • Body Heat
- • The Body Snatcher
- • Bombers B-52
- • Bonjour Tristesse
- • Bonnie and Clyde

BODY AND SOUL (1981)
★★

Leon Isaac Kennedy

Leon Isaac Kennedy stars as an earnest boxer who shelves a promising medical career in an effort to win big bucks by vying for the championship. This uninspired remake of the 1947 John Garfield classic lacks any sort of vitality and comes across in a rather undramatic way. Muhammad Ali is in the film as the aspiring champ's adviser, and he adds some levity merely playing himself. Jayne Kennedy and Peter Lawford also star. **Director**—George Bowers. (R)
109 minutes

BODY HEAT (1981)
★★★

William Hurt
Kathleen Turner

Lawrence Kasdan triumphantly debuts as director of this sultry movie, which smacks of such '40s *films noirs* as *Double Indemnity*. It drips with steamy atmospherics and lavishly dwells on passion and treachery. Hurt stars as an affable, second-rate lawyer who is lured into killing the well-heeled husband of a seductive woman, played by Turner. Again, Hurt demonstrates his fine acting ability. As for Turner, she's not so hot. (R)   *113 minutes*

Hurt and Turner in Body Heat.

THE BODY SNATCHER (1945)
★★★

Henry Daniell
Boris Karloff
Bela Lugosi

A blood-chilling horror story about a doctor in 19th-century Scotland who

Bela Lugosi (right) gets instructions from Boris Karloff in The Body Snatcher.

experiments with bodies supplied by grave robbers. Lots of good creepy atmosphere in this Val Lewton thriller, with Karloff and Lugosi at their sinister best. The film is based on a familiar story by Robert Lewis Stevenson and is executed in an inventive manner. Edith Atwater and Russell Wade are also in the cast. **Director**—Robert Wise.   *77 minutes b&w*

BOMBERS B-52 (1957)
★★

Karl Malden
Marsha Hunt
Efrem Zimbalist, Jr.
Natalie Wood

Routine romantic melodrama set against a military aircraft background. Zimbalist is a young pilot who wants to marry a fellow officer's daughter, played by Wood; Malden, as Wood's father, objects. The outcome is predictable. Spectacular shots of flying bombers are interspersed amid the domestic scenes. Also with Dean Jagger and Don Kelly. **Director**—Gordon Douglas.   *106 minutes*

BONJOUR TRISTESSE (1957)
★★★

David Niven
Deborah Kerr
Jean Seberg

An elegant-looking film based on the Françoise Sagan novel about a teenage girl who resents her philandering father's mistress. Tragedy results when the daughter tries to break up the romance. The film is set against the lavish background of the French Riviera. The script is a little melodramatic but entertaining nevertheless. Kerr is outstanding, with help from Niven and Seberg. Mylene Demongeot, Geoffrey Horne, Juliette Greco, and Martita Hunt are also in the cast. **Director**—Otto Preminger.
94 minutes

BONNIE AND CLYDE (1967)
★★★★

Warren Beatty
Faye Dunaway
Michael J. Pollard

A vivid, penetrating, and stylish film biography of the notorious bank robbers who terrorized mid-America at the depth of the Great Depression. The exciting production seems to have a bit of everything—grim drama, comedy at the right moments, social commentary, and suspense. Stunning direction by Arthur Penn is complemented by the brilliant acting of Beatty and Dunaway in the title roles. The film was a huge box-office success and a pacesetter of modern gangster movies. Pollard, Gene Hackman, Estelle Parsons, Gene Wilder, and Denver Pyle are excellent in supporting roles. **Academy Awards**—Parsons, best supporting actress; Burnett Guffey, cinematography. **Nominations**—best picture; Penn, best director; Beatty, best actor; Dunaway, best actress; Hackman, best supporting actor; David Newman and Robert Benton, best story and screenplay (written directly for the screen).   *111 minutes*

Warren Beatty and Faye Dunaway play bank robbers in Bonnie and Clyde.

BON VOYAGE (1962)
★★

Fred MacMurray
Jane Wyman

MacMurray plays a middle-class father who takes his family on vacation to Paris. Slow-paced, lightweight Disney fare about a family dealing with a variety of comic events. One of the misadventures is dad getting trapped in the Paris sewer system. It's an interesting tour of the French capital, however. Michael Callan, Tommy Kirk, and Deborah Walley are in the cast. **Director**—James Neilson.   *133 minutes*

BOOMERANG (1947)
★★★★

Dana Andrews
Jane Wyatt
Lee J. Cobb

A priest in a New England community is murdered, and a determined prosecuting attorney saves an innocent man from false conviction. The actual guilty person isn't apprehended although the audience knows who did it. This brilliant and fascinating drama is based on a true story and produced in semidocumentary form. First-class entertainment, with stylish direction and outstanding acting. Arthur Kennedy, Sam Levene, and Ed Begley also star. **Director**—Elia Kazan. **Academy Award Nomination**—Richard Murphy, writing (screenplay).

88 minutes b&w

BOOM TOWN (1940)
★★★

Clark Gable
Spencer Tracy
Claudette Colbert
Hedy Lamarr

A big-name cast livens up this action-packed drama of oil drillers who bring in black gold. Entertainment and excitement run high in a slick blending of romance, comedy, and suspense. Gable, Tracy, Colbert, and Lamarr top the cast. Frank Morgan, Chill Wills, and Lionel Atwill also lend a hand. **Director**—Jack Conway. **Academy Award Nomination**—Harold Rosson,

AUDREY HEPBURN

Born in 1929 in Brussels of Irish-Dutch parents, Audrey Hepburn lived in the Netherlands during World War II and later moved to London to study dance at the Rambert Ballet School. She made her stage debut in 1948, as a ballerina in the musical High Button Shoes, *and later danced in* Sauce Tartare. *After some initial film roles in Britain, France, and Holland, Hepburn was chosen to play the starring role in* Gigi, *which Anita Loos had converted into a Broadway hit play. Then William Wyler saw an earlier screen test Hepburn had made for Paramount and demanded her for the princess in* Roman Holiday *(1953), opposite Gregory Peck; her performance brought her an Academy Award.*

Although Hepburn has appeared in many earlier movies, Roman

Holiday *really began her striking screen career, including such early successes as Billy Wilder's* Sabrina *(1954), King Vidor's* War and Peace *(1956), Stanley Donen's* Funny Face *(1957), and Wilder's* Love in the Afternoon *(1957). On Broadway, she also starred in* Ondine, *for which she won the Drama Critics' Award. Her co-star was Mel Ferrer, whom she married at the end of the play's run.*

In 1957, Hepburn appeared in Mayerling *with Ferrer and Raymond Massey. One of her best portrayals was in Fred Zinnemann's* The Nun's Story *(1959). Other films from the early 1960s were* The Unforgiven *(1960),* Breakfast at Tiffany's *(1961),* The Children's Hour *(1962),* Charade *(1963), and* Paris When It Sizzles *(1964).*

Hepburn was then chosen over Julie Andrews, who played Eliza on Broadway, for the expensive film version of My Fair Lady *(1964). She then co-starred with Peter O'Toole in* How To Steal a Million *(1966), with Albert Finney in* Two for the Road *(1966), and in the thriller* Wait Until Dark *(1967). Lately, she has appeared in* Robin and Marian *(1976) and* Bloodline *(1979).*

Hepburn's marriage to Ferrer ended in 1968, and, a year later, she married Andrea Dotti, an Italian psychiatrist.

cinematography (black and white).
120 minutes b&w

THE BORDER (1982)
★★★

Jack Nicholson

Nicholson brings considerable richness to his working-stiff characterization of a border patrol officer involved with corruption. The movie intelligently details the plight of illegal Mexican workers with sharp contrasts between their condition and the materialistic life-style of some Americans. Occasionally, the film is marred by its excessive commercial leanings, yet the suspense and passion shine through. Valerie Perrine and Harvey Keitel are excellent in supporting roles. Also

with Warren Oates and Elpidia Carrillo. **Director**—Tony Richardson. (R)
107 minutes

BORDERLINE (1980)
★★

Charles Bronson

Bronson plays a border patrol officer on the trail of illegal aliens from Mexico. There's potential for some socially significant moviemaking. But alas, the film only halfheartedly examines the sorry plight of exploited Mexicans. Most of the time, the film is just another action vehicle, with Bronson seeking revenge for the killing of a fellow officer. Bronson does his usual credible job, but his inspiration seems merely borderline. **Director**—Gerrold Freedman. (R)   *97 minutes*

B
- Born Again
- Born Free
- Born Yesterday
- The Boston Strangler
- Boulevard Nights
- Bound for Glory
- A Boy and His Dog

BORN AGAIN (1978)
★

**Dean Jones
Anne Francis**

An awkward drama of Charles Colson's Watergate misadventures and later conversion to Christianity. Jones, himself a born-again Christian, plays the former Nixon hatchet man with pious enthusiasm; he's hardly convincing. Neither are the other cardboard characterizations associated with the Watergate affair. Harry Spillman, however, relieves some of the seriousness with a funny—and probably unintentional—parody of Richard Nixon. Also with Jay Robinson, Dana Andrews, and Raymond St. Jacques. **Director**—Irving Rapper. (PG)
110 minutes

BORN FREE (1966)
★★★

**Virginia McKenna
Bill Travers
Geoffrey Keen**

Pleasant family film based on Joy Adamson's best-selling book about the lioness Elsa, who was raised as a pet and then returned to the jungle. Photography of the animals, and especially of the lion's efforts to adapt to the wilds of Kenya, is impressive. Travers and McKenna star as the game warden and his wife who managed the retraining of Elsa. **Director**—James Hill. **Academy Award**—best song ("Born Free," John Barry and Don Black); Barry, best original score.
95 minutes

BORN YESTERDAY (1950)
★★★★

**Judy Holliday
Broderick Crawford
William Holden**

Holliday is sensational in this screen adaptation of Garson Kanin's hit Broadway play on the *Pygmalion* theme. She plays a dumb blond (what else?), the girlfriend of a wealthy scrap dealer, played by Crawford. She starts out for education and sophistication and then falls in love with her tutor,

played by Holden. The film brims with subtle humor and witty dialogue; the top cast turns in hilarious performances. Howard St. John also stars. **Director**—George Cukor. **Academy Award**—Holliday, best actress. **Nominations**—best picture; Cukor, best director; Albert Mannheimer, writing (screenplay).
103 minutes b&w

THE BOSTON STRANGLER (1968)
★★★

**Tony Curtis
Henry Fonda**

Curtis gives an effective performance as the maniac who murdered several women in Boston in the mid-60s. The semidocumentary film drags at times, but it remains a startling rendition of Gerold Frank's book about the brutal sex killings allegedly committed by Albert De Salvo, a deranged plumber. The compelling account follows the criminal's grisly deeds, his arrest, and his trial. George Kennedy and Sally Kellerman also star. **Director**—Richard Fleischer.
118 minutes

BOULEVARD NIGHTS (1979)
★★

**Richard Yniguez
Marta Du Bois
Danny De La Paz**

Mexican-American youths of East Los Angeles cruise the neon-lit streets and wage gang warfare. The film tries so hard to be the Chicano version of *West Side Story* or *Saturday Night Fever* that it loses sight of its characters. A cast of unknowns do only a fair acting job. Flash and gloss seem to be more important here than story development. **Director**—Michael Pressman. (R)
102 minutes

BOUND FOR GLORY (1976)
★★★

**David Carradine
Ronny Cox**

The great folksinger Woody Guthrie is played with slow and heartfelt perfection by Carradine. And director Hal Ashby carefully provides a stunning, detailed portrait of the Great Depres-

In Bound for Glory, *David Carradine portrays American folksinger Woody Guthrie.*

sion of the 1930s. The story follows Guthrie's separation from his poverty-stricken family, his experience with political activism among California's migrant laborers, and his initial radio career. The 2½-hour film doesn't build dramatically and rambles too often, yet Guthrie's social consciousness shines through. There's fine support from Melinda Dillon. Also with Gail Strickland, John Lehne, and Ji-Tu Cumbuka. (PG) **Academy Award**—Haskell Wexler, cinematography. **Nominations**—best picture; Robert Getchell, best screenplay adaptation.
147 minutes

A BOY AND HIS DOG (1975)
★

**Don Johnson
Susanne Benton
Jason Robards, Jr.
Tiger (the dog)**

A mixed breed of a film set in the 21st century when the Earth's surface has been reduced to a wasteland after World War IV. A young man and his talking dog, played by Tiger, prowl about looking for food and sex. The man, played smartly by Johnson, is lured into a weird subterranean city ruled by a dictatorship led by Robards. Director L. Q. Jones is still in the puppy stage with this one, which is at times stimulating and at times mildly revolting. Also with Tim McIntire and Charles McGraw. (R)
87 minutes

- Boy, Did I Get a Wrong Number
- Boy on a Dolphin
- The Boys From Brazil
- The Boys in Company C
- The Boys in the Band
- The Boy With Green Hair
- Brannigan
- Brass Target

B

BOY, DID I GET A WRONG NUMBER (1966)
★

**Bob Hope
Elke Sommer
Phyllis Diller**

Silly, unfunny Hope outing, with the comedian as a real estate agent who tries to call his wife and instead gets hooked up with a movie star, played by Sommer. The dopey script generates little in the way of laughs, and the production is mostly an embarrassment for Hope and the rest of the cast. It's a wrong number, indeed. Also with Marjorie Lord and Cesare Danova. **Director**—George Marshall.

99 minutes

BOY ON A DOLPHIN (1957)
★★

**Alan Ladd
Sophia Loren**

Striking photography of the Greek islands, the sparkling sea, and the statuesque beauty of Loren are the main attractions of this otherwise routine adventure involving sunken treasure. Loren plays a Greek skin diver who uncovers a lost artifact. An archaeologist and an ambitious art collector join the recovery operations. Clifton Webb and Laurence Naismith are also in the cast. **Director**—Jean Negulesco.

113 minutes

THE BOYS FROM BRAZIL (1978)
★★

**Gregory Peck
Laurence Olivier
James Mason**

Peck and Olivier star in this weird drama that exploits the current interest in cloning. In this case, the evil Dr. Josef Mengele, who conducted sadistic human experiments in Nazi death camps, is on the loose in South America with a scheme to produce 94 copies of Adolf Hitler. Mengele is played by Peck; Olivier plays a Jewish Nazi-hunter. There are moments of suspense here and there, but the shaky story, based on Ira Levin's best-selling novel, lapses into silliness.

Laurence Olivier and Gregory Peck struggle to the death in The Boys From Brazil.

Also with Lilli Palmer, Uta Hagen, Denholm Elliott, and Steven Guttenberg. **Director**—Franklin Schaffner. (R) **Academy Award Nomination**—Olivier, best actor.

123 minutes

THE BOYS IN COMPANY C (1978)
★★

**Stan Shaw
Andrew Stevens
James Canning**

This drama about Marine warfare in Vietnam starts off on the right foot with an authentic account of boot-camp training. When the scene shifts to Southeast Asia, however, the story falls apart. The characters, played by an unfamiliar cast, are World War II stereotypes who mostly shout and screech at one another. The climax concerns an absurd soccer match that looks like a cheap rip-off of the football game from *M*A*S*H*. Lee Ermey, an ex-Marine drill instructor originally hired as a consultant, came up with the best acting job—playing his former real-life role. Also with Michael Lembeck and Craig Wasson. **Director**—Sidney J. Furie. (R)

127 minutes

THE BOYS IN THE BAND (1970)
★★★

**Frederick Combs
Leonard Frey
Cliff Gorman**

This impressive film version of Mart Crowley's successful Broadway play about homosexuality is full of emotion, an honest exposure of feelings, and the right touch of humor. The rather confined production concerns a homosexual birthday party to which a heterosexual is inadvertently invited. Fine acting and efficient direction keep the story moving right up to a stunning ending. Also with Laurence Luckinbill, Kenneth Nelson, and Reuben Greene. **Director**—William Friedkin. (R)

120 minutes

THE BOY WITH GREEN HAIR (1948)
★★★

**Dean Stockwell
Pat O'Brien**

A captivating drama with a social message opposing the senselessness of war. After an air raid takes the life of his parents, a boy's hair turns green. The boy, played by Stockwell, becomes an outcast, but he wins the sympathy of other war orphans. Fine acting overcomes some of the muddle in the plot. O'Brien stands out as a likable grandfather. Also with Robert Ryan and Barbara Hale. **Director**—Joseph Losey.

82 minutes

BRANNIGAN (1975)
★★

**John Wayne
Richard Attenborough
Judy Geeson**

Wayne stars as Brannigan, a Chicago cop who goes to London to retrieve a criminal. The plot is a bit overdrawn and familiar, but the London setting is a nice change of pace for Wayne. You can expect the regular round of slug-fests and other macho action typical of the Duke, even though he seems old for this role. Attenborough does well as a Scotland Yard detective whose style is at odds with the American's. Also with Mel Ferrer, Ralph Meeker, and John Vernon. **Director**—Douglas Hickox. (PG)

111 minutes

BRASS TARGET (1978)
★

**John Cassavetes
Sophia Loren
George Kennedy**

Plodding film based on the dubious theory that Gen. George S. Patton was

(Continued)

51

B
- The Bravados
- Bread and Chocolate
- Breaker! Breaker!
- Breaker Morant
- Breakfast at Tiffany's

ELIZABETH TAYLOR

Elizabeth Taylor is perhaps as well known for her off-screen romances, marriages, and divorces as she is for her acting talent and beauty. She was born in 1932 in London of American parents who returned to the United States in 1939 and settled in Los Angeles.

Enchantingly beautiful at age 10, Taylor made her screen debut in 1942 in There's One Born Every Minute. *The following year, she signed on with MGM, where she made a number of films as a child star and then continued on through the '60s in numerous dramatic roles.*

Her personal life was tumultuous almost from the start. She married hotel heir Nick Hilton at the age of 17 and divorced him a few months later.

In 1952, actor Michael Wilding became her second husband. They parted in 1957, and she then married film producer Michael Todd.

Taylor's relationship with Todd was probably the most significant in her life. Todd, however, died in the crash of his private plane in 1958.

A year later, Taylor married singer Eddie Fisher, only to divorce him in 1964, when she fell in love with Richard Burton during the filming of Cleopatra.

Her relationship with Burton was the subject of considerable publicity throughout the '60s and '70s. After a divorce, remarriage, and a second divorce from Burton, she married U.S. Senator John Warner. This seventh marriage failed in 1981, when the couple separated.

Taylor won her first Oscar as best actress for Butterfield 8 *(1960), and she won her second Academy Award for* Who's Afraid of Virginia Woolf? *(1966).*

Among her other notable movies are Lassie Come Home *(1943),* National Velvet *(1944),* Life With Father *(1947),* Father of the Bride *(1950),* A Place in the Sun *(1951),* Rhapsody *(1954),* Giant *(1956),* Cat on a Hot Tin Roof *(1958),* The Taming of the Shrew *(1967), and* A Little Night Music *(1978).*

(Continued)
assassinated rather than killed in a car accident. Kennedy plays old Blood-and-Guts as if the famous commander was a drill sergeant. Robert Vaughn, Max Von Sydow, Patrick McGoohan, and Bruce Davison are also in the cast. They shuffle through their parts as if bored with the silly script, which is based on Frederick Nolan's novel of historical speculation. **Director**—John Hough. (PG)   111 minutes

THE BRAVADOS (1958)
★★

Gregory Peck
Joan Collins
Stephen Boyd

After four brutes rape and kill a man's wife, the widower embarks on a man-hunt to revenge the crime. Peck stars in this downtrodden western as the seeker of justice. But he becomes as despicable as the killers in his zeal for success. The production is handsome, but the execution of the story is uneven and plodding at times. Also with Albert Salmi, Henry Silva, and Lee Van Cleef. **Director**—Henry King.
98 minutes

BREAD AND CHOCOLATE (1978)
★★★

Nino Manfredi

Italian director Franco Brusati's bittersweet satire takes a hard look at the plight of migrant workers. The story, told with pathos and humor, concerns a disorganized Italian waiter, played by Manfredi, who painfully tries to fit in among the stuffy and orderly Swiss. Our hero, at times, resembles Charlie Chaplin's woeful tramp. Brusati illus-trates the agony of the outsider with force and intelligence. In Italian with English titles. (No MPAA rating)
108 minutes

BREAKER! BREAKER! (1977)
★

Chuck Norris

Martial arts whiz Norris stars in this shabby drama, which exploits the interest in heavy trucking, CB radio, and chop-socky action. The simple plot concerns the efforts of Norris, aided by some of his buddies, to rescue his kid brother from a remote town where sadistic citizens harass unsuspecting truckers. Cardboard acting and inept direction drag down the mediocre screenplay; it could only appeal to those who haven't outgrown comic books. Also with George Murdock and Terry O'Connor. **Director**—Don Hulette. (PG)   86 minutes

BREAKER MORANT (1981)
★★★★

Edward Woodward
Jack Thompson
John Waters

This film from Australia is a stirring courtroom drama set during the Boer War. Three officers tragically become scapegoats of a hypocritical British military. There are obvious parallels to Vietnam and references to the ambiguities of warfare ("We were only following orders."). The film shines with strongly developed characters. There's a powerhouse performance by Woodward in the title role, and Bruce Beresford's crisp direction is on target. Also with Charles Tingwell. (No MPAA rating) **Academy Award Nomination**—Jonathan Hardy, David Stevens, and Beresford, best screenplay (adapted from another medium).
106 minutes

BREAKFAST AT TIFFANY'S (1961)
★★★★

Audrey Hepburn
George Peppard

A stylish and witty film version of Truman Capote's cosmopolitan story

- Breakheart Pass
- Breaking Away
- The Breaking Point
- Brewster McCloud
- Brewster's Millions
- The Bribe
- The Bride Came C.O.D.

B

about a New York writer, played by Peppard, who has some kooky neighbors, including a daffy call girl. The lively production is graced with hilarious scenes, memorable performances, and colorful characterizations. There's a madcap party sequence that is unforgettable. Hepburn is charming and funny as the modish Holly Golightly. Henry Mancini wrote the score, which includes the award-winning "Moon River." Also with Patricia Neal, Martin Balsam, John McGiver, Buddy Ebsen, and Mickey Rooney. **Director**—Blake Edwards. **Academy Award**—Mancini, best song. **Nominations**—Hepburn, best actress; George Axelrod, best screenplay (based on material from another medium).   *115 minutes*

BREAKHEART PASS (1976)
★★★

Charles Bronson
Ben Johnson
Richard Crenna

The film is mainly set on an old woodburning steam train chugging through picturesque mountain country. The ever-faithful Bronson is on board as a federal agent in disguise trying to track down a stolen arms shipment. The train is crawling with villains, corpses, and mystery. Shades of *Murder on the Orient Express*. Only in this case, the setting is the West in the 1870s. There's an intricate plot, but the film is a solidly entertaining whodunit packed with suspense and action. It's based on Alistair MacLean's book. Also with Jill Ireland, Charles Durning, and Archie Moore. **Director**— Tom Gries. (PG)   *95 minutes*

BREAKING AWAY (1979)
★★★★

Dennis Christopher
Dennis Quaid
Daniel Stern
Jackie Earle Haley

A simple, charming little comedy with a big heart and a gentle touch. It's about four working-class boys in Bloomington, Indiana, who challenge the college stuffed shirts in a grueling bike race. The cast is unknown, but director Peter Yates obtains sparkling performances all around. Christopher

Dennis Christopher is a rider who idolizes Italian bike champs in Breaking Away.

is especially delightful as a first-class rider who idolizes Italian bike champs. The climactic yet predictable big race will leave you elated and cheering. Also with Barbara Barrie and Paul Dooley. **Academy Award**—Steve Tesich, best screenplay (written directly for the screen). **Nominations**—best picture; Yates, best director; Barrie, best supporting actress. (PG)   *100 minutes*

THE BREAKING POINT (1950)
★★

John Garfield
Patricia Neal

Garfield portrays a desperate charterboat skipper who falls in with criminals and transports some illicit cargo. The script, based on Ernest Hemingway's *To Have and Have Not*, is slightly tedious, but the film is partially salvaged by the superb performances of Garfield and Juano Hernandez, who plays Garfield's first mate. Also with Phyllis Thaxter and Wallace Ford. **Director**—Michael Curtiz.   *97 minutes*

BREWSTER McCLOUD (1970)
★★★

Bud Cort
Sally Kellerman

This is a far-out, slapstick comedy as only director Robert Altman can create one. Brewster is an oddball character who wants to fly—with man-made

wings—inside the Houston Astrodome. When he tries, he kills himself. Altman sets up many striking scenes—some of them are bizarre, some of them are funny, and some of them are funny and bizarre. Cort, in the title role, is effectively kooky. Also with Michael Murphy, William Windom, Shelley Duvall, and Stacy Keach. (R)   *105 minutes*

BREWSTER'S MILLIONS (1945)
★★

Dennis O'Keefe

A familiar comedy, adequately done, about a young man, played by O'Keefe, who inherits a million dollars and knocks himself out trying to spend it in two months so he can inherit even more. Bright, fast-paced mirth with a fine cast helping out with the spending spree. It should happen to you. Also with Helen Walker, Eddie "Rochester" Anderson, and June Havoc. **Director**—Allan Dwan.
            79 minutes b&w

THE BRIBE (1949)
★★

Robert Taylor
Ava Gardner

Taylor plays a G-man who pursues some criminals in Latin America and falls in love with sultry Gardner, the wife of one of the bad guys. Glossy, pretentious claptrap, which entertains on a rather low level. The usually competent players aren't at their best although the crooks are impressively menacing. Also with Charles Laughton, Vincent Price, and John Hodiak. **Director**—Robert Z. Leonard.
            98 minutes b&w

THE BRIDE CAME C.O.D. (1941)
★★★

Bette Davis
James Cagney

Davis and Cagney star in this workable comedy in which the talent salvages a cornball script. Cagney is a charter pilot who must deliver runaway bride Davis, but the plane crashes. Guess who falls in love with
(Continued)

B
- Bride of Frankenstein
- The Bridge of San Luis Rey
- The Bridge on the River Kwai
- The Bridges at Toko-Ri
- A Bridge Too Far
- Brief Encounter

(Continued) whom? This is Davis's first comedy role. She's not bad, and she improved her skills in subsequent pictures. Supporting players include Harry Davenport, Jack Carson, and Stuart Erwin. **Director**—William Keighley.

92 minutes b&w

In The Bride Came C.O.D., *James Cagney and Bette Davis discuss her prickly situation.*

BRIDE OF FRANKENSTEIN
(1935)
★★★★

Boris Karloff
Elsa Lanchester

Baron Frankenstein is coerced into reviving the monster and constructing a mate. This classic horror film, a sequel to *Frankenstein,* is better than the first film in many respects. It is expertly laced with wit, black comedy, pathos, and thrills galore. Karloff is back in his striking monster getup, and Lanchester is superb in dual roles; she plays the macabre mate of the monster and Mary Shelley. Also with Colin Clive, Valerie Hobson, and Ernest Thesiger. **Director**—James Whale. *80 minutes b&w*

THE BRIDGE OF SAN LUIS REY
(1944)
★★

Lynn Bari
Alla Nazimova
Louis Calhern

Painful, plodding film, based on Thornton Wilder's novel, about five people who are killed when a flimsy bridge in Peru collapses. A priest investigates the cause of the mishap and the reasons why the people were on the bridge at the moment of collapse. It's a hard pull for the cast and the director. The players also include Francis Lederer, Akim Tamiroff, and Donald Woods. **Director**—Rowland V. Lee. *85 minutes b&w*

THE BRIDGE ON THE RIVER KWAI (1957)
★★★★

Alec Guinness
Jack Hawkins
William Holden
Sessue Hayakawa

A superb war drama distinguished by magnificent acting and direction and an out-of-the-ordinary approach to its subject. Guinness stands out as a determined British commanding officer captured by the Japanese. He spurs his men to construct a railway bridge in Burma for their captors to maintain morale and demonstrate British engineering superiority; then he can't bear to see his own creation blown up by his own side. The film is blessed with gripping action, suspense, and a compelling script that bristles with ironies. The film is based on Pierre Boulle's novel. **Director**—David Lean. **Academy Awards**—best picture; Lean, best director; Guinness, best actor; Boulle, best screenplay (based on material from another medium); Jack Hildyard, cinematography. **Nomination**—Hayakawa, best supporting actor. *161 minutes*

Alec Guinness plays a determined British officer in The Bridge on the River Kwai.

THE BRIDGES AT TOKO-RI
(1954)
★★★

William Holden
Grace Kelly
Mickey Rooney

A powerful film about the adventures of a pilot during the Korean Conflict and the impact of the separation on his family. The action-packed thriller, based on James E. Michener's novel, is a cut above the usual war drama, with some impressive statements to make about fighting, comradeship, and family. Fine performances from Holden, Rooney, and Kelly. Also with Fredric March, Robert Strauss, and Charles McGraw. **Director**—Mark Robson.

104 minutes

A BRIDGE TOO FAR (1977)
★★

Dirk Bogarde
James Caan
Michael Caine
Sean Connery

It seems as if an entire regiment of movie notables appears in this $26-million epic based on Cornelius Ryan's best-seller about a disastrous Allied offensive during World War II. However, the Joseph E. Levine production is just another massive war movie mired in noise and confusion. Hardly any of the big American or British stars are on screen long enough to establish audience involvement. At an almost three-hour length, *A Bridge Too Far* is a movie too long. Also with Robert Redford, Elliott Gould, Laurence Olivier, and Ryan O'Neal. **Director**—Richard Attenborough. (PG) *175 minutes*

BRIEF ENCOUNTER (1946)
★★★★

Celia Johnson
Trevor Howard

A touching and sensitive love story that works surprisingly well in light of its familiar theme. A housewife, played by Johnson, has an affair with a local doctor, played by Howard. It ends abruptly when he takes a job in another country. Outstanding crafts-

- Brigadoon
- Bring Me the Head of Alfredo Garcia
- The Brink's Job
- Broadway
- Broken Arrow
- Broken Lance
- Bronco Billy

B

manship in all quarters has produced a classic romantic drama, with memorable love scenes that are a pleasure to watch. Also with Stanley Holloway and Joyce Carey. The film is based on Noel Coward's play. **Director**—David Lean. **Academy Award Nominations**—Lean, best director; Johnson, best actress; Anthony Havelock-Allan, Lean, and Ronald Neame, best writing (screenplay). *86 minutes b&w*

BRIGADOON (1954)
★★★

**Gene Kelly
Cyd Charisse
Van Johnson**

Gene Kelly and Van Johnson discover a magical Scottish village in Brigadoon.

Pleasant and charming film version of the Alan Jay Lerner and Frederick Loewe Broadway musical about two Americans—Kelly and Johnson—who discover a magical Scottish village that comes to life for a day every 100 years. Kelly and Charisse handle the dancing with grace and style, and the music is invigorating. The sets look artificial, but that doesn't distract much from the entertainment. Jimmy Thompson, Elaine Stewart, and Barry Jones have supporting roles. **Director**—Vincente Minnelli. *108 minutes*

BRING ME THE HEAD OF ALFREDO GARCIA (1974)
★

**Warren Oates
Gig Young**

A blood-and-gore drama about a Mexican seeking revenge on the person who seduced his daughter. Director Sam Peckinpah serves up his usual spread of violence garnished with plenty of gruesome details. However, the action is somewhat slow for this sort of outing. Isela Vega, Robert Webber, Emilio Fernandez, Helmut Dantine, and Kris Kristofferson are also in the cast. (R) *112 minutes*

THE BRINK'S JOB (1978)
★★

**Peter Falk
Robert Boyle**

The $2.7-million Brink's stickup in Boston was called "the crime of the century." This flippant account of the celebrated 1950 caper comes off as a petty theft. William Friedkin, who gave us the exciting *French Connection*, directs with scant energy or spirit. After sitting through this movie, you'll probably feel that you've been robbed. Also with Allen Goorwitz, Warren Oates, and Gena Rowlands. (PG) *103 minutes*

BROADWAY (1942)
★★★

**George Raft
Pat O'Brien**

Raft takes us down memory lane to the Prohibition era when he danced in nightclubs. Gangsters, bootleggers, chorus girls, and speakeasies are the backdrops for this colorful drama, which involves a murder. Raft plays himself and does some dancing. O'Brien plays a cop, and Broderick Crawford is effective as a tough gangster. Also with S. Z. Sakall and Janet Blair. **Director**—William A. Seiter. *90 minutes b&w*

BROKEN ARROW (1950)
★★★

**James Stewart
Jeff Chandler
Debra Paget**

A serious western drama, with Stewart as an Army scout sympathetic to the Indians and trying to promote peace and understanding between the redskins and the whites. The film is interesting because it doesn't present the Indians as cardboard characters; Chandler is impressive as Apache Chief Cochise, and Paget does well as Stewart's Indian wife. A few brisk action scenes perk up the straightaway narrative. Will Geer and Jay Silverheels co-star. **Director**—Delmer Daves. **Academy Award Nominations**—Chandler, best supporting actor; Michael Blankfort, writing (screenplay); Ernest Palmer, cinematography (color). *92 minutes*

BROKEN LANCE (1954)
★★★

**Spencer Tracy
Richard Widmark**

Tracy is effective as the patriarch of a fading cattle empire who grapples with family conflicts. The taut western drama, remade from *House of Strangers*, also offers a fine performance by Widmark as the unlikable eldest son. Robert Wagner and Jean Peters manage the romantic interlude. Other fine supporting performances from Hugh O'Brien, E. G. Marshall, and Katy Jurado. **Director**—Edward Dmytryk. **Academy Award**—Philip Yordan, writing (motion picture story). **Nomination**—Jurado, best supporting actress. *96 minutes*

BRONCO BILLY (1980)
★★★

**Clint Eastwood
Sondra Locke**

In Bronco Billy, *Clint Eastwood is the star and owner of a rickety Wild West show.*

A sweet-natured, low-key comedy with Eastwood as star and owner of a rickety Wild West show. The predict-
(Continued)

B
- The Brood
- Brother, Can You Spare a Dime?
- Brothers
- Brubaker
- Brute Force
- Buck Privates
- Buck Privates Come Home
- Buck Rogers in the 25th Century

(Continued)
able plot is strictly corn, but Eastwood has fashioned a warmhearted character, which keeps the film at a respectable comic level. Eastwood's "Billy" is a big kid, living in a fantasy world, who is sentimentally concerned about his likable ragtag troupe and his small-fry fans. Eastwood, who has played his Dirty Harry character to the hilt, is a charming "Mr. Clean." **Director**—Eastwood. (PG) *119 minutes*

THE BROOD (1980)
★★

Oliver Reed
Samantha Eggar

An effective yet overly grotesque Canadian-made horror film, written and directed by David Cronenberg, who borrowed freely from such shockers as *Night of the Living Dead*. Eggar plays a mental patient under the care of a bizzare doctor, played by Reed. She gives birth to strange children, who murder a number of people, including her mother and father. Cronenberg builds adequate suspense, but there's plenty of plodding amid the gore. (R) *90 minutes*

BROTHER, CAN YOU SPARE A DIME? (1975)
★★

This documentary takes you down memory lane via film clips and popular songs. The film, mainly about the Depression in the United States, dwells on such celebrities as James Cagney, W. C. Fields, FDR, and Al Jolson. A good try, but it can't quite make it. **Director**—Philippe Mora. (PG) *103 minutes b&w*

BROTHERS (1977)
★★★

Bernie Casey
Vonetta McGee

A dramatized semidocumentary, based on the love affair between black activist Angela Davis and George Jackson, one of the famed Soledad Brothers. The script is oversimplified and loaded in favor of the Jackson-Davis cause. Still, the film is an effective and jolting statement against racism, injustice, and the indignities of prison life. Casey in the Jackson role and McGee in the part of Davis display forceful and convincing characterizations. The film is a sober and refreshing departure from such black exploitation vehicles as *Superfly*. **Director**—Arthur Barron. (R) *104 minutes*

BRUBAKER (1980)
★★

Robert Redford
Yaphet Kotto
Murray Hamilton

Redford stars as a reform-minded prison warden, who halts corruption and torture only to be dismissed by the political establishment. Redford starts out as a prisoner to secretly witness the brutality. But when he soon reveals his identity, the film loses impact; the grim drama ends and sentimental sermonizing begins. **Director**—Stuart Rosenberg. (R) **Academy Award Nomination**—screenplay (written directly for the screen): W. D. Richter (screenplay), Richter and Arthur Ross (story). *131 minutes*

BRUTE FORCE (1947)
★★★★

Burt Lancaster
Charles Bickford

Exceptional big-house melodrama that lives up to its title with graphic detail of prison environment. Six desperate convicts plan to break out, getting revenge against a sadistic guard captain along the way. Tough, savage action leads up to a smashing climax. The fine cast also features Hume Cronyn, Ella Raines, Yvonne De Carlo, Ann Blyth, Howard Duff, and Sam Levene. **Director**—Jules Dassin. *96 minutes b&w*

BUCK PRIVATES (1941)
★★★

Bud Abbott
Lou Costello

Abbott and Costello join the Army, and after an energetic romp of escapades, they accidentally become heroes. This is typical service comedy corn with some romantic subplots thrown in, but it works for Abbott and Costello. This was one of their first starring films, and their success won them promotions as the top sergeants of movie comedy. Lee Bowman, Alan Curtis, Jane Frazee, Nat Pendleton, and the Andrews Sisters round out the cast. **Director**—Arthur Lubin. *84 minutes b&w*

BUCK PRIVATES COME HOME (1946)
★★

Bud Abbott
Lou Costello

Abbott and Costello muster out of the Army and care for a European war orphan. This is a rather flimsy slapstick comedy and certainly not at the level of *Buck Privates*. However, the film perks up considerably with a chase sequence at the finale. Beverly Simmons, Tom Brown, and Nat Pendleton co-star. **Director**—Charles T. Barton. *77 minutes b&w*

BUCK ROGERS IN THE 25TH CENTURY (1979)
★★

Gil Gerard
Pamela Hensley
Erin Gray

This is a film based on the sci-fi comic strip character, but there's more inspiration from *Star Wars*. You'll see space hardware galore, a climactic shootout among rocket ships, and a pixie robot that's an obvious rip-off of R2-D2. The

Gil Gerard plays the title role in Buck Rogers in the 25th Century *with tongue in cheek.*

- Bucktown
- Buddy Buddy
- The Buddy Holly Story

- Buffalo Bill and the Indians, or Sitting Bull's History Lesson
- Bug

- The Bugs Bunny/Road Runner Movie
- Bugsy Malone
- Bullit

B

film looks dazzling most of the time thanks to the snappy direction of Daniel Haller. Small fry should be able to handle the simple good-guy/bad-guy plot and take delight in the wise-cracks of Gerard, who plays the title role. (PG)   *89 minutes*

BUCKTOWN (1975)
(no stars)

**Fred Williamson
Pam Grier**

A black exploitation movie about a cool and tough man who returns to his hometown to try to wipe out "honky" corruption. There's a silly script with lots of violence and a dash of sex. Also with Thalmus Rasulala, Tony King, and Bernie Hamilton. **Director—**Arthur Marks. (PG)   *94 minutes*

BUDDY BUDDY (1981)
★★

**Jack Lemmon
Walter Matthau**

What a team: Billy Wilder directing Matthau and Lemmon in this farce about a hit man trying to bump off a stool pigeon while a suicidal schnook keeps interfering with the assassination plan. Matthau plays the hood, and Lemmon is the schnook—and what a disappointment. The comedy material is consistently off stride and only manages to generate a few smiles. It's all sadly trite and strained; not what anyone would expect from the folks responsible for hits like *The Fortune Cookie*. Paula Prentiss and Klaus Kinski co-star. (R)   *96 minutes*

THE BUDDY HOLLY STORY
(1978)
★★★★

**Gary Busey
Don Stroud**

A first-rate, realistic film biography of the talented rockabilly composer-musician who introduced such '50s hits as "Peggy Sue" and "That'll Be the Day." Lanky, toothsome Busey, in the title role, lights up the screen with his energetic musical and dramatic performance. The story follows Holly's career beginning as a roller

Gary Busey stars in The Buddy Holly Story, *a film biography of the rockabilly composer-musician.*

rink musician in Texas to his death at 22 in a plane crash. Best of all is the way the film captures the joy and enthusiasm of early rock 'n' roll and its effect on young people. **Director—**Steve Rash. (PG) **Academy Award Nomination**—Busey, best actor.
114 minutes

BUFFALO BILL AND THE INDIANS, OR SITTING BULL'S HISTORY LESSON (1976)
★★★

**Paul Newman
Joel Grey**

Robert Altman's intelligent and penetrating study of the legendary showbiz hero of the late 1800s shows Buffalo Bill as an egotistical, inflated product of publicity. The film is also about genocide committed against the Indians. Newman gives a keen and often amusing performance in the title role. Frank Kaquitts plays an impressive, silent, and dignified Sitting Bull, who was signed to appear in Buffalo Bill's Wild West Show. There are some uneven and dreary moments, which lessen the film's impact. But it succeeds in its creativity and its reexamination of history. Also with Kevin McCarthy, Burt Lancaster, and Geraldine Chaplin. **Director—**Altman. (PG)   *120 minutes*

BUG (1975)
(no stars)

**Bradford Dillman
Joanna Miles**

A rather absurd story about foot-long insects that pour out of a fissure in a farmer's field after an earthquake. The abominable buggers start fires and other assorted chaos. Also with Rich-

ard Gilliland and Jamie Smith Jackson. **Director—**Jeannot Szwarc. (PG)
100 minutes

THE BUGS BUNNY/ ROAD RUNNER MOVIE (1979)
★★★

**Bugs Bunny
Road Runner
Daffy Duck
Wile E. Coyote
Porky Pig**

Now you can really indulge yourself in an hour and a half of nonstop fun with Bugs, Daffy, Wile E. Coyote, and other stars from the Warner Brothers cartoon stable. Animator Chuck Jones has compiled scenes from numerous cartoons and has included several complete short features. There's about 20 minutes of new animation with Bugs as narrator. It's a nostalgic, colorful parade of great animated comedy—that's what's up, Doc! (G)
92 minutes

BUGSY MALONE (1976)
★★★

**Scott Baio
Florrie Dugger
Jodie Foster**

An ingeniously conceived and lavish '20s gangster movie played entirely by kids whose average age is 12. Most of the youngsters perform rather well, dressed in pinstriped double-breasted suits and flapper outfits. The tommy guns splatter their victims with whipped cream. Veteran actress Foster (age 14) is outstanding as a brassy showgirl. The film is made with care and affection, yet it's top-heavy with old movie clichés, and momentum is lost toward the end. Also with John Cassisi and Martin Lev. **Director—**Alan Parker. (G)   *93 minutes*

BULLITT (1968)
★★★★

**Steve McQueen
Jacqueline Bisset
Robert Vaughn**

Stylish, stirring detective thriller with McQueen smartly cast as a San Fran-
(Continued)

(Continued)

cisco cop trying to put the lid on underworld activity. A key witness in McQueen's charge is killed, and he tracks down the murderers. The action-packed drama, graced by efficient direction, ends in a classic car chase that is well above the ordinary. The fine supporting cast includes Don Gordon, Robert Duvall, and Simon Oakland. **Director**—Peter Yates.

113 minutes

BUNDLE OF JOY (1956)
★★

Debbie Reynolds
Eddie Fisher

Reynolds and Fisher star in this thin and occasionally cute musical comedy remade from *Bachelor Mother*. Reynolds plays a department store clerk, who discovers an abandoned child; people suspect that her boyfriend, played by Fisher, is the father. Fisher sings some forgettable songs, and the cast milks a few laughs from the script. Also with Adolphe Menjou, Melville Cooper, and Tommy Noonan. **Director**—Norman Taurog. *98 minutes*

THE BURNING (1981)
(no stars)

Brian Matthews
Leah Ayres

A cheaply made potboiler that blatantly rips off *Friday the 13th* and a few other horror movies. In this film, the killer is a camp counselor who was badly burned because of a prank. Now disfigured, he returns to the camp where he murders young people with large garden shears. The film overflows with red herrings, the direction is uninspired, and the acting isn't so hot either. **Director**—Tony Maylan. (R) *90 minutes*

BURNT OFFERINGS (1976)
★★★

Karen Black
Oliver Reed

Skillful direction from Dan Curtis produces a lot of chills and tension in this thriller about a family who rents a creepy old mansion for the summer.

There are solid performances, too, from Black, Reed, Lee Montgomery, and Bette Davis. Clichés are sprinkled throughout the plot, and the ending is predictable. But the eerie goings-on at that rambling murderous house and the mystery behind the locked door on the top floor will keep moviegoers on the edges of their seats. Also with Burgess Meredith and Eileen Heckart. (PG) *115 minutes*

BUS STOP (1956)
★★★

Marilyn Monroe
Don Murray

Monroe displays competent acting talent as well as her familiar sex appeal in this comedy-drama about ordinary people. She plays a voluptuous cafe singer who entices a naïve cowboy, played by Murray, while his friends urge him not to get involved. The film, based on William Inge's play, offers an entertaining mixture of sensitive drama and comic moments. Betty Field stands out as a waitress. Eileen Heckart, Arthur O'Connell, Hope Lange, and Hans Conried co-star. **Director**—Joshua Logan. **Alternate Title**—*Wrong Kind of Girl*. **Academy Award Nomination**—Murray, best supporting actor. *96 minutes*

BUSTIN' LOOSE (1981)
★★

Richard Pryor
Cicely Tyson

Pryor stars as a small-time thief who shepherds some rascally children to the West Coast in a rickety bus. Pryor

In Bustin' Loose, Richard Pryor meets an unexpected guard dog.

fans will love some of his funny skits. His self-parodying style has great charm, but as the script gains sentimentality, his talents are undermined; the tone becomes domesticated and even tacky. The kids are precocious (clones of *The Bad News Bears?*). Tyson is a social worker and the unlikely romantic interest of Pryor. **Director**—Oz Scott. (R) *94 minutes*

BUTCH AND SUNDANCE: THE EARLY DAYS (1979)
★★

William Katt
Tom Berenger

This prequel to *Butch Cassidy and the Sundance Kid* explores how the two outlaws met and some of their preliminary escapades. Berenger and Katt are in the title roles, but there's no special chemistry between them as we witnessed with Paul Newman and Robert Redford in the original, which was made 10 years earlier. The prequel also lacks spirit and style, and the script is as hollow as a drainpipe. It seems their early days were dreary days. **Director**—Richard Lester. (PG) *110 minutes*

BUTCH CASSIDY AND THE SUNDANCE KID (1969)
★★★★

Paul Newman
Robert Redford
Katherine Ross

This humorous and cheerful western offers a full complement of film excellence: superb direction, winning performances, effective comedy, and the memorable tune "Raindrops Keep Fallin' on My Head." Newman and Redford strike up perfect chemistry together as clownish outlaws with a sheriff's posse always one step behind. The appealing movie begins energetically and never flags. There is enthusiastic support from Ross, Strother Martin, Jeff Corey, and Cloris Leachman. **Director**—George Roy Hill. (PG) **Academy Awards**—William Goldman, best story and screenplay (based on material not previously published or produced); Conrad Hall, cinematography. **Nominations**—best picture; Hill, best director. *110 minutes*

★ STAR PROFILE

- Butterfield 8
- Butterflies Are Free
- Bye Bye Birdie
- By Love Possessed
- By the Light of the Silvery Moon

B

BUTTERFIELD 8 (1960)
★★

Elizabeth Taylor
Laurence Harvey

The only thing going for this routine melodrama is a slick performance by Taylor as a high-priced call girl who longs to get out of the profession. The film, based on John O'Hara's novel, starts off awkwardly and never really picks up steam. Harvey is impressive as Taylor's Mr. Right. There's adequate support, too, from Dina Merrill, Mildred Dunnock, and Betty Field. **Director**—Daniel Mann. **Academy Award**—Taylor, best actress. **Nomination**—Joseph Ruttenberg and Charles Harten, cinematography (color).

108 minutes

BUTTERFLIES ARE FREE (1972)
★★★

Goldie Hawn
Edward Albert

Hawn stars in this lighthearted film as a flighty actress who falls in love with a blind young man next door. Then she has to deal with his overprotective mother. Based on Leonard Gershe's Broadway play, the film adaptation is somewhat confined, but good acting by the top cast overcomes the drawback. Hawn is perfectly cast, and Eileen Heckart is brilliant as the possessive mother. Albert plays the blind man. **Director**—Milton Katselas. **Academy Award**—Heckart, best supporting actress. **Nomination**—Charles B. Lang, cinematography.

109 minutes

Goldie Hawn, Eileen Heckart, and Edward Albert star in the comedy Butterflies Are Free.

BYE BYE BIRDIE (1963)
★★★

Janet Leigh
Dick Van Dyke
Ann-Margret

A teenage singing sensation gives his final TV show before leaving for military service. This frothy musical is based on the Broadway show and features some pleasant numbers, including "Put on a Happy Face." Van Dyke is good as a songwriter, and Paul Lynde and Maureen Stapleton are impressive as frantic parents. The film should have special appeal for younger audiences. Also with Bobby Rydell and Ed Sullivan. **Director**—George Sidney.

112 minutes

BY LOVE POSSESSED (1961)
★★

Lana Turner
Efrem Zimbalist, Jr.

A dour melodrama about a successful but lonely New England lawyer, played by Zimbalist, who has an affair with the restless wife of his partner. Turner plays the wife. The cast is presentable, but the soapy script is rather unmoving. This film is based loosely on a James Gould Cozzens novel. Jason Robards, Jr., Barbara Bel Geddes, George Hamilton, and Thomas Mitchell co-star. **Director**—John Sturges.

116 minutes

BY THE LIGHT OF THE SILVERY MOON (1953)
★★★

Doris Day
Gordon MacRae

A pleasant musical-comedy vehicle tailor-made for Day, who has lots of old-fashioned songs to sing. The film is set in a small American town just after World War I, and it involves family problems with a returning soldier. MacRae is a fine singing partner for Day. The screenplay, which is a sequel to *On Moonlight Bay*, is based on a Booth Tarkington story. Leon Ames, Rosemary DeCamp, and Mary Wickes co-star. **Director**—David Butler.

101 minutes

RICHARD DREYFUSS

Born in Brooklyn in 1947, Richard Dreyfuss began his acting career in Los Angeles community theater after his family moved to California in 1956.

After graduating from Beverly Hills High School, he briefly attended San Fernando Valley State College and then worked for two years as a clerk in a Los Angeles hospital to fulfill his conscientious objector status during the Vietnam War. By the late '60s, Dreyfuss was commuting from coast to coast doing Broadway, off-Broadway, and improvisational comedy as well as guest appearances on television. He made his film debut in Hello Down There (1968), but gained prominence with his sensitive performance as a college-bound boy in American Graffiti (1973).

Dreyfuss drew further praise for his portrait of an aggressive youth in Montreal's Jewish ghetto in The Apprenticeship of Duddy Kravitz (1974). Starring roles in Jaws (1975), Inserts (1975), and Close Encounters of the Third Kind (1976) led to his romantic lead in The Goodbye Girl (1977), which brought him the Oscar at the age of 29. Some of his recent movies include The Competition (1980) and Whose Life Is It Anyway? (1982).

After winning an Academy Award, Dreyfuss also began an ongoing relationship with the Shakespearean Company in Lennox, Massachusetts; he played Cassius in the Brooklyn Academy of Music production of Julius Caesar and Iago in Othello twice, the first time at the Alliance Theatre in Atlanta with Paul Winfield as Othello.

C
- Cabaret
- Cabin in the Sky
- Caboblanco
- Cactus Flower
- Caddie
- The Caddy
- Caddyshack
- Cafe Express

C

CABARET (1972)
★★★★

Liza Minnelli
Joel Grey
Michael York

Smashing, masterful musical with the showstopping performance of Minnelli as Sally Bowles, an American singer working in Berlin on the eve of World War II. The multitalented Minnelli proves to be a fantastic actress as well as a singer-dancer, and she's complemented nicely by Bob Fosse's stylish direction and choreography. The film loosely follows the Broadway musical, based on Christopher Isherwood's stories, but the script also relies on the plot of *I Am a Camera*. The political backdrop of Hitler's Germany is handled intelligently. Also with Helmut Griem, Fritz Wepper, and Marisa Berenson. (PG) **Academy Awards**—Bob Fosse, best director; Minnelli, best actress; Grey, best supporting actor; Geoffrey Unsworth, cinematography. **Nomination**—Jay Allen, best screenplay (based on material from another medium). *123 minutes*

In Cabaret, *Liza Minnelli portrays Sally Bowles, a singer working in Berlin.*

CABIN IN THE SKY (1943)
★★★

Eddie "Rochester" Anderson
Ethel Waters
Lena Horne

God and the Devil compete for the soul of a gambling man in this delightful musical, which features an all-black cast. The film doesn't quite live up to the play, but it's energetic and engrossing nevertheless. The superb cast also includes Cab Calloway and Louis Armstrong. With such giants of entertainment on board, it's watchable indeed. **Director**—Vincente Minnelli. *99 minutes b&w*

CABOBLANCO (1980)
(no stars)

Charles Bronson
Fernando Rey
Jason Robards, Jr.

This is an inept, lamebrained rehash of *Casablanca*. This time the setting is Peru, and Bronson is in the Humphrey Bogart role as owner of a small nightclub. Rey replaces Claude Rains as the corrupt law official, Robards subs for Paul Henreid, and Dominique Sanda has the Ingrid Bergman part. All are less than adequate here. The plot has them double- and triple-crossing one another in the search for gold aboard a sunken ship. The audience, however, gets the real double-cross. **Director**—J. Lee Thompson. (R) *87 minutes*

CACTUS FLOWER (1969)
★★

Ingrid Bergman
Walter Matthau
Goldie Hawn

Despite the fine cast, this film version of the Broadway comedy doesn't hold up. Matthau plays a dentist in love with his nurse, who is played by Bergman. She drops her defensive attitude when she discovers he's sincere. Bergman is miscast for this sort of part, and the starchy dialogue is a noticeable drawback. But Hawn shines as the dentist's mistress, who is forsaken for the nurse. Also with Jack Weston, Vito Scotti, and Irene Hervey. **Director**—Gene Saks. (PG) **Academy Award**—Hawn, best supporting actress. *103 minutes*

CADDIE (1981)
★★

Helen Morse

A well-intentioned but pedestrian Australian biographical film about a struggling single woman who supports two young children while working as a barmaid during the '20s and '30s. The sets are handsome and authentic-looking, but the story really goes nowhere. Morse stars as the resolute, independent lass who becomes involved in several on-again, off-again romances that are as interesting as the affairs in a soap opera that has gone on too long. **Director**—Donald Crombie. (No MPAA rating) *107 minutes*

THE CADDY (1953)
★★

Dean Martin
Jerry Lewis

Martin and Lewis star in this film about golf. The production is organized in a series of vignettes, with Lewis as a golf enthusiast trying to build up Martin's game. This is certainly not the best the pair has to offer, but there are some good moments and Martin sings, "That's Amore." Donna Reed, Fred Clark, and Barbara Bates co-star. **Director**—Norman Taurog. *95 minutes b&w*

CADDYSHACK (1980)
★

Chevy Chase
Ted Knight
Rodney Dangerfield
Bill Murray

There are silly high jinks on the golf links with Chase, Knight, Dangerfield, and Murray engaging in crude jokes that mostly misfire. There's only a ghost of a plot—something about a polite but poor caddy trying to wheedle help for a college scholarship from an influential club member. Generally, the film is a series of dopey throwaway vignettes that poke fun at the WASPy country club set. **Director**—Harold Ramos. (R) *98 minutes*

CAFE EXPRESS (1981)
★★

Nino Manfredi

Manfredi, star of *Bread and Chocolate*, plays a gypsy coffee vendor aboard a train who is chased by the cops as if he

● The Caine Mutiny ● California Split
● Calamity Jane ● California Suite
● California Dreaming ● Caligula
● Call Me Bwana

C

were public enemy number one. Manfredi is a charming con artist, bravely outmaneuvering the authorities and hoodwinking the passengers. But the situations, shot almost entirely aboard the train, are rather confining. The jokes generate only smiles where belly laughs would do. In Italian with English titles. **Director**—Nanni Loy. (No MPAA rating)   *105 minutes*

THE CAINE MUTINY (1954)
★★★★

**Humphrey Bogart
José Ferrer
Van Johnson**

A powerful adaptation of Herman Wouk's gripping Pulitzer Prize novel of Navy officers who rebel against the neurotic captain of a destroyer escort during World War II. This absorbing film offers exciting action and first-class performances, which graphically portray the frustrations and character traits of the subjects. Bogart is especially memorable as the unhinged skipper. The film ends in a smashing court-martial climax with the resolution of justice under question. Also with Fred MacMurray, E. G. Marshall, Lee Marvin, and Tom Tully. **Director**—Edward Dmytryk. **Academy Award Nominations**—best picture; Bogart, best actor; Tully, best supporting actor; Stanley Roberts, writing (screenplay).   *125 minutes*

Humphrey Bogart is Queeg, the paranoid captain in The Caine Mutiny.

CALAMITY JANE (1953)
★★★

**Doris Day
Howard Keel**

A pleasant, energetic musical that's just the right vehicle for Day, who stars in the title role. Doris plays the rough-and-ready frontier girl with plenty of vigor. She's tamed by Keel, who co-stars as Wild Bill Hickok. The film is a little on the order of *Annie Get Your Gun*. It has a pleasant score, including the Oscar-winning song, "Secret Love." Phil Carey, Allyn McLerie, Dick Wesson, and Paul Harvey lend support. **Director**—David Butler.   *101 minutes*

CALIFORNIA DREAMING (1979)
★

**Glynnis O'Connor
Seymour Cassel**

A raunchy, adolescent beach-party film about the so-called carefree lifestyle of youthful southern California. There's lots of surfing, volleyball, boozing, and sex . . . all of which, we are told by the meager story line, are necessary for the character development of young people. The mostly unknown players are competent and look attractive in swimsuits, but the film has all the depth and perspective of a second-rate TV comedy series. **Director**—John Hancock. (R) *92 minutes*

CALIFORNIA SPLIT (1974)
★★★

**Elliott Gould
George Segal**

Uneven but cheerful and entertaining comedy especially suited for those who like director Robert Altman's unique style. Gould and Segal are compulsive gamblers who become fast friends and go on a spree together. Altman manages to present these oddball characters in a way that's touching and amusing. Ann Prentiss and Gwen Welles are effective as a couple of amateur hookers. Also with Joseph Walsh and Bert Remsen. (R)

109 minutes

CALIFORNIA SUITE (1978)
★★

**Jane Fonda
Alan Alda
Maggie Smith
Michael Caine
Walter Matthau
Elaine May
Richard Pryor
Bill Cosby**

A bevy of top film stars talk, talk, talk in this Neil Simon comedy, set in the Beverly Hills Hotel. This movie version of the Broadway stage production is changed from four separate playlets to a cohesive story, but the effect is a labored, ragged barrage of wisecracks. There's top-notch acting, but even the good performances wear thin from the tiresome dialogue, which sounds like incessant bickering after a while. **Director**—Herbert Ross. (PG) **Academy Award**—Smith, best supporting actress. **Nomination**—Simon, best screenplay adaptation. *103 minutes*

CALIGULA (1980)
(no stars)

**Malcolm McDowell
Peter O'Toole
John Gielgud**

Penthouse magazine publisher Bob Guccione produced this vulgar $17-million porno spectacle set in first-century Rome. It's a lengthy smorgasbord of explicit sex, mixed with assorted horrors, such as disembowelment, castration, decapitation, and strangulation. Just watching this mess can be a real workout. **Director**—Giovanni Tinto. (No MPAA rating)   *150 minutes*

CALL ME BWANA (1962)
★★

**Bob Hope
Anita Ekberg**

Hope goes to Africa to find a lost space capsule and tries to elude foreign agents. Typical Hope farce with some effective jokes, but not quite enough to sustain the movie. Ekberg and Edie Adams are just lovely to look at.
(Continued)

C

- Call Me Madam
- Call Me Mister
- Call Northside 777
- Camelot
- Can-Can
- The Candidate
- Candleshoe

(Continued)
Lionel Jeffries, Percy Herbert, and Paul Carpenter are also in the cast. **Director**—Gordon Douglas.

103 minutes

CALL ME MADAM (1953)
★★★★

**Ethel Merman
Donald O'Connor
George Sanders
Vera-Ellen**

Merman belts out Irving Berlin songs with her typical gusto in this lively and colorful film version of the Broadway musical. She plays an energetic Washington party-giver ("the hostess with the mostess"), who is appointed U.S. Ambassador to Lichtenberg. Merman is supported by a splendid cast. Some of the political jokes, however, are out-of-date. Also with Billy de Wolfe, Helmut Dantine, and Walter Slezak. **Director**—Walter Lang. *117 minutes*

CALL ME MISTER (1951)
★★

**Betty Grable
Dan Dailey**

Dailey, a GI stationed in Japan, goes AWOL to join his show-biz wife, played by Grable, who is dancing and singing with the USO. This version isn't as effective as the Broadway musical, but there are some good moments in the predictable screenplay. Danny Thomas, Dale Robertson, and Richard Boone have supporting parts. **Director**—Lloyd Bacon. *95 minutes*

CALL NORTHSIDE 777 (1948)
★★★

**James Stewart
Lee J. Cobb
Helen Walker**

Stewart plays a determined Chicago reporter. He painstakingly uncovers evidence to free a man who was convicted of murder 11 years earlier. The compelling semidocumentary thriller, based on a true story, is executed with impressive atmosphere and excellent acting. Stewart's step-by-step assembly of the facts is handled with pacing that builds suspense toward a satisfy-

Richard Harris (right) stars in the musical Camelot, *the story of King Arthur and his knights.*

ing climax. Also with E. G. Marshall, Kazia Orzazewski, and Betty Garde. **Director**—Henry Hathaway.

111 minutes b&w

CAMELOT (1967)
★★

**Richard Harris
Vanessa Redgrave**

An overblown, overstuffed version of the successful Lerner and Loewe Broadway musical that strains for style and charm, but never makes it. Harris and Redgrave star in the classic story of King Arthur and his gallant knights. The acting is fine, but no one really does justice to the memorable songs. And Joshua Logan's glossy direction lacks imagination. David Hemmings, Lionel Jeffries, and Franco Nero are also in the cast. **Academy Award Nomination**—Richard H. Kline, cinematography. *181 minutes*

CAN-CAN (1960)
★★

**Frank Sinatra
Shirley MacLaine**

This shallow version of the Cole Porter musical stars Sinatra as a 19th-century Parisian lawyer, who defends a nightclub entertainer, played by MacLaine, for performing an allegedly lewd dance. Sinatra doesn't seem to be with it, and MacLaine is miscast. Maurice Chevalier and Louis Jourdan add their charm, but it's not enough to prop up

the sagging script. Some memorable songs are featured though, including "C'est Magnifique," "I Love Paris," and "Just One of Those Things." Also with Juliet Prowse and Leon Belasco. **Director**—Walter Lang. *131 minutes*

THE CANDIDATE (1972)
★★★

**Robert Redford
Peter Boyle**

Redford plays a liberal lawyer from California, who runs for senator and discovers there are more than issues and ideals at stake. He has a firm hand on the part and seems right at home in this probing and honest political satire that captures the flavor of the campaign trail. The film maintains its vibrant energy to the very end. Don Porter and Melvyn Douglas are effective in supporting roles. **Director**—Michael Ritchie. (PG) **Academy Award**—Jeremy Larner, best story and screenplay (based on factual material or material not previously published). *110 minutes*

CANDLESHOE (1977)
★★★

**Jodie Foster
Helen Hayes
David Niven**

A charming sugarplum from Walt Disney. Foster is a streetwise orphan who poses as a lost heiress in the estate of Hayes to find a hidden family trea-

- Cannonball
- The Cannonball Run
- Can't Stop the Music

- Cape Fear
- Capone
- Capricorn One
- Captain Horatio Hornblower

C

sure. Niven plays the butler and three other characters with obvious relish. With such a first-rate cast and the winning Disney formula of comedy and suspense, it's fun and merriment all the way. Of course, there's a happy ending. Also with Leo McKern, Veronica Quilligan, and Ian Sharrock. **Director**—Norman Tokar. (G)
101 minutes

CANNONBALL (1976)
★

David Carradine
Bill McKinney

This is another car-wreck saga with special appeal to the crash crowd. This orgy of screeching tires and bashed fenders involves a race from Los Angeles to New York with $100,000 for the winner. Carradine and McKinney lead the convoy across the continent, leaving a wake of flaming wrecks. Directed by Paul Bartel, who seems to specialize in such hysteria. Also with Veronica Hamel, Judy Canova, and Gerrit Graham. (PG)
93 minutes

THE CANNONBALL RUN (1981)
★★

Burt Reynolds

Reynolds and many of his pals star in yet another reckless-driving movie on the order of *Smokey and the Bandit*. The story concerns a coast-to-coast car race that defies the country's speed laws.

In The Cannonball Run, *Burt Reynolds drives a disguised van in a madcap race.*

But this theme is so worn by now that the film runs out of steam long before the cars can cross the finish line. A steady stream of cornball gags accompany the crashes and breakdowns. The good breezy fun of the *Smokey* outings is sorely missing. **Director**—Hal Needham. (PG)
95 minutes

CAN'T STOP THE MUSIC (1980)
★★★

Village People
Valerie Perrine
Bruce Jenner

A brassy, eye-popping rock musical that features the Village People, who blast out some hot numbers, including their show-stopping "YMCA." The music does stop occasionally to make way for a silly plot that's reminiscent of old MGM musicals. But then it's back to the music and the film is flying high with razzle-dazzle songs, crisp choreography, and glittering costumes. There's no energy crisis here. Also with Steve Guttenberg. **Director**—Nancy Walker. (PG)
118 minutes

CAPE FEAR (1962)
★★★

Gregory Peck
Robert Mitchum
Polly Bergen

A grim thriller with moderate suspense about an ex-convict who seeks revenge on the lawyer he believes responsible for his prison sentence. Mitchum plays the sadistic bad guy who threatens to rape the wife of lawyer Peck. The wife is played by Bergen. The performances are convincing. The film, based on a John D. MacDonald novel, is set in the bayous of the Deep South. Martin Balsam, Jack Kruschen, Lori Nelson, and Telly Savalas also star. **Director**—J. Lee Thompson.
106 minutes b&w

CAPONE (1975)
★★

Ben Gazzara
Susan Blakely

A film biography of Scarface Al, from his rise to power in Chicago to his

imprisonment for tax evasion. There's lots of blood and gunfighting, laced with some *Godfather* treatment. It's a familiar and sometimes tedious gangster saga, but the action moves along efficiently. Also with Harry Guardino, John Cassavetes, Sylvester Stallone, and Frank Campanella. **Director**—Steve Carver. (R)
101 minutes

CAPRICORN ONE (1978)
★★★

Elliott Gould
James Brolin
Karen Black
Telly Savalas

James Brolin, O. J. Simpson, and Sam Waterston in Capricorn One.

NASA tries to pull off a fake landing on Mars in this rip-snorting action melodrama, starring Gould and Brolin. The plot is rather farfetched, but there's no doubt about the suspense and excitement. A chase sequence with two helicopters and a cropdusting plane piloted by Savalas just may have you on the edge of your seat. Peter Hyams's direction is nicely paced. Also with Brenda Vaccaro, O. J. Simpson, Hal Holbrook, and Sam Waterston. (PG)
124 minutes

CAPTAIN HORATIO HORNBLOWER (1951)
★★★

Gregory Peck
Virginia Mayo

Peck plays Hornblower, the 19th-century English naval hero who outmaneuvers the Spanish and the French during the Napoleonic wars. Peck sweats and strains in this sprawling sea epic, but he manages to look
(Continued)

⭐ **STAR PROFILE**

C
- Captain Lightfoot
- The Captain's Paradise
- The Car
- Caravans
- Carbon Copy

(Continued)

valiant. The colorful film, based on the C. M. Forester novels, also features Robert Beatty, James Robertson Justice, and Denis O'Dea in supporting roles. **Director**—Raoul Walsh.

117 minutes

CAPTAIN LIGHTFOOT (1955)
★★

Rock Hudson
Barbara Rush

Hudson plays an Irish rebel adventurer in this handsome costume drama filmed in Ireland. The film is set in the time of the Irish rebellion in the 19th century. Rush is fine as the female lead, but Hudson looks like he would rather be cavorting with Doris Day. Also with Jeff Morrow, Kathleen Ryan, Finlay Currie, and Denis O'Dea. **Director**—Douglas Sirk.   *92 minutes*

THE CAPTAIN'S PARADISE (1953)
★★★

Alec Guinness
Yvonne De Carlo
Celia Johnson

A fine droll comedy starring Guinness as a ferry boat skipper who has a wife at each end of his route. Guinness expertly fills the role with his usual measure of dry wit played rather straight-faced. De Carlo and Johnson are perfectly cast as the unsuspecting wives, who accommodate the contrasting aspects of the captain's personality. It's a great sophisticated romp. Bill Fraser and Charles Goldner also star. **Director**—Anthony Kimmins.   *80 minutes b&w*

THE CAR (1977)
★★

James Brolin
Kathleen Lloyd
Ronny Cox

Here's further exploitation of the heavy scare movie in the *Jaws* tradition. In this case, it's a menacing, driverless, automobile that terrorizes a small Southwestern town by running down most of the cast. The performances are amateurish, the dialogue is

silly and thin, but the film delivers the required forceful tension and energy. The monstrous, mysterious car upstages the human actors. Also with John Marley and R. G. Armstrong. **Director**—Elliot Silverstein. (PG)

95 minutes

CARAVANS (1978)
★★

Anthony Quinn
Jennifer O'Neill

This film, based on James Michener's tale of desert nomads, has the trappings of an epic: elegant photography, colorful native dances, and so on. But when the plot gets moving, it's evident there's scant drama and low credibility. The story deals with the search for an American woman, played by O'Neill, who is living with a desert

PETER O'TOOLE

Peter O'Toole was born in 1932, in Connemara, County Galway, Ireland, and spent his childhood in Kerry, Dublin, Gainsborough, and, finally, Leeds. Following two years of National Service in the Royal Navy, he won a scholarship to the Royal Academy of Dramatic Art.

O'Toole's first professional engagement was with the Bristol Old Vic Company, and during the 3½ years that followed, he played 73 different roles. O'Toole made his West End (the London equivalent of Broadway) debut in the musical Oh, My Papa, and later toured England in The Holiday, in which the young Welsh actress, Sian Phillips, played the part of his sister. They married and had two children.

In 1959, O'Toole was named "Actor of the Year" for his performance as Charlie Bamforth in

tribe, led by Quinn. O'Neill, who constantly encounters sand storms and camels, looks as if she is ready to pose for *Vogue*. Incredible. Also with Michael Sarrazin, Christopher Lee, Joseph Cotten, and Barry Sullivan. **Director**—James Fargo. (PG)

·*123 minutes*

CARBON COPY (1981)
★★

George Segal
Susan Saint James

Segal stars as a successful businessman who had an affair with a black woman long ago, and now his black son comes knocking on his door. This silly comedy confronts racial prejudice in a rather absurd manner as Segal faces numerous problems because of the revelation. However, the

the West End play The Long, the Short and the Tall; while appearing in this play, he made his film debut with a small part in Kidnapped. O'Toole was then signed by Jules Buck for the role of a young Scots Guards lieutenant in The Day They Robbed the Bank of England (1960). During this period, O'Toole and producer Buck formed Keep Films, Ltd., their own production company.

O'Toole then starred at the Stratford-on-Avon Memorial Theatre, playing in three roles—Shylock in The Merchant of Venice, Petruchio in The Taming of the Shrew, and Thersites in Troilus and Cressida. In 1960, he was asked to play the title role in Lawrence of Arabia (1962), a film that won awards around the world and made O'Toole an international star. Although he has yet to win an Oscar, he has been nominated more than half a dozen times.

O'Toole's list of film credits also includes Becket (1964), Lord Jim (1965), What's New Pussycat? (1965), How To Steal a Million (1966), The Lion in Winter (1968), Goodbye, Mr. Chips (1969), Murphy's War (1970), Under Milk Wood (1971), The Ruling Class (1971), Rosebud (1975), and The Stunt Man (1980).

- Carnal Knowledge
- Carny
- Carousel
- The Carpetbaggers
- Carrie
- Car Wash

C

George Segal in Carbon Copy, *a "black" comedy.*

cliché-strewn film ends on a happy note. Also with Jack Warden, Denzel Washington, and Paul Winfield. **Director**—Michael Schultz. (PG)
92 minutes

CARNAL KNOWLEDGE (1971)
★★★

**Jack Nicholson
Arthur Garfunkel
Candice Bergen
Ann-Margret**

Writer Jules Feiffer and director Mike Nichols team up to explore the sexual attitudes and problems of the American male as seen through the experiences of two men from college to middle-age. Nicholson and Garfunkel do well as the main subjects in this uneven comedy-drama that strikes out in new directions. Ann-Margret deserves applause for her shining role as Nicholson's coquettish mistress. Also with Rita Moreno, Cynthia O'Neal, and Carol Kane. (R) **Academy Award Nomination**—Ann-Margret, best supporting actress. *97 minutes*

CARNY (1980)
★★

**Jodie Foster
Gary Busey
Robbie Robertson**

A brassy, semidocumentary look at carnival life, with perceptive performances by Foster, Busey, and Robertson. Director Robert Kaylor captures the grimy atmosphere of carny life. Unfortunately, a feeble script fritters away the talents of the energetic cast. Busey is fascinating as a dunk-tank bozo, and Foster sheds some of her former innocence in her role as a bored teenager who joins the show. But the film bogs down in an unfocused romantic triangle and finally ends on an unsatisfying note. (R) *106 minutes*

CAROUSEL (1956)
★★★

**Gordon MacRae
Shirley Jones**

A handsome film musical based on Ferenc Molnár's play *Liliom*, with the memorable Rodgers and Hammerstein music pleasantly adapted. MacRae plays a gruff carnival barker who wants a better way of life when he marries a modest girl, played by Jones. Tragedy, however, gets in the way of his ambition. MacRae and Jones sing beautifully, and the photography is stunning. Songs include "If I Loved You" and "You'll Never Walk Alone." Also with Cameron Mitchell, Robert Rounseville, and Gene Lockhart. **Director**—Henry King. *128 minutes*

THE CARPETBAGGERS (1964)
★★★

**George Peppard
Carroll Baker
Alan Ladd**

A brash young man takes over an aircraft manufacturing business and then pyramids his fortune into other ventures, including moviemaking. This film version of the Harold Robbins novel, which parallels the career of Howard Hughes, is made in a garish fashion, but it's entertaining nevertheless. Peppard portrays the eccentric industrialist. This was Ladd's last film. Also with Martin Balsam, Bob Cummings, Elizabeth Ashley, Lew Ayers, and Archie Moore. **Director**—Edward Dmytryk. *150 minutes*

CARRIE (1976)
★

**Sissy Spacek
Piper Laurie**

An uneven horror tale about a weird teenage girl who is tormented by her

Sissy Spacek plays the title role in Carrie.

high school classmates. She finally uses her power of telekinesis in revenge. Director Brian De Palma has tried to fashion a sort of *Death Wish* with overtones of Alfred Hitchcock-type suspense, but the scheme hardly works. The film is scary and taut for only a brief moment at the end; most of the time it's awkward and puzzling. Also with William Katt, John Travolta, and Amy Irving. (R) **Academy Award Nominations**—Spacek, best actress; Laurie, best supporting actress.
97 minutes

CAR WASH (1976)
★

**Richard Pryor
Irwin Corey
Franklyn Ajaye
George Carlin**

(Continued)

Customers and workers of Car Wash, *a comedy about a typical zany day at a Los Angeles car wash.*

C
- Casablanca
- Casanova Brown
- Casanova's Big Night
- The Cassandra Crossing
- Cass Timberlane
- Cat and Mouse
- Cat Ballou

(Continued)

Zany characters jive, work in rhythm, and play jokes on one another in this noisy comedy about a day at a Los Angeles car wash. There's a certain formlessness to this lively pop film, much in the style of *American Graffiti*. But it's hardly in keeping with *Graffiti*'s depth. Not much happens dramatically—two of the biggest gags involve a dog that relieves itself on the driveway and a boy who throws up all over his mother's car. The cast consists mostly of unknown players. Directed by Michael Schultz, who was responsible for *Cooley High*. (PG)   *97 minutes*

CASABLANCA (1943)
★★★★

**Humphrey Bogart
Ingrid Bergman
Claude Rains
Paul Henreid**

Crackling intrigue, tingling romance, and a superb moody atmosphere make this taut melodrama one of the best World War II films. Bogart, in a memorable performance, is in top form as the owner of a dingy Casablanca nightclub. He helps an old flame, played by Bergman, and her underground leader-husband, played by Henreid, escape the Nazis. This classic, witty thriller seems to earn more appreciation as time goes by. Also with Conrad Veidt, S. Z. Sakall, Peter Lorre, and Sydney Greenstreet. **Director**—Michael Curtiz. **Academy Awards**—best picture; Curtiz, best director; Julius J. Epstein, Philip G. Epstein, and Howard Koch, best writing (screenplay). **Nominations**—Bogart, best actor; Rains, best supporting actor; Arthur Edeson, cinematography (black and white).
102 minutes b&w

Ingrid Bergman and Humphrey Bogart share a newspaper in the film classic Casablanca.

CASANOVA BROWN (1944)
★★

**Gary Cooper
Teresa Wright**

Mediocre comedy starring Cooper as a divorced professor who learns that his former wife, played by Wright, is pregnant just as he is about to remarry. The cast tries hard to squeeze some amusement from the material, but they often seem to overwhelm it. Also with Frank Morgan and Anita Louise. **Director**—Sam Wood.
94 minutes b&w

CASANOVA'S BIG NIGHT (1954)
★★

**Bob Hope
Joan Fontaine**

Hope plays a tailor's apprentice who masquerades as the great Italian lover and winds up in some intriguing comic situations. This film is the last of Hope's lavish costume farces, and it generally wastes his talents. However, just his presence is good for some laughs. The film plods haphazardly despite the supporting efforts of Basil Rathbone, Raymond Burr, and Audrey Dalton. **Director**—Norman McLeod.
86 minutes

THE CASSANDRA CROSSING (1977)
★

**Sophia Loren
Burt Lancaster
Richard Harris
Ava Gardner**

This tedious film, directed by George Pan Cosmatos and produced by Carlo Ponti, is another all-star disaster epic filled with strained and hokey situations. It's mainly about 1,000 disease-exposed passengers trapped on board an express train heading for a rickety bridge somewhere in Poland. Loren, Harris, Lancaster, and others are hopelessly miscast. The cardboard script is loaded with dreary interpersonal problems. Half the train hurtles to destruction in a final special-effects gimmick. As for the deadly germs, they mutate to something like an annoying cold, which is similar to sitting through this movie. Also with Martin Sheen, O. J. Simpson, and John Philip Law. (PG)   *127 minutes*

CASS TIMBERLANE (1947)
★★★

**Spencer Tracy
Lana Turner**

Tracy plays a judge in a midwestern community who marries a young working-class girl, played by Turner, and strives to keep up with her youthful ways. This nicely mounted drama, based on the Sinclair Lewis novel, offers Tracy an ideal, sympathetic role. Although the story is not among Lewis's best, it is played out well on the screen. The fine cast also includes Zachary Scott, Tom Drake, Mary Astor, and Albert Dekker. **Director**—George Sidney.   *119 minutes b&w*

CAT AND MOUSE (1978)
★★

**Michele Morgan
Jean-Pierre Aumont
Serge Reggiani**

French filmmaker Claude Lelouch is at his usual playfulness with this thriller about the mysterious death of a wealthy businessman, played by Aumont. Reggiani is a police inspector looking for the murderer. The complex plot may be too confusing at times because it's muddled with too many flashbacks and subplots. But it's a challenge for armchair detectives. The ravishing Morgan, who plays the widow and prime suspect, heads an excellent cast. In French with English titles. **Director**—Lelouch. (PG)
107 minutes

CAT BALLOU (1965)
★★★

**Jane Fonda
Lee Marvin**

Marvin is marvelous as a whiskey-soaked, over-the-hill gunslinger, who is hired to eliminate a vicious killer. He plays the role of the killer, too. This unusual western spoof features Fonda

- Catch-22
- The Catered Affair
- The Cat From Outer Space
- Cat on a Hot Tin Roof
- Cattle Annie and Little Britches
- Caught in the Draft
- Caveman

C

in the title role, as a young outlaw who employs the gunslinger. The smart screenplay contributes to the mirth and the direction is on the money. Michael Callan, Nat King Cole, Stubby Kaye, Dwayne Hickman, and Reginald Denny are in supporting roles. **Director**—Eliot Silverstein. **Academy Award**—Marvin, best actor. **Nomination**—Walter Newman and Frank R. Pierson, best screenplay (based on material from another medium).

96 minutes

CATCH-22 (1970)
★★★★

**Alan Arkin
Martin Balsam
Richard Benjamin
Art Garfunkel**

This wry black comedy, based on Joseph Heller's popular novel, is one of the best antiwar films. The story concerns a medium-bomber group in the Mediterranean during World War II. One by one, officers are killed in various ways. Arkin leads the gallery of outsized characters by playing Yossarian, a desperate and logical flyer who strives to be classified insane so he can avoid going on bombing missions. Other fine performances are given by Jack Gilford, Buck Henry, Bob Newhart, Paula Prentiss, Anthony Perkins, Jon Voight, Martin Sheen, and Orson Welles. **Director**—Mike Nichols. (R)   *122 minutes*

THE CATERED AFFAIR (1956)
★★★

**Bette Davis
Ernest Borgnine
Debbie Reynolds
Rod Taylor**

The wife of a Bronx taxi driver wants her daughter to be married in style, but the planned affair is more than the family can afford. This intelligent comedy, which is adapted from Paddy Chayefsky's TV play, succeeds much in the style of *Marty*. Davis is excellent as the overreaching mother, and Reynolds is effective as the daughter. Borgnine plays Davis's husband. Barry Fitzgerald and Dorothy Stickney also star. **Director**—Richard Brooks.

93 minutes b&w

THE CAT FROM OUTER SPACE
(1978)
★★★

**Ken Berry
Sandy Duncan
McLean Stevenson**

In The Cat From Outer Space, *Ken Berry and Sandy Duncan introduce spacecat Jake to Lucy Belle.*

Walt Disney Productions joins the space movie race with this delightful film about a cat from another planet, who makes an emergency landing on Earth. The handsome feline—named Jake—encounters adventure and excitement galore as he attempts to return to the planet of the pussycats with the help of space scientists Berry and Duncan. The plot is predictable, but the special effects and fast pacing should delight the youngsters. Goes down easily with plenty of popcorn. Also with Harry Morgan, Roddy McDowall, and Ronnie Schell. **Director**—Norman Tokar. (G)

104 minutes

CAT ON A HOT TIN ROOF
(1958)
★★★★

**Elizabeth Taylor
Paul Newman
Burl Ives**

This film version of Tennessee Williams's powerful play about a patriarchal Southern family is somewhat stage-bound, but is entertaining on many levels. Taylor is excellent as the wife of a frustrated young man, played by Newman, who's under the control of his dying father. Ives is convincing as "Big Daddy," the overwhelming plantation owner, and the

rest of the cast turns in credible performances. Also with Jack Carson, Judith Anderson, and Madeleine Sherwood. **Director**—Richard Brooks. **Academy Award Nominations**—best picture; Brooks, best director; Newman, best actor; Taylor, best actress; Brooks and James Poe, best screenplay (based on material from another medium); William Daniels, cinematography (color).   *108 minutes*

CATTLE ANNIE AND LITTLE BRITCHES (1981)
★★★

**Burt Lancaster
Rod Steiger
Amanda Plummer**

The western movie gets a comic kick in the pants with this lighthearted tale of two teenage girls who try to inject some spirit into the fading Doolin-Dalton gang. The cast is impeccable. Lancaster is magnificent as the aging outlaw boss. Steiger is brittle and eloquent as the U.S. marshal. And watch out for Plummer as Annie; this young actress, making her screen debut, gives class and dazzle to the spunky character. **Director**—Lamont Johnson. (PG)   *95 minutes*

CAUGHT IN THE DRAFT (1941)
★★★

**Bob Hope
Dorothy Lamour**

One of Hope's better comedies. There are plenty of well-timed gags and nice support from a good cast. Bob is a movie star who resists joining the Army, but he accidentally enters the service at last. A sprightly, funny service comedy for its time. Effective performances, too, from Lynne Overman, Clarence Kolb, and Eddie Bracken. **Director**—David Butler.   *82 minutes*

CAVEMAN (1981)
★★

**Ringo Starr
Dennis Quaid**

A feeble spoof of our prehistoric ancestors, who defend themselves
(Continued)

C
- Chain Lightning
- The Champ
- Champion
- The Changeling
- A Change of Seasons
- The Chant of Jimmie Blacksmith
- Chapter Two

Atouk (Ringo Starr) is leader of a group of misfit primitives in the comedy Caveman.

(Continued)

against dinosaurs and discover fire, the slingshot, love, and jealousy. The broad slapstick comedy is sort of a primitive version of Mel Brooks's *Silent Movie*, with some campy special effects tossed in. The tribesmen are cartoon characters who don't actually speak; they grunt bits of strange dialogue, which becomes tiresome before long. The Flintstones are funnier and more colorful. Also with Shelley Long, Jack Gilford, and John Matuszak. **Director**—Carl Gottlieb. (PG)

91 minutes

CHAIN LIGHTNING (1950)
★★

**Humphrey Bogart
Eleanor Parker**

Bogart plays a World War II flyer who adapts to the new and faster jet aircraft when the war ends. There are nice scenes of the jets in action, but Bogey can't keep a shallow script airborne. Also, he has more trouble trying to deal with Parker than he does with the new planes. Raymond Massey, Richard Whorf, and James Brown are also in the cast. **Director**—Stuart Heisler.

94 minutes b&w

THE CHAMP (1979)
★

**Jon Voight
Faye Dunaway
Ricky Schroder**

The tear-drenched Wallace Beery-Jackie Cooper tale of 1931 returns to the screen, with Voight as the has-been boxer and moppet Schroder as his adoring son. Along comes the boy's mother, played by Dunaway, after a seven-year absence to claim her child. What follows is such unrestrained pathos that any honest drama is drowned in its wake. Director Franco Zeffirelli doesn't spare a single gimmick to wrench tears from the viewer, but under the slick veneer is a distinct staleness. Also with Jack Warden, Arthur Hill, Strother Martin, Joan Blondell, and Elisha Cook. (PG)

121 minutes

CHAMPION (1949)
★★★★

**Kirk Douglas
Arthur Kennedy
Lola Albright**

A stylish, rousing fight film based on the Ring Lardner short story. Douglas is in the title role as a determined boxer, who bulldozes his way to the top, alienating friends and relatives along the way. He then dies as the result of a boxing match. Obviously, the story is a cliché by now, but it's nicely handled and acted with much energy. A good role for Douglas and effective backup from Kennedy, Albright, Marilyn Maxwell, and Ruth Roman. **Director**—Mark Robson. **Academy Award Nominations**—Douglas, best actor; Kennedy, best supporting actor; Carl Foreman, writing (screenplay); Frank Planer, cinematography (black and white).

99 minutes b&w

THE CHANGELING (1980)
★★★

**George C. Scott
Trish Van Devere
Melvyn Douglas**

A haunted Victorian mansion. Strange noises in the night. A piano plays by itself. An eerie seance. The dusty room in the attic. Déjà vu? Perhaps. But director Peter Medak adds stylish and chilling dimensions to this stock material that would frighten Dracula's mother. Scott, who rents the spooky old house, unravels a 70-year-old murder mystery with the help of a venge-ful spirit. Scott and Douglas contribute strong performances to make this a relentlessly suspenseful story. Also with John Colicos and Jean Marsh. (R)

109 minutes

A CHANGE OF SEASONS (1980)
★★

**Shirley MacLaine
Anthony Hopkins
Bo Derek**

MacLaine, Hopkins, and Derek star in this compex comedy about the sexual revolution. When professor Anthony has an affair with fetching student Bo, wife Shirley fights back by having an affair with the young campus carpenter. The plot gets even more involved, and what's supposed to be satire becomes just silly and absurd. MacLaine turns in a fine performance; as for Bo, she's still only a sex symbol. Also with Michael Brandon and Mary Beth Hurt. **Director**—Richard Lang. (R)

102 minutes

THE CHANT OF JIMMIE BLACKSMITH (1980)
★★★

Tommy Lewis

This handsome, compelling Australian film explores racism through the experience of an earnest half-caste young man, who violently rebels after being exploited by white employers. The film bulges with excessive detail and plot. Nevertheless, director Fred Schepisi effectively hammers home a sense of helplessness and rage at the upshot of the encroachment of European culture on the Aborigines. Lewis is effective in the title role. (No MPAA rating)

122 minutes

CHAPTER TWO (1979)
★★

**James Caan
Marsha Mason
Valerie Harper**

Neil Simon brings this semiautobiographical Broadway play to the screen. It's the story of a successful writer, played by Caan, who remarries

- Charade
- The Charge of the Light
  Brigade

- Chariots of Fire
- Charley and the Angel
- Charley's Aunt
- Charlie Bubbles

C

After a whirlwind courtship, James Caan and Marsha Mason tie the knot in Chapter Two.

shortly after his first wife's death, but guilt plagues his efforts to settle into an earnest romance. Simon's glib lines undercut the serious scenes. Caan is miscast, but Mason, as his second wife, grabs the full flavor of her role. As well she might, because she's the second Mrs. Simon. Also with Joseph Bologna. **Director**—Robert Moore. (PG) **Academy Award Nomination**—Mason, best actress. *124 minutes*

CHARADE (1963)
★★★★

**Cary Grant
Audrey Hepburn**

Grant is suave as usual in this romantic comedy set in glittering Paris. Hepburn plays a widow whose late husband stashed away a fortune. Some bad guys want the money, and they believe Audrey knows where it's hidden. Along comes handsome Grant offering help and sympathy, but is he really on her side? It's lightweight fare patterned after Hitchcock's style, and it keeps moving along. The excellent supporting cast includes Walter Matthau, James Coburn, and George Kennedy. **Director**—Stanley Donen. *113 minutes*

THE CHARGE OF THE LIGHT BRIGADE (1968)
★★

**Trevor Howard
John Gielgud
David Hemmings**

This handsome drama is well acted, but fails to come across. It's built on the events at the time of the 1854 battle at Balaclava, Turkey, during the Cri-

mean War, when the British were defeated by the Russians. The film makes an antiwar statement and offers an impressive battle scene, but it stumbles into plot potholes too often. Richard Williams's special animated portions help a little. The cast includes Vanessa Redgrave and Jill Bennett. **Director**—Tony Richardson. (PG) *141 minutes*

CHARIOTS OF FIRE (1981)
★★★

**Ben Cross
Ian Charleson**

Ben Cross, as running ace Harold Abrahams, breaks the tape in Chariots of Fire.

A handsome, well-made drama based on the true story of two English champion runners, who compete in the 1924 Paris Olympics. Hugh Hudson, directing his first theatrical film, magnificently assembles a flowing narrative brimming with believable characters and stunning period detail. Cross is fine as running ace Harold Abrahams, who competes to compensate for religious bigotry. Charleson does nicely as fleet-footed Eric Liddell, who runs for the glory of God. The film also offers a nice contrast to the contemporary megabucks sports business. (PG) *123 minutes*

CHARLEY AND THE ANGEL (1974)
★★

**Fred MacMurray
Cloris Leachman
Harry Morgan**

Rather typical Walt Disney sentimental piece about a small-town merchant, played by MacMurray, who mellows his attitude toward his family when he finds out he only has a short time to live. Morgan plays the angel. There are some amusing moments and a predictably happy ending, but the expected Disney warmth seems trumped up. The plot partially follows the events of *On Borrowed Time*. Also with Kurt Russell, Kathleen Cody, and Vincent Van Patten. **Director**—Vincent McEveety. (G) *93 minutes*

CHARLEY'S AUNT (1941)
★★★

**Jack Benny
Kay Francis**

Benny hams it up with glee in this familiar Victorian farce about the Oxford student who impersonates a rich maiden aunt to help out a roommate. The comedy is strained at times, but it's a good opportunity to observe the great Benny do his stuff. Other cast members are also in top form, including James Ellison, Anne Baxter, Laird Cregar, and Edmund Gwenn. **Director**—Archie Mayo. *81 minutes b&w*

CHARLIE BUBBLES (1968)
★★★

**Albert Finney
Billie Whitelaw
Liza Minnelli**

Finney directs and stars in this clever fantasy about a young man who suddenly becomes very wealthy, only to find boredom with the emptiness of an artificial environment. The film is sometimes slow and uneven, but it offers a fascinating character sketch and some effective scenes of the man inundated by pointless electronic gadgets. Minnelli turns in a good act-
(Continued)

C
• Charlie Chan and the Curse
  of the Dragon Queen
• Charly

• The Cheap Detective
• Cheaper by the Dozen

WARREN BEATTY

Born Warren Beaty in Richmond, Virginia, in 1937, Beatty first came to the attention of critics with his acclaimed Broadway debut in William Inge's play, A Loss of Roses.

His first film as an actor was Splendor in the Grass (1961), directed by Elia Kazan. This was followed by José Quintero's The Roman Spring of Mrs. Stone (1961), John Frankenheimer's All Fall Down (1962), Robert Rossen's Lilith (1965), and Arthur Penn's Mickey

One (1965). Penn also directed Beatty's production of Bonnie and Clyde (1967). This was followed by George Stevens' The Only Game In Town (1969), Robert Altman's McCabe and Mrs. Miller (1971), Richard Brooks's $ (1972), and Alan J. Pakula's The Parallax View (1974). Beatty also appeared in Shampoo (1975), which he produced and co-wrote with Robert Towne. After an appearance in Mike Nichols's The Fortune (1975), Beatty produced, co-wrote, co-directed, and starred in the box-office hit Heaven Can Wait (1978). He then produced, directed, wrote, and starred in Reds (1981).

During his career, Beatty has received more than 10 Academy Award nominations, including two for best screenplay, three for best actor, two for directing, and three as the producer of the best picture.

He is the younger brother of actress Shirley MacLaine.

(Continued)

ing job as Finney's secretary. The ending is sort of a letdown when Finney tries to return to his original lifestyle. Colin Blakely, Timothy Garland, and Alan Lake are also in the cast. (R)   *91 minutes*

CHARLIE CHAN AND THE CURSE OF THE DRAGON QUEEN (1981)
★

**Peter Ustinov
Richard Hatch
Lee Grant
Angie Dickinson
Roddy McDowall**

The redoubtable Oriental detective is called out of retirement to solve some bizarre murders in San Francisco. But curses, this high-budget feature is a low-level comedy overloaded with slapstick routines. Ustinov as grandpa Chan is rather good—at least in solving the drawing-room caper. But Grant, Dickinson, Hatch, and McDowall waste their talents with embarassing situations that are supposed to be comic. Also with Brian Keith and Rachel Roberts. **Director—Clive Donner. (PG)   97 minutes**

CHARLY (1968)
★★★

**Cliff Robertson
Claire Bloom
Lilia Skala**

Robertson's stellar performance dominates this tale of a mentally retarded baker who becomes a genius after submitting to a new surgical technique. It's based on Daniel Keyes's *Flowers for Algernon*. The screenplay, however, is overly sentimental and somewhat unconvincing—especially during a romantic interlude between Charly and an intelligent woman, played by

Bloom, after the operation has taken effect. Also with Leon Janney and Dick Van Patten. **Director**—Ralph Nelson. **Academy Award**—Robertson, best actor. (PG)   *106 minutes*

THE CHEAP DETECTIVE (1978)
★★★

**Peter Falk
Ann-Margret
Sid Caesar
Louise Fletcher**

Writer Neil Simon fondly parodies a slew of Humphrey Bogart melodramas of the '40s, with wit, humor, and a good-natured elbow-poke to the ribs. The timing doesn't always work well and the plot tries to cover too much ground, but the Simon dialogue, loaded with stalwart one-liners, goes down easily. The blue-ribbon cast has a fine time carving up *The Maltese Falcon*, *Casablanca*, and *The Big Sleep*. Falk leads the pack with a priceless imitation of Bogart. Also with Nicol Williamson, Eileen Brennan, Stockard Channing, Dom DeLuise, James Coco, and many other stars. **Director**—Robert Moore. (PG)   *92 minutes*

CHEAPER BY THE DOZEN (1950)
★★★

**Clifton Webb
Myrna Loy**

Webb is perfectly cast as Frank Gilbreth, the patriarch who ran his large family with the same discipline and efficiency that he applied to motion and time study methods for industry. The lilting comedy, set in the '20s, is

Clifton Webb, Myrna Loy, and the rest of the clan in the comedy Cheaper by the Dozen.

- Cheaper to Keep Her
- Cheech and Chong's Next Movie
- Cheech and Chong's Nice Dreams
- Cheyenne Autumn
- The Cheyenne Social Club
- The Chicken Chronicles
- Chief Crazy Horse

C

based on the popular book by two of the 12 Gilbreth children. This is definitely one of Webb's best performances, set in a somewhat corny but funny framework. Loy is exceptionally good, too, as the stalwart mother of the family. Other cast members include Jeanne Crain, Edgar Buchanan, Barbara Bates, and Mildred Natwick. **Director**—Walter Lang. *86 minutes*

CHEAPER TO KEEP HER (1980)
★

Mac Davis

A silly and offensive comedy-drama that awkwardly pokes fun at women, Mexican-Americans, and homosexuals. Davis, in a wasted effort, plays a roguish detective hired by a female lawyer to track down men who skip their alimony payments. Davis tries to make like Burt Reynolds. But, saddled with such shabby material, he just makes frivolous comedy. The film is nothing more than a cheap shot. **Director**—Ken Annakin. (R) *92 minutes*

CHEECH AND CHONG'S NEXT MOVIE (1980)
★

Cheech Marin
Thomas Chong

Another chapter in the silly misadventures of Cheech and Chong of counterculture comedy fame. The scroungy, pot-smoking duo carry their inane antics to a welfare office, a massage parlor, the home of a wealthy family, and finally into space, all the while mumbling their repetitious and dopey dialogue. It's a sort of stoned version of a Marx Brothers comedy that wouldn't work even if they were acting sober. Unfortunately, this wasn't their last movie. **Director**—Chong. (R) *99 minutes*

CHEECH AND CHONG'S NICE DREAMS (1981)
★★

Cheech Marin
Thomas Chong

A third round of spaced-out high jinks from "Los Guys," whose brand of humor seems to improve with age. This time the maestros of the marijuana set peddle their wares from an ice cream truck and engage in a variety of disjointed situations. The film is short on plot, and many skits are merely silly. But this outing is executed with the typical unflagging hazy humor that will surely appeal to the turned-on set. As Cheech might say, "Hey man, this is a groovy movie." **Director**—Chong. (R) *88 minutes*

CHEYENNE AUTUMN (1964)
★★★

Richard Widmark
Carroll Baker
Karl Malden

Director John Ford's sprawling epic western tells the harrowing story of starving Indians trekking from their barren Oklahoma reservation to their original home, 1,500 miles away in Wyoming. The Indians also have to fight the U.S. Cavalry, which wants them to stay put. The handsome production features fine acting by Widmark, Baker, and Malden. Also with Dolores Del Rio, Ricardo Montalban, Gilbert Roland, Sal Mineo, and Victor Jory. There are nice cameos, too, from James Stewart and Edward G. Robinson. However, the historical drama seems rather ponderous after a while. **Academy Award Nomination**— William Clothier, cinematography (color). *160 minutes*

Richard Widmark is flanked by two cavalrymen in Cheyenne Autumn, *director John Ford's epic about a 1,500-mile Indian trek.*

THE CHEYENNE SOCIAL CLUB (1970)
★★

James Stewart
Henry Fonda
Shirley Jones

Stewart and Fonda running a brothel on the western frontier? That's good for some laughs, but there aren't enough of them in this comedy, which offers too many clichés and too much adolescent humor. A shoot-out at the end perks things up, but what we really need are some bawdy girls and some bawdy jokes that work. Jones plays the madam of the house. Also with Sue Anne Langdon, Robert Middleton, and Arch Johnson. **Director**— Gene Kelly. (PG) *102 minutes*

THE CHICKEN CHRONICLES (1977)
★

Steven Guttenberg
Ed Lauter
Lisa Reeves

A trite and silly comedy about high school life in the late '60s among affluent teenagers in Beverly Hills. The plot touches on moral statements about the Vietnam War, the drug scene, sexual liberation, and absentee parents. The acting by the mostly young cast is second-rate. Phil Silvers is on board as the owner of a chicken take-out joint at which some of the youngsters work. Also with Meridith Baer and Gino Baffa. **Director**— Francis Simon. (PG) *95 minutes*

CHIEF CRAZY HORSE (1954)
★★

Victor Mature
Suzan Ball
John Lund

Mature is in the title role as the famous Indian chief who leads his braves at the Little Big Horn and defeats General Custer. The clichéd western, which is seen from the side of the Indians, involves the chief's dealings with an Army officer. Mature is convincing as the tough Indian warrior. *(Continued)*

C
● The Children
● The Children of Theater Street
● The Children's Hour
● China Doll
● The China Syndrome
● Chinatown
● Chitty Chitty Bang Bang

(Continued)
Also with Keith Larsen and Ray Danton. **Director**—George Sherman.

86 minutes

THE CHILDREN (1980)
★

Martin Shakar
Gil Rogers
Gale Garnett

A nuclear power plant releases a radioactive mist that turns some schoolchildren into monsters. The nasty tykes commit such despicable acts as killing their parents with deadly hugs. It's a cheaply made, lackluster horror film with a predictable script, dreadful acting, and the usual amount of gore. These kids should neither be seen nor heard. **Director**—Max Kalmanowicz. (R)   *90 minutes*

THE CHILDREN OF THEATER STREET (1978)
★★

This Soviet-American documentary takes us behind the scenes of Leningrad's famous Kirov Ballet School. The photography is beautiful, but the film plods too often. Grace Kelly's narration is loaded with clichés. The movie, which follows the experiences of three young dancers, is perhaps of special interest for ballet lovers. **Directors**—Robert Dornhelm and Earle Mack. (No MPAA rating)   *100 minutes*

THE CHILDREN'S HOUR (1961)
★★★

Audrey Hepburn
Shirley MacLaine

MacLaine and Hepburn star in this touching drama about a malicious schoolgirl. She alleges that her teachers are lesbians, causing them untold grief. The film, based on Lillian Hellman's play, was originally filmed as *These Three*. The explicit treatment of lesbianism was somewhat daring at the time of release, but the theme has lost impact. Yet the movie is compelling, and Hepburn and MacLaine are exceptional as the maligned teachers. There is good support from James Gar-

ner, Miriam Hopkins, and Fay Bainter. **Director**—William Wyler. **Academy Award Nominations**—Bainter, best supporting actress; Franz F. Planer, cinematography (black and white).

108 minutes b&w

CHINA DOLL (1958)
★

Victor Mature
Li Li Hua
Bob Mathias

Soggy, romantic story about a World War II pilot who accidentally buys a Chinese maid. They eventually get married, but are both killed in the war. Then their daughter comes to the United States. Mature and Hua star, but they cannot overcome the dull script. Ward Bond and Stuart Whitman are also in the cast. **Director**—Frank Borzage.   *88 minutes b&w*

THE CHINA SYNDROME (1979)
★★★★

Jane Fonda
Jack Lemmon
Michael Douglas

A nuclear power plant goes on the fritz and touches off a dangerous confrontation. This dynamite thriller stars Fonda and Lemmon. Fonda gives a super performance as an ambitious "Brenda Star" TV newswoman. Lemmon, meanwhile, performs convincingly as the plant engineer with a

Jane Fonda, playing a TV reporter, witnesses a near-disaster in The China Syndrome.

nagging conscience. Director James Bridges maintains relentless tension from the start right up to the hair-raising climax. It's classic entertainment that packs a wallop and makes a vivid social observation. Also with Scott Brady, James Hampton, Peter Donat, and Wilford Brimley. (PG) **Academy Award Nominations**—Lemmon, best actor; Fonda, best actress; Mike Gray, T. S. Cook, and James Bridges, best screenplay (written directly for the screen).

123 minutes

CHINATOWN (1974)
★★★★

Jack Nicholson
Faye Dunaway
John Huston

Compelling and suspenseful private-eye yarn filled with all sorts of goodies in the spirit of Hammett-Chandler mysteries. Nicholson is excellent as the Los Angeles gumshoe who becomes involved over his head in an intricate web of murder and political corruption concerning a fortune in land and water rights. He's led into this complex situation by the beautiful Dunaway as femme fatale extraordinaire. Director Roman Polanski handles the 1930s atmosphere with exceptional skill. Also with Perry Lopez, John Hillerman, and Diane Ladd. (R) **Academy Award**—Robert Towne, best original screenplay. **Nominations**—best picture; Polanski, best director; Nicholson, best actor; Dunaway, best actress; John A. Alonzo, cinematography.

131 minutes

CHITTY CHITTY BANG BANG (1968)
★★

Dick Van Dyke
Sally Ann Howes

Van Dyke and the rest of the cast mainly waste their time with this flimsy children's fantasy-musical about an inventor who produces a flying car. Nothing seems to click, including the special effects and a score that features many forgettable songs. There are a few scenes for the kids to laugh at, but it's pretty tame stuff. The script is based on a book by

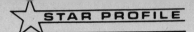

Ian Fleming. Anna Quayle, Gert Frobe, Lionel Jeffries, Benny Hill, and James Robertson Justice also star. **Director**—Ken Hughes. (G)

145 minutes

THE CHOIRBOYS (1977)

★

**Perry King
Don Stroud
James Woods**

A vulgar, cheap-looking, black comedy based on one of Joseph Wambaugh's best-selling novels about Los Angeles cops. The inept production is a series of rambling vignettes sprinkled with adolescent sex jokes and coarse cut-ups. The direction by Robert Aldrich is chaotic, and the acting is amateurish. Also with Charles Durning, Louis Gossett, Jr., and Tim McIntire. **Director**—Aldrich. (R)

119 minutes

C.H.O.M.P.S. (1979)

★

**Wesley Eure
Valerie Bertinelli
Conrad Bain**

You've heard of the Bionic Man? Well, here's the bionic pooch, which closely resembles *Benji*. The corny plot has to do with a local burglar alarm company on the threshold of bankruptcy. An eager-beaver employee, played by Eure, designs the dauntless robot dog, a feat that saves the company and wins the affection of the boss's daughter, played by Bertinelli. The silly outing resembles many an outdated TV sitcom. You might as well watch reruns of *Mr. Ed*. Also with Chuck McCann, Red Buttons, Hermione Baddeley, and Jim Backus. **Director**—Don Chaffey. (PG)

89 minutes

THE CHOSEN (1978)

★

**Kirk Douglas
Agostina Belli**

Douglas plays an industrialist who gets all tangled up with the Antichrist and nuclear power plants. Even a nice fellow like Kirk can't rescue the confused plot that must have been cooked

up by the Devil himself. Douglas, of course, goes on to save the world from nuclear destruction, but this film hardly saves his reputation as a respected actor. Simon Ward, Anthony Quayle, and Virginia McKenna are in supporting roles. **Director**—Alberto De Martino. (R)

105 minutes

CHRISTMAS IN CONNECTICUT (1945)

★★

**Barbara Stanwyck
Dennis Morgan
Sydney Greenstreet**

Stanwyck stars in this lightweight farce. She's a newspaper columnist who invites a war hero, played by Morgan, to her home for Christmas to impress her editor, played by Greenstreet. Since she has no family, she must assemble one for the occasion.

ROBERT MITCHUM

Robert Mitchum's first film was a role as a bad guy in a Hopalong Cassidy western in 1940. He had small roles in a number of movies after that, but didn't catch the attention of audiences until 1944, when he appeared in the low-budget movie When Strangers Marry *and in a supporting role in* Thirty Seconds Over Tokyo.

Born in Bridgeport, Connecticut, in 1917, Mitchum dropped out of school when he was 14 and worked as a deckhand on a salvage vessel. During the Depression, he worked his way across the country. His sister introduced him to the Long Beach Theater Guild, where he began as a stagehand and only later became an actor, performing in The Petrified

The cast succeeds in making the most of this froth, which offers a few good moments. But there's not enough going on to really impress the audience. Also with Reginald Gardiner, S. Z. Sakall, and Robert Shayne. **Director**—Peter Godfrey.   *101 minutes*

CHU CHU AND THE PHILLY FLASH (1981)

★

**Alan Arkin
Carol Burnett**

Arkin and Burnett waste their talents and energy as two bedraggled characters in this plodding, no-laughs comedy set in San Francisco. Burnett plays a luckless entertainer, and Arkin is a derelict who was once a pro baseball player. They accidentally meet when they stumble onto some secret documents belonging to underworld

(Continued)

Forest *and* Remember the Day. *He also wrote children's plays, comedy material, and organized a road tour for astrologist Carroll Richter.*

During the late '40s, better roles in Till the End of Time *(1946),* Undercurrent *(1946),* Crossfire *(1947),* Desire Me *(1947),* Out of the Past *(1947),* Rachel and the Stranger *(1948),* Blood on the Moon *(1948), and* The Red Pony *(1949) made him a box-office favorite.*

Some of Mitchum's other films include My Forbidden Past *(1951),* His Kind of Woman *(1951),* Angel Face *(1953),* River of No Return *(1954),* Track of the Cat *(1954),* Not as a Stranger *(1955),* Heaven Knows, Mr. Allison *(1957), and* Fire Down Below *(1957). Under Charles Laughton's direction, he starred in James Agee's* The Night of the Hunter *(1955), which became one of the first cult films.*

In more recent years, Mitchum starred in The Sundowners *(1960),* The Longest Day *(1960),* Ryan's Daughter *(1971),* Farewell, My Lovely *(1975),* The Last Tycoon *(1976),* The Amsterdam Kill *(1978), and* The Big Sleep *(1978). When he's not making a motion picture, Mitchum lives in northern California.*

C
- The Cincinnati Kid
- Cinderfella
- Circle of Iron
- Citizen Kane
- Citizens Band
- City of Women
- City on Fire

Burnett in Chu Chu and the Philly Flash.

(Continued)

characters. Arkin mopes through the movie wearing a raincoat so soiled that even Lieutenant Columbo would reject it. Burnett talks and yells a lot. **Director**—David Lowell Rich. (PG)

100 minutes

THE CINCINNATI KID (1965)
★★★

Steve McQueen
Edward G. Robinson
Ann-Margret
Tuesday Weld

McQueen does rather well in the title role, as a roving poker player who likes big games with big stakes. It's sort of *The Hustler* of card games. A big card game at the finale adds a dimension to the adventure. However, the romantic interludes don't fare as well. This film version of Richard Jessup's novel is set in the late '30s in New Orleans. There's nice support from the talented cast, which also includes Karl Malden, Joan Blondell, Rip Torn, Jack Weston, and Cab Calloway. **Director**—Norman Jewison. *113 minutes*

CINDERFELLA (1960)
★★

Jerry Lewis
Ed Wynn
Judith Anderson

Lewis puts his comic twist on the classic fairy tale, and the whole film

turns into a pumpkin. The production is lavish, but Lewis's jokes are rather ordinary. There's lots of talk between gags, and the musical sequences are uninspired. There may be some enjoyment if you're a big Lewis fan; otherwise, there's not much to laugh at. Also with Anna Maria Alberghetti and Count Basie. **Director**—Frank Tashlin. *91 minutes*

CIRCLE OF IRON (1979)
★

David Carradine
Jeff Cooper
Christopher Lee

What's a fine actor like Carradine doing in this pretentious mishmash of a martial arts movie? He plays a blind flute player and several other characters we meet on the road to ultimate wisdom. His acting is heads above the dopey script, which must have been inspired by fortune cookie messages. The phony philosophy is accompanied by the standard chop-socky antics, complete with lots of grunts and heavy breathing. There are cameos by Eli Wallach and Roddy McDowall. **Director**—Richard Moore. (R)

102 minutes

CITIZEN KANE (1941)
★★★★

Orson Welles
Joseph Cotten
Everett Sloane

Welles's masterpiece is about a tyrannical newspaper publisher who built a

Orson Welles, playing a Hearst-like publisher, stars in Citizen Kane, *his first and best film.*

vast empire. Every moment of the story, which parallels the career of William Randolph Hearst, is filled with intelligence, excitement, and pure entertainment. Welles wrote, directed, and starred in this magnificent production, which broke new ground in cinematic craftsmanship. Seeing it today is still a remarkable experience, and it surely will remain a gem among Hollywood's offerings. Also stars George Coulouris, Dorothy Comingore, Paul Stewart, and Agnes Moorehead. **Academy Award**—Herman J. Mankiewicz and Welles, best writing (original screenplay). **Nominations**—best picture; Welles, best director; Welles, best actor; Gregg Toland, cinematography (black and white).

119 minutes b&w

CITIZENS BAND
See Handle With Care

CITY OF WOMEN (1981)
★★★

Marcello Mastroianni
Ettore Manni
Anna Prucnal

Director Federico Fellini takes on women's lib as only Fellini can, with bombastic dream sequences that parade onward with exuberance and extravagance. Mastroianni is ideally cast as the maestro's alter ego, who stumbles on a feminist convention. Here, he's attacked as a spy and at last rescued by a macho man. Despite the usual Fellini flamboyance, the film is devoid of drama. However, serious Fellini fans may still rejoice. Also with Katren Gebelein and Donatella Damiani. (No MPAA rating)

140 minutes

CITY ON FIRE (1979)
(no stars)

Barry Newman
Susan Clark

A deliberately set fire at an oil refinery engulfs an entire city in this poorly conceived, dull disaster movie. Despite all that burning real estate, the sketchy characterizations and trite dialogue would seem more at home on daytime soap operas. There's also an ugly fixation on grisly details, with

- Clash of the Titans
- The Class of Miss MacMichael
- Cleopatra
- Cleopatra Jones and the Casino of Gold
- The Clock
- A Clockwork Orange
- Close Encounters of the Third Kind

C

plenty of sickening close-ups of horribly burned bodies. The wasted cast includes such Hollywood old-timers as Henry Fonda, Ava Gardner, Leslie Nielsen, and Shelley Winters. **Director**—Alvin Rakoff. (R) *101 minutes*

CLASH OF THE TITANS (1981)
★★★

**Harry Hamlin
Judi Bowker**

Greek mythology is the basis for this spirited, romantic adventure, featuring many glorious monsters created by special-effects wiz Ray Harryhausen. Square-jawed Hamlin plays Perseus, who engages in assorted daring feats to save his lady love, played by Bowker, from being sacrificed to the huge sea monster, the Kraken. Perseus gets around with the help of Pegasus, the flying horse. He valiantly battles a two-headed wolf, a giant vulture, and a woman whose stare can kill. **Director**—Desmond Davis. (PG)

120 minutes

Ammon (Burgess Meredith) examines Perseus' (Harry Hamlin) sword in Clash of the Titans.

THE CLASS OF MISS MACMICHAEL (1979)
★★

**Glenda Jackson
Oliver Reed**

Jackson, projecting her veddy proper British manner, plays a dedicated teacher who struggles with a roomful of unruly teenagers. It's her and the kids against the world and an authoritative principal, overplayed by Reed. This theme has been worn thin on the screen and on TV, and the situations are predictable. Jackson and most cast members do a serviceable job. Also

with Michael Murphy and Rosalind Cash. **Director**—Silvio Narizzano. (R)   *99 minutes*

CLEOPATRA (1963)
★★

**Elizabeth Taylor
Richard Burton
Rex Harrison**

This historical drama was much heralded prior to its release, but turned out to be a horrendous disappointment. Despite its tremendous expense and length, there's perhaps less than an hour's worth of decent entertainment. Taylor, in the title role, is lovely to look at, but that's it. Harrison is good as Caesar, but Burton as Anthony turns in an uneven performance. Also with Pamela Brown, Roddy McDowall, Martin Landau, and Michael Hordern. **Director**—Joseph L. Mankiewicz. **Academy Award**—Leon Shamroy, cinematography (color). **Nomination**—Harrison, best actor.(G)

243 minutes

CLEOPATRA JONES AND THE CASINO OF GOLD (1975)
★★

**Tamara Dobson
Stella Stevens**

This is a black exploitation film in which a six-foot-two, high-kicking, martial arts-trained, lady narcotics agent takes on a Dragon Lady in Macao. There's lots of kung fu action, but a limited plot. Also with Norman Fell and Caro Kenyatta. **Director**—Chuck Bail. (R)   *96 minutes*

THE CLOCK (1945)
★★★

**Judy Garland
Robert Walker**

Garland stars in this frothy romantic drama as a New York City secretary. She meets a soldier, played by Walker, and marries him before his 24-hour leave is up. During their whirlwind courtship, the lovebirds meet an assortment of pleasant characters. Garland is charming as ever, but she doesn't sing. James Gleason, Lucille Gleason, Keenan Wynn, and Marshall

Thompson are also in the cast. **Director**—Vincente Minnelli.

90 minutes b&w

A CLOCKWORK ORANGE (1971)
★★★★

**Malcolm McDowell
Patrick Magee
Michael Bates**

Stanley Kubrick's perceptive dark satire about the future isn't as good as his *Dr. Strangelove*, but it hits the mark with plenty of impact. The film was adapted from Anthony Burgess's novel. The scene is 21st-century England, where gangs of young hoodlums run rampant, and ordinary citizens are afraid to venture far from their homes. A young murderer returns to society after being brainwashed by the authorities in a prison experiment and finds that the violent nature of society has increased. The film is generously laced with stark images and a chilling political message about the future. Also with Adrienne Corri, Aubrey Morris, and James Marcus. (R) **Academy Award Nominations**—best picture; Kubrick, best director; Kubrick, best screenplay (based on material from another medium).   *136 minutes*

CLOSE ENCOUNTERS OF THE THIRD KIND (1977)
★★★★

**Richard Dreyfuss
François Truffaut
Melinda Dillon**

Steven Spielberg's $19-million epic about UFOs begins somewhat inco-
(Continued)

Richard Dreyfuss in Close Encounters of the Third Kind.

C
- The Clown
- Cluny Brown
- Coal Miner's Daughter
- Coast to Coast
- The Collector
- Coma

(Continued)

herently. The film lapses even more toward the middle. But wait. The final portion—when earthlings and extra-terrestrial beings rendezvous on a Wyoming mountain—suddenly flares to a dazzling climax. The special effects are stunning, and Spielberg's awesome imaginative effort comes into full focus. The faults are forgiven. It's sensational. Also with Teri Garr, Cary Guffey, and Bob Balaban. (PG) **Academy Award Nominations**—Spielberg, best director; Dillon, best supporting actress. *135 minutes*

THE CLOWN (1953)
★★

Red Skelton
Jane Greer

Skelton has a rare dramatic role in this sentimental version of *The Champ*. He plays a has-been comic who is urged by his son to make a comeback. Skelton handles the part well, but he's better off working with comedy. There's adequate support from Tim Considine and Loring Smith. **Director**—Robert Z. Leonard. *92 minutes b&w*

CLUNY BROWN (1946)
★★★

Jennifer Jones
Charles Boyer

This is a fine, pleasing romantic comedy, set in England just before World War II. Jones plays a plumber's niece who falls in love with a Czech refugee, played by Charles Boyer. The film works well as a spoof of the upper class, and it's helped by buoyant characterizations. Expertly directed by Ernst Lubitsch. Richard Haydn, Una O'Connor, and Peter Lawford give good support. *100 minutes b&w*

COAL MINER'S DAUGHTER
(1980)
★★★★

Sissy Spacek
Tommy Lee Jones

Spacek gives a stunning, virtuoso performance in the title role of this rags-to-riches biography of Loretta Lynn, the country singer superstar. First-rate

In Coal Miner's Daughter, *Sissy Spacek plays Loretta Lynn, a girl who becomes a singing star.*

support from Jones, as Lynn's everlovin' manager husband, also moves the film along, even when the screenplay seems to lose some energy. Director Michael Apted captures the authentic detail of Appalachia in a careful documentary style. It's a winning film, filled with plenty of heart, hope, and some surprisingly good singing from Spacek. Also with Beverly D'Angelo, Levon Helm, and Phyllis Boyens. (PG) **Academy Award**—Spacek, best actress. **Nominations**—best picture; Tom Rickman, best screenplay (adapted from another medium). *124 minutes*

COAST TO COAST (1980)
★★

Dyan Cannon
Robert Blake

Blake and Cannon barrel across the country in a huge trailer truck while various enemies intercept them along the way. This action-comedy is nothing more than another routine variation of such cat-and-mouse chase films as *Smokey and the Bandit*. Blake and Cannon, who seem to be imitating Burt Reynolds and Sally Field, ham it up with gusto. But it's a forgettable trip. Also with Quinn Redeker. **Director**—Joseph Sargent. (PG) *95 minutes*

THE COLLECTOR (1965)
★★★

Terence Stamp
Samantha Eggar

An unusual story about a strange young man who collects butterflies and decides to add a beautiful art student, played by Eggar, to his collection. Stamp is convincing as the disturbed youth who kidnaps Eggar and keeps her in his basement. The suspense builds nicely under the fine direction of William Wyler. The chilling drama is based on John Fowles's popular novel. Maurice Dallimore and Mona Washbourne have supporting roles. **Academy Award Nominations**—Wyler, best director; Eggar, best actress; Stanley Mann and John Kohn, best screenplay (based on material from another medium). *119 minutes*

COMA (1978)
★★

Geneviève Bujold
Michael Douglas

When the full moon rose in the sky and Court Dracula and the Wolf Man

Geneviève Bujold seeks clues to a conspiracy at an experimental lab in Coma.

● The Comancheros
● Come Back, Little Sheba
● Come Blow Your Horn

● The Comedians
● The Comedy of Terrors
● Come Fill the Cup
● Comes a Horseman

C

prowled about, it scared the daylights out of you. This horror story, which takes place in a Boston hospital, is scary enough, too, but the fun and satisfaction are absent. Bujold is a resident surgeon, who unravels a sinister plot to send healthy patients into irreversible comas and then steal their organs for transplants. The mystery unfolds amid the antiseptic glare of modern institutions with little style, imagination, or humor. Dr. Frankenstein, where are you? Also with Elizabeth Ashley, Rip Torn, and Richard Widmark. Michael Crichton directed this film, which is based on his novel. (PG)   *113 minutes*

THE COMANCHEROS (1961)
★★★

**John Wayne
Stuart Whitman**

Wayne is right at home in this rough, tough western, as a Texas Ranger who is determined to rid the territory of a gang supplying guns and whiskey to the Indians. Whitman plays a gambler-prisoner forced to tag along with Wayne. The Duke gets involved with some lively gunplay, yet there's just the right amount of levity mixed in with the action. Big John and the rest of the cast seem to be having an enjoyable time with the material. Also with Lee Marvin, Bruce Cabot, Nehemiah Persoff, and Ina Balin. **Director**—Michael Curtiz.   *107 minutes*

COME BACK, LITTLE SHEBA (1952)
★★★★

**Shirley Booth
Burt Lancaster**

Top-notch performances propel this emotionally charged drama about a slovenly housewife trying to cope with her alcoholic husband. The film, based on the William Inge play, is somewhat stagebound, but effective nevertheless. Booth is splendid as the wife, and Lancaster is superb as the husband. Terry Moore and Richard Jaeckel are fine in supporting roles. **Director**—Daniel Mann. **Academy Award**—Booth, best actress. **Nomination**—Moore, best supporting actress.   *99 minutes b&w*

COME BLOW YOUR HORN (1962)
★★★

**Frank Sinatra
Tony Bill
Lee J. Cobb
Molly Picon**

Sinatra plays a swinging bachelor with a stable of girls, who teaches his younger brother the ways of the world. The Neil Simon play is successfully transposed to the screen, with the funny characters and funny lines firmly intact. Ol' Blue Eyes is well cast as the bachelor, and Bill plays the awestruck kid brother with conviction. Cobb and Picon are good as anxious parents. Sinatra sings the title song. Jill St. John, Barbara Rush, and Dan Blocker have supporting roles. **Director**—Bud Yorkin.   *112 minutes*

THE COMEDIANS (1967)
★★

**Richard Burton
Elizabeth Taylor
Alec Guinness
Peter Ustinov**

A champagne cast can't do much with this labored and awkward film version of Graham Greene's novel about politics and violence in Haiti under the rule of Papa Doc Duvalier. Burton and Taylor play odd characters involved with intrigue. The clumsy, cliché-heavy script seems to overwhelm the acting, and the direction lacks inspiration. Supporting players include Lillian Gish, Paul Ford, Roscoe Lee Browne, Raymond St. Jacques, James Earl Jones, and Cicely Tyson. **Director**—Peter Glenville.   *160 minutes*

THE COMEDY OF TERRORS (1963)
★★

**Vincent Price
Peter Lorre
Boris Karloff
Basil Rathbone**

This spoof of the macabre features a quartet of horror-film greats. Although there are a few effective scenes, the film falls short of expecta-

tions. Price plays a sinister undertaker who schemes to increase his business by hastening the demise of prospective clients. They should have buried the script instead. Joe E. Brown and Joyce Jameson are also in the cast. **Director**—Jacques Tourneur.   *88 minutes*

COME FILL THE CUP (1951)
★★★

**James Cagney
Phyllis Thaxter**

A solid performance by Cagney graces this melodrama. Cagney plays an ex-newspaperman trying to cure himself of alcoholism and get his life back together. He also tries to help the son of his boss, who has ties to gangsters. There's fine support from Gig Young, who plays the son—a tipsy playboy. Raymond Massey and James Gleason are also in the cast. **Director**—Gordon Douglas.   *113 minutes b&w*

COMES A HORSEMAN (1978)
★★

**Jane Fonda
James Caan
Jason Robards, Jr.**

Young, struggling ranchers stand up to a cattle baron and oil industrialists. Sound familiar? It's a version of a theme for countless westerns of yesteryear, and they've used it again here with middling results. Only this time, they've blended in some sensitivity
(Continued)

Jane Fonda and James Caan are embroiled in a land battle in Comes a Horseman.

C
- Come to the Stable
- Comin' at Ya
- Coming Home

RAY MILLAND

Since arriving in Hollywood in 1932, Ray Milland has been a busy actor, making more than 130 motion pictures. Born Reginald Truscott-Jones in Neath, Wales, Milland went to school at Kings College, the University of Wales, and, for a short time, at Cambridge. Originally intending to make the army his career, he spent four years in the British Army's Household Cavalry Life Guards. He later turned to acting, playing several juvenile roles.

In 1929, Milland appeared in his first film, The Plaything. In 1931, before he was to appear opposite Beatrice Lillie in Charlot's Revue in
London, he was signed to a MGM contract. After a few unproductive years in Hollywood, however, his option was dropped and he returned home. Later, he returned to Hollywood and so impressed Paramount executives that he was signed to a long-term contract.

In 1946, Milland won an Academy Award, the New York Film Critics' Award, and the first Cannes Film Festival Award for his performance as an alcoholic in The Lost Weekend. His other screen credits include Beau Geste (1939), Arise My Love (1941), Skylark (1941), The Major and the Minor (1942), Reap the Wild Wind (1942), Lady in the Dark (1944), The Uninvited (1944), The Big Clock (1948), So Evil My Love (1948), Alias Nick Beal (1949), The Thief (1952), Dial M for Murder (1954), Love Story (1970), and The Last Tycoon (1976).

Milland directed and starred in A Man Alone (1955), Lisbon (1956), and the two TV series Meet Mr. McNulty (1953-1955) and Markham (1959). He also appeared in the popular television mini-series Rich Man, Poor Man.

(Continued)
and added a dash of modern feminism. The film walks most of the time when it should gallop, despite the strong performances by the cast. Fonda plays a rancher, Caan is the rescuer, and Robards plays the cattle baron. Also with George Grizzard, Robert Farnsworth, and Jim Davis. **Director**—Alan J. Pakula. (PG) **Academy Award Nomination**—Farnsworth, best supporting actor.

118 minutes

COME TO THE STABLE (1949)
★★★

Loretta Young
Celeste Holm

Young and Holm star in this charming, heartwarming film about two French nuns who seek support to build a children's hospital in a New England town. The duo is perfectly suited for their parts, and they exude considerable grace and sweetness in
this tasteful production. Henry Koster directs with simplicity and efficiency. Also with Hugh Marlowe, Elsa Lanchester, Mike Mazurki, and Regis Toomey. **Academy Award Nominations**—Young, best actress; Holm, Lanchester, best supporting actress; Clare Boothe Luce, writing (motion picture story); Joseph LaShelle, cinematography (black and white).

94 minutes b&w

COMIN' AT YA (1981)
★★

Tony Anthony

It does, indeed, in this 3-D film, which revives the technique briefly used in the early '50s. It'll probably be fuzzy on the small screen, though. The plot is a brutal western about a young man, played by Anthony, who rescues his wife from the clutches of some grubby white slavers. But the story is more of an opportunity to wow the audience with a steady stream of objects that
seem to fly off the screen—flaming arrows, bats, snakes, rats, swords, even a yo-yo. It's still merely a novelty that probably will fade quickly. **Director**—Ferdinando Baldi. (R)

91 minutes

COMING HOME (1978)
★★

Jon Voight
Jane Fonda

Fonda apparently conceived this post-Vietnam melodrama, but where is the snap and spirit one would expect from a film associated with such a celebrated war protestor? The Vietnam experience seems more of a backdrop to the soapy and confusing love story about a Marine captain's wife, played by Fonda, who has an affair with a paraplegic Vietnam veteran, played by Voight. There are appealing performances by Fonda, Voight, and Bruce Dern in the major roles, but the ideas are foggy, and the film doesn't hit home. Also with Robert Carradine, Penelope Milford, and Robert Ginty. **Director**—Hal Ashby. (R) **Academy Awards**—Voight, best actor; Fonda, best actress; Nancy Dowd (story), Waldo Salt and Robert Jones (screenplay), best original screenplay. **Nominations**—best picture; Ashby, best director; Dern, best supporting actor; Milford, best supporting actress.

127 minutes

Jon Voight and Jane Fonda share a tender moment in Coming Home.

- Command Decision
- The Competition
- Compulsion
- The Concorde—Airport '79
- Condorman
- Conduct Unbecoming
- Coney Island
- Confrontation
- A Connecticut Yankee in King Arthur's Court

C

COMMAND DECISION (1948)
★★★

Clark Gable
Walter Pidgeon
Van Johnson

This gripping World War II drama focuses on the top brass who must make the distressing decisions that will send many men to their deaths. Gable is the general who huddles with his staff to discuss the strategy for bombing missions over Nazi Germany. This straightforward adaptation of William Haines's Broadway play also features Brian Donlevy, John Hodiak, Edward Arnold, and Charles Bickford. **Director**—Sam Wood.
112 minutes b&w

THE COMPETITION (1980)
★★

Richard Dreyfuss
Amy Irving

He (Dreyfuss) is a brilliant young classical pianist. She (Irving) is also a musical prodigy. They fall in love while vying for top honors in a piano competition. Beethoven and Prokofiev get a workout at the keyboards, but this overlong love story is drab and predictable. It's also bogged down with half-baked subplots that contribute to the film's awkwardness. Dreyfuss and Irving are convincing as dedicated musicians, but they don't seem to hit the right notes as young lovers. Also with Lee Remick and Sam Wanamaker. **Director**—Joel Oliansky. (PG)
129 minutes

COMPULSION (1959)
★★★

Dean Stockwell
Bradford Dillman

The infamous Leopold-Loeb murder case of the '20s is brought to the screen with solid performances and impressive direction. The plot mainly concerns the murder trial of the two brilliant but twisted Chicago students. The students, played by Stockwell and Dillman, are put on trial for killing a young boy for thrills. Orson Welles stands out in a cameo role as defense lawyer Clarence Darrow. And there are fine performances, too, from Diane Varsi, E. G. Marshall, and Martin Milner. **Director**—Richard Fleischer.
103 minutes b&w

THE CONCORDE—AIRPORT '79 (1979)
★★

Alain Delon
Susan Blakely
Robert Wagner
Sylvia Kristel

The *Airport* saga continues. This time it's the supersonic Concorde jet, which encounters assorted hair-raising mishaps. The special effects are praiseworthy, but the plot, which mainly concerns an arms sale scandal, is rather déjà vu. The usual gallery of oddball characters is on board for the globe-trotting flight. The large cast also includes George Kennedy, Eddie Albert, Bibi Andersson, and Martha Raye. **Director**—David Lowell Rich. (PG)
113 minutes

CONDORMAN (1981)
★★

Michael Crawford
Barbara Carrera

From the Walt Disney studios comes a flimsy parody of James Bond adventures, which features striking scenery from exotic locations and an adolescent, plodding script. Crawford plays a cartoonist who occasionally dresses up like the comic-book hero he has created. He's drawn into a CIA caper, in which he helps a beautiful Russian agent, played by Carrera, defect. Of course, he uses all the wonderful gadgets and schemes that he dreamed up for his comic strip. **Director**—Charles Jarrott. (PG)
90 minutes

CONDUCT UNBECOMING (1975)
★★★★

Michael York
Richard Attenborough
Trevor Howard

This magnificent British film, taken from the successful play by Barry England, smartly explodes myths about duty, valor, and honor in Victorian India. The suspenseful drama deals with the kangaroo trial of a young, aristocratic lieutenant, who is accused of attacking the widow of an officer. Excellent cinematography enhances the rich atmosphere. Also with Stacy Keach, Susannah York, Christopher Plummer, James Faulkner, and James Donald. **Director**—Michael Anderson. (PG)
107 minutes

CONEY ISLAND (1943)
★★★

Betty Grable
Cesar Romero
George Montgomery

Grable struts and sings in this glossy, lighthearted period musical set at the turn of the century. She's a saloon songstress; Montgomery and Romero—two showmen—vie for her attention. Later remade by Grable as *Wabash Avenue*. Also with Phil Silvers and Matt Briggs. **Director**—Walter Lang.
96 minutes

CONFRONTATION (1976)
★★

This is a Swiss-made documentary that probes a touchy issue of conscience: Should neutrality be maintained in the face of blatant evil? The point is illustrated by the true story of a young Jewish medical student, David Frankfurter, who assassinates a Swiss-Nazi party organizer. It's an intelligent and penetrating film, but it sadly lacks drama. Frankfurter is brilliantly played by Peter Bollag. **Director**—Rolf Lyssy. In German with English titles. (No MPAA rating)
115 minutes b&w

A CONNECTICUT YANKEE IN KING ARTHUR'S COURT (1949)
★★★

Bing Crosby
Rhonda Fleming
William Bendix

Crosby is an engaging Sir Boss in this jazzed-up musical version of the
(Continued)

William Bendix and Bing Crosby in A Connecticut Yankee in King Arthur's Court.

(Continued)
classic Mark Twain comedy. Bing is a blacksmith, who's transported back in time to Camelot, where Merlin declares him a wizard. Bing sings some forgettable tunes, yet he handles the acting chores with aplomb. Also with Cedric Hardwicke and Murvyn Vye, who are fine in supporting roles. **Director**—Tay Garnett. *107 minutes*

THE CONSTANT NYMPH (1943)
★★★

Joan Fontaine
Charles Boyer

Fontaine is in top form as a young girl in love with a sophisticated musician, played smartly by Boyer. Top-notch performances by other cast members enhance this well-produced drama. Also with Alexis Smith, Brenda Marshall, Charles Coburn, Dame May Whitty, and Peter Lorre. **Director**—Edmund Goulding. **Academy Award Nomination**—Fontaine, best actress. *112 minutes b&w*

CONTINENTAL DIVIDE (1981)
★★

John Belushi
Blair Brown

Belushi plays a gruff Chicago newspaper columnist. Brown plays a brainy, reclusive ornithologist, working to save the bald eagle. They meet high in the Rocky Mountains. They argue. They fall in love. They part. They are in love again. This is a rather typical romantic comedy setup that Tracy and Hepburn handled so nicely so often. Belushi and Brown play interesting characters, but they're too diverse to be believable. The film strains to be witty, but much of it is for the birds. Also with Allen Goorwitz, Carlin Glynn, and Tony Ganios. **Director**—Michael Apted. (PG)
103 minutes

Blair Brown and John Belushi are in love—at times—in Continental Divide.

THE CONVERSATION (1974)
★★★★

Gene Hackman
John Cazale
Frederick Forrest
Cindy Williams

Compelling, fresh mystery-drama about a determined wiretap expert, played by Hackman, who finally is bugged by his own conscience when he goes too far. Director Francis Ford Coppola, who also wrote the screenplay, hits home with this absorbing story in light of Watergate. The plot involves murder, but the theme also focuses on the loss of privacy and the erosion of democracy as new technologies are misused. Hackman digs into his role with straight-faced discipline. Also with Allen Garfield, Teri Garr, and Harrison Ford. (PG) **Academy Award Nominations**—best picture; Coppola, best original screenplay. *113 minutes*

CONVICTS FOUR (1962)
★★

Ben Gazzara
Vincent Price

An unusual film about a convict who is spared from execution and then becomes rehabilitated by developing skills as a painter. Gazzara plays the central character, based on the autobiography of John Resko. The production is a curious blend of drama, documentary, and character study, which begins with determination, but then trails off into uncertainty. Broderick Crawford and Rod Steiger appear briefly in cameo roles. Others in the cast include Stuart Whitman, Ray Walston, Jack Kruschen, and Sammy Davis, Jr. **Director**—Millard Kaufman. **Alternate Title**—*Reprieve*.
106 minutes b&w

CONVOY (1978)
★★

Kris Kristofferson
Ali MacGraw
Ernest Borgnine

Scores of huge trailer trucks barrel across the screen to the tune of C. W.

- Coogan's Bluff
- Cooley High
- Cool Hand Luke
- Coonskin
- Copacabana
- Cornbread, Earl and Me
- Corvette Summer

C

Ali MacGraw and Kris Kristofferson in Convoy, *a film about a truckers' revolt.*

McCall's trucker ballad. Director Sam Peckinpah romanticizes the freewheeling, cowboy image of these drivers and, as expected, pours on the violent action. Logic and good taste are often left stranded by the roadside. Also with Burt Young, Madge Sinclair, and Franklyn Ajaye. (PG)   *110 minutes*

COOGAN'S BLUFF (1968)
★★★

**Clint Eastwood
Lee J. Cobb
Susan Clark**

Big, bad Eastwood plays an Arizona deputy sheriff who comes to New York City and tries to retrieve an escaped murderer, played by Don Stroud. After the thug slips away from him, Eastwood resorts to western-style methods, to the chagrin of the city cops, to recapture his man. Cobb plays a city detective. Lots of fast-paced action and good character contrasts enliven the production. Also with Tisha Sterling, Betty Field, and Tom Tully. **Director**—Don Siegel. (PG)   *100 minutes*

COOLEY HIGH (1975)
★★★★

**Glynn Turman
Lawrence-Hilton Jacobs
Garrett Morris**

The film is a bit like *American Graffiti*, but this time it's the story of black adolescents on Chicago's near North Side in 1964. Instead of cruising the main drag in flashy automobiles, they get together under elevated trains and hitch free rides on the backs of buses. Impressively written and directed, the film is blessed with the exceptional talents of Turman, Jacobs, and Morris. Also with Cynthia Davis, Corin Rogers, and Maurice Leon Havis. **Director**—Michael Schultz. (PG)
107 minutes

COOL HAND LUKE (1967)
★★★★

**Paul Newman
George Kennedy**

Forthright, gripping drama about a chain-gang prisoner, played by Newman, who has a burning determination to maintain his individualism despite his compromising situation. Newman's portrayal is stunning, and he's backed to the hilt with an award-winning performance by Kennedy, who plays the vicious chain-gang overseer. There are some subtle references to Christ in this well-made production. Also with Jo Van Fleet, J. D. Cannon, Lou Antonio, Robert Drivas, and Strother Martin. **Director**—Stuart Rosenberg. **Academy Award**—Kennedy, best supporting actor. **Nominations**—Newman, best actor; Don Pearce and Frank R. Pierson, best screenplay (based on material from another medium). (PG)   *126 minutes*

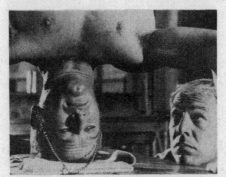

Paul Newman plays the title role in Cool Hand Luke; *George Kennedy is a chain-gang supervisor.*

COONSKIN (1975)
★

This movie is a blend of live action and animation from director Ralph Bakshi, who produced the X-rated feature cartoons *Heavy Traffic* and *Fritz the Cat*. *Coonskin* is about three black characters who leave the South for Harlem and try to take over the rackets. It's generally a dull story, filled with grotesque characters. The film has provoked denunciations from the Congress of Racial Equality and other black organizations for portraying blacks as stereotypes. The voices of Barry White, Scatman Crothers, and Charles Gordone are used. (R)
83 minutes

COPACABANA (1947)
★

**Groucho Marx
Carmen Miranda**

Not much doing in this uninspired musical-comedy involving nightclub performers. Things go awry when a girl with two different acts is needed for both parts at the same time. Even Marx in a key role can't save this one. Also with Steve Cochran and Andy Russell. **Director**—Alfred E. Green.
91 minutes b&w

CORNBREAD, EARL AND ME (1975)
★★★

**Moses Gunn
Bernie Casey
Rosalind Cash**

A sensitive story about a college-bound black basketball star, who is accidentally killed by the police. This urban tragedy and courtroom drama is a far cry from the typical black exploitation film. However, it's flawed by some uneven directing. Also with Madge Sinclair, Keith Wilkes, and Tierre Turner. **Director**—Joe Manduke. (PG)   *95 minutes*

CORVETTE SUMMER (1978)
★★

**Mark Hamill
Annie Potts
Eugene Roche**

Hamill of *Star Wars* fame plays a naïve high-school boy in love with a flashy car and an equally flashy would-be
(Continued)

(Continued)

hooker, played by Potts. This unusual, breezy, and innocuous film is primarily aimed at teen audiences. Director Matthew Robbins keeps the action moving along, but the picture often stumbles over too much silliness. Also with Kim Milford and Richard McKenzie. (PG) *105 minutes*

COUNT DRACULA AND HIS VAMPIRE BRIDE (1978)
★

**Chrisopher Lee
Peter Cushing**

Moviemakers won't let Count Dracula rest in peace as long as there are a few more dollars to be made. This version has the Count, played by veteran bloodsucker Lee, plotting to annihilate mankind with biological warfare. It's all familiar vampire doings, by now unexciting and silly. Cushing plays the good professor, who puts an end to the sinister scheme. **Director**—Alan Gibson (R) *87 minutes*

THE COUNTRY GIRL (1954)
★★★

**Bing Crosby
Grace Kelly**

Fantastic performances by Crosby and Kelly enhance this absorbing drama about an alcoholic singer trying to make a comeback. When Bing, formerly feeling sorry for himself, is stimulated to get back on his feet, wife Grace demonstrates her support. The film, which is adapted from the play by Clifford Odets, features some songs by Ira Gershwin and Harold Arlen. Also with William Holden, Anthony Ross, and Gene Reynolds. **Director**—George Seaton. **Academy Awards**—Kelly, best actress; Seaton, writing (screenplay). **Nominations**—best picture; Seaton, best director; Crosby, best actor; John F. Warren, cinematography (black and white). *104 minutes b&w*

COUNT YOUR BLESSINGS (1959)
★★

**Deborah Kerr
Maurice Chevalier
Rossano Brazzi**

Unworkable comedy of manners about an English girl, played by Kerr, who marries a wealthy Frenchman, played by Brazzi, during World War II. The conflict separates them, and when they are united, their nine-year-old son learns his father is a philanderer. The plot limps along with occasional levity by the commentary of Chevalier. His charm, however, is only a slight blessing. Also with Mona Washbourne, Martin Stephens, Ronald Squire, and Tom Helmore. **Director**—Jean Negulesco. *102 minutes*

COUP DE TÊTE (1980)
★★

Patrick Dewaere

François, an ill-tempered soccer player framed for rape, gets revenge on the stuffy citizens of a small French town. François is played by Dewaere. Directed by Jean-Jacques Annaud (*Black and White in Color*), this light satire starts off with promise, but it's too uncertain in outlook. The jokes are rather broad and don't have much effect. Dewaere seems a little too high-handed at times to play the part of a nonconformist. In French with English titles. **Alternate Title**—*Hothead*. (No MPAA rating) *90 minutes*

JOHN WAYNE

John Wayne's fabulous screen exploits and long film career began with his first leading role, in Raoul Walsh's The Big Trail *(1930). From that time on, the rugged popular star invariably rang a happy tune at theater box offices around the world.*

Known to his friends and fellow workers as Duke, Wayne was born Marion Michael Morrison in Winterset, Iowa, in 1907. His father's illness forced the family to move to California. After recovering his health, his father, a pharmacist, opened a drugstore in Glendale.

Wayne graduated from Glendale High School, where he was a football star and a talented debater. He received a scholarship to the University of Southern California, where he played on the championship football team.

His entry into motion pictures was completely unplanned. During summer vacations he worked as a property man at what was then the Fox Film Corporation. He became acquainted with director John Ford, who was impressed with the young man and prodded him into taking a small role in Hangman's House *(1928). After this minor debut, Wayne went back to props.*

Director Raoul Walsh took Wayne out of the property department permanently by giving him his new name and entrusting him with the leading role in The Big Trail *(1930). In the '30s, Wayne starred in about 100 westerns. In fact, he became the screen's first singing cowboy in a series of westerns, even though he couldn't carry a tune.*

In 1939, Wayne's role of the Ringo Kid in Ford's Stagecoach *finally let him achieve stardom.*

During the next three decades, Wayne starred in numerous movies, including The Long Voyage Home *(1940),* Seven Sinners *(1940),* Red River *(1948),* She Wore a Yellow Ribbon *(1949),* Sands of Iwo Jima *(1949),* The Quiet Man *(1952),* The High and the Mighty *(1954),* The Searchers *(1956),* Rio Bravo *(1959),* The Alamo *(1960),* McLintock! *(1963),* In Harm's Way *(1965),* El Dorado *(1967), and* True Grit *(1969), for which he finally received the Academy Award after appearing in hundreds of films.*

Before his death in 1979, Wayne made another 10 films, including Rio Lobo *(1970),* The Cowboys *(1972),* Cahill *(1973),* Rooster Cogburn *(1975), and* The Shootist *(1976).*

- The Court Jester
- The Court Martial of Billy Mitchell
- The Courtship of Eddie's Father
- Cousin, Cousine
- Cover Girl
- Cowboy
- The Cowboys

C

THE COURT JESTER (1955)
★★★★

**Danny Kaye
Glynis Johns
Basil Rathbone**

Kaye is a knockout in this superb, made-to-order comedy set in medieval times. The delightful romp, which spoofs costume movies, has Kaye posing as a jester to infiltrate a plot against the king. There are all sorts of effective comic situations, decorated with delightful tunes and well-staged action. The fine supporting cast includes Angela Lansbury, Mildred Natwick, Cecil Parker, Edward Ashley, and Robert Middleton. **Director—** Norman Panama and Melvin Frank.
101 minutes

THE COURT MARTIAL OF BILLY MITCHELL (1955)
★★★

**Gary Cooper
Rod Steiger
Ralph Bellamy**

Straightforward but slow-paced account of the prophetic American general who accused his superiors of being unprepared for invasion and was subsequently court-martialed. His warning came almost two decades prior to the sneak attack on Pearl Harbor. Cooper is convincing in the title role. The film concludes effectively in a stirring courtroom sequence. Also with Charles Bickford, Elizabeth Montgomery, Fred Clark, and Darren McGavin. **Director—**Otto Preminger. **Academy Award Nomination—** Milton Spirling and Emmett Lavery, writing (story and screenplay).
100 minutes

James Daly, Ralph Bellamy, and Gary Cooper in The Court Martial of Billy Mitchell.

THE COURTSHIP OF EDDIE'S FATHER (1962)
★★★

**Glenn Ford
Ronnie Howard
Shirley Jones**

A rather cute, teary-eyed comedy that is handled well for this sort of material. Ford plays the title role of a man who loses his wife. His young son plays cupid so the family can have a new mom. There's just the right measure of humor and sentimentality to maintain the film's charming aspects most of the way through. Other fine cast members include Stella Stevens and Dina Merrill. **Director—**Vincente Minnelli.
117 minutes

COUSIN, COUSINE (1975)
★★★★

**Marie-Christine Barrault
Victor Lanoux**

Marie-Christine Barrault, Victor Lanoux, Marie-France Pisier, and Guy Marchand in Cousin, Cousine.

This pleasant romantic comedy about French social mores, directed by Jean-Charles Tacchella, stops a step or two short of turning into a farce. Barrault and Lanoux turn in brilliant performances as cousins—by marriage— who first become friends and eventually fall in love. They finally have an affair when all their friends and relatives assume they are doing just that. The romance is performed with such charm that you might find yourself rooting for adultery. Also with Marie-France Pisier, Guy Marchand, Ginette Garcin, and Sybil Maas. (No MPAA rating) **Academy Award Nominations—**Barrault, best actress; Tacchella and Daniele Thompson, best original screenplay.
95 minutes

COVER GIRL (1944)
★★★

**Rita Hayworth
Gene Kelly**

A lively, toe-tapping musical with the spectacular dancing of Kelly and the memorable music of Jerome Kern. Hayworth stars as a chorus girl, who breaks out of the chorus line to become a magazine cover model. That's it for the simple plot. The strength here is Kelly's solo numbers and a fine supporting role by Eve Arden as a wisecracking secretary. The score includes "Long Ago and Far Away." Also with Phil Silvers, Lee Bowman, Jinx Falkenburg, Otto Kruger, and Ed Brophy. **Director—** Charles Vidor.
107 minutes

COWBOY (1958)
★★★

**Jack Lemmon
Glenn Ford**

Generally pleasant western yarn, based on *On the Trail*, the autobiography of Frank Harris. It concerns a lad who becomes a cowboy and then discovers it's not the glamorous life he envisioned. Lemmon plays Harris, and Ford stars as his trail boss. Good western atmosphere out where the cattle roam. Also with Anna Kashfi, Brian Donlevy, Dick York, Richard Jaeckel, and King Donovan. **Director—**Delmer Daves.
92 minutes

THE COWBOYS (1972)
★

**John Wayne
Roscoe Lee Browne**

Wayne stars in this drab and overly violent western, as a cattleman who is forced to recruit 11 schoolboys for his roundup after his regular drovers quit. The youngsters become killers to revenge the death of their boss. Big John isn't bad in a few scenes, but he has fared better with this genre. Also with Bruce Dern, Colleen Dewhurst, and Slim Pickens. (PG) **Director—**Mark Rydell.
128 minutes

C

- The Crash of Silence
- The Creature From the Black Lagoon
- Crime and Passion
- Criss Cross
- Critic's Choice
- Cromwell
- Crossed Swords
- Crossfire

THE CRASH OF SILENCE

See Mandy

THE CREATURE FROM THE BLACK LAGOON (1954)
★★★

Richard Carlson
Julie Adams
Richard Denning

Surprisingly effective sci-fi thriller—originally a 3-D movie—about some explorers who discover a half-man/half-fish monster, which emerges from a lagoon adjacent to the Amazon River. This B-movie is rife with clichés and hokey horror gimmicks, but it delivers plenty of chills. It's sort of the cream of the crop of camp. Sequels include *Revenge of the Creature* and *The Creature Walks Among Us*. Also with Antonio Moreno, Nestor Paiva, and Ricou Browning. **Director**—Jack Arnold. (G)   *79 minutes*

CRIME AND PASSION (1976)
(no stars)

Omar Sharif
Karen Black
Joseph Bottoms

Director Ivan Passer, who is credited with sensitive and well-made films (*Law and Disorder; Born to Win*) is out of character with this disoriented mixture of sex and murder. It's also an embarrassment for Sharif and Black. Sharif plays an international financier, whose sexual appetite escalates when faced with fiscal disaster. Black plays his willing Girl Friday. This scenario somehow is supposed to be funny—it isn't. Also with Bernhard Wicki. (R)
92 minutes

CRISS CROSS (1948)
★★★

Burt Lancaster
Yvonne De Carlo
Dan Duryea

A brooding, suspenseful cops-and-robbers film about an armored-car guard who gets mixed up in a heist and is double-crossed by his ex-wife and friends. Lancaster does a commendable job, and Duryea plays a villain extraordinaire who is out to get Lancaster. Also with Stephen McNally, Richard Long, and Alan Napier. **Director**—Robert Siodmak.
87 minutes b&w

CRITIC'S CHOICE (1963)
★★

Bob Hope
Lucille Ball
Marilyn Maxwell

Hope plays a hard-nosed drama critic, whose wife, played by Ball, writes a play that he gives an unflattering review. This screen adaptation of Ira Levin's Broadway play can't be saved by such talented performers, so the film comes off as a lopsided and limp vehicle. Some of the supporting players have better moments than the leads. Also with Rip Torn, Jim Backus, and Marie Windsor. **Director**—Don Weis.   *100 minutes*

CROMWELL (1970)
★★

Richard Harris
Alec Guinness
Robert Morley

A good-looking, but ponderous, historical drama at the time of Britain's 17th-century civil war and the rise to power of Oliver Cromwell, who became a revolutionary and then a dictator. The events include the execution of Charles I and some notable battle scenes. Harris handles the title role unconvincingly, while Guinness plays an acceptable King Charles. This subject may be tough to grasp in some school textbooks, but you don't expect the same treatment on the screen. Supporting players include Frank Finlay, Dorothy Tutin, and Patrick Magee. **Director**—Ken Hughes. (G)
140 minutes

CROSSED SWORDS (1978)
★★★

Mark Lester
Oliver Reed
Raquel Welch
Ernest Borgnine
George C. Scott
Rex Harrison
Charlton Heston

A likable, robust, costume adventure, based on Mark Twain's classic, *The Prince and the Pauper*. A champagne cast enlivens the handsome saga about a ragged street urchin who trades identities with young Prince Edward of England. There's lots of derring-do and swashbuckling action to delight the kids and accompanying adults. **Director**—Richard Fleischer. (PG)
113 minutes

CROSSFIRE (1947)
★★★★

Robert Young
Robert Mitchum
Robert Ryan

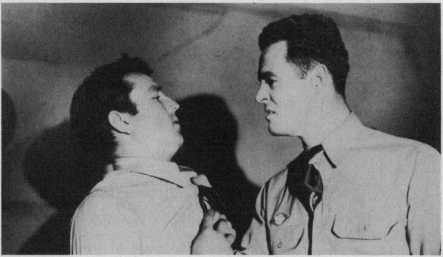

Robert Ryan (right) warns Steve Brodie not to expose him in Crossfire.

A taut, exciting melodrama about an unhinged, bigoted soldier who murders a Jew in a New York City hotel and is pursued by the police. This landmark film is one of the first to deal so directly with racial prejudice. The film was shot mostly at night, and this technique contributes to its moody atmosphere. Fine performances are given by a top cast that also includes Gloria Grahame, Paul Kelly, Sam Levene, Jacqueline White, and Steve Brodie. **Director**—Edward Dmytryk. **Academy Award Nominations**—best picture; Dmytryk, best director; Ryan, best supporting actor; Grahame, best supporting actress; John Paxton, writing (screenplay). *86 minutes b&w*

CROSS OF IRON (1977)
★★

James Coburn
Maximilian Schell
James Mason

Sam Peckinpah's first World War II movie is a puffed-up cliché about a small detachment of German soldiers fighting on the Russian front. Peckinpah, as can be expected, trowels on heavy doses of gore and violence—some of it in slow motion—while he skips lightly over plot, dialogue, and acting. There are dull and uneven performances from Coburn, Schell, and Mason. The film lasts two hours, which is more than enough time to inflict battle fatigue on any audience. Also with David Warner, Senta Berger, and Klaus Lowitsch. (R)
120 minutes

THE CRUEL SEA (1953)
★★★★

Jack Hawkins
Donald Sinden
Stanley Baker

A compelling screen adaptation of Nicholas Monsarrat's best-selling novel about the rigors aboard a British corvette in the North Atlantic during World War II. The taut drama depicts the dangers of encountering convoy-hunting Nazi subs as well as dealing with harsh weather. There are strong characterizations of the officers and men, too. Also with John Stratton, Denholm Elliott, John Warner, and

Bruce Seton. **Director**—Charles Frend. **Academy Award Nomination**—Eric Ambler, writing (screenplay). *126 minutes b&w*

CRUISING (1980)
★★★

Al Pacino
Paul Sorvino
Karen Allen

William Friedkin (*The Exorcist; The French Connection*) takes us on a grim tour of New York City's freaky leather bars. Pacino plays a young detective who infiltrates this bizarre fringe of the homosexual world to flush out a killer. It's strong stuff, which may disturb some. But it's also a relentlessly gripping detective story with excellent performances by Pacino and a first-rate supporting cast. Friedkin doesn't attempt to explain this kinky way of life, yet he makes his point with subtle images. Also with Richard Cox and Don Scardino. (R) *106 minutes*

Al Pacino, as Steve Burns, infiltrates homosexual haunts to find a killer in Cruising.

CRY TERROR (1958)
★★★

James Mason
Rod Steiger
Inger Stevens

Mason and Steiger are good in this taut drama about a tricky extortion scheme, which involves a kidnapping. Suspense is turned up full volume with Steiger as a crafty criminal who forces Mason, an electronics expert, to
(Continued)

CARY GRANT

Cary Grant was born Archibald Alexander Leach in 1904 in Bristol, England. He ran away from a poverty-stricken home at 13 to join an acrobatic troupe as a song-and-dance man. The troupe came to New York in 1920, and Grant stayed on to work as a lifeguard at Coney Island. In 1923, he returned to England to work in musical comedies, and he caught the attention of Arthur Hammerstein who brought him back to New York to appear in Golden Dawn, a Broadway musical.

Grant then went on to Hollywood and made his film debut in This Is the Night (1932). After starring in supporting roles, he established his reputation as a debonair leading man, usually in screwball comedies. For more than three decades, he was a leading box-office draw. Although he never won an Academy Award for a specific performance, Grant received a special Oscar in 1970.

Grant has been married five times. His fourth wife, Dyan Cannon, bore him a daughter when he was past 60. In the mid '60s, he retired from movies and became an executive for a cosmetics company.

Grant's many films include She Done Him Wrong (1933), The Awful Truth (1937), Topper (1937), Bringing Up Baby (1938), Gunga Din (1939), My Favorite Wife (1940), His Girl Friday (1940), The Philadelphia Story (1940), Arsenic and Old Lace (1944), Notorious (1946), Mr. Blandings Builds His Dream House (1948), To Catch a Thief (1955), An Affair to Remember (1957), Indiscreet (1958), North By Northwest (1959), Charade (1963), and his last movie, Walk, Don't Run (1966).

C
- Cry, the Beloved Country
- Cuba
- Cul-de-Sac
- The Curse of Frankenstein
- Cutter and Bone
- Cyrano de Bergerac

(Continued)
aid him with the caper. Stevens plays Mason's wife. New York City locations add to the tense atmosphere. Also with Angie Dickinson, Jack Klugman, Neville Brand, and Jack Kruschen. **Director**—Andrew Stone.

96 minutes b&w

CRY, THE BELOVED COUNTRY (1951)
★★★

**Canada Lee
Sidney Poitier**

Crisp drama and tense moments highlight this screen version of Alan Paton's novel about apartheid in South Africa. A black preacher travels to the city where he finds the black population living in dreadful poverty. This vivid account of the conditions separating the races is treated with candor and intelligence. The fine cast also includes Charles Carson, Charles McRae, and Joyce Carey. **Director**—Zoltan Korda.   *96 minutes b&w*

CUBA (1979)
★★

**Sean Connery
Brooke Adams**

Martin Balsam and Sean Connery discuss plans to harass and kill rebels in Cuba.

Cuba is about to succumb to Fidel Castro's revolution. The atmosphere is rich with vivid images of the corrupt and decaying Batista regime, but the movie is defeated by a weak script and numerous undefined characters. Connery plays a well-dressed British mercenary, who halfheartedly fights for Batista and pursues an old flame, played by Adams. Connery never earnestly swings into action—either on the battlefield or with the sultry Adams, who portrays a wealthy Cuban beauty. Also with Chris Sarandon, Denholm Elliot, Jack Weston, and Hector Elizondo. **Director**—Richard Lester. (R)   *121 minutes*

CUL-DE-SAC (1966)
★★★

**Lionel Stander
Donald Pleasence
Jack MacGowran**

Roman Polanski's terse direction propels this black comedy, which is set on a lonely island. Two fugitive gangsters hide out in a rambling castle and terrorize the inhabitants, a fey middle-aged man and his gorgeous wife. There are some bland moments, but the film works well overall. Also with Françoise Dorleac, William Franklyn, and Jacqueline Bisset.

111 minutes b&w

THE CURSE OF FRANKENSTEIN (1957)
★★

**Peter Cushing
Christopher Lee**

Another chapter in the tale of the famous monster, with Cushing and Lee in the key roles. This version lays on the gore, thus sacrificing some wit and stylish atmosphere. But there are a few effective scary moments of note. Yet the 1931 original and the sequels of that era remain the best. Boris Karloff, where are you? Also with Hazel Court, Robert Urquhart, and Valerie Gaunt. **Director**—Terence Fisher.

83 minutes

CUTTER AND BONE (1981)
★

**Jeff Bridges
John Heard**

Bridges and Heard star in this peculiar murder mystery, which expends considerable energy and ends up nowhere. Bridges is Bone, a young free-wheeling southern Californian, who is falsely accused of murdering a high school girl. Heard plays Cutter, a slightly loony Vietnam vet, who works up an absurd scheme to clear Bone. The entire screenplay and dialogue are absurd as well, and the film bogs down in utter confusion. Also with Lisa Eichorn, Ann Dusenberry, and Stephen Elliott. **Director**—Ivan Passer. (R)   *109 minutes*

CYRANO DE BERGERAC (1950)
★★★★

**José Ferrer
Mala Powers**

An exceptional moving performance by Ferrer in the title role says it all, in this film version of Edmond Rostand's classic love story, which is set in the 17th century. Cyrano is the poet with the long nose who writes tender love letters to a beautiful lady for his friend. However, Cyrano genuinely loves the woman, too. Powers plays the Lady Roxanne. Ferrer requires little help to make this film worthwhile. Also with William Prince and Morris Carnovsky.

- Daddy Long Legs
- Dakota
- The Dam Busters
- Damien—Omen II
- Damnation Alley
- Damn Yankees
- Darby O'Gill and the Little People

C·D

Director—Michael Gordon. **Academy Award**—Ferrer, best actor.

112 minutes b&w

D

DADDY LONG LEGS (1955)
★★

Fred Astaire
Leslie Caron

The energetic dancing of Astaire and Caron top this romantic musical about a French orphan girl who is secretly supported by a rich playboy. Fred's the playboy, and Leslie's the waif. The production, however, is too long and somewhat awkward. The film, based on Jean Webster's popular novel, has sly references to the classic *Cinderella* story. Also with Fred Clark, Thelma Ritter, Terry Moore, and Larry Keating. **Director**—Jean Negulesco.

126 minutes

DAKOTA (1945)
★★

John Wayne
Vera Hruba Ralston

Typical western yarn with Wayne in the saddle and immersed in a territorial conflict involving a railroad line. The Duke handles the job with ease, and lovely Ralston, who plays a railway tycoon's daughter, is by his side. Other characters are played adequately by Walter Brennan, Ward Bond, and Ona Munson. **Director**—Joseph Kane.

82 minutes b&w

THE DAM BUSTERS (1954)
★★★★

Michael Redgrave
Richard Todd

Gripping, straightforward World War II account of the development of the RAF's skip-bombing technique, which was used to blow up the Ruhr dams in 1943 to cripple some vital German industries. An intense climate of suspense and danger builds as the British execute their plan step by step. Fine acting and impressive special effects enhance the production. Also with

In The Dam Busters, *Michael Redgrave and Richard Todd ponder a tough mission.*

Ursula Jeans, Derek Farr, Patrick Barr, and Basil Sydney. **Director**—Michael Anderson.

125 minutes b&w

DAMIEN—OMEN II (1978)
★★

William Holden
Lee Grant

Damien, that little demon from *The Omen*, is now 13 and living with his rich uncle in Chicago. After Damien is through this time, about a dozen victims are murdered in the most grisly fashion. The movie has a slick look; a good cast, led by Holden and Grant, is effective. Jonathan Scott-Taylor is Damien. But the film is burdened with much tedious dialogue interspersed with warmed-over mayhem. And the Devil apparently isn't finished making money for Hollywood. Thus the ending leaves the door open for *Omen III*. Also with Lew Ayres, Sylvia Sidney, and Robert Foxworth. **Director**—Don Taylor. (R)

107 minutes

DAMNATION ALLEY (1977)
★

Jan-Michael Vincent
George Peppard

Plodding and silly adventure about a tiny band of nuclear war survivors, who trek across the U.S. continent searching for signs of life. The acting is second-rate. Considerable emphasis is on special effects, which come off as half-baked and phony-looking. Also with Dominique Sanda and Paul Winfield. **Director**—Jack Smight. (PG)

91 minutes

DAMN YANKEES (1958)
★★★

Gwen Verdon
Tab Hunter

This is a competent film version of the hit Broadway musical about a baseball fan who becomes a star player with the help of the Devil. Verdon tops the cast lineup as the temptress Lola, with lively dancing and singing. And she especially upstages Hunter, who plays the critical role of the spectacular athlete. Tab strikes out when it comes to the footwork and the songs, but Ray Walston is an amusing Devil. Famous songs include "You've Got to Have Heart" and "Whatever Lola Wants." Also with Russ Brown and Shannon Bolin. **Directors**—George Abbott and Stanley Donen.

110 minutes

In Damn Yankees, *Gwen Verdon tempts Tab Hunter and sings "Whatever Lola Wants."*

DARBY O'GILL AND THE LITTLE PEOPLE (1959)
★★★

Albert Sharpe
Janet Munro

A breezy Walt Disney fantasy based on an Irish folk tale. Darby, played by Sharpe, is a caretaker who tells tall tales and becomes involved with leprechauns. The Disney special effects are outstanding, and there's a lively script to keep the kids anchored to their seats. The fine cast also includes

(Continued)

D
- Darby's Rangers
- The Dark
- The Dark at the Top of the Stairs
- The Dark Mirror
- Dark Passage
- Darktown Strutters
- Darling
- David and Bathsheba
- David and Lisa

(Continued)
Jimmy O'Dea, Sean Connery, and Jack MacGowran. **Director**—Robert Stevenson. (G)   *90 minutes*

DARBY'S RANGERS (1957)
★★

James Garner
Etchika Choureau
Jack Warden

Garner plays Maj. William Darby, the heroic commander who led assaults in North Africa and Italy during World War II. The troops experience frontline action and romantic interludes. This rather uneven film has some adequate moments. Also with Edward Byrnes, Venetia Stevenson, and David Janssen. **Director**—William Wellman.   *121 minutes b&w*

THE DARK (1979)
★★

William Devane
Cathy Lee Crosby

A fiend with laser-beam eyes stalks Los Angeles and does its grisly work on a few citizens. Nothing really novel or terribly scary here. Devane plays a writer whose daughter is a victim of the fiend. After a few preliminary chilling scenes, the film lapses into just another run-of-the-mill Hollywood monster flick. At last, an army of cops arrive to blast away with relentless firepower until the creature disappears. Also with Keenan Wynn and Vivian Blaine. **Director**—John (Bud) Cardos. (R)   *92 minutes*

THE DARK AT THE TOP OF THE STAIRS (1960)
★★★

Robert Preston
Dorothy McGuire

William Inge's play about family life in a small Oklahoma town in the '20s is expertly produced for the screen with much of the emotions unfettered. Preston stars as the father, and McGuire plays the wife with proper stateliness. However, Eve Arden, Angela Lansbury, and Shirley Knight stand out in supporting roles. **Director**—Delbert Mann. **Academy Award**

Nomination—Knight, best supporting actress.   *124 minutes*

THE DARK MIRROR (1946)
★★★

Olivia de Havilland
Lew Ayres

A taut, clever whodunit about identical twins, one of whom is a murderess. De Havilland is excellent playing the roles of the twins. Ayers plays a doctor who is faced with the challenge of identifying the killer. Lots of suspense in the offing. Also with Thomas Mitchell, Richard Long, Charles Evans, and Gary Owen. **Director**—Robert Siodmak. **Academy Award Nomination**—Vladimir Pozner, writing (original story).
85 minutes b&w

DARK PASSAGE (1947)
★★★

Humphrey Bogart
Lauren Bacall

Bogart plays a man who escapes from the big house and then tries to prove he didn't kill his wife. He masks his identity with plastic surgery and hides out with Bacall. Not one of the best Bogey-Bacall films, but it entertains only because of the stars' professionalism and their magnetic appeal. The plot, however, is rather farfetched. There are good performances from Agnes Moorehead, Tom D'Andrea, Bruce Bennett, and Houseley Stevenson. **Director**—Delmer Daves.
106 minutes b&w

DARKTOWN STRUTTERS (1975)
(no stars)

Trina Parks
Norman Bartold

A hectic and pointless comedy-satire. It's about a group of black women, who pursue a male gang and a fried-ribs kingpin who has kidnapped some blacks. There's lots of racing around on motorcycles through Los Angeles's Watts section, but not much else. **Director**—William Witney. (PG)
90 minutes

DARLING (1965)
★★★★

Julie Christie
Dirk Bogarde

A slick, stylish, and cynical drama about an ambitious London model who succeeds socially by having a series of affairs. Quite a perceptive and honest approach to contemporary morals, all graced with the brilliant performance of Christie, the efficient direction of John Schlesinger, and plenty of smart dialogue. Also with Laurence Harvey and Alex Scott. **Academy Awards**—Christie, best actress; Frederic Raphael, best story and screenplay (written directly for the screen). **Nominations**—best picture; Schlesinger, best director.
127 minutes b&w

DAVID AND BATHSHEBA (1952)
★★

Gregory Peck
Susan Hayward

This is a rather routine Bible epic that's top-heavy with impressive sets and gorgeous costumes. However, someone neglected to work diligently on the script, so the film drags along without much excitement. Peck and Hayward, who lead the cast, don't seem to have their hearts in the project. The familiar plot has to do with King David's love for the wife of one of his soldiers. His majesty, played by Peck, conspires to have the man killed in battle. Hayward plays Bathsheba. Also with Raymond Massey, Jayne Meadows, and Francis X. Bushman. **Director**—Henry King.   *116 minutes*

DAVID AND LISA (1962)
★★★★

Keir Dullea
Janet Margolin

An earnest and touching low-budget film that works beautifully because of its poignant script, efficient direction, and fine acting by a novice cast. The plot concerns two mentally ill teenagers at a private institution who share a bond of mutual understanding. Dul-

★ STAR PROFILE

- Dawn of the Dead
- Day of the Animals
- The Day of the Dolphin
- The Day of the Jackal

D

Keir Dullea and Janet Margolin portray troubled teenagers in David and Lisa.

lea and Margolin are exceptionally good as the troubled youngsters. Howard da Silva stands out as an understanding doctor. Neva Patterson, Clifton James, and Richard McMurray round out the cast. **Director—Frank Perry. Academy Award Nominations**—Perry, best director; Eleanor Perry, best screenplay (based on material from another medium).

94 minutes b&w

DAWN OF THE DEAD (1979)
★★

Gaylen Ross
Ken Foree

Director George Romero whips up the horror and gore again in this sequel to his 1968 *Night of the Living Dead*. This film, however, lacks the shock of its predecessor. But Romero outdoes himself with lavish grisly events, such as flesh being torn apart, severed heads, and spurting blood. An army of cannibalistic zombies invade a suburban shopping mall where our heroes slaughter them in an orgy of mayhem. The plot and acting are inconsequential; the emphasis is on blood and guts. Also with Scott Reiniger and David Emge. (No MPAA rating)

125 minutes

DAY OF THE ANIMALS (1977)
★★

Christopher George
Lynda Day George
Leslie Nielsen
Michael Ansara

Bears, wolves, large birds, and packs of dogs go crazy and attack a group of mountain hikers. The story is absurd, and the performances by the humans are routine at best. But there are some terrifying and convincing shots of the stalking critters. It's a movie about animals for animals; send your dog or cat to see this one. Also with Richard Jaeckel. **Director**—William Girdler. (PG)

98 minutes

THE DAY OF THE DOLPHIN
(1973)
★★

George C. Scott
Trish Van Devere

A so-so thriller about a marine biologist, played by Scott, who trains dolphins to talk and becomes entangled in a plot to assassinate the President. Despite the big money and top talent involved, the film doesn't come off. There's a bit of comedy and suspense here and there, but the proceedings mostly suffer from the blahs. Also with Paul Sorvino, Fritz Weaver, John Korkes, and Edward Herrmann.

Director—Mike Nichols. (PG)

104 minutes

THE DAY OF THE JACKAL
(1973)
★★★

Edward Fox
Cyril Cusack

Frederick Forsyth's suspenseful novel about an OAS attempt to assassinate Charles de Gaulle is adapted for the screen with all the thrills neatly intact. Fox plays the role of the professional killer who is hired by some conspiring French generals for the dastardly deed. Tension mounts as the police step up their manhunt while the assassin prepares for his strike. Good supporting acting, excellent pacing, and impressive European locations add to the professional production. TV commercials, however, can ruin the pace. Michel Lonsdale, Eric Porter, Delphine Seyrig, and Alan Badel also star. **Director**—Fred Zinnemann. (PG)

142 minutes

SALLY FIELD

Norma Rae (1979) catapulted Sally Field into the ranks of popular and critically acclaimed young actresses. Her multifaceted portrayal of a young working-class woman struggling to unionize the textile mill in the small southern town where she lives received rave reviews and brought her the Academy Award as best actress.

Born in Pasadena, California, in 1946, Field became a favorite of TV audiences in the mid '60s and early '70s when she starred in three successive series—Gidget, The Flying Nun, and The Girl With Something Extra. But it wasn't until her motion-picture debut in 1976—as a health spa receptionist in Stay Hungry—that Field was taken seriously as a first-rate dramatic actress.

Subsequently, she was selected for the title role in Sybil, a TV mini-series based on the true story of a schizophrenic woman tormented by multiple personality. The production was a critical and ratings smash and earned Field the Emmy Award for best actress in a drama special.

Next, Field co-starred with Burt Reynolds in Smokey and the Bandit (1977). Since then, Field has also starred with Henry Winkler in Heroes (1977), re-teamed with Reynolds in The End (1978) and Hooper (1978), starred opposite Michael Caine in Irwin Allen's Beyond the Poseidon Adventure (1979), acted with Reynolds in Smokey and the Bandit II (1980), co-starred with Tommy Lee Jones in Back Roads (1980), and starred with Paul Newman in Absence of Malice (1981).

D
- The Day of the Locust
- Days of Heaven
- Days of Wine and Roses
- D-Day the Sixth of June
- Dead and Buried
- Deadline, USA
- The Deadly Affair

THE DAY OF THE LOCUST
(1975)

★★

Donald Sutherland
William Atherton
Karen Black

An overblown and alternately brilliant and disappointing movie based on Nathanael West's novel of Hollywood in the '30s. There are good performances by Burgess Meredith as an old vaudevillian and Billy Barty as a macho dwarf, but West's keen description of the wretchedness of dashed hopes on the fringes of Hollywood's dream factories is poorly interpreted. Also with Geraldine Page, Richard A. Dysart, and Bo Hopkins. **Director**—John Schlesinger. (R) **Academy Award Nominations**—Meredith, best supporting actor; Conrad Hall, cinematography. *140 minutes*

DAYS OF HEAVEN (1978)

★★

Richard Gere
Brooke Adams

Writer-director Terrence Malick's spectacular art film is a technical achievement of exquisite photography and beautiful images. But alas, a skimpy plot, shallow characters, and a lack of drama lead to disappointment. The story, set in 1916, is about three poverty-stricken vagabonds, who become involved with a wealthy Texas wheat farmer. This production might have worked better in the days of silent movies. Also with Linda Manz, Sam Shepard, and Robert Wilke. (PG) **Academy Award**—Nestor Almendros, cinematography. *95 minutes*

DAYS OF WINE AND ROSES
(1962)

★★★★

Jack Lemmon
Lee Remick

A brilliant, uncompromising drama about a public relations man, played by Lemmon, who becomes disillusioned with his work, turns to drink, and leads his wife down the alcoholic path. Remick plays the wife. Lemmon

In Days of Wine and Roses, *Jack Lemmon and Lee Remick give compelling performances.*

and Remick are at their acting best, and there's professional work from all quarters—direction, script, and supporting roles. The film is compelling from beginning to end, dwelling relentlessly on stark realism. Charles Bickford, Jack Klugman, Alan Hewitt, Tom Palmer, and Jack Albertson costar. **Director**—Blake Edwards. **Academy Award Nominations**—Lemmon, best actor; Remick, best actress. *117 minutes b&w*

D-DAY, THE SIXTH OF JUNE
(1956)

★★★

Robert Taylor
Richard Todd
Dana Wynter
Edmond O'Brien

Two officers—one an American, the other British—fall in love with the same girl during the time of the World War II Normandy invasion. Taylor and Todd are the rivals; Wynter is the girl. The film is highlighted by impressive action scenes. The romantic plot is rather familiar, but it's executed with above-average flair. **Director**—Henry Koster. *106 minutes*

DEAD AND BURIED (1981)
(no stars)

James Farentino
Jack Albertson

The folks who gave us *Alien* present this grisly horror film, but don't count on seeing the quality and style of their initial sci-fi thriller. This time they go right for the stomach with some grotesque and sensational murders in a small town. Farentino plays a sheriff who attempts to solve the killings; Albertson is a strange coroner. Victims meet horrible deaths—a hypodermic needle into the eye, a deadly injection of acid, burial alive, and so on. The makeup people take all the bows in this one. **Director**—Gary A. Sherman. (R) *93 minutes*

DEADLINE, USA (1952)
★★★

Humphrey Bogart
Kim Hunter
Ethel Barrymore

Bogart stars in this terse drama as a courageous newspaper editor who promotes stories about an influential criminal and then must struggle to prevent his superiors from bending to intimidation. Bogey is enjoyable, and there are good dramatic scenes with him and Ethel Barrymore, who plays the publisher. Hunter plays Bogey's ex-wife. Some newspaper clichés here and there, but not enough to spoil the fun. Also with Ed Begley, Paul Stewart, Warren Stevens, Martin Gabel, and Jim Backus. **Director**—Richard Brooks. *87 minutes b&w*

THE DEADLY AFFAIR (1967)
★★★

James Mason
Simone Signoret

A gripping whodunit, with Mason as a British agent investigating the appar-

- Deadly Blessing
- Deadly Hero
- Dead of Night
- Dead Reckoning
- Dear Detective
- Dear Inspector
- Death Hunt
- Death of a Salesman

D

ent suicide of a colleague and uncovering a nest of spies. The film is nicely plotted, with suspense relentlessly building at an even pace. The story is based on the John Le Carré novel *Call for the Dead*. Mason is convincing, and he's backed up nicely with good acting by Signoret, Maximilian Schell, Lynn Redgrave, and Max Adrian. **Director**—Sidney Lumet. *106 minutes*

DEADLY BLESSING (1981)
★

Ernest Borgnine

This is a strange horror story about some mysterious deaths among a religious sect called the Hittites. A farmer is run over by his own tractor, and others are murdered with knives, snakes, and spiders. It's not certain who does the killing in this illogical film, yet there are many suspects for the perpetrator, referred to as "the incubus" by the Hittites. Borgnine is interesting as the fanatical religious leader. **Director**—Wes Craven. *102 minutes*

DEADLY HERO (1976)
★

Don Murray
Diahn Williams
James Earl Jones

Murray portrays a psychotic New York City cop, who kills a black mugger and shakedown artist. Williams plays a mugging victim; Jones is her attacker. Moments of suspense occasionally perk up the thin script, and the moody photography of the metropolitan jungle adds some color. But it still comes off as a rather commonplace melodrama. Also with Lilia Skala, George S. Irving, and Cochata Ferrell. **Director**—Ivan Nagy. (R) *102 minutes*

DEAD OF NIGHT (1946)
★★★★

Mervyn Johns
Roland Culver

A superior bone-chilling thriller about a man who has strange dreams that appear to interconnect with the dreams of other people. The film is composed of five stories of the supernatural, which are blended well for the utmost in eerie atmosphere and suspenseful thrills. It's all topped off with fine acting. Also stars Michael Redgrave, Googie Withers, Antony Baird, Judy Kelly, and Sally Ann Howes. **Directors**—Alberto Cavalcanti, Basil Dearden, Robert Hamer, and Charles Crichton. *104 minutes b&w*

DEAD RECKONING (1947)
★★★

Humphrey Bogart
Lizabeth Scott

Bogart plays a World War II veteran who investigates the murder of his friend, during a trip to Washington to receive a medal. Standard *film noir* fare, but it's enhanced by some good acting, especially Bogey's reliable performance as a tough character. Also with Morris Carnovsky, William Prince, and Wallace Ford. **Director**—John Cromwell. *100 minutes b&w*

DEAR DETECTIVE (1978)
★★★

Annie Girardot
Philippe Noiret

French director Philippe De Broca's frisky comedy-suspense film, with Girardot and Noiret as unlikely lovers, moves at a brisk pace. Noiret is a middle-aged professor of Greek, and she, alas, is France's equivalent of Lieutenant Columbo who solves a series of crimes. It's not one of De Broca's best, but his droll humor is effective. Annie bags a murderer and gets her man too. Also with Catherine Aric and Paulette Dubost. In French with English titles. **Alternate Title**—*Dear Inspector*. (No MPAA rating) *105 minutes*

DEAR INSPECTOR
See Dear Detective

DEATH HUNT (1981)
★★★

Charles Bronson
Lee Marvin

Granite-hard Bronson and grizzled, rawhide-tough Marvin are matched in

In Death Hunt, *Charles Bronson plays a trapper who's wrongly accused of murder.*

this action-packed adventure filmed in northern Canada. Marvin is a whiskey-soaked Mountie on the brink of retirement, who reluctantly pursues a quiet trapper, played by Bronson, who is wrongly accused of murder. Both stars portray larger-than-life adversaries who gradually develop respect for one another. It's an old-fashioned story, set in the '30s amid perilous terrain, with heroes worth cheering. **Director**—Peter Hunt. (R) *96 minutes*

DEATH OF A SALESMAN (1951)
★★★★

Fredric March
Kevin McCarthy
Mildred Dunnock
Cameron Mitchell

Arthur Miller's powerful and heartfelt drama is brought to the screen with all the emotion and pathos of the magnificent Broadway play. March has never been better as the indelible Willy Loman, the over-the-hill traveling salesman who confronts the disappointment of his career and commits suicide. Flashbacks are cleverly used to bring out an extra dimension of this great American classic tragedy. Dunnock plays Loman's wife; McCarthy and Mitchell play his sons. Also with *(Continued)*

D
- Death on the Nile
- Death Play
- Death Ship
- Death Weekend
- Death Wish
- Deception
- The Deep

Cameron Mitchell, Fredric March, and Kevin McCarthy in Death of a Salesman.

(Continued)

Howard Smith, Royal Beal, and Jesse White. **Director**—Laslo Benedek. **Academy Award Nominations**—March, best actor; McCarthy, best supporting actor; Dunnock, best supporting actress; Frank Planer, cinematography (black and white).

112 minutes b&w

DEATH ON THE NILE (1978)
★★★★

**Peter Ustinov
Bette Davis
David Niven
Mia Farrow
Angela Lansbury
George Kennedy
Maggie Smith**

Celebrated Belgian sleuth Hercule Poirot, played by Ustinov, encounters suspects galore as he unravels a murder mystery on a Nile River cruise as only Dame Agatha Christie could tell it. A big first-rate cast, elegant settings, and lively acting add up to a charming, old-fashioned movie whodunit. Old pros Davis and Lansbury ham it up and steal a number of scenes on the way to an intriguing ending, where the droll Monsieur Poirot unmasks the killer of a beautiful heiress. Also with Jack Warden, Lois Chiles, and Olivia Hussey. **Director**—John Guillermin. (PG)   *140 minutes*

DEATH PLAY (1976)
★

**Karen Leslie
Michael Higgins
James Keach**

Several New York legitimate theater actors star in this low-budget and uneven backstage drama, about the tangled affairs of various characters who stage a Broadway comedy. Leslie gives an impressive performance of a young, high-strung actress who is murdered at the film's end. Other roles are nondescript, and the plot is a series of clichés. **Director**—Arthur Storch. (PG)   *86 minutes*

DEATH SHIP (1980)
★

George Kennedy

A ludicrous horror movie about a haunted ship, once used as a floating torture chamber by the Nazis, that prowls the Atlantic looking for victims. Despite numerous gruesome scenes—rotting corpses strapped to racks and so on—there's scant sense of suspense or thrills. It's just so much floating garbage. Kennedy, stalwart veteran of many disaster films, leads a shipwrecked cast. **Director**—Alvin Rakoff. (R)   *91 minutes*

DEATH WEEKEND
See The House by the Lake

DEATH WISH (1974)
★★★

**Charles Bronson
Hope Lange**

In New York City, muggers brutally rape the wife and daughter of a placid businessman, who then launches a one-man vigilante crusade against numerous thugs he encounters on the streets. The script is farfetched. How could one man be confronted by so many attackers in such a short time? However, director Michael Winner pulls out the stops, and the film is watchable to the end. Bronson is at his best as the stone-faced citizen out for revenge. Also with Vincent Gardenia, Stuart Margolin, and Stephen Keats. (R)   *94 minutes*

DECEPTION (1946)
★★★

**Bette Davis
Claude Rains**

Davis and Rains shine in this stylish but sloshy melodrama, set against the background of classical music. Rains is a wealthy pianist who loves Davis, but she weds her former boyfriend, played by Paul Henreid. That makes Claude jealous, indeed. Good acting all around, but Henreid is upstaged by the dynamic performances of Davis and Rains. Also with John Abbott and Benson Fong. **Director**—Irving Rapper.   *112 minutes b&w*

THE DEEP (1977)
★★

**Robert Shaw
Jacqueline Bisset**

Peter *(Jaws)* Benchley wrote this underwater adventure, but if you're

Peter Ustinov (third from left) plays Belgian sleuth Hercule Poirot in Death on the Nile.

- The Deer Hunter
- The Defiant Ones
- Deliverance
- Delusions of Grandeur
- Demetrius and the Gladiators
- Demon Seed

D

looking for *Son of Jaws*, forget it. Spectacular underwater photography is the only virtue in this rather shallow production, which concerns a scramble for sunken treasure off the Bermuda coast. Most of the dialogue and acting is wooden. Peter Yates directed as if he was seasick most of the time. So-so acting jobs by Nick Nolte and Bisset; a realistic performance from Shaw. Also with Louis Gossett and Eli Wallach. (PG) *123 minutes*

THE DEER HUNTER (1978)
★★★★

Robert De Niro
John Cazale
John Savage
Meryl Streep
Christopher Walken

Director Michael Cimino's protracted film about the Vietnam experience is extraordinarily powerful and original. Cimino uncorks a fascinating multitude of emotions and insights about war and violence. Essentially, the story deals with three young steelworkers from a small Pennsylvania town who are devastated by the horror of the war. Superb performances by De Niro, Walken, and Streep. Also with George Dzunda and Chuck Aspegren. (R) **Academy Awards**—best picture; Cimino, best director; Walken, best supporting actor. **Nominations**—De Niro, best actor; Streep, best supporting actress; Cimino, Louis Garfinkle, and Quinn K. Redeker (story) and Deric Washburn (story and screenplay), best original screenplay. *183 minutes*

Robert De Niro in The Deer Hunter, *a film about the Vietnam experience.*

THE DEFIANT ONES (1958)
★★★★

Tony Curtis
Sidney Poitier

An inspired racial drama, with Curtis and Poitier as escaped convicts who are chained together and attempt to flee a police dragnet. This is powerful stuff that deals squarely with hatred. There are some superbly powerful performances and well-paced action. Director Stanley Kramer outdoes himself with a great job. Théodore Bikel, Cara Williams, and Lon Chaney, Jr., turn in fine supporting performances. **Academy Award**—Nathan Douglas and Harold Jacob Smith, best story and screenplay (written directly for the screen). **Nominations**—best picture; Kramer, best director; Curtis, Poitier, best actor; Bikel, best supporting actor; Williams, best supporting actress. *97 minutes b&w*

DELIVERANCE (1972)
★★★★

Burt Reynolds
Jon Voight
Ned Beatty

Four well-to-do young men embark on a canoe trip down a swift Georgia river, but their weekend outing turns into a nightmare when they're set upon by some sadistic mountain men. The engrossing film, adapted by James Dickey from his novel, offers lucid contrasts between the haves and have-nots, and it brims with suspense and terror. Superb direction and tight editing enhance the thrilling and terrifying adventure. Exceptionally good acting from Voight, Reynolds, Beatty, Ronny Cox, Billy McKinney, and Herbert Coward. **Director**—John Boorman. (R) **Academy Award Nominations**—best picture; Boorman, best director. *109 minutes*

DELUSIONS OF GRANDEUR (1975)
★★

Yves Montand
Louis De Funes

Montand and De Funes star in this slapstick comedy about royal intrigue in the 17th-century court of the King of Spain. De Funes plays a corrupt, incompetent tax minister, and Montand is his valet. The film is well made and there are plenty of good laughs, yet smooth continuity is lacking. At times, Montand seems out of place in this comedy role. **Director**—Gerard Oury. In French with English titles. (No MPAA rating) *85 minutes b&w*

DEMETRIUS AND THE GLADIATORS (1954)
★★

Victor Mature
Susan Hayward
Michael Rennie

Humdrum sequal to *The Robe*, with Mature hamming it up as a slave in possession of Christ's garment. Emperor Caligula, played by Jay Robinson, wants it. The hokey script dwells on heroics rather than religiousness. There is some worthwhile action in the arena with the gladiators battling away. The costumes and sets—probably left over from *The Robe*—are impressive. Also with Debra Paget, Anne Bancroft, Richard Egan, Ernest Borgnine, and Barry Jones. **Director**—Delmer Daves. *101 minutes*

DEMON SEED (1977)
★★★

Julie Christie
Fritz Weaver

Proteus IV is an ultra-sophisticated computer capable of philosophical decisions and creativity. It wants to perpetuate itself in the flesh by impregnating a human female. Just how this feat is accomplished evolves into a bizarre and intriguing science-fiction tale that's sort of a cross between *Rosemary's Baby* and *2001: A Space Odyssey*. Christie is excellent as the reluctant object of the electronic brain's affections. The story is preposterous, but it's smartly executed with effective direction by Donald Cammell, top-notch special effects, and a haunting climax. Also with Gerrit Graham, Berry Kroeger, and Lisa Lu. (R) *94 minutes*

D
- The Desert Fox
- The Desert Rats
- The Desert Song
- Desire Under the Elms
- The Desk Set
- The Desperate Hours
- Desperate Living

James Mason (center) portrays German Field Marshal Erwin Rommel in The Desert Fox.

THE DESERT FOX (1951)
★★★

**James Mason
Jessica Tandy
Cedric Hardwicke**

Mason is fantastic as German Field Marshal Erwin Rommel in this film biography, which follows his defeat in North Africa and his disillusionment on his return to Nazi Germany. The engrossing drama features some stunning desert location scenes. Mason followed up his Rommel role in *The Desert Rats*. Also with Luther Adler, Everett Sloane, Leo G. Carroll, George Macready, and Richard Boone. **Director**—Henry Hathaway.

88 minutes b&w

THE DESERT RATS (1953)
★★★

**Richard Burton
James Mason**

A well-made follow-up to *The Desert Fox*, with Mason once again portraying German Field Marshal Erwin Rommel. This exciting war drama is seen from the Allied side, with Burton leading Australian troops against Nazi armor in the siege of Tobruk. There are impressive battle scenes, with Burton doing a fine acting job. There's good support, too, from Robert Newton as a soldier who was a professor in civilian life. Also with Robert Douglas, Torin Thatcher, and Chips Rafferty. **Director**—Robert Wise. **Academy Award Nomination**—Richard Murphy, best writing (story and screenplay).

88 minutes b&w

THE DESERT SONG (1953)
★★

**Gordon MacRae
Kathryn Grayson**

A third film version of Sigmund Romberg's endurable operetta with MacRae and Grayson acceptably singing and acting in the key roles. The score offers "The Riff Song" and "One Alone." The setting is Africa, and MacRae plays the leader of the Riffs, who fight some evil tribesmen. Steve Cochran, Raymond Massey, and William Conrad are also in the cast. **Director**—Bruce Humberstone.

110 minutes

DESIRE UNDER THE ELMS (1958)
★★

**Sophia Loren
Anthony Perkins
Burl Ives**

Slow-paced and stagey screen version of Eugene O'Neill's play about conflicts of a New England farm family in the 19th century. Loren is out of her element as an elderly farmer's young wife who falls in love with her stepson. There are a few minor moments of visible drama, but most of the film is rather murky. Perkins plays the young stepson; Ives is the father. Frank Overton, Pernell Roberts, and Anne Seymour also star. **Director**—Delbert Mann.

111 minutes b&w

THE DESK SET (1957)
★★★

**Spencer Tracy
Katharine Hepburn**

Tracy and Hepburn head up this adult comedy, which is based on William Marchant's play. The chemistry is perfect, and the sparks fly. She runs a broadcast company's reference section. He's an efficiency expert who wants to improve the operation. They fight. They fall in love. Plenty of good dialogue and laughs along the way. Supporting roles are played by Joan Blondell, Gig Young, and Dina Merrill. **Director**—Walter Lang.

103 minutes

THE DESPERATE HOURS (1955)
★★★

**Humphrey Bogart
Fredric March
Arthur Kennedy**

Three escaped convicts hide out in the home of a typical family and hold them hostage. A suspenseful battle of wits ensues, with Bogart as good as usual, playing one of the cons. Fine performances, too, from Martha Scott, Dewey Martin, and Gig Young. Based on the Joseph Hayes novel and play. **Director**—William Wyler.

112 minutes b&w

DESPERATE LIVING (1977)
(no stars)

A revolting, pointless episode by Director John Waters, the sultan of bad taste, who is responsible for the similarly disgusting *Pink Flamingos*. The action includes sadism, emasculation, assorted murders, and vomiting. The film is obviously desperate, but it's certainly not for the living. (No MPAA rating)

90 minutes

- Desperate Siege
- Destination Tokyo
- Destroyer
- Destry Rides Again
- The Detective
- Detective Story
- The Devil and Max Devlin
- The Devil and Miss Jones

D

DESPERATE SIEGE
See Rawhide

DESTINATION TOKYO (1943)
★★★

Cary Grant
John Garfield
Alan Hale

In Destination Tokyo, *Cary Grant is skipper of a U.S. submarine that slips into Tokyo Bay.*

Taut, World War II action adventure, with Grant skippering a submarine, which slips into Tokyo Bay. Good suspense and professional acting heighten this enjoyable wartime drama. There is fine interplay among the crew members as tension mounts. Garfield and Dane Clark come across as colorful submariners. Faye Emerson and John Forsythe are also in the cast. **Director**—Delmer Daves.
135 minutes b&w

DESTROYER (1943)
★★

Edward G. Robinson
Glenn Ford

Robinson plays an old salt who ships out on a destroyer and clashes with the younger sailors. A routine and predictable flag-waving film with below-par production values. Ford is on board as a novice seaman with his own methods of doing things, but Robinson emerges as the real pro. Marguerite Chapman, Edgar Buchanan, and Leo Gorcey contribute sup-

port. **Director**—William A. Seiter.
99 minutes b&w

DESTRY RIDES AGAIN (1939)
★★★★

James Stewart
Marlene Dietrich
Brian Donlevy

A first-class classic western, loaded with such goodies as rousing action, suspense, satire, pathos, and even some fine musical numbers. Stewart is superb as a polite sheriff, who gets fed up with local rowdiness and corruption and decides to clean up the town. Dietrich is also great as a saloon dancer who sings "See What the Boys in the Back Room Will Have." This Hollywood gem spawned several imitators, but this version is still champ. Lively acting jobs, too, from Charles Winninger, Samuel S. Hinds, and Jack Carson. **Director**—George Marshall.
94 minutes b&w

THE DETECTIVE (1968)
★★★

Frank Sinatra
Lee Remick
Ralph Meeker

Sinatra makes the most of the sleazy material as he plays a tough New York City detective involved in the murder of a homosexual. The film is further helped along with smart dialogue and quick pacing. Remick does good work, and there is other able support from Jacqueline Bisset, Jack Klugman, Horace MacMahon, William Windom, Tony Musante, and Al Freeman. Based on Roderick Thorp's best-selling novel. **Director**—Gordon Douglas.
114 minutes

DETECTIVE STORY (1951)
★★★★

Kirk Douglas
Eleanor Parker
William Bendix

Douglas is excellent as a tough city detective whose sense of morality and honesty erodes after contact with criminals for so long. The setting is mostly a day in a New York City police precinct station. The film, adapted

from Sidney Kingsley's fine Broadway play, retains much of its impact on the screen. Joseph Wiseman and Lee Grant are good as thieves, Bendix turns in a fine performance as a police sergeant, and Parker is magnificent as Douglas's neglected wife. Also with Cathy O'Donnell, George Macready, and Horace MacMahon. **Director**—William Wyler. **Academy Award Nominations**—Wyler, best director; Parker, best actress; Grant, best supporting actress; Philip Yordan and Robert Wyler, writing (screenplay).
103 minutes b&w

THE DEVIL AND MAX DEVLIN (1981)
★★★

Elliott Gould
Bill Cosby

Gould plays Max Devlin, a grumpy Los Angeles landlord who escapes eternal damnation by conning three innocents into signing their souls over to Satan. Cosby plays the Devil. The plot is rather familiar (*Heaven Can Wait*; *Angel On My Shoulder*), and the ending is predictable. But this Disney production is executed with warmth and a decent amount of suspense. There are endearing performances, too—especially from Gould, who works like the devil to secure the confidence of his young victims. **Director**—Steven Stern. (PG)   *96 minutes*

THE DEVIL AND MISS JONES (1941)
★★★

Jean Arthur
Charles Coburn

A delightful comedy filled with captivating moments and social awareness. Coburn is exceptionally effective as a department store owner who masquerades as a clerk in his own establishment to solve problems among his employees. The humor is rather old-fashioned, but it retains its impact. Robert Cummings, Spring Byington, S. Z. Sakall, and William Demarest also star. **Director**—Sam Wood. **Academy Award Nominations**—Coburn, best supporting actor; Norman Krasna, writing (original screenplay).   *97 minutes b&w*

D
- The Devil Is a Woman
- The Devil's Playground
- The Devil's Rain
- The Devil Within Her
- Dial M for Murder
- Diamond Head
- Diamond Horseshoe
- Diamonds
- Diary of a Mad Housewife

THE DEVIL IS A WOMAN (1975)
★

Glenda Jackson

A half-baked and shallow drama, which takes place in a religious hostel in Rome. Jackson plays Sister Geraldine, an autocratic nun who stages group confessions for prominent sinners. Undistinguished performances all around. Damiano Damiani is director and creator of the story. (R)
83 minutes

THE DEVIL'S PLAYGROUND (1981)
★★

Simon Burke
Arthur Dignam
Nick Tate
Charles McCallum

This Australian film by director Fred Schepisi is filled with good intentions, but it isn't particularly moving. The somewhat autobiographical story, set in a Catholic seminary, involves the sexual awakening of a 13-year-old boy, played by Burke, who is studying for the priesthood. He's caught between temptations of the flesh and controls imposed by the brothers, who are also tormented by such restrictions. The performances are decent, with Dignam, Tate, and McCallum standing out. (No MPAA rating) *107 minutes*

THE DEVIL'S RAIN (1975)
(no stars)

Ernest Borgnine
Eddie Albert
Ida Lupino

This is an occult film about devil worshippers in Mexico. It's a plodding, stupid story unbefitting the cast members. Stay out of the rain. Also with William Shatner, Keenan Wynn, and John Travolta. **Director**—Robert Fuest. (PG) *85 minutes*

THE DEVIL WITHIN HER (1976)
★

Joan Collins

This British-made film is another con-

coction on *The Exorcist* and *Rosemary's Baby* themes. Collins plays a dancehall performer who gives birth to a devil-possessed baby after she rejects the advances of a dwarf. The absurd story drags on, with the angelic-looking baby—in between naps and late-night bottle feedings—methodically knocking off his nurse, his pediatrician, and his parents. It's all about as thrilling as a case of diaper rash. Mediocre direction by Peter Sasdy. (R)
90 minutes

DIAL M FOR MURDER (1954)
★★★

Ray Milland
John Williams
Grace Kelly

Ray Milland, Robert Cummings, Grace Kelly, and John Williams in Dial M for Murder.

Alfred Hitchcock adapted Frederick Knott's Broadway mystery drama for the screen with good results, but this isn't among Hitchcock's greatest efforts. A man (Milland) plots his wife's death to inherit money, but the scheme goes awry, and the police investigate. Kelly plays the wife; Williams is the police inspector. Also with Robert Cummings and Anthony Dawson. (PG) *105 minutes*

DIAMOND HEAD (1962)
★★

Charlton Heston
Yvette Mimieux
George Chakiris

Heston stars as an overbearing Hawaiian plantation owner whose stubbornness makes things difficult for his family. The film, based on Peter Gilman's novel, comes off as a rather dazzling soap opera, with the cardboard characters involved in run-on

conflicts. The tropical settings are easy on the eyes, but the script is predictable and labored. Supporting players also include France Nuyen, James Darren, Aline MacMahon, and Richard Loo. **Director**—Guy Green.
107 minutes

DIAMOND HORSESHOE (1945)
★★★

Betty Grable
Dick Haymes

A lavish musical with some old pros doing their stuff in Billy Rose's famous night spot. The routine plot has Grable playing a nightclub singer who chucks fame and fortune to marry a struggling medical student, played by Haymes. "The More I See You" is among the musical numbers. William Gaxton, Phil Silvers, Beatrice Kay, Carmen Cavallaro, and Margaret Dumont also participate in the frolic. **Director**—George Seaton. *104 minutes*

DIAMONDS (1976)
★

Robert Shaw
Richard Roundtree

A weak, confused, illogical plot and a dumb ending tarnish any luster that Shaw brings to this joint Israeli-Swiss film. The story is about a London diamond merchant who plans to steal diamonds from an apparently supersecure safe in an Israeli diamond exchange. At literally the last moment, the would-be crook decides not to be a thief. Many fans of this sort of caper may wish they decided not to see this film. Also stars Barbara Seagull and Shelley Winters. **Director**—Menahem Golan. (PG) *101 minutes*

DIARY OF A MAD HOUSEWIFE (1970)
★★★★

Carrie Snodgress
Richard Benjamin

Thoroughly enjoyable satirical story of a husband-pecked and bored housewife who has an affair with an arrogant writer, played convincingly by Frank Langella. Snodgress gives an excellent performance as the wife. Smart

• The Diary of Anne Frank
• Die Laughing
• A Different Story
• The Dirty Dozen
• Dirty Harry
• The Disappearance
• A Dispatch From Reuters

D

dialogue, snappy direction, and fine performances are everywhere in this insightful look at a deteriorating contemporary marriage. Benjamin is also on target as the self-centered, over-reaching husband whose law career founders. Lorraine Gullen and Frannie Michel contribute supporting work. **Director**—Frank Perry. (R) **Academy Award Nominations**—Snodgress, best actress. *95 minutes*

THE DIARY OF ANNE FRANK (1959)
★★★★

Millie Perkins
Joseph Schildkraut
Shelley Winters
Ed Wynn

In The Diary of Anne Frank, *Millie Perkins and Richard Beymer pass the time.*

Moving and gripping account of a family of Dutch Jews who hide from the Nazis in a factory loft for two years. The film faithfully follows the Broadway play, based on the meticulous and touching diary of the young girl who eventually died in a Nazi concentration camp. Perkins, in the title role, looks a lot like the real Anne, but her performance isn't up to the role. But the film never falters, thanks to good direction and fine supporting acting. Also with Lou Jacobi, Richard Beymer, and Diane Baker. **Director**—George Stevens. **Academy Awards**—Winters, best supporting actress; William C. Mellor, cinematography (black and white). **Nominations**—best picture; Stevens, best director; Wynn, best supporting actor. *170 minutes b&w*

DIE LAUGHING (1980)
★

Robby Benson
Charles Durning

Benson co-wrote and stars in this dopey comedy-mystery, about a San Francisco cabdriver who wants to be a rock singer. The trivial plot involves the murder of a nuclear scientist and the pursuit of a spider monkey who knows the formula for an atomic weapon. Unfortunately, Benson is a poor singer. And that's no laughing matter, because the intent of the film is just the opposite. Linda Grosvenor, Elsa Lanchester, and Bud Cort are in supporting roles. **Director**—Jeff Werner. (PG) *108 minutes*

A DIFFERENT STORY (1978)
★

Perry King
Meg Foster

Here's a new twist to the odd-couple theme: A boy falls in love with a girl, but they're both gay. An interesting proposition, perhaps, but the situation here is handled clumsily. The story drags on and on with all the charm of a mechanical soap opera. King and Foster work hard in the lead roles, but the superficial script prevents them from portraying believable characters. Also with Valerie Curtin, Peter Donat, and Richard Bull. **Director**—Paul Aaron. (R) *108 minutes*

THE DIRTY DOZEN (1967)
★★★★

Lee Marvin
Jim Brown
Ernest Borgnine
John Cassavetes
Robert Ryan
Charles Bronson

Slam-bang, overly violent World War II adventure with an intriguing angle on combat. Twelve convicts, most of them murderers, get out of prison in exchange for their services in an Army commando unit, where they're trained to kill on a different level. It's professionally done, with lots of tough, he-man action scenes. Director Robert Aldrich doesn't neglect character development, and he offers some insights into the personalities of these unusual recruits. Marvin and Cassavetes stand out among the cast, which also includes Donald Sutherland, George Kennedy, and Richard Jaeckel. **Academy Award Nomination**—Cassavetes, best supporting actor. *150 minutes*

DIRTY HARRY (1971)
★★

Clint Eastwood
Harry Guardino

Harry Guardino and Clint Eastwood discuss plans to catch a killer in Dirty Harry.

Eastwood stars as a San Francisco supercop who stops at nothing to bring in a man wanted for sniper killings. All stops are out to exploit violence and self-righteousness, with Eastwood at his steely-eyed best. The film packs a big punch, but it's overbearing. It spawned some sequels: *Magnum Force* and *The Enforcer*. The cast also includes Reni Santoni, John Vernon, and Andy Robinson. **Director**—Don Siegel. (R) *103 minutes*

THE DISAPPEARANCE (1981)
★

Donald Sutherland
Christopher Plummer
John Hurt
David Hemmings

Some talented actors waste their skills in this meandering drama about a professional hit man whose wife suddenly disappears. Sutherland, who plays the paid killer, carries most of the burden, while Plummer, Hurt, and Hemmings have brief throwaway parts. The direction is uninspired, the plot is confusing, and the ending is annoyingly vague. **Director**—Stuart Cooper. (R) *88 minutes*

A DISPATCH FROM REUTERS (1940)
★★★

Edward G. Robinson
Edna Best
Eddie Albert

An interesting and informative film biography about the man who
(Continued)

D
- Distance
- Distant Thunder
- Divine Madness
- Divorce American Style
- Doctor Dolittle
- Doctor No

(Continued)
founded Europe's first news service. Robinson does a fine acting job as Reuter, and production details are first class. However, the film could use more drama. Also with Gene Lockhart, Otto Kruger, Nigel Bruce, and

CHARLTON HESTON

Charlton Heston is perhaps best known as the idol of epics, portraying an athletic and strong-jawed hero in many classic Hollywood adventures.

Heston was born in 1924 in Evanston, Illinois. He studied drama at Northwestern University and worked at several Chicago radio stations before joining the U.S. Air Force.

After his discharge, Heston appeared on Broadway in Anthony and Cleopatra *and then starred in several classic roles in television specials.*

In 1950, he went to Hollywood and made his film debut in Dark City. *Soon he was portraying such historical figures as Moses, Michelangelo, and El Cid. For the title role in* Ben Hur *(1959), he won the Oscar as best actor.*

Some of Heston's movies include The Greatest Show on Earth *(1952),* The Private War of Major Benson *(1955),* The Ten Commandments *(1956),* The Wreck of the Mary Deare *(1959),* 55 Days at Peking *(1963),* The Greatest Story Ever Told *(1965),* The War Lord *(1965),* Khartoum *(1965),* Planet of the Apes *(1967),* Will Penny *(1968),* Julius Caesar *(1970),* Antony and Cleopatra *(1971),* The Three Musketeers *(1973),* Two Minute Warning *(1976), and* Gray Lady Down *(1978).*

Albert Basserman. **Director**—William Dieterle. *90 minutes b&w*

DISTANCE (1976)
★★★

Paul Benjamin
Elija Pokkinen

A sensitive and admirable little film about a black sergeant at a Georgia Army post in the 1950s. The soldier is married to a white German girl, and their relationship is deteriorating. The screenplay, by Jay Castle, offers touching human characterizations and thoughtful issues. There's top-notch acting by Benjamin as the sergeant and Pokkinen, a Finnish actress, as his wife. James Wood and Bibi Besch are excellent in other key roles. **Director**—Anthony Lover. (No MPAA rating) *93 minutes*

DISTANT THUNDER (1975)
★★★★

This vivid and powerful film by Indian director Satyajit Ray is about a famine that took the lives of five million people in 1943. The story, set in a remote Bengali village, focuses on the impact among the villagers as their rice supply is slowly depleted. The crisis prompts the social awakening of a pompous village Brahmin. Richly photographed, and exquisitely performed and directed. In Bengali with English titles. (No MPAA rating) *100 minutes b&w*

DIVINE MADNESS (1980)
★★

Bette Midler

Midler belts out an assortment of musical numbers, struts about in wild costumes, and tells raunchy jokes in this concert film that intimately displays her extraordinary talents. The Divine Miss M demonstrates amazing energy and showmanship that should please her fans. But some of the songs are unappealing, and the pacing is often uneven. The result is a mixture of Midler's magical madness and many irritating lapses in her performance. **Director**—Michael Ritchie. (R) *94 minutes*

DIVORCE AMERICAN STYLE
(1967)
★★★★

Dick Van Dyke
Debbie Reynolds

The great talents of writer-producer Norman Lear and director Bud Yorkin combine for this stinging and stylish satire on suburban marriage and family problems. Van Dyke and Reynolds star as the upper-middle-class Los Angeles couple who are on the verge of splitting, but conclude they're in for more trouble if they divorce. This is a highly entertaining film with good performances all around. Others in the cast are Jason Robards, Jr., Jean Simmons, Van Johnson, Joe Flynn, Shelley Berman, Lee Grant, and Tom Bosley. **Academy Award Nomination**—Robert Kaufman and Lear, best story and screenplay (written directly for the screen). *109 minutes*

DOCTOR DOLITTLE (1967)
★★

Rex Harrison
Anthony Newley
Samantha Eggar

Overlong fantasy musical based on the novels of Hugh Lofting, about the magnificent veterinary doctor who can talk to animals. Some animals may get a kick out of this one, but for *Homo sapiens*, it's a charmless, plodding affair. The songs are forgettable; the acting is lackluster. Harrison is in the title role with support from Newley, Eggar, Richard Attenborough (rather good as Mr. Blossom), and Peter Bull. **Director**—Richard Fleisher. **Academy Award Nominations**—best picture; Robert Surtees, cinematography. *152 minutes*

DOCTOR NO (1962)
★★★★

Sean Connery
Ursula Andress
Jack Lord

This first in the popular James Bond superspy thriller series is one of the best. Connery plays British secret agent 007, who tries to save the world

● Dr. Strangelove: Or, How I Learned To Stop Worrying and Love the Bomb
● Doctor Zhivago
● Dog Day Afternoon
● Dogs of War

D

from a powerful fiend operating from a base in the West Indies. The film sparkles with fabulous tongue-in-cheek humor, snappy action, gorgeous girls, exotic hardware, and beautiful locales. After this success, Ian Fleming's indestructible hero just kept coming back to the screen for more adventures. Also with Joseph Wiseman, Bernard Lee, John Kitzmiller, Lois Maxwell, and Anthony Dawson. **Director**—Terence Young. (PG)
111 minutes

DR. STRANGELOVE: OR, HOW I LEARNED TO STOP WORRYING AND LOVE THE BOMB (1964)
★★★★

**Peter Sellers
George C. Scott
Peter Bull
Sterling Hayden**

Director Stanley Kubrick's towering black comedy seems to become more poignant and pertinent as time marches on. The plot concerns a fanatical U.S. general who launches a nuclear attack on Russia. And when a bomber cannot be recalled, the U.S. sadly awaits devastating retaliation. Sellers, in the best acting job of his career, is magnificent in three memorable roles—the U.S. President, a British officer, and a creepy nuclear scientist. Other fabulous portrayals abound, with Hayden, Scott, Keenan Wynn, and Slim Pickens leading the way. Kubrick's perceptive view of our fragile security in the nuclear age is presented with biting humor and suspense. It's remarkable, classic moviemaking. Also with James Earl Jones and Tracy Reed. **Academy Award**

Nominations—best picture; Kubrick, best director; Sellers, best actor; Kubrick, Peter George, and Terry Southern, best screenplay (based on material from another medium). (PG)
93 minutes b&w

DOCTOR ZHIVAGO (1965)
★★★★

**Omar Sharif
Julie Christie
Rod Steiger
Alec Guinness**

An exquisite historical film with spectacular production detail based on Boris Pasternak's novel about Russia at the time of the Revolution. The movie seems overextended on various levels, yet it offers some engrossing moments and fine performances by a good cast. The plot concerns a Russian doctor who's forced into the army and longs for the woman he loves. The big-name cast also includes Tom Courtenay, Rita Tushingham, Ralph Richardson, and Geraldine Chaplin. **Director**—David Lean. (PG) **Academy Awards**—Robert Bolt, best screenplay (based on material from another medium); Freddie Young, cinematography (color). **Nominations**—best picture; Lean, best director; Courtenay, best supporting actor. *192 minutes*

DOG DAY AFTERNOON (1975)
★★★★

**Al Pacino
John Cazale
Charles Durning**

A true story based on a bungled bank heist in Brooklyn on a hot summer

In Dog Day Afternoon, *John Cazale and Al Pacino try to rob a bank, but bungle the job.*

day. It's a thrilling, energetic circus of a movie, packing comedy and tension. Brilliant acting by Pacino as the bisexual robber out to get money for a sex-change operation for his boyfriend, played by Chris Sarandon. There are other shining characterizations by a large supporting cast, which also includes Sully Boyar and James Broderick. **Director**—Sidney Lumet. (R) **Academy Award Nominations**—best picture; Lumet, best director; Pacino, best actor; Sarandon, best supporting actor; Frank Pierson, best original screenplay. *130 minutes*

DOGS OF WAR (1981)
★★★

**Christopher Walken
Colin Blakely
Tom Berenger**

Steely-eyed, mysterious Jamie Shannon, played by Walken, runs a dial-a-mercenary service from his seedy New York City apartment. He and his pals are dispatched to overthrow an Idi Amin-type dictatorship. The final combat scenes are executed with stunning shoot-em-up flourish. The film, based on the Frederick Forsyth novel, never fully explores the psychology of soldiers of fortune. But director John Irvin, in his first feature movie, puts together a taut and intelligent action adventure, with smashing perform-
(Continued)

In this scene from Dr. Strangelove, *Peter Sellers (center) plays the title role.*

D
- A Doll's House
- A Doll's House
- The Domino Principle
- Donovan's Reef

- Don't Answer the Phone
- Don't Bother To Knock
- Don't Go in the House
- Don't Go Near the Water

Tom Berenger plays Drew, a tough, gun-happy mercenary in The Dogs of War.

(Continued)
ances by Walken, Blakely, and Berenger. (R) *102 minutes*

A DOLL'S HOUSE (1973)
★★★

Claire Bloom
Anthony Hopkins

Ibsen's 19th-century play about women's liberation is handled with efficient direction and good acting. Bloom and Hopkins do well in the key roles; Bloom is Nora, the mousey wife who declares her independence when her husband approaches death. Supporting roles are performed by Ralph Richardson, Denholm Elliott, Anna Massey, and Edith Evans. (G)
95 minutes

A DOLL'S HOUSE (1973)
★★

Jane Fonda
Trevor Howard

Fonda takes a shot at playing Nora, the shy 19th-century housewife who strikes out for liberation from her overbearing husband. This should have been a piece of cake for Jane, but she handles the Ibsen character rather unevenly. Howard, however, does better as Dr. Rank. The movie's statement on behalf of women's liberation

doesn't come over too clearly. Also stars David Warner and Edward Fox. **Director**—Joseph Losey. (G)
103 minutes

THE DOMINO PRINCIPLE
(1977)
★

Gene Hackman
Candice Bergen
Richard Widmark

Hackman plays a convict who's sprung from prison by a powerful intelligence organization that wants his assistance in an assassination job. It's never explained in this incoherent and humdrum movie who the victim is, what the conspiracy is about, who is behind this nameless secret agency, or why we should even care. Also with Mickey Rooney, Edward Albert, and Eli Wallach. A bad mark for director Stanley Kramer, who is known for better filmmaking. (R) *97 minutes*

DONOVAN'S REEF (1963)
★★★

John Wayne
Lee Marvin
Jack Warden

There's fun and frolic with this broad comedy about some war veterans who reside on a Pacific island. Their carefree life is interrupted when a daughter of one of the men pays them a visit. Everyone has a fine time with the bouncy comedy and spirited action. Also in the cast are Dorothy Lamour, Elizabeth Allen, Cesar Romero, and Mike Mazuki. **Director**—John Ford.
108 minutes

DON'T ANSWER THE PHONE
(1980)
(no stars)

James Westmoreland
Flo Gerrish
Ben Frank
Nicholas Worth

A dismal, unsavory exploitation film about a muscular psychopathic killer who prowls Los Angeles preying on women. This potboiler offers shabby performances by Westmoreland, Frank, and Worth, and atrocious writing and direction by Robert Hammer. Any opportunity for suspense is discarded when the killer is identified early in the film. The movie was initially tagged *The Hollywood Strangler*, but no matter what they call it, it's still a wrong number. (R) *94 minutes*

DON'T BOTHER TO KNOCK
(1952)
★★

Marilyn Monroe
Richard Widmark

Monroe stars as an unhinged girl hired as a babysitter in a hotel, who threatens to kill the youngster in her care. A tough act for Monroe at the outset of her career. She's stuck with a shabby, absurd script. Veteran actor Widmark fares only slightly better, as a tough but nice guy who comes to the rescue. Anne Bancroft is on hand in a throwaway part. Jeanne Cagney, Donna Corcoran, Elisha Cook, Jr., Gloria Blondell, and Jim Backus also star. **Director**—Roy Baker.
76 minutes b&w

DON'T GO IN THE HOUSE
(1980)
(no stars)

Dan Grimaldi
Ruth Dardick
Robert Osth

This is an absurd horror exploitation film that merely dwells on gruesome events and fails to generate genuine suspense or terror. The shabby plot concerns a mama's boy who lures young women to his house where he burns their nude bodies. The audience is likely to get burned by such nonsense. Take the advice in the title—don't go. **Director**—Joseph Ellison. (R) *82 minutes*

DON'T GO NEAR THE WATER
(1957)
★★

Glenn Ford
Fred Clark
Gia Scala

An adolescent service comedy about a World War II public relations operation on an exotic South Pacific island.

● Don't Look Now   ● The Double McGuffin
● Dossier 51   ● Down the Ancient Stairs
● Double Indemnity ● Dracula (1931)
● A Double Life   ● Dracula (1979)

D

The uneven farce offers moments of amusement with equal amounts of boredom. The film is based on William Brinkley's novel. Also with Anne Francis, Eva Gabor, Romney Brent, Mickey Shaughnessey, and Keenan Wynn. **Director**—Charles Walters.

107 minutes

DON'T LOOK NOW (1973)
★★★

**Donald Sutherland
Julie Christie**

Daphne du Maurier's suspense story is handled with eerie style and a bit of artiness by director Nicolas Roeg, who filmed against the spooky winter background in Venice. A young British couple try to contact their young daughter, killed in an accident, through a medium. Their attempt only leads to further tragedy. Fine performances by Sutherland and Christie, with support from Hilary Mason, Clelia Mantania, and Massimo Serrato. (R)   *110 minutes*

DOSSIER 51 (1978)
★★

**François Marthouret
Claude Marcault
Phillippe Rouleau**

Director Michel Deville is overwhelming with his obsession with technical gadgetry and jargon in this spy caper. The film examines blatant invasion of privacy, as intelligence agents go all out to gather information on a French diplomat. Deville goes through these elaborate motions without suspense or drama, turning the film into an overblown gimmick. In French with English titles. (No MPAA rating)

108 minutes

DOUBLE INDEMNITY (1944)
★★★★

**Fred MacMurray
Barbara Stanwyck
Edward G. Robinson**

This is one of the best *films noirs* of the '40s. It's based on the James M. Cain novel of conspiracy and murder. MacMurray plays an insurance salesman conned into killing the husband of a

Barbara Stanwyck and Fred MacMurray board a train in Double Indemnity.

fetching beauty, played by Stanwyck, to collect the insurance money. Director Billy Wilder coaxes dynamite performances from the entire cast, and the film effectively captures the seedy surroundings associated with the plot. Robinson also stands out as MacMurray's boss, who cracks the case. There's double suspense and triple excitement. Also with Tom Powers, Porter Hall, and Jean Heather. **Academy Award Nominations**—best picture; Wilder, best director; Stanwyck, best actress; John Seitz, cinematography (black and white).   *107 minutes b&w*

A DOUBLE LIFE (1947)
★★★★

**Ronald Colman
Shelley Winters**

Colman gives one of the best performances of his career, as a Shakespearean actor whose off-stage life imitates his theater role. Colman, who is playing the role of Othello, kills a woman he believes to be Desdemona. The electrifying melodrama is laced with effective suspense and crackling dialogue. Fine support from Winters, Signe Hasso, Edmond O'Brien, and Millard Mitchell. **Director**—George Cukor. **Academy Award**—Colman, best actor. **Nominations**—Cukor, best director; Ruth Gordon and Garson Kanin, writing (original screenplay).

103 minutes b&w

THE DOUBLE McGUFFIN (1979)
★★★

**Ernest Borgnine
George Kennedy
Elke Sommer**

A band of teenagers foil an assassination plot in this comedy adventure by

director Joe Camp, better known for his shaggy dog series starring *Benji*. The kids, mostly unknowns, do an exceptional job of keeping the film at a lively level of fun and mystery. The story is farfetched, but the pace is energetic, and Camp's execution is impressive. Borgnine, Kennedy, and Sommer help out as the adult heavies. Also with Rod Browning, Dion Pride, and Lisa Whelchel. (PG)   *89 minutes*

DOWN THE ANCIENT STAIRS (1975)
★

Marcello Mastroianni

This is a familiar melodrama, set in Mussolini's Italy in the 1930s. It's about a power-hungry psychiatrist in a mental institution who is perhaps as insane as the patients. The doctor, played by Mastroianni, hunts for a virus he believes causes schizophrenia and engages in assorted sexual escapades. The movie suffers from a shallow screenplay and plodding dialogue. **Director**—Mauro Bolognini. (R)   *110 minutes*

DRACULA (1931)
★★★★

**Bela Lugosi
David Manners
Helen Chandler**

This classic screen adaptation of Bram Stoker's haunting novel remains the granddaddy of horror films. Lugosi is fantastic as the Transylvanian vampire who travels to London looking for blood. The strange misty atmosphere drives home the chills. Actually, the film is somewhat slow and uneven. Yet, for some uncanny reason, this version continues to cast its spell. Many sequels and imitations have gone in its wake. Also with Dwight Frye and Edward Van Sloan. **Director**—Tod Browning. *84 minutes b&w*

DRACULA (1979)
★★★

**Frank Langella
Laurence Olivier
Donald Pleasence**

(Continued)

D
- The Dragon Flies
- Dragon Seed
- Dragonslayer
- Dreamer
- A Dream of Passion
- Dressed To Kill
- Drive-In

(Continued)

The evil count from Transylvania is on the prowl for more blood in this lavish, moody, and scary production starring Langella in the title role. At times, Langella is too sexy and sensual to be menacing. But there are enough howling wolves, squeaking bats, and murky graveyards to give a zombie the shivers. Olivier plays Dr. Van Helsing with conviction. It's an excellent rendition of the ageless fable, but the 1931 Bela Lugosi version is still top Drac. Also with Kate Nelligan, Trevor Eve, and Janine Duvitski. **Director**—John Bedham. (R)   *109 minutes*

THE DRAGON FLIES (1975)
★★

**Jimmy Wang Yu
George Lazenby
Rebecca Gilling**

A martial-arts adventure about a Hong Kong police inspector who goes to Australia to bring back a member of the drug underworld. Lots of kung fu action for those who enjoy such sport. **Director**—Brian Smith.   *102 minutes*

DRAGON SEED (1944)
★★

**Katharine Hepburn
Walter Huston**

This meandering film version of Pearl Buck's novel has good intentions but evolves in an artificial manner. Peasants in a Chinese village battle the Japanese invaders. However, there are some intense moments among all the flag-waving. Hepburn tops the cast, but she's not up to par here. Also with Turhan Bey, Agnes Moorehead, Akim Tamiroff, J. Carrol Naish, and Aline MacMahon. **Directors**—Jack Conway and Harold S. Bucquet. **Academy Award Nominations**—MacMahon, best supporting actress; Sidney Wagner, cinematography (black and white).   *144 minutes b&w*

DRAGONSLAYER (1981)
★★

Peter MacNicol

A Dark Ages fairy tale that's partly flawed with mediocre acting and a

Sorcerer's apprentice Peter MacNicol plunges a lance into the dragon in Dragonslayer.

tedious script. Young MacNicol plays a sorcerer's apprentice who is called upon to slay a fearsome flying dragon; it seems that the citizens are fed up with appeasing the beast by sacrificing virgins. The super special effects are the real stars. When that huge, fire-breathing dragon goes into action, the story comes alive. But that's rather late in the film. **Director**—Matthew Robbins. (PG)   *108 minutes*

DREAMER (1979)
★★

**Tim Matheson
Susan Blakely
Jack Warden**

Remember Paul Newman shooting a wicked game of pool in *The Hustler?* How about those boxing movies, like *Rocky*, where an unknown contender struggles to win the big fight? Well, here they've given this treatment to bowling, without much style or depth. There's some authentic detail about kegling and the Americana that surrounds it. Yet the story lacks real dramatic tension or credible moral conflict to give the characters stature. Also with Richard B. Shull, Barbara Stuart, and Pedro Gonzalez-Gonzalez. **Director**—Noel Nosseck. (PG)   *86 minutes*

A DREAM OF PASSION (1978)
★

**Melina Mercouri
Ellen Burstyn**

Burstyn turns in a brief but superb performance as a half-mad American woman who murders her three children because of her husband's infidel-

ity. And that's about the only redeeming facet of this otherwise tedious tragedy, which involves the legitimate theater performance of *Medea*, the ancient Greek play with a similar infanticide theme. Mercouri displays an inflated ego in her role as the on-stage Medea who becomes involved with the American woman. Also with Andreas Voutsinas and Despo Diamantidou. **Director**—Jules Dassin. In Greek with English titles. (R)
106 minutes

DRESSED TO KILL (1980)
★★

**Michael Caine
Angie Dickinson
Nancy Allen**

Director Brian De Palma liberally borrows from Alfred Hitchcock's *Psycho* and other classics for this slick but shallow suspense movie about a transvestite who attacks women with a straight razor. De Palma sets up several impressive sequences and displays dazzling camera technique. But the characters are vague and uninteresting, despite decent performances by Caine, Dickinson, and Allen. The film offers much style but little substance. (R)   *105 minutes*

DRIVE-IN (1976)
★★★

**Lisa Lemole
Glen Morshower
Gary Cavagnaro**

This easygoing, low-budget production focuses on youths at a drive-in theater in a rural Texas town. Much of the plot is composed of bits stolen from *American Graffiti* and *The Last Picture Show*, but the results are appealing. A bumbling stickup, a gang rumble, and troubled romance are confronted at the drive-in location. Meanwhile, the big screen features its own version of catastrophe in *Disaster '76*, which is a blend of *Jaws*, *The Towering Inferno*, and *The Poseidon Adventure*. A lot of fresh and unknown faces make up the lively cast. Also with Billy Milliken, Lee Newsom, and Regan Kee. **Director**—Rod Amateau. (PG)
96 minutes

• The Driver   • Drum   • Duel in the Sun   **D**
• The Drowning Pool   • The Duchess and the   • The Duellists
           Dirtwater Fox   • Dumbo

THE DRIVER (1978)
★

Ryan O'Neal
Bruce Dern
Isabelle Adjani

This pretentious film glorifies the driver of a getaway car. It's filled with squealing tires, preposterous smash-'em-up car chase scenes, and dialogue so absurd that it's unintentionally funny. O'Neal is The Driver, Dern is The Detective who pursues him, and Adjani is The Player, a mysterious gambler who serves as an alibi for O'Neal. Their acting careers suffer as many dents as the wrecked cars. Also with Ronee Blakely, Matt Clark, and Felice Orlandi. **Director**—Walter Hill. (R)   *90 minutes*

THE DROWNING POOL (1975)
★★

Paul Newman
Joanne Woodward
Tony Franciosa

Tony Franciosa tries to best Paul Newman, in The Drowning Pool.

Newman plays a second installment of his portrayal of Ross MacDonald's Lew Harper, the 1950s-era private eye. It's a listless workout against the backdrop of some colorful surroundings of New Orleans and its bayou countryside. The talented cast, however, can't rescue the film. Also with Murray Hamilton, Melanie Griffith, and Richard Jaeckel. **Director**—Stuart Rosenberg. (PG)   *108 minutes*

DRUM (1976)
(no stars)

Warren Oates
Ken Norton

This contemptible exploitation film about slavery in the antebellum South is a sequel to the financially successful *Mandingo*. Norton plays a slave on a Louisiana slave-breeding plantation. He's a fine athlete, but no actor. The plot is mostly concerned with titillation and encompasses beatings, castration, and homosexuality—all in bad taste. Also stars Yaphet Kotto and Pam Grier. Directed by Steve Carver and produced by Dino De Laurentiis, who removed his name from the credits. (R)   *110 minutes*

THE DUCHESS AND THE DIRTWATER FOX (1976)
★

George Segal
Goldie Hawn

A period western strung together with mostly corny gags that leads nowhere. Hawn plays a dance-hall hooker who teams up with Segal, a bumbling card shark. Segal is trying to escape from bank robbers whose $40,000 he has stolen. Hawn and Segal seem to work well together at times, but such moments are too few. This film seems as if it might have been better off as a 15-minute animated cartoon. Also with Conrad Janis, Thayer David, and Roy Jenson. **Director**—Melvin Frank. (PG)   *103 minutes*

DUEL IN THE SUN (1946)
★★★★

Jennifer Jones
Joseph Cotten
Gregory Peck
Lionel Barrymore
Lillian Gish

Big, sprawling epic western with the influence of writer-producer David O. Selznick very much in evidence. The plot centers on a half-breed Indian girl, played by Jones, who sparks rivalry between two brothers—Cotten and Peck—when she comes to reside in the home of a powerful cattle rancher. The film boasts some great romantic scenes and rousing action—especially a bizarre gun battle in the finale. Barrymore and Gish are exceptional in supporting roles. Also with Walter Huston, Herbert Marshall, Charles Bickford, and Otto Kruger. Based on Niven Busch's novel. **Director**—King Vidor. **Academy Award Nominations**—Jones, best actress; Gish, best supporting actress.
138 minutes

THE DUELLISTS (1978)
★★

Keith Carradine
Harvey Keitel
Albert Finney

Screen adaptation of the Joseph Conrad short story about two Hussar officers, played by Carradine and Keitel, who fight a protracted series of duels during the Napoleonic wars. Director Ridley Scott has taken meticulous care in reconstructing the period. The lavish production abounds with elegant settings and breathtaking vistas. But the film comes up tragically short with a dull script and stiff dialogue. The principal characters seem rather awkward and unconvincing. Also with Edward Fox, Cristina Raines, and Robert Stephens. (PG)   *101 minutes*

DUMBO (1941)
★★★★

Memorable and touching Walt Disney cartoon feature, about the baby circus elephant with ears so big that he can use them as wings and fly. This project represents the studio at the peak of its creative years. Unforgettable scenes include the crows' song and the drunken nightmare. Voices include
(Continued)

Dumbo is a baby circus elephant with ears so big he can use them as wings and fly.

D·E
- The Eagle Has Landed
- The Earthling
- Earthquake
- Easter Parade
- East of Eden
- East Side, West Side

(Continued)
Sterling Holloway, Edward Brophy, and Verna Felton. **Director**—Ben Sharpsteen.   *64 minutes*

E

THE EAGLE HAS LANDED
(1977)
★★★

Michael Caine
Donald Sutherland
Robert Duvall

In The Eagle Has Landed, *Donald Sutherland is an enemy spy smoothing the way for a Nazi mission.*

Caine, Sutherland, and Duvall deliver first-rate performances in director John Sturges's film about a Nazi plot to kidnap Winston Churchill. There's a fair amount of suspense, drama, and battle action to overcome occasional plot potholes. The well-paced screenplay is based on Jack Higgins's novel. The photography is spectacular, especially the scenes on the beautiful Norfolk coast of England. Also with Jenny Agutter, Donald Pleasence, and Anthony Quayle. (PG)   *123 minutes*

THE EARTHLING (1981)
★

William Holden
Ricky Schroder

Schroder plays a recently orphaned city boy who learns to survive in the Australian wilderness with the help of Holden, a cantankerous old man who returns to his birthplace to die. This muddled, cliché-strewn film pretends to be sentimental, but it can't fool anyone. However, there's no denying the appealing nature photography of the Australian bush country, with kangaroos and wallabies romping over the exquisitely beautiful landscape. Also with Jack Thompson and Olivia Hamnett. **Director**—Peter Collinson. (No MPAA rating)   *97 minutes*

EARTHQUAKE (1975)
★★

Charlton Heston
Ava Gardner
Lorne Greene
Marjoe Gortner
George Kennedy

This disaster film has a dumb script and lackluster acting, but great visual and aural effects. There are disasters galore as a massive earthquake strikes Los Angeles. Also with Richard Roundtree, Geneviève Bujold, Lloyd Nolan, Walter Matthau, and Sensurround. **Director**—Mark Robson. (PG)   *129 minutes*

Charlton Heston tries to help office workers in a skyscraper escape in Earthquake.

EASTER PARADE (1948)
★★★★

Judy Garland
Fred Astaire
Peter Lawford
Ann Miller

MGM's golden age of musicals was at its peak with this delightfully entertaining film, brimming with Irving Berlin's fabulous songs. The trivial plot has Astaire avoiding dance part-

Judy Garland and Fred Astaire stroll down the avenue in Easter Parade.

ner Miller, while he latches on to new sensation Garland. Everyone is at perfection; sit back and enjoy. Also with Jules Munshin. **Director**—Charles Walters.   *109 minutes*

EAST OF EDEN (1955)
★★★★

Raymond Massey
James Dean
Julie Harris

A splendid film version of John Steinbeck's novel, focusing on a teenager's torment over the lack of love from his father. Dean proves his superb acting ability in his starring debut as the rebellious adolescent. Jo Van Fleet is also magnificent as the boy's mother, who operates a brothel. Director Elia Kazan skillfully lays on the emotion and develops the characters to perfection. Also with Dick Davalos, Burl Ives, and Albert Dekker. **Academy Award**—Van Fleet, best supporting actress. **Nominations**—Kazan, best director; Dean, best actor; Paul Osborn, writing (screenplay).   *115 minutes*

EAST SIDE, WEST SIDE (1949)
★★

James Mason
Barbara Stanwyck
Van Heflin
Ava Gardner

Slick soap opera, set among New York City's upper crust. Mason and Stan-

★ STAR PROFILE

- Easy Rider
- Eat My Dust!
- Edge of the City
- Edison, the Man
- Edward, My Son

E

wyck are a wealthy couple with marital problems involving Gardner and Heflin. There's some entertainment value thanks to the stylish treatment and a professional cast. But the story, based on Marcia Davenport's novel, is rather artificial. Also with Gale Sondergaard, Cyd Charisse, Nancy Davis, and William Conrad. **Director**—Mervyn Le Roy.

108 minutes b&w

EASY RIDER (1969)
★★★★

Peter Fonda
Dennis Hopper
Jack Nicholson

Dennis Hopper and Peter Fonda are two freewheeling bikers in Easy Rider.

A trend-setting movie about two hippies who cross the Southwest on motorcycles and meet disaster at the hands of trigger-happy rednecks. This remarkable and unusual film seems to be a metaphor of the times with its casual statements on hatred and a society that for some is too structured and too organized. Hopper and Fonda are exceptionally good as the freewheeling bikers. Nicholson is great as a tipsy small-town lawyer, who goes along for the ride. Also with Luana Anders, Robert Walker, and Karen Black. **Director**—Hopper. **Academy Award Nominations**—Nicholson, best supporting actor; Fonda, Hopper, and Terry Southern, best story and screenplay (based on material not previously published or produced). (R)

94 minutes

EAT MY DUST! (1976)
★★★

Ron Howard
Christopher Norris

Teenagers should enjoy this car-chase comedy starring Howard and Norris.

The plot is simple. The teenage son of a small-town California sheriff swipes a stock car and takes a blonde for a joyride; the sheriff recruits a bumbling posse of cars to chase the madcap pair. The result is a demolition derby with no injuries. The wrecks and stunts are well done, and the photography is attractive. Also with Warren Kemmerling, Dave Madden, and Rance Howard. Directed and written by Charles Griffith. (PG)   *90 minutes*

EDGE OF THE CITY (1957)
★★★★

Sidney Poitier
John Cassavetes
Jack Warden

An exciting, gripping melodrama, filmed on the docks of New York City much in the style of *On the Waterfront*. Poitier and Cassavetes play longshoremen who confront a brutal and bigoted union boss, portrayed convincingly by Warden. The film, which has something significant to say about racial integration, is based on Robert Alan Aurther's TV play, *A Man Is Ten Feet Tall*. Also with Kathleen Maguire, Ruby Dee, and Robert Simon. **Director**—Martin Ritt.   *85 minutes b&w*

EDISON, THE MAN (1940)
★★★

Spencer Tracy
Rita Johnson

Straightforward and slightly sentimental film biography of America's most famous inventor, made as a sequel to *Young Tom Edison*. The script traces Edison's life from his obscure years in poverty to his emergence as genious inventor of the light bulb and the phonograph. Good casting of Tracy in the title role. There's earnest support from Charles Coburn, Gene Lockhart, and Lynne Overman. **Director**—Clarence Brown. **Academy Award Nomination**—Hugo Butler and Dore Schary, writing (original story).   *107 minutes b&w*

EDWARD, MY SON (1948)
★★

Spencer Tracy
Deborah Kerr

An overbearing and somewhat artificial screen adaptation of a compelling play about a wealthy man's unbecom-

(Continued)

LAURENCE OLIVIER

Sir Laurence Olivier, born in Dorking, England, in 1907, is acknowledged by many to be the preeminent actor of the age. He's also well known for his directing and producing credits. Olivier has received two Academy Awards and has been nominated eight other times.

Olivier had appeared in movies for nine years before his first Oscar nomination in 1939 for his performance in Wuthering Heights, *one of his most famous roles.*

Olivier also received Oscar nominations for his performances in Rebecca *(1940),* Henry V *(1946),* Richard III *(1956),* The Entertainer *(1960),* Othello *(1965),* Sleuth *(1972),* Marathon Man *(1976), and* The Boys From Brazil *(1978). Olivier is also credited as the man who brought plays of Shakespeare to the screen and made them successful with movie audiences. In fact, in 1946 he received a special Academy Award for outstanding achievement as actor, producer, and director in bringing* Henry V *to the screen. In 1948, he won the Oscar for* Hamlet, *a film that he also produced and directed.*

In 1970, Sir Laurence was granted a Life Peerage by Her Majesty Queen Elizabeth II of England, and Lord Olivier became the first actor to be so honored.

Some of his most recent movies include The Jazz Singer *(1980) and* Clash of the Titans *(1981).*

E
- The Egg and I
- The Eiger Sanction
- El Cid
- El Dorado
- The Electric Horseman
- The Elephant Man

(Continued)

ing conduct toward his son. Tracy, as the unscrupulous father, seems ill at ease in an unsuitable role. Kerr plays his distraught wife, and there is support from Ian Hunter, James Donald, Leueen McGrath, and Mervyn Johns. **Director**—George Cukor.

112 minutes b&w

THE EGG AND I (1947)
★★★

Claudette Colbert
Fred MacMurray

Colbert and MacMurray are effective in this warm comedy about a city couple who buy a chicken farm and struggle with numerous problems. The film is notable for introducing Marjorie Main and Percy Kilbride as Ma and Pa Kettle. The script is based on Betty McDonald's popular book. Also with Louise Allbritton, Richard Long, and Billy House. **Director**—Chester Erskine.

104 minutes b&w

THE EIGER SANCTION (1975)
★★

Clint Eastwood
George Kennedy

Jonathan Hemlock, played by Eastwood, is hired to assassinate the killers of an American agent. Most of the year Hemlock teaches art, but on vacation he's a secret agent who works for a government organization. He uses the money he earns from his missions to buy works of art. Generally, it's a dreary film, with all the clichés of suspense thrillers thrown in. The film, based on one of Trevanian's popular novels, is set in the Swiss Alps; the Eiger is a Swiss peak. Some vitality and humor from the supporting cast, which includes Vonetta McGee, Jack Cassidy, and Heidi Bruhl. **Director**—Eastwood. (R)   *128 minutes*

EL CID (1961)
★★★

Charlton Heston
Sophia Loren
Raf Vallone

Sprawling, opulent period epic with none other than Heston portraying the

Charlton Heston and Sophia Loren in El Cid, *about the hero who rid Spain of the Moors.*

legendary hero who rid Spain of the Moors in the 11th century. The magnificent spectacle features an eyeful of flashy costumes, impressive settings, and big battle scenes. The script, however, doesn't live up to the visual splendor. The cast also includes Geraldine Page, Hurd Hatfield, Gary Raymond, Herbert Lom, and John Fraser. **Director**—Anthony Mann.

184 minutes

EL DORADO (1966)
★★★

John Wayne
Robert Mitchum

Big John straps on his shootin' irons and helps his friend, a drunken sheriff played by Mitchum, fight a crooked cattle baron. Director Howard Hawks whips together this funny, action-packed, old-fashioned western, based loosely on his *Rio Bravo*. Not the best of Hawks's features, but it's likable. James Caan, Charlene Holt, Michele Carey, and Ed Asner are also in the cast.   *126 minutes*

THE ELECTRIC HORSEMAN (1979)
★★★★

Robert Redford
Jane Fonda

Redford and Fonda generate the right chemistry together in this winning

film that roasts conglomerates and consumer manipulation. Redford is a hard-drinking ex-rodeo star, who sells out to a giant company to promote breakfast cereal. Outraged at the abuse of a multimillion-dollar racehorse, he dramatically kidnaps the animal. Fonda, in a TV news reporter role similar to the one she played in *The China Syndrome*, pursues him through the picturesque Rocky Mountains. Also with Valerie Perrine, Willie Nelson, and John Saxon. **Director**—Sidney Pollack. (PG)   *120 minutes*

THE ELEPHANT MAN (1980)
★★★★

Anthony Hopkins
John Hurt
Anne Bancroft
John Gielgud

John Hurt, playing the title role in The Elephant Man, *at Liverpool Street Station.*

The story of John Merrick, the hideously deformed sideshow freak with the soul of an angel, is presented on film with dignity and compassion. Director David Lynch enhances the drama with a graceful texture and precisely captures the mood of Victorian England. But it's the magnificent performance of Hurt in a most difficult title role that really expresses the humanity and gentleness of this grotesque young man. Also with Wendy Hiller. (PG) **Academy Award Nominations**—best picture; Hurt, best actor; Lynch, best director; Christopher De Vore, Eric Bergren, and Lynch, best screenplay (adapted from another medium).   *125 minutes b&w*

- Elephant Walk
- Elmer Gantry
- Embryo
- Emmanuelle, Joys of a Woman
- The Emperor Waltz
- Empire of the Ants
- The Empire Strikes Back

E

ELEPHANT WALK (1954)
★★

Elizabeth Taylor
Peter Finch

Taylor stars as the new wife of a Ceylon tea plantation owner who has difficulty adjusting to her new environment. Liz looks beautiful, and there's an impressive elephant stampede finale; otherwise, the film is merely a puffed-up soap opera with a rather confused script. Finch plays the wealthy tea planter. Also with Dana Andrews and Abraham Sofaer. **Director**—William Dieterle.   *103 minutes*

ELMER GANTRY (1960)
★★★★

Burt Lancaster
Jean Simmons
Arthur Kennedy
Shirley Jones

Lancaster is fantastic as the hypocritical evangelist in this exciting and absorbing screen version of the Sinclair Lewis novel. The film brims with first-class performances by all involved. And there are some memorable scenes with Simmons as an ambitious lady preacher, Kennedy as a sharp newspaper reporter, and Jones as Gantry's former girl friend turned prostitute. It's an intensive piece of work that grabs you early and won't let go. Also with Dean Jagger, Edward Andrews, and Patti Page. **Director**—Richard Brooks. **Academy Awards**—Lancaster, best actor; Jones, best supporting actress; Brooks, best screenplay (based on material from another medium). **Nomination**—best picture.   *146 minutes*

EMBRYO (1976)
★

Rock Hudson
Diane Ladd

An absurd variation of the Frankenstein theme, with Hudson as a doctor who injects a human fetus with a growth hormone. A little more than a week later, there's a full-grown, beautiful woman who can play chess. Of course, Rock falls in love with her, but then things turn sour as they did with Frankenstein's monster. The producers will just have to make a sequel: *Bridegroom of Embryo*, or something like that. Also with Barbara Carrera, Roddy McDowall, and Anne Schedeen. **Director**—Ralph Nelson. (PG)   *104 minutes*

EMMANUELLE, JOYS OF A WOMAN (1976)
★★

Sylvia Kristel

Kristel returns in this sequel to the financially successful first *Emmanuelle*. The soft-core sex tale again takes place in the Far East and concerns a wealthy and liberated couple dedicated to extramarital sex. Settings are elegant, Kristel is fetching, and there's plenty of sexual activity. And, as in most films of this sort, the screenplay is amateurish and uninteresting. **Director**—Francis Giacobetti. (X)   *100 minutes*

THE EMPEROR WALTZ (1948)
★★

Bing Crosby
Joan Fontaine

Crosby stars as a phonograph salesman trying to get an order from Emperor Franz Joseph of Austria. This rather oddball operetta is pleasing in spots, but it carries scant impact. Also, director Billy Wilder is out of place with this sort of puffed-up material. The script is merely routine, and the music is forgettable. Others in the cast include Roland Culver and Richard Haydn.   *106 minutes*

EMPIRE OF THE ANTS (1977)
★★

Joan Collins
Robert Lansing

Some ants get into radioactive waste, quickly grow as large as police dogs, and then viciously attack humans. This B-grade sci-fi film was routinely produced, directed, and written by Bert I. Gordon, who seems hung up on H. G. Wells stories. Most of the dialogue is ridiculous, but there's some suspense generated as the humans attempt to escape from the bloodthirsty insects. Also with Albert Salmi, John David Carson, and Robert Pine. (PG)   *90 minutes*

THE EMPIRE STRIKES BACK (1980)
★★★★

Mark Hamill
Harrison Ford
Carrie Fisher
Billy Dee Williams

Space-opera maestro George Lucas, creator of *Star Wars*, scores again with another lulu of a fantasy adventure in a galaxy far, far away. It's a worthy and sumptuous sequel, with action galore and imaginative special effects that are special indeed. Old friends are
(Continued)

In The Empire Strikes Back, *Han Solo and friends await their fate.*

E

- The Enchanted Cottage
- The End
- Endless Love
- End of the Game
- The Enemy Below
- The Enforcer (1951)
- The Enforcer (1976)
- The Entertainer
- Enter the Dragon

(Continued)
back—Luke Skywalker, Han Solo, Chewbacca, R2-D2, C-3PO—gallantly adventuring among the stars and planets. And there's a startling plot twist involving archvillain Darth Vader. Also with Alec Guinness, David Prowse, Frank Oz, and Anthony Daniels. To be continued. **Director**—Irvin Kershner. (PG)
124 minutes

THE ENCHANTED COTTAGE
(1945)
★★★

**Dorothy McGuire
Robert Young**

An agreeable romantic fantasy that works well despite a syrupy and sentimental script. Young is a disfigured war veteran, and McGuire is a plain young girl. They discover beauty and love in each other. Is it really the enchantment of the New England cottage where they meet? Sensitive direction by John Cromwell pulls it off. Herbert Marshall, Mildred Natwick, Hillary Brooke, and Spring Byington also star. *91 minutes b&w*

THE END (1978)
★★

**Burt Reynolds
Sally Field
Dom DeLuise**

How can a story about a man about to die be something to laugh about? Reynolds strains hard in this endeavor, but doesn't succeed. That lovable nut, DeLuise, steals many a scene. But mostly, the film is an embarrassing attempt at gallows humor. In this case, the end doesn't come soon enough. Also with Joanne Woodward, Kristy McNichol, Robby Benson, David Steinberg, Norman Fell, and Carl Reiner. **Director**—Reynolds. (R)
100 minutes

ENDLESS LOVE (1981)
★

**Brooke Shields
Martin Hewitt**

This syrupy, soap-opera movie, based on Scott Spencer's sultry novel, stars Shields and Hewitt as obsessive, ill-fated teenage lovers. The screenplay, which begins with passionate puppy love, shifts midway to tragedy, embroiling the youngsters and their families in unbearable distress. Shields and Hewitt are impressively pretty, but there's hardly any acting talent between them. The erratic direction of Franco Zeffirelli merely emphasizes the film's puffed-up sentimentality. Endless nonsense. (R) *115 minutes*

END OF THE GAME (1976)
★

**Martin Ritt
Jon Voight
Robert Shaw
Jacqueline Bisset**

A confused plot and a lot of overacting dull the edge in this story of intrigue and murder. Ritt, better known as a director, plays a rumpled Swiss detective who pursues an acquaintance wanted for a murder committed 30 years ago. Along the way there's an excess of murky detail, more murder, and a surprise ending. **Director**—Maximilian Schell. (PG) *106 minutes*

THE ENEMY BELOW (1957)
★★★

**Robert Mitchum
Curt Jurgens
Theodore Bikel**

An absorbing World War II action drama. An American destroyer and a German U-boat stalk one another in the South Atlantic. Interest is maintained throughout, thanks to gripping underwater action, notable photography, and impressive special effects. Lots of tense moments heighten the suspense. Also with David Hedison, Russell Collins, and Doug McClure. **Director**—Dick Powell. *98 minutes*

THE ENFORCER (1951)
★★★

**Humphrey Bogart
Everett Sloane**

Bogart portrays a determined district attorney in this semidocumentary crime thriller, about the smashing of a gang of hired killers known as Murder, Inc. The suspenseful film is relentless in its attention to realism. Sharp dialogue and good pacing enhance the quality. Bogey is at his best, and he gets top support from Zero Mostel, Ted de Corsia, King Donovan, and Roy Roberts. **Director**—Bretaigne Windust. *87 minutes b&w*

THE ENFORCER (1976)
★

**Clint Eastwood
Tyne Daly
Harry Guardino**

Eastwood, in this third Dirty Harry Callahan film, takes on a gang of San Francisco political terrorists. There's blood, gore, and howling sirens galore, as Harry, waving his .44 magnum, blows people's heads off. This time, his partner is a woman police officer, played by Daly. The witless plot comes off as a worn-out copy of the previous adventures of the self-righteous homicide cop. Also with Bradford Dillman, John Mitchum, and DeVeren Bookwalter. **Director**—James Fargo. (R) *96 minutes*

THE ENTERTAINER (1960)
★★★★

Laurence Olivier

The magnificent Olivier is at his best in the role of a second-rate comedian with a bloated ego, in the twilight of his career. This screen version of John Osborne's play is obviously stagey, but Olivier's triumphant performance overcomes any obstacle. He brilliantly brings to bear the tragedy of this man with large expectations and little talent to achieve them. The atmosphere of a seedy seaside resort adds to the characterization. The fine supporting cast includes Roger Livesey, Alan Bates, Albert Finney, and Joan Plowright. **Director**—Tony Richardson. **Academy Award Nomination**—Olivier, best actor. *96 minutes b&w*

ENTER THE DRAGON (1973)
★★★

**Bruce Lee
John Saxon**

A surprisingly good martial-arts action

● Equus
● The Errand Boy
● Escape From Alcatraz

● Escape From Fort Bravo
● Escape From New York
● Escape to Athena

E

Bruce Lee, the wizard of kung fu, does his thing to help smash a drug-smuggling ring in Enter the Dragon.

film, with kung fu wiz Lee kicking up a storm. He's hired by British agents to infiltrate a remote fortress and smash a drug-smuggling operation. Forget about any logical script; it's the action that counts here. And this is a king-size portion of chop-socky. Also with Shih Kien, Jim Kelly, and Bob Wall. **Director**—Robert Clouse. (R)
99 minutes

EQUUS (1977)
★★

**Richard Burton
Peter Firth**

Peter Shaffer's prizewinning psychological play loses much of its emotional impact and imagination in the transfer from stage to screen. Director Sidney Lumet has perhaps injected too much realism into this story, about the relationship between a psychiatrist and a troubled stable boy who blinds six horses. The performances, however, are excellent all around. Burton plays the psychiatrist with steady fortitude; Firth brings depth and persuasiveness to his role as the boy. Also with Colin Blakely, Joan Plowright, and Harry Andrews. (R) **Academy Award Nominations**—Burton, best actor; Firth, best supporting actor.
138 minutes

THE ERRAND BOY (1961)
★★

**Jerry Lewis
Brian Donlevy**

Typical Lewis silliness, with the comedian playing a bumbling paperhanger

on the rampage in a Hollywood studio. There are sight gags galore—a few effective ones and many more that fall flat. Fans of Lewis, if there are any still around, may get a bang out of this. Sig Ruman, Fritz Feld, and Doodles Weaver are also involved with the nonsense. **Director**—Lewis.
92 minutes b&w

ESCAPE FROM ALCATRAZ
(1979)
★★★

**Clint Eastwood
Patrick McGoohan**

Eastwood, looking mean and lean, stars in this tough and realistic prison film, which ranks with such classics as *White Heat* and *Brute Force*. Producer-director Don Siegel is in top form, creating tension and the grim mood of prison life. There's fine supporting work, too, especially from McGoohan as the cold-hearted warden. Richard Tuggle's efficient screenplay is based on the actual escape of three prisoners from "the Rock" in 1962. Also with Roberts Blossom and Jack Thibeau. (PG)
112 minutes

ESCAPE FROM FORT BRAVO
(1953)
★★★

**William Holden
Eleanor Parker
John Forsythe**

Better-than-average western yarn, with Holden as the commanding officer of a Union fort in Arizona during the Civil War. Some Confederates try to escape, but they're attacked by Indians who don't distinguish between adversaries of the North and the South. The climactic redskin ambush sequence is tense, indeed. Also with William Demarest and Polly Bergen. **Director**—John Sturges.
98 minutes

ESCAPE FROM NEW YORK
(1981)
★★

**Kurt Russell
Ernest Borgnine**

It's 1997, and New York City is a

walled-in, escape-proof prison, populated by thousands of criminals and loonies. John Carpenter (*Halloween; The Fog*) dreamed up this mindless melodrama, which features characters and action of exceptional viciousness and violence. In the midst of this ominous hellhole, the President's plane crash-lands, and a cunning criminal, played by Russell, masterminds the rescue in trade for his freedom. Also with Isaac Hayes. (R)
99 minutes

ESCAPE TO ATHENA (1979)
★

**Roger Moore
David Niven
Elliott Gould**

Stefanie Powers and Elliott Gould in Escape to Athena, *a drama set in occupied Greece, where commandos pave the way for an invasion.*

A feeble war melodrama, with undistinguished performances, a ludicrous script, and bland direction. The story is set in occupied Greece, where a band of Allied commandos paves the way for the oncoming invasion. The film tries to be humorous in a ridiculous way that seems to say warfare is fun and games. Moore, Niven, and other film notables plod through their routines as if their minds are more on their paychecks than their lines. Also with Stefanie Powers, Richard Roundtree, Claudia Cardinale, and William Holden. **Director**—George Pan Cosmatos. (PG)
101 minutes

E
- The Europeans
- Everything I Have Is Yours
- Everything You Always Wanted to Know About Sex (But Were Afraid To Ask)
- Every Which Way But Loose
- The Evil of Frankenstein
- Excalibur
- Excuse My Dust
- Executive Suite

THE EUROPEANS (1979)
★★★

**Lee Remick
Robin Ellis**

Henry James's novel, which contrasts American and European cultures, is tastefully adapted to the screen as a literate comedy of manners. Remick and Ellis are sophisticated Europeans—brother and sister—who move in with their staid New England cousins. Remick is lovely and plays the Baroness Munster with grace. The New England autumn countryside is photographed in full glory, and the 1850 period is meticulously recreated. Also with Wesley Addy, Tim Choate, and Lisa Eichorn. **Director**—James Ivory. (No MPAA rating)

90 minutes

EVERYTHING I HAVE IS YOURS (1952)
★★

**Marge Champion
Gower Champion
Dennis O'Keefe**

Marge and Gower Champion star in this routine musical that perks up only when the stars go through their dance routines. The uneventful plot has the dance team on the brink of Broadway success only to discover that Marge is pregnant. This sort of thing is well-outdated. Also with Eduard Franz. **Director**—Robert Z. Leonard.

92 minutes

EVERYTHING YOU ALWAYS WANTED TO KNOW ABOUT SEX (BUT WERE AFRAID TO ASK) (1972)
★★★

**Woody Allen
Lynn Redgrave
Anthony Quayle
John Carradine
Lou Jacobi**

Director Allen lampoons sex in a series of inventive comic sketches; some of them work, some fizzle. But those that succeed are a howl. Segments include a giant female breast, Gene Wilder as a doctor attracted to a sheep, Redgrave modeling a chastity belt, and a tour of the male body with Woody portraying a sperm. Loosely based on Dr. David Reuben's book. Others in the cast are Louise Lasser, Tony Randall, and Burt Reynolds. (R)

87 minutes

EVERY WHICH WAY BUT LOOSE (1978)
★

**Clint Eastwood
Sondra Locke**

Clint Eastwood shares a beer with his hairy sidekick in Every Which Way But Loose.

Eastwood, seemingly tired of his *Dirty Harry* character, tries to latch on to Burt Reynolds's good-ol'-boy routine in this dim-witted comedy. Eastwood earns money in pickup fistfights, travels with a cute orangutan, and is chased by mean cops and a gang of motorcycle toughs. The orangutan upstages the actors, which says it all about this film. Also with Geoffrey Lewis, Beverly D'Angelo, and Ruth Gordon. **Director**—James Fargo. (R)

119 minutes

THE EVIL OF FRANKENSTEIN (1964)
★★

**Peter Cushing
Peter Woodthorpe**

Another episode in the notorious monster series; this one lacks the style and impact of Boris Karloff's portrayals. Cushing plays Dr. Frankenstein, who returns to his laboratory where he finds the monster, played by Kiwi Kingston, frozen in ice. Terror ensues when the monster thaws out and rampages through the community. Also with Sandor Eles, Duncan Lamont, and Katy Wild. **Director**—Freddie Francis.

87 minutes

EXCALIBUR (1981)
★★

**Nigel Terry
Nicol Williamson**

Knights of the Round Table, dressed in full battle armor, clankety-clank through this handsome but ponderous retelling of the Arthurian legend. King Arthur, Lancelot, Merlin, Guinevere, and other inhabitants of Camelot—played solemnly by an unfamiliar cast—plod through scenes of chivalry, adultery, grisly battlefield slaughter, sorcery, and finally a bit of Holy Grailing. The film smacks of a medieval version of *Star Wars*, without the razzle-dazzle. Also with Helen Mirren, Nicholas Clay, and Cherie Lunghi. **Director**—John Boorman. (R)

140 minutes

EXCUSE MY DUST (1951)
★★

**Red Skelton
Sally Forrest**

Skelton stars as an automobile inventor in this mild and pleasant musical comedy. Red is in love with a livery stable owner's daughter, played by Forrest. The old man gets upset when Red unwraps a horseless carriage. Some funny moments, but it's lightweight stuff. Macdonald Carey and William Demarest provide support. **Director**—Roy Rowland. *82 minutes*

EXECUTIVE SUITE (1954)
★★★

**Fredric March
William Holden
June Allyson
Barbara Stanwyck
Walter Pidgeon**

Effective screen treatment of Cameron Hawley's book about wheeling and dealing in the boardroom of a big company. When the president dies, the vice-presidents vie for control, and tension mounts. The story also explores some domestic matters, but the thrust is on corporate power. A big-name cast delivers the goods. Also with Shelley Winters, Paul Douglas, Louis Calhern, Dean Jagger, and Nina Foch. **Director**—Robert Wise. **Acad-**

- Exodus
- The Exorcist
- Exorcist II: The Heretic
- Experiment in Terror
- Eye for an Eye
- Eye of the Devil

E

emy Award Nominations—Foch, best supporting actress; George Folsey, cinematography (black and white).

104 minutes b&w

EXODUS (1960)
★★★

Paul Newman
Eva Marie Saint
Ralph Richardson
Peter Lawford
Lee J. Cobb
Sal Mineo

This sprawling epic, based on Leon Uris's chronicle about the formation of the state of Israel, offers some exciting moments with the struggling settlers. However, the direction is often heavy-handed, with some wooden performances distracting from the flow. A shorter version might have worked better; after three hours it ends on a tiresome note. Yet it's a well-intended historical film. The cast also includes John Derek, Hugh Griffith, David Opatoshu, and Martin Milner. **Director**—Otto Preminger. **Academy Award Nominations**—Mineo, best supporting actor; Sam Leavitt, cinematography (color). *213 minutes*

THE EXORCIST (1973)
★★★★

Ellen Burstyn
Max Von Sydow
Jason Miller
Linda Blair

A highly commercial and extremely effective fright film, based on William Peter Blatty's best-selling novel, about a young girl possessed by demons. Director William Friedkin goes to extremes to keep you on the edge of

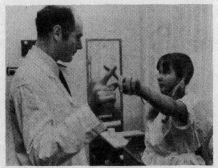

Linda Blair is tested for physical problems in The Exorcist, *a highly effective fright film.*

your seat from beginning to end. The film's compelling aspects are derived from sensational tricks as well as chilling suspense; it's a humdinger of a horror experience. Blair is good as the bedeviled child, and Miller is memorable as the priest who attempts to rid her of the evil spirits. Also with Lee J. Cobb, Kitty Winn, and Jack MacGowran. **Academy Award**—Blatty, best screenplay (based on material from another medium). **Nominations**—best picture; Friedkin, best director; Burstyn, best actress; Miller, best supporting actor; Blair, best supporting actress; Owen Roizman, cinematography. (R) *121 minutes*

EXORCIST II: THE HERETIC (1977)
★★

Richard Burton
Linda Blair
Louise Fletcher

This overstuffed sequel isn't up to the scary effectiveness of the original. It's just so much warmed-over, supernatural mumbo jumbo inspired by the initial story. The angelic-faced Blair is now four years older and still bothered by a demon. Burton plays a priest assigned to wrestle with it. He seems very busy chasing the devil to all parts of the globe, but actually there's not much happening. Also stars Max Von Sydow, Kitty Winn, James Earl Jones, and Ned Beatty. **Director**—John Boorman. (R) *120 minutes*

EXPERIMENT IN TERROR (1962)
★★★

Glenn Ford
Lee Remick
Ross Martin

Ford and Remick head the cast of this gripping thriller, effectively mounted against the background of San Francisco. Ford is convincing as an FBI agent fast on the trail of a criminal who terrorizes a bank teller, played by Remick, and kidnaps her sister as part of a robbery scheme. Martin is the villain; Stefanie Powers plays the sister. Lots of meticulous detail and suspense are used effectively by director Blake Edwards. Also with Ned Glass and Roy Poole. *123 minutes b&w*

EYE FOR AN EYE (1981)
★★

Chuck Norris

Chuck Norris, star of Eye for an Eye, *prepares for a showdown.*

Martial-arts champ Norris takes on scores of bad guys packing guns and knives in his quest for revenge on the killers of his pals. But even as chop-socky films go, this one is uninspired and rather subdued. The routine plot features Norris as a San Francisco cop on the trail of murderous drug peddlers. He single-handedly faces a platoon of foes and is challenged by an Oriental thug twice his size, but the outcome is predictable. **Director**—Steve Carver. (R) *106 minutes*

EYE OF THE DEVIL (1967)
★

David Niven
Deborah Kerr

Some top actors waste their time and talents with this dreary thriller about spooky events in a French castle. Niven plays a nobleman who suddenly leaves Paris to visit his family's ancestral home. The atmosphere is more sullen than suspenseful. Not worth the strain on anyone's eyes. Others in the cast include Flora Robson, Donald Pleasence, David Hemmings, and Sharon Tate. **Director**—J. Lee Thompson. *92 minutes b&w*

E·F

- Eye of the Needle
- Eyes of a Stranger
- Eyes of Laura Mars
- Eyewitness
- A Face in the Crowd
- The Facts of Life
- Fade to Black
- Fail-Safe

EYE OF THE NEEDLE (1981)
★★★

Donald Sutherland
Kate Nelligan

This absorbing, suspenseful World War II spy thriller, based on Ken Follett's popular novel, combines a balanced working of romance and intrigue in war-torn England. Sutherland plays a master Nazi spy, who strives to smuggle out secrets of the impending Allied invasion of Europe. But he's thwarted in a breathtaking climax by beautiful Nelligan, who plays the wife of a crippled British pilot. Nelligan gives extraordinary warmth, intelligence, and excitement to her part. **Director**—Richard Marquand. (R) *111 minutes*

EYES OF A STRANGER (1981)
(no stars)

Lauren Tewes

Lauren Tewes in Eyes of a Stranger, *a horror film.*

A shabby horror film about a madman who rapes and murders young women, and sometimes carves up their boyfriends. The assembly-line brutality is tiresome and offensive. The story is loaded with trumped-up situations, clichés, and red herrings. Tewes of TV's *Love Boat* plays a Nancy Drew-type TV news hen who chases the killer. We've seen it all before. **Director**—Ken Wiederhorn. (R) *85 minutes*

EYES OF LAURA MARS (1978)
★★★

Faye Dunaway
Tommy Lee Jones

The world of chic fashion photography is the setting for this classy who-dunit. There are suspects galore to keep the audience guessing right up to the moment of the clever ending. Dunaway, in the title role, puts it all together as the trendy photographer who has horrifying premonitions of murder. Director Irvin Kershner's even-handed direction, effective eerie backdrops, and superb casting also contribute to this sharp-edged thriller. Also with Brad Dourif. (R)
103 minutes

EYEWITNESS (1981)
★★

William Hurt
Sigourney Weaver

Director Peter Yates and writer Steve Tesich, conceivers of the hit *Breaking Away*, collaborate again with this romantic mystery. But this time, their effort is flawed by a farfetched plot that's loaded with red herrings. Yet there are charming performances by Hurt and Weaver. Hurt portrays a soft-spoken janitor who discovers a murder victim and woos the beautiful, sophisticated TV reporter covering the crime story; Weaver plays the reporter. The two are as fresh and appealing together as Bogart and Bacall in their prime. Also with Christopher Plummer, James Woods, Irene Worth, and Steven Hill. (R)
102 minutes

F

A FACE IN THE CROWD (1957)
★★★★

Andy Griffith
Lee Remick
Walter Matthau
Patricia Neal

Griffith is outstanding as a small-town yokel who becomes a celebrated TV wit after a manipulating reporter, played by Neal, discovers him and promotes his career. Budd Schulberg's script is on target in its perception of the entertainment business. Griffith's convincing performance and fine supporting work adds dimension to the fascinating melodrama. Also with Anthony Franciosa, Percy Waram, and Marshall Neilan. **Director**—Elia Kazan. *126 minutes b&w*

THE FACTS OF LIFE (1960)
★★★

Bob Hope
Lucille Ball

Hope and Ball team up in this romantic comedy; the result is lots of good laughs. The two comic pros play middle-aged suburbanites who have a brief extramarital fling. It's an effective poke at American middle-class values, done with finesse and only a small amount of slapstick. Hope and Ball are supported expertly by Ruth Hussey, Don Defore, Louis Nye, and Philip Ober. **Director**—Melvin Frank. **Academy Award Nominations**—Norman Panama and Frank, best story and screenplay (written directly for the screen); Charles B. Lang, Jr., cinematography (black and white).
103 minutes b&w

FADE TO BLACK (1980)
★★

Dennis Christopher

Christopher, the young biker in *Breaking Away*, plays a weird young man whose obsession with movies leads him to a spree of killings. He dresses up as Dracula, Hopalong Cassidy, and other movie immortals to carry out his revenge on various enemies. He most often imagines himself to be James Cagney playing Cody Jarrett in *White Heat*. But unlike such classics, this film is uneven, with mediocre acting. It's touted as a thriller but is more often silly than scary. **Director**—Vernon Zimmerman. (R) *100 minutes*

FAIL-SAFE (1964)
★★★★

Henry Fonda
Walter Matthau
Dan O'Herlihy

An earnest and sober drama about the impending horrors and terrible decisions to be made after an American bomber is accidentally ordered to drop atomic bombs on Moscow. The theme is similar to the black comedy *Dr. Strangelove*, but here the point is made with gripping seriousness. First-rate performances all around. Also with Frank Overton, Fritz Weaver, Edward Binns, and Larry Hagman. **Director**—Sidney Lumet.   *111 minutes b&w*

THE FALLEN IDOL (1949)
★★★★

**Ralph Richardson
Michele Morgan
Bobby Henrey**

Graham Greene's short story is turned into a terse and stylish film that works on many levels. The plot involves a young ambassador's son who respects the family butler. When the servant's bitchy wife dies accidentally, the boy innocently focuses suspicion on his friend. The film offers an intelligent view of human emotions, with professional acting and efficient direction helping to make the point. The fine cast also includes Sonia Dresdel and Jack Hawkins. **Director**—Carol Reed. **Academy Award Nominations**—Reed, best director; Greene, writing (screenplay).   *94 minutes b&w*

FALLING IN LOVE AGAIN (1980)
★★

**Elliott Gould
Susannah York
Kaye Ballard**

Steven Paul—producer, writer, and director—completed this amateurish romantic comedy when he was 22. It's about a middle-aged Californian who grew up in the Bronx in the '40s and longingly returns there for a brief stroll down memory lane. Characters are warm and sympathetic, yet the corny screenplay is predictable. A noble first try for young Paul. Still, the outcome is unsatisfying. (PG)   *103 minutes*

FAME (1980)
★★★★

**Eddie Barth
Irene Cara
Gene Anthony Ray**

An extraordinary film about students at New York's High School of the Performing Arts. Structured in semidocumentary vignettes, the film virtually

DIANE KEATON

Born in Los Angeles, in 1949, Diane Keaton was raised in nearby Santa Ana, where she attended grammar and high schools. Even as a teenager, she was interested in acting and appeared in a number of high school productions.

Keaton majored in drama at Santa Ana College, where she began her theatrical career by playing a wide variety of roles in productions ranging from contemporary musicals to Shakespeare. Her summers were spent performing in stock company productions of such plays as The Importance of Being Ernest; Little Mary Sunshine; Oklahoma!; Kiss Me, Kate; The Sound of Music; Bye, Bye Birdie; and Oh! What a Lovely War.

She moved to New York City, where she studied at the Neighborhood Playhouse and in 1968 made her first professional stage appearance, replacing Lynn Kellogg in the Broadway production of Hair.

Keaton's next Broadway assignment was co-starring with Woody Allen in his hit play Play It Again, Sam; in 1970, she made her motion-picture debut in Lovers and Other Strangers.

Since then, Keaton's film credits have included the role of Al Pacino's wife in The Godfather (1972) and The Godfather—Part II (1974), the recreation of her stage performance in the movie version of Play It Again, Sam (1972), and five other motion pictures with Woody Allen—Sleeper (1974), Love and Death (1975), Annie Hall (1977), Interiors (1978), and Manhattan (1979). For her performance in Annie Hall, she won the Oscar as best actress. After Annie Hall, Keaton played Theresa Dunn, the lead in Richard Brooks's film version of Judith Rossner's best-selling novel, Looking for Mr. Goodbar (1977).

Keaton also appeared in two 1976 comedies, I Will, I Will . . . For Now and Walter and Harry Go to New York. In the same year, she returned to the New York stage in Israel Horovitz's off-beat comedy, The Primary English Class. Her most recent films are Reds (1981), which won her another Oscar nomination, and Shoot the Moon (1982).

overflows with joy, emotion, comedy, energy, and inspiration as it follows the budding performers from initial auditions to graduation. The cast is mostly young unknowns who display incredible talent. Director Alan Parker (*Midnight Express*) deserves credit for the film's amazing charm and zest. (R)

In Fame, Hilary, played by Antonia Franceschi, displays her eloquent ballet style.

Academy Award Nomination—Christopher Gore, best screenplay (written directly for the screen).   *133 minutes*

FAMILY PLOT (1976)
★

**Karen Black
Bruce Dern**

Director Alfred Hitchcock is still at it with this suspense-comedy about two pair of con artists who get involved over a family fortune. It's the old master's 56th film. Unfortunately, it's out of character with his great features of yore. A complicated and shallow screenplay by Ernest Lehman fails to produce the expected degree of ten-
(Continued)

(Continued)

sion, although there are several moments of fun and interest. Also with Barbara Harris, William Devane, Cathleen Nesbitt, and Ed Lauter. (PG) *120 minutes*

THE FAN (1981)
★★

Lauren Bacall
James Garner

Solid, brilliant acting by Bacall is the only high point of this routine suspense-thriller. As a Broadway star who is terrorized by an embittered fan, Bacall enlivens the part with the style and energy that marked her career opposite Humphrey Bogart. The story is a notch above the usual horror fare, but much appeal is frittered away by awkward handling of the psychotic young man whose adoration and rejection turns to murder. Garner is wasted in a secondary role. **Director**—Edward Bianchi. (R) *95 minutes*

FANCY PANTS (1950)
★★★

Bob Hope
Lucille Ball

Bob Hope gives Lucille Ball some advice as she ponders her next shot in Fancy Pants.

None other than Hope is all dressed up and posing as a butler to bring proper manners to a frontier town. With Ball on board, fun and laughs galore are guaranteed in this remake of *Ruggles of Red Gap*. There are a few slow moments now and then, but the stars trod on in one of their better vehicles. Bruce Cabot, Eric Blore, and Jack Kirkwood help with supporting roles. **Director**—George Marshall. (G) *92 minutes*

FANNY (1961)
★★★

Charles Boyer
Maurice Chevalier
Leslie Caron

This standard version of three Marcel Pagnol films, about a girl in Marseilles involved with a sailor, is effectively carried along by the charm of a marvelous cast and beautiful photography. Boyer and Chevalier give colorful performances, and they are aided by the beautiful Caron. The songs from the Broadway musical version are used here only as background music. Also with Horst Buchholz, Georgette Anys, and Lionel Jeffries. **Director**—Joshua Logan. **Academy Award Nominations**—best picture; Boyer, best actor; Jack Cardiff, cinematography (color). *133 minutes*

FANTASIA (1940)
★★★★

A rare, innovative animated feature from Walt Disney that combines classical music with cartoons. The music of Bach, Tchaikovsky, Stravinsky, Beethoven, Moussorgsky, and other masters is presented under the direction of Leopold Stokowski and the Philadelphia Orchestra. The cartoon interpretations are especially inspiring. And this brilliant production serves as a wonderful introduction—especially for children—to the world of great classical music. **Supervisor**—Ben Sharpsteen. **Academy Awards**—special awards to Walt Disney, William Garity, John N. A. Hawkins, Leopold Stokowski, and RCA. (G) *135 minutes*

FANTASTIC VOYAGE (1966)
★★★★

Stephen Boyd
Raquel Welch
Edmond O'Brien
Donald Pleasence

Here's a truly unusual science-fiction feature that's entertaining and informative. A scientist needs delicate brain surgery after an assassination attempt, so a medical team is shrunk to the size of bacteria and enters his bloodstream to perform the vital work. The photography, special effects, and animation are of the first order, and the action and suspense never let up. It's a fantastic trip, indeed. Also with Arthur Kennedy, Arthur O'Connell, and William Redfield. **Director**—Richard Fleischer. *100 minutes*

THE FAR COUNTRY (1955)
★★★

James Stewart
Walter Brennan

Cattleman Stewart, looking tall in the saddle and stoic, drives his herd to Alaska and finds trouble along the way. It's a solid adventure story, set handsomely against the Alaskan outback. Stewart is reliably effective, and there's an excellent supporting part by Brennan. Also with Ruth Roman, Jay C. Flippen, Corinne Calvet, and Harry Morgan. **Director**—Anthony Mann. *97 minutes*

FAREWELL, MY LOVELY (1944)
★★★★

Dick Powell
Claire Trevor

In Farewell, My Lovely, *Dick Powell is hot on the trail of a gangster's girl friend.*

A stylish and engrossing film based on Raymond Chandler's private-eye yarn. Powell is excellent as Philip Marlowe, the battered gumshoe, on the trail of a gangster's girl friend. And director Edward Dmytryk effectively brings out the rundown, moody atmosphere of a decaying big city. It's a remarkable *film noir* that sets the pace for more to come. Also with Anne Shirley, Mike Mazurki, and Otto Kruger. **Alternate Title**—*Murder, My Sweet.* *95 minutes b&w*

- Farewell, My Lovely (1975)
- Far From the Madding Crowd
- The Farmer
- The Farmer's Daughter
- Fast Break
- Fat City
- Father Goose
- Father of the Bride

F

FAREWELL, MY LOVELY (1975)
★★

Robert Mitchum
Charlotte Rampling

This film version of Raymond Chandler's novel portrays the efforts of detective Philip Marlowe, played by Mitchum, to find the lost love of an ex-con. The search involves a maze of multiple murders, blackmail, larceny, and prostitution. But the film, in an effort to link the 1940s with contemporary life-styles, spoils the hard-boiled character Chandler created so well, and thus deadens the spirit of the story. Rampling is an ersatz Lauren Bacall; Jack O'Halloran plays the ex-con. Also with John Ireland and Sylvia Miles. **Director**—Dick Richards. (R) **Academy Award Nomination**—Miles, best supporting actress. *97 minutes*

FAR FROM THE MADDING CROWD (1967)
★★

Julie Christie
Peter Finch
Alan Bates
Terence Stamp

An overlong and somewhat plodding screen treatment of Thomas Hardy's novel about a beautiful English farm girl who affects the lives of three men. Christie is out of step as the head-strong beauty, although Finch and Bates perform well as two of the objects of her desire. However, the film boasts exceptional production values with exquisite photography and a stirring score. Also with Prunella Ransome. **Director**—John Schlesinger. (PG) *169 minutes*

THE FARMER (1977)
★

Gary Conway
Angel Tompkins

A World War II combat hero returns to his dilapidated Georgia farm, becomes involved with gangsters, and engages in a self-righteous outpouring of bloody violence. The plot leans on *Death Wish*, but it is ineptly directed and poorly performed. Conway, in the title role, is no Charles Bronson. There's a look of sleaziness and viciousness about the entire production. Also with Michael Dante and George Memmbli. **Director**—David Berlatsky. (R) *98 minutes*

THE FARMER'S DAUGHTER (1947)
★★★★

Loretta Young
Joseph Cotten

A smartly made comedy-drama about a willful servant girl, played by Young, who runs for the congressional seat occupied by her boss. It's an effective treatment of the *Cinderella* theme, with a top cast providing excellent performances at every turn. Also with Ethel Barrymore, Charles Bickford, and Harry Davenport. **Director**—H. C. Potter. **Academy Award**—Young, best actress. **Nomination**—Bickford, best supporting actor. *97 minutes b&w*

FAST BREAK (1979)
★★

Gabriel Kaplan

Kaplan of television's *Welcome Back, Kotter* series stars in his first feature film, which looks more like a TV sitcom. He plays a basketball coach at an obscure Nevada college, who puts together a winning team comprised of misfits recruited from New York City streets. Kaplan's role isn't far removed from his familiar TV character. Sandor Stern's screenplay clips cheerfully along right up to the predictable ending. Also with Howard Sylvester and Mike Warren. **Director**—Jack Smight. (PG) *107 minutes*

FAT CITY (1972)
★★★

Stacy Keach
Jeff Bridges
Susan Tyrell

Keach brilliantly portrays an over-the-hill boxer trying to get back on his feet in this touching film adapted from Leonard Gardner's novel. The setting is a small California town, and the story incisively explores the frustrations and heartbreaks of poor people. Fine supporting work by Bridges and Tyrell builds interest in the characters. John Huston's direction is on target, and it's among his best efforts. Also with Candy Clark and Nicholas Colasanto. (PG) **Academy Award Nomination**—Tyrell, best supporting actress. *96 minutes*

FATHER GOOSE (1964)
★★★

Cary Grant
Leslie Caron
Trevor Howard

This ordinary half-baked farce is salvaged mainly because of the special charms of Grant, who stars as a South Seas beach bum during World War II. Cary's part-time mission is to spot aircraft for the Australian navy, but then a beautiful French schoolteacher (Caron) and her pupils arrive, and the fun begins. **Director**—Ralph Nelson. **Academy Award**—S. H. Barnett (story), Peter Stone and Frank Tarloff (screenplay), best story and screenplay (written directly for the screen). *115 minutes*

FATHER OF THE BRIDE (1950)
★★★★

Spencer Tracy
Joan Bennett
Elizabeth Taylor

Spencer Tracy and Joan Bennett are among the stars in the lighthearted Father of the Bride.

A fantastic middle-class comedy, graced with a champagne cast and a witty script. Tracy is in top form as the happy but frustrated father faced with organizing and financing his daugh-
(Continued)

F
- Fatso
- Fear No Evil
- Fedora
- Fellini's Casanova
- Femmes Fatales
- ffolkes
- F for Fake
- Fiddler on the Roof

(Continued) ter's wedding. And the bride is none other than Taylor at her loveliest. Also with Don Taylor, Billie Burke, Leo G. Carroll, and Russ Tamblyn. **Director**—Vincente Minnelli. **Academy Award Nominations**—best picture; Tracy, best actor; Frances Goodrich and Albert Hackett, writing (screenplay). *93 minutes b&w*

FATSO (1980)
★★

Dom DeLuise
Anne Bancroft

This flabby satire, about a fat man who struggles in vain to stop eating, may make you hungry, but there's not enough comic nourishment for honest entertainment. DeLuise is often funny and appealing as the overweight protagonist. Yet he cannot overcome the thin script by Bancroft, who debuts as writer and director. She fails to maintain the proper balance between humor and pathos. (PG) *94 minutes*

FEAR NO EVIL (1981)
(no stars)

Stefan Arngrim

Writer-director Frank LaLoggia dishes up a muddled concoction of horror and religion, mostly inspired by *The Exorcist* and *The Omen*, in his first feature film. The ill-conceived story concerns a teenage lad, played by Arngrim, who is the reincarnation of Lucifer. He raises all sorts of hell among his high-school classmates and local citizens. Devilish events include a crucifixion, a glowing cross, and Lucifer giving folks the whammy with laser-beam eyes. All this and bad acting too is enough evil to fear. (R) *94 minutes*

FEDORA (1979)
★★

William Holden
Marthe Keller

Director Billy Wilder's romantic melodrama is about a Garbo-like screen goddess, played by Keller, who retires at the height of her fame and beauty to live in seclusion on a remote Greek island with her "secret." The film is reminiscent of the director's 1950 success, *Sunset Boulevard*. Even Holden stars again to narrate the tragic tale in the same ironic tone. Wilder's satiric observations and comic touches can still be entertaining, but they've lost their bite over the years. Also with Hildegarde Knef, José Ferrer, Frances Sternhagen, Henry Fonda, and Michael York. (PG) *114 minutes*

FELLINI'S CASANOVA (1977)
★★

Donald Sutherland
Tina Aumont
Cicely Browne

Director Federico Fellini's 2½-hour epic about the fabled 18th-century Venetian is a ponderous essay that reflects the director's own alienation from his subject. The film is strung together with repetitive and joyless scenes of a man who makes love like a robot. An eyepopping production design adds a measure of dazzle to this otherwise chilly spectacle. Sutherland, his face grotesquely rearranged, has the title role. Also with John Karlsen. (R) *158 minutes*

FEMMES FATALES (1977)
★★

Jean-Pierre Marielle
Jean Rochefort

Clumsy and callous French satire about a gynecologist and a pimp who unsuccessfully try to escape from women. There are a few funny moments and interesting scenes before the film disintegrates. Bertrand Blier's direction is stiff, but the story is partially shored up by decent acting from Marielle and Rochefort in the lead roles. Marielle plays the doctor, and Rochefort plays the pimp. In French with English titles. (No MPAA rating) *81 minutes b&w*

FFOLKES (1980)
★★★

Roger Moore
James Mason
Anthony Perkins

Hijackers threaten to blow up a North

Underwater expert Rufus ffolkes, played by Roger Moore, prepares to submerge in ffolkes.

Sea oil-drilling rig and a billion-dollar production platform. Moore, as an eccentric underwater commando, outsmarts the terrorists and saves the British empire from untold humiliation; he's delightful as an adventurer who loves cats and distrusts women. He undertakes his daring assignment with unblinking cockiness. Suspense is relentless as the hours tick off toward the impending disaster. Mason and Perkins are credible in supporting roles. Also with Michael Parks and Jeremy Clyde. **Director**—Andrew V. McLaglen. (PG) *99 minutes*

F FOR FAKE (1977)
★★★

Director Orson Welles conducts a playful and cynical tour of the world of fakery, forgery, and imposters in this semidocumentary that may itself be a put-on. Master of ceremonies Welles concentrates on the deceptions of literary forger Clifford Irving and art forger Elmyr de Hory. Welles suggests that the signature on a piece of art isn't as important as the work itself. The film is engrossing and clever. (No MPAA rating) *85 minutes*

FIDDLER ON THE ROOF (1971)
★★★

Topol
Norma Crane
Leonard Frey
Molly Picon

A worthy screen version of the longrunning Broadway musical, with the rousing songs intact. Topol plays Tevye, the Jewish dairyman in the small Russian village who deals with

★ STAR PROFILE

- The Fiendish Plot of Dr. Fu Manchu
- The Fifth Floor
- The 5th Musketeer
- Fighter Squadron
- Fighting Mad

F

family problems and the strain of persecution by the authorities. He's not quite as good as Zero Mostel, but he's convincing, and his "If I Were a Rich Man" song comes off quite well. Also with Paul Mann, Rosalind Harris, and Michele Marsh. The rooftop fiddling is by Isaac Stern. **Director**—Norman Jewison. (G) **Academy Award**—Oswald Morris, cinematography. **Nominations**—best picture; Jewison, best director; Frey, best supporting actor. *180 minutes*

THE FIENDISH PLOT OF DR. FU MANCHU (1980)
★★

Peter Sellers

The last film starring the late great Sellers is a weak and disappointing attempt at comedy. It's obviously not the fault of the beloved comedian, who once more plays multiple roles with his usual versatile skill. *The Fiendish Plot* has a flat, no-laugh plot that concerns the efforts of master-criminal Dr. Fu Manchu to steal one of England's crown jewels. The direction and script aren't up to par for one of the movie industry's most prolific comic talents. **Director**—Piers Haggard. (PG) *100 minutes*

THE FIFTH FLOOR (1980)
★

Dianne Hull
Bo Hopkins

Hopkins and Hull star in this shabby melodrama that leans on *One Flew Over the Cuckoo's Nest*. Hull plays a sane woman who is wrongly committed to a psychiatric ward; Hopkins is a sinister nurse. The doctors and nurses in the institution seem as insane as any of the patients. The film is a tasteless concoction of second-rate acting and direction, predictable shock scenes, and stretches of boredom. Also with Patti D'Arbanville. **Director**—Howard Avedis. (R) *87 minutes*

THE 5TH MUSKETEER (1979)
★

Beau Bridges
Sylvia Kristel
Ursula Andress

Here's another remake of Alexandre Dumas's *The Man in the Iron Mask*. This lavish costume drama offers flashing swordplay and an international cast, but there's a lack of suspense, a lifeless plot, and absurd dialogue. Beau Bridges doubles as Louis XIV and his twin brother, Philippe, who struggle for the crown of France. Andress, as Louis's mistress, is often in a state of semi-undress when decked out in low-cut dresses. The diverting title is an apparent attempt to benefit from Richard Lester's stylish *Musketeer* series. Also with Cornel Wilde, Ian McShane, Lloyd Bridges, Alan Hale, Jr., and José Ferrer. **Director**—Ken Annakin. (PG) *103 minutes*

FIGHTER SQUADRON (1948)
★★

Edmond O'Brien
Robert Stack

Standard World War II action story with some good air combat sequences. O'Brien plays a gung ho pilot who takes unusual risks. The script is loaded with clichés. Also with John Rodney, Henry Hull, Walter Reed, and Rock Hudson (in his first film). **Director**—Raoul Walsh. *96 minutes*

FIGHTING MAD (1976)
★★★

Peter Fonda

The formula vengeance plot, which served *Death Wish* and *Walking Tall*, is effectively used in this action drama set in rural Arkansas. Fonda plays a young man who returns to the family ranch and wages a one-man battle against crooked strip-mining interests.
(Continued)

SISSY SPACEK

Sissy Spacek was born in Quitman, Texas, in 1950. She was christened Mary Elizabeth, but her older brothers called her Sissy and the name stuck.

At Quitman High, Spacek was a cheerleader, played drums in the band, and worked on the school paper. In rural Quitman, she was able to own a horse and became an oustanding rider. At that time, Spacek dreamed of a career as a singer-musician. She sang with a choral group and taught guitar for 50 cents an hour.

Her parents encouraged her professional aspirations and gave her permission to seek a career in New York City, where she first lived with her cousin, Rip Torn, and his wife, Geraldine Page. Spacek's visions of musical stardom, however, didn't materialize. Instead, she earned a living as a photographic model and attended acting classes under Lee Strasberg.

Spacek made her professional film debut in a small role in Prime Cut *(1972) with Lee Marvin and Gene Hackman. Next she was cast in* The Girls of Huntington House *(1973), a TV movie of the week, and played the role of Ginger in* Ginger in the Morning *(1973).*

Spacek was hailed as the most talented young actress in years for her portrayal of a naïve 15-year-old girl swept off her feet by a psychotic youth in Badlands *(1973). She was a guest star in two episodes of* The Waltons *television series, then won more honors for the television version of Tennessee Williams's* The Migrants *(1974) with Cloris Leachman. This was followed by the title role in the television movie* Katherine *(1975). Other feature film assignments include* Carrie *(1976),* Welcome to L.A. *(1976), and* Raggedy Man *(1981).*

She won an Academy Award for her moving portrayal of country singer Loretta Lynn in Coal Miner's Daughter *(1980). Her early musical training came in handy on this film in which she did her own singing and guitar-playing.*

F
- The Fighting O'Flynn
- The Fighting Seabees
- The Fighting 69th
- Final Chapter—Walking Tall
- The Final Conflict
- The Final Countdown
- Fingers
- Finian's Rainbow

(Continued)

The script is filled with holes large enough to drive a bulldozer through. But there's plenty of emotion and non-stop violent action to satisfy audiences who relish such fare. Also with Lynn Lowry, John Doucette, and Philip Carey. Written and directed by Jonathan Demme. (R)   *90 minutes*

THE FIGHTING O'FLYNN (1949)
★★

Douglas Fairbanks, Jr.
Helena Carter

Fairbanks plays the title role with robust energy. He's a poor Irish swashbuckler who interferes with Napoleon's invasion scheme. But all in all, it's a low-level adventure, with the rest of the cast not up to Fairbanks's high spirits. The film is based on Justin McCarthy's novel. Also with Richard Greene, Patricia Medina, and Arthur Shields. **Director**—Arthur Pierson.
94 minutes b&w

THE FIGHTING SEABEES (1944)
★★★

John Wayne
Susan Hayward
Dennis O'Keefe

Wayne is involved with the Navy's construction battalion, busy repairing installations and fighting the Japanese during World War II. There's plenty of action for Wayne fans, with a romantic subplot occasionally breaking the pace. The good cast also includes William Frawley, Duncan Renaldo, and Addison Richards. **Director**—Edward Ludwig.   *100 minutes b&w*

THE FIGHTING 69TH (1940)
★★★

James Cagney
Pat O'Brien

A schmaltzy World War I film, with Cagney hamming it up as a tough Irish trooper who becomes a hero. The tale packs plenty of spirit, some rough-and-tumble comedy, ripsnorting battle scenes, and corny sentiment. It's pure Hollywood-style entertainment. Also with George Brent, Jeffrey Lynn, Alan Hale, and Dennis Morgan. **Director**—William Keighley.   *90 minutes b&w*

FINAL CHAPTER—WALKING TALL (1977)
★★★

Bo Svenson

Svenson continues with his impressive job as a heroic Tennessee sheriff in this third screen installment on the life of Buford Pusser. This chapter covers crusading sheriff Pusser's success in selling his life's story to a Hollywood producer and his efforts to wipe out a gambling joint owned by the local crime boss. As usual, the violence is overdone, but the movie delivers for Pusser fans. Also with Margaret Blye, Forrest Tucker, and Lurene Tuttle. **Director**—Jack Starrett. (R)   *112 minutes*

THE FINAL CONFLICT (1981)
★★

Sam Neill

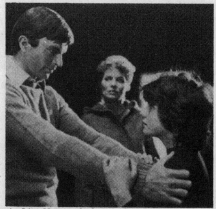

As Lisa Harrow looks on, Sam Neill as Damien Thorn exercises his evil powers on Barnaby Holm.

Neill plays Damien, the Devil, in this third installment of the *Omen* series. This time, Damien is head of an international conglomerate; he attempts to track down Jesus Christ, who he believes has been reborn. There are the standard violent gore sequences and more of the preposterous horror plot that's rather shopworn by now. This film concludes the trilogy; apparently, Hollywood has decided to give the Devil a rest and the rest of us a break from such nonsense. **Director**—Graham Baker. (R)   *100 minutes*

THE FINAL COUNTDOWN (1980)
★★★

Kirk Douglas
Martin Sheen
Katharine Ross
James Farentino

The USS *Nimitz*, the mighty nuclear-powered aircraft carrier, is thrown back in time and confronts the fateful Japanese attack on Pearl Harbor. This clever plot idea generates rousing drama and excitement. And the authentic technical nature of the film provides rich and colorful details of the ship's awesome power. Douglas is outstanding as the *Nimitz*'s skipper, who is faced with the dilemma of whether he should meddle with history. **Director**—Don Taylor. (PG)
103 minutes

FINGERS (1978)
★

Harvey Keitel
Jim Brown

Keitel dominates this strange and confusing melodrama, about an aspiring concert pianist who becomes caught up in gangland violence. Keitel is hardly up to the task and gives a performance that displays a lack of insight. The pointless screenplay by writer-director James Toback doesn't develop any characters worth caring about. Only the gritty New York City background elicits interest. Also with Tisa Farrow and Michael V. Gazzo. (R)
91 minutes

FINIAN'S RAINBOW (1968)
★★★

Fred Astaire
Petula Clark

Uneven and overdone film version of the Broadway musical, which combines social statements with Irish fantasy. The pacing and dialogue seem out of kilter, yet this colorful production still offers plenty of entertainment with the memorable music and the great talents of Astaire in a key role. Also with Tommy Steele, Keenan Wynn, Barbara Hancock, Al Freeman,

- Firepower
- The First Deadly Sin
- First Family
- First Love
- First Monday In October
- The First Nudie Musical
- Fish Hawk
- The Fish That Saved Pittsburgh

F

Jr., and Don Francks. **Director—** Francis Ford Coppola. *145 minutes*

FIREPOWER (1979)
★

Sophia Loren
James Coburn
O. J. Simpson

Producer-director Michael Winner put together this action-adventure with a heavy dose of explosions, fires, and shootings. All the hubbub seems to be about the tracking down of a Howard Hughes-type tycoon who is hiding out in the Caribbean. The violent episodes drown out the plot, and the film lapses into tiresome confusion. Also with Eli Wallach, Anthony Franciosa, and George Grizzard. (R)   *104 minutes*

THE FIRST DEADLY SIN (1980)
★

Frank Sinatra
Faye Dunaway

Sinatra, ending a long pause from theatrical films, plays his familiar detective role in this dull and disappointing outing. Sinatra departs somewhat from his tough *Tony Rome* character to portray a mellow, close-to-retired cop—a role appropriate to his current age. Dunaway is wasted as Sinatra's dying wife. He entertains her by reading a children's book at her bedside, but she keeps falling asleep—so might the audience. **Director—** Brian Hutton. (R)   *112 minutes*

FIRST FAMILY (1981)
★★

Bob Newhart
Gilda Radner
Harvey Korman

What we need is some comic relief from politics, but this satire about an American Presidential administration doesn't fill the bill. Director Buck Henry's screenplay has a few hilarious moments, yet most of the gags fall flat, and some are in poor taste. Newhart plays the frustrated President, who cultivates diplomatic relations with a small African nation; Radner is his sex-starved daughter, and Korman is a flustered United Nations ambassador.

All have had better opportunities to display their comic talents. (R)   *104 minutes*

FIRST LOVE (1977)
★

William Katt
Susan Dey

This is an adolescent soap opera about a college student's search for true love. The story, which takes place on a fictitious college campus, is bland and gloomy much of the time. There's a lot of sexual activity going on, but it's overlaid with silly dialogue and squeaky-clean romantic sentiment. Katt and Dey star as the young lovers. Also with John Heard and Beverly D'Angelo. **Director—**Joan Darling. (R)   *92 minutes*

FIRST MONDAY IN OCTOBER
(1981)
★★★

Walter Matthau
Jill Clayburgh

In First Monday in October, *Jill Clayburgh helps Walter Matthau with his dinner.*

Matthau and Clayburgh shine in this breezy comedy, based on the stage play, about the first woman appointed to the United States Supreme Court. Although Clayburgh is the center of attention as a conservative appointee from California, it's Matthau who steals the film as a wisecracking liberal associate justice, on the order of the late William O. Douglas. The two exchange funny and clever dialogue as they debate constitutional issues. **Director—**Ronald Neame. (R)   *98 minutes*

THE FIRST NUDIE MUSICAL
(1977)
★★★

Bruce Kimmel
Cindy Williams
Stephen Nathan

This naughty double parody of porno movies and '30s musicals is often silly and amateurish, but it's loaded with eager young talent and hilarious musical numbers that make up for the deficiencies. It's a raunchy, sexual laugh-in. There's some nudity, but this doesn't detract from the gleeful appeal. Kimmel wrote the screenplay and music, co-directed, and has a leading part. Also with Diana Canova and Leslie Ackerman. (R)   *100 minutes*

FISH HAWK (1981)
★★

Will Sampson
Charlie Fields

Sampson stars as a drunken, outcast Indian, who redeems himself when called on to hunt down a marauding bear. The film, which is a rather tepid adventure tale, also concerns the sentimental relationship between a farm boy, played by Fields, and the imposing Indian. Acting is substantial, and the atmosphere is touching and warm, but the movie is never compelling. **Director—**Donald Shebib. (G)   *97 minutes*

THE FISH THAT SAVED PITTSBURGH (1979)
★★★

Julius Irving
James Bond III
Stockard Channing
Jonathan Winters
Meadowlark Lemon

A basketball team is on the skids, and it can only be saved by astrology. So, in this funny and imaginatively drawn spoof, the team is reorganized with a wacky bunch of players, all born under the astrological sign of Pisces (The Fish). Channing is the astrologer who draws their horoscopes and coaches them to a championship. Bas-
(Continued)

F
- F.I.S.T.
- Five Card Stud
- Five Easy Pieces
- Five Fingers
- Five Weeks in a Balloon
- The Fixer
- The Flame and the Arrow

(Continued)

ketball greats Irving and Lemon turn in some fancy court work while Winters adds some humorous moments. **Director**—Gilbert Moses. (PG) *102 minutes*

F.I.S.T. (1978)
★★★

Sylvester Stallone
Rod Steiger
Peter Boyle

An ambitious, handsome melodrama, about a truckers' union, beginning in idealism and ending in corruption. Stallone is appealing as a two-fisted Jimmy Hoffa-like character, but the charm of his *Rocky* is missing. Director Norman Jewison's style evokes those early Warner Brothers social dramas. The entire cast is excellent. Also with Melinda Dillon, Tony Lo Bianco, and David Huffman. (PG) *145 minutes*

FIVE CARD STUD (1968)
★

Dean Martin
Robert Mitchum
Inger Stevens

So-so western mystery with an unfortunate case of the blahs. Martin stars as a gambler in a poker game. One by one, the game's participants are killed. The predictable film also features Roddy McDowall, Katherine Justice, John Anderson, and Yaphet Kotto. They're all dealt bad hands by director Henry Hathaway. *103 minutes*

FIVE EASY PIECES (1970)
★★★★

Jack Nicholson
Karen Black
Susan Anspach

Nicholson is at his best in this inspired film that vividly observes middle-class values. He's a rather gifted musician from a wealthy, neurotic family, who drops out to work in oil fields and drift about the country. The story is somewhat influenced by *Easy Rider*, but it has memorable moments that are most original. There are winning support-

Jack Nicholson runs into a bit of trouble in an oil field in Five Easy Pieces.

ing parts all around, with Black, Anspach, and Helena Kallianiotes outstanding. Also with Lois Smith, Billy Green Bush, and Fannie Flagg. Bob Rafelson's direction packs a wallop. (R) **Academy Award Nominations**—best picture; Nicholson, best actor; Black, best supporting actress; Rafelson and Adrien Joyce, best story and screenplay (based on factual material or material not previously published). *98 minutes*

FIVE FINGERS (1952)
★★★★

James Mason
Danielle Darrieux
Michael Rennie

Mason stands out in this gripping espionage thriller set in Turkey during World War II. He plays a British diplomat's butler who peddles military information to the Germans. The compelling story is brought off in convincing semidocumentary style, and it's loaded with suspense. Based on the book *Operation Cicero*, a true story. Nice acting, too, from the supporting cast, which also includes Walter Hampden, Michael Pate, and Richard Loo. **Director**—Joseph L. Mankiewicz. **Academy Award Nomina-**
tions—Mankiewicz, best director; Michael Wilson, writing (screenplay). *108 minutes b&w*

FIVE WEEKS IN A BALLOON (1962)
★★

Cedric Hardwicke
Peter Lorre
Red Buttons

A pedestrian and strained comedy adventure, based on the Jules Verne story about a balloon expedition to claim territory in Africa in 1862. The comedy situations fall flat, and the script is rife with clichés. However, the film is kept aloft occasionally by the cast. Also with Fabian, Richard Hayden, and Billy Gilbert. **Director**—Irwin Allen. *101 minutes*

THE FIXER (1968)
★★

Alan Bates
Dirk Bogarde

This screen adaptation of Bernard Malamud's prizewinning novel doesn't come into sharp focus. However, it does offer some entertainment thanks to the fine acting. Bates performs extraordinarily well as a poor handyman in csarist Russia, who is imprisoned and humiliated relentlessly on trumped-up charges. Bogarde plays a sympathetic defense attorney. Also with Georgia Brown and Hugh Griffith. **Director**—John Frankenheimer. *132 minutes*

THE FLAME AND THE ARROW (1950)
★★★

Burt Lancaster
Virginia Mayo

A colorful costume drama set in medieval Italy. Lancaster performs with energy as a lusty rebel leading a campaign against evil forces. Lancaster, who goes all out with some of his best gymnastics, has the lovely Mayo by his side. Robert Douglas, Aline MacMahon, and Nick Cravat are also in the cast. **Director**—Jacques Tourneur. *88 minutes*

- Flame of the Barbary Coast
- Flamingo Road
- Flash Gordon
- The Flight of the Phoenix
- The Flim Flam Man
- Flipper
- Flower Drum Song

F

FLAME OF THE BARBARY COAST (1945)
★★

Ann Dvorak
John Wayne

An adequate western comedy-drama set in San Francisco at the time of the 1906 earthquake. Wayne plays a gambling hall owner falling in love with a saloon singer, played by Dvorak. This film may be interesting for Wayne fans, but the low-key action doesn't exactly set the screen on fire. Also with Joseph Schildkraut, William Frawley, and Virginia Grey. **Director**—Joseph Kane. *91 minutes b&w*

FLAMINGO ROAD (1949)
★★

Joan Crawford
Zachary Scott
Sydney Greenstreet

The screenplay is rather farfetched in this film version of Robert Wilder's novel about a carnival dancer involved with politicians in a small town. However, Crawford, as the tough entertainer, does rather well in this role, which suits her style. Greenstreet plays a crooked politician. Also with David Brian, Gertrude Michael, and Gladys George. **Director**—Michael Curtiz. *94 minutes b&w*

FLASH GORDON (1980)
★★

Sam Jones
Max Von Sydow
Melody Anderson

An overblown, overbudgeted extravaganza, based on those heroic space-opera serials of the '30s. For all the glitter and lavish special effects, this puffed-up version isn't as much fun as the B-movie matinee cliffhangers. Platinum blond, pretty-boy Jones is in the title role; he has no screen presence. Only Von Sydow, as the menacing Emperor Ming, carries off his role with aplomb. Buster Crabbe, where are you? Also with Topol and Ornella Muti. **Director**—Mike Hodges. (PG) *110 minutes*

James Stewart and passengers seek a way to survive in The Flight of the Phoenix.

THE FLIGHT OF THE PHOENIX (1965)
★★★★

James Stewart
Richard Attenborough
Hardy Kruger
Peter Finch

A plane carrying an oil-drilling crew crash-lands in the Arabian desert, and the survivors use their wits and primitive skills to rebuild the plane and fly to safety. Tension mounts dramatically, and there are fine character studies of the desperate men. Stewart is right at home as the pilot, and there are other sterling performances by the cast, which also includes Dan Duryea, Ernest Borgnine, Ian Bannen, and George Kennedy. Director Robert Aldrich puts it all together in grand style. **Academy Award Nomination**—Bannen, best supporting actor. *149 minutes*

THE FLIM FLAM MAN (1967)
★★

George C. Scott
Michael Sarrazin
Sue Lyon

This lightweight comedy is improved some by the lively performance of Scott, who plays a rascally con man working small towns. Scott gives it his best shot, but the entertainment values flag after awhile. Sarrazin also does rather well as a young military deserter who joins Scott and learns that too much honesty gets in the way. Also with Harry Morgan, Jack Albertson, Alice Ghostley, and Albert Salmi. **Director**—Irvin Kershner. *104 minutes*

FLIPPER (1963)
★★

Chuck Connors
Luke Halpin

Routine animal adventure about a boy in Florida who rescues a wounded dolphin; they soon become great friends. Halpin is fine as the plucky lad. Nice fluff for the kids, but adults will probably find it tiresome. This film led to two sequels and a TV series. Also with Kathleen Maguire and Connie Scott. **Director**—James B. Clark. *87 minutes*

FLOWER DRUM SONG (1961)
★★

Nancy Kwan
James Shigeta

A mildly entertaining screen version of the Rodgers and Hammerstein Broadway musical about life and love in San Francisco's Chinatown. The staging is colorful, the choreography is adequate, and the songs are good, but nothing is memorable. And it goes on

(Continued)

F
- Flying Leathernecks
- Flying Tigers
- FM
- The Fog
- The Food of the Gods
- Foolin' Around
- Forbidden Planet

James Shigeta (center) watches as Miyoshi Umeki speaks to Nancy Kwan in Flower Drum Song.

(Continued)

too long. Also with Juanita Hall, Benson Fong, Miyoshi Umeki, James Soo, and Sen Yung. **Director**—Henry Koster.

133 minutes

FLYING LEATHERNECKS (1951)
★★

**John Wayne
Robert Ryan**

Wayne takes to the skies as a martinet Marine officer in World War II. There are some striking battle scenes against Japanese forces, but a poor script keeps most of the drama grounded. A standard macho performance by the Duke, with support from Ryan, Janis Carter, Don Taylor, and Jay C. Flippen. **Director**—Nicholas Ray.

102 minutes

FLYING TIGERS (1942)
★★★

**John Wayne
John Carroll**

Wayne and company join the famous Flying Tiger squadron in China to fight the Japanese. Lots of good aerial combat scenes, with some time off for Wayne to romance an attractive nurse. The standard World War II clichés and heroics abound in this wartime movie, but it's exciting all the way. As usual, Big John is no pussycat. Also with Anna Lee, Paul Kelly, and Mae Clarke. **Director**—David Miller.

100 minutes b&w

FM (1978)
★★

**Michael Brandon
Eileen Brennan
Alex Karras
Cleavon Little
Martin Mull**

A silly youth film, about the tribulations of a fictitious popular rock radio station. The DJs and their loyal fans go on a rampage, all because the guys from the business office try to wring extra profits from the good vibes. The hollow plot doesn't hold up too well, but there's plenty of rock music— including some impressive numbers by Linda Ronstadt—to brighten things up now and then. Also with Cassie Yates and Norman Lloyd. **Director**—John A. Alonzo. (PG) *105 minutes*

THE FOG (1980)
★★★

**Adrienne Barbeau
Hal Holbrook
Janet Leigh
Jamie Lee Curtis**

Director John Carpenter, who brought us the grisly and overbearing *Halloween*, strikes again with this traditional yet effective chiller. Carpenter is no Hitchcock, but he certainly is improving his ability to spin a scary tale. Leigh, Curtis, and Holbrook are residents of a seaside town in California, where a supernatural fog carries ashore ghosts from a century-old shipwreck to wreak revenge. Also with John Houseman. (R) *91 minutes*

THE FOOD OF THE GODS (1976)
★

**Marjoe Gortner
Pamela Franklin
Ida Lupino**

Rats, worms, and wasps grow to 10 times their normal size after eating some mysterious goop that oozes out of the ground. It's supposed to be scary when these overgrown critters attack people, but the script and special effects are so inept and absurd that it's mostly laughable. The story is based on part of H. G. Wells's novel of the same name. Also with Ralph Meeker and John McLiam. Bert I. Gordon produced, directed, and wrote the screenplay for this fiasco. (PG)

88 minutes

FOOLIN' AROUND (1980)
★★

**Gary Busey
Annette O'Toole**

Down-to-earth farm boy, played by Busey, courts and wins a well-heeled coed, played by O'Toole, after showing up the girl's snooty fiancé. The entire cast, which includes Cloris Leachman, Eddie Albert, and Tony Randall, performs with enthusiasm. But this predictable romantic plot has been exhaustively run through the Hollywood mill. It's yesterday's cold mashed potatoes. **Director**—Richard T. Heffron. (PG) *103 minutes*

FORBIDDEN PLANET (1956)
★★★

**Walter Pidgeon
Anne Francis
Leslie Nielsen**

An above-average sci-fi adventure, stylishly executed with imagination and just the right touch of humor. The plot is loosely based on Shakespeare's *The Tempest*. A team of scientists visits a remote planet to make contact with previous explorers and finds a sinister one-man empire in control. Pidgeon is the reclusive survivor of the pioneer-

- Force of Evil
- Force 10 From Navarone
- Foreign Correspondent
- Forever Amber
- For Love of Ivy
- For Me and My Gal
- The Formula

F

ing explorers; Francis plays his daughter. You will notice effective use of Robby the Robot. Could this be the father of R2-D2? Excellent performances by Pidgeon, Francis, and Nielsen in the key roles. The cast also includes Warren Stevens, Jack Kelly, Richard Anderson, and Earl Holliman. **Director**—Fred McLeod Wilcox. (G)
98 minutes

As robot Robby waits, Leslie Nielsen talks to Walter Pidgeon and Anne Francis in Forbidden Planet.

FORCE OF EVIL (1948)
★★★

John Garfield
Thomas Gomez

A striking crime drama about the numbers racket, vividly filmed against the background of New York City. Garfield is excellent, portraying an involved man desperately trying to break away from crime. Expertly directed, with lots of sharp atmosphere and smart dialogue. Beatrice Pearson, Roy Roberts, and Marie Windsor also star. **Director**—Abraham Polonsky.   *78 minutes b&w*

FORCE 10 FROM NAVARONE
(1978)
★★★

Robert Shaw
Harrison Ford

Familiar war adventure billed as a continuation—not a sequel—of *The Guns of Navarone*. Lots of goodies for action fans: suspense, narrow escapes, spectacular destruction of a dam and a bridge, and other impressive special effects. Our heroes are a mixed bag of Allied commandos assigned to harass the Nazis in Yugoslavia. Shaw is good as an American major. Some appeal-

Franco Nero plays a Yugoslavian officer in Force 10 From Navarone.

ing humor is occasionally offset by stretched credibility. Also with Edward Fox, Franco Nero, Barbara Bach, and Richard Kiel. **Director**—Guy Hamilton. (PG)   *118 minutes*

FOREIGN CORRESPONDENT
(1940)
★★★★

Joel McCrea
Laraine Day
Herbert Marshall

Alfred Hitchcock is at his best with this edge-of-your-seat tale of an American reporter in Europe, who's hot on the trail of spies. The master builds suspense to a glorious crescendo and spices the film nicely with effective atmospherics. Some of the memorable scenes include a murder attempt in Westminster Cathedral and a plane crash. McCrea is excellent in the title role, and there's fine supporting work from Day, Marshall, Albert Basserman, Edmund Gwenn, George Sanders, Robert Benchley, and Harry Davenport. **Academy Award Nominations**—best picture; Basserman, best supporting actor; Charles Bennett and Joan Harrison, writing (original screenplay); Rudolph Maté, cinematography (black and white).
120 minutes b&w

FOREVER AMBER (1947)
★★

Linda Darnell
Cornel Wilde
George Sanders

Kathleen Winsor's steamy novel about an ambitious woman in 17th-century England gets half-baked treatment on the screen. The production is handsome, but the script plods along, only

to perk up for brief spells with some lively scenes. The players seem unenthusiastic most of the time. Darnell plays a girl trying to make good at the court of Charles II. Also with Richard Greene, Richard Haydn, Jessica Tandy, Robert Coote, and Leo G. Carroll. **Director**—Otto Preminger.
138 minutes

FOR LOVE OF IVY (1968)
★★

Sidney Poitier
Abby Lincoln

An ill-conceived, although well-intentioned, romance concerning a black maid and her bid to better her condition. When Ivy, played by Lincoln, decides to quit her job to go to secretarial school, the family pressures a congenial black man, played by Poitier, to be her boyfriend in hope of keeping her on the job. Also with Beau Bridges, Carroll O'Connor, Nan Martin, and Laurie Peters. **Director**—Daniel Mann.   *100 minutes*

FOR ME AND MY GAL (1942)
★★★

Judy Garland
Gene Kelly
George Murphy

This is a marvelously entertaining old-fashioned musical with a star-studded cast. The routine plot, set prior to World War II, has two vaudeville hoofers trying to make the big time while grappling with romantic problems. Look for the great songs and dancing with Garland, Murphy, and Kelly, who is starring in his first film. Horace McNally, Keenan Wynn, and Ben Blue also grace the cast. **Director**—Busby Berkeley.

104 minutes b&w

THE FORMULA (1980)
★★

George C. Scott
Marlon Brando
Marthe Keller

Scott plays a police detective who pursues an intricate trail of clues and murders that leads to the inner sanctum of
(Continued)

F
- Fort Apache
- Fort Apache, The Bronx
- For the Love of Benji
- The Fortune
- The Fortune Cookie
- Forty Pounds of Trouble
- For Whom the Bell Tolls

(Continued)

Big Oil and a secret formula for producing synthetic fuel. Scott's investigation also leads to a tense confrontation with an oil tycoon, played by Brando, who magnificently steals the few scenes in which he appears. But alas, Steve Shagan's cumbersome screenplay, adapted from his best-selling novel, is as complicated as the piping at an oil refinery. Also with Beatrice Straight, John Gielgud, and G. D. Spradin. **Director**—John G. Avildsen. (R) *117 minutes*

FORT APACHE (1948)
★★★

Henry Fonda
John Wayne
Shirley Temple

A handsome and somewhat thoughtful epic western that plays out slowly with more attention to character than to action. Fonda excels as a gung ho Army colonel whose stubbornness irritates his troops and also prompts trouble with the Indians. Wayne plays a practical officer under Fonda's command. Moments of comedy appear occasionally. The cast also includes Ward Bond, Pedro Armendariz, John Agar, Anna Lee, and Victor McLaglen. **Director**—John Ford.
127 minutes b&w

FORT APACHE, THE BRONX (1981)
★★★★

Paul Newman
Edward Asner

A powerful, realistically portrayed drama involving an embattled police

Paul Newman, followed by Ken Wahl, chases a suspect in Fort Apache, the Bronx.

station house in one of New York's most poverty-stricken and crime-ridden neighborhoods. The film is more than a routine cops and bad guys story; it offers a moving and impressive view of the urban decay and the people intimately affected. Newman gives a first-rate performance as a veteran cop who struggles with his thankless assignments and his conscience. Also with Kathleen Beller and Rachel Ticotin. **Director**—Daniel Petrie. *125 minutes*

FOR THE LOVE OF BENJI (1977)
★★

This sequel to *Benji* has the lovable pooch leading a merry chase through the streets and back alleys of Athens, Greece, while caught up in a CIA caper. The confusing plot doesn't seem to matter. The film concentrates on the scraggly mutt, who is able to outperform the human actors. But mainly it's a dog's-eye view of the world, which involves the legs of a lot of people. Written and directed by Joe Camp. (G) *84 minutes*

THE FORTUNE (1975)
★★★★

Jack Nicholson
Warren Beatty
Stockard Channing

A funny tale about two con men who covet the fortune of a dim-witted New York heiress. Inspired directing by Mike Nichols of slick, pencil-moustached Beatty; his seedy side-kick, Nicholson; and Channing, the lamebrained, filthy-rich heiress. The film is set in the '20s and mostly in southern California. Channing scores as a refreshing and accomplished comic actress. Also with Florence Stanley, Richard B. Shull, and John Fiedler. (PG) *88 minutes*

THE FORTUNE COOKIE (1966)
★★★★

Walter Matthau
Jack Lemmon

This insightful Billy Wilder comedy effectively satirizes middle-class values

and the pursuit of success. Lemmon is perfectly cast as a TV cameraman who's slightly injured during a football game. But it's Matthau who really ties the film together. He delivers a superb memorable performance as "Whiplash Willie," the shyster lawyer brother-in-law who schemes to collect outrageous personal-injury claims from the insurance company. Ron Rich, Cliff Osmond, Judi West, and Lurene Tuttle perform in supporting roles. **Academy Award**—Matthau, best supporting actor. **Nomination**—Wilder and I.A.L. Diamond, best story and screenplay (written directly for the screen). *125 minutes b&w*

FORTY POUNDS OF TROUBLE (1963)
★★

Tony Curtis
Phil Silvers
Suzanne Pleshette

Cutesy, sentimental romantic comedy, with Curtis as a casino manager who grudgingly looks after an abandoned six-year-old girl. Of course, complications follow. This obvious reworking of *Little Miss Marker* is routine at best, helped now and then by some decent acting and some spirited chases through Disneyland. Also with Larry Storch, Howard Morris, and Edward Andrews. **Director**—Norman Jewison. *106 minutes*

FOR WHOM THE BELL TOLLS (1943)
★★★★

Gary Cooper
Ingrid Bergman

Ernest Hemingway's classic adventure of the Spanish Civil War is presented with high drama and mounting suspense. Cooper is at his best, as an American mercenary who helps a scruffy band of peasants engaged in blowing up a bridge. Bergman is winning as the object of Cooper's affections. Effectively directed, with first-rate supporting performances by Katina Paxinou, Akim Tamiroff, Arturo de Cordova, and Joseph Calleia. **Director**—Sam Wood. **Academy Award**—Paxinou, best supporting actress. **Nominations**—best picture;

- For Your Eyes Only
- Foul Play
- The Fountainhead
- Four Friends
- The Four Horsemen of the Apocalypse
- The Four Musketeers
- The Four-Poster
- The Four Seasons

F

Cooper, best actor; Bergman, best actress; Tamiroff, best supporting actor; Ray Rennahan, cinematography (color). *170 minutes*

FOR YOUR EYES ONLY (1981)
★★★

Roger Moore

Roger Moore, as James Bond, fires at henchmen of the villainous Kristatos in For Your Eyes Only.

Once again British secret agent James Bond, played by Moore, saves the world—this time outrunning and outfoxing his enemies on ski slopes, under water, and on the face of a vertical cliff. This 12th adventure in the popular series isn't the most exuberant; the villains aren't as terrifying as in past escapades, and the women aren't as sexy. But there are still plenty of hair-raising thrills with the usual lavish hardware and Bond suaveness. Good show, 007. Carry on. **Director—** John Glen. (PG) *127 minutes*

FOUL PLAY (1978)
★★

Goldie Hawn
Chevy Chase

Saucer-eyed Hawn is the best thing going for this action comedy, set in San Francisco. Her warm and mature performance as an innocent librarian caught up in a scheme to assassinate the Pope overshadows the entire movie. Chase plays a detective. The plot seems as if it was written by a computer; it steals from a half-dozen Hitchcock films and ends with an all-too-familiar car chase episode. Also with Burgess Meredith, Dudley Moore, and Rachel Roberts. **Director—**Colin Higgins. (PG) *116 minutes*

THE FOUNTAINHEAD (1949)
★★

Gary Cooper
Patricia Neal
Raymond Massey

An uneven screen adaptation of Ayn Rand's novel about an idealistic architect who bucks big business and makes sacrifices for the sake of principle. The script offers philosophical symbols that don't often register. Cooper plays the architect with some credibility, but he seems ill at ease half the time. Also with Kent Smith and Robert Douglas. **Director—**King Vidor. *114 minutes b&w*

FOUR FRIENDS (1981)
★★

Craig Wasson
Jodi Thelen
Michael Huddleston
Jim Metzler

Screenwriter Steven Tesich, who gave us the exhilarating *Breaking Away*, misses the mark with this grand tour of the turbulent '60s, as seen through the experiences of a young man from East Chicago, played by Wasson. Tesich's partly autobiographical story is intelligent and somewhat perceptive, but his jigsaw-puzzle script packs in too many underdeveloped and incoherent episodes; the pieces never come together, and many of the characters are out of focus. Also with Lois Smith and Reed Birney. **Director—**Arthur Penn. (R) *115 minutes*

THE FOUR HORSEMEN OF THE APOCALYPSE (1961)
★★

Glenn Ford
Ingrid Thulin
Charles Boyer

Overblown and awkward updating of the 1921 silent film, which starred Rudolph Valentino. This version concerns an Argentine family's involvement in World War II, with members fighting on both sides. The script and the direction are no help to the actors, who approach their assignments with seemingly little enthusiasm. The cast also includes Paul Henreid, Lee J. Cobb, Paul Lukas, and Yvette Mimieux. **Director—**Vincente Minnelli. *153 minutes*

THE FOUR MUSKETEERS (1975)
★★★

Michael York
Oliver Reed
Frank Finlay
Richard Chamberlain
Raquel Welch
Faye Dunaway
Charlton Heston

This sequel to *The Three Musketeers* has the same swashbuckling cast as the original. It is, however, lighter, funnier, and less burdensome than the first film. Both were filmed simultaneously. Also stars Christopher Lee, Simon Ward, and Geraldine Chaplin. **Director—**Richard Lester. (PG) *108 minutes*

THE FOUR-POSTER (1952)
★★★

Rex Harrison
Lilli Palmer

Excellent performances by Harrison and Palmer liven up this comic story of a married couple's life, with scenes played about their bed. The script is pleasingly adapted from the successful Broadway play by Jan de Hartog. A nice touch is using animated cartoons to connect the scenes. **Director—**Irving Reis. *103 minutes b&w*

THE FOUR SEASONS (1981)
★★★

Alan Alda
Carol Burnett
Sandy Dennis
Rita Moreno
Jack Weston

Alda wrote, directed, and stars in this warm and friendly salute to the middle-aged and the middle-class. The low-key comedy involves three couples who vacation together at *(Continued)*

Jack Weston, Bess Armstrong, Alan Alda, Rita Moreno, and Len Cariou in The Four Seasons.

(Continued)
various locales. Alda overuses dialogue; the result is a rather stagey production. But a game cast injects ample humor and appeal in this good-natured slice of ordinary life. (PG)

107 minutes

THE FOX AND THE HOUND (1981)
★★

A new generation of Walt Disney animators made this $12-million cartoon feature, about the deteriorating friendship of two animals. The film is full of obvious Disney playfulness and sentimentality. Yet the tone is often heavy-handed and overly serious, especially

Cartoon characters appearing in Walt Disney Productions' The Fox and the Hound.

in dealing with a parable on race relations. Somehow, that special Disney magic hasn't been fully realized by the new generation. Voices include those of Mickey Rooney, Kurt Russell, Pearl Bailey, and Jack Albertson. **Director—** Art Stevens. (G) *83 minutes*

FOXES (1980)
★★★

**Sally Kellerman
Jodie Foster**

A moving and highly realistic story about the social and emotional problems of four teenage girls growing up in Los Angeles. Foster and Kellerman head a cast of mostly unknowns, but every performance is convincing. The film succeeds in depicting the adolescent world beset by the inadequacies of home and school. This portrait is the dark side of *American Graffiti.* **Director—** Adrian Lyne. (R)

106 minutes

FRAMED (1975)
★★

Joe Don Baker

A professional gambler, played by Baker, is railroaded into prison and emerges, with fists swinging and guns blazing, in pursuit of the bad guys who framed him. Perhaps there's too

much gore and violence for some—an ear shot off, a knife driven through a hand—but the film is adequately constructed and guaranteed to keep you awake. Also with Conny Van Dyke, Gabriel Dell, and John Marley. **Director—**Phil Karlson. (R) *106 minutes*

FRANKENSTEIN (1931)
★★★★

**Boris Karloff
Colin Clive
Mae Clarke**

This is the granddaddy of horror films and still one of the most haunting and effective around. With somber mood and misty background, the film, based on Mary Shelley's fascinating novel, tells the tale of the determined scientist who recreates human life in the form of a monster assembled from corpses. Karloff is impressive as the mistreated monster who terrorizes the local community. And there are other fine performances by Clive, Clarke, and Edward Van Sloan. This film spawned a slew of sequels and launched its stars and director on their way to further fame. **Director—**James Whale. *71 minutes b&w*

FRANKENSTEIN MEETS THE WOLF MAN (1943)
★★★

**Lon Chaney, Jr.
Ilona Massey
Bela Lugosi**

The Wolf Man, alias Lawrence Talbot, takes a trip in hope of finding a cure to

Lon Chaney, Jr., as Lawrence Talbot, finds the frozen monster in Frankenstein Meets the Wolf Man.

- Frankenstein '70
- Fraternity Row
- Freaky Friday
- The French Connection
- French Connection II
- The French Lieutenant's Woman
- French Postcards

F

his moon madness, but all he finds is Frankenstein's monster on the loose. Chaney and Lugosi team up for the horror high jinks, and it's all done with stylish atmospherics. However, Lugosi isn't too convincing as the monster. Also with Patrick Knowles, Maria Ouspenskaya, and Lionel Atwill. **Director**—Roy Neill.

73 minutes b&w

FRANKENSTEIN '70 (1958)
★

**Boris Karloff
Tom Duggan**

Almost all talk and few scares in this limp film, which doesn't do justice to the famous name. The silly plot has a TV crew, led by Duggan, using the gloomy Castle Frankenstein to make a horror feature, while the Baron is involved with his own monster work. Karloff is around, but he can't rescue the effort. Also with Jana Lund. **Director**—Howard Koch. *83 minutes b&w*

FRATERNITY ROW (1977)
★★★

**Peter Fox
Gregory Harrison
Scott Newman**

The script for this sobering drama began as a student filmmaking project and evolved into an intelligent movie aimed at exposing the excesses and hypocrisy of college fraternity life. The film is set in the mid '50s at a small Eastern college. The young novice cast does rather well—especially Newman, as a sadistic frat brother, and Harrison, as an idealistic pledge who suffers under the hazing system. Also with Nancy Morgan and Robert Emhardt. There's sensitive direction from newcomer Thomas J. Tobin. (PG) *101 minutes*

FREAKY FRIDAY (1977)
★★

**Barbara Harris
Jodie Foster**

Harris and Foster play a frustrated 35-year-old mother and a tomboy teenage daughter who mysteriously switch places for a day. This Disney family comedy is chock full of formula slapstick and Freudian undertones. Harris and Foster turn on their talent and charm to salvage several scenes that would otherwise misfire because of the repetitive screenplay. As with most latter-day Disney fare, it's harmless fun with a few laughs here and there—if you stay alert to catch them. Also with John Astin, Patsy Kelly, Dick Van Patten, and Sorrell Booke. **Director**—Gary Nelson. (G) *95 minutes*

THE FRENCH CONNECTION (1971)
★★★★

**Gene Hackman
Roy Scheider**

Slam-bang cops-and-smugglers film, filled with exciting action, mounting suspense, and colorful characterizations, and played to the hilt. The semidocumentary story is based on the experiences of New York City detectives who broke up a lucrative narcotics operation. Featured is one of the screen's most exciting and nerve-jangling chases, with a car pursuing a subway train. Hackman, Scheider, and Fernando Rey perform outstandingly. Also with Tony Lo Bianco and Marcel Bozzuffi. **Director**—William Friedkin. (R) **Academy Awards**—best picture; Friedkin, best director; Hackman, best actor; Ernest Tidyman, best screenplay (based on material from another medium). **Nominations**—Scheider, best supporting actor; Owen Roizman, cinematography. *104 minutes*

FRENCH CONNECTION II (1975)
★★★

**Gene Hackman
Fernando Rey**

Hackman again plays detective Popeye Doyle, on leave from the New York City Police Department to battle the French police and the underworld. He takes Marseilles by storm, while on the trail of his old dope-dealing enemy. This sequel has its own distinct style and more concentration on mood and the supercharged character of Popeye. Also with Bernard Fresson and Jean-Pierre Castaldi. **Director**—John Frankenheimer. (R) *104 minutes*

THE FRENCH LIEUTENANT'S WOMAN (1981)
★★★

**Meryl Streep
Jeremy Irons**

Sarah Woodruff (Meryl Streep) waits for lover Charles Smithson in The French Lieutenant's Woman.

A handsomely mounted period drama, based on John Fowles's romantic Victorian novel. The novel uses asides to make social comments; the film uses a story-within-a-story structure, about a filmmaking company with parallel involvements of the players on and off the screen. Streep plays the title role, as a young woman with a tarnished reputation who entices a wealthy Englishman, played by Irons; the two are also lovers in their own characters. It's an intelligent, inventive production, yet at times it leans toward the pretentious. **Director**—Karel Reisz. (R) *127 minutes*

FRENCH POSTCARDS (1979)
★★★

**Miles Chapin
Blanche Baker**

Gloria Katz and Willard Huyck, the screenwriters for *American Graffiti*, continue to come up with adolescent adventures in this sunny and likable

(Continued)

HUMPHREY BOGART

Humphrey Bogart, in a long and distinguished acting career, established the image of the lonely, brooding, cynical antihero. He was born in 1899 in New York City, the son of a surgeon. Bogart attended Phillips Academy with the intention of studying medicine at Yale, but he was expelled because of disciplinary problems and joined the U.S. Navy, serving during World War I. While he was in the Navy, he received the injury to his lip that left him with his trademark lisp.

After his discharge, Bogart went to work in the theater, initially as an office boy and finally as a stage manager. In 1920, he tried acting with limited success; he played various minor stage roles. In 1930, he was offered a chance to star in a 10-minute short titled Broadway's Like That.

Bogart made his motion-picture debut in A Devil With Women (1930), and during the early '30s he combined secondary film roles with acting assignments on Broadway. In 1935, he portrayed Duke Mantee, a gangster, in the Broadway production of The Petrified Forest. Warner Brothers bought the film rights, and Bogart demonstrated his acting ability by repeating his stage role in the movie, which became a hit.

In the latter part of the '30s, Bogart starred in more than 25 films, primarily in gangster roles. Then in 1941, he established his legendary qualities with a smashing performance in High Sierra. This was followed by his fabulous portrayal of private-eye Sam Spade in The Maltese Falcon (1941). Perhaps his best-remembered role was the cynical and mysterious Rick of Casablanca (1942). This film gave him a new image—the intriguing and sexy leading man.

Casablanca, which won an Oscar for best picture, remains one of Hollywood's most enduring classics. Incidentally, the original actor scheduled to play the role of Rick was Ronald Reagan.

While making To Have and Have Not (1943), he fell in love with and married his co-star Lauren Bacall, who became his fourth wife.

In the '50s, Bogart displayed his acting skills in such movies as The African Queen (1951) and The Caine Mutiny (1954). He received the Oscar as best actor for The African Queen. In 1957, soon after completing The Harder They Fall, he died.

Some of Bogart's other movies include Marked Woman (1937), Dead End (1937), Angels With Dirty Faces (1938), The Roaring Twenties (1939), Across the Pacific (1942), Sahara (1943), The Big Sleep (1946), The Treasure of the Sierre Madre (1947), Key Largo (1948), The Enforcer (1951), Beat the Devil (1954), The Barefoot Contessa (1954), and The Left Hand of God (1955).

(Continued)

tale of American students in Paris. The film gets a lot of its zing from the talents of some eager young newcomers; Chapin is especially pleasing as a shy American who gets an ego boost from a charming French girl, played by Valerie Quennessen. There are a few problems with plot and too many characters, but the film ends refreshingly. Also with David Marshall Grant and Marie-France Pisier. **Director—Huyck. (PG)** *92 minutes*

FRENZY (1972)
★★★

Jon Finch
Alex McCowen
Barry Foster

Director Alfred Hitchcock does it again with this gripping tale about an innocent man tagged as the London Strangler because of circumstantial evidence. The plot is déjà vu, but the maestro adds his unique touches and comes up with a good thriller. A cast of unknowns delivers the goods with style and just the right amount of savory black humor. Foster plays the strangler, and Finch plays the innocent man. Anthony Shaffer's taut screenplay is based on Arthur La Bern's novel *Goodby Piccadilly, Farewell Leicester Square*. Also with Vivien Merchant, Barbara Leigh-Hunt, and Anna Massey. (R) *116 minutes*

FREUD (1962)
★★★

Montgomery Clift
Larry Parks
Susannah York

Straightforward, intelligent film biography of the founder of psychoanalysis. The story dwells on the treatment of a boy with a mother fixation and Freud's early efforts to find acceptance for his revolutionary methods. Clift gives a sensitive performance in the title role. Others in the cast include Eileen Herlie, David McCallum, and Susan Kohner. **Director—John Huston.** *140 minutes b&w*

FRIDAY FOSTER (1975)
(no stars)

Pam Grier

Grier stars as a swinging woman photographer, a character based on the comic strip. She's chased by mysterious assassins amid a barrage of gunfire. There are corpses everywhere and gore galore in this typical low-grade, black exploitation adventure, which whizzes along at a breakneck pace. Yaphet Kotto, Godfrey Cambridge, Eartha Kitt, Jim Backus, and Thalmus Rasulala co-star. **Director—Arthur Marks. (R)** *89 minutes*

FRIDAY THE 13TH (1980)
★★

Betsy Palmer
Adrienne King
Harry Crosby

A diabolical murderer stalks a summer camp, dispatching several young counselors in bloody, bizarre fashion

- Friday the 13th—Part II
- Friendly Persuasion
- The Frisco Kid
- From Here to Eternity
- From Noon Til Three
- From Russia With Love

F

within a day's time. Director Sean Cunningham offers a few suspenseful moments, but most of the story is handled in a routine, unconvincing style. The young novice players act out their parts with appeal despite the wooden dialogue. (R)   *95 minutes*

FRIDAY THE 13TH—PART II (1981)
★

**Amy Steel
John Furey
Adrienne King**

This sequel to the commerically successful horror movie revisits the New Jersey summer camp for more grisly slaughter. There are a few romantic interludes among the young counselors; then it's time for assembly-line murder by a hooded killer with a mother fixation. He systematically dispatches his victims by garroting, an ax to the head, and other horrifying means aimed at increasing the shock effect. Will there be a Part III? Give us a break. **Director**—Steve Miner. (R)
87 minutes

FRIENDLY PERSUASION (1956)
★★★★

**Gary Cooper
Dorothy McGuire
Anthony Perkins**

A beautiful and sensitive story of a peace-loving Quaker family in Indiana whose lives are disrupted by the Civil War. Cooper and McGuire do well as the mother and father, but there's an especially winning performance by Perkins as their son. The outlook is perhaps a bit too sentimental, yet it's a fine piece of work. William Wyler's direction is on target. Also with Marjorie Main, Richard Eyer, and Robert Middleton. **Academy Award Nominations**—best picture; Wyler, best director; Perkins, best supporting actor.
139 minutes

THE FRISCO KID (1979)
★★

**Gene Wilder
Harrison Ford**

Wilder plays a befuddled Polish rabbi

who sets off across the United States on horseback in 1850 to head a congregation in San Francisco. Wilder occasionally does well with this overdrawn ethnic joke, but the story is jagged and predictable, and fizzles just when we expect the gags to really sizzle. Part of the problem seems to be director Robert Aldrich, who's home on the range with action westerns, but not with this sort of comedy. Also with William Smith, Ramon Bieri, and Penny Peyser. (PG)   *122 minutes*

FROM HERE TO ETERNITY (1953)
★★★★

**Burt Lancaster
Deborah Kerr
Frank Sinatra
Donna Reed**

First-rate, compelling drama about Army life in Hawaii on the eve of World War II. This screen version of James Jones's best-selling novel comes across with power and passion, thanks to sterling performances and taut direction. Lancaster and Kerr head the cast, but the supporting performances of Sinatra and Reed highlight the film. Also with Montgomery Clift, Ernest Borgnine, Philip Ober, and Mickey Shaughnessy. **Director**—Fred Zinnemann. **Academy Awards**—best picture; Zinnemann, best director; Sinatra, best supporting actor; Reed, best supporting actress; Daniel Taradash, writing (screenplay); Burnett Guffey, cinematography (black and white). **Nominations**—Clift, Lancaster, best actor; Kerr, best actress.   *118 minutes b&w*

FROM NOON TIL THREE (1977)
★★★

**Charles Bronson
Jill Ireland**

Director Frank Gilroy's little comic western stars Bronson in an unconventional satirical role; he plays a two-bit bandit who holes up in a plush Victorian mansion belonging to an attractive and kooky widow, played by Ireland. The story is cheerful, mildly funny, and intelligent, although it takes a long time to make its point. Bronson's remarkable straight performance manages to be amusing. (PG)
100 minutes

FROM RUSSIA WITH LOVE (1963)
★★★★

**Sean Connery
Robert Shaw**

More good rollicking spy adventures in this second James Bond film caper. This time secret agent 007 is on the hit list of a Russian agent, played by Shaw, who also wants possession of a Russian coding machine. But don't worry. Our hero, played by Connery, takes care of the bad guys on a speeding train; he even deals with Lotte Lenya, who plays a vicious spy out for his scalp. It's all accomplished in high style and with tongue-in-cheek humor against exotic Istanbul and Venice backgrounds. Also with Pedro Armendariz, Daniela Bianchi, Bernard Lee, Eunice Gayson, and Lois Maxwell. **Director**—Terence Young. (PG)
118 minutes

While Burt Lancaster listens, Frank Sinatra gives Mongomery Clift a piece of his mind in From Here To Eternity.

F
- From the Terrace
- The Front
- The Fugitive Kind
- The Fuller Brush Girl
- The Fuller Brush Man
- The Funhouse
- Funny Face

FROM THE TERRACE (1960)
★★

Paul Newman
Joanne Woodward
Myrna Loy

Good-looking but leaden treatment of John O'Hara's novel, about family problems among the upper crust in Pennsylvania. Newman, Woodward, and Loy give adequate performances, but the film goes on too long, and the characters aren't developed with much interest. Also in the cast are Ina Balin, Leon Ames, George Grizzard, Patrick O'Neal, and Elizabeth Allen. **Director**—Mark Robson. *144 minutes*

THE FRONT (1976)
★★★★

Woody Allen
Zero Mostel
Herschel Bernardi

Here's a bold, entertaining, and moving comedy-drama about the entertainment industry's painful experience with the political witch-hunts of the '50s. Allen is outstanding as a goggle-eyed schlemiel who fronts for blacklisted TV writers by submitting their scripts under his name. Many involved with this film—director Martin Ritt, screenwriter Walter Bernstein, and performers Mostel, Bernardi, Joshua Shelley, and Lloyd Gough—were themselves blacklisted. This uncompromising look at that tragic period is handled with intelligence, feeling, and humor. Also with Michael Murphy and Remak Ramsay. (PG) **Academy Award Nomination**—Bernstein, best original screenplay.
94 minutes

Woody Allen testifies before a House Committee in The Front.

THE FUGITIVE KIND (1959)
★★

Marlon Brando
Anna Magnani
Joanne Woodward

This is a gloomy Tennessee Williams drama, based on his play *Orpheus Descending*. Brando stars as a footloose young man who becomes involved with women in a strange Southern town; Magnani and Woodward are the objects of his desires. Even with such heavyweights in the cast, the film never takes off. Victor Jory and Maureen Stapleton also star. **Director**—Sidney Lumet. *135 minutes b&w*

THE FULLER BRUSH GIRL
(1950)
★★

Lucille Ball
Eddie Albert

Lucille Ball tries to make a sale to the bridge club in The Fuller Brush Girl.

Ball stars in the title role, as an enthusiastic cosmetics saleslady who gets tangled up with murders and thieves. Typical slapstick stuff, with Lucy cutting up with delight. It's worthwhile if you love Lucy; otherwise, forget it. Supporting cast also includes Carl Benton Reid, Gale Robbins, Lee Patrick, Jeff Connell, and Jerome Cowan. **Director**—Lloyd Bacon. *85 minutes b&w*

THE FULLER BRUSH MAN
(1948)
★★

Red Skelton
Janet Blair

Skelton dishes up the slapstick as an eager-beaver door-to-door salesman who becomes involved in murder. Predictable stuff, with some meandering, but it's well suited for Red. Lots of fun if you enjoy this sort of comedy. Don McGuire and Adele Jergens also co-star. **Director**—S. Sylvan Simon.
93 minutes b&w

THE FUNHOUSE (1981)
★★

Elizabeth Berridge
Shawn Carson
Jeanne Auston

Director Tobe Hooper, who established his horror-cult credentials with the frightful *Texas Chainsaw Massacre*, serves up another ration of gore, but this time there's too much nonsense mixed in with the terror. Four teenagers spend the night in an elaborate carnival funhouse where they are terrorized by a vile monster. Before the sun comes up, blood and dead bodies are strewn all over the place. Hooper puts his imagination and bizarre style into full force, but the film is deflated by amateurish performances. (R)
95 minutes

FUNNY FACE (1957)
★★★★

Fred Astaire
Audrey Hepburn

This is among the best of the Astaire musicals, with the dean of dancing turning in some fancy footwork to the beat of great Gershwin tunes. Fred plays a fashion photographer who meets a rather colorless bookstore clerk (Hepburn) and turns her into a glamorous fashion model. Sparkling Parisian locations enhance the stylish production. Kay Thompson, Michel Auclair, and Suzy Parker perform well in supporting roles. **Director**—Stanley Donen. *103 minutes*

- Funny Girl
- Funny Lady
- A Funny Thing Happened on the Way to the Forum
- Fun With Dick and Jane
- The Fury
- Futureworld
- Gable and Lombard

F·G

FUNNY GIRL (1968)
★★★★

**Barbra Streisand
Omar Sharif
Walter Pidgeon**

Streisand is perfectly cast as comedienne Fanny Brice in this glimmering musical. And she gives it her best shot, belting out a slew of show-stopping tunes with exceptional gusto. The Jule Styne-Bob Merrill score is first-rate; "Don't Rain On My Parade" and "People" are memorable. This was Streisand's film debut, and she proves that she's a powerhouse performer. The fine supporting cast also includes Kay Medford and Anne Francis. **Director**—William Wyler. (G) **Academy Award Nominations**—best picture; Streisand, best actress; Medford, best supporting actress; Harry Stradling, cinematography.
155 minutes

FUNNY LADY (1975)
★★

**Barbra Streisand
James Caan
Omar Sharif
Ben Vereen**

This sequel to *Funny Girl* involves the further adventures of Fanny Brice, again as depicted by Streisand. There are a few comic moments, and the film is occasionally shored up by the shining talents of the great Streisand. But when she stops singing, the picture limps along amid phony Hollywood-type romantic suffering and unconvincing characterizations. Also with Roddy McDowall and Larry Gates. **Director**—Herbert Ross (PG)
137 minutes

A FUNNY THING HAPPENED ON THE WAY TO THE FORUM (1966)
★★★

**Zero Mostel
Phil Silvers**

Mostel is fabulous in this musical comedy set in ancient Rome. Zero plays a scheming slave in the home of a wealthy family; he's trying hard to gain his freedom. Richard Lester directs with plenty of style and pep, and there's no shortage of good laughs. Most of the supporting roles are also performed excellently, with Silvers, Michael Crawford, Jack Gilford, Michael Horder, and Beatrix Lehmann in top form. The film is adapted from the Broadway production, with the score of Stephen Sondheim mostly intact. *99 minutes*

FUN WITH DICK AND JANE (1977)
★★★

**Jane Fonda
George Segal**

In Fun With Dick and Jane, *George Segal is stunned as his front lawn is repossessed.*

Segal and Fonda are cheerful and intensely funny in this social comedy about a middle-class couple who turn to crime when the husband loses his job as an aerospace engineer. Both perform resourcefully and work hard to keep the laughter flowing in their perky slapstick routines. The story is as contemporary as the latest recession, and it pecks at some vulgar aspects of middle-class values. The supporting cast is excellent, especially Ed McMahon, who plays Segal's former employer. Also with Dick Gautier and Allan Miller. **Director**—Ted Kotcheff. (PG) *95 minutes*

THE FURY (1978)
★

**Kirk Douglas
John Cassavetes
Carrie Snodgress**

Brian De Palma, who directed *Carrie*, uses the parapsychic gimmick again in this gruesome, blood-drenched chiller. The absurd and confusing script concerns a teenager with telekinesis power—the ability to move objects by will—who is kidnapped by a super-secret government agency. De Palma lays on plenty of slick action, but there isn't an ounce of logic in this story, and he only succeeds in insulting the intelligence of his audience. Douglas, Cassavetes, and Snodgress are on board to the detriment of their reputations. Also with Amy Irving and Charles Durning. (R) *118 minutes*

FUTUREWORLD (1976)
★

**Peter Fonda
Blythe Danner
Arthur Hill**

This sequel to *Westworld* is pretty much an ordinary sci-fi adventure—high on computers, robots, and other hardware, and low on drama and thoughtful plot development. Delos, the Disneylike technological paradise, is revisited. Things are expected to run much smoother than when haywire circuitry caused robots to kill the customers in *Westworld*, but as could be expected, investigative reporters Fonda and Danner discover a worse situation. Yul Brynner, who had a significant role as a *Westworld* robot, is back in this film for a token appearance. Also with John Ryan and Stuart Margolin. **Director**—Richard Heffron. (PG) *104 minutes*

G

GABLE AND LOMBARD (1976)
★

**James Brolin
Jill Clayburgh**

This cliché-soaked recap of the lives of Clark Gable and Carole Lombard lacks emotion or that special electricity of the legendary stars. There's little help from the actors, too. Brolin, as Gable, comes off as a mediocre nightclub impressionist and sounds more like Walter Brennan. Clayburgh plays Lombard. Why not watch the real Gable and Lombard? Also with Allen
(Continued)

G • Gaby
• Gaily, Gaily
• Galaxina
• Galaxy of Terror
• Gallipoli
• Gambit
• Gang War
• Gaslight

(Continued)
Garfield, Red Buttons, and Joanne Linville. **Director**—Sidney J. Furie. (R)
131 minutes

GABY (1956)
★★

**Leslie Caron
John Kerr**

Caron and Kerr star in this tepid remake of *Waterloo Bridge*. It's the romantic story of a ballerina, played by Caron, who's in love with a soldier about to be sent into battle in World War II. Kerr plays the soldier. The film is rather too melodramatic and not as good as the original. Also with Cedric Hardwicke, Taina Elg, and Margalo Gillmore. **Director**—Curtis Bernhardt.
97 minutes

GAILY, GAILY (1969)
★★★

**Beau Bridges
Melina Mercouri**

A winning film biography about the early career of Ben Hecht, the colorful Chicago journalist. The film's script is somewhat uneven, but the early 1900s settings are impressive, and the production is executed with just the right amount of humor. Bridges gives an appealing performance of Hecht as a determined cub reporter. And he's assisted nicely by Mercouri, who plays the warmhearted madam of a Chicago bordello. Also with Brian Keith, George Kennedy, Hume Cronyn, Margot Kidder, Melodie Johnson, and Wilfrid Hyde-White. (PG) **Director**—Norman Jewison.
117 minutes

GALAXINA (1981)
★

Dorothy R. Stratten

A flimsy, adolescent spoof of galactic films, with a surplus of silly dialogue and a critical shortage of laughs. The late Dorothy R. Stratten, a former *Playboy* Playmate, is in the title role, as a gorgeous robot who pilots a spacecraft. She can't act, and she isn't even as sexy as could be expected. Wooden performances and cardboard characters prevail amid the gleaming space

In Galaxina, Dorothy R. Stratten plays the title role, as a robot who falls in love.

hardware, and the action never even reaches orbit. **Director**—William Sachs. (R)
95 minutes

GALAXY OF TERROR (1982)
★

**Edward Albert
Erin Moran
Ray Walston**

This thinly plotted sci-fi adventure is about astronauts who attempt to rescue a spaceship on a strange planet and are attacked by reptilelike monsters. The script, much on the order of *Alien*, is absurd, and the characters are strictly cardboard. In one sequence, a female astronaut is raped by a giant worm. How low can a movie scene go? **Director**—B. D. Clark. (R)
80 minutes

GALLIPOLI (1981)
★★★

**Mark Lee
Bill Kerr
Mel Gibson**

Australian director Peter Weir fashions a handsome and intimate historical film that deals intelligently with the exploitations of youthful zeal, ambition, and innocence. Lee and Gibson are convincing as two athletic young men who enlist in the Australian army and fight in the disastrous World War I battle of Gallipoli. Weir concentrates primarily on personal relationships, and the story unfortunately lacks drama and urgency. Nevertheless, his provocative statement is most memorable. Also with Bill Hunter and John Morris. (PG)
110 minutes

Mel Gibson is one of the young Australians who fights the battle of Gallipoli.

GAMBIT (1966)
★★★

**Michael Caine
Shirley MacLaine**

A nifty crime caper, with Caine as a determined but rather inept thief out to steal a valuable statue from a wealthy man. He has the help of MacLaine, cast effectively as a mysterious Eurasian woman he hires to participate in the heist. The script is spotty, but it maintains an entertaining pace right to the end. Also with Herbert Lom, Roger C. Carmel, and John Abbott. **Director**—Ronald Neame.
109 minutes

GANG WAR
See Odd Man Out

GASLIGHT (1944)
★★★

**Charles Boyer
Ingrid Bergman**

Dated but still entertaining drama about a man attempting to drive his

- Gator
- The Gauntlet
- The Geisha Boy
- The Gene Krupa Story

- Geneviève
- Genghis Khan
- Gentleman Jim
- Gentleman's Agreement

G

wife mad. A top cast turns in stylish performances to bring out the chills. The screenplay is based on Patrick Hamilton's play. Also with Joseph Cotten, Dame May Whitty, and Angela Lansbury. **Director**—George Cukor. **Academy Award**—Bergman, best actress. **Nominations**—best picture; Boyer, best actor; Lansbury, best supporting actress; Joseph Ruttenberg, cinematography (black and white). *144 minutes b&w*

GATOR (1976)
★★

**Burt Reynolds
Jack Weston
Lauren Hutton**

Reynolds is mischievous moonshiner Gator McClusky in this choppy follow-up to his lucrative *White Lightning* movie. This time, Gator is recruited to infiltrate the organization of a backwater county crime boss. Reynolds also is the director and handles the job in an uneven manner. There are moments of excitement and drama interlaced with unsophisticated humor, contrived action sequences, and lethargic romantic scenes. There are, however, interesting character portrayals by Weston, Hutton, and Jerry Reed. Also with Alice Ghostley, Mike Douglas, and Dub Taylor. (PG) *116 minutes*

In Gator, Burt Reynolds portrays mischievous moonshiner Gator McClusky.

THE GAUNTLET (1978)
★★

**Clint Eastwood
Sondra Locke**

Eastwood is director and star of this caper about a hard-drinking detective who risks all to bring a Las Vegas hooker, played by Locke, to Phoenix to testify against the mob. Eastwood's character here is a departure from his familiar *Dirty Harry* routine. The film's action and violence are at par, with narrow escapes in assorted vehicles, including a motorcycle and an armored bus. The comic book storyline is unbelievable. It's Eastwood's stylish mayhem that seems to count. Also with Pat Hingle, William Prince, and Bill McKinney. (R) *109 minutes*

THE GEISHA BOY (1958)
★★

Jerry Lewis

Lewis plays a bumbling magician traveling with a USO troupe in the Far East. Typical Lewis high jinks prevail, with a number of effective sight gags generating some laughs—but not enough to sustain interest. Lewis strains a little too much, and at times the film lapses into sentimentality. Also with Marie MacDonald, Sessue Hayakawa, Barton MacLane, and Suzanne Pleshette. **Director**—Frank Tashlin. *98 minutes*

THE GENE KRUPA STORY (1959)
★

Sal Mineo

Ill-conceived and grossly miscast film biography of the famous drummer. Mineo plays the title role, and that's a mistake. The story follows Krupa's rocky career and includes his involvement with drugs. There are, however, some good musical numbers. Others in the cast include Susan Kohner, James Darren, Susan Oliver, Shelly Manne, and Buddy Lester. **Director**—Don Weis. *101 minutes b&w*

GENEVIÈVE (1954)
★★★★

**Dinah Sheridan
John Gregson
Kay Kendall
Kenneth More**

A warm British comedy done with exceptional skill and care. It involves a good-natured cross-country race between two couples, in vintage cars. Along the way, there are many charming and memorable moments, brilliantly executed by a delightful cast. Kendall stands out in some saucy comedy scenes. And there are other delicious performances from Sheridan, Gregson, More, Geoffrey Keen, Joyce Grenfell, Reginald Beckwith, and Arthur Wontner. **Director**—Henry Cornelius. **Academy Award Nomination**—William Rose, writing (story and screenplay) *86 minutes*

GENGHIS KHAN (1964)
★★

**Omar Sharif
Stephen Boyd
Françoise Dorléac**

A passable historical epic with some good action scenes, but hung up by a script loaded with nonsense. The plot follows the Chinese warrior's rise to power and his campaign of revenge against his old enemy Jamuga, who murdered Genghis Khan's father. Moments of decent acting stand out among the routine. Cast also includes James Mason, Robert Morley, Telly Savalas, and Eli Wallach. **Director**—Henry Levin. *126 minutes*

GENTLEMAN JIM (1942)
★★★

**Errol Flynn
Alan Hale**

Flynn is in the title role of this pleasant film biography of famous 1890s boxer Jim Corbett. Flynn's portrayal offers just the right amount of dash and comedy in the role of this colorful hero, who fought when the sport was prohibited in some areas. Jack Carson, Alexis Smith, and Ward Bond are also among the co-stars. **Director**—Raoul Walsh *104 minutes*

GENTLEMAN'S AGREEMENT (1947)
★★★★

**Gregory Peck
Dorothy McGuire
John Garfield**

Fascinating and powerful story about
(Continued)

G
- Gentlemen Prefer Blondes
- Georgy Girl
- Gestapo
- Get Charlie Tully
- Get Out Your Handkerchiefs
- Get Rollin'
- Getting Straight
- The Ghost and Mrs. Muir

Dorothy McGuire and Gregory Peck have a tête-à-tête in Gentleman's Agreement.

(Continued)

a journalist, played by Peck, who poses as a Jew and encounters much hatred. The film, based on Laura Hobson's intelligent novel, was rather startling at the time of its release, and it's still compelling. Fine acting all around, with Celeste Holm outstanding as a lonely fashion editor. Cast also includes Anne Revere, June Havoc, Albert Dekker, Jane Wyatt, and Dean Stockwell. **Director**—Elia Kazan. **Academy Awards**—best picture; Kazan, best director; Holm, best supporting actress. **Nominations**—Peck, best actor; McGuire, best actress; Moss Hart, writing (screenplay).

118 minutes b&w

GENTLEMEN PREFER BLONDES (1953)
★★★

**Jane Russell
Marilyn Monroe**

Monroe and Russell are right at home in this agreeable musical-comedy, about a couple of Little Rock tootsies off to Paris to snag rich husbands. You can forget the dopey plot and keep your eyes on the girls, who sing songs like "Diamonds Are a Girl's Best Friend." Charles Coburn adds a touch of comedy to the splashy proceedings. Based on the Broadway musical of the '20s. Also with Tommy Noonan and George Winslow. **Director**—Howard Hawks. *91 minutes*

GEORGY GIRL (1966)
★★★★

**Lynn Redgrave
James Mason**

Redgrave is marvelous in the role of an awkward young girl who chucks her bizarre life-style and marries a wealthy

widower old enough to be her father. Mason plays the widower. The charming comedy-drama examines contemporary attitudes and develops entertaining characterizations along the way. The entire cast performs splendidly, with an exceptional supporting role by Charlotte Rampling as Redgrave's freewheeling roommate. Alan Bates and Bill Owen also star. **Director**—Silvio Narizzano. **Academy Award Nominations**—Redgrave, best actress; Mason, best supporting actor; Ken Higgins, cinematography (black and white). *100 minutes b&w*

GESTAPO
See Night Train to Munich

GET CHARLIE TULLY (1977)
★★★

**Dick Emery
Ronald Fraser**

This wacky, delightful British comedy stars Emery as an unflappable con man. He and his associate, played by Fraser, engage in a variety of schemes to relieve some important figures of their fortunes. The film, somewhat in the spirit of the *Carry On* series of movies, is full of old jokes, yet it's still funny and refreshing. Emery is energetic and droll in the title role; Fraser's support is superb. **Director**—Cliff Owen. (PG) *97 minutes*

GET OUT YOUR HANDKERCHIEFS (1978)
★★★★

**Gerard Depardieu
Patrick Dewaere
Carole Laure**

An exhilarating, audacious comedy by French director Bertrand Blier. Two bumbling pals can't understand why the beautiful wife of one of them is down in the dumps, but a precocious 13-year-old boy knows what the woman wants. Blier's observation of the feminine mystique has never been so funny. The subject of the film could have been offensive, but it's carried off with cool intelligence. Also with Michel Serreault and Eleonore Hirt. In French with English titles. (No MPAA rating). **Academy Award**—best foreign-language film. *109 minutes*

GET ROLLIN' (1980)
★★

**Pat "the Cat" Richardson
Vincent Brown**

A clattering, uneven semidocumentary about people who take rollerskating seriously. The players are all excellent skaters who perform to blasting disco music at the Empire Roller Dome in Brooklyn. But when it comes to acting, they're rather amateurish, and the sketchy script doesn't help matters. The film sustains interest when it concentrates on some spirited and colorful skating, but after a while it all rolls downhill. Richardson and Brown show off their skating skills. **Director**—J. Terrance Mitchell. (No MPAA rating) *85 minutes b&w*

GETTING STRAIGHT (1970)
★★

**Elliott Gould
Candice Bergen**

A dated and only occasionally interesting comedy-drama about political radicalism of the '60s and '70s. Gould plays a veteran who returns to college as a student and is torn between idealism and the conventional attitude of the administration. An on-campus confrontation between the students and the cops comes off badly. Also with Jeff Corey, Max Julien, and Robert F. Lyons. **Director**—Richard Rush. (R) *125 minutes*

THE GHOST AND MRS. MUIR (1947)
★★★

**Gene Tierney
Rex Harrison**

Engaging and charming comedy about a widow, played by Tierney. She lives by the sea and strikes up a romance with the ghost of a sea captain, played by Harrison. It's a handsomely produced fantasy, with the proper measure of sentimentality included. Also with George Sanders, Edna Best, Vanessa Brown, Robert Coote, Anna Lee, and Natalie Wood. **Director**—Joseph L. Mankiewicz.

104 minutes b&w

- Ghost Story
- Giant
- Gidget
- Gigi
- Gilda
- Gilda Live
- The Girl Can't Help It

G

GHOST STORY (1981)
★

**John Houseman
Fred Astaire
Melvyn Douglas
Douglas Fairbanks, Jr.**

Four old men are haunted by a ghastly deed they committed 50 years ago, and a mysterious woman suddenly appears to seek revenge. The topic seems menacing, but the story quickly bogs down with trite fright effects, unimpressive atmospherics, and other failed attemps to scare. The film resembles a fluffed-up version of cheap horror films like *Friday the 13th*. Houseman, Astaire, Douglas, and Fairbanks, as the elderly gentlemen, try to give the production some class, but they waste their talents. **Director**—John Irvin. (R) *110 minutes*

GIANT (1956)
★★★★

**Elizabeth Taylor
Rock Hudson
James Dean
Carroll Baker**

This sprawling epic, based on the novel by Edna Ferber, is about a Texas family involved in cattle ranching. The

James Dean in Giant, *a sprawling epic based on the novel by Edna Ferber.*

film is rendered with style and fine acting by a good cast. Hudson and Dean are excellent as competitors for the love of beautiful Taylor. Director George Stevens expertly develops a feeling for the period and the lives of the characters who achieved success from the land. There's fine supporting work, too, from Baker, Sal Mineo, Mercedes McCambridge, Chill Wills, Dennis Hopper, and Rod Taylor. This was Dean's last picture. **Academy Award**—Stevens, best director. **Nominations**—best picture; Dean, Hudson, best actor; McCambridge, best supporting actress; Fred Guiol and Ivan Moffat, writing (best screenplay—adapted). (G) *197 minutes*

GIDGET (1959)
★★

**Sandra Dee
Cliff Robertson
James Darren**

Fluffy teenage comedy-adventure has Dee in the title role, making goo-goo eyes at a surfer, played by Darren; but mom and dad are skeptical of the romance. Robertson plays a beach bum. This original feature led to several *Gidget* sequels. Also with Doug McClure, Toby Baker, Arthur O'Connell, and Yvonne Craig. **Director**—Paul Wendkos. *95 minutes*

GIGI (1958)
★★★★

**Leslie Caron
Louis Jourdan
Maurice Chevalier**

Colorful and delightful Lerner and Loewe musical, graced with memorable songs and fine acting. Caron is ideal in the part of a young French girl who becomes a stunning woman and charms a handsome rake, played by Jourdan. The film, however, is best remembered for the performance of Chevalier as Gigi's guardian; he sings "Thank Heaven for Little Girls." The costumes and turn-of-the-century Paris settings are wonderful. Co-stars Hermione Gingold, Jacques Bergerac, Eva Gabor, and John Abbott. **Director**—Vincente Minnelli. **Academy Awards**—best picture; Minnelli, best director; Alan Jay Lerner, best screen-

play (based on material from another medium); Joseph Ruttenberg, cinematography (color). (G) *116 minutes*

GILDA (1946)
★★★★

**Rita Hayworth
Glenn Ford
George Macready**

A moody drama set in South America, with Ford as a gambling man emotionally involved with his boss's wife, played fetchingly by Hayworth. Macready plays Ford's boss. Rita is at her loveliest, and she sings "Put the Blame on Mame." Typical Hollywood atmospheric melodrama of the '40s era. Also with Steve Geray and Joseph Calleia. **Director**—Charles Vidor.

110 minutes b&w

GILDA LIVE (1980)
★★

Gilda Radner

Radner runs through her familiar repertoire of characters—including Rhonda Weiss, Roseanne Roseannadanna, and Lisa Loopner—as filmed from her one-woman Broadway show and as seen on television. Some of the skits of broad parody are lively while other numbers drag. But there's really nothing here that's any better than what has been on TV. Don Novello joins in with his Father Guido Sarducci act and, at times, outdoes Radner. **Director**—Mike Nichols. (R) *90 minutes*

THE GIRL CAN'T HELP IT (1956)
★★

**Jayne Mansfield
Tom Ewell**

Mansfield stars in this routine comedy as the girl friend of a mobster. She plays the role of a dumb blonde being promoted for stardom by press agent Ewell. There are many sight gags and some comic pokes at Jayne's famous figure. A number of rock 'n' roll stars, including Little Richard and Fats Domino, are featured. Also with Julie London and Ray Anthony. **Director**—Frank Tashlin. *97 minutes*

⭐ STAR PROFILE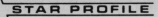

G
- Girl Crazy
- Girl Friends
- Give 'em Hell, Harry!
- Give My Regards To Broadway
- Gizmo

GIRL CRAZY (1943)
⭐⭐⭐

**Judy Garland
Mickey Rooney**

Judy Garland is flanked by Mickey Rooney (left) and Tommy Dorsey in Girl Crazy.

Garland and Rooney belt out some fabulous Gershwin numbers in this romantic musical. Rooney plays a rich young man from the East, sent off to a remote southwestern school to take his mind off girls, but Garland is there and the fun begins. Other fine talent includes Guy Kibbee, Gil Stratton, Rags Ragland, June Allyson, Nancy Walker, and Tommy Dorsey and his band. **Director**—Norman Taurog.
99 minutes b&w

GIRL FRIENDS (1978)
⭐

**Melanie Mayron
Eli Wallach
Bob Balaban
Anita Skinner**

Producer-director Claudia Weill's first feature film is an amateurish and overly emotional study of loneliness in the big city. This theme has been done many times before, and Weill doesn't add any new dimensions. Mayron stars as a young neurotic photographer, who is shaken when her roommate leaves to be married. Also with Viveca Lindfors. (No MPAA rating)
86 minutes

GIVE 'EM HELL, HARRY! (1975)
⭐⭐⭐

James Whitmore

Whitmore's moving, one-man stage show about Harry S Truman is captured on film via videotape. Despite an awkward beginning and technical hurdles, Whitmore's presentation of the feisty, plain-spoken 33rd President is entertaining. **Director**—Steve Binder. (No MPAA rating) **Academy Award Nomination**—Whitmore, best actor.
102 minutes

GIVE MY REGARDS TO BROADWAY (1948)
⭐⭐

**Dan Dailey
Charles Winninger**

Flimsy musical, about a veteran vaudeville hoofer, played by Winninger, trying to make a comeback even though this type of entertainment is on the wane. The creaky plot involves a lot of sentimentality about the love affairs of the vaudevillian's children. A few familiar songs are featured; otherwise it's a drag. Also included in the cast are Fay Bainter, Charles Ruggles, and Nancy Guild. **Director**—Lloyd Bacon.
89 minutes

GIZMO (1980)
⭐⭐⭐

Hare-brained inventions have a field day in this zany and cheerful documentary, compiled by *Village Voice* columnist Howard Smith. Film clips show goggles with windshield wipers, an electric fork to turn spaghetti, rickety flying machines that go kerplunk, a commuter airplane that ejects passengers at their destinations, and so on. Perhaps these loony schemes

CLINT EASTWOOD

Clint Eastwood is best known for his portrayals of a heroic man of action in both westerns and detective adventures in the late '60s. In the late '70s, he easily shifted into some comedy features with Every Which Way But Loose, *where one of his co-stars was an appealing orangutan. Eastwood has since successfully directed many of his own movies, and he's the founder of Malpaso Productions, his own production company.*

Eastwood was born in San Francisco in 1930. After high school, he worked as a lumberjack, a service station attendant, and served in the Army. In 1955, he went to Hollywood where he played bit parts in films like Francis in the Navy *and* Revenge of the Creature.

In 1958, his career was further established when he was offered a significant part in the TV western series Rawhide, *which ran until 1965. Eastwood then went to Italy and starred in a trio of Sergio Leone westerns known for their emphasis on violence—*A Fistful of Dollars *(1964),* For a Few Dollars More *(1965), and* The Good, The Bad, and The Ugly *(1966).*

Returning to Hollywood, Eastwood enhanced his reputation even more as a lean, no-nonsense, independent tough guy. His brutish Dirty Harry *(1971) and some sequels perhaps best exemplified this image. However, Eastwood's violent image mellowed in the late '70s and early '80s, when he starred in several action comedies, such as* Every Which Way But Loose *(1978),* Any Which Way You Can *(1980), and* Bronco Billy *(1980).*

Some of Eastwood's other movies include Hang 'Em High *(1968),* Coogan's Bluff *(1968),* Play Misty for Me *(1971),* High Plains Drifter *(1973),* Magnum Force *(1973),* Thunderbolt and Lightfoot *(1974), and* The Enforcer *(1976).*

- The Glass Bottom Boat
- The Glass Menagerie
- The Glenn Miller Story
- A Global Affair
- Gloria
- The Go-Between
- The Goddess
- The Godfather

G

didn't bring fame and fortune to their inventors, but displayed here, they leave us with a laugh or two. (G)

77 minutes b&w/color

THE GLASS BOTTOM BOAT (1966)
★★

**Doris Day
Rod Taylor
Arthur Godfrey**

Routine foolishness, with Day as a widow who becomes involved with a spy ring. This flimsy farce bulges with unworkable slapstick and gags that fall flat. Godfrey is rather pleasant, as the captain of the title boat and Doris's father. Taylor plays a businessman and Doris's love interest. Paul Lynde, John McGiver, Edward Andrews, Eric Fleming, and Dom DeLuise co-star. **Director**—Frank Tashlin. *110 minutes*

THE GLASS MENAGERIE (1950)
★★★

**Gertrude Lawrence
Jane Wyman
Kirk Douglas
Arthur Kennedy**

Good film rendition of Tennessee Williams's thoughtful stage play. The drama is about a lonely crippled girl and her strained relationship with her mother, who lives a life of fantasy. There are many touching moments brought out by good acting from a top cast. Efficiently directed by Irving Rapper. *107 minutes b&w*

THE GLENN MILLER STORY (1954)
★★★

**James Stewart
June Allyson**

Sentimental and romantic film biography of the popular big-band leader of the '30s and '40s. Stewart is exceptionally convincing in the title role, and Allyson is fine as Miller's wife. However, it's Miller's fabulous music that really carries the film. Worthwhile, indeed, if you love the Miller sound; there's plenty of it here. Also with Harry Morgan, Frances Langford, Charles Drake, Louis Arm-

In The Glenn Miller Story, James Stewart (right) plays the role of the big-band leader.

strong, and Gene Krupa. **Director**—Anthony Mann. **Academy Award Nomination**—Valentine Davies and Oscar Brodney, writing (story and screenplay). (G) *116 minutes*

A GLOBAL AFFAIR (1963)
★★

Bob Hope

Not-so-hot Hope affair, with comic situations that don't suit the comedian's style. Bob plays a United Nations staffer charged with looking after a baby abandoned in the UN building. The task becomes complicated when the female representatives of many countries want to claim the child. Also stars Yvonne de Carlo, Michele Mercier, John McGiver, Lilo Pulver, and Robert Sterling. **Director**—Jack Arnold.

84 minutes b&w

GLORIA (1980)
★★

**Gena Rowlands
Juan Adames**

Rowlands, in the title role, plays a tough-talking, quick-on-the-trigger ex-gun moll who is forced to protect an eight-year-old Puerto Rican boy marked for assassination by gangsters, even though she says she doesn't like the kid. Rowlands's performance is credible and appealing as the hard-bitten dame who suddenly discovers her mother instincts. But director John Cassavetes' threadbare screenplay is farfetched. And there's a lot of desperate chasing around New York City, which finally becomes tiresome. Also with Buck Henry and Julie Carmen. (PG) **Academy Award Nomination**—Rowlands, best actress. *123 minutes*

THE GO-BETWEEN (1970)
★★★

**Alan Bates
Julie Christie
Dominic Guard**

A beautiful and moody movie, set in turn-of-the-century England, involving a boy who passes love letters between an aristocratic woman and a farmer. Harold Pinter's screenplay is touching, and the production is mounted handsomely. Christie and Bates play the unlikely lovers with tenderness; Guard plays the boy. A most unusual and richly rewarding film. Cast also includes Michael Redgrave, Michael Gough, Margaret Leighton, and Edward Fox. **Director**—Joseph Losey. *116 minutes*

THE GODDESS (1958)
★★★★

**Kim Stanley
Lloyd Bridges**

Stanley is exceptionally appealing as a beauty from a small town seeking fame as a Hollywood sex symbol, but mostly finding heartache. Paddy Chayefsky's biting and intelligent script is partially based on the career of Marilyn Monroe. Parts of the film are slightly overwrought, but it's all held nicely together by Stanley's brilliant portrayal and other fine acting jobs. Also with Steven Hill and Betty Lou Holland. **Director**—John Cromwell. **Academy Award Nomination**—Chayefsky, best story and screenplay (writing directly for the screen).

105 minutes b&w

THE GODFATHER (1972)
★★★★

**Marlon Brando
Al Pacino
Robert Duvall
James Caan**

A brilliant and exciting epic crime drama, masterfully fashioned by director Francis Ford Coppola from Mario Puzo's best-selling novel. The engrossing plot follows the career of a Mafia leader and the struggle for power be-
(Continued)

G
- The Godfather, Part II
- God Is My Co-Pilot
- God's Little Acre
- Godspell
- Godzilla vs. Megalon
- Go for Broke
- Going Ape

(Continued)

tween his family and rival family organizations. Exceptional acting by a champagne cast is evident throughout. And the drama, suspense, and character development are of the highest order. The film is more than just a compelling gangster saga; it's also a fascinating study of the struggle for achievement and success in America. Memorable performances by Brando, Pacino, Duvall, Caan, Richard Castellano, and Diane Keaton. (R) **Academy Awards**—best picture; Brando, best actor; Puzo and Coppola, best screenplay (based on material from another medium). **Nominations**—Coppola, best director; Caan, Duvall, Pacino, best supporting actor. *175 minutes*

THE GODFATHER, PART II (1974)
★★★★

**Al Pacino
Robert Duvall
Diane Keaton
Robert De Niro
John Cazale**

A worthy sequel to the first film. This continuation of the epic saga fills in the early life of family patriarch Don Corleone and then picks up the story after his death, with young Michael (Pacino) taking control and expanding the crime empire. Engrossing scenes and sensational acting abound. Pacino is excellent, and De Niro, somewhat underplaying his part, is outstanding as young Don Vito, establishing his family and power at the turn of the century. Duvall, Keaton, Cazale, Talia Shire, Lee Strasberg, and Michael Gazzo are terrific in supporting roles. **Director**—Francis Ford Coppola. (R) **Academy Awards**—best picture; Cop-

In The Godfather, Part II, Al Pacino (right) listens to advice from Lee Strasberg.

pola, best director; De Niro, best supporting actor; Coppola and Mario Puzo, best screenplay (adapted from other material). **Nominations**—Pacino, best actor; Gazzo, Strasberg, best supporting actor; Shire, best supporting actress. *200 minutes*

GOD IS MY CO-PILOT (1945)
★★★

**Dennis Morgan
Dane Clark
Raymond Massey**

Better-than-average air-combat film, set in the Pacific during World War II. The plot involves fighting scenes with the Flying Tigers. There are some predictable moments among the good drama and action scenes. Also with Alan Hale, Andrea King, Donald Woods, John Ridgely, and Craig Stevens. **Director**—Robert Florey.
89 minutes b&w

GOD'S LITTLE ACRE (1958)
★★

**Robert Ryan
Aldo Ray
Tina Louise
Buddy Hackett**

Watered-down screen version of Erskine Caldwell's novel, although some good acting and characterizations are featured. Ryan is effective as the patriarch of a family of poor Georgia farmers. He brings even more misery to the family in his desperate and unproductive search for gold on his land. Louise is fetching and convincing as a cheating wife. Also with Jack Lord, Fay Spain, and Vic Morrow. **Director**—Anthony Mann. (PG)
110 minutes b&w

GODSPELL (1973)
★★

**Victor Garber
David Haskell
Jerry Sroka**

The life of Jesus, set as a rock musical in contemporary New York, is performed with much pep and enthusiasm, but fails to provoke interest in the story. A band of hippie disciples follows their leader to the beat of num-

erous musical numbers, composed splendidly by Stephen Schwartz. The young cast performs well with their dancing and singing, but the production runs out of steam before long. Also with Robin Lamont and Lynne Thigpen. **Director**—David Greene.
102 minutes

GODZILLA VS. MEGALON (1976)
★★★

**Katsuhiko Sasaki
Hiroyuki Kawase**

This imaginative comic-book film from Japan has the good Tyrannosaurus Godzilla defending Tokyo from the ravages of similar prehistoric monsters. The film's storyline is rather appealing, and the technical effects are superb. And, would you believe, the violence is low-keyed. Lots of fun for the kiddies and even some adults. Also with Yutaka Hayashi and Robert Dunham. **Director**—Jun Fukuda. (G)
80 minutes

GO FOR BROKE (1951)
★★★

**Van Johnson
Lane Nakano
George Miki**

Johnson plays the commander of Nisei troops—Americans of Japanese ancestry—fighting in Europe during World War II. Good action and interesting characterizations come off well in this unusual war movie. Also with Akira Fukunaga, Warner Anderson, and Gianna Canale. **Director**—Robert Pirosh. **Academy Award Nomination**—Pirosh, writing (story and screenplay). *93 minutes b&w*

GOING APE (1981)
★

Tony Danza

Monkeyshines paid off in Clint Eastwood's *Every Which Way But Loose*, but even orangutans need a decent script and imaginative support from their human co-stars. Here, the monkeys and the audience are shortchanged. Danza plays a goofy young man who inherits three monkeys from his father

● Going in Style ● The Golden Voyage of
● Going My Way   Sinbad
● Goin' South ● Goldfinger
● Goldengirl   ● Gone With the Wind

G

and must protect them from harm so he can collect $5 million. The shopworn gag lineup includes a routine car chase and pie-throwing antics. You'll have more fun at the zoo. **Director—**Jeremy Joe Kronsberg. (PG)

87 minutes

GOING IN STYLE (1980)
★★

**George Burns
Art Carney
Lee Strasberg**

Three senior citizens, frustrated with idleness and the limits of Social Security, plan and execute a bank robbery. Burns, Carney, and Strasberg play the aged robbers. The film comments on the problems of the aging, and the three old pros turn in appealing performances, but the story is predictable and unconvincing. Limp direction by newcomer Martin Brest makes the movie itself appear caught in the aging process—more drama and more comic energy are badly needed. Also with Charles Hallahan and Pamela Payton-Wright. (PG) *96 minutes*

GOING MY WAY (1944)
★★★★

**Bing Crosby
Barry Fitzgerald**

Bing Crosby and Barry Fitzgerald in Going My Way, *Leo McCarey's sentimental comedy.*

Crosby is perfectly cast in this sentimental comedy, as a young priest in a New York slum parish. Fitzgerald also shines as the elderly pastor who is finally charmed by the personable newcomer. Bing, perhaps at the top of his film career, sings "Swinging On a Star" and "Too-ra-Loo-ra-Loo-ra." Many delightful scenes throughout. Good supporting work is provided by

Rise Stevens, Frank McHugh, Gene Lockhart, James Brown, and Porter Hall. **Director—**Leo McCarey. **Academy Awards—**best picture; McCarey, best director; Crosby, best actor; Fitzgerald, best supporting actor; McCarey, writing (original story). **Nomination—**Lionel Lincoln, cinematography (black and white).

126 minutes b&w

GOIN' SOUTH (1978)
★★

**Jack Nicholson
Mary Steenburgen**

Thin, uneven comedy western with none other than Nicholson in the saddle, as a scruffy outlaw who escapes the gallows by marrying a prim spinster, played by Steenburgen. Nicholson, who also directed, hams it up and essentially wastes his own remarkable talent on such hokey material. The film begins with promise, but never gets going. John Belushi, Christopher Lloyd, and Veronica Cartwright also star. (PG) *109 minutes*

GOLDENGIRL (1979)
★★★

**Susan Anton
Curt Jurgens
James Coburn**

An intelligent, stylish melodrama about a statuesque young woman who is systematically groomed to be an Olympic track star. Tall, willowy Anton sparkles in the title role and contributes most to the movie's suc-

Susan Anton, playing an Olympic contender, leads the competition in Goldengirl.

cess. Coburn is especially good as a slick sports agent. Jurgens is fine, too, as Anton's adopted father, a doctor who once performed medical research under the Nazis. Also with Robert Culp, Leslie Caron, Harry Guardino, and Jessica Walter. **Director—**Joseph Sargent. (PG) *104 minutes*

THE GOLDEN VOYAGE OF SINBAD (1973)
★★★

**John Philip Law
Caroline Monroe**

Lively reworking of the Sinbad story, with the adventurer dueling with a magician. The fantasy progresses in grand style, and it's beautifully enhanced by Ray Harryhausen's magnificent trick photography, which brings to life the figurehead of a ship and other inanimate objects. Also with Tom Baker, Douglas Wilmer, and John Garfield, Jr. **Director—**Gordon Hessler. (G) *105 minutes*

GOLDFINGER (1964)
★★★★

**Sean Connery
Honor Blackman
Gert Frobe**

Among the best of the James Bond adventures, with agent 007, played by Connery, stopping a sinister gold smuggler from plundering Fort Knox. Frobe plays the title role. The slick production brims with the expected spread of gadgetry, beautiful women, menacing villians, and lots of tongue-in-cheek humor. The indestructable Bond ties it up smartly in a spectacular climax. Harold (Oddjob) Sakata, Bernard Lee, Shirley Eaton, and Lois Maxwell join in the fun. **Director—**Guy Hamilton. (PG) *112 minutes*

GONE WITH THE WIND (1939)
★★★★

**Clark Gable
Vivien Leigh
Olivia de Havilland
Leslie Howard**

This stirring romantic spectacle is among the best and most memorable
(Continued)

G
- The Gong Show Movie
- Goodbye Again
- Goodbye Columbus
- The Goodbye Girl
- Good Guys Wear Black
- Good Neighbor Sam
- Good News

(Continued)

of all Hollywood productions. Based on Margaret Mitchell's compelling novel of the South during the Civil War, the epic tells the story of an aristocratic plantation family and its involvement with the war. Leigh is magnificent as Scarlett O'Hara, the spoiled beauty, and Gable is at his best as the dashing Rhett Butler. Many other sterling performances abound. Producer David O. Selznick went all out to provide the utmost in film entertainment. It's a tremendous movie that absolutely defies its title. It seems this masterpiece will be with us forever. Also with Thomas Mitchell, Barbara O'Neil, Hattie McDaniel, Butterfly McQueen, Victory Jory, and Ona Munson. **Director**—Victor Fleming. **Academy Awards**—best picture; Fleming, best director; Leigh, best actress; McDaniel, best supporting actress; Sidney Howard, writing (screenplay); Ernest Haller and Ray Rennahan, cinematography (color). **Nominations**—Gable, best actor; De Havilland, best supporting actress. (G)
220 minutes

THE GONG SHOW MOVIE
(1980)
★★

Chuck Barris

Barris, TV's *Gong Show* impresario, has more latitude for his vulgar, nutty acts on the less-restricted movie screen. And he seems to be having a good time, sending such low comedy to new depths. There's enough comic ammunition to keep *Gong* fans chuckling, but the film's plot is rather flimsy. Barris, who directed, stars as himself. He plays a poor soul driven to the brink of a nervous breakdown by loonies clamoring to perform for him and by the constant threat of his show's cancellation because of poor taste. (R)
89 minutes

GOODBYE AGAIN (1961)
★★

Ingrid Bergman
Anthony Perkins

Overwrought, weepy melodrama about a fortyish woman having an af-

fair with a young law student. Bergman plays the woman; Perkins plays the student. This so-called woman's film, based on Françoise Sagan's novel, is nicely photographed against a Paris background, but it's typical, tearful, soap-opera stuff—a two-hanky movie, perhaps. Supporting players include Yves Montand, Jessie Royce Landis, Diahann Carroll, and Jackie Lane. **Director**—Anatole Litvak.
120 minutes b&w

GOODBYE COLUMBUS (1969)
★★★★

Richard Benjamin
Ali MacGraw

On-target screen version of Philip Roth's insightful look at a status-seeking Jewish family in suburban New York. The romantic drama centers on a young librarian from the Bronx who falls for a spoiled college girl from a *nouveau riche* family. Benjamin is superb in his film debut as the librarian, and MacGraw is excellent as the snobbish young woman with whom he becomes disillusioned. An opulent wedding sequence—for the girl's brother—is a gem. First-class supporting performances from Jack Klugman, Nan Martin, Michael Meyers, and Lori Shelle. **Director**—Larry Peerce. (R)
105 minutes

THE GOODBYE GIRL (1977)
★★

Richard Dreyfuss
Marsha Mason
Quinn Cummings

Neil Simon's romantic comedy is a boy-meets-girl formula movie, about an over-the-hill dancer and a struggling actor who share a New York apartment. This latest wrinkle in the odd-couple theme is loaded with cornball wisecracks, a lot of whining, and verbal sparring. To no one's surprise, the boy, played by Dreyfuss, finally gets the girl, played by Mason. Who cares? **Director**—Herbert Ross. (PG) **Academy Award**—Dreyfuss, best actor. **Nominations**—best picture; Mason, best actress; Cummings, best supporting actress; Simon, best original screenplay.
110 minutes

GOOD GUYS WEAR BLACK
(1979)
★

Chuck Norris

A dull martial-arts adventure based on commando operations in Vietnam. Karate champ Norris handles most of the heavy action, but he really doesn't get warmed up until the film is more than half over. The scripting and character development are at low levels. Anne Archer, James Franciscus, Jim Backus, and Dana Andrews are also in the cast. **Director**—Ted Post. (PG)
96 minutes

GOOD NEIGHBOR SAM (1964)
★★

Jack Lemmon

Lemmon stars in this drawn-out comedy, as an advertising man pretending to be the husband of a gorgeous divorcée living next door. Romy Schneider plays the divorcée. Good comic opportunities are frittered away by an unworkable script and gags that seem repetitious. Lemmon has some funny moments, but there's not enough substance to develop a satisfying film. Edward G. Robinson appears in a cameo role. Also with Senta Berger, Mike Connors, Edward Andrews, Dorothy Provine, Louis Nye, and Joyce Jameson. **Director**—David Swift.
130 minutes

GOOD NEWS (1947)
★★★

June Allyson
Peter Lawford

A lively, toe-tapping college musical, based on the popular Broadway hit of the '30s, with a professional cast giving it their best shot. The minor plot concerns a football game intermingled with various campus romances. But the music is the thing, and there are plenty of snappy tunes, such as "Varsity Drag" and "The French Lesson." Allyson is fantastic belting out the numbers. Also with Patricia Marshall, Joan McCracken, and Mel Torme. **Director**—Charles Walters.
95 minutes

• Good Sam
• Go Tell the Spartans
• Go West

• The Graduate
• Grand Theft Auto
• The Grapes of Wrath

G

GOOD SAM (1948)
★★

**Gary Cooper
Ann Sheridan**

A listless comedy that falls apart despite the efforts of Cooper in the title role. He portrays a hopeless soft touch whose charity drives him to financial ruin. Director Leo McCarey seems to be trying hard, but he can't get this lengthy production together. Also with Ray Collins, Edmund Lowe, Joan Lorring, and Ruth Roman.
114 minutes b&w

GO TELL THE SPARTANS (1978)
★★

Burt Lancaster

Burt Lancaster commands military advisors in South Vietnam in Go Tell the Spartans.

Lancaster plays an Army major who commands a detachment of military advisers, futilely defending an outpost in South Vietnam. Lancaster and the novice supporting cast make an earnest effort, but the story seems incompatible with post-war moods. Overall, the movie plods under the burden of heavy-handed symbolism and irony. Also with Craig Wasson, Marc Singer, Jonathan Goldsmith, and Joe Unger. **Director**—Ted Post. (R)
114 minutes

GO WEST (1940)
★★★

Marx Brothers

Groucho, Harpo, and Chico hit the trail and take on the western bad guys. A rather uneven comedy most of the way through until the smashing finale. Then it's the Marx Brothers in all their glory, as they take a moving train apart. It's certainly worth the trip. John Carroll, Diana Lewis, and Robert Barratt co-star. **Director**—Edward Buzzell.
82 minutes b&w

THE GRADUATE (1967)
★★★★

**Anne Bancroft
Dustin Hoffman
Katherine Ross**

A milestone masterpiece about a young college graduate who has an affair with the wife of his father's partner. Underneath it all, the story intelligently reveals the youth's intense feelings—that his success in college was primarily for the benefit of his wealthy, status-seeking parents—and he strives to establish his own set of values. The film entertains on many levels, with great moments of charm, humor, suspense, and drama. Hoffman nailed down a brilliant acting career, in this his film debut, as the young graduate. Bancroft plays the seductive older woman; Ross plays her daughter, with whom Hoffman falls in love. Also with Murray Hamilton and William Daniels. Mike Nichols's direction is a triumph. (PG) **Academy Award**—Nichols, best director. **Nominations**—best picture; Hoffman, best actor; Bancroft, best actress; Ross, best supporting actress; Calder

In The Graduate, *Dustin Hoffman has the title role, and Anne Bancroft plays the seductive older woman.*

Willingham and Buck Henry, best screenplay (based on material from another medium); Robert Surtees, cinematography. *105 minutes*

GRAND THEFT AUTO (1977)
★

**Ron Howard
Nancy Morgan
Marion Ross**

This is another childish and dim-witted car-smash-'em-up story. This one involves a young eloping couple who generate a trail of assorted wrecked vehicles when chased from Los Angeles to Las Vegas. Morgan plays the female lead; Howard is the male lead and the director—he's not good at either task. Also with Pete Isacksen and Barry Cahill. (PG) *84 minutes*

THE GRAPES OF WRATH (1940)
★★★★

**Henry Fonda
Jane Darwell
John Carradine**

Henry Fonda drives his family out of the Dust Bowl to California in The Grapes of Wrath.

A magnificent film, based on John Steinbeck's moving account of poor Oklahoma farmers, moving from the Dust Bowl to California during the Depression to reestablish their lives. Brilliant acting by a superb cast. The film, which brims with unforgettable moments of drama and poignant characterizations, reveals considerable compassion for poor, honest people struggling for dignity against seemingly insurmountable odds. Also with Charley Grapewin, Dorris Bowdon, and Russell Simpson. **Director**—John Ford. **Academy Awards**—Ford, best director; Darwell, best supporting
(Continued)

G
- The Grass Is Greener
- Gray Lady Down
- Grease
- Greased Lightning
- The Great Bank Hoax
- The Great Bank Robbery
- The Great Caruso
- The Great Dictator

(Continued)
actress. **Nominations**—best picture; Fonda, best actor; Nunnally Johnson, writing (screenplay).

128 minutes b&w

THE GRASS IS GREENER (1960)
★★★

**Cary Grant
Deborah Kerr
Robert Mitchum**

Stylish comedy of manners with an air of slow-paced staginess about it, yet it's enlivened by good performances. Grant and Kerr play a noble English couple. Their marriage is upset when an American millionaire, played by Mitchum, enters the picture. Based on a play by Hugh and Margaret Williams. Also with Jean Simmons and Moray Watson. **Director**—Stanley Donen. *105 minutes*

GRAY LADY DOWN (1978)
★★

**Charlton Heston
David Carradine
Stacy Keach**

What happens when an American nuclear sub is rammed by a freighter and sinks off the coast of Connecticut? The U.S. Navy, of course, comes to the official rescue with all sorts of wonderful gadgets, stiff upper lips, and disaster-movie clichés. Heston, who has seen better days riding chariots, plays the fearless sub skipper; Keach is one of his officers. Carradine plays a nonconformist officer and a designer of a diving craft who saves the day just before the sub's oxygen supply—and the audience's patience—wears out. Also with Ned Beatty and Ronny Cox. **Director**—David Greene. (PG) *111 minutes*

GREASE (1978)
★★★★

**John Travolta
Olivia Newton-John
Stockard Channing**

A zesty dandy of a musical, based on the long-running Broadway hit show about a 1950s high school class. Travolta and Newton-John star as the

Olivia Newton-John catches up with John Travolta during training in Grease.

sentimental teenage sweethearts. Both can really do their stuff in the way of dancing, singing, and acting. The excellent musical numbers are well-staged and come off with high spirits. The talented supporting cast does an impressive job. Channing, as the tough girl with a heart of gold, steals a few scenes. Also with Jeff Conaway, Didi Conn, Eve Arden, and Sid Caesar. **Director**—Randal Kleiser. (PG) *110 minutes*

GREASED LIGHTNING (1977)
★★★

**Richard Pryor
Beau Bridges**

Pryor gives a cool and subtle performance in this action-filled biography of Wendell Scott, the first black stock-car racing champion. The zesty pace is captured nicely by director Michael Schultz. Bridges contributes effective support as a local driver who joins Scott's crew. The film might have been better with more emphasis on character; however, it's still good entertainment with a significant social message. Also with Pam Grier, Cleavon Little, and Vincent Gardenia. (PG) *94 minutes*

THE GREAT BANK HOAX (1979)
★

**Richard Basehart
Burgess Meredith
Ned Beatty**

Bumbling bank officers in a small town try to cover up an embezzlement by staging a robbery. It's supposed to be

comedy, but you'll probably find more laughs in a life insurance policy. Basehart, Beatty, and Meredith play stereotyped characters who come close to the style of The Three Stooges. Such antics may have gone over in the early days of filmmaking; now, it's just so much silliness. Also with Paul Sand and Michael Murphy. **Director**—Joseph Jacoby. (PG) *89 minutes*

THE GREAT BANK ROBBERY (1969)
★★

**Kim Novak
Zero Mostel
Clint Walker**

This western spoof can't make it up the hill, even with the talents of Mostel, who plays a scheming bank robber in the town of Friendly. He also has to compete with other outlaws who have their eyes on the loot. There are a few agreeable moments here and there, but it's not so great. Also with Claude Akins, Akim Tamiroff, and Larry Storch. **Director**—Hy Averback. (PG) *98 minutes*

THE GREAT CARUSO (1951)
★★★

**Mario Lanza
Ann Blyth**

Lanza plays the famous Italian tenor in this handsome film biography, embellished slightly with fiction. The production lacks sufficient drama, and the dialogue is somewhat stiff; yet the settings are colorful, and Lanza sings a wide variety of opera numbers. He's not as great as Caruso, but he does an adequate job. Also with Dorothy Kirsten, Jarmila Novotna, and Carl Benton Reid. **Director**—Richard Thorpe. (G) *109 minutes*

THE GREAT DICTATOR (1940)
★★★

**Charles Chaplin
Paulette Goddard
Jack Oakie**

Effective spoof of Adolf Hitler with Chaplin in a dual role; he plays a Jewish barber and Adenoid Hynkel, the dictator of Tomania. Oakie is also outstanding as Benzino Napaloni, the ruler of the rival country of Bacteria. Chaplin's unique satire focuses on humanity by way of his familiar slapstick routine. Also with Reginald Gardiner, Henry Daniell, Billy Gilbert, and Maurice Moscovich. **Director—** Chaplin. **Academy Award Nominations**—best picture; Chaplin, best actor; Oakie, best supporting actor; Chaplin, writing (original screenplay). (G) *129 minutes b&w*

THE GREAT ESCAPE (1963)
★★★★

James Garner
Steve McQueen
Richard Attenborough
James Donald
Charles Bronson

Slam-bang action adventure, about Allied prisoners attempting to bust out of a German POW camp during World War II. The film is based on a true story. A top cast keeps the excitement moving and building despite the film's length. There's an especially daring sequence with McQueen on a motorcycle, trying to reach freedom. Also with Donald Pleasence. James Coburn, and David McCallum. **Director**—John Sturges. *173 minutes*

THE GREATEST (1977)
★★★★

Muhammed Ali
Ernest Borgnine
Robert Duvall

Boxing great Ali plays himself as no one else could in this charming movie biography, which recounts his career from Cassius Clay of Louisville to the bombastic world heavyweight cham-

In The Greatest, *who else but Muhammed Ali could play himself?*

pion of the '70s. Ali proves he can be a good actor; his performance matches that of the fine supporting cast. It's an old-fashioned upbeat movie, with Ali's colorful personality dominating scene after scene. There's a winning script by Ring Lardner, Jr., and excellent direction by Tom Gries. Also with John Marley, James Earl Jones, Roger E. Mosley, Ben Johnson, and Paul Winfield. (PG) *101 minutes*

THE GREATEST SHOW ON EARTH (1952)
★★★

Betty Hutton
Cornel Wilde
James Stewart
Charlton Heston

Director Cecil B. DeMille takes us to the circus and uncorks some thrilling excitement and drama in this slick, expensive production. The film brims with amusing cameos, especially Stewart dressed up as a clown. A train wreck climax is sort of a letdown. Also with Dorothy Lamour, Gloria Grahame, Lyle Bettger, Henry Wilcoxon, Emmett Kelly, and John Ringling North. **Academy Awards**—best picture; Frederic M. Frank, Theodore St. John, and Frank Cavett, writing (motion picture story). **Nomination**— DeMille, best director. *153 minutes*

THE GREATEST STORY EVER TOLD (1965)
★★

Max Von Sydow
Dorothy McGuire
Claude Rains
José Ferrer
David McCallum
Charlton Heston

Overlong and unwieldy telling of the story of Christ. Von Sydow does an earnest job in the role of Jesus, but much of this plodding epic is taken up with many unworkable bit parts. For example, there's John Wayne as a Roman officer involved with the details of the Crucifixion. The elaborate settings look too perfect, too unreal—sort of like a series of Christmas cards. It's hardly the greatest picture ever made. Also with Sidney Poitier, Donald Pleasence, Roddy Mc-

Dowall, Carroll Baker, Van Heflin, Shelley Winters, Ed Wynn, Telly Savalas, and Angela Lansbury. **Director**—George Stevens. (G) *225 minutes*

GREAT EXPECTATIONS (1946)
★★★★

John Mills
Bernard Miles
Finlay Currie
Martita Hunt
Valerie Hobson

A scene from Great Expectations, *a first-class screen adaptation of Charles Dickens's classic.*

A first-class screen adaptation of the beloved Charles Dickens classic. All the interesting characters, faithfully portrayed by a top cast, are brought brilliantly to life under the superb guidance of director David Lean. The film also boasts detailed settings and fine photography. There have been other attempts to film this story of the poor orphan boy who becomes a gentleman, thanks to the help of a mysterious escaped convict, but this version is tops. Superb performances are given by Mills, Hobson, Currie, Hunt, Alec Guinness, and Jean Simmons. **Academy Award**—Guy Green, cinematography (black and white). **Nominations**—best picture; Lean, best director; Lean, Ronald Neame, and Anthony Havelock-Allan, writing (screenplay). *118 minutes*

G
• The Great Gatsby
• The Great Imposter
• The Great Lie
• The Great McGinty
• The Great McGonagall
• The Great Muppet Caper

THE GREAT GATSBY (1974)
★★

**Robert Redford
Mia Farrow
Karen Black**

Mia Farrow and Robert Redford in The Great Gatsby, *based on F. Scott Fitzgerald's novel.*

This third rendition of F. Scott Fitzgerald's novel of the Roaring Twenties is lavishly mounted, but the story and characters lack compelling interest. Redford, in the title role, is the hustling bootlegger who has everything except the woman he loves. He does an adequate job, but his performance is forgettable. Also with Scott Wilson, Bruce Dern, Sam Waterston, and Lois Chiles. **Director**—Jack Clayton. (PG)
146 minutes

THE GREAT IMPOSTER (1960)
★★★

**Tony Curtis
Raymond Massey
Karl Malden**

Curtis stars in the title role, as the incredible con artist, Ferdinand Waldo Demara, who successfully posed as a naval doctor, a prison warden, and a teacher. Curtis is right at home in this striking episodic tale, and the film maintains interest throughout. Also co-starring Edmund O'Brien, Arthur O'Connell, Gary Merrill, and Frank Gorshin. **Director**—Robert Mulligan.
112 minutes b&w

THE GREAT LIE (1941)
★★★★

**Bette Davis
Mary Astor
George Brent**

This rather complex and talky soap-opera story is spruced up nicely, thanks to the supremely bitchy performances of Davis and Astor. Davis marries the man (Brent), who used to be married to Astor. Astor, meanwhile, is pregnant, and when Brent dies in a plane crash, Davis rears the child as her own. Soap fans should have fun sorting out this one. The film is set against a background of classical music. Lucile Watson, Hattie McDaniel, and Grant Mitchell also star. **Director**—Edmund Goulding. **Academy Award**—Astor, best supporting actress.
107 minutes b&w

THE GREAT McGINTY (1940)
★★★★

**Brian Donlevy
Akim Tamiroff**

Smashing debut for writer-director Preston Sturges, who fashioned this biting political satire. Donlevy plays a bum who gains political power and then lets it slip away. This inventive film gets its point across with unusual efficiency and a liberal amount of snappy dialogue; it starts with a bang and never lets up. Some good supporting players add to the fun. Also with Muriel Angelus, Louis Jean Heydt, and William Demarest. **Academy Award**—Sturges, writing (original screenplay).

83 minutes b&w

THE GREAT McGONAGALL (1975)
★★

**Spike Milligan
Peter Sellers**

This comedy about a 19th-century Scotsman, who fails as a weaver and then as a poet, is put together by the BBC's *Goon Show* players. Although the story has its touching and hilarious moments, the film generally falls flat, despite the first-class talents of Milligan as the poet McGonagall and Sellers as Queen Victoria. The *Goon Show* was a British radio series in the 1950s, and it's obviously difficult to transpose this sort of comedy to the screen. **Director**—Joseph McGrath. (No MPAA rating)
95 minutes

THE GREAT MUPPET CAPER (1981)
★★

Miss Piggy, Kermit the Frog, Fozzi Bear, and other adorable Muppet characters crack a London jewel heist in this cheerful musical-melodrama. The incomparable Miss Piggy steals scenes as star of an Esther Williams water ballet and in a Busby Berkeley nightclub

In The Great Muppet Caper, *Miss Piggy lends her charm and grace to a water ballet.*

● The Great Race
● The Great Santini
● The Great Scout and Cathouse Thursday
● The Great Train Robbery

EDWARD G. ROBINSON

Edward G. Robinson was best known for various gangster roles, initially stemming from his triumphant portrayal of Caesar Enrico Bandello, a tough small-time hood who rises to the top of a mob in the 1930 classic Little Caesar. *However, his range of acting skills was sufficient for effective roles in many categories.*

Robinson was born Emanuel Goldenberg in Bucharest, Rumania, in 1893. His family came to the United States in 1902, and he spent his childhood on New York's Lower East Side. He studied acting at New York City College and starred on Broadway for many years. Robinson appeared in his first film in 1923.

After the introduction of sound in movies, Robinson's film career prospered. Aside from his many roles in underworld films, he displayed impressive acting talent in Dr. Ehrlich's Magic Bullet (1940) and A Dispatch From Reuters (1940), both film biographies.

During the '50s, Robinson's career suffered when he was associated with communist groups in America, but he was cleared of allegations after testifying before the House Un-American Activities Committee.

Robinson was fairly active in films during the '60s, but primarily in supporting roles. He died in 1973, shortly before he was to receive a special Academy Award.

Some of Robinson's many other films include Five Star Final (1931), A Slight Case of Murder (1938), The Amazing Dr. Clitterhouse (1938), Brother Orchid (1940), The Sea Wolf (1941), Double Indemnity (1944), Scarlet Street (1945), All My Sons (1948), Key Largo (1948), House of Strangers (1949), Two Weeks in Another Town (1962), The Cincinnati Kid (1965), Grand Slam (1967), *and* Soylent Green (1973).

O'Keefe plays his son. **Director**—Lewis John Carlino. (PG) **Academy Award Nominations**—Duvall, best actor; O'Keefe, best supporting actor. *115 minutes*

THE GREAT SCOUT AND CATHOUSE THURSDAY (1976)
★

Lee Marvin
Oliver Reed
Kay Lenz

Marvin stars as a legendary vagabond scout out to collect $60,000 from a wealthy ex-friend in Colorado about 1908. The slapstick western comedy tries to reach for the successful *Cat Ballou* brass ring, but falls flat on its face. The film is loaded down with hokey situation gags and a tedious plot. Marvin, however, does a fair enough job as the aging brawler. Also with Robert Culp, Elizabeth Ashley, and Strother Martin. **Director**—Don Taylor. (PG)
102 minutes

THE GREAT TRAIN ROBBERY (1979)
★★★★

Sean Connery
Donald Sutherland
Lesley-Anne Down

Connery plays the charming rascal who pulled off England's first re-
(Continued)

Sean Connery checks his watch while planning a heist in The Great Train Robbery.

---

production. The film is rather uncertain as to its intended audience; some of the humor is childish, but many gags are aimed at adults. The puppet characters perform with a live cast, including Charles Grodin and Diana Rigg. **Director**—Jim Henson. (G)
95 minutes

THE GREAT RACE (1965)
★★

Jack Lemmon
Tony Curtis
Peter Falk
Natalie Wood

The first New York-to-Paris automobile race, set in the early 1900s, is the centerpiece of this comedy; it's uneven and strained, but it manages to offer a few funny moments. Some gimmicky slapstick is notable—a barroom brawl and a climactic pie-throwing melee. But after a while, it becomes tiresome. Lemmon plays Pro-

fessor Fate, a dastardly villain; Curtis is the Great Leslie, a dashing hero in a white suit. Also with George Macready, Ross Martin, Vivian Vance, Keenan Wynn, and Larry Storch. **Director**—Blake Edwards.
150 minutes

THE GREAT SANTINI (1980)
★★★

Robert Duvall
Blythe Danner
Michael O'Keefe

An affecting, modest movie about a gung ho Marine fighter pilot, who presides over his family with the same pile-driving authority he used on his squadron. The setting is peacetime in the early '60s, and the focus is on family stress and a father-son conflict. Duvall plays the title role with a dynamic, overwhelming performance that makes this perplexing character totally believable and moving.

G
• The Great Waldo Pepper
• The Great White Hope
• The Greek Tycoon
• The Green Berets
• Green Dolphin Street
• Green for Danger
• Green Mansions
• Grizzly

(Continued)
corded moving-train heist in 1855. Writer-director Michael Crichton, working from his own best-selling novel, serves up dazzling excitement and spicy wit, wrapped in the elegant detail of early Victorian England. Sutherland is an amusing accomplice, along with Down, who radiates sex appeal and beauty to rival Marilyn Monroe. It's great movie entertainment, alive with classy action and spine-tingling suspense. Also with Alan Webb, Malcolm Terris, and Robert Lang. (PG)   *111 minutes*

THE GREAT WALDO PEPPER (1975)
★★

**Robert Redford
Bo Svenson
Bo Brundin
Susan Sarandon**

A former World War I pilot dreams of air combat against a German ace he never fought during the war. He realizes his dream at last when he gets a stunt-flying job in Hollywood and meets the German—also a stunt pilot. The flying sequences are impressive, but some of the dialogue and events are ludicrous. Redford stars as the pilot. Also with Margot Kidder and Geoffrey Lewis. George Roy Hill directed and produced. (PG)
107 minutes

THE GREAT WHITE HOPE (1970)
★★★★

**James Earl Jones
Jane Alexander**

A high-voltage film biography of Jack Johnson, the black heavyweight boxing great who won the world title in 1908. Jones and Alexander repeat their Broadway roles on screen. The film is faithful to the play, and details much of the pain and humiliation Johnson suffered because of his affair with a white woman, played by Alexander. Jones is magnificent in the central role, nicely portraying this fascinating character. Lou Gilbert, Joel Fleullen, Chester Morris, Robert Webber, and Hal Holbrook star in supporting roles. **Director**—Martin Ritt. (PG) **Academy**

Award Nominations—Jones, best actor; Alexander, best actress.
101 minutes

THE GREEK TYCOON (1978)
★★

**Anthony Quinn
Jacqueline Bisset**

This trashy film blatantly exploits the headlines and gossip columns about Jackie and Aristotle Onassis. The producers obviously spent a fortune on lush settings and fancy clothes, but apparently pinched pennies on a dull script. Quinn and Bisset plod through their roles as the world's most glamorous couple. The supporting cast, including Raf Vallone and Edward Albert, adds to the tedium. **Director**—J. Lee Thompson. (R)   *106 minutes*

THE GREEN BERETS (1968)
★

**John Wayne
David Janssen
Jim Hutton**

This overblown and undernourished war movie, made at the height of the Vietnam war, is nothing more than flagwaving mumbo jumbo at its worst. Wayne plays a Special Forces colonel, with all his gung ho flourishes, leading troops against the enemy. It's a very shallow treatment of an extremely complex situation. Also with Aldo Ray, Raymond St. Jacques, Jack Soo, and Bruce Cabot. **Director**—Wayne.   *141 minutes*

GREEN DOLPHIN STREET (1947)
★★

**Lana Turner
Richard Hart
Donna Reed**

Slick but humdrum period romantic drama set in New Zealand in the 19th century. Turner and Reed play sisters who want to marry the same man. The situation sets off all sorts of absurd complications. The tedium is relieved by a climactic earthquake. Also with Edmund Gwenn and Van Heflin. **Director**—Victor Saville.
141 minutes b&w

GREEN FOR DANGER (1946)
★★★★

**Alastair Sim
Sally Gray
Trevor Howard**

Smartly made whodunit that neatly mixes mystery and comedy in an English hospital during World War II. Sim is at his witty best as a determined detective who nails an operating-table murderer after some careful sleuthing. There's some effective humor at the right moments. The top cast also includes Rosamund John, Leo Genn, Megs Jenkins, and Judy Campbell. **Director**—Sidney Gilliat.
93 minutes b&w

GREEN MANSIONS (1959)
★★

**Anthony Perkins
Audrey Hepburn
Lee J. Cobb**

W. H. Hudson's intriguing romantic fantasy doesn't adapt comfortably to the screen. Perkins plays a young adventurer who enters a South American rain forest, where he encounters a mysterious nature girl and falls in love with her. Hepburn isn't up to the role of Rima, a beautiful nymph dedicated to protecting the jungle wildlife. However, some effective scenes shine through. Also with Sessue Hayakawa and Henry Silva. **Director**—Mel Ferrer.   *104 minutes*

GRIZZLY (1976)
★

**Christopher George
Andrew Prine**

Another shabby attempt to capitalize on the success of *Jaws*. This grizzly weighs a ton and eats young girls, a horse, and some hunters. That's enough reason to give the bear indigestion, close down the national park, and call out the troops, who finish him off with a rocket. There's little in the way of action, suspense, or intelligent dialogue. At least Winnie the Pooh had better manners. Also with Richard Jaeckel and Joan McCall. **Director**—William Girdler. (PG)   *92 minutes*

- The Group
- Guadalcanal Diary
- Guess Who's Coming to Dinner?
- The Gumball Rally
- Gunfight at the OK Corral
- The Gunfighter

G

THE GROUP (1966)
★★★

**Joanna Pettet
Candice Bergen
Jessica Walter
Joan Hackett**

A decent adaptation of Mary McCarthy's novel that overcomes much of the soap-opera aspects of the story. The plot follows the lives of eight women who were graduated from Vassar in 1933. An earnest effort is made to flesh out the characters. Fascinating performances from Pettet, Hackett, Walter, Shirley Knight, and Kathleen Widdoes. Also with Elizabeth Hartman, Larry Hagman, and Hal Holbrook. **Director**—Sidney Lumet. *150 minutes*

GUADALCANAL DIARY (1943)
★★★

**Preston Foster
Lloyd Nolan
William Bendix**

A top World War II action adventure, with the Marines slugging it out to capture a strategic base in the Pacific. It's a bit heavy on the heroics and flag-waving, but that's to be expected from this wartime film, based on Richard Tregaskis's book. The fine cast also includes Richard Conte, Anthony Quinn, and Richard Jaeckel. **Director**—Lewis Seiler. *93 minutes b&w*

GUESS WHO'S COMING TO DINNER? (1967)
★★★★

**Spencer Tracy
Katharine Hepburn
Katharine Houghton
Sidney Poitier**

A wealthy San Francisco white girl (Houghton) becomes engaged to a black man (Poitier), and announces their plans to her parents, who are considered very liberal-minded—or are they? The film is somewhat confined and overly cautious with its touchy subject. However, the picture succeeds primarily because of the adroit performances of Hepburn and Tracy as the perplexed elders. It's their

Hal Holbrook and Shirley Knight in The Group, *based on Mary McCarthy's novel.*

last appearance together, and they present a sumptuous acting feast, indeed. Also with Cecil Kellaway, Beah Richards, and Roy E. Glenn, Sr. **Director**—Stanley Kramer. **Academy Awards**—Hepburn, best actress; William Rose, best story and screenplay (written directly for the screen). **Nominations**—best picture; Kramer, best director; Tracy, best actor; Kellaway, best supporting actor; Richards, best supporting actress. *112 minutes*

THE GUMBALL RALLY (1976)
★

**Michael Sarrazin
Normann Burten
Gary Busey**

Kooky characters from every walk of life race their souped-up vehicles from New York to California in defiance of the 55-mile-an-hour speed limit. The skimpy plot and the adolescent comic situations quickly run out of gas while the autos noisily roar on, leaving a trail of contrived smash-ups. There's a limit to what can be done with scenes of passing cars, and after a while, the film becomes as tedious as a rush-hour traffic jam. **Director**—Chuck Bail. (PG) *107 minutes*

GUNFIGHT AT THE OK CORRAL (1957)
★★★

**Burt Lancaster
Kirk Douglas**

Doc Holiday (Douglas) and Wyatt Earp (Lancaster) team up to take on the Clanton gang. A slick, action-packed western that's a bit overwrought, but delivers the goods with style and suspense. Fine performances by a first-class cast heighten the interest. Also with Rhonda Fleming, Jo Van Fleet, John Ireland, and Lee Van Cleef. **Director**—John Sturges. *122 minutes*

THE GUNFIGHTER (1950)
★★★

**Gregory Peck
Helen Westcott**

Peck is outstanding in this inventive western. He plays a gunfighter who would like to quit, but his past keeps catching up with him. The finely
(Continued)

Poitier, Houghton, and Hepburn in Guess Who's Coming to Dinner?

G·H

- Gunga Din
- The Guns of Navarone
- Guyana: Cult of the Damned
- Guys and Dolls
- Gypsy
- Hail the Conquering Hero
- Hair

(Continued)
crafted screenplay is believable, and it's done with a lot more care than your average shoot-'em-up. Also with Karl Malden, Skip Homeier, Millard Mitchell, and Jean Parker. **Director—** Henry King. **Academy Award Nomination—**William Bowers and André de Toth, writing (motion picture story). *84 minutes b&w*

GUNGA DIN (1939)
★★★★

Cary Grant
Victor McLaglen
Douglas Fairbanks, Jr.
Sam Jaffe

Rudyard Kipling's memorable poem becomes a splendid action adventure with just the right amount of comic touches. Grant, Fairbanks, and McLaglen are comrades-in-arms in India, fighting a native revolt. The film brims with sweeping battle scenes, swashbuckling derring-do, and a cheerful, fun-filled outlook. Director George Stevens coaxes great performances from the entire cast; Jaffe is particularly memorable as the smiling, loyal water boy. Also with Joan Fontaine, Robert Coote, and Edwardo Ciannelli. *117 minutes b&w*

THE GUNS OF NAVARONE (1961)
★★★★

Gregory Peck
David Niven
Stanley Baker
Anthony Quinn

A high-powered World War II action yarn, based on an Alistair MacLean novel, brought off nicely by a top cast.

Gregory Peck (second from right) prepares to lead the mission in The Guns of Navarone.

Allied commandos embark on a do-or-die mission to silence big German guns perched high on a cliff-top fortress along the Aegean Sea. Suspense builds at a near-perfect pace, and it all leads to a ripsnorting, explosive climax. Also with Anthony Quayle, James Darren, Gia Scala, and James Robertson Justice. **Director—**J. Lee Thompson. **Academy Award Nominations—**best picture; Thompson, best director; Carl Foreman, best screenplay (based on material from another medium). *159 minutes*

GUYANA: CULT OF THE DAMNED (1980)
(no stars)

Stuart Whitman
Gene Barry
John Ireland

The mass suicide at Jonestown in Guyana is exploited in this shabby and inept semidocumentary that was hastily put together in Mexico and Panama. There's little effort to explain the reasons for the tragedy, or to probe the cult leader's personality. Scenes are narrated by the off-camera voice of someone described as a cult follower. Whitman plays Jim Johnson (the film's name for Jim Jones). Hollywood notables, such as Joseph Cotten and Yvonne De Carlo, show up in minor roles. **Director—**René Cardona, Jr. (R) *90 minutes*

GUYS AND DOLLS (1955)
★★★★

Frank Sinatra
Marlon Brando
Jean Simmons
Vivian Blaine

An entertaining musical-comedy, based on Damon Runyon's story about a gambler who takes a sucker bet that he can date a prudish Salvation Army girl, played by Simmons. Brando is miscast as the determined Romeo. However, the film succeeds marvelously because of saucy Runyonesque characters, played to the hilt by perfectly cast supporting actors. Sinatra is outstanding as the proprietor of "the oldest established, permanent floating crap game in New York." Also with Stubby Kaye, Sheldon

Leonard, B. S. Pully, Robert Keith, and George E. Stone. **Director—** Joseph L. Mankiewicz. *149 minutes*

GYPSY (1962)
★★

Rosalind Russell
Natalie Wood

Undernourished musical taken from the Broadway production about the career of Gypsy Rose Lee and her energetic stage mother. The main problem is Wood in the title role; she's an unlikely stripteaser, indeed. The Jule Styne-Stephen Sondheim score is appealing, but it sounded better on the stage. Russell is okay as the mother, but the part was made for Ethel Merman, who brought the character to life on Broadway. Also with Karl Malden and James Milhollin. **Director—**Marvyn Le Roy. *149 minutes*

H

HAIL THE CONQUERING HERO (1944)
★★★★

Eddie Bracken
Ella Raines
William Demarest

Rip-roaring satire, starring Bracken as a military reject who is thought to be a war hero when he returns to his small-town home. This hearty comedy tickles the funnybone and offers some serious points to ponder as well. All hail writer-director Preston Sturges for a first-class job. There are effective supporting roles by Demarest, Raines, Franklin Pangborn, Raymond Walburn, and Alan Bridge. **Academy Award Nomination—**Sturges, writing (original screenplay). *101 minutes b&w*

HAIR (1979)
★★★

John Savage
Treat Williams
Beverly D'Angelo

Director Milos Forman reworks the

- The Hallelujah Trail
- Halloween
- Halloween II
- Halls of Montezuma
- Hamlet
- The Hand
- Handle With Care
- Hangar 18

H

Treat Williams dances at a high-society party in this scene from Hair.

'60s "tribal love-rock musical" with effective screen results. The film is sometimes incoherent and slow-paced, but the big musical numbers burst forth with energy and euphoria. There are some impressive show-stoppers, such as a song-and-dance sequence when the flower children break up a high-society party. Also with Annie Golden, Dorsey Wright, and Don Dacus. (PG)   *121 minutes*

THE HALLELUJAH TRAIL (1965)
★

Burt Lancaster
Lee Remick

Lancaster and Remick star in this heavy-going comedy-western that seems to plod on forever. Lancaster rides shotgun on a shipment of whiskey bound for Denver, and Remick is a temperance crusader with other ideas for the booze. A band of Indians also want to get their hands on the goods. The humor never clicks, and Remick and Lancaster seem ill at ease with the material. If you can sit through nearly three hours of this nonsense, then hallelujah! Also with Brian Keith, Jim Hutton, Donald Pleasence, and Martin Landau. **Director**—John Sturges.
167 minutes

HALLOWEEN (1978)
★★

Donald Pleasence
Jamie Lee Curtis

A maniac escapes from a mental hospital to stalk and kill young women on Halloween night. The silly script offers minimal logic, but there are scares and suspense galore. Director John Carpenter builds the terrifying atmo-

sphere with deft skill. The cast is mainly composed of novice actors. Curtis, daughter of Tony Curtis and Janet Leigh, is effective as an intended victim. Also with Nancy Loomis and P. J. Soles. (R)   *93 minutes*

HALLOWEEN II (1981)
★★

Donald Pleasence
Jamie Lee Curtis

More corpses pile up in this sequel, as a zombielike maniac prowls the corridors of a small hospital and performs gruesome unauthorized surgery on the staff. Plenty of inventive tricks heighten suspense and induce scares, but the film also drips with unnecessary gore and features a mechanical style of dispatching victims. Once again, scream-queen Curtis is pursued and terrorized, and narrowly escapes. Pleasence co-stars as a beleagured psychiatrist. **Director**—Rick Rosenthal. (R)   *92 minutes*

HALLS OF MONTEZUMA (1950)
★★

Richard Widmark
Jack Palance

The Marines hit the beaches in the Pacific during World War II and defeat the enemy in a blaze of heroics. The film is recruiting-poster stuff, with lots of comic-book-type action and characterizations to match. It's all done to the beat of the Marine Corps Hymn. Widmark and Palance head the competent cast, which also includes Reginald Gardiner, Robert Wagner, Karl Malden, Richard Boone, Skip Homeier, and Jack Webb. **Director**—Lewis Milestone.   *113 minutes*

HAMLET (1948)
★★★★

Laurence Olivier
Eileen Herlie
Basil Sydney
Jean Simmons

Even if you find Shakespeare heavy going, you'll probably appreciate this absorbing screen version of his magnificent play. Olivier stars as the melancholy Dane, and it's one of the

greatest film performances of all time. Direction, also by Olivier, is on target, too; he presents the great drama with clarity and effective moody atmospherics. The Bard of Avon himself would be proud of this fine movie. Also with Felix Aylmer and Norman Wooland. **Academy Awards**—best picture; Olivier, best actor. **Nominations**—Olivier, best director; Simmons, best supporting actress.
153 minutes b&w

THE HAND (1981)
★★★

Michael Caine

Clever, stylish psychological thriller about a cartoonist, played by Caine, whose severed hand becomes a symbol of uncontrolled rage and frustration. The disembodied hand, lost in an auto accident, follows Caine from location to location, perpetrating a chain of murderous events. The film is heavily laced with Freudian clichés, yet it's an impressive showcase for Caine's solid, unwavering performance. Oliver Stone wrote and directed this feature with amazing skill. (R)   *104 minutes*

HANDLE WITH CARE (1977)
★

Paul Le Mat
Candy Clark

This slaphappy comedy revolves around the Citizens Band radio craze, and it borrows much of its style from *American Graffiti*. The film is cluttered with numerous plotlets, which give it a muddled tone. The script mainly involves the problems of a bigamous trucker and a lad who tries to enforce the regulations governing CB radio operation. Also with Ann Wedgeworth and Marcia Rodd. **Director**—Jonathan Demme. (PG) **Alternate Title**—*Citizens Band*.   *98 minutes*

HANGAR 18 (1981)
★

Darren McGavin
Robert Vaughn

The U.S. Air Force captures a flying saucer and hides it from the public,
(Continued)

H
- Hang 'em High
- The Hanging Tree
- Hanover Street
- Hans Christian Andersen
- The Happiest Days of Your Life
- Happy Birthday, Gemini

(Continued)

thus causing assorted crises for government agencies and many lost lives. The main reason for such super-secrecy, according to this pretentious movie, is fear that the President—facing an election—would lose credibility if he revealed the spacecraft's existence. The not-so-special effects include scenes of the UFO, which look as if they were taken from close-ups at a five-and-dime toy department. It's a close encounter of the absurd kind. Also with Gary Collins. **Director**—James L. Conway. (PG) *93 minutes*

HANG 'EM HIGH (1968)
★★

Clint Eastwood
Inger Stevens
Ed Begley

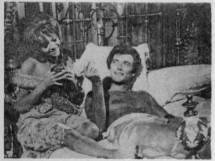

Arlene Golonka and Clint Eastwood in Hang 'em High, *a western about revenge.*

Eastwood stars as a victim of a lynching party who survives the noose and then sets out for revenge on the nine men who tried to kill him. The film offers a double dose of brutality, much in the manner of a spaghetti western. The slick production moves along fairly well, with adequate performances throughout. Also with Pat Hingle, James MacArthur, Arlene Golonka, Bruce Dern, and Dennis Hopper. **Director**—Ted Post. (PG) *114 minutes*

THE HANGING TREE (1959)
★★★

Gary Cooper
Maria Schell

A doctor who murdered his philandering wife tries to get his life back on track in a Montana frontier mining town. Cooper plays the doctor. Along the way, he helps a blind girl, played by Schell. It's an intelligent western drama, enhanced by fine photography and realistic background detail. Cooper is impressive in this serious portrayal. Also with George C. Scott, Karl Malden, and Ben Piazza. **Director**—Delmer Daves. *106 minutes*

HANOVER STREET (1979)
★

Harrison Ford
Lesley-Anne Down

An American bomber pilot has a secret love affair with a married British nurse amid the London blitz of 1943. Ford is the pilot; Down plays the nurse. More tears and war-film clichés fall than enemy bombs in this unbelievable turkey. Such excess sentimentality may have worked during the frantic World War II years, but now this sort of mush seems absurd. The acting doesn't help the limp screenplay by writer-director Peter Hyams. (PG) *105 minutes*

HANS CHRISTIAN ANDERSEN (1952)
★★★

Danny Kaye

Kaye is ideally suited to the title role in this appealing children's fantasy, about a poor shoemaker-storyteller who makes dancing slippers for a ballerina and then falls in love with her. The colorful production comes across with a thick coating of sugar, yet the score is appealing. Danny sings such favorites as "Thumbelina" and "Ugly Duckling." Jeanmaire, Farley Granger, and John Qualen co-star. **Director**—Charles Vidor. *112 minutes*

THE HAPPIEST DAYS OF YOUR LIFE (1950)
★★★★

Alastair Sim
Margaret Rutherford
Joyce Grenfell

A cast of great British character players has a field day with this energetic comedy. There are fun and laughs galore when some schoolgirls are mistakenly quartered at a boy's boarding school. A first-rate, effective adaptation for the screen of John Dighton's popular post-war play. Also with Richard Wattis, Guy Middleton, Muriel Aked, and Edward Rigby. **Director**—Frank Launder. *81 minutes b&w*

HAPPY BIRTHDAY, GEMINI (1980)
★

Rita Moreno
Madeline Kahn

A shrill and, at times, offensive screen version of the award-winning Broadway comedy, *Gemini*. It's about a college student from a working-class Italian-American family, who faces a

Danny Kaye plays the title role in Hans Christian Andersen, *a children's fantasy.*

- Happy Birthday to Me
- The Happy Ending
- The Happy Hooker
- The Happy Hooker Goes to Washington
- The Happy Time
- Happy Times
- Hardcore
- A Hard Day's Night
- The Harder They Fall
- Hardly Working

H

sexual identity crisis. The characters, which fit comfortably on stage, are blown out of proportion on the screen, with much overacting and screaming at one another. Kahn and Moreno are wasted in leading roles. Director Richard Benner guides the film with the grace of a drunken sailor. Also with Robert Viharo and Alan Rosenberg. (R)   *112 minutes*

HAPPY BIRTHDAY TO ME (1981)
★

Melissa Sue Anderson

A muddled, listless teenage horror story involving six gory killings at a snobbish prep school. Students are brutally murdered at regular intervals by various means, including a shish kebab skewer jammed down a young man's throat. At the center of this mayhem is a frantic young girl, played by Anderson, who once had a birthday party and all the invited guests failed to show. The performances are consistently second-rate, and the method of resolving the murder mystery only adds to the confusion. **Director**—J. Lee Thompson. (R)   *120 minutes*

THE HAPPY ENDING (1969)
★★

Jean Simmons
John Forsythe

Simmons is convincing as a frustrated woman who chucks her marriage of 16 years to find a new life. This glossy production transcends its soap-opera mentality with an adequate number of interesting moments. The top cast also include Shirley Jones, Lloyd Bridges, Teresa Wright, Dick Shawn, Nanette Fabray, Bobby Darin, and Tina Louise. **Director**—Richard Brooks. **Academy Award Nomination**—Simmons, best actress.   *112 minutes*

THE HAPPY HOOKER (1975)
★★

Lynn Redgrave
Jean-Pierre Aumont

This story about Xaviera Hollander, distinguished by Lynn Redgrave's excellent characterization, is a comedy about greed and lust with some amusing behind-the-scenes looks at the kinky world of hookers. Also with Lovelady Powell and Nicholas Pryor. **Director**—Nicholas Sgarro. (R)   *96 minutes*

THE HAPPY HOOKER GOES TO WASHINGTON (1977)
★

Joey Heatherton

This is a second shabby screen installment, loosely based on the life of Xaviera Hollander, the notorious madame. Heatherton, in the title role, is hardly convincing. While bit players in the film unblushingly shed their clothes, Joey stays modestly covered. The plot, involving sexual escapades in the nation's capital, is absurd and adolescent. George Hamilton and Phil Foster also star. **Director**—William Levey. (R)   *89 minutes*

THE HAPPY TIME (1952)
★★★

Charles Boyer
Louis Jourdan

A nifty family situation comedy concerning the day-to-day lives of French Canadians in the 1920s. Boyer is appealing as the father of this odd-ball group, involved in various comic interpersonal relationships. Jourdan plays an uncle. It's smartly directed by Richard Fleischer, with pleasant performances all around. Others in the cast include Bobby Driscoll, Linda Christian, and Marsha Hunt.   *94 minutes b&w*

HAPPY TIMES
See The Inspector General

HARDCORE (1979)
★★★

George C. Scott
Peter Boyle

A religious businessman from Grand Rapids, Michigan, searches for his teenage daughter who has fallen in with pornographic filmmakers. The businessman is played by Scott. Boyle plays a hardboiled detective who helps in the search. Writer-director Paul Schrader gives us a hard-hitting, vivid tour of the sleazy sex-for-sale underworld. He also presents a chilling contrast between complacent Middle American culture and the seamy big-city jungle. Boyle and Scott are convincing in this intelligent drama, which contains some heart-rending moments. Also with Season Hubley, Dick Sargent, and Leonard Gaines. (R)   *108 minutes*

A HARD DAY'S NIGHT (1964)
★★★★

The Beatles

The Beatles—George, Paul, John, and Ringo—star in this surprisingly sensational comedy, which revolves around their hectic schedule during a trip to London. The mop tops demonstrate that they can excell at clowning as well as singing, and the madcap affair comes off with enormous energy and good humor. There's also plenty of favorite Beatle songs. Wilfred Brambell and Victor Spinetti co-star. **Director**—Richard Lester.   *85 minutes b&w*

THE HARDER THEY FALL (1956)
★★★

Humphrey Bogart
Rod Steiger

Bogart is reliably good, as a press agent who blows the whistle on unethical dealings in the prizefight business. The searing drama, based on Budd Schulberg's novel, is sympathetic to athletes who are controlled by selfish managers. Steiger is also on board with a decent acting job. This is Bogey's last feature film. Also stars Jan Sterling, Mike Lane, and Max Baer. **Director**—Mark Robson.   *109 minutes b&w*

HARDLY WORKING (1981)
★★

Jerry Lewis

Lewis brings back his familiar repertoire of slapstick comedy in this story of a circus clown who loses his job and then bungles his way through a variety of other occupations. There are a
(Continued)

H
- ● Hard Times
- ● Harlan County, U.S.A.
- ● Harold and Maude
- ● Harper
- ● Harper Valley PTA

(Continued) few amusing episodes, but much of the humor is repetitious and merely desperate. Some of the gags are recycled from his earlier movies, and many of the new routines are uninspired. Scattered about are some serious moments that don't seem to fit in this confusing and uneven movie. **Director**—Lewis. (PG) *91 minutes*

HARD TIMES (1975)
★★★

Charles Bronson
James Coburn

It's 1936, the midst of the Depression. The place: New Orleans. Bronson plays a moody, silent loner who earns a living—such as it is—by illegal bare-knuckle prizefighting. It's a gripping and exciting action drama that's also frequently funny. Coburn does well as the shifty fight manager. Also with Jill Ireland and Strother Martin. A winning debut by director Walter Hill. (PG) *97 minutes*

HARLAN COUNTY, U.S.A. (1976)
★★★★

This powerful, passionate documentary about a strike by coal miners has as much excitement going as any fictional drama. It's a pro-miner film that mainly revolves around a brutal confrontation in Brookside, Kentucky, in 1973. The film also illuminates a broader portrait of perilous mining conditions over the years and the corruption of some elements of organized labor and some managements. It's an impressive debut for Barbara Kopple who directed the project during a three-year period. (No MPAA rating) **Academy Award**—documentary feature. *103 minutes*

HAROLD AND MAUDE (1972)
★★★

Bud Cort
Ruth Gordon

A nutty black comedy that has evolved into a cult film. Cort plays a strange young man who often contemplates

ROBERT DE NIRO

Robert De Niro was born in New York City's tough Lower East Side, in Little Italy, in 1945. As a child, he was extremely shy, but, at the age of 10, he played the role of the Cowardly Lion in a school production of The Wizard of Oz.

By 16, De Niro had dropped out of high school and had earned his first paycheck on a tour of high schools in the New England and New York area in Chekov's The Bear. *He then spent 15 years learning his craft from such drama teachers as Stella Adler, Luther James, Lee Strasberg's Actors' Studio, and the American Workshop.*

De Niro made his motion picture debut in The Wedding Party *(1969), directed by Brian De Palma. He co-starred with Shelley Winters in* Bloody Mama *(1970) for producer Roger Corman. In 1971, he made* The Gang That Couldn't Shoot Straight, *the film that first showed he was star material. He then received recognition for his performance as the dying ballplayer in* Bang the Drum Slowly *(1973). Also released that same year was Martin Scorsese's* Mean Streets, *a powerful film that won him the best supporting actor award of the New York Film Critics Circle.*

Some of De Niro's other movies include The Godfather—Part II *(1974),* Taxi Driver *(1976),* The Deer Hunter *(1978),* Raging Bull *(1980), and most recently* True Confessions *(1981). De Niro won an Academy Award for his portrayal of middleweight boxing champion Jake La Motta in* Raging Bull.

death. He pals around with an equally odd 79-year-old adventurous woman, hilariously portrayed by Gordon. The two fall in love; she shows him a picture of herself and it's a sunflower; she commits suicide but shows him how to live. Weird as it is, this campy outing is done with style, wit, and spirit, thanks to an inventive screenplay by Colin Higgins and Hal Ashby's perceptive direction. Also with Vivian Pickles, Cyril Cusack, Charles Tyner, and Ellen Geer. (PG) *92 minutes*

HARPER (1966)
★★★

Paul Newman
Lauren Bacall

A fast-paced detective yarn somewhat on the order of Bogart-type gumshoe capers of the '40s. It's based on John Ross MacDonald's novel *The Moving Target.* Director Jack Smight strains to capture the *film noir* flavor, but doesn't quite succeed; however, the fine cast carries it along in high style. Newman is Lew Harper, a private eye hired to track down the missing husband of a rich California woman, played by Bacall. He's a slick bird dog who gets himself into a variety of scrapes along the way. Other players include Julie Harris, Shelley Winters, Janet Leigh, Robert Wagner, and Arthur Hill. *121 minutes*

HARPER VALLEY PTA (1979)
★★★

Barbara Eden
Ronny Cox
Nanette Fabray

Inspired by the '60s pop tune of the same name, this light comedy pokes fun at snootiness and hypocrisy. Eden plays the sexy mom in miniskirts who wreaks revenge on some stuffy PTA board members in Harper Valley, Ohio. Most of the gags work quite well; an especially funny scene has three pink elephants marching in on astonished town drunkard Pat Paulsen. Also with Susan Swift, Louis Nye, and John Fiedler. **Director**—Richard Bennett. (PG) *93 minutes*

- Harry and Tonto
- Harry and Walter Go to New York
- Harvey
- The Harvey Girls
- The Hasty Heart
- A Hatful of Rain
- Hawaii

H

HARRY AND TONTO (1974)
★★★

Art Carney
Ellen Burstyn

After being evicted, a New York senior citizen and his cat Tonto take a sentimental journey to Chicago, and a variety of funny and sad episodes occur along the way. Carney, in the title role, makes the character shine with affection and pathos. It's a lovely trip that never runs out of interesting events and scenery. There's good support from Burstyn, Chief Dan George, Geraldine Fitzgerald, and Larry Hagman. **Director**—Paul Mazursky. (PG) **Academy Award**—Carney, best actor. **Nomination**—Mazursky and John Greenfeld, best original screenplay.
115 minutes

HARRY AND WALTER GO TO NEW YORK (1976)
★

James Caan
Elliott Gould

Caan and Gould play a couple of talentless vaudeville entertainers named Harry and Walter, who go to New York to organize the heist of a Massachussetts bank. What's supposed to be funny turns out pathetic and embarrassing; like The Three Stooges, Caan and Gould scream, jump, pinch, and pull each other's ears, and strain their professional reputations. There's also clumsy direction by Mark Rydell. New York is in enough trouble; Harry and Walter should have stayed home. Also with Michael Caine, Diane Keaton, and Charles Durning. (PG)
123 minutes

HARVEY (1950)
★★★★

James Stewart
Josephine Hull

Mary Chase's touching play about a middle-aged tippler with an imaginary huge white rabbit as his companion comes to the screen with all the wonderful dialogue and memorable moments firmly in place. Stewart is wonderful as the gentle Elwood P.

In Harvey, James Stewart is a tippler who's pals with a huge imaginary white rabbit.

Dowd, under pressure by his relatives to enter a mental hospital. Hull also stands out as the perplexed sister who is constantly apologizing for Dowd's nutty behavior. The engrossing story wisely questions the true definition of insanity. There are other good performances from Victoria Horne, Peggy Dow, Cecil Kellaway, and Jesse White. **Director**—Henry Koster. **Academy Award**—Hull, best supporting actress. **Nomination**—Stewart, best actor.
104 minutes b&w

THE HARVEY GIRLS (1946)
★★★

Judy Garland
Ray Bolger

A delightful musical about young women who go west to be waitresses for a 19th-century restaurant chain operating in frontier communities. Much of the script is nonsense, but this drawback is more than redeemed by good performances and a memorable score. "Atchison, Topeka and the Santa Fe" is among the songs. Garland and Bolger head the fine cast, which also includes John Hodiak, Preston Foster, Angela Lansbury, and Marjorie Main. **Director**—George Sidney.
101 minutes

THE HASTY HEART (1949)
★★★

Richard Todd
Patricia Neal

Touching story about an overbearing Scottish soldier who's brought to an army hospital in Burma. The attitudes toward him drastically change when

it's discovered that he will soon die. Todd is especially convincing as the young trooper. The film is based on John Patrick's play, which worked slightly better on the stage. Other cast members include Ronald Reagan and Orlando Martins. **Director**—Vincent Sherman. **Academy Award Nomination**—Todd, best actor.
104 minutes b&w

A HATFUL OF RAIN (1957)
★★★

Eva Marie Saint
Don Murray

A powerful story about a young man, played by Murray, who becomes addicted to drugs, and how his deteriorating condition affects his family and friends. Fine acting by a competent cast highlights this searing drama, which was one of the first to examine addiction with intelligence and understanding. Based on Michael V. Gazzo's Broadway play. Also with Anthony Franciosa, Lloyd Nolan, and Howard da Silva. **Director**—Fred Zinnemann.
109 minutes b&w

HAWAII (1966)
★★★

Max Von Sydow
Julie Andrews
Richard Harris

Mammoth film epic based on portions of James Michener's ambitious historical novel, about the intrusion of western culture on native Hawaiians in the early 1800s. The narrative flow is handled in a choppy fashion, but the acting is adequate, and the production is presented with lavish care. Von Sydow stars in the key role of a young missionary who tries to impose his
(Continued)

Jocelyn Lagarde gives it to Max Von Sydow in the epic film Hawaii.

(Continued)

religious dogma on the islanders. Also with Jocelyn Lagarde, Carroll O'Connor, and Gene Hackman. **Director—** George Roy Hill. **Academy Award Nominations**—Jocelyn Lagarde, best supporting actress; Russell Harlan, cinematography (color). *186 minutes*

THE HAWAIIANS (1970)
★★

Charlton Heston
Tina Chen
Geraldine Chaplin

This continuation of the James Michener chronicle brings the story up to the 1900s. However, this portion doesn't work too well, because the spectacular production takes in too many episodes in one bite. Heston stars as a businessman who comes to the islands and encounters a mixture of good fortune, disease, revolution, destruction, and anguish over morality. The huge cast also includes John Philip Law, Mako, Alec McCowen, and Ann Knight. **Director—**Tom Gries. (PG) *132 minutes*

HAWMPS! (1976)
★

James Hampton
Christopher Connelly
Slim Pickens

Slapstick comedy of the Old West, when camels were briefly used in Texas to replace U.S. Cavalry horses. Adults will probably find the film tiresome, but there are plenty of laughs for the kids. There's a big saloon brawl, a comic shootout, and a camel vs. horse race. But it all drags on for nearly two hours, and even the youngsters will begin to nod at the end. Also with Jack Elam and Denver Pyle. Produced and directed by Joe Camp, who also presented *Benji*. (G) *113 minutes*

HEAD OVER HEELS (1979)
★★

John Heard
Mary Beth Hurt

Joan Micklin Silver's adaptation of Ann Beattie's novel *Chilly Scenes of Winter* is a rather uninteresting movie about some uninteresting people. Charles, played by Heard, is a bachelor who has a dull job as a reports analyst. He falls in love with a librarian, played by Hurt, who is married to a dull husband. There's a lot of cutesy dialogue. He wins her. He loses her. He wins her back again. After a while, who cares? Also with Peter Riegert and Kenneth McMillan. (PG) *97 minutes*

THE HEARSE (1980)
★★

Trish Van Devere
Joseph Cotten

Van Devere plays a daring divorcée who moves into an old house, and before long she's up to her neck with wicked ghosts from the past. Among the evil demons who pursue her is the chauffeur of the vehicle from the film's title. Cotten is effective as a grumpy lawyer who presents obstacles to Van Devere's taking legal possession of the house. The film offers enough frightening moments, but it's really just another routine twist to the haunted-house movie. Also with Perry Lang. **Director—**George Bowers. (PG) *95 minutes*

HEART BEAT (1980)
★★

Nicky Nolte
Sissy Spacek
John Heard

The '50s beat generation is explored rather timidly in this biographical film about novelist Jack Kerouac (*On the Road*) and his friends Neal and Carolyn Cassady. The story is engaging and stylish at times, as it delves into the nonconforming life-styles of the characters. But too often the loosely constructed movie wanders off the road and fritters away dramatic impact. Nolte, as the freewheeling Neal Cassady, turns in a sizzling performance that provides some much-needed energy. Spacek plays Carolyn, and Heard plays Kerouac. **Director—** John Byrum. (R) *109 minutes*

HEARTBEEPS (1981)
★

Andy Kaufman
Bernadette Peters

A romantic comedy about robots that seems to have been written by a computer and could only be appreciated by someone with a mechanical brain. Kaufman and Peters play amorous robots who meet at a repair facility and venture into the wide world where they encounter similar creatures. One of them, called "Catskill," spouts Henny Youngman one-liners; another is "Crimebusters," which looks like a tank. There's enough mechanical corn generated here to overload anyone's memory bank. **Director—**Allan Arkush. (PG) *88 minutes*

THE HEARTBREAK KID (1972)
★★★★

Charles Grodin
Cybill Shepherd
Jeannie Berlin

Neil Simon's compelling screenplay, based on Bruce Jay Friedman's play, is alternately funny and sad—but either way, it cuts to the bone. Grodin plays a cocky young man on his honeymoon, who abruptly abandons his bride to pursue a seemingly more attractive girl. The situation is outrageous, but it's carried off with intelligence and played to the hilt for impact. Berlin is effective as the ditched newlywed, and Shepherd is fine as the new love interest. Eddie Albert and Audra Lindley have good supporting roles. **Director—**Elaine May. (PG) **Academy Award Nominations**—Albert, best supporting actor; Berlin, best supporting actress.

106 minutes

THE HEART IS A LONELY HUNTER (1968)
★★★

Alan Arkin
Sondra Locke

Arkin gives a moving performance as a kindhearted deaf-mute who resides in a small southern town. Based on the compelling novel by Carson McCul-

● Heartland
● Hearts of the West
● Heaven Can Wait
● Heaven Knows, Mr. Allison
● Heaven's Gate
● Heavy Metal

H

lers, the film sensitively touches on isolation and cruelty. Locke plays a girl who befriends Arkin. It's all brought together nicely by a professional cast that also includes Stacy Keach, Cicely Tyson, and Laurinda Barrett. **Academy Award Nominations**—Arkin, best actor; Locke, best supporting actress. *125 minutes*

HEARTLAND (1981)
★★★

Conchata Ferrell
Rip Torn

The stars of Heartland, *a film chronicling pioneer life in 1910 America.*

Plucky spirit of American pioneer life is richly portrayed in this low-budget but handsomely made film chronicle set in 1910. The unpretentious story concerns a poor young widow, played by Ferrell, who signs on as housekeeper for a stoic Wyoming rancher, played by Torn, and eventually marries him. Megan Folsom plays Ferrell's daughter. All performances are remarkable, and the directing effort by Richard Pearce—his first—beautifully captures the challenges and hardships of frontier life without being overly sentimental. Also with Barry Primus and Lilia Skala. (PG) *93 minutes*

HEARTS OF THE WEST (1975)
★★★★

Jeff Bridges
Alan Arkin
Andy Griffith

A warm, merry movie about an Iowa farm boy who goes to Hollywood in the '30s to become a cowboy actor and write western movies. Bridges plays the hero with style and charm, and there are other excellent performances

by Arkin and Griffith. The film is artistically directed by Howard Zieff, who has a keen appreciation of moviemaking of that era. In all, it's a well-blended mixture of color, romance, suspense, nostalgia, and comedy. Also with Blythe Danner, Donald Pleasence, and Richard B. Schull. (PG) *102 minutes*

HEAVEN CAN WAIT (1978)
★★★★

Warren Beatty
Julie Christie
Jack Warden
Dyan Cannon

Beatty's remake of the 1941 comedy-drama *Here Comes Mr. Jordon* is a cheerful gem of a movie, brimming with priceless moments and inspired dialogue. It's about an enthusiastic football quarterback who dies prematurely and returns to earth as a powerful industrialist. Beatty is sensational in the leading role and works harmoniously with the marvelous cast. Although the film is a retread, it's contemporary in most respects and shines with its own madcap personality; it satisfies. Also with Charles Grodin, James Mason, Buck Henry, and Vincent Gardenia. (PG) **Academy Award Nominations**—best picture; Beatty and Henry, best director; Beatty, best actor; Warden, best supporting actor; Cannon, best supporting actress; Elaine May and Beatty, best screenplay adaptation; William Fraker, cinematography. *100 minutes*

In Heaven Can Wait, *Warren Beatty plays an athlete who's summoned before his time.*

HEAVEN KNOWS, MR. ALLISON (1957)
★★★

Robert Mitchum
Deborah Kerr

Mitchum and Kerr perform well together in this mildly preposterous and predictable film. The story is set on a Pacific island during World War II. He's a gruff Marine corporal; she's a mild-mannered nun; together they conspire to outfox the Japanese. Doesn't this seem a little like *The African Queen?* John Huston directs with style and skill. *105 minutes*

HEAVEN'S GATE (1981)
★★

Kris Kristofferson
Isabelle Huppert
Christopher Walken
John Hurt

Michael Cimino's $40-million epic western about 1890 Johnson County, Wyoming, cattle wars is still muddled and overblown despite improvements from editing and voice-over narration. Kristofferson stars as a Harvard-educated federal marshal, who sides with poor settlers marked for search-and-destroy extermination by wealthy landowners. His role and others are ill-defined and mostly incoherent. It seems as if Cimino's theme of the corrupting influence of money and power has also corrupted the movie itself. (R) *219 minutes*

HEAVY METAL (1981)
★

A brash, crude animated anthology, based on the grotesque fantasy magazine. The various segments deal with sword-and-sorcery, violence, sex, science fiction, drugs, and mysticism—all tied together with ear-blasting rock music. Those who like that sort of thing might enjoy it. The cartoon fantasies are bridged by a luminous green ball that represents evil. It's a heavy trip that begins with a bang and gradually runs out of energy. **Director**—Gerald Potterton. (R) *90 minutes*

H
- Hedda
- The Heiress
- He Knows You're Alone
- Hellfighters
- Hell Night
- Hello, Dolly!

HEDDA (1976)
★★

Glenda Jackson

The talented Jackson dominates this film version of Ibsen's *Hedda Gabler* with a steely and intelligent performance, playing the bored and impatient woman who wrecked the lives of the men who pursued her. It's a first-class acting job, but the movie itself is stale and unmoving. Trevor Nunn directed and wrote the screenplay, based on the Royal Shakespeare production. The transferral from stage presentation to screen is strained. Also with Peter Eyre and Jennie Linden. (PG) *104 minutes*

THE HEIRESS (1949)
★★★★

Olivia de Havilland
Montgomery Clift

De Havilland is brilliant as a plain, lonely, but rich spinster who is wooed by a sly, charming fortune-seeker, played by Clift. The smartly styled film, set in turn-of-the-century New York, is based on Henry James's play, *Washington Square*. All parts are played out nicely, with Ralph Richardson, Miriam Hopkins, Vanessa Brown, Mona Freeman, and Ray Collins in supporting roles. **Director**—William Wyler. **Academy Award**—De Havilland, best actress. **Nominations**—best picture; Wyler, best director; Richardson, best supporting actor; Leo Tover, cinematography (black and white).
115 minutes b&w

HE KNOWS YOU'RE ALONE (1980)
★

Don Scardino
Caitlin O'Heaney

This is a cheaply made horror film that concentrates on mindless bloodletting and gore and ignores logic. A knife-wielding maniac carves up brides-to-be. The bodies quickly pile up and so do the flaws, such as shabby acting, clumsy pacing, and shallow character development. This nonsense was put together by novice director Armand Mastroianni, who is said to be a cousin of the well-known Italian actor. (R)
92 minutes

HELLFIGHTERS (1969)
★★

John Wayne
Jim Hutton
Katharine Ross

This sophomoric action yarn about rough-tough men who battle oil-well fires is upgraded a half-notch by the presence of Wayne. Big John leads his crew against the flames and finds time to deal with woman problems, too. Some action scenes have noticeable class. Also with Vera Miles, Bruce Cabot, and Barbara Stuart. **Director**—Andrew V. McLaglen. (G) *121 minutes*

HELL NIGHT (1981)
★

Linda Blair

This film is more teenage love-and-terror fare, cranked off the Hollywood-horror assembly line with a minimum of inspiration and talent. Some fraternity pledges spend their initiation night at a haunted house where survivors of a family murder 12 years ago take their revenge on the youths. The usual head-choppings and other gory deaths go on until most of the kids are eliminated. Blair is the only familiar player, and she escapes the massacre. **Director**—Tom DeSimone. (R) *101 minutes*

HELLO, DOLLY! (1969)
★★★

Barbra Streisand
Walter Matthau
Michael Crawford

Big, brassy musical, based on the Broadway success about a New York matchmaker in the early 1900s who ends up getting married herself. Streisand plays the title role in her usual powerhouse style, but she's obviously too young for the part. However, all is forgiven when she turns up the volume and belts out some enjoyable songs with exceptional gusto. Louis Armstrong is on board, too, adding immeasurably to the frolic. Armstrong and Streisand team up to sing the title song. The film is based on Thornton Wilder's play *The Matchmaker*. Other cast members include E. J. Peaker and Marianne McAndrew. **Director**—Gene Kelly. (G) **Academy Award Nominations**—best picture; Harry Stradling, cinematography. *129 minutes*

Barbra Streisand (center) conspires to match two couples in Hello, Dolly!

● Hellzapoppin
● Hennessy
● Henry V
● Herbie Goes Bananas
● Herbie Goes to Monte Carlo
● Here Comes Mr. Jordan
● Here Comes the Tigers

H

HELLZAPOPPIN (1941)
★★★

Ole Olsen
Chic Johnson

Olsen and Johnson present a screen version of their madcap Broadway burlesque show, and the results are pleasingly funny. The zany duo decides to make a movie, and they cook up their own plot as they progress. A few gags misfire, but most of them score high on the laugh meter. It's great fun if you enjoy the '40s-era brand of humor. The supporting cast also features Hugh Herbert, Martha Raye, and Mischa Auer. **Director**—H. C. Potter. *84 minutes b&w*

HENNESSY (1975)
★★

Rod Steiger

A peace-loving Irishman, whose wife and child have been accidentally killed in a battle in Belfast, renounces his pacifism and seeks revenge on the Royal Family and the British Parliament. Steiger plays the title role. It's a slow-moving melodrama that exploits rather harmlessly one's emotions about assassination. There are several unbelievable situations, such as the ease with which Steiger assumes the identity of a Member of Parliament he has kidnapped. There is some clever use of newsreel footage of the Royal Family in conjunction with the fictional story. Also with Lee Remick, Trevor Howard, and Richard Johnson. **Director**—Don Sharp. (PG) *103 minutes*

HENRY V (1946)
★★★★

Laurence Olivier
Robert Newton

No one does Shakespeare like Olivier, and he triumphs here as both director and lead actor. The production is presented as an example of a play at the Globe Theatre in the early 1600s, and then it brilliantly evolves as a contemporary screen rendition. Olivier's acting is magnificent, and the film offers many glorious moments; the battle scenes, splendidly photographed in color, are engrossing. It's a masterpiece of moviemaking. Also with Leslie Banks, Esmond Knight, Leo Genn, Renée Asherson, and Ralph Truman. **Director**—Olivier. **Academy Award Nominations**—best picture; Olivier, best actor. *137 minutes*

HERBIE GOES BANANAS (1980)
★★

Cloris Leachman
Charles Martin Smith
Harvey Korman

The fourth chapter in Disney's adventures of the lovable and almost-human Volkswagen Beetle has Herbie on a trip to Latin America where he (it) engages in a bullfight and, as expected, foils the bad guys. The initial *Love Bug* film was a hit and subsequent installments were relatively successful, but alas, Herbie has run out of gas. The gags are rather familiar by now and generate only minimal amusement. **Director**—Vincent McEveety. (G) *100 minutes*

HERBIE GOES TO MONTE CARLO (1977)
★★

Dean Jones
Don Knotts
Julie Sommers

Herbie, the lovable Volkswagen Beetle with a mind of its own, is the star of this third in the series of *Love Bug* movies. This time, Herbie is involved in a European auto race, and falls for a cute blue Lancia named Giselle. The formula Disney slapstick is guaranteed to produce squeals from the small fry; there's some nice scenery for the adults. Also with Roy Kinnear and Jacque Marin. **Director**—Vincent McEveety. (G) *91 minutes*

HERE COMES MR. JORDAN (1941)
★★★★

Robert Montgomery
Evelyn Keyes

This is an inventive comedy-fantasy about a boxer who dies in a plane crash by mistake, and is sent to Earth

Robert Montgomery and Edward Everett Horton in Here Comes Mr. Jordan.

to occupy someone else's body. Montgomery plays the prizefighter who dies before his time. The film's novel twist about heaven and death works on many levels and sustains interest and comic vitality to the end; the theme has been reused in many subsequent movies. Also with Claude Rains, Rita Johnson, Edward Everett Horton, James Gleason, and Donald MacBride. **Director**—Alexander Hall. **Academy Award**—Harry Segall, writing (original story). **Nominations**—best picture; Hall, best director; Montgomery, best actor; Gleason, best supporting actor; Joseph Walker, cinematography (black and white). *93 minutes b&w*

HERE COME THE TIGERS (1978)
★

Richard Lincoln
James Zvanut
Samantha Grey

This is a low-budget spinoff from *The Bad New Bears*; it strains at slapstick, but doesn't deliver. This warmed-over copy of the Little League epic has a kid karate champ and a deaf pitcher who bring the team success. An unfamiliar cast of meager talent plods through the acting chores with minimal energy. These Tigers are merely pussycats. Also with William Caldwell and Manny Lieberman. **Director**—Sean S. Cunningham. (PG) *90 minutes*

H
- Here Come the Waves
- A Hero Ain't Nothin' But a Sandwich
- Hero at Large
- Heroes
- Hester Street
- The Hiding Place
- Hide in Plain Sight
- The High and the Mighty

HERE COME THE WAVES (1944)
★★★

Bing Crosby
Betty Hutton

Bouncy World War II musical morale-builder, with Crosby in the Navy and romancing identical twin Waves. Hutton plays the twins. As expected, there's not much plot, but there are plenty of good songs. Bing sings "Accent-tchu-ate the Positive" and more. Sonny Tufts co-stars in his first singing role. Also with Ann Doran and Gwen Crawford. **Director**—Mark Sandrich.
98 minutes b&w

A HERO AIN'T NOTHIN' BUT A SANDWICH (1978)
★

Cicely Tyson
Paul Winfield
Larry B. Scott

This frank family film, about a 13-year-old boy who grapples with a drug problem, is made in the tradition of such films as *Sounder* and *Lilies of the Field*. Tyson and Winfield give decent performances, but they're often upstaged by Scott, 16, as the intelligent but troubled youth. Scott knows how to turn on the charm and warmth at the correct moments. The movie, however, is preachy and pedantic. Also with Helen Martin and Glynn Turman. **Director**—Ralph Nelson. (PG)
105 minutes

HERO AT LARGE (1980)
★★

John Ritter
Anne Archer

Ritter of TV's *Three's Company* plays a struggling actor in New York City, who becomes an instant hero when he foils a robbery attempt. At the time, he was wearing a comic-book hero outfit for a movie promotion. Ritter is at his easygoing best, as the young man in the superhero suit who can save the world. But midway, the script runs out of steam, and what charm there is deteriorates into excessive sentimentality. Unfortunately, a good idea gets pushed too far. Archer plays the girl next door. Also with Kevin McCarthy. **Director**—Martin Davidson. (PG)
98 minutes

HEROES (1977)
★

Henry Winkler
Sally Field

Winkler and Field co-star in this erratic and poorly written story about the escapades of a troubled Vietnam veteran. Winkler, making his film debut, has trouble shaking off his television image of "The Fonz" and adapting to the big screen. Field, however, evokes energy and charm in her part as Winkler's companion. The film comes off as an exhausting commercial television drama, which doesn't work well. Also with Harrison Ford and Val Avery. **Director**—Jeremy Kagan. (PG)
113 minutes

HESTER STREET (1975)
★★★

Stevens Keats
Carol Kane

Joan Micklin Silver wrote and directed this compassionate movie about Jewish immigrants struggling to adapt to the New World at the turn of the century. The story concerns a young immigrant, played by Keats, who is charmed with the ways of his new country. His wife, played by Kane, arrives later with their son and finds assimilation painful. The plot is familiar, but the performances are keen and extraordinary. Also with Mel Howard, Dorrie Kavanaugh, and Doris Roberts. Mostly in Yiddish with English titles. (PG) **Academy Award Nomination**—Kane, best actress. *92 minutes b&w*

THE HIDING PLACE (1975)
★

Julie Harris
Eileen Heckart
Arthur O'Connell

This film, elaborately produced by the Billy Graham Association, is based on a true account of a Dutch Christian family who led an underground operation in Holland to assist Jews during World War II. Here is a splendid opportunity to develop an exciting and moving movie; instead, the film plods along somewhat in the manner of an overlong sermon. The action hardly gets moving in situations that must have been suspenseful indeed. Also with Jeanette Clift and Robert Rietty. Filmed in the Netherlands and Great Britain. **Director**—James F. Collier. (PG)
145 minutes

HIDE IN PLAIN SIGHT (1980)
★★

James Caan
Jill Eikenberry

Caan directs and stars in this restrained drama about a divorced factory worker's frustrating efforts to locate his children, who are in hiding under the government's Witness Relocation Program, which is designed to protect witnesses from criminal retaliation. This is Caan's directorial debut, and he handles the assignment at a sluggish pace. The film, based on a true story, needs a shot of adrenalin. But the supporting cast is especially good, and Caan manages to depict ordinary people with authenticity. Also with Robert Viharo, Kenneth McMillan, and Danny Aiello. (PG)
91 minutes

THE HIGH AND THE MIGHTY (1954)
★★★★

John Wayne
Robert Newton
Robert Stack

A gripping drama about a crippled airliner trying to reach safety during a long flight over the Pacific. The nervous passengers, contemplating a crash-landing in the ocean, reveal their emotions. Wayne is effective as a co-pilot who keeps his cool. See *Airplane* for a terrific parody of this pioneer *Airport* film. Also with Doe Avedon, Claire Trevor, Laraine Day, Jan Sterling, Phil Harris, Sidney Blackmer, and David Brian. **Director**—William Wellman. **Academy Award Nominations**—Wellman, best director; Claire Trevor, Jan Sterling, best supporting actress. *147 minutes*

- High Anxiety
- High-Ballin'
- High Barbaree
- High Noon
- High Plains Drifter
- High Risk
- High Sierra
- High Society

H

HIGH ANXIETY (1978)
★★★

**Mel Brooks
Madeline Kahn
Cloris Leachman
Harvey Korman**

Comedy maestro Brooks parodies Alfred Hitchcock suspense films, such as *Psycho* and *Vertigo*, with glee while also spoofing modern psychiatry. The howls and belly laughs of his *Blazing Saddles* are missing, but there are ample zany comic situations from beginning to end. Brooks is director, producer, star, and even songwriter. Korman, Leachman, and Kahn chip in with funny performances. It's a sure cure for anyone's blues, blahs, or anxiety. Also with Dick Van Patten, Ron Carey, and Howard Morris. (PG)
94 minutes

HIGH-BALLIN' (1978)
★★

**Peter Fonda
Jerry Reed**

Fonda and Reed are good guys who fight a gang of hijackers trying to put the squeeze on independent truckers. The action-adventure sends 18-wheelers careening through snowstorms in some daring chase scenes. The dialogue is rather pat, and the story line isn't original, but there's lots of flashy action along with some decent performances. Also with Helen Shaver and Chris Wiggins. Filmed in Canada. **Director**—Peter Carter. (PG)
100 minutes

HIGH BARBAREE (1947)
★★

**Van Johnson
June Allyson**

Two Navy pilots crash in the Pacific Ocean, and one reveals the story of his life while they wait for rescue. It's a rather flimsy story featuring a decent cast, and it can't sustain itself because of poor dialogue and a lack of inspired plotting. Also with Thomas Mitchell and Marilyn Maxwell. **Director**—Jack Conway.
91 minutes b&w

HIGH NOON (1952)
★★★★

**Gary Cooper
Grace Kelly**

Gary Cooper and Grace Kelly embrace in High Noon, *one of the period's best westerns.*

One of the best westerns of the period, with tight-lipped Cooper doing a sensational job as a determined lawman who bravely faces the bad guys alone when the town's citizens cop out. The production is well done, with suspense mounting in well-paced steps. It's high drama, indeed. Kelly is memorable as Coop's bride-to-be, and there's fine support from Thomas Mitchell, Lloyd Bridges, Otto Kruger, Lon Chaney, Katy Jurado, and Henry Morgan. **Director**—Fred Zinnemann. **Academy Award**—Cooper, best actor. **Nominations**—best picture; Zinnemann, best director; Carl Foreman, writing (screenplay).
85 minutes b&w

HIGH PLAINS DRIFTER (1973)
★★

**Clint Eastwood
Verna Bloom**

Eastwood is the director and star of this overly violent western. He plays a mysterious drifter who comes to a small town, terrorizes the people, and then stays on to shoot it out with some criminals just out of jail. The half-serious, semi-supernatural film comes off as a parody of Eastwood's own style. Also with Marianna Hill, Mitchell Ryan, Jack Ging, and Stefan Gierasch. (PG)
105 minutes

HIGH RISK (1981)
★★★

**James Brolin
Bruce Davison
Chick Vennera
Cleavon Little**

A clever, lighthearted adventure about four "nice guys" who steal $5 million from a Columbian drug kingpin and then encounter unexpected obstacles during their escape. Writer-director Stewart Raffill offers an efficient script with a proper portion of humor amid the action. The film is nicely cast, with Brolin, Davison, Vennera, and Little as the unlikely heroes, and James Coburn, Ernest Borgnine, and Anthony Quinn in effective cameo roles. (R)
94 minutes

HIGH SIERRA (1941)
★★★

**Humphrey Bogart
Ida Lupino**

An interesting crime drama about a veteran gangster, played by Bogart, operating in the California mountain country. The cliché-laden script stays above water thanks to Bogey's fine performance as Mad Dog Earle, a ruthless killer who can muster some moments of kindness. Lupino is his moll. Also with Joan Leslie, Alan Curtis, Arthur Kennedy, Henry Hull, and Henry Travers. **Director**—Raoul Walsh.
100 minutes b&w

HIGH SOCIETY (1955)
★★★

**Bing Crosby
Grace Kelly
Frank Sinatra
Celeste Holm**

This musical version of *The Philadelphia Story* comes over well despite some heavy-going moments. Crosby stars as a man of means who tries to stop his ex-wife, played by Kelly, from remarrying. Sinatra and Holm play reporters who becomes involved in the affair.
(Continued)

H
- The Hindenburg
- His Girl Friday
- His Majesty O'Keefe
- History of the World—Part I
- Hitler
- Hobson's Choice
- Hold Back the Dawn
- Holiday Inn

(Continued)
Cole Porter's score adds pleasure to the proceedings. Also stars Louis Armstrong, Louis Calhern, John Lund, and Sidney Blackmer. **Director**—Charles Walters.   *107 minutes*

THE HINDENBURG (1976)
★★

George C. Scott
Anne Bancroft
Burgess Meredith

This is a disaster formula movie about the German dirigible that exploded while docking at Lakehurst, New Jersey, in 1937. The special effects are impressive, and for some this alone may prove worthwhile, but the script slowly blimps along, and the suspense is lighter than air. Scott stars as a Nazi security agent on board to identify a possible saboteur. Also with William Atherton, Roy Thinnes, Charles Durning, and Gig Young. **Director**—Robert Wise. (PG)   *125 minutes*

HIS GIRL FRIDAY (1940)
★★★★

Rosalind Russell
Cary Grant

A howlingly funny version of *The Front Page*, brought off at a fast clip and with a cast of pros giving it their all. Grant is great as a scheming editor. Russell is a riot as a prima donna reporter—in the Hildy Johnson role—tracking down a murder story. Lots of good live-wire supporting players add to the fun. Also with Ralph Bellamy, Gene Lockhart, Porter Hall, Ernest Truex, Clarence Kolb, Roscoe Karns, and Billy Gilbert. **Director**—Howard Hawks.   *92 minutes b&w*

HIS MAJESTY O'KEEFE (1953)
★★

Burt Lancaster

Lancaster swashbuckles around some islands in the South Seas helping the natives fend off pirates. Adequate action and a bit of romance make up the adventure film, but Lancaster doesn't reach his full potential here. Also with Joan Rice, André Morell,

Benson Fong, Philip Ahn, and Grant Taylor. **Director**—Byron Haskin.
92 minutes

HISTORY OF THE WORLD— PART I (1981)
★★★

Mel Brooks
Dom DeLuise
Madeline Kahn
Harvey Korman

Gregory Hines and Mel Brooks take on Nero's legions in History of the World—Part I.

Funnyman Brooks rewrites history with comic pokes at the Roman Empire, the Spanish Inquisition, and the French Revolution. Brooks stars in various roles and generates a fair portion of belly laughs and inspired comic situations. However, many skits are undermined by excessive crudeness. The comedy is rather uneven, so Brooks earns only a "B" for his history report. **Director**—Brooks. (R)
92 minutes

HITLER (1961)
★★

Richard Basehart

Basehart stars in the title role as the bloodthirsty Nazi fuhrer. The film traces Hitler's career from his early adult life to his defeat and suicide in his Berlin bunker. This film biography treads rather lightly on a subject that deserves more insight, and Basehart isn't all that convincing as the

mad dictator. Others in the cast include Mario Emo, Martin Kosleck, and John Banner. **Director**—Stuart Heisler.   *107 minutes b&w*

HOBSON'S CHOICE (1954)
★★★

Charles Laughton
Brenda de Banzie
John Mills

Laughton sparkles in this family comedy, based on a play by Harold Brighouse, as a strong-willed boot-smith in the 1890s who tries to control the lives of his daughters. It's a breezy and spirited film, played in the best style of British humor. All of the performances fall nicely into place. Also with Richard Wattis and Daphne Anderson. **Director**—David Lean.
107 minutes b&w

HOLD BACK THE DAWN (1941)
★★★

Charles Boyer
Olivia de Havilland

Boyer is in top form as a refugee from Nazi Germany who marries a schoolteacher in Mexico merely to gain entrance to the United States. De Havilland plays the teacher. It's a moving wartime melodrama, stylishly produced and heightened by fine acting and direction. The cast also includes Paulette Goddard, Victor Francen, Walter Abel, and Rosemary De Camp. **Director**—Mitchell Leisen. **Academy Award Nominations**—best picture; De Havilland, best actress; Leo Tover, cinematography (black and white).   *115 minutes b&w*

HOLIDAY INN (1942)
★★★

Bing Crosby
Fred Astaire

Crosby sings and Astaire dances up a storm in this colorful musical. The routine romantic plot concerns competition between partners of a hotel—Crosby and Astaire—for the attention of a woman. However, the magnificent Irving Berlin score is the real cause for interest here, with Bing crooning "White Christmas." Also with Walter Abel, Marjorie Reynolds, Virginia Dale, and Louise Beavers. **Director**—Mark Sandrich. **Academy Award Nomination**—Berlin, writing (original story).   *101 minutes*

HOLLYWOOD BOULEVARD (1977)
★

Candice Rialson

Here's a grade-B movie that's a spoof of grade-B movies. The result: just another shabby and silly grade-B movie from the Roger Corman factory. Rialson stars as an aspiring actress who breaks into low-budget films and becomes involved with a number of perilous situations, including some bizarre murders. Also with Mary Woronov and Rita George. **Directors**—Joe Dante and Allan Arkush. (R)   *83 minutes*

HOLLYWOOD CANTEEN (1944)
★★

Joan Leslie
Robert Hutton
Dane Clark
Janis Paige

A galaxy of Hollywood stars make guest appearances in this review of the entertainment community's supporting efforts during World War II. Some of the music is pleasant, but the story goes nowhere. It's about a soldier hankering for a date with a pretty girl. Other luminaries include Joan Crawford, Bette Davis, the Andrews Sisters, Jack Benny, Eddie Cantor, Roy Rogers, Sidney Greenstreet, Peter Lorre, and Barbara Stanwyck. **Director**—Delmer Daves.
123 minutes b&w

THE HOLLYWOOD KNIGHTS (1980)
★★

Fran Drescher
Stuart Pankin
Tony Danza

California teenagers pull off some outrageous monkeyshines on Halloween night in 1965 to protest the closing of their favorite drive-in restaurant. Most
(Continued)

Bing Crosby, Marjorie Reynolds, and Fred Astaire in the colorful musical Holiday Inn.

BETTE DAVIS

Bette Davis, who was the queen of the movie box office in the late '30s and throughout most of the '40s, was born Ruth Elizabeth Davis in 1908 in Lowell, Massachusetts. In high school, her ambition was to be an actress, but her initial attempts to succeed in this profession were met with disappointment.

During 1930, she was turned down by MGM, but eventually she was granted some small parts at Universal. At Warner Brothers, her career began to improve as the result of hard work and her demands for better parts, but she continued to work in many films that were beneath her talents.

She began to be accepted as an actress of star quality in 1935 when she earned an Oscar for Dangerous, but she was later suspended by Warners for rejecting a role, and she went to England to star in some films there. The studio enforced its contract, but after the legal battles, Davis was offered better roles.

Her career prospered throughout the '40s and most of the '50s, as she primarily played the formidable and bitchy woman who cherished her independence.

In the late '50s, her career faltered, but she made an amazing comeback in the early '60s with effective portrayals in What Ever Happened to Baby Jane? (1962), and Hush . . . Hush, Sweet Charlotte (1964).

Davis won the American Film Institute's Life Achievement Award in 1977, the first woman to attain the honor.

Some of her memorable films include Of Human Bondage (1934); The Petrified Forest (1936); Jezebel (1938), for which she received an Oscar; The Little Foxes (1941); All About Eve (1950); and Death on the Nile (1978).

H
- The Hollywood Strangler
- Hombre
- Home of the Brave
- Hondo
- Honeysuckle Rose
- Honky Tonk Freeway
- Hooper

Robert Wuhl makes an unscheduled appearance at a school function in The Hollywood Knights.

(Continued)

of the pranks are aimed at harassing authoritative adults. A few jokes go over, but much of the movie, which looks like a combination of *American Graffiti* and *Animal House*, is merely ill-conceived silliness. Also with Robert Wuhl and Michelle Pfeiffer. **Director**—Floyd Mutrux. (R)   *91 minutes*

THE HOLLYWOOD STRANGLER
See Don't Answer the Phone

HOMBRE (1967)
★★★

Paul Newman
Diane Cilento
Fredric March

An engrossing western drama, starring Newman as a young white man brought up by Indians. The film picks up steam when Newman boards a stagecoach and helps the passengers in an encounter with outlaws. An

In the engrossing western drama Hombre, *Paul Newman holds bandits at bay.*

intelligent script and interesting characterizations mix well with suspense and action. There's also a thread of moral considerations running through the production. Also with Richard Boone, Martin Balsam, Barbara Rush, and Cameron Mitchell. **Director**—Martin Ritt.   *111 minutes*

HOME OF THE BRAVE (1949)
★★★

Frank Lovejoy
Lloyd Bridges

A compelling drama set during World War II, about a black soldier who suffers from the intolerance of his white fellow comrades-in-arms. The film had more impact at the time of its release, but it's still watchable. Based on the play by Arthur Laurents. Also with James Edwards, Jeff Corey, and Steve Brodie. **Director**—Mark Robson.
86 minutes b&w

HONDO (1953)
★★★

John Wayne
Geraldine Page

An out-of-the-ordinary western drama about a cavalry soldier who discovers a widow and her son living in an isolated part of Texas and stays to defend them against an Indian attack. Wayne plays the solider, of course. Violence is toned down and warm characterizations are played up in this interesting story that takes on some of the aspects of *Shane*. Page is excellent in her film-debut role as the plucky widow. Ward Bond, James Arness, and Michael Pate also star. Originally a 3-D film. **Director**—John Farrow. **Academy Award Nomination**—Page, best supporting actress.   *84 minutes*

HONEYSUCKLE ROSE (1980)
★★

Willie Nelson
Dyan Cannon
Amy Irving
Slim Pickens

Nelson picks a mean guitar and sings rousing country-western songs. He does a lot of that rather well in this

Slim Pickens looks on as Willie Nelson slakes his thirst in Honeysuckle Rose.

film, but when the music stops there's only a wisp of a plot—mostly borrowed from *Intermezzo*—about Nelson's infidelity while on the road. The scenario is a rather dull hillbilly soap opera. Cannon plays the long-suffering wife and sings country with style and gusto. **Director**—Jerry Schatzberg. (PG)   *119 minutes*

HONKY TONK FREEWAY (1981)
★

Beau Bridges
William Devane

Director John Schlesinger (*Midnight Cowboy*) can't deliver the goods in this uneven, silly, and meandering comedy. The flimsy story mainly concerns efforts of citizens to secure a highway off-ramp at their small Florida town. Meanwhile, the film detours all over the country collecting some uninteresting people—and some animals—who finally converge on this community. Everyone has a few gags to play with, but most fall flat. (R)
107 minutes

HOOPER (1978)
★★

Burt Reynolds
Jan-Michael Vincent
Sally Field

Reynolds plays the greatest Hollywood stuntman of his time; he's being challenged by a younger man, played by Vincent. This movie-within-a-movie should please most fans of Reynolds, who plays his raucous, wise-guy char-

- Hopscotch
- The Horn Blows at Midnight
- The Hospital
- Hotel Paradiso

- Hothead
- Hot Lead and Cold Feet
- Hot Potato
- Hot Stuff

H

acter to the hilt. There's a variety of well-executed stunts—car crashes, a chariot race, and a helicopter jump. However, the pedestrian story takes the edge off the action, and many of the stunts have been performed in other films. By now, they look familiar and unexciting. Also with Brian Keith and John Marley. **Director**—Hal Needham. (PG)   *100 minutes*

HOPSCOTCH (1980)
★★

Walter Matthau
Glenda Jackson

Matthau stars as a disillusioned CIA agent who writes an embarrassing exposé about his bumbling colleagues and then leads them on a cat-and-mouse chase. The ever-appealing Matthau gives it his rumpled best, with Jackson adding a touch of class as his wily accomplice. The film can't seem to make up its mind whether it's a comedy or a drama. At times, the mood is straightforward, but then the movie lapses into silly slapstick. Also with Ned Beatty. **Director**—Ronald Neame. (R)   *104 minutes*

THE HORN BLOWS AT MIDNIGHT (1945)
★★

Jack Benny
Alexis Smith

Benny stars in this slapstick farce as an angel assigned to destroy Earth with blasts from Gabriel's horn. Benny took delight in panning this film, but it's a lot better than he made it out to be. The plot leans heavily on *Here Comes Mr. Jordan*. Also with Franklin Pangborn, Guy Kibbee, Dolores Moran, Reginald Gardiner, and Margaret Dumont. **Director**—Raoul Walsh.
          78 minutes b&w

THE HOSPITAL (1971)
★★★★

George C. Scott
Diana Rigg

A biting black comedy that firmly skewers incompetence and misman-agement within the medical profession as seen at a large city hospital. Paddy Chayefsky's award-winning screenplay digs into its subject with the force of a jackhammer, as a series of mishaps cause chaos and death. Scott is magnificent as a disillusioned chief doctor, and he gets plenty of professional support. Also with Barnard Hughes, Richard Dysart, and Nancy Marchand. **Director**—Arthur Hiller. (PG) **Academy Award**—Chayefsky, best story and screenplay (based on factual material or material not previously published). **Nomination**—Scott, best actor.   *101 minutes*

HOTEL PARADISO (1966)
★★

Alec Guinness
Gina Lollobrigida

A capable cast flounders around in this uneven romantic farce, set in Paris at the turn of the century. The story concerns various love affairs and comic mix-ups at a seedy hotel. The production is handsomely mounted, but the direction leaves much to be desired. Also with Robert Morley, Akim Tamiroff, and Peggy Mount. **Director**—Peter Glenville.
          96 minutes

HOTHEAD
See Coup de Tête

HOT LEAD AND COLD FEET (1978)
★★

Jim Dale
Darren McGavin
Karen Valentine

This comedy western by the Disney studio plods along on its flat feet, trying to amuse the kids and adults; it generally fails in both categories. British comic Dale plays three characters, a cantankerous old land dealer and his two sons, who compete for their inheritance. Don Knotts and Jack Elam are on board with top billing, but actually they're assigned to cameo roles. **Director**—Robert Butler. (G)
          90 minutes

HOT POTATO (1976)
★

Jim Kelly
George Memmoli
Geoffrey Binney

A chop-socky adventure with a half-baked plot, concerning the rescue of a U.S. Senator's daughter who is held captive in a Southeast Asian country. A trio of American special agents, sent in for the retrieval, kick and karate-chop their way through hordes of Oriental bad guys. The action is a let-down compared with most kung fu productions; *Hot Potato* is just a lot of cold borsht. Directed and written by Oscar Williams. (PG)   *87 minutes*

HOT STUFF (1979)
★★★

Dom DeLuise
Suzanne Pleshette
Jerry Reed

A surprised Dom DeLuise and an amused Jerry Reed; they play cops in Hot Stuff.

DeLuise directs and stars in this good-natured screwball comedy about some Miami cops who catch petty thieves through a fencing front. The script is silly and predictable, but DeLuise has assembled a fine cast of character actors to help him keep the fun and laughter perking from start to finish. It's the style of visual slapstick in which DeLuise excels, and he often steals the show. Pleshette and Reed do well as his partners in the undercover setup. Also with Luis Avalos and Ossie Davis. (PG)   *87 minutes*

H
- Houdini
- Houseboat
- The House by the Lake
- House Calls
- A House Is Not a Home
- House of Frankenstein
- House of Usher
- House of Wax

HOUDINI (1953)
★★★

**Tony Curtis
Janet Leigh**

Straight-down-the-middle film biography of the famous escape artist, with Curtis handling the title role with skill. The story, however, seems embellished some to underline the romantic aspects of Houdini's life. Interest is constantly maintained as Houdini gets involved with more and more difficult tricks. Leigh is good as the ever-faithful wife. Torin Thatcher and Sig Rumann also star. **Director**—George Marshall. *106 minutes*

HOUSEBOAT (1958)
★★★

**Cary Grant
Sophia Loren**

Grant and Loren make the sparks fly in this predictable but charming comedy. He's a widower residing in a houseboat with three children. She comes on board as a maid and provides some motherly love for the kids, yet she's really a woman with social standing. Guess who falls in love with whom? Martha Hyer, Eduardo Ciannelli, and Harry Guardino perform very well in supporting roles. **Director**—Melville Shavelson. **Academy Award Nomination**—Jack Rose and Shavelson, best story and screenplay (written directly for the screen). *110 minutes*

THE HOUSE BY THE LAKE (1977)
★★

**Brenda Vaccaro
Don Stroud**

A grisly suspense drama about four sadistic punks who terrorize a playboy dentist and his girl friend at a remote hideaway in Ontario, Canada. This mindless exploitation of bloody violence depicts a rape and deaths by drowning, fire, slashed throat, and shotgun. The cast is convincing, especially Stroud as the leader of the hoodlums and Vaccaro as the rape victim who eventually gets revenge. But there's too much emphasis on wanton terror as a form of entertainment. Also with Chuck Shamata and Richard Ayres. Written and directed by William Fruet. **Alternate Title**—*Death Weekend*. (R) *89 minutes*

HOUSE CALLS (1978)
★★★

**Walter Matthau
Glenda Jackson
Art Carney
Richard Benjamin**

Glenda Jackson keeps Walter Matthau on his toes in the romantic comedy House Calls.

A lightweight romantic comedy that is firmly secured with the charm of Matthau and the steel demeanor of Jackson. Matthau is good as a middle-aged swinging surgeon—recently widowed—who falls for strong-minded Jackson—recently divorced. The uneven script has a moderate case of the clichés, but the one-liners and laughs roll along with ease. Carney gets some mileage out of his part as the senile chief of surgery. Also with Candice Azzara and Dick O'Neill. **Director**—Howard Zieff. (PG) *98 minutes*

A HOUSE IS NOT A HOME (1964)
★

**Shelley Winters
Robert Taylor**

This is a film biography of Polly Adler, New York's notorious madame. The shabby-looking production is brought off in a most dreary manner—no style and scant energy. Polly herself would surely be disappointed. Also with Broderick Crawford and Cesar Romero. **Director**—Russell Rouse. *198 minutes b&w*

HOUSE OF FRANKENSTEIN (1944)
★★★

**Boris Karloff
John Carradine
Lon Chaney, Jr.**

Universal Pictures once more rallies its monsters for sinister work. Karloff stars as an evil scientist and manager of a freak show who rejuvenates Frankenstein's creation and the Wolf Man and sets out to pay back those who crossed him. A regular cast of horror heavies gives it their best shot. Also with George Zucco, J. Carrol Naish, and Lionel Atwill. **Director**—Erle C. Kenton. *71 minutes b&w*

HOUSE OF USHER (1960)
★★★

Vincent Price

Effective horror tale based on the classic Edgar Allen Poe chiller. Price heads the cast as a member of Usher, the family involved in various forms of madness and terror. Director Roger Corman puts it together with impressive style. Also with Myrna Fahey, Mark Damon, and Harry Ellerbe. *79 minutes*

HOUSE OF WAX (1953)
★★★

**Vincent Price
Carolyn Jones**

Vincent Price, in the wheelchair, stars in House of Wax. *Recognize Charles Bronson?*

- The House on 92nd Street
- How Green Was My Valley
- The Howling
- How the West Was Won

- How To Beat the High Cost of Living
- How To Marry a Millionaire
- How To Murder Your Wife

H

Adequate remake of *The Mystery of the Wax Museum*, with Price striking terror into the hearts of the innocent. He effectively plays the owner of a wax museum. After it's destroyed in a fire, he rebuilds his exhibit using dead bodies. The film was initially shot in 3-D, and many of the gimmicks have this process in mind. Also with Phyllis Kirk, Frank Lovejoy, Paul Picerni, and Charles Buchinski (Bronson). **Director**—André de Toth.   *88 minutes*

THE HOUSE ON 92nd STREET (1945)
★★★★

William Eythe
Lloyd Nolan
Signe Hasso

A fast-paced spy thriller set in New York City during World War II, with the FBI bearing down on Nazi agents seeking to steal atomic bomb secrets. This is a smartly styled production that effectively uses a combination of documentary technique and exciting drama. It set the trend for subsequent "realistic" films like *The Naked City*. Also with Gene Lockhart and Leo G. Carroll. **Director**—Henry Hathaway. **Academy Award**—Charles G. Booth, writing (original story). *88 minutes b&w*

HOW GREEN WAS MY VALLEY (1941)
★★★★

Walter Pidgeon
Maureen O'Hara
Roddy McDowall
Donald Crisp

Touching and heartwarming drama of life in a Welsh coal-mining town. The plot is rather flat, but memorable and moving moments abound. Much effort was lavished on exquisite production detail, giving eloquent class to the film, which is based on Richard Llewellyn's novel. Cast also includes Barry Fitzgerald, Sara Allgood, and John Loder. **Director**—John Ford. **Academy Awards**—best picture; Ford, best director; Crisp, best supporting actor; Arthur Miller, cinematography (black and white). **Nominations**—Allgood, best supporting actress; Philip Dunne, writing (screenplay). *118 minutes b&w*

THE HOWLING (1981)
★★

Dee Wallace

A tongue-in-cheek horror film where practically the entire cast turns into yelping werewolves. Wallace plays an attractive TV reporter who goes to a secluded Esalen-like spa to unwind. Before long, she's face-to-face with monstrous werewolves who seem to pop out of the woodwork. A hat tip to special-effects whiz Rob Bottin for creating the scary, blood-drooling beasts with menacing fangs and hairy skulls. As for the acting and silly script, there's nothing to howl about. **Director**—Joe Dante. (R)   *92 minutes*

HOW THE WEST WAS WON (1963)
★★

Debbie Reynolds
Carroll Baker
Lee J. Cobb
Henry Fonda

Overlong, over-cast epic that follows the pioneering efforts of several generations of an adventurous farming family from New England across the continent. The trail is strewn with clichés and half-baked episodes. The production, however, is done lavishly, but such lavishness loses impact on TV screens. Cast also includes Karl Malden, Carolyn Jones, Gregory Peck, George Peppard, James Stewart, and John Wayne. Spencer Tracy narrates. **Directors**—Henry Hathaway, John Ford, and George Marshall. **Academy Award**—James R. Webb, best story and screenplay (written directly for the screen). **Nominations**—best picture; William H. Daniels, Milton Krasner, Charles Lang, Jr., and Joseph LaShelle, cinematography (color). *155 minutes*

HOW TO BEAT THE HIGH COST OF LIVING (1980)
★★

Susan Saint James
Jessica Lange
Jane Curtin

Three seemingly respectable young women burglarize a shopping mall because inflation has deflated their life-styles. This listless comedy is a variation of *Fun With Dick and Jane*, but hardly as funny. Rising prices are no laughing matter, especially in this film. Saint James, Curtin, and Lange play the bungling, thieving threesome who pull off the caper. Also with Richard Benjamin and Eddie Albert. **Director**—Robert Scheerer. (PG)   *110 minutes*

HOW TO MARRY A MILLIONAIRE (1953)
★★★

Lauren Bacall
Marilyn Monroe
Betty Grable
William Powell

Fun-filled comedy with Bacall, Monroe, and Grable perfectly cast as schemers out to trap wealthy men as husbands. The stars lend plenty of sparkle to the amicable proceedings, set in New York City, and there are plenty of lavish settings to heighten the frolic. It all leads to a happy ending, with the girls getting more than they intended. Also with Cameron Mitchell, David Wayne, and Rory Calhoun. **Director**—Jean Negulesco. *96 minutes*

HOW TO MURDER YOUR WIFE (1965)
★★★★

Jack Lemmon
Virna Lisi
Terry-Thomas

Smart, sophisticated comedy with wry comic situations clicking off nicely at a fast pace. Lemmon is great as a bachelor comic-strip writer who wakes up one morning after a wild party to find himself unexpectedly married to beautiful Lisi. He thinks of ways to get rid of her. And when she vanishes, the police believe he murdered her. A top supporting cast contributes to the fun. Eddie Mayehoff plays a lawyer friend, and Terry-Thomas is a wise-cracking butler. Sidney Blackmer and Clair Trevor also star. It's murderously funny. **Director**—Richard Quine. *118 minutes*

H
- How To Succeed in Business Without Really Trying
- The Hucksters
- Hud
- The Human Comedy
- The Human Factor (1975)
- The Human Factor (1980)
- Humanoids From the Deep

HOW TO SUCCEED IN BUSINESS WITHOUT REALLY TRYING (1967)
★★★★

Robert Morse
Rudy Vallee
Michele Lee

Morse superbly repeats his Broadway role as an ambitious window washer who gets to be president of a large corporation through cunning rather than energy and talent. Many of the delights from the stage musical, based on Shepard Mead's book, are kept intact. Frank Loesser's songs are appealing, and the effective gags fall into place with perfection. A success, indeed. Also with Anthony Teague and Maureen Arthur. **Director**—David Swift. *119 minutes*

THE HUCKSTERS (1947)
★★★

Clark Gable
Deborah Kerr
Ava Gardner

The advertising business is skewered in this impressive film drama based on Frederic Wakeman's insightful novel. Gable does well as an advertising executive who becomes frustrated by questionable methods of the profession; Sidney Greenstreet is nicely cast as a tyranical soap company president. The story gets to the point and stays there. Also with Adolphe Menjou, Keenan Wynn, and Edward Arnold. **Director**—Jack Conway. *115 minutes b&w*

HUD (1963)
★★★★

Paul Newman
Patricia Neal
Melvyn Douglas

Newman gives an excellent character portrayal as the irresponsible son of a hardworking Texas rancher. The powerful film takes a hard look at interpersonal family relationships and the deterioration of moral values. Neal stands out as the wise housekeeper who readily perceives the complex problems; Douglas is also fine as the

Robert Morse (left) in How To Succeed in Business Without Really Trying.

harassed father. Martin Ritt's direction hits the mark. Also with Brandon de Wilde and John Ashley. **Academy Awards**—Neal, best actress; Douglas, best supporting actor; James Wong Howe, cinematography (black and white). **Nominations**—Martin Ritt, best director; Paul Newman, best actor; Irving Ravetch and Harriet Frank, best screenplay (based on material from another medium).
112 minutes b&w

THE HUMAN COMEDY (1943)
★★★

Mickey Rooney
Frank Morgan
James Craig

This screen adaptation of William Saroyan's novel is moving although it goes overboard at times with sentimentality. Touching characterizations are simply portrayed in this slice of life in small-town America during World War II. Rooney heads the cast of what seems to be a version of the *Andy Hardy* series. Also with Marsha Hunt,

Mickey Rooney (right) heads the cast of The Human Comedy.

Fay Bainter, Van Johnson, and Donna Reed. **Director**—Clarence Brown. **Academy Award**—Saroyan, writing (original story). **Nominations**—best picture; Brown, best director; Rooney, best actor; Harry Stradling, cinematography (black and white).
117 minutes b&w

THE HUMAN FACTOR (1975)
★

George Kennedy
John Mills

An American computer expert, working with NATO in Italy, stalks and kills a group of radicals who assassinated his family. It's a poor reworking of the vigilante angle of *Death Wish*. The film suffers from limp direction, unmoving performances, and a wobbly script. Kennedy's talent is wasted in the leading role. Co-stars Raf Valone and Rita Tushingham. **Director**—Edward Dmytryk. (R)
96 minutes

THE HUMAN FACTOR (1980)
★★

Richard Attenborough
Derek Jacobi
Nicol Williamson

Espionage is, in all likelihood, a routine job carried out by drab civil servants. If such is the case, this Otto Preminger film of Graham Greene's topical novel is close to home. Williamson plays a mild-mannered double agent who leaks secrets to the Russians. The story is intelligent, and the cast of fine British actors is impressive; but a dose of James Bond excitement is badly needed. Also with Robert Morley, John Gielgud, and Ann Todd. (R) *115 minutes*

HUMANOIDS FROM THE DEEP (1980)
★★

Doug McClure
Ann Turkel
Vic Morrow

Amphibious beasts invade a fishing village, where they kill the men and rape the women. The monsters resemble relatives of *The Creature From the*

★ STAR PROFILE

- Humoresque
- The Hunchback of Notre Dame
- The Hunter
- Hurricane
- Hurry Sundown

H

Black Lagoon, and the silly plot is the formula stuff that served so many sci-fi films in the '50s. But because it's the '80s, the horror comes embellished with a fair amount of nudity. There's also an environmental angle about construction of a cannery that would spoil the coastline. **Director**—Barbara Peeters. (R)   *80 minutes*

HUMORESQUE (1946)
★★★

Joan Crawford
John Garfield

Crawford stars as a wealthy patron of the arts who sponsors a promising violinist, played by Garfield. At times, the screenplay smacks of a soap opera, but exquisite settings and superb acting elevate the film to a higher level. A classical-music backdrop and some funny antics from Oscar Levant add to the quality. And there's a slam-bang tragic ending. Also with J. Carrol Naish, Craig Stevens, and Ruth Nelson. **Director**—Jean Negulesco.
125 minutes b&w

THE HUNCHBACK OF NOTRE DAME (1939)
★★★

Charles Laughton
Cedric Hardwicke
Maureen O'Hara
Edmond O'Brien

The classic Victor Hugo story receives superior screen treatment with impressive sets, costumes, and direction, aimed at recreating the mood of medieval Paris. And there's great acting to match, with Laughton as the deformed bell-ringer who rescues a gypsy girl from the clutches of a mob. It's a worthy remake of the silent version with Lon Chaney. Also with Thomas Mitchell and Harry Davenport. **Director**—William Dieterle.
117 minutes b&w

THE HUNTER (1980)
★★

Steve McQueen
Eli Wallach

McQueen plays a modern-day bounty hunter who risks his neck tracking

GREGORY PECK

Gregory Peck was born in La Jolla, California, in 1916, and began acting while attending the University of California at Berkeley. He then moved to New York, where he appeared with the Neighborhood Playhouse for two years before making his Broadway debut in Emlyn Williams's Morning Star *in 1942.*

During the next two years, while Peck spent most of his time playing a double role in the play The Willow and I, *he received some movie offers. Finally, he accepted one from scriptwriter Casey Robinson to co-star as a Russian guerrilla in*

down bail-jumpers. It's a dirty job that only someone desperate for money would undertake, and McQueen sloshes through this film as if he's desperate for a paycheck. A jumbled script and too many undeveloped characters keep things at a low boil, but the story perks up during some spectacular chase scenes. However, there's not enough originality or style to prevent McQueen's star image from being tarnished. Also with Kathryn Harrold and Ben Johnson. **Director**—Buzz Kulik. (PG)   *97 minutes*

HURRICANE (1979)
★★

Jason Robards, Jr.
Mia Farrow
Max Von Sydow
Trevor Howard

Dino De Laurentiis's $20-million romantic epic, filmed in Bora Bora, is boring, boring. The script is based on the engaging Nordhoff and Hall novel about ill-fated lovers. But here the story plods, characters are one-

Days of Glory (1943).

Peck's first screen appearance resulted in instant recognition, and soon 20th-Century Fox cast him as the gentle Scottish missionary in The Keys of the Kingdom *(1944), a role that brought him an Academy Award nomination. He then starred in* The Valley of Decision *(1944) opposite Greer Garson. Both this film and his next,* Spellbound *(1945), were among the top money-makers of the year, and* Duel in the Sun *(1946) and* The Yearling *(1946) were equally big hits the following year.*

He also starred in Gentleman's Agreement *(1947),* Twelve O'Clock High *(1949),* The Gunfighter *(1950),* The Man in the Grey Flannel Suit *(1956), and* The Big Country *(1958).*

In 1963, Peck finally received an Oscar as best actor for his performance as the liberal country lawyer in To Kill a Mockingbird. *Since then, Peck has made many films, including* Arabesque *(1966),* Marooned *(1969),* The Omen *(1976),* MacArthur *(1977), and* The Boys From Brazil *(1978).*

dimensional, and the silly dialogue makes the actors appear foolish. The storm is impressive, but the rest is just tedious nonsense. Also with Dayton Ka'ne. **Director**—Jan Troell. (PG)
119 minutes

HURRY SUNDOWN (1967)
★

Jane Fonda
Michael Caine
Rex Ingram
Diahann Carroll

Director Otto Preminger butchers this film drama, based on a best-selling novel by K. B. Gilden. Although the murky production boasts a superior cast and some lavish settings, it lapses into absurdity only a few minutes from the starting gate. The story concerns racial problems in a small Georgia community. In getting to the ending, this one doesn't hurry fast enough. Cast also includes Burgess Meredith, Faye Dunaway, Beah Richards, and George Kennedy.
142 minutes

H·I
- Hush... Hush Sweet Charlotte
- Hustle
- The Hustler
- I Am a Camera
- Ice Castles
- I Confess
- Icy Breasts

HUSH... HUSH SWEET CHARLOTTE (1965)
★★★

**Bette Davis
Olivia de Havilland
Joseph Cotten**

A stylish chiller about a lonely woman, played by Davis. She's set upon by her cousin and her boyfriend, who both want her property. The plot borrows liberally from *Whatever Happened to Baby Jane*, but it's watchable to the end. The acting by a pro cast is reliably good, and Robert Aldrich's direction achieves the desired macabre effect. Also with Cecil Kellaway, Mary Astor, Victor Buono, and Agnes Moorehead. *133 minutes b&w*

HUSTLE (1975)
★★

**Burt Reynolds
Catherine Deneuve**

An intriguing, fast-moving but disjointed cop movie about the investigation of the death of a young woman of middle-class origins. Reynolds plays a tough and suave detective who discovers that the dead woman has been exploited by a corrupt and powerful lawyer. The plot hopscotches confusingly from one situation to another; only at the end, and too late, does it all seem to make sense. Deneuve plays a high-class prostitute sentimentally attached to Reynolds. With Ben Johnson, Eddie Albert, Paul Winfield, Eileen Brennan, and Ernest Borgnine. **Director**—Robert Aldrich. (R) *120 minutes*

THE HUSTLER (1961)
★★★★

**Paul Newman
Jackie Gleason
George C. Scott**

Newman gives a terrific character portrayal of a hustling pool shark whose game is spoiled when he meets the woman he loves, played by Piper Laurie. The film offers impressive atmosphere of the world of seedy pool halls, and there's effective suspense during the pool matches. Watch for an

In The Hustler, *Paul Newman (left) portrays a pool shark who meets a tough opponent.*

unusual dramatic performance by Gleason as the venerable Minnesota Fats. Gleason plays it straight and subdued, and he's terrific. Good acting jobs, too, by Scott, Laurie, and Myron McCormick. **Director**—Robert Rossen. **Academy Award**—Eugene Shuftan, cinematography (black and white). **Nominations**—best picture; Robert Rossen, best director; Newman, best actor; Laurie, best actress; Gleason, Scott, best supporting actor; Sidney Carroll and Rossen, best screenplay (based on material from another medium). *135 minutes b&w*

I

I AM A CAMERA (1955)
★★★

**Julie Harris
Laurence Harvey**

Harris and Harvey play young adventurers in Berlin just prior to World War II. Harris is excellent as a freewheeling English girl; Harvey, as an English author who records events in the German capital, matches her performance. This romantic comedy is a fine, intelligent rendition of Christopher Isherwood's stories. The plot is also the basis for the Broadway musical and film *Cabaret*. Also with Shelley Winters, Ron Randell, and Patrick McGoohan. **Director**—Henry Cornelius. *98 minutes b&w*

ICE CASTLES (1979)
★★

**Lynn-Holly Johnson
Robby Benson**

A pretty girl from a small town in Iowa gets a crack at an Olympic skating medal, but is accidentally blinded on the brink of success. Yet she skates on with the encouragement of the boy she left behind. Johnson plays Alexis, the blinded skater; Benson is her sympathetic boyfriend. This schmaltzy story is aimed right at the tear ducts, so bring along a *big* handkerchief. The characters, however, are fuzzy, and the film seems to lose steam at crucial moments. The big attraction is newcomer Johnson; she does some good figure skating and impressive acting. Also with Colleen Dewhurst, Tom Skerritt, and Jennifer Warren. **Director**—Donald Wrye. (PG) *109 minutes*

I CONFESS (1953)
★★★

**Montgomery Clift
Anne Baxter**

A murderer confesses his crime to a priest, played by Clift, who upholds the sanctity of the confessional even though he becomes a suspect in the murder. This Canadian-made mystery, directed by Alfred Hitchcock, isn't among his best, yet it's entertaining, mainly because of the moody atmosphere set against the background of Quebec. Clift's acting is adequate, and the story never gets out of control. Also with Brian Aherne, Karl Malden, and Dolly Haas. *94 minutes b&w*

ICY BREASTS (1975)
★★★

**Mireille Darc
Claude Brasseur**

Director Georges Lautner has fashioned an effective psychological suspense-drama. It's about a woman, played by Darc, who is recently released from a mental institution and is bent on murdering the men in her life. A TV writer, played by Brasseur, falls in love with her, unaware of her murderous intent. The suspense remains intact, and most of the acting is relatively good; there are several profoundly scary scenes. Filmed on the French Riviera. In French with English titles. (No MPAA rating) *105 minutes b&w*

- The Idolmaker
- I Dood It!
- . . . If

- If Ever I See You Again
- If It's Tuesday, This Must Be Belgium

- I Hate Blondes
- I'll Be Seeing You
- I'll Cry Tomorrow

I

THE IDOLMAKER (1980)
★★★

Ray Sharkey
Peter Gallagher
Paul Land

Peter Gallagher is taught a simple dance routine by Ray Sharkey in The Idolmaker.

An energetic and compelling drama about a hard-driving promoter of rock singers during the late '50s. Sharkey is superb in the title role as a sharp-eyed manager, whose dynamic behind-the-scenes manipulations create teenybopper idols on the order of Frankie Avalon and Fabian. The film presents the rock 'n' roll era in colorful detail. Gallagher and Land are fine as pop singers whose looks are more vital to stardom than their musical abilities. **Director**—Taylor Hacksford. (PG)
119 minutes

I DOOD IT! (1943)
★★

Red Skelton
Eleanor Parker

In this rather sophomoric slapstick comedy, Skelton plays a tailor who romances a movie star, played by Parker. The overlong film offers too much strained humor, but there are some memorable musical numbers, including "Take a Chance on Love." Red is known for better work. Also with John Hodiak, Lena Horne, and Jimmy Dorsey. **Director**—Vincente Minnelli. *102 minutes b&w*

. . . IF (1969)
★★★★

Malcolm McDowell
David Wood

Searing, intelligent drama set in an English boarding school, where students rebel against harsh discipline. Director Lindsay Anderson cleverly portrays this school setting as an allegory for similar adult situations. A fine cast of pros and nonprofessional actors hammer home the powerful message with perfection. Also with Richard Warwick, Peter Jeffrey, Christine Noonan, and Robert Swann. (R)
111 minutes

IF EVER I SEE YOU AGAIN (1978)
★★

Joe Brooks
Shelley Hack

This is a syrupy, over-sentimental love story. Writer-director-composer-producer-star Brooks plays an advertising man who is reunited with his college sweetheart, played by Hack. Brooks—a sometime ad man himself—serves up this formula boy-meets-girl scenario against a background of romantic songs that sound a lot like television commercials. Much of the acting is so-so, but there's an interesting minor performance by newspaper columnist Jimmy Breslin, who plays a music contractor. Also with Jerry Keller and George Plimpton. (PG) *105 minutes*

IF IT'S TUESDAY, THIS MUST BE BELGIUM (1969)
★★★

Suzanne Pleshette
Ian McShane
Mildred Natwick
Norman Fell

Fast-paced comedy about American vacationers on a whirlwind tour of seven European countries in 18 days. All sorts of hilarious adventures occur along the route, including some unexpected romantic situations. Apparently, this group didn't leave home without their sense of humor. Also

with Murray Hamilton, Michael Constantine, Sandy Baron, Peggy Cass, and Marty Ingels. **Director**—Mel Stuart. (G) *98 minutes*

I HATE BLONDES (1981)
★★★

Enrico Montesano
Jean Rochefort

Montesano, Italy's answer to Woody Allen, hams it up for plenty of laughs in this breezy slapstick comedy. Montesano plays a mild-mannered ghost-writer of tough-guy detective novels who becomes entangled in actual crimes unwittingly. Rochefort, the suave French actor, eases the farce along as the eminent author for whom Montesano writes. It's mainly farcical floss, enhanced with some clever sight gags. In Italian with English titles. **Director**—Giorgio Capitani. (No MPAA rating) *89 minutes*

I'LL BE SEEING YOU (1944)
★★

Ginger Rogers
Joseph Cotten

Rogers plays a convicted killer allowed to go home for the Christmas holidays. She meets and falls in love with a mentally ill soldier, played by Cotten. A good cast gets involved with some interesting scenes in this wartime romance, but the overripe sentimentality intervenes much too often. Also with Shirley Temple, Spring Byington, Tom Tully, and Chill Wills. **Director**—William Dieterle.
85 minutes b&w

I'LL CRY TOMORROW (1955)
★★★★

Susan Hayward
Richard Conte
Eddie Albert
Jo Van Fleet

This is a powerful film biography of Lillian Roth, recounting her marital affairs and her bout with the bottle. Hayward's superb portrayal of the '30s stage and film star gives the production an incisive sense of realism, and she gets excellent support from Van
(Continued)

I
- I Love You, Alice B. Toklas
- I'm All Right Jack
- Imitation of Life
- Improper Channels
- In Cold Blood
- The Incredible Melting Man
- The Incredible Sarah

(Continued)

Fleet as Roth's despondent mother. Roth's husbands are played by Conte, Albert, and Don Taylor. **Director—**Daniel Mann. **Academy Award Nominations**—Hayward, best actress; Arthur Arling, cinematography (black and white). *117 minutes b&w*

I LOVE YOU, ALICE B. TOKLAS (1968)
★★★

**Peter Sellers
Jo Van Fleet
Leigh Taylor-Young**

What's this? Sellers as a hippie? Yes, indeed, and he's in top form as a Los Angeles lawyer with an overbearing mother, played by Van Fleet. Sellers decides to chuck it all to join the dropped-out generation. He then finds truth and happiness with his new lady-love, played by Taylor-Young. There are many excellent comic moments and even a subtle message in the film. Also with Joyce Van Patten, David Arkin, and Herb Edelman. **Director**—Hy Averback.
93 minutes

I'M ALL RIGHT JACK (1960)
★★★★

**Ian Carmichael
Peter Sellers
Terry-Thomas
Richard Attenborough**

Spirited satire about the world of work, set in England in the '50s. The film touches on the questionable practices of both labor and management. The plot focuses on a youthful bumbler, played by Carmichael. He gets a factory job, provokes a strike, and is caught up in a controversy between the workers and the bosses. Sellers is memorable as an oafish labor official. Also with Dennis Price and Margaret Rutherford. **Director**—John Boulting. *104 minutes b&w*

IMITATION OF LIFE (1959)
★★

**Lana Turner
Juanita Moore**

Slick reworking of the Fannie Hurst tearjerker. Turner plays the beauty who becomes a successful actress only to find disappointment in her personal relationships; Moore is the black servant who shares her life with Turner. Moore's life is tragic because her daughter, played by Susan Kohner, passes for white. The racial aspect, however, gets shoved aside. The 1934 version, starring Claudette Colbert, worked better. Also with John Gavin, Sandra Dee, and Robert Alda. **Director**—Douglas Sirk. **Academy Award Nominations**—Moore, Kohner, best supporting actress. *124 minutes*

IMPROPER CHANNELS (1981)
★★

**Alan Arkin
Mariette Hartley**

Computers and bureaucracy are the villains in this uneven, screwball comedy. Arkin and Hartley become tangled in red tape when their daughter accidentally bumps her head and an officious social worker charges child abuse. Arkin and Hartley handle their roles with moderate appeal, but the material never gives them the opportunity to sustain comic momentum. There are a few laughs along the way, but more are needed. **Director**—Eric Till. (PG) *92 minutes*

IN COLD BLOOD (1967)
★★★★

**Robert Blake
Scott Wilson**

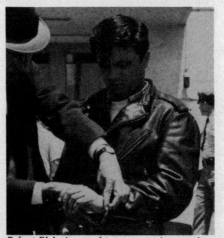

Robert Blake is one of two ex-cons in custody for killing a farm family in In Cold Blood.

First-class film rendition of Truman Capote's book about two young ex-convicts who brutally kill a Kansas farm family. The semidocumentary account digs deep into motives, characterizations, and the stark contrasts between the life-styles of the killers and the victims. The horrible murders, life on the run, capture, and execution are handled in taut step-by-step fashion for the maximum realistic effect. Blake and Wilson are excellent as the desperate killers. Also with John Forsythe, Paul Stewart, Gerald S. O'Loughlin, and Jeff Corey. **Director**—Richard Brooks. **Academy Award Nominations**—Brooks, best director; Brooks, best screenplay (based on material from another medium); Conrad Hall, cinematography. *134 minutes b&w*

THE INCREDIBLE MELTING MAN (1978)
(no stars)

Alex Rebar

An astronaut, played by Rebar, returns to earth with a strange disease that causes his body to melt. He goes about chomping on humans and dripping gobs of goo everywhere. This foolishness is supposed to be scary, but it only succeeds in being disgusting. Dull acting by a cast of unknowns, trite dialogue, and poor editing add up to an incredibly bad movie. Also with Burr DeBenning and Myron Healey. **Director**—William Sachs. (R) *86 minutes*

THE INCREDIBLE SARAH (1976)
★

Glenda Jackson

Jackson, who plays the remarkable and eccentric Sarah Bernhardt in this film, goes through some 40 costume changes and almost as many temper tantrums. Despite such lavishness and energy, this attempt at biography is no more than a series of humdrum vignettes, which fails to illuminate the legendary showmanship of the French actress. Also with Daniel Massey and Douglas Wilmer. **Director**—Richard Fleischer. (PG) *106 minutes*

- The Incredible Shrinking Man
- The Incredible Shrinking Woman
- Indiscreet
- I Never Promised You a Rose Garden
- I Never Sang for My Father
- In God We Trust
- Inherit the Wind

I

THE INCREDIBLE SHRINKING MAN (1957)
★★★

Grant Williams

A superior sci-fi thriller despite its modest budget. Williams plays a scientist exposed to a radioactive fog; he shrinks to a minute size, where he views the world from a new perspective. Inventive trick photography makes it all happen with exceptional interest and suspense. And there's even a decent script to heighten the proceedings. Incredible, indeed. Also stars Randy Stuart, April Kent, and Paul Langton. **Director**—Jack Arnold.   *81 minutes b&w*

THE INCREDIBLE SHRINKING WOMAN (1981)
★★

Lily Tomlin
Charles Grodin

In The Incredible Shrinking Woman, *Lily Tomlin tries to prepare dinner for her family.*

Tomlin plays a modern housewife who shrinks to Barbie Doll proportions because of an intolerance to chemical additives in household products. Grodin is her bewildered husband. Tomlin is a first-rate comedienne, but her talents are subdued by a half-baked script that doesn't reach its potential as social satire on American consumerism. There are a few moments of inspired comedy; the rest is just so much dead air. Cast also

includes Ned Beatty. **Director**—Joe Schumacher. (PG)   *88 minutes*

INDISCREET (1958)
★★★

Cary Grant
Ingrid Bergman

Charming upper-crust comedy about a dashing American diplomat romancing a beautiful actress in London. Grant and Bergman are the perfect couple for this sort of ritzy, sophisticated production, enhanced with lush sets. The film is reliably based on Norman Krasna's play *Kind Sir*; Krasna also wrote the screenplay. Also with Phyllis Calvert, Cecil Parker, David Kossoff, and Megs Jenkins. **Director**—Stanley Donen.

100 minutes

I NEVER PROMISED YOU A ROSE GARDEN (1977)
★★

Bibi Andersson
Kathleen Quinlan

This sincere story, set in a psychiatric hospital, is about a young girl's fight against madness. The film is loaded with good intentions, but it's excessively grim and often confusing; don't expect another *One Flew Over the Cuckoo's Nest*. Yet there are impressive performances by Quinlan, as the disturbed girl, and Andersson, as her faithful psychiatrist. It's an exhausting movie, one more likely to be admired than enjoyed. Adapted from Joanne Greenberg's 1964 best-selling novel. Also with Reni Santoni, Susan Tyrell, and Signe Hasso. **Director**—Anthony Page. (R)   *96 minutes*

I NEVER SANG FOR MY FATHER (1970)
★★★

Melvyn Douglas
Gene Hackman

Douglas and Hackman are a fine acting duo in this moving film version of Robert Anderson's play. Hackman is a middle-aged man who tries to cope with his strong-willed father, played by Douglas. The old man is proud and sassy, even though he's in his 80's.

There are intelligent and profound character studies all around; the mood, however, is depressing. Co-stars Dorothy Stickney and Estelle Parsons. **Director**—Gilbert Cates. (PG) **Academy Award Nominations**—Douglas, best actor; Hackman, best supporting actor; Anderson, best screenplay (based on material from another medium).   *92 minutes*

IN GOD WE TRUST (1980)
★

Marty Feldman

Strained comedy with banjo-eyed Feldman as a Trappist monk on the prowl for some fast cash to pay the monastery's debts. Out in the wicked world—Los Angeles—innocent Marty encounters a blustering television evangelist and a kindhearted prostitute. He also meets "God"—played by Richard Pryor—in the form of that big computer in the sky. What we don't meet are situations that make us laugh. **Director**—Feldman.

97 minutes

INHERIT THE WIND (1960)
★★★★

Spencer Tracy
Fredric March

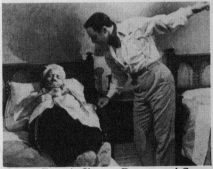

Spencer Tracy is Clarence Darrow, and Gene Kelly is a reporter in Inherit the Wind.

A fascinating slice of American history is brought brilliantly to the screen as an adaptation of the Jerome Lawrence/Robert E. Lee play, about the famous 1925 Scopes "monkey trial" in Tennessee. Tracy and March are superb as Clarence Darrow and William Jennings Bryan, respectively. They argue the merits of Darwin's theory of evolu-
(Continued)

I • The In-Laws • In Praise of Older Women
• The Innocent • In Search of Noah's Ark
• The Inn of the Sixth • Inserts
  Happiness • Inside Daisy Clover

(Continued)

tion passionately. The sultry atmosphere of a small-town courtroom in midsummer adds to the realism. Excellent supporting work by Dick York, Gene Kelly, Florence Eldridge, Elliott Reid, and Harry Morgan. **Director**—Stanley Kramer. **Academy Award Nominations**—Tracy, best actor; Nathan E. Douglas and Harold Jacob Smith, best screenplay (based on material from another medium); Ernest Laszlo, cinematography (black and white). *127 minutes b&w*

THE IN-LAWS (1979)
★★★

Peter Falk
Alan Arkin

Peter Falk and Alan Arkin are a funny twosome in the wacky comedy The In-Laws.

Falk and Arkin team up for laughs galore in this wacky and hilarious comedy about a New York dentist who unwittingly becomes involved with his future father-in-law who claims to be a CIA agent. Arkin plays the dentist; Falk plays the CIA man. Andrew Bergman, who collaborated with Mel Brooks in *Blazing Saddles*, has come up with a gem of a comic script; it falters occasionally, but at the right moments it escalates to provoke side-splitting laughter. Falk and Arkin make an effective and funny twosome. Also with Richard Libertini, Nancy Dussault, Penny Peyser, and Arlene Golonka. **Director**—Arthur Hiller. (PG) *103 minutes*

THE INNOCENT (1979)
★

Giancarlo Giannini

This Luchino Visconti film, completed shortly before his death, is rich in the velvety detail of the Roman upper class at the turn of the century, but that's the only positive thing that can be said. The heavy drama rambles on about an aristocratic philanderer who commits infanticide and then suicide. Giannini, in the lead role, wades bravely through the tedium. Laura Antonelli plays his wife, and Jennifer O'Neill plays his mistress; both women plod along with him. In Italian with English titles. (No MPAA rating.) *115 minutes*

THE INN OF THE SIXTH HAPPINESS (1958)
★★★

Ingrid Bergman
Curt Jurgens
Robert Donat

Engrossing drama set in China just prior to World War II. Bergman does a fine acting job as an English girl who becomes a brave missionary. She shepherds children through enemy lines and carries on a romance with Jurgens. Donat, in his last film, is notable in the role of a mandarin. An exciting happy ending wraps it up nicely. Other performers are Athene Seyler, Ronald Squire, and Richard Wattis. **Director**—Mark Robson. **Academy Award Nomination**—Robson, best director. *158 minutes*

IN PRAISE OF OLDER WOMEN (1979)
★

Tom Berenger
Karen Black
Susan Strasberg
Alexandra Stewart

An awkward soft-core porno film, set in Hungary and Canada, about a boy's sexual experiences with older women. Berenger, as the lad who strikes out with girls his own age, doesn't light any fires. Instead, he carries on with some married women played by Black, Strasberg, and Stewart, who appear semi-nude. Most of the sex scenes are embarrassing rather than erotic. Also with Helen Shaver and Marilyn Lightstone. **Director**—George Kaczender. (R) *108 minutes*

IN SEARCH OF NOAH'S ARK (1977)
★

A pedantic and boring documentary about the possible discovery of the remains of Noah's ark atop Mount Ararat on the Turkish-Soviet border. An assortment of so-called experts beats around the scholarly bush, and the presentation lacks conviction of proof. Viewers are advised to be in search of a better film. **Director**—James L. Conway. (G) *95 minutes*

INSERTS (1976)
★

Richard Dreyfuss
Jessica Harper

Despite its MPAA rating, this film is hardly pornographic, as might be expected; it's hardly a movie either. It's about making pornographic movies in the '30s. Dreyfuss stars as a has-been director who, in desperation, resorts to shooting porno flicks in his living room. The film never leaves this setting, and it drones on for almost two hours in sheer tedium. Harper plays a woman who tries to cure Dreyfuss's withdrawal from life. Also with Bob Hoskins and Veronica Cartwright. **Director**—John Byrum.(X) *117 minutes*

INSIDE DAISY CLOVER (1965)
★★

Natalie Wood
Robert Redford

Wood plays the title role in this half-baked story of a young movie star's hard-pressed Hollywood career in the '30s. Redford plays a troubled matinee idol. Many of the characters are wet cardboard—Wood included. Christopher Plummer, however, does well as a bombastic studio boss. A few moments shine through in this film, but not enough to be satisfying; the film is mostly style and little substance. Also with Ruth Gordon and Roddy MacDowall. **Director**—Robert Mulligan. **Academy Award Nomination**—Gordon, best supporting actress. *128 minutes*

- Inside Moves
- The Inspector General
- Interiors

- Intermezzo
- International Velvet
- In the Heat of the Night

I

INSIDE MOVES (1980)
★★

**John Savage
David Morse**

A sentimental drama about regulars at a neighborhood bar, where all are afflicted with some sort of physical ailment. Savage plays a cripple who helps his bartending buddy, played by Morse, obtain a knee operation that opens the door to a successful basketball career. The acting is fine, and the main characters are sort of Rocky Balboas of the handicapped. The plot, however, is rather corny and loosely constructed—a situation that detracts from the film's compassion for its characters. Also with Diana Scarwid and Amy Wright. **Director**—Richard Donner. (PG) **Academy Award Nomination**—Scarwid, best supporting actress. *113 minutes*

THE INSPECTOR GENERAL
(1949)
★★★

Danny Kaye

Top-of-the-line star vehicle for Kaye masquerading as an important official in 19th-century Russia. Kaye turns on the charm and the energy in this good-looking comedy of errors, tarnished only by a few plodding moments. Co-stars Walter Slezak, Barbara Bates, Elsa Lanchester, and Gene Lockhart. **Director**—Henry Koster. **Alternate Title**—*Happy Times*. *101 minutes*

INTERIORS (1978)
★★

**Diane Keaton
Geraldine Page**

With daughters and son-in-law looking on, Geraldine Page opens gifts in Interiors.

John Savage and David Morse become friends at Max's Bar in Inside Moves.

Woody Allen's first serious drama as writer-director is so relentlessly gloomy that it doesn't succeed as entertainment. The style parallels Ingmar Bergman's, but the substance is noticeably sterile. The painful story involves a round robin of intense emotional crises in a wealthy New York family. Excellent acting by Page, Keaton, Maureen Stapleton, and E. G. Marshall. A noble try, Woody, but please stick to comedy. (PG) **Academy Award Nominations**—Page, best actress; Stapleton, best supporting actress; Allen, best original screenplay. *99 minutes*

INTERMEZZO (1939)
★★★

**Ingrid Bergman
Leslie Howard**

A well-done love story about a famous married violinist, played by Howard, who falls hopelessly in love with a young pianist, played by Bergman. The movie gets right to the point and offers fine moments of charm and sentimentality. There's good acting all around, and Bergman is impressive in her English-speaking debut. Others in the cast are John Halliday, Edna Best, and Cecil Kellaway. **Director**—Gregory Ratoff. *69 minutes b&w*

INTERNATIONAL VELVET
(1978)
★★★

**Tatum O'Neal
Christopher Plummer
Nanette Newman**

O'Neal stars in this warm and handsome sequel to *National Velvet*, the 1944 girl-meets-horse movie, which featured young Elizabeth Taylor. Velvet, now grown up and played in this film by Newman, resides in the picturesque English countryside. Along comes O'Neal, who plays her orphaned niece. Tatum takes a liking to a magnificent colt and wins a gold medal in the exciting Olympic equestrian competition. Plummer plays Newman's lover. Also with Anthony Hopkins and Dinsdale Landen. **Director**—Bryan Forbes. (PG) *127 minutes*

Sarah (Tatum O'Neal) and her horse Arizona Pie in International Velvet.

IN THE HEAT OF THE NIGHT
(1967)
★★★★

**Sidney Poitier
Rod Steiger**

Poitier plays a highly professional big-city homicide detective on a visit to a backwater Mississippi town. A murder is committed, and he joins forces with a bigoted police chief to solve the case. Steiger is exceptional as the pompous policeman who learns some professional crime-solving methods from the black cop. Director Norman Jewison brings out their personality clash with amazing skill, and the film, an insightful study of prejudices and life-styles in the South, is wrapped up neatly by classy acting all around. Top supporting jobs from Lee Grant, Warren Oates, Quentin Dean, William Schallert, and Scott Wilson. **Academy Awards**—best picture; Steiger, best actor; Stirling Silliphant, best *(Continued)*

I • Intruder in the Dust
• Invasion of the Body
Snatchers (1956)

• Invasion of the Body
Snatchers (1978)
• Invitation to a Gunfighter

• The IPCRESS File
• Iphigenia
• I Remember Mama

(Continued)
screenplay (based on material from another medium). **Nomination—** Jewison, best director. *110 minutes*

INTRUDER IN THE DUST (1949)
★★★★

**Juano Hernandez
Elizabeth Patterson
David Brian**

A gripping drama, enhanced by indelible characterizations, about a black man who is wrongfully accused of murder. He's rescued from a lynch mob by a boy and an old woman who find the real killer. Hernandez is the accused black, and Brian and Patterson are his rescuers. The film, based on William Faulkner's novel, works as a fine mystery as well as straightforward social observation. There's topnotch acting with well-paced direction. Also with Claude Jarman, Jr., Porter Hall, and Will Geer. **Director**—Clarence Brown.

87 minutes b&w

INVASION OF THE BODY SNATCHERS (1956)
★★★★

**Kevin McCarthy
Dana Wynter**

An amazingly good sci-fi thriller considering it's a low-budget film with a relatively unknown cast. A small American town is invaded by strange pods from space, and a sinister force takes over the bodies of the residents. The production progresses smartly with intelligence and mounting suspense. A classic of its time. Also with Larry Gates, King Donovan, Carolyn Jones, and Sam Peckinpah. **Director**—Don Siegel. *80 minutes b&w*

INVASION OF THE BODY SNATCHERS (1978)
★★★

**Donald Sutherland
Brooke Adams**

The 1956 sci-fi classic gets a coat of gloss and some flashy new thrills in this remake by director Philip Kauf-

In *Invasion of the Body Snatchers*, *Brooke Adams and Donald Sutherland are puzzled as they examine an unfamiliar blossom.*

man. Aliens arrive on earth in the form of strange seed pods to replace humans, but this time the setting is San Francisco instead of a small town. Sutherland stands out as a beleaguered public health officer who tries to unscramble the mystery. The film slows down a bit about midway, but there are enough scary scenes to keep the chills flowing to the end. Kevin McCarthy, who played the Sutherland role in the original film, and Don Siegel, the director of the 1956 version, both appear in cameo roles. Also look for Robert Duvall in a bit part. Also with Jeff Goldblum, Veronica Cartwright, and Leonard Nimoy. (PG) *115 minutes*

INVITATION TO A GUNFIGHTER (1964)
★★

**Yul Brynner
George Segal**

There's more talk than action in this tepid western drama about a community that recruits a gunman to do some dirty work. The characterizations come off rather pat despite the efforts of a decent cast. Also with Janice Rule, Brad Dexter, and Pat Hingle. **Director**—Richard Wilson. *92 minutes*

THE IPCRESS FILE (1965)
★★★

**Michael Caine
Nigel Green**

Taut, relentlessly absorbing espionage caper, based on Len Deighton's novel, with Caine perfectly cast as Harry Palmer, a low-key secret agent who tracks a missing scientist behind the Iron Curtain and discovers one of his superiors is a spy. Sidney J. Furie's efficient direction upholds the tension throughout the film, and the script is plotted for maximum suspense. The film led to two sequels. Also stars Guy Doleman, Sue Lloyd, and Gordon Jackson. *92 minutes*

IPHIGENIA (1977)
★★★

**Tatiana Papamoskou
Irene Papas**

This Euripides drama transforms nicely to the screen, illuminating the power and passion of the classic Greek tragedy. It's the story of King Agamemnon, who is forced to sacrifice his daughter, Iphigenia, to appease the gods and assure favorable passage for his fleet to Troy. Fourteen-year-old Papamoskou is magnificent as the martyred daughter. Also with Costa Kazakos. Classy direction by Michael (*Zorba the Greek*) Cacoyannis. In Greek with English titles. (No MPAA rating) **Academy Award Nomination**—best foreign-language film.

127 minutes

I REMEMBER MAMA (1948)
★★★★

**Irene Dunne
Barbara Bel Geddes**

A nice bit of sentimental nostalgia as a novelist remembers growing up with her stouthearted Norwegian family, struggling to attain the American dream in San Francisco. Dunne is wonderful as the energetic mother whose devotion and fortitude keeps the family on an even keel; Bel Geddes plays the novelist. The film is filled with rich details of growing up wisely. Other good performances by Oscar Homolka, Edgar Bergen, Philip Dorn, Ellen Corby, and Cedric Hardwicke. **Director**—George Stevens. **Academy Award Nominations**—Dunne, best actress; Homolka, best supporting actor; Bel Geddes, Corby, best supporting actress; Nicholas Musuraca, cinematography (black and white).

134 minutes b&w

● Irma La Douce
● I Sent a Letter to My Love
● Island in the Sky
● The Island of Dr. Moreau

● Islands in the Stream
● Is Paris Burning?
● It Happened One Night
● It Happens Every Spring

I

IRMA LA DOUCE (1963)
★★★

Shirley MacLaine
Jack Lemmon

The delightful Broadway musical, without music, is done up for the screen with style and flavor. Writer-director Billy Wilder succeeds with this comic romp about a Paris cop, played by Lemmon, who falls in love with a prostitute, played by MacLaine. Lemmon is in top form, and he's matched by the spirited performance of MacLaine as the sweet, good-natured trollop. Nonstop fun, especially for adult audiences. Co-stars Lou Jacobi, Herschel Bernardi, Joan Shawlee, and Bruce Yarnell. **Academy Award Nominations**—MacLaine, best actress; Joseph LaShelle, cinematography (color). *146 minutes*

I SENT A LETTER TO MY LOVE (1981)
★★★

Jean Rochefort
Simone Signoret

Rochefort plays a cripple confined to a wheelchair; Signoret is the spinster who cares for him. Inadvertently, they reveal their intimate feelings of love, compassion, and loneliness. The poignant screenplay brims with emotion and suspense while proceeding smoothly with a gently comic spirit. Signoret and Rochefort work extraordinarily well together. Rochefort, with his sad eyes and shy smile, gives a triumphant performance. **Director**—Moshe Mizrahi. In French with English titles. (No MPAA rating) *96 minutes*

ISLAND IN THE SKY (1953)
★★★

John Wayne
Lloyd Nolan

Adequate adventure about the survival of a crew from a transport plane, forced to land in the frozen wastes of Greenland. The story is enhanced by impressive photography, and the action and suspense are elevated by the talents of Wayne. Also with Walter Abel, Allyn Joslyn, Andy Devine, and James Arness. **Director**—William Wellman. *109 minutes b&w*

THE ISLAND OF DR. MOREAU (1977)
★★

Burt Lancaster
Michael York

In 1933, this adaptation of the H. G. Wells horror fantasy was called *The Island of Lost Souls*. Then, it starred Charles Laughton as a sinister scientist who tries to breed animals into humans and vice-versa. This $6 million remake is a nice try with Lancaster in the title role, but alas, the strange critters aren't as creepy, and the atmosphere is hardly ghoulish. The horror movies just don't work the same as when Boris Karloff, Bela Lugosi, and their like were around. Also with Nigel Davenport and Barbara Carrera. **Director**—Don Taylor. (PG) *104 minutes*

ISLANDS IN THE STREAM (1977)
★★

George C. Scott
David Hemmings
Claire Bloom

This introspective movie version of Ernest Hemingway's novel begins

George C. Scott stars as a famous painter and sculptor in Islands in the Stream.

with feeling, but peters out awkwardly. Scott plays the artist-hero—a self-exiled sculptor whose marriages have failed—with gruff macho spirit. But the film doesn't justify the Hemingway prose, and the story drifts and plods out of control. Also with Susan Tyrrell, Michael-James Wixted, and Gilbert Roland. **Director**—Franklin J. Schaffner. (PG) *105 minutes*

IS PARIS BURNING? (1965)
★★

Leslie Caron
Gert Frobe
Charles Boyer
Yves Montand
Orson Welles

Meandering and overblown all-star epic account of the efforts to prevent the destruction of Paris by the retreating Germans in World War II. The story is put together as a succession of vignettes, and the film is loaded with half-baked cameos that only provoke annoyance and lead to dreariness. All in all, not so hot. Also with Alain Delon, Jean-Pierre Cassel, Kirk Douglas, Glenn Ford, and Robert Stack. **Director**—René Clément. *173 minutes b&w*

IT HAPPENED ONE NIGHT
See State Fair

IT HAPPENS EVERY SPRING (1949)
★★★

Ray Milland
Jean Peters

A chemistry professor, played by Milland, becomes an unlikely pitching ace after he discovers a formula that makes baseballs repel wood, including baseball bats. Milland handles the part with skill and coaxes plenty of chuckles and smiles from the buoyant material. It's as enjoyable as watching your favorite team win, with the pitcher hurling a no-hitter. Also stars Paul Douglas, Ed Begley, Ted de Corsia, and Ray Collins. **Director**—Lloyd Bacon. **Academy Award Nomination**—Shirley W. Smith and Valentine Davies, writing (motion picture story). *80 minutes b&w*

I
- It Lives Again
- It's Alive!
- It's A Mad Mad Mad Mad World
- It's a Wonderful Life
- It's My Turn
- Ivanhoe
- I Wanna Hold Your Hand

IT LIVES AGAIN (1978)
(no stars)

Frederic Forrest
Kathleen Lloyd

Murderous mutant babies return for more bloody rampaging in this sequel to the financially successful horror film *It's Alive!* Writer-director Larry Cohen again overindulges with silliness and bad taste. Awkward performances, led by Forrest and Lloyd, are in keeping with the tacky plot. Also with John Ryan and John Marley. (R)

91 minutes

IT'S ALIVE! (1977)
★

John Ryan
Sharon Farrell

This movie is some nonsense about a weird newborn baby with long fangs that goes on a killing spree, beginning with the doctors and nurses in the delivery room. The acting is awful, the dialogue is silly, and the music by Bernard Herrmann is overdone. However, director-producer-writer Larry Cohen manages a few moments of suspense and a mild comment on the overuse of drugs. Also with Andrew Duggan and Guy Stockwell. (PG)

91 minutes

IT'S A MAD MAD MAD MAD WORLD (1963)
★★

Spencer Tracy
Jimmy Durante
Milton Berle
Sid Caesar
Ethel Merman

An overlong, overblown frontal assault on the funnybone, with virtually every Hollywood comedian getting in their licks. The 2½-hour romp is about a mad scramble to recover hidden loot from a robbery. Tracy plays a detective trying to recover the booty. All sorts of wild chases and slapstick antics abound, with the stunts outshining the acting most of the time. It's okay for a while, but it gets tiresome. The large cast also includes Buddy Hackett, Mickey Rooney, Dick Shawn, Jack Benny, Jerry Lewis, Terry-Thomas, Phil Silvers, Edie Adams, Jonathan Winters, and many more. **Director**—Stanley Kramer.

162 minutes

IT'S A WONDERFUL LIFE (1946)
★★★★

James Stewart
Henry Travers
Donna Reed

James Stewart and Donna Reed, two stars in the sentimental film It's a Wonderful Life.

This is perhaps Frank Capra's best film; it shows his uniquely warm and charming blend of humor. Stewart is superb as a small-town businessman who beats his brains out most of his life. When he decides to end it all because he thinks he's a failure, a guardian angel, played by Travers, comes to Earth to show him his accomplishments. Reed plays Stewart's wife. It is film sentimentality done to perfection and displayed with a silver lining; a Christmas favorite, and it's a wonderful movie. Also with Lionel Barrymore, Thomas Mitchell, Ward Bond, and Gloria Grahame. **Academy Award Nominations**—best picture; Capra, best director; Stewart, best actor.

129 minutes b&w

IT'S MY TURN (1980)
★★

Jill Clayburgh
Michael Douglas
Charles Grodin

Clayburgh plays a successful math professor, trying to resolve her career and her love life in this vague comedy-drama. The performances are engaging, but Eleanor Bergstein's muddled screenplay keeps the film on the level of a soap opera. Finally, the movie just stops in its tracks, dangling all sorts of unanswered questions. Douglas and Grodin co-star as Clayburgh's lovers of the moment—one in New York, the other in Chicago. Also with Beverly Garland. **Director**—Claudia Weill. (PG)

91 minutes

IVANHOE (1952)
★★★

Robert Taylor
Joan Fontaine
Elizabeth Taylor

A splendid costume adventure, based on Sir Walter Scott's colorful tale of brave knights and fair damsels in medieval England. Robert Taylor plays the title role, galloping off on daring assignments and romancing beautiful Liz and lovely Joan. It's all done to a "T," with lavish sets and striking photography. The script, however, could have been better. Also stars Emlyn Williams, George Sanders, Robert Douglas, and Sebastian Cabot. **Director**—Richard Thorpe. **Academy Award Nominations**—best picture; F. A. Young, cinematography (color).

106 minutes

I WANNA HOLD YOUR HAND (1978)
★★

Nancy Allen
Bobby DiCicco
Mark McClure

In I Wanna Hold Your Hand, *a group of teens get caught in Beatles-induced hysteria.*

● I Want To Live!
● I Was a Male War Bride
● I Was a Teenage Werewolf
● I Will, I Will . . . For Now

● I Wonder Who's Kissing Her Now
● Jabberwocky
● The Jackpot

I·J

A group of teenagers try to crash into the Beatles's New York hotel suite when the famous mop tops pay their first visit to America to appear on *The Ed Sullivan Show*. If you haven't been weaned away from *Archie* comics, you might find this adolescent slapstick comedy worthwhile. The film, set in 1964, is a series of silly routines and raucous chases, performed mainly by an unfamiliar young cast. First-time director Robert Zemeckis tries to copy the freewheeling spirit of *American Graffiti*, but he doesn't achieve that quality or style. (PG)   *104 minutes*

I WANT TO LIVE! (1958)
★★★★

Susan Hayward
Simon Oakland

Smashing crime drama, based on the case of Barbara Graham, who was executed in the gas chamber for murder amid debate over the severity of her punishment. Hayward gives a tour-de-force performance as the tough prostitute, and the production is neatly assembled for maximum impact by director Robert Wise. Especially compelling are the details of the execution. The film offers a moving plea for the abolition of capital punishment. Good supporting efforts by Oakland, Virginia Vincent, Theodore Bikel, and Philip Coolidge. **Academy Award**—Hayward, best actress; **Nominations**—Wise, best director; Nelson Gidding and Don Mankiewicz, best screenplay (based on material from another medium); Lionel Linden, cinematography (black and white).
120 minutes b&w

I WAS A MALE WAR BRIDE (1949)
★★★

Cary Grant
Ann Sheridan

The title may sound absurd, but this energetic comedy really clicks. Grant plays a French army officer who gets all dressed up in women's clothing as part of a scheme to join Sheridan, his American WAC wife, on a return trip to the United States. Grant and Sheridan are hilarious, and they have a fine, funny script to work with. Also

with Marion Marshall and Randy Stuart. **Director**—Howard Hawks.
105 minutes b&w

I WAS A TEENAGE WEREWOLF (1957)
★★★

Michael Landon
Whit Bissell

A low-budget monster movie that has unexpected style. A doctor uses a delinquent youth as a guinea pig for some experiments. Unfortunately, the young man, played by Landon, becomes a werewolf. It's an interesting mixture of horror and humor. And who can forget that crazy title? Also with Yvonne Leslie and Guy Williams. **Director**—Gene Fowler, Jr.
76 minutes b&w

I WILL, I WILL . . . FOR NOW (1976)
(no stars)

Elliott Gould
Diane Keaton

Victoria Principal and Elliott Gould chat over groceries in I Will, I Will . . . For Now.

A stale and wretched sex farce right out of the Doris Day-Rock Hudson comedies of the '50s. Gould and Keaton play a rich, hip New York couple who get involved with a sex clinic, a contract marriage, and extramarital affairs. The film is full of adolescent gags that consistently fall flat. Norman Panama, who wrote and directed comedies back in the '40s, directed this one and helped with the writing. It's a poor job that just doesn't work today. He's obviously out of touch with current realities. Also with Paul Sorvino, Victoria Principal, and Robert Alda. (R)   *96 minutes*

I WONDER WHO'S KISSING HER NOW (1947)
★★★

Mark Stevens
June Haver

This film is a pleasant film biography of 1890s songwriter Joseph E. Howard. It works mainly because of its great music; the plot, embellished with some fiction, is merely routine. A talented cast, however, helps bring it along. Also stars Martha Stewart, Reginald Gardiner, Lenore Aubert, William Frawley, and Gene Nelson. **Director**—Lloyd Bacon.   *104 minutes*

J

JABBERWOCKY (1977)
★★

Michael Palin
Max Wall

A shabby-looking medieval farce; a second cousin to *Monty Python and the Holy Grail*, but hardly achieving its quality. Occasionally, there are flashes of honest humor, which are quickly drowned in a confused outpouring of adolescent slapstick and bad taste. The wobbly script involves knights, a king, grubby peasants, a bumbling hero, and a vile monster—the Jabberwock. Also with Deborah Fallender, John Le Mesurier, and Annette Badland. Written and directed by Terry Gilliam. (No MPAA rating)   *100 minutes*

THE JACKPOT (1950)
★★★

James Stewart
Barbara Hale

An ordinary guy wins a pile of money on a radio quiz show. After he attains notoriety, his life changes drastically. The film is a rather low-key comedy, adequately handled for a steady stream of amusing moments. Stewart excels as the winner who gets a fair share of headaches along with extra income. Others in the cast include James Gleason, Fred Clark, Alan Mowbray, and Natalie Wood. **Director**—Walter Lang.   *85 minutes b&w*

J
- Jacob, the Liar
- Jane Eyre
- Jaws
- Jaws 2
- The Jazz Singer
- J. D.'s Revenge

JACOB, THE LIAR (1977)
★★

Vlastimil Brodsky

Heartwarming yet listless tragicomedy made in East Germany about Jews in a Polish ghetto under Nazi control. Jacob, decently played by Brodsky, boosts morale among the doomed inhabitants by inventing stories about nearby Russian victories. The film is well-intentioned, but lacks much-needed drama and depth. Direction, scripting, and cinematography are pedestrian. Also with Erwin Geschonneck and Manuela Simon. **Director**—Frank Beyer. In German with English titles. (No MPAA rating) **Academy Award Nomination**—best foreign-language film. (1976)   95 minutes

JANE EYRE (1944)
★★★★

**Joan Fontaine
Orson Welles**

Charlotte Brontë's classic romantic story, set in Victorian times, is faithfully reproduced for the screen with the skillful use of brooding atmospherics. Fontaine heads the cast of this deliberately paced production about an unfortunate orphan girl who becomes a governess for a wealthy Englishman and gets involved with mystery and romance. Also with Margaret O'Brien, Henry Daniell, John Sutton, Agnes Moorehead, and Elizabeth Taylor. **Director**—Robert Stevenson.   96 minutes b&w

JAWS (1975)
★★★★

**Robert Shaw
Roy Scheider
Richard Dreyfuss**

A man-eating shark comes to dine at a Long Island, New York, summer resort. The film has been designed to scare the hell out of you and may become a classic in the style of *King Kong* and *Frankenstein*. There's fine acting by Dreyfuss, Shaw, and of course, the Great White Shark—a 25-foot mechanical marvel. Shaw plays an expert shark hunter, Dreyfuss is an ichthy-

Richard Dreyfuss, who plays an ichthyologist, cools off in shark-infested waters in Jaws.

ologist, and Scheider is the area's police chief. Clever directing by Steven Spielberg. Adapted from the novel by Peter Benchley. Also with Lorraine Gary, Murray Hamilton, and Carl Gottlieb. **Academy Award Nomination**—best picture. (PG)
124 minutes

JAWS 2 (1978)
★★

**Roy Scheider
Lorraine Gary**

This sequel to the big moneymaking shark movie offers a moderate ration of excitement, when the huge mechanical man-eater swallows some skin divers or chomps on some sailboating teenagers. But this time it's all done without the imagination and slick style that director Steven Spielberg lavished on the original film. The

In Jaws 2, *Lorraine Gary and Roy Scheider leave a celebration at a Holiday Inn.*

plot, which is mostly a threadbare rehash of the initial *Jaws* theme, never quite builds to a satisfying climax. Scheider again plays the resort community's embattled police chief. Also with Murray Hamilton, Joseph Mascolo, and Jeffrey Kramer. **Director**—Jeannot Szwarc. (PG)   117 minutes

THE JAZZ SINGER (1980)
★★

**Neil Diamond
Laurence Olivier
Lucie Arnaz**

Pop singer Diamond stars as the cantor's son who pursues a show business career in this cliché-filled remake of the 1927 original melodrama that featured Al Jolson. Instead of singing "Mammy," Diamond belts out "Love on the Rocks" and other pop tunes; he's obviously a better singer than actor. But there are energetic performances from Olivier, as the heartbroken father, and from Arnaz, as the young woman who promotes Diamond's career. Also with Catlin Adams. **Director**—Richard Fleischer. (PG)   115 minutes

Laurence Olivier and Neil Diamond play father and son in The Jazz Singer.

J. D.'S REVENGE (1976)
★★

**Glynn Turman
Lou Gossett**

Gore and violence dominate this black-themed thriller about a young law student possessed by the spirit of a slain hoodlum. Turman works hard in the lead role, and there's stylish support from Gossett as a revivalist minister. Professional direction from Arthur Marks and a tight script also help keep the film moving smartly, but much of the material is too far-out to be taken seriously. Also with Joan Pringle, David McKnight, and Carl Crudup. (R)   *95 minutes*

JENNIFER (1978)
★★

Lisa Pelikan

A schoolgirl who is harassed by her classmates gets revenge through her mysterious powers of telekinesis. This poor relation to *Carrie* has a few suspenseful moments, but mainly it's predictable stuff. Pelikan is fair in the title role, and Amy Johnston steals a few scenes as Jennifer's main tormentor. Also with Bert Convy, John Gavin, and Nina Foch. **Director**—Brice Mack. (PG)   *90 minutes*

THE JERK (1979)
★★

**Steve Martin
Bernadette Peters**

In The Jerk, Steve Martin is Navin Johnson; he's not too bright, but very enthusiastic.

Wild and crazy Martin, in his first starring feature film, lives up to his title role; but he's a silly jerk, not so much a funny jerk. In this rather harmless story, Steve—the son of a poor, black sharecropper—leaves home at age 35 to take a series of odd jobs, becomes wealthy, and finally loses his fortune. If you're alert, you can catch a few good gags, but most of the humor is merely idiotic. Jerry Lewis did this sort

of material with more energy and style. Also with Catlin Adams, Mabel King, and Richard Ward. **Director**—Carl Reiner. (R)   *104 minutes*

JESUS (1980)
★★

**Brian Deacon
John Kirsh**

The producers of this straightforward film on the life of Christ knocked themselves out for the sake of authenticity. The movie was actually shot in the Holy Land, and the screenplay is adapted almost verbatim from the Gospel of Luke; yet Hollywood occasionally manages to creep in. British actor Deacon, who plays the role of Jesus, looks like he just emerged from a beauty shop. There's about as much drama here as in a Sunday school lesson. Also with Rivka Noiman and Yossef Shiloah. Alexander Scourby narrated. **Director**—Peter Sykes. (G)   *117 minutes*

JESUS CHRIST SUPERSTAR
(1973)
★★

**Ted Neeley
Carl Anderson**

A rather uneven screen version of the Broadway rock opera, filmed on location in the Holy Land. The story of Christ is enacted to the beat of rock music and with some contemporary trappings. It's certainly an oddball way of presenting a portion of the Scriptures. The cast does a good job, and the music is invigorating, especially if you happen to like this style. Also with Yvonne Elliman and Barry Dennen. **Director**—Norman Jewison. (G)   *103 minutes*

JEZEBEL (1938)
★★★★

**Bette Davis
Henry Fonda**

Davis is sensational in this excellent melodrama, as a southern belle with a knack for manipulating the men in her life. Fonda plays her fiancé. The film also abounds with other pluses, including a smart script, stylish direc-

tion, and superb photography. It packs plenty of dramatic power, and Davis gives it an extra shot of adrenalin. Other excellent performances from George Brent, Margaret Lindsay, Donald Crisp, Fay Bainter, Spring Byington, and Eddie Anderson. **Director**—William Wyler. **Academy Awards**—Davis, best actress; Bainter, best supporting actress. **Nominations**—best picture; Ernest Haller, cinematography.   *104 minutes b&w*

JOAN OF ARC (1948)
★★

**Ingrid Bergman
José Ferrer**

So-so treatment of the classic story based on Maxwell Anderson's play, with a general feeling of pretentiousness throughout the lavish production. Bergman stars as Joan, the French peasant girl who led military campaigns against British forces and was eventually burned as a heretic. Bergman and the rest of the cast seem to be suffering from a bout of tired blood. Also with George Coulouris, Francis L. Sullivan, Gene Lockhart, Ward Bond, John Ireland, and J. Carrol Naish. **Director**—Victor Fleming. **Academy Award**—Joseph Valentine, William V. Skall, and Winton Hoch, cinematography (color). **Nominations**—Bergman, best actress; Ferrer, best supporting actor.   *145 minutes*

JOE (1970)
★★★★

**Peter Boyle
Dennis Patrick**

(Continued)

Peter Boyle, playing loudmouth foundry worker Joe Curran, stops at a bar in Joe.

J
- Joe Panther
- Johnny Belinda
- The Joker Is Wild
- The Jolson Story

(Continued)

An uncanny, haunting film about a loudmouth foundry worker and a well-heeled advertising executive who become unlikely friends and end up killing some hippies. Boyle gives a vivid performance as the raging, Archie Bunker-type reactionary, and Patrick is convincing as the smooth ad man. The compelling story makes a strong social statement about hatred and bigotry, and the message is hammered home by the similarities and the stark contrasts in the two characters. The film, which is humorous in some respects, ends on a sad note. Also stars Audrey Caire and Susan Sarandon. **Director**—John G. Avildsen. (R) **Academy Award Nomination**—Norman Wexler, best story and screenplay (based on factual material or material not previously published).

107 minutes

JOE PANTHER (1976)
★★

Ray Tracey
A. Martinez

This film, suitable for the whole family, is based on the Zachard Ball novel about a Seminole Indian youth who must prove his manhood by fighting a huge alligator. In some respects, it's almost a children's version of *Jaws*, with some gripping gator-fighting scenes. Much of the film, though, deals with the young Indian's attempt to find acceptance in Florida's white culture, and here the story falls flat, despite decent performances by Tracey in the title role and Martinez as his best friend. Also with Brian Keith, Ricardo Montalban, and Cliff Osmond. **Director**—Paul Krasny. (G)

110 minutes

JOHNNY BELINDA (1948)
★★★

Jane Wyman
Lew Ayres

Wyman gives a magnificent performance as a deaf-mute who is raped; Ayres is effective as a doctor involved with the young girl. This film is highly dramatic and touching, with authentic-looking surroundings of the small fishing village. Wyman seems to

PAUL NEWMAN

Paul Newman has been a major film star for more than two decades. Oscar-nominated for his riveting characterizations in Cat on a Hot Tin Roof *(1958),* The Hustler *(1961),* Hud *(1963),* Cool Hand Luke, *(1967) and* Absence of Malice *(1981), Newman has also starred in such successes as* Somebody Up There Likes Me *(1956),* The Long, Hot Summer *(1958),* The Young Philadelphians *(1959),* From the Terrace *(1960),* Sweet Bird of Youth *(1962),* Harper *(1966),* Winning *(1969),* The Towering Inferno *(1974), and* Slap Shot *(1977), as well as in two of the most popular films in movie history,* Butch Cassidy and the Sundance Kid *(1969), and* The Sting *(1973).*

Born in 1925 and raised in Cleveland, the second son of a business executive, Newman entered Ohio's Kenyon College to major in economics, but left to serve three years in the Navy during World War II. After he returned to Kenyon, he became seriously interested in acting.

A season of summer stock followed his graduation in 1949, but the death of his father forced Newman back to Cleveland to manage the family business. After 18 months, he turned the business over to his brother and entered Yale Drama School. Later, he went to New York, where he was accepted into Lee Strasberg's Actors' Studio and played the role of Alan Seymour in the Broadway production of Picnic, *in which he met Joanne Woodward, his second wife. During the play's 14-month run, he was placed under contract by Warner Brothers studio.*

Disappointed in his film debut as a Greek slave in The Silver Chalice *(1954), Newman was released from his contract and returned to New York to appear in the Broadway hit,* The Desperate Hours.

Hollywood beckoned again, and after his first solid film hit in 1956—as Rocky Graziano in Somebody Up There Likes Me—*he was catapulted to stardom.*

say it all with her eyes. Also with Charles Bickford, Agnes Moorehead, Stephen McNally, and Jan Sterling. **Director**—Jean Negulesco. **Academy Award**—Wyman, best actress. **Nominations**—best picture; Negulesco, best director; Ayres, best actor; Bickford, best supporting actor; Moorehead, best supporting actress; Irmgard Von Cube and Allen Vincent, writing (screenplay); Ted McCord, cinematography (black and white).

103 minutes b&w

THE JOKER IS WILD (1957)
★★★

Frank Sinatra
Mitzi Gaynor

Sinatra portrays nightclub singer Joe E. Lewis of the roaring '20s who had problems with gangsters. This atmospheric film biography is carried off

with adequate energy, and it offers Ol' Blue Eyes an opportunity to belt out some favorite tunes, including "All the Way." Gaynor and Jeanne Crain are fine as objects of Sinatra's affections. Also with Eddie Albert, Beverly Garland, and Jackie Coogan. **Director**—Charles Vidor.

123 minutes b&w

THE JOLSON STORY (1946)
★★★

Larry Parks
William Demarest

A highly successful film biography of the '20s superstar who might have been a cantor, but became one of the greatest singing entertainers of the century. Parks superbly portrays the great performer, with the real Jolson dubbing in his voice for a slew of popular songs, including "Swanee"

- Jonah—Who Will Be 25 in the Year 2000
- Joseph Andrews
- Journey Into Fear
- Journey to the Center of the Earth
- Judgment at Nuremberg
- Julia

J

and "April Showers." It's a first-class show on the subject of show business. Also with Evelyn Keyes, Ludwig Donath, Tamara Shayne, and Scotty Beckett. **Director**—Alfred Green. **Academy Award Nominations**—Parks, best actor; Demarest, best supporting actor; Joseph Walker, cinematography (color). *128 minutes*

JONAH—WHO WILL BE 25 IN THE YEAR 2000 (1976)
★★★

Jean-Luc Bideau
Myriam Boyer

A jaunty Swiss comedy about eight friends who were active in political distrubances of the late '60s and who still uphold utopian ideals. The film, rich with irony, is somewht too talky. Set in Geneva, with a superb cast. Also with Jacques Denis, Rufus, and Miou-Miou. **Director**—Alain Tanner. In French with English titles. (No MPAA rating) *110 minutes*

JOSEPH ANDREWS (1978)
★

Ann-Margret
Peter Firth

Director Tony Richardson, who brought us the delightful *Tom Jones*, falls flat on his face with this similar 18th-century costume tale. It's about a young footman, played by Firth, who is the object of the lustful desires of Lady Booby, his employer; she's played by Ann-Margret. Firth's Andrews character is rather uninteresting. The film is mostly a noisy jumble of tasteless arguing and brawling. And, although the pace is upbeat, the overall tone is tedious. Also with Michael Hordern and Beryl Reid. (R) *103 minutes*

JOURNEY INTO FEAR (1942)
★★★★

Joseph Cotten
Dolores del Rio

This gripping spy caper, based on the Eric Ambler novel, is ablaze with atmospherics and embellishments as only Orson Welles could dream them up. The story concerns a cat-and-

mouse situation during World War II, with an American munitions expert trying to escape from the clutches of enemy agents in Turkey. There are spine-tingling pursuits and tense confrontations, all expertly concocted for maximum shock. Also with Welles, Jack Moss, Agnes Moorehead, and Ruth Warrick. **Director**—Norman Foster and Welles. *71 minutes b&w*

JOURNEY TO THE CENTER OF THE EARTH (1959)
★★★

James Mason
Arlene Dahl
Pat Boone

James Mason and Pat Boone in Journey to the Center of the Earth.

Outlandish but enjoyable sci-fi nonsense, based on the Jules Verne fantasy about a Scottish professor and colleagues who enter an extinct volcano in Iceland and travel to the Earth's core. The special effects are the big thing here, with some good performances and a modest touch of humor. Also with Peter Ronson, Diane Baker, and Thayer David. **Director**—Henry Levin. *132 minutes*

JUDGMENT AT NUREMBERG (1961)
★★★★

Spencer Tracy
Marlene Dietrich
Burt Lancaster
Richard Widmark
Maximilian Schell

A distinguished film treatment of the famous 1948 trial of Nazi bigwigs

Spencer Tracy and Marlene Dietrich in the powerful drama Judgment at Nuremberg.

accused by the Allies of terrible crimes against humanity. It's intelligently done in semidocumentary style and graced with powerful performances. Primarily, the film confronts that nagging rationalization for such outrageous behavior: "We were only following orders." Schell is outstanding as a defense attorney, and Tracy is effective as the court's presiding judge. Also with Judy Garland, Montgomery Clift, William Shatner, Edward Binns, and Werner Klemperer. **Director**—Stanley Kramer. **Academy Awards**—Schell, best actor; Abby Mann, best screenplay (based on material from another medium). **Nominations**—best picture; Kramer, best director; Tracy, best actor; Clift, best supporting actor; Garland, best supporting actress; Ernest Laszlo, cinematography (black and white). *178 minutes b&w*

JULIA (1977)
★★

Jane Fonda
Vanessa Redgrave

Fred Zinnemann (*High Noon*) directed this handsome but bland period film,
(Continued)

In Julia, *Vanessa Redgrave plays the title role, and Jane Fonda stars as Lillian Hellman.*

J
- Julius Caesar
- Jumping Jacks
- The Jungle Book
- Just a Gigolo
- Just Before Nightfall
- Just Crazy About Horses
- Just Tell Me What You Want
- Just You and Me, Kid

(Continued)

based on Lillian Hellman's memoir of a friendship between two brilliant and strong-willed young women. Keen and subtle performances by Fonda, Redgrave, and the fine supporting cast are short-circuited by a lack of passion, drama, and suspense in the screenplay, but the film, set on the eve of World War II, still has some appeal. Also with Jason Robards, Maximilian Schell, and Hal Holbrook. **Academy Awards**—Robards, best supporting actor; Redgrave, best supporting actress. **Nominations**—best picture; Zinnemann, best director; Fonda, best actress. (PG)   *118 minutes*

JULIUS CAESAR (1953)
★★★★

**John Gielgud
James Mason
Marlon Brando**

Excellent acting by a top cast and a sumptuous production do justice to Shakespeare's compelling tragedy about conspiracy and revenge in the Roman Empire. Joseph L. Mankiewicz's direction captures the mood of this moment in history as imagined by the great bard. Mason, as Brutus, and Gielgud, as Cassius, stand out in key roles. Brando plays Marc Antony, and Louis Calhern is Julius Caesar. Also with Greer Garson, Deborah Kerr, Edmond O'Brien, and George Macready. **Academy Award Nominations**—best picture; Brando, best actor; Joseph Ruttenberg, cinematography (black and white).

121 minutes b&w

JUMPING JACKS (1952)
★★★

**Dean Martin
Jerry Lewis**

Martin and Lewis join the Army and sign up for paratrooper duty. Plenty of funny sight gags come along at a fast clip in predictable style, and the boys and the audience have a jolly time. However, the U.S. Airborne takes awhile to recover from the frolic. Co-stars Mona Freeman, Robert Strauss, and Don Defore. **Director**—Norman Taurog.   *96 minutes*

THE JUNGLE BOOK (1942)
★★

Sabu

This children's story by Rudyard Kipling is produced for the screen with lavish detail, but the script is rather farfetched and stilted. Sabu stars as the lad who befriends animals in the Indian jungle and learns their ways. It's probably heavy going for adults, but tolerable for the kids. Also with Joseph Calleia, John Qualen, Frank Puglia, and Rosemary DeCamp. **Director**—Zoltan Korda.

109 minutes

JUST A GIGOLO (1981)
★★

**David Bowie
Kim Novak
Curt Jurgens
Marlene Dietrich**

Bowie, Novak, Jurgens, and Dietrich star in this bizarre, baroque comedy set in post-World War I Germany. The story centers on Bowie as an aristocratic Prussian war vet who drifts in and out of menial jobs before becoming a gigolo. The performances are impressive, but the material is so uneven and loosely constructed that there's scant satisfaction from such notable talent. Dietrich, looking somewhat sad and uneasy, sing-talks the title song. **Director**—David Hemmings. (R)   *105 minutes*

JUST BEFORE NIGHTFALL (1975)
★★★

Michel Bouquet

Director Claude Chabrol's elegant suspense drama is about a French advertising executive who kills his mistress. He escapes police detection, and he's forgiven by his wife and best friend—husband of the victim—but he cannot escape his own need to be punished. Top performance by Bouquet. Also with Stephan Audran and François Perier. In French with English titles. (PG)   *100 minutes b&w*

JUST CRAZY ABOUT HORSES (1979)
★★★

This is an affectionate documentary about breeding, training, selling, and racing horses, but it's just as much about the upper-crust people who are obsessed with the equestrian life. The film is a fascinating observation, but perhaps most enjoyable for people who are—as the title says—crazy about horses. There are explicit scenes of breeding horses and births of foals. Narrated by Tammy Grimes. **Directors**—Tim Lovejoy and Joe Wemple. (PG)   *105 minutes*

JUST TELL ME WHAT YOU WANT (1980)
★★

**Ali MacGraw
Alan King**

King is Max Herschel, a pushy tycoon who's as childish as he is shrewd in this mean-spirited romantic comedy. Despite all the trappings of elegance, King still comes off as a stand-up nightclub comedian. The meager plot involves an attempt by Max's mistress, played by MacGraw, to break away from his domination. Sidney Lumet directs with determined frenzy. There are a few funny moments, but all the shouting and bullying becomes tiresome. Also with Peter Weller, Myrna Loy, Dina Merrill, and Keenan Wynn. (R)   *112 minutes*

JUST YOU AND ME, KID (1979)
★★

**George Burns
Brooke Shields**

Lovable Burns plays a retired vaudeville performer who befriends a pretty 14-year-old orphan, played by Shields. As long as Burns does what comes naturally—ticking off one-liners and doing the old soft shoe—there's some appeal. Aside from that, it's a rather half-baked, lethargic comedy. Shields's stiff performance pales against the warm glow of the venerable old trooper. In this case, it's definitely age

- The Kentuckian
- Kentucky Fried Movie
- Key Largo
- Khartoum
- The Kidnapping of the President
- The Killer Elite

J·K

George Burns and Brooke Shields in the comedy Just You and Me, Kid.

before beauty. Also with Lorraine Gary, Nicholas Coster, Burl Ives, and Ray Bolger. **Director**—Leonard Stern. (PG)   *95 minutes*

K

THE KENTUCKIAN (1955)
★★★

Burt Lancaster

This is a frontier adventure set in the early 1800s with Lancaster, a Kentucky backwoodsman, braving the elements to establish a new home in Texas. The film offers some interesting moments of rugged action, romance, and even a bit of humor. Some decent acting contributes to the interesting tale. Supporting players include Dianne Foster, Diana Lynn, Walter Matthau, Una Merkel, and John Carradine. **Director**—Lancaster.   *104 minutes*

KENTUCKY FRIED MOVIE (1977)
★★

**Evan Kim
Master Bong Soo Han**

A mixed-bag of youth-oriented, satirical sketches on the order of *The Groove Tube* and *Tunnelvision*. The film, divided into 22 segments, takes on TV newscasts, martial-arts and porno movies, and commercials. Some of the skits are clever and funny, but frequent doses of bad taste spoil the fun. The project is the outgrowth of the Kentucky Fried Theater, a satirical group formed at the University of Wisconsin. There are cameos by Bill Bixby, Henry Gibson, Donald Sutherland, and George Lazanby. **Director**—John Landis. (R)   *90 minutes*

KEY LARGO (1948)
★★★★

**Humphrey Bogart
Edward G. Robinson
Lauren Bacall
Claire Trevor**

Tense, electrifying gangster yarn set in the Florida Keys, with Bogart and Robinson making the sparks fly as adversaries. Robinson plays a sinister criminal who holds a group of people captive at a remote hotel during a violent coastal storm; Trevor plays his moll. Bogey is an ex-GI who stands up to Robinson's intimidation. Director John Huston precisely captures the dramatic mood and coaxes excellent performances from the cast. Also with Lionel Barrymore and Thomas Gomez. **Academy Award**—Trevor, best supporting actress.   *101 minutes*

Humphrey Bogart, Claire Trevor, and Lauren Bacall in the gangster yarn Key Largo.

KHARTOUM (1966)
★★

**Charlton Heston
Laurence Olivier**

This slice of history, concerning England's involvement with the Arab nations in the late 19th century, is highlighted with some well-staged battle scenes, but it gets bogged down by too much dialogue. It stars Heston as General Charles "Chinese" Gordon, who meets his match against Arab warriors led by the Mahdi, played by Olivier. There's good acting by these two, but there's not enough depth to their characters. Also with Richard Johnson, Ralph Richardson, Hugh Williams, Nigel Green, and Johnny Sekka. **Director**—Basil Dearden. **Academy Award Nomination**—Robert Ardrey, best story and screenplay (written directly for the screen).   *134 minutes*

THE KIDNAPPING OF THE PRESIDENT (1980)
★★

**William Shatner
Hal Holbrook
Van Johnson
Ava Gardner**

Terrorists abduct the President of the United States during a visit to Toronto and hold him captive in an explosive-filled armored car. This Canadian-made movie stirs up moderate suspense as authorities press their rescue plans. But the improbable plot is riddled with clichés and dumb dialogue that consistently spoils the atmosphere. Shatner plays the man in charge of rescuing the President. Holbrook plays the President with conviction, and there are stylish performances from Johnson as the Vice President and Gardner as Holbrook's wife. **Director**—George Mendeluk. (R)   *113 minutes*

THE KILLER ELITE (1975)
★★

**James Caan
Robert Duvall**

A farfetched action drama about Japanese terrorists who try to kill an anti-Communist Chinese leader. There's a smorgasbord of violence involving the CIA, with guns, machine guns, karate, swords, and kung fu. It's somewhat similar to *Three Days of the Condor*—only the screenplay is thinner. It stars Caan and

(Continued)

In The Killer Elite, *a crippled James Caan prepares to counter an attacker.*

(Continued)
Duvall as a team of gun-toting operatives who eventually wind up on opposite sides. Also with Gig Young, Arthur Hill, and Bo Hopkins. **Director**—Sam Peckinpah. (PG)

122 minutes

KILLER FISH (1979)
★

**Lee Majors
Karen Black**

Just when it seems the waters have been fished clean of horror ideas, they come up with this nasty number made in Brazil. Some thieves steal a pile of emeralds from a mining company and stash the loot in a lake infested with flesh-eating piranha. The piscatorial predators eat most of the cast—just punishment for uttering so much absurd dialogue. Also with Margaux Hemingway, James Franciscus, Marisa Berenson, and Gary Collins. **Director**—Anthony M. Dawson. (PG)

101 minutes

KILLER FORCE (1976)
★★★

**Peter Fonda
Telly Savalas**

A fairly entertaining action drama about a bunch of desperados out to steal several million dollars worth of diamonds from a South American diamond syndicate. Fonda plays a double agent in the plan to rob the company. Savalas, menacing and coldhearted, is the company's security boss. The desert dunes bristle with security gadgets and armed patrols, which the diamond thieves must penetrate to reach the diamonds. The plot is hardly convincing, but the fast-paced action makes up for such drawbacks. Also with Hugh O'Brian, Christopher Lee, Maud Adams, and O. J. Simpson. **Director**—Val Guest. (R)

101 minutes

THE KILLERS (1946)
★★★★

**Burt Lancaster
Edmond O'Brien**

A high-voltage crime drama, smartly directed, professionally acted, and partially based on an Ernest Hemingway short story. A prizefighter is killed in a small town, and an insurance investigator finds out why. The suspense is handled with skill. Also with Ava Gardner, Albert Dekker, Sam Levene, and William Conrad. **Director**—Robert Siodmak. **Academy Award Nominations**—Siodmak, best director; Anthony Veiller, writing (screenplay). *105 minutes b&w*

THE KILLING OF A CHINESE BOOKIE (1976)
★

Ben Gazzara

John Cassavetes, who scored with *A Woman Under the Influence*, fizzles in directing this pointless tale about the sleazy world of nightclub entertainers. Cosmo Vitelli, played by Gazzara, is the owner of a Hollywood strip joint who pays off a gambling debt to the mob by bumping off a Chinese bookie. Gazzara's performance as the hit man is shallow, and the story fails to generate much interest. Also with Timothy Agoglia Carey and Seymour Cassel. (R)

136 minutes

KIM (1951)
★★★

**Errol Flynn
Dean Stockwell**

Rudyard Kipling's tale of the English lad reared in 19th-century India among the Hindus is presented with energy and color. Stockwell plays the title role, as the young adventurer who becomes involved with intrigue and uprisings. Lots of lively action for the kids, and it's rather tolerable for the adults, too. Flynn co-stars, with assists from Paul Lukas, Robert Douglas, Thomas Gomez, and Cecil Kellaway. **Director**—Victor Saville.

112 minutes

KIND HEARTS AND CORONETS (1949)
★★★★

**Alec Guinness
Dennis Price**

Guinness has a field day playing eight

Dennis Price is the scheming young man in Kind Hearts and Coronets.

roles in this stylish black comedy set in Edwardian England. A scheming young man, played by Price, decides that the family fortune belongs to him, and he attempts to achieve his goal by knocking off the competing heirs. It's all done rather cleverly with a liberal amount of wit and irony. Also with Valerie Hobson, Joan Greenwood, and Miles Malleson. **Director**—Robert Hamer. *104 minutes b&w*

THE KING AND I (1956)
★★★

**Deborah Kerr
Yul Brynner**

A lavish musical, based on the Broadway production *Anna and the King of Siam*. Good acting and the Rodgers and Hammerstein music add up to pleasant entertainment; but the film doesn't achieve the high spirits of the stage version. Kerr does well as the perplexed young widow hired to teach the children of the stubborn Siamese monarch, played by Brynner. Brynner gives a powerful performance, and he's credible, indeed, as the mighty ruler with whom Kerr eventually falls in love. There are also some terrific songs, including "Hello Young Lovers" and "Getting To Know You." Also stars Rita Moreno, Martin Benson, Alan Mowbray, and Goeffrey Toone. **Director**—Walter Lang. **Academy Award**—Brynner, best actor. **Nominations**—best picture; Lang, best director; Kerr, best actress; Leon Shamroy, cinematography (color).

133 minutes

- King Kong (1933)
- King Kong (1976)
- King of Hearts
- The King of Marvin Gardens
- King of the Gypsies
- King of the Mountain
- King Solomon's Mines

K

KING KONG (1933)
★★★★

Robert Armstrong
Fay Wray

A thrill-packed monster movie that has achieved screen-classic status, thanks to the imaginative and skillful use of special effects and on-target direction. A giant ape is brought from the jungle to New York, where it escapes and causes havoc in the city; the memorable climax on the Empire State Building is a masterpiece. Wray stars as the beauty the beast finds irresistable. Also with Bruce Cabot and Frank Reicher. **Directors**—Merian C. Cooper and Ernest Schoedsack.

100 minutes b&w

KING KONG (1976)
★★★★

Jeff Bridges
Jessica Lange

The big beast in King Kong *gives Dwan, played by Jessica Lange, a big hand.*

Kong still reigns as king in this $24-million retread of the 1933 classic. The lavish Dino De Laurentiis production is substantially faithful in spirit and imagery to this enduring fantasy of beauty and the beast. In fact, the update contains noticeable improvements: suberb special effects, richer characters, and a polished contemporary script. It's old-time movie magic that's intimate, amusing, sentimental, adventuresome, and marvelous fun all the way. Also with Charles Grodin and John Randolph. **Director**—John Guillermin. (PG) *134 minutes*

KING OF HEARTS (1967)
★★★★

Alan Bates
Geneviève Bujold

A smashing, thought-provoking antiwar movie with a satirical punch that's unforgettable. Bates plays a Scottish soldier in World War I, sent on a mission to defuse a bomb in a French town. All the inhabitants have fled except the inmates of an insane asylum, and they turn out to be more rational than those engaged in fighting the war. Bujold is a dancer who's an asylum inmate. Directed and acted with exceptional style, the film has become a cult favorite. Co-stars Pierre Brasseur and Jean-Claude Brialy. In French with English titles. **Director**—Philippe De Broca. *102 minutes*

THE KING OF MARVIN GARDENS (1972)
★★

Jack Nicholson
Bruce Dern
Ellen Burstyn

An out-of-kilter bittersweet comedy about two brothers, played by Nicholson and Dern, who long to achieve the American dream, but their ways and means aren't enough to reach the goal. Nicholson is excellent as a radio talk-show host, and Dern is impressive as a small-time operator with big ideas. Burstyn plays an aging beauty. But this overly talky film misses the mark. Director Bob Rafelson, whose earlier effort was *Five Easy Pieces*, isn't up to the level of that film here. Also with Julia Anne Robinson and Scatman Crothers. (R) *104 minutes*

KING OF THE GYPSIES (1978)
★★

Sterling Hayden
Eric Roberts
Shelley Winters

This is a contemporary story of a feuding gypsy family, based on Peter Maas's book. There are some fascinating moments, but mostly the film is disorganized and unconvincing. There's an encouraging debut by

In King of the Gypsies, *Eric Roberts protects Brooke Shields from Judd Hirsch.*

Roberts as the young rebel who struggles to escape from the bizarre gypsy world, but Hayden, Winters, Judd Hirsch, and Susan Sarandon are miscast in stereotyped roles. Also with Annette O'Toole and Brooke Shields. It was a good opportunity for an exciting film, but writer-director Frank Pierson missed the mark. (R) *112 minutes*

KING OF THE MOUNTAIN (1981)
★★

Harry Hamlin

Young men race their souped-up sports cars down winding Mulholland Drive in Los Angeles, drink whiskey straight from the bottle, and challenge their male egos. A few end up in flaming wrecks, and sometimes the cops show up. This pointless melodrama appears to be a vague throwback to those James Dean movies of the '50s. In this case, the cars are fast, but the plot is slow. Hamlin stars as the top speedster with the fastest Porsche in the West. **Director**—Noel Nosseck. (R) *90 minutes*

KING SOLOMON'S MINES (1950)
★★★★

Stewart Granger
Deborah Kerr

Ripsnorting adventure in darkest Africa, with Granger and Kerr heading an exploration team to find Kerr's missing husband and lost diamond mines. The impressive-looking production, based on H. Rider Haggard's novel, is nicely paced and leads to a magnificent climax, and there's ade-
(Continued)

K
- King's Row
- Kismet (1944)
- Kismet (1955)
- Kiss Me Kate
- Kiss of Death
- Kiss Tomorrow Goodbye
- Kitty

(Continued)

quate excitement and suspense along the way. Also with Richard Carlson, Hugo Haas, and Lowell Gilmore. **Director**—Compton Bennett. (PG) **Academy Award**—Robert Surtees, cinematography (color). **Nomination**—best picture. *102 minutes*

KING'S ROW (1942)
★★★★

Ann Sheridan
Robert Cummings

Ann Sheridan, Robert Cummings, and a bedridden Ronald Reagan in King's Row.

A penetrating look at a small American community at the turn of the century, with pettiness and anxieties laid bare. The story unfolds as an early-century *Peyton Place*, with much style and high drama. Superb characterizations abound, and there's plenty of fine acting throughout. Also with Ronald Reagan, Claude Rains, Charles Coburn, and Judith Anderson. **Director**—Sam Wood. **Academy Award Nominations**—Wood, best director; James Wong Howe, cinematography (black and white). *127 minutes b&w*

KISMET (1944)
★★★

Ronald Colman
Marlene Dietrich

Adequate telling of the Arabian Nights fable, with a good cast doing its utmost. The production, starring Colman and Dietrich, has a lot of polish, and there's a striking dance scene with Marlene all aglow in gold body paint. The proceedings could use a bit of levity, but it's worthwhile viewing nevertheless. Also with James Craig, Edward Arnold, Harry Davenport,

and Florence Bates. **Director**—William Dieterle. *100 minutes*

KISMET (1955)
★★

Howard Keel
Ann Blyth

Disappointing film version, starring Keel and Blyth, of the hit musical stage production of romance and intrigue in Old Baghdad. Alexander Borodin's beautiful music comes over nicely, but the story is off stride. It's nice to listen to, but barely watchable. Also with Vic Damone, Monty Woolley, Dolores Gray, Sebastian Cabot, and Jack Elam. **Director**—Vincente Minnelli. *113 minutes*

KISS ME KATE (1953)
★★★

Howard Keel
Kathryn Grayson

A perky backstage musical taken from the Broadway hit and filled with Cole Porter's delightful tunes. Keel and Grayson portray married thespians performing in Shakespeare's *Taming of the Shrew* adapted for music. It's decked out nicely with energetic dancing, a touch of comedy, and such great songs as "So In Love," "Wunderbar," and "Brush Up Your Shakespeare," Also among the cast are Ann Miller, Keenan Wynn, Bobby Van, James Whitmore, Tommy Rall, and Bob Fosse. **Director**—George Sidney. *109 minutes*

KISS OF DEATH (1947)
★★★★

Victor Mature
Richard Widmark

Taut, moody gangster thriller played to the hilt for suspense. A thief rats on his pals, and then a ruthless hit man trails him to get revenge. There are outstanding performances by Mature and by Widmark, who is perfectly cast as the giggling, psychopathic killer. Remade as *The Fiend Who Walked the West*. Also with Brian Donlevy, Karl Malden, Mildred Dunnock, and Coleen Gray. **Director**—Henry Hathaway. **Academy Award Nominations**—

Victor Mature (center) doing time in the taut gangster thriller Kiss of Death.

Widmark, best supporting actor; Eleazar Lipsky, writing (original story). *98 minutes b&w*

KISS TOMORROW GOODBYE (1950)
★★★

James Cagney
Barbara Payton

Cagney plays his typical gangster role in this violent drama that's watchable mainly because of the star's performance. The film, however, isn't up to the level of Cagney's *White Heat*. Here, the tough guy plays an escaped convict who marries and then embarks on some gun-blazing holdups. Also with Ward Bond, Luther Adler, Steve Brodie, and Helena Carter. **Director**—Gordon Douglas. *102 minutes b&w*

KITTY (1945)
★★★

Paulette Goddard
Ray Milland

Another version of the *Pygmalion* story. Set in 18th-century London, the film stars Goddard as a poor girl who becomes a well-mannered woman with the help of an artist, played by Milland. The film is well made and there is excellent use of costumes and period detail. Goddard's performance is tops, and she's nicely assisted by Milland, Cecil Kellaway, Constance Collier, Reginald Owen, Patric Knowles, and Sara Allgood. **Director**—Mitchell Leisen. *103 minutes b&w*

★ STAR PROFILE

- Kitty Foyle
- Klute
- Knightriders
- Knute Rockne—All American
- Kramer Vs. Kramer

K

KITTY FOYLE (1940)
★★★★

Ginger Rogers

An above-average love story with a fine performance by Rogers as a working girl who has romantic problems. The film is expertly adapted from Christopher Morley's dramatic novel, and it features other good performances from Dennis Morgan, Eduardo Ciannelli, Gladys Cooper, and James Craig. **Director**—Sam Wood. **Academy Award**—Rogers, best actress. **Nominations**—best picture; Wood, best director; Dalton Trumbo, writing (screenplay).

108 minutes b&w

KLUTE (1971)
★★★★

Jane Fonda
Donald Sutherland

Donald Sutherland, a small-time cop, falls in love with call-girl Jane Fonda in Klute.

Fonda gives a smashing performance as a sophisticated call girl in this gripping crime thriller. The story involves a small-town cop, played by Sutherland, who comes to New York City to locate a missing friend. During his investigation, he meets Fonda and falls in love with her. Fonda portrays her character expertly, with much credibility and colorful detail, and the film offers some insightful character studies. Also with Charles Cioffi, Roy Scheider, Jean Stapleton, and Rita Gam. **Director**—Alan J. Pakula. (R) **Academy Award**—Fonda, best actress. **Nomination**—Andy and Dave Lewis, best story and screenplay (based on factual material or material not previously published).

114 minutes

KNIGHTRIDERS (1981)
★★

Ed Harris
Gary Lahti

George Romero (*Night of the Living Dead*) applies the legend of King Arthur to modern-day knights who tour the country staging jousting contests on motorcycles. Harris and Lahti star in a cast of largely unknown actors. The performances are adequate, and the motorcycle stunts are well coordinated, yet there's meager dramatic impetus as these gasoline-propelled warriors pursue honor and glory atop their Harley-Davidsons. In fact, it's rather tame in contrast to Romero's former bloodletting horror excesses. Also with Tom Sauini and Amy Ingersoll. (R)   *145 minutes*

KNUTE ROCKNE—ALL AMERICAN (1940)
★★★

Pat O'Brien
Gale Page

This memorable film biography of the famous Notre Dame football coach is perhaps most intriguing since Ronald Reagan became President. O'Brien is very convincing as the determined coach, and Reagan is adequate as George Gipp, the team's star player. The story is rather predictable, with considerable emphasis on gridiron glory. The script contains the indelible locker room plea: ". . . win it for the Gipper!" Unfortunately, this scene is cut from TV prints due to legal problems. Also co-stars Donald Crisp and Albert Bassermann.   *98 minutes b&w*

KRAMER VS. KRAMER (1979)
★★★★

Dustin Hoffman
Meryl Streep
Jane Alexander
Justin Henry

A love story about the love of a father and son who really get to know each other when the wife and mother abruptly walks out on them. Hoffman plays the father, Henry is his son, and Streep is the woman trying to find her-

ALEC GUINNESS

Sir Alec Guinness is a versatile stage actor who became a spectacular screen star. He performed Shakespeare on stage and starred as Disraeli, the Pope, Hitler, King Charles I, and Obi-Wan Kenobi in Star Wars *(1977) in films. He also excelled in comedy, with superbly droll performances in such movies as* The Lavender Hill Mob *(1951) and* The Captain's Paradise *(1952).*

Guinness was born in London in 1914. He started out as an advertising copywriter before studying acting. In the '30s, he was in various stage productions with the Old Vic; in 1941, he joined the British navy, in which he served as an officer.

After World War II, Guinness began a serious film career. He soon became proficient in playing multiple roles in a single movie. In Kind Hearts and Coronets *(1949), he amazed audiences by playing eight roles, but it was as a stiff-upper-lipped British officer in* The Bridge on the River Kwai *(1957) that he won an Oscar for best actor. In 1959, Queen Elizabeth II knighted Guinness for his outstanding work on the stage and in movies.*

Some of his other memorable films include Great Expectations *(1946),* Oliver Twist *(1948),* The Mudlark *(1950),* The Man in the White Suit *(1951),* Our Man in Havana *(1959),* Lawrence of Arabia *(1962),* Doctor Zhivago *(1966),* The Comedians *(1967), and* Brother Sun, Sister Moon *(1973).*

self; Alexander plays a concerned family friend. Ordinarily, such fare is grist for flimsy soap operas, but this film is blessed with insight, sensitivity, and intelligence; it also dissects a number *(Continued)*

K·L

- La Cage Aux Folles
- La Cage Aux Folles II
- The Lacemaker
- The Lady Eve

- Lady Hamilton
- Lady in a Cage
- Lady in Cement
- Lady in the Dark

In Kramer vs. Kramer, *Dustin Hoffman discovers the joys of fatherhood.*

(Continued)

of current social problems relentlessly. Hoffman, Streep, and six-year-old Henry are in rare form. Also with Howard Duff and George Coe. **Director**—Robert Benton. (PG) **Academy Awards**—best picture; Benton, best director; Hoffman, best actor; Streep, best supporting actress; Benton, best screenplay (adapted from another medium). **Nominations**—Henry, best supporting actor; Alexander, best supporting actress; Nestor Alemdros, cinematography. *105 minutes*

L

LA CAGE AUX FOLLES (1979)
★★★★

**Ugo Tognazzi
Michel Serrault**

What do you do when you're in love with a beautiful, respectable girl, and your father is a homosexual who lives with a drag queen? Bring her folks over to meet your folks, of course. And that's when all the outrageous fun begins in this brilliant farce, which won France's version of the Oscar. Skilled performances and keen comic timing by Tognazzi and Serrault as the gay duo make this film a great comedy. In French with English titles. (R) **Director**—Edouard Molinaro. **Academy Award Nominations**—Molinaro, best director; Francis Veber, Molinaro, Marcello Danon, and Jean Poiret, best screenplay (adapted from another medium). *99 minutes*

LA CAGE AUX FOLLES II (1981)
★★

**Ugo Tognazzi
Michel Serrault**

Serrault, as the temperamental drag queen, and Tognazzi, as the straight lover, return in this so-so sequel to the successful French comedy. This time, the duo is mixed up in a drab and predictable secret-agent melodrama with missing microfilm and several corpses. Serrault and Tognazzi generate some funny moments, but it's formula stuff without the relentlessly clever ingredients that made the first film a hit. In French with English titles. **Director**—Edouard Molinaro. (R) *100 minutes*

Michel Serrault and Ugo Tognazzi in La Cage Aux Folles II, *a French comedy.*

THE LACEMAKER (1977)
★★★

**Isabelle Huppert
Yves Beneyton**

Swiss director Claude Goretta's gentle and delicate film is about a tragic affair between mismatched lovers. Huppert dominates the film, with a warmly appealing performance as the sweet-natured beauty parlor assistant who is eventually dismissed by her lover, an intellectual student played by Beneyton. The material is familiar, but Goretta's masterful touch adds the extra sensitivity needed. (No MPAA rating) *108 minutes*

THE LADY EVE (1941)
★★★★

**Barbara Stanwyck
Henry Fonda**

Lively, witty, romantic farce, done in an engaging manner by director Preston Sturges for nonstop mirth. Stanwyck stars as a con artist who tries to pull a fast one on a seemingly gullible rich man, played by Fonda. The spoof progresses at a fast pace, and the laughs come at a gallop. Nice work by Stanwyck and Fonda, with expert support from Charles Coburn, Eugene Pallette, William Demarest, and Eric Blore. **Academy Award Nomination**—Monckton Hoffe, writing (original story). *97 minutes b&w*

LADY HAMILTON
See That Hamilton Woman

LADY IN A CAGE (1964)
★★

Olivia de Havilland

Overwrought suspense story about a rich woman trapped in an elevator by some young thugs who vandalize her apartment. There are some tense moments, but most of the film is pretentious and somewhat unsavory. De Havilland is wasted as the harassed and vulnerable widow. Supporting roles are played by James Caan, Ann Sothern, and Jeff Corey. **Director**—Walter Grauman. *97 minutes b&w*

LADY IN CEMENT (1968)
★★

**Frank Sinatra
Raquel Welch**

More adventures in the life of private-eye Tony Rome. This time the film is dressed up with an added portion of flashy sex and violence. Sinatra again plays the hip gumshoe, and he's on the trail of a killer after discovering a woman's corpse with its feet anchored in cement. There are predictable and plodding proceedings, bogged down with heavy-handed embellishments. Welch and Lainie Kazan add the glamour, with support from Richard Conte and Dan Blocker. **Director**—Gordon Douglas. (PG) *93 minutes*

LADY IN THE DARK (1944)
★★★

Ginger Rogers

A lavish and colorful romantic comedy about a woman magazine editor who

● Lady Sings the Blues
● La Grande Bourgeoise
● The Land That Time Forgot

● Laserblast
● Lassie Come Home
● The Last Angry Man
● The Last Detail

L

suffers mental anguish over the men in her life. Rogers, in the starring role, turns on the charm as the perplexed career girl. And there are ample comic moments for the entire cast, which also features Ray Milland, Warner Baxter, Jon Hall, Mischa Auer, and Barry Sullivan. Adapted from Moss Hart's Broadway musical, but lacking many of the songs. **Director**—Mitchell Leisen. *100 minutes*

LADY SINGS THE BLUES (1972)
★★★

Diana Ross
Billy Dee Williams

Diana Ross and Billy Dee Williams in Lady Sings the Blues, *a film about Billie Holiday.*

The tumultuous and tragic life of singing great Billie "Lady Day" Holiday is portrayed with amazing clarity and style by Ross, a singing sensation in her own right. This film biography seems light on facts and heavy on drama, but it's high-level entertainment nevertheless, thanks to Ross's grasp of the role. She belts out the tunes in convincing style, and her straight acting is impressive, too. Williams plays her husband. Also with Richard Pryor and Sid Melton. **Director**—Sidney J. Furie. (R) **Academy Award Nominations**—Ross, best actress; Terence McCloy, Chris Clark, and Suzanne de Passe, best story and screenplay (based on factual material or material not previously published). *144 minutes*

LA GRANDE BOURGEOISE (1977)
★★

Giancarlo Giannini
Catherine Deneuve
Fernando Rey

Intellectual but sluggish story about a turn-of-the-century murder and scan-

dal that involved a prominent family in Bologna, Italy. A handsome cast is headed by Giannini, Deneuve, and Rey, but their excellent performances are lost in the confusion and shallowness of the screenplay. Director Mauro Bolognini's lush, soft-focus photography mutes much of the drama. In Italian with English titles. (No MPAA rating) *115 minutes*

THE LAND THAT TIME FORGOT (1975)
★★

Doug McClure

The film, based on an Edgar Rice Burroughs novel, is about German submariners and survivors of a British ship who discover a lost continent where prehistoric beasts roam. A trite and confusing script, but impressive special effects that may appeal to children more than adults. Also with John McEnery, Susan Penhaligon, and Keith Barron. **Director**—Kevin Connor. (PG) *91 minutes*

LASERBLAST (1978)
★

Kim Milford
Cheryl Smith
Roddy McDowall

This low-budget, slipshod horror movie tries to force the plot angles of *Carrie* within a sci-fi framework. A nice kid from California, who is teased a lot, discovers an alien's laser gun in the desert and goes on a revenge spree. The special effects are unconvincing, and the second-string cast turns in inadequate performances. Sci-fi fans would be better off seeing *Star Wars* one more time. Also with Keenan Wynn and Ron Masock. **Director**—Michael Raye. (PG) *90 minutes*

LASSIE COME HOME (1943)
★★★★

Roddy McDowall
Elizabeth Taylor
Donald Crisp

Big tug at the heartstrings with this sentimental tale about a poor family that must sell its faithful collie, but the

loyal dog makes a brave journey back to its familiar home. This is a family film of the highest order, and it spawned a lot of sequels and a TV series. The remarkable cast also includes Edmund Gwenn, Dame May Whitty, Elsa Lanchester, and, of course, Lassie. **Director**—Fred M. Wilcox. **Academy Award Nomination**—Leonard Smith, cinematography (color). *88 minutes*

THE LAST ANGRY MAN (1959)
★★★★

Paul Muni

Sensitive story, adapted from Gerald Green's book, about an elderly family doctor in a poor Brooklyn neighborhood, who is more concerned with the welfare of his impoverished patients than with making lots of money. The film makes a strong statement about commercialism within the professions, which obviously rings true about other corners of society. Muni, in his last screen role, is excellent as the idealistic physician. There's good support, too, from David Wayne, Betsy Palmer, and Luther Adler. **Director**—Daniel Mann. **Academy Award Nomination**—Muni, best actor.

100 minutes b&w

THE LAST DETAIL (1973)
★★★★

Jack Nicholson
Otis Young
Randy Quaid

A true-to-life, bittersweet comedy about justice without mercy in the Navy. Two senior petty officers—Nicholson and Young—escort a
(Continued)

Otis Young and Jack Nicholson play two senior petty officers in The Last Detail.

L
• The Last Embrace
• The Last Flight of Noah's Ark
• The Last Hard Men
• The Last Hurrah
• The Last Married Couple in America
• The Last Metro

(Continued)

young sailor accused of petty theft on a two-day trip to the Portsmouth, New Hampshire, brig. En route, they take pity and treat him to a last fling before his imprisonment. Nicholson shines as the tough but sympathetic career man; Quaid is outstanding as the hapless sailor whose impending punishment doesn't fit the crime. And there are excellent character studies throughout. Also with Clifton James, Carol Kane, and Michael Marty. **Director**—Hal Ashby. (R) **Academy Award Nominations**—Nicholson, best actor; Quaid, best supporting actor; Robert Towne, best screenplay (based on material from another medium). *104 minutes*

THE LAST EMBRACE (1979)
★★

Roy Scheider
Janet Margolin

Janet Margolin and Roy Scheider are troubled lovers in The Last Embrace.

Scheider plays a worried-looking government agent who believes someone is about to kill him. Margolin is a graduate student who mysteriously enters his life. Scheider and Margolin are excellent; they build suspense by virtue of their acting talents. But director Jonathan Demme's romantic thriller is meager, illogical, and often confusing. The movie winds up at the edge of Niagara Falls; by that time, the story seems all wet. Also with Sam Levene, John Glover, and Christopher Walken. (R) *102 minutes*

THE LAST FLIGHT OF NOAH'S ARK (1980)
★★

Elliott Gould
Geneviève Bujold
Ricky Schroder
Tammy Lauren

Disney's takeoff on the well-known Bible story is a pat and predictable adventure film where kids once more get their way with adults. Gould and Bujold crash-land on a Pacific island in a lumbering B-29 full of animals and a couple of stowaway kids; the kids are Schroder and Lauren. They all finally escape by converting the plane into a ship, and they take the animals along at the youngsters' insistence. The animals should have stayed behind. Also with Vincent Gardenia. **Director**—Charles Jarrott. (G) *97 minutes*

THE LAST HARD MEN (1976)
★★

Charlton Heston
James Coburn

Vengeance is the theme of this routine western, set in Arizona in the early 1900s. Coburn plays a half-breed Navajo who lures a retired lawman, played by Heston, to a slow and gruesome death. The plot gallops occasionally, but most often it moves at a slow walk. Coburn and Heston, however, are convincing as the hard-boiled adversaries. Some of the vivid brutality may be hard on the audience. Also with Barbara Hershey, Christopher Mitchum, and Michael Parks. **Director**—Andrew V. McLaglen. (R) *98 minutes*

THE LAST HURRAH (1958)
★★★★

Spencer Tracy
Jeffrey Hunter

Entertaining account of big-city politics, with Tracy expertly portraying a mayor who holds power through shrewdness. Tracy is completely at ease in the role, and he receives top support from a veteran cast. Adapted from Edwin O'Connor's novel, inspired by the career of Boston Mayor

James Curley. Also co-stars Pat O'Brien, Basil Rathbone, Edward Brophy, Donald Crisp, James Gleason, John Carradine, Jeffrey Hunter, Dianne Foster, and Wallace Ford. **Director**—John Ford.

121 minutes b&w

THE LAST MARRIED COUPLE IN AMERICA (1980)
★★

George Segal
Natalie Wood

In The Last Married Couple in America, *Natalie Wood tells George Segal it's over.*

Segal and Wood are Jeff and Mari of Los Angeles, who observe their friends' marriages breaking up and wonder if they're next. The predictable TV-sitcom screenplay is only mildly amusing as it examines the despair of the sexual revolution. The acting, however, is well above the material; Wood is especially good with her comic assignment. And there are some classy scenes with Richard Benjamin, Dom DeLuise, and Valerie Harper. **Director**—Gilbert Cates. (R) *103 minutes*

THE LAST METRO (1981)
★★★

Catherine Deneuve
Heinz Bennent

Director François Truffaut (*The 400 Blows; Jules and Jim*) scores again with this affecting story of backstage theater life during the Nazi occupation of Paris. Beautiful Deneuve runs a small Paris theater by proxy for her husband, a Jewish director who goes into

• Last of the Red Hot Lovers
• The Last Picture Show
• The Last Remake of Beau Geste
• The Last Romantic Lover
• Last Tango in Paris
• The Last Tycoon

L

hiding. He's played by Bennent. Gerard Depardieu is splendid as a rakish actor who turns out to be quite a patriot. A fine supporting cast adds to this charming slice-of-life drama of love and heroism. Also with Jean-Louis Richard, Jean Poiret, and Sabine Haudepin. In French with English titles. (No MPAA rating)

130 minutes

LAST OF THE RED HOT LOVERS (1972)
★★

Alan Arkin

So-so film version of Neil Simon's stage comedy about the owner of a seafood restaurant who attempts an extramarital fling with three women. Arkin, in the title role, manages to arouse a few smiles as the klutzy Don Juan, but there isn't enough comic energy to sustain the film. All in all, it's not so hot. Also with Paula Prentiss, Sally Kellerman, and Renée Taylor. **Director**—Gene Saks. (PG)

98 minutes

THE LAST PICTURE SHOW (1971)
★★★

Timothy Bottoms
Jeff Bridges
Cybill Shepherd
Ben Johnson

A nostalgic look at life in a small Texas town in the early '50s, as seen through the experiences of some high-school students. This film is a bit short on drama and plot, but there are fine, engrossing characterizations and exquisite atmospheric detail; the film is somewhat of a low-key *American Graffiti*. First-class performances by Bottoms, Bridges, Shepherd, Johnson, Cloris Leachman, and Ellen Burstyn. **Director**—Peter Bogdanovich. (R) **Academy Awards**—Johnson, best supporting actor; Leachman, best supporting actress. **Nominations**—best picture; Bogdanovich, best director; Bridges, best supporting actor; Burstyn, best supporting actress; Larry McMurtry and Bogdanovich, best screenplay (based on material from another medium); Robert Surtees, cinematography.

114 minutes b&w

THE LAST REMAKE OF BEAU GESTE (1977)
★★

Marty Feldman
Ann-Margret
Michael York
Peter Ustinov

Digby (Marty Feldman) has a daring jailbreak foiled in The Last Remake of Beau Geste.

Pop-eyed Feldman strikes out on his own as star, director, and writer of this parody of Foreign Legion films, but he's left stranded in the desert. The uneven picture gallops about in fits and starts—at times funny, more often just strained silliness. Feldman borrows generously from his mentor, Mel Brooks, but his execution is heavy-handed and reckless. Some of the barren stretches are shored up by a first-rate cast that also includes Trevor Howard, James Earl Jones, Terry-Thomas, and Henry Gibson. (PG)

83 minutes

THE LAST ROMANTIC LOVER (1979)
★★★

Gerard Ismael
Dayle Haddon

An amusing and charming comedy about a French lion-tamer who reluctantly enters a male beauty contest organized by a bitchy magazine editor. As a prize, the lion-tamer wins a week with the woman of his choice. Guess who? Ismael plays the lion-tamer, and Haddon plays the editor. The compli-

cations of this arrangement lead to plenty of fun as our hero demonstrates he's quite the romantic lover indeed. In French with English titles. **Director**—Just Jaeckin. (R)   *100 minutes*

LAST TANGO IN PARIS (1973)
★★★

Marlon Brando
Maria Schneider

Controversial sex film about a middle-aged American widower and a young French girl who have a torrid love affair. Brando and Schneider play the couple in love. The patchy story is engrossing, but at times it's rather dull. Still, there are a few extraordinary scenes, and, in a most difficult role, Brando gives one of his best performances. Schneider also performs well. The uncut version depicts anal intercourse. The film co-stars Jean-Pierre Léaud. **Director**—Bernardo Bertolucci. (X) **Academy Award Nominations**—Bertolucci, best director; Brando, best actor.   *129 minutes*

Maria Schneider and Marlon Brando dance in the controversial Last Tango in Paris.

THE LAST TYCOON (1976)
★

Robert De Niro
Tony Curtis
Robert Mitchum
Jack Nicholson

Lethargy pervades this screen version of F. Scott Fitzgerald's unfinished novel about the flourishing Hollywood of the '30s. De Niro plays the film producer who's working himself to death. The all-star cast, including De Niro, Curtis, Mitchum, and Nicholson, is essentially wasted in muted roles. The production is a

(Continued)

L
- The Last Waltz
- The Last Wave
- Las Vegas Lady
- The Late George Apley
- The Late Great Planet Earth
- The Late Show
- Laura

(Continued)

meandering and wistful story with no real climax. Harold Pinter wrote the screenplay. Also with Ingrid Boulting, Donald Pleasence, Jeanne Moreau, and Ray Milland. **Director**—Elia Kazan. (PG)   *125 minutes*

THE LAST WALTZ (1978)
★★

The Band
Bob Dylan
Neil Young

Robbie Robertson, the leader of The Band, in the rock documentary The Last Waltz.

Martin Scorsese directed this rock music documentary, focusing on the farewell concert by The Band in 1976 in San Francisco. Interviews with the group's members are interspersed among the musical numbers, which come on at full blast of Dolby stereo. Dylan, Young, Joni Mitchell, Neil Diamond, Muddy Waters, and Eric Clapton join in with some rousing songs. It's a film for aficionados, but it does little to illuminate that dazzling era of rock music. Also with Van Morrison and Emmylou Harris. (No MPAA rating)   *117 minutes*

THE LAST WAVE (1978)
★★

Richard Chamberlain

This is a pretentious story about an Australian lawyer, played by Chamberlain, who defends Aborigines accused of ritual murder and becomes involved with their tribal mysteries. Director Peter Weir can't get the events organized, so the film comes over as so much mumbo jumbo. There are, however, moments of effective suspense. Also with Olivia Hammett, Frederick Parslow, Vivian Gray, and David Gulpilil. (No MPAA rating)   *106 minutes*

LAS VEGAS LADY (1976)
(no stars)

Stella Stevens
Stuart Whitman

The movie is about three girls who relieve a crooked Las Vegas casino manager of his loot. This film suffers from uninspired acting and direction, an unimaginative script, and little suspense. It was shot amid the glitter of the Circus Circus casino in Las Vegas, and it's far from a winner. Also with George DeCenzo and Lynne Moody. **Director**—Noel Nosseck. (PG)   *87 minutes*

THE LATE GEORGE APLEY (1946)
★★★

Ronald Coleman
Peggy Cummins

Mildy entertaining film based on John P. Marquand's satirical novel about an aristocratic Boston family. It's a sturdy, adequate family comedy, but without any particular snap. There are, however, some good performances by the cast, which also includes Edna Best, Vanessa Brown, Richard Haydn, and Charles Russell. **Director**—Joseph L. Mankiewicz.   *98 minutes b&w*

THE LATE GREAT PLANET EARTH (1979)
★

Live it up, folks—according to this quasi-documentary, worldwide destruction will be upon us before we know it. The film refers to the Bible, and a few eminent scientists, too, about our ultimate demise—atomic blasts, floods, starvation, and earthquakes. Grim stuff, indeed, but hardly convincing. Based on the book by Hal Lindsey. Orson Welles narrates. **Director**—Robert Amram. (PG)   *90 minutes*

THE LATE SHOW (1977)
★★★

Art Carney
Lily Tomlin

Art Carney and Lily Tomlin star in the comedy-mystery The Late Show.

Writer-director Robert Benton creates oodles of rich and unforgettable characters in this latter-day version of the '40s private-eye movie. Carney is sensational as an over-the-hill gumshoe who pursues the killer of an old colleague. He's matched by Tomlin's winning performance as his loony sidekick who dabbles in show biz, astrology, and Eastern religions. The top-heavy and complex plot is difficult to unravel, but it pays off in atmosphere rather than in detective-story thrills. Also with Bill Macy, Eugene Roche, Joanna Cassidy, John Considine, and Howard Duff. (PG) **Academy Award Nomination**—Benton, best original screenplay.   *94 minutes*

LAURA (1944)
★★★★

Dana Andrews
Clifton Webb
Gene Tierney

A gripping murder mystery that's full of surprise, suspense, and atmosphere. A lovely girl, played by Tierney, is supposedly murdered, and a determined detective, played by Andrews, uncovers more than he expected. Webb is outstanding as a cynical columnist. It's a fascinating, classic whodunit with a mature outlook. Also with Judith Anderson, Vincent Price, Dorothy Adams, and Grant Mitchell. **Director**—Otto Preminger. **Academy Award**—Joseph LaShelle, cinematography (black and white). **Nominations**—Preminger, best director; Webb, best supporting actor.

85 minutes

THE LAVENDER HILL MOB
(1952)
★★★★

**Alec Guinness
Stanley Holloway**

A lively, droll comedy full of sharp wit and smart dialogue. Guinness triumphs as a mild-mannered bank clerk who engineers a clever scheme to steal a fortune in gold bullion from an armored car. The hilarity is relentless, and it ends with an effective, rollicking chase sequence. In this case, crime doesn't pay, but there's a big reward in the laughter. See if you can spot Audrey Hepburn. Also co-stars Sidney James, Alfie Bass, Marjorie Fielding, and John Gregson. **Director**—Charles Crichton. **Academy Award**—T.E.B. Clarke, writing (story and screenplay). **Nomination**—Guinness, best actor. *82 minutes b&w*

LAWMAN (1970)
★★★

**Burt Lancaster
Robert Ryan
Lee J. Cobb**

A top cast helps this grim western story about a showdown between a marshal determined to arrest some lawbreakers and the local citizens who resist his efforts. Lancaster is good as the duty-bound lawman, and Cobb is convincing as the cattleman whose hired hands are involved with the killing of an old man. Also with Sheree North, Robert Duvall, Joseph Wiseman, Alber Salmi, John McGiver, and J. D. Cannon. **Director**—Michael Winner. (PG) *99 minutes*

LAWRENCE OF ARABIA (1962)
★★★★

**Peter O'Toole
Omar Sharif
Arthur Kennedy**

Grandiose epic about the exploits of enigmatic British adventurer T. E. Lawrence in the Middle East during World War I. The film features stunning photography, excellent performances, and an intelligent script; however, it offers little insight into Lawrence, a complex and mysterious character. O'Toole is outstanding in the title role, and there's impressive supporting work from Sharif, Kennedy, Claude Rains, Donald Wolfit, Anthony Quinn, Anthony Quayle, Alec Guinness, and José Ferrer. The spectacle, however, loses some of its impact on the small screen. **Director**—David Lean. **Academy Awards**—best picture; Lean, best director; Fred A. Young, cinematography (color).

Nominations—O'Toole, best actor; Sharif, best supporting actor; Robert Bolt, best screenplay (based on material from another medium).

221 minutes

LEADBELLY (1976)
★★★

Roger E. Mosley

An engaging biography of black bluesman Huddie "Leadbelly" Ledbetter who's known best for his songs "Goodnight Irene," "The Rock Island Line," and "The Midnight Special." Mosley plays the title role convincingly, although he occasionally seems too polished; the real Leadbelly spent much of his chaotic life serving time on prison chain gangs and singing in brothels. The film, however, is beautifully photographed and captures much of the old Deep South atmosphere. Gordon Parks directs with much feeling and dwells on *(Continued)*

INGRID BERGMAN

Known for her beauty, charm, energy, and superb acting ability, Ingrid Bergman is a popular screen actress and leading lady in American and Swedish films. Born in 1915 in Stockholm, Sweden, she was orphaned at an early age and was reared by relatives. After graduation from high school, she studied at the Royal Dramatic Theater School in Stockholm and became a major Swedish screen star by the mid '30s.

Producer David O. Selznick brought her to Hollywood in 1939 to star in an American version of Intermezzo, *and she was well on her way to becoming a popular film and stage actress in America.*

Bergman's career gained impetus with remarkable performances in Casablanca *(1943),* For Whom the Bell Tolls *(1943),* Gaslight *(1944),* Notorious *(1946), and* Joan of Arc *(1948). She received an Oscar as best actress for* Notorious. *In 1949, her popularity nose-dived after she left her dentist husband for director Roberto Rossellini. Public indignation over the affair prevented her appearance in American films for some seven years, but all was forgiven when she starred in* Anastasia, *filmed in London in 1956, for which she won another Oscar as best actress.*

Her marriage to Rossellini was dissolved in 1958, and she married Swedish producer Lars Schmidt and moved to Europe. From time to time, she continues to make films, and she won an Oscar as best supporting actress for her role in Murder on the Orient Express *(1974).*

Some of Bergman's other major films include Spellbound *(1945),* Saratoga Trunk *(1945),* The Bells of St. Mary's *(1945),* Indiscreet *(1958),* The Inn of the Sixth Happiness *(1958),* Cactus Flower *(1969),* A Matter of Time *(1976), and* Autumn Sonata *(1978).*

L
- Left Hand of God
- The Legacy
- The Legend of the Lone Ranger
- Le Magnifique
- The Lemon Drop Kid
- Lenny

(Continued)
Leadbelly's music, which is sung by HiTide Harris. Also with James E. Brodhead and John McDonald. (PG)
126 minutes

LEFT HAND OF GOD (1955)
★★

**Humphrey Bogart
Gene Tierney
Lee J. Cobb**

Bogart stars as an American pilot posing as a Catholic priest in China just after World War II. He gets involved with a renegade warlord, played by Cobb, who is immersed in conflict. The drama plods along, but it's watchable because of the top cast, which is much better than the material. Also co-stars E. G. Marshall, Agnes Moorehead, and Benson Fong. **Director**—Edward Dmytryk.
87 minutes

THE LEGACY (1979)
★

**Katharine Ross
Sam Elliott**

Katharine Ross uses her powers to prevent Sam Elliott from being killed in The Legacy.

Ross and Elliott are Los Angeles architects who travel to England to study a stately mansion inhabited by followers of Satan. In this dreary horror film, numerous gruesome deaths are offered to heighten the shock effect: a man is burned to a crisp, another has his throat brutally slashed, and someone else chokes to death. All this is sickening—not scary. The Devil's power is finally passed to Ross; let's hope she doesn't use it to make another movie like this. Also with John Standing, Ian Hogg, and Margaret Tyzack. **Director**—Richard Marquand. (R) *100 minutes*

THE LEGEND OF THE LONE RANGER (1981)
★

**Klinton Spillsbury
Michael Horse**

Klinton Spilbury portrays the Masked Rider of the Plains, and Michael Horse plays Tonto in The Legend of the Lone Ranger.

The legend is better off dormant if this bland version is the best that can be done with it. This straight-faced western tells the story of the well-known champion of justice—why he put on a mask and chose to fight crime. But the film is so out of kilter and so innocuous that some of the serious dialogue provokes unintentional laughter. Clean-cut Spillsbury plays the title role; Horse plays Tonto. Neither makes much impact. Who was that masked man? Who cares? Also with Jason Robards and Christopher Lloyd. **Director**—William A. Frakar. (PG)
98 minutes

LE MAGNIFIQUE (1976)
★

**Jean-Paul Belmondo
Jacqueline Bisset**

French director Philippe De Broca (*King of Hearts; That Man From Rio*) falls flat with this tepid spoof of the James Bond character. Belmondo plays two roles—a Walter Mittyish pulp writer and a dashing spy hero. There's an obvious lack of energy, and much of the humor misfires. Bisset plays the spy's assistant and neighbor. (No MPAA rating) *86 minutes*

THE LEMON DROP KID (1951)
★★★

**Bob Hope
Marilyn Maxwell**

Lots of laughs and lots of sentiment in this well-made film, based on a Damon Runyon story. Hope plays a bookie who's in hock with the mob, and he must pay or face the consequences. Bob is right at home in this colorful vehicle set in New York City during the Christmas season. "Silver Bells" is the memorable song. Also with Lloyd Nolan, Jane Darwell, Andrea King, Fred Clark, and Jay C. Flippen. **Director**—Sidney Landfield.
91 minutes b&w

LENNY (1974)
★★★★

**Dustin Hoffman
Valerie Perrine**

Hoffman gives a powerhouse performance as the controversial nightclub performer Lenny Bruce, known best for his obscene monologues. The biographical film follows Lenny's rocky career, from his meager beginning to many run-ins with the law, and finally to his death from an overdose of drugs. Perrine is convincing as the faithful wife, stripper Honey Harlowe, who suffers along with her husband. Jan Miner, Stanley Beck, and Gary Morton also star. **Director**—Bob Fosse. (R) **Academy Award Nomina-**

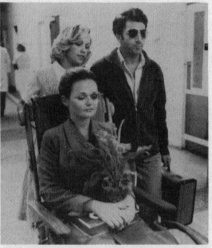
Dustin Hoffman accompanies a battered Valerie Perrine in the biographical film Lenny.

- Lepke
- Let Joy Reign Supreme
- Let No Man Write My Epitaph
- Let's Do It Again
- Let's Scare Jessica to Death
- The Letter
- Letter From an Unknown Woman
- A Letter to Three Wives

L

tions—best picture; Fosse, best director; Hoffman, best actor; Perrine, best actress; Julian Barry, best screenplay (adapted from other material); Bruce Surtees, cinematography.

111 minutes b&w

LEPKE (1975)
★

Tony Curtis

Curtis plays Louis (Lepke) Buchalter, who becomes boss of Murder, Inc., after World War I. The movie suffers from a lackluster screenplay. Also with Anjanette Comer, Michael Callan, Warren Berlinger, and Milton Berle. **Director**—Menahem Golan. (R)
110 minutes

LET JOY REIGN SUPREME (1977)
★★★

Philippe Noiret
Jean Rochefort
Marina Vlady

Director Bertrand Tavernier's second film is a handsome and detailed mosaic of pre-revolutionary France, a time when corruption and debauchery ran wild. The film is confusing at times, but it's nevertheless a witty, intelligent, and provocative semi-documentary drama of crucial events that led to the Revolution. In French with English titles. (No MPAA rating)
120 minutes

LET NO MAN WRITE MY EPITAPH (1960)
★★

James Darren
Shelley Winters

A second-rate sequel to *Knock on Any Door* that also focuses on the squalor of slum living. Darren stars as a poor youth with ambitions to be a classical pianist, but the harshness of his environment becomes an obstacle. Winters plays his drug-addicted mother. Some top players live up to their reputations in this film. Also with Burl Ives, Sal Mineo, Jean Seberg, Ricardo Montalban, and Ella Fitzgerald. **Director**—Philip Leacock.
106 minutes b&w

LET'S DO IT AGAIN (1975)
★★★

Sidney Poitier
Bill Cosby

Two lodge brothers—Poitier and Cosby—raise money for a new temple and raise lots of laughs, too, by fixing a prizefight and ripping off the mob. It's reminiscent of an Amos 'n' Andy comic adventure, only brought up to contemporary standards and tastes. Cosby is a howl, and Poitier makes an effective straight man. A fine supporting cast also includes Calvin Lockhart, Jimmie Walker, Ossie Davis, and Denise Nicholas. **Director**—Poitier. (PG)
112 minutes

LET'S SCARE JESSICA TO DEATH (1971)
★★

Zohra Lampert
Barton Heyman

Routine horror tale about a woman who recuperates from a nervous breakdown in an old country home where she hears strange sounds and sees creepy visions. There's enough here to generate a few screams, but there's nothing remarkable. Also with Kevin O'Connor and Mari-Claire Costello. **Director**—John Hancock. (PG)
89 minutes

THE LETTER (1940)
★★★★

Bette Davis
Herbert Marshall

Davis is outstanding as a woman who killed a man—apparently in self-defense—but a letter she wrote tells a different story. This Somerset Maugham story, set in Malaya, is well done and features some first-class performances; Davis is especially convincing. William Wyler's direction is on target. Also with James Stephenson, Sen Yung, Frieda Inescort, and Gale Sondergaard. **Academy Award Nominations**—best picture; Wyler, best director; Davis, best actress; Stephenson, best supporting actor; Gaetano Gaudio, cinematography (black and white). *95 minutes b&w*

In Let's Do It Again, *Sidney Poitier and Bill Cosby rip off the mob to raise money.*

LETTER FROM AN UNKNOWN WOMAN (1948)
★★★★

Joan Fontaine
Louis Jourdan

A superior tearjerker about a woman who's madly in love with a suave, callow pianist, but he doesn't sincerely return her affection. Stunningly produced and set in Vienna, with the charm of the city much in evidence. Fontaine plays the woman, and Jourdan is the dashing musician. Also with Mady Christians, Art Smith, and Marcel Journet. **Director**—Max Ophuls.
89 minutes b&w

A LETTER TO THREE WIVES (1948)
★★★★

Jeanne Crain
Ann Sothern
Linda Darnell

Three women receive a letter from a mutual friend that says she has run off with one of their husbands, but doesn't say which. The wives react by reexamining their marriages in a series of flashbacks. There's lots of ironic revelations, with expert direction and some fine acting from a good cast. Also with Kirk Douglas and Paul Douglas. A superior achievement from writer-director Joseph L. Mankiewicz. **Academy Awards**—Mankiewicz, best director; Mankiewicz, writing (screenplay). **Nomination**—best picture. *102 minutes b&w*

L
- Lies My Father Told Me
- The Life and Times of Grizzly Adams
- Life at the Top
- Lifeboat
- Lifeguard
- The Life of Brian
- Life With Father

LIES MY FATHER TOLD ME
(1975)
★★★

Yossi Yadin
Len Birman
Jeffrey Lynas

A warm, colorful story about the close relationship between a six-year-old Jewish boy and his grandfather, a junk man, in Montreal during the 1920s. The boy's father is an unsuccessful inventor who constantly seeks financial help from the bearded and deeply religious grandfather. There's sensitive direction by Jan Kada and appealing performances from Lynas, Birman, and Yadin. Also with Marilyn Lightstone. (PG) **Academy Award Nomination**—Ted Allen, best original screenplay. *102 minutes*

THE LIFE AND TIMES OF GRIZZLY ADAMS (1976)
★★

Dan Haggerty

The story of James Adams, a late-1800s trapper-mountaineer, who supposedly befriended lots of animals, including a big bear, while exiled in the wilderness. Disney-type sweetness and sentimentality abounds, but it's hardly a believable tale. The animals come off as polished actors, and a bearded Haggerty makes an impressive denizen of the forest. Filmed in Utah's Wasatch Mountains. Also with Don Shanks, Lisa Jones, and Marjorie Harper. **Director**—Richard Friedenberg. (G) *93 minutes*

LIFE AT THE TOP (1965)
★★

Laurence Harvey
Jean Simmons

This sequel to the well-made *Room at the Top* is routine and predictable at best, although there are a few worthwhile scenes. The story continues 10 years later, with Joe Lampton, played by Harvey, married to the daughter of his boss. He's financially secure, but restless and unhappy, and involved in an affair. Harvey's performance is adequate, and he gets worthy support from Simmons as his unhappy wife.

Also with Honor Blackman, Michael Craig, Margaret Johnston, Donald Wolfit, and Robert Morley. **Director**—Ted Kotcheff. *117 minutes b&w*

LIFEBOAT (1944)
★★★

Tallulah Bankhead
Walter Slezak

Hume Cronyn, Mary Anderson, John Hodiak, and William Bendix are among the survivors of a U-boat attack in Lifeboat.

Searing drama about survivors of a passenger ship, which was sunk by a German submarine during World War II. A group of passengers, including the commander of the attacking U-boat, are adrift together at sea and lay their emotions bare. Director Alfred Hitchcock handles the confined and stressful situation with amazing skill and extracts excellent performances from an interesting cast. Bankhead is outstanding as a pampered wealthy woman, and Slezak is convincing as the Nazi skipper. Also with Henry Hull, John Hodiak, Canada Lee, and William Bendix. **Academy Award Nominations**—Hitchcock, best director; John Steinbeck, writing (original story); Glen MacWilliams, cinematography (black and white). *96 minutes b&w*

LIFEGUARD (1976)
★★

Sam Elliott
Anne Archer
Kathleen Quinlan

Lifeguards, unlike blondes, don't have more fun—at least when they're over the hill at age 32. This is a rather somber sociological study of such an aging southern California beach boy who exists as a perennial adolescent. Ron

Koslow's lucid screenplay adroitly explores a series of personal conflicts, but without sufficient passion or energy. Elliott does well in the title role. Also with Stephen Young, Steve Burns, and Parker Stevenson. **Director**—Daniel Petrie. (PG) *96 minutes*

THE LIFE OF BRIAN (1979)
★★★

Graham Chapman
John Cleese
Terry Gilliam
Eric Idle
Terry Jones
Michael Palin

Those rascals, England's Monty Python comic troupe, have really done it this time. They parody the story of Christ in this outrageous and hilarious comedy that stops at nothing in taking apart various biblical legends. Chapman plays Brian of Nazareth, a ne'er-do-well Judean, who is reluctantly chosen messiah. There are moments of drab awkwardness in the comic storm, but many routines are masterpieces of satire and burlesque. **Director**—Jones. (R) *93 minutes*

Michael Palin (center) portrays a pompous Pilate in The Life of Brian.

LIFE WITH FATHER (1947)
★★★★

William Powell
Irene Dunne

Charming and handsomely mounted screen version of the Broadway hit play about coming of age in turn-of-

- Li'l Abner
- Lilies of the Field
- Limelight
- The Lion in Winter
- A Lion Is in the Streets
- Lion of the Desert
- Lipstick

L

the-century New York under the influence of an eccentric patriarch. Powell is outstanding as the irascible head of the family, and Dunne does well as his long-suffering wife. The film is based on Clarence Day's book and the Lindsay and Crouse stage production. Others in the cast include Edmund Gwenn, Zasu Pitts, Elizabeth Taylor, Martin Milner, and Jimmy Lydon. **Director**—Michael Curtiz. **Academy Award Nominations**—Powell, best actor; Peverell Marley and William V. Skall, cinematography (color).

118 minutes

LI'L ABNER (1959)
★★★

Leslie Parrish
Peter Palmer
Stubby Kaye

Al Capp's wonderful cartoon characters come to life on the screen with plenty of energy and color, as taken from the Broadway musical. The comedy is strictly cornpone, but the music and dance numbers are done with extraordinary vigor. Palmer is believable in the title role, Parris is fetching as Daisy Mae, and Kaye makes a good Marryin' Sam. Other denizens of Dogpatch include Howard St. John, Julie Newman, Stella Stevens, Robert Strauss, and Billie Hayes. **Director**—Melvin Frank. *113 minutes*

LILIES OF THE FIELD (1963)
★★★★

Sidney Poitier
Lilia Skala

Charming, sentimental drama starring Poitier as a jack-of-all-trades who helps a group of German nuns, led by Skala, build a chapel in New Mexico. The film is done on a small scale, but it offers a large portion of enjoyment, especially for Poitier's Oscar-winning performance. Ralph Nelson's direction is nicely paced. Also with Lisa Mann, Isa Crino, and Stanley Adams. **Academy Award**—Poitier, best actor. **Nominations**—best picture; Skala, best supporting actress; James Poe, best screenplay (based on material from another medium); Ernest Haller, cinematography (black and white).

94 minutes b&w

LIMELIGHT (1952)
★★★★

Charles Chaplin
Claire Bloom

The wonderful skills of Chaplin are in full evidence in this touching love story set in London. Chaplin is charming and sentimental as a broken-down musical-hall comedian who prevents the suicide of a ballerina, played by Bloom. There are many tender and compassionate scenes as only Chaplin could envision them. Bloom's brilliant performance is a fine compliment to the heartwarming production. Buster Keaton, Sydney Chaplin, and Nigel Bruce also star. **Director**—Charles Chaplin. *144 minutes b&w*

THE LION IN WINTER (1968)
★★★★

Katharine Hepburn
Peter O'Toole

Fantastic acting by O'Toole and Hepburn adorns this splendid drama set in medieval England. O'Toole is a magnificent Henry II, and Hepburn is tremendous as Eleanor of Aquitaine. They are lovers who square off on Christmas Eve as the fate of the throne is debated. There are some dry moments, but many high-powered scenes dominate the film. Also with Jane Merrow, John Castle, and Anthony Hopkins. **Director**—Anthony Harvey. **Academy Awards**—Hepburn, best actress; James Goldman, best screenplay (based on material from another medium). **Nominations**—best picture; Harvey, best director; O'Toole, best actor.

134 minutes

A LION IS IN THE STREETS (1953)
★★★

James Cagney

Cagney gives a striking portrayal of a power-hungry politician with humble roots in this intense drama, which leans somewhat on *All the King's Men*. The plot goes astray now and then, but there's enough energy in the production to sustain interest. An expected climax has Cagney caught up in corruption, which brings on his decline; it's among Cagney's best roles. Also with Barbara Hale, Anne Francis, Warner Anderson, Jeanne Cagney, and Lon Chaney, Jr. **Director**—Raoul Walsh. *88 minutes*

LION OF THE DESERT (1981)
★★★

Anthony Quinn
Oliver Reed

In Lion of the Desert, *Anthony Quinn is a Bedouin hero who battles Mussolini's Fascists.*

Quinn plays a wise and majestic Bedouin warrior who wages a relentless and effective guerrilla campaign against the Italian occupiers of Libya from 1912 to 1931. Reportedly costing more than $30 million, the film is of epic proportions, with sweeping battle scenes of the determined Bedouins at times humiliating the well-equipped Fascist troops. A thread of propaganda runs through the spectacle, but this doesn't detract from its superb vigor and style. **Director**—Moustapha Akkad. (PG) *160 minutes*

LIPSTICK (1976)
★

Margaux Hemingway
Chris Sarandon

This disappointing film about rape is a bad debut for Margaux Hemingway. A beautiful photographer's model, *(Continued)*

L
- Lisztomania
- Little Big Man
- Little Caesar
- Little Darlings
- The Little Foxes
- The Little Girl Who Lives Down the Lane

In Lipstick, *Margaux Hemingway comforts her younger sister Mariel.*

(Continued)

played by Margaux, is raped by a shy music teacher. After the rapist goes free and attacks her younger sister, she arms herself with a rifle and seeks revenge. Mariel Hemingway, Margaux's 14-year-old sister, plays her sister in the film, and delivers a surprisingly impressive performance. Also with Anne Bancroft, Perry King, and Robin Gammell. **Director—** Lamont Johnson (R)   *89 minutes*

LISZTOMANIA (1975)
★★

Roger Daltrey

Ken Russell wrote and directed this glittering and noisy movie, which portrays Franz Liszt and Richard Wagner as the pop stars of their time. At first, it's amusing, but quickly becomes overblown and garish. Daltrey, who starred in *Tommy*, plays Liszt. Ringo Starr portrays the Pope. Also with Sara Kestelman, Paul Nicholas, Fiona Lewis, and John Justin. (R)
105 minutes

LITTLE BIG MAN (1970)
★★★★

Dustin Hoffman

Episodic western tale seen through the experiences of 121-year-old Jack Crabb, the sole survivor of Custer's last stand, who is played by Hoffman. The compelling film offers a grand tour of a portion of American history with liberal doses of satire and pathos. Perhaps this is a milestone film because it treated American Indians with genuine understanding. The complex story climaxes with Custer's defeat at the Little Big Horn. Also stars Martin Balsam, Faye Dunaway, Chief Dan George, and Richard Mulligan. Directed with extraordinary care by Arthur Penn. (PG) **Academy Award Nomination**—George, best supporting actor.   *147 minutes*

LITTLE CAESAR (1930)
★★★★

Edward G. Robinson

More than 50 years later, this classic gangster movie is still fascinating. Robinson is magnificent as Enrico Bandello, the ruthless killer who takes over a gang of criminals and then is gunned down by the cops. The pace is fast, the story is exciting, and it even features a special style of sly humor. A young-looking Edward G. did such a convincing job with the role that he became identified with the character throughout his career. Also with Douglas Fairbanks, Jr., Glenda Farrell, William Collier, Jr., Stanley Fields, and Sidney Blackmer. **Director—** Mervyn Le Roy. **Academy Award Nomination**—Francis Faragoh and Robert N. Lee, writing (adaptation).
77 minutes b&w

LITTLE DARLINGS (1980)
★

Kristy McNichol
Tatum O'Neal

Tatum O'Neal and Kristy McNichol play two girls who come of age in Little Darlings.

How times have changed. Young Elizabeth Taylor's main concern in the '40s was whether National Velvet would win the crucial horse race. But in this shabby movie, teenagers McNichol and O'Neal race to see which one will be the first to lose her virginity. The youngsters are appealing, and they are certainly better than the simpleminded script. Despite the sexual titillation and exploitation, the ending is socially redeeming; yet the film leaves a bad aftertaste. Andy Hardy, where are you? Also with Kris Erickson and Armand Assante. **Director—**Ronald Maxwell. (R)   *92 minutes*

THE LITTLE FOXES (1941)
★★★★

Bette Davis
Herbert Marshall
Teresa Wright

High drama with sharp characterizations about a Southern family involved in various nasty schemes. Davis is the formidable head of this clan of connivers, and she's at her bitchy best. The film is expertly adapted from Lillian Hellman's play. Other fine performances by Marshall, Wright, Dana Andrews, Dan Duryea, Charles Dingle, and Patricia Collinge. **Director**—William Wyler. **Academy Award Nominations**—best picture; Wyler, best director; Davis, best actress; Collinge, best supporting actress; Hellman, writing (screenplay).
116 minutes b&w

THE LITTLE GIRL WHO LIVES DOWN THE LANE (1977)
★★★

Jodie Foster
Martin Sheen
Alexis Smith

Foster comes across with a first-rate performance in this provocative thriller. She plays a composed and independent 13-year-old who dispatches a few nasty adults with aplomb. The script is flawed in part, but the suspense is good, and there's a moving love affair between Foster and Scott Jacoby, who supports her endeavors. Also with Mort Shuman. **Director**—Nicholas Gessner. (PG)
94 minutes

- Little Miss Marker
- A Little Night Music
- A Little Romance
- The Littlest Horse Thieves
- Live and Let Die
- Logan's Run
- Lolita

L

LITTLE MISS MARKER (1980)
★★★

Walter Matthau
Julie Andrews
Tony Curtis

Julie Andrews, Walter Matthau, and little Sara Stimson in Little Miss Marker.

Matthau is excellent as the grumpy gambler Sorrowful Jones, in this fourth version of Damon Runyon's sentimental tale. Originally, it starred Shirley Temple. In this film, new-comer Sara Stimson plays the cute kid left in the care of Sorrowful as an IOU (or marker) for a gambling debt. Matthau's special style of sour, cynical humor saves the unlikely story. There's a great comic scene where "bought" jockeys knock themselves out restraining their mounts so a long shot can win. Andrews plays a once-wealthy socialite, and Curtis is a gangster. Also with Bob Newhart. **Director**—Walter Bernstein. (PG)
112 minutes

A LITTLE NIGHT MUSIC (1978)
★★

Elizabeth Taylor
Diana Rigg

This film version of the hit Broadway musical doesn't transfer successfully to the screen. The production looks elegant, but it's uneven, slow, and flat-footed. Even Taylor, somewhat plump and matronly, isn't that effective as the seductive Desiree Armfeldt. Stephen Sondheim's enchanting music and lyrics shine through and lift the spirits at times. Also with Len Cariou, Hermione Gingold, and Lesley-Anne Down. **Director**—Harold Prince. (PG)
124 minutes

A LITTLE ROMANCE (1979)
★★

Laurence Olivier
Arthur Hill
Sally Kellerman

Director George Roy Hill's comedy of puppy love in Paris is too cute and often trite. Two teenagers, the son of a taxi driver and a rich American girl, run off to Venice to kiss under the Bridge of Sighs. The kids are played by Thelonious Bernard and Diane Lane. The couple is helped on the romantic escapade by a softhearted pickpocket, played by Olivier. The kids are win-some while the great Olivier, in a Maurice Chevalier role, hams it up shamelessly. Kellerman and Hill are wasted as Lane's concerned parents. Also with Broderick Crawford. (PG) **Academy Award Nomination**—Allan Burns, best screenplay (adapted from another medium). *108 minutes*

Diane Lane, Laurence Olivier, and Thelonious Bernard in A Little Romance.

THE LITTLEST HORSE THIEVES (1977)
★★★

Alastair Sim
Peter Barkworth

A trio of charming children come to the rescue of pit ponies slated for the glue factory when new machinery is introduced in a small English mining town. The pleasant Walt Disney adventure, set in picturesque York-shire, is rather bland, but the story relates well to children and their feel-ings toward animals. The film also makes a modest statement about the working conditions of miners. The children—Andrew Harrison, Benjie Bolgar, and Chloe Franks—handle their parts with sentimental appeal. Also with Maurice Colbourne and

Susan Tebbs. **Director**—Charles Jar-rott. (G) *104 minutes*

LIVE AND LET DIE (1973)
★★★

Roger Moore
Yaphet Kotto
Jane Seymour

Moore stars as superspy James Bond in this eighth agent 007 film, with the usual doses of tongue-in-cheek humor, wonderful gadgets, and sexy women. This time, our hero is after a formidable drug dealer, operating out of exotic Caribbean territory. It's pretty much the same sort of wild chases, narrow escapes, and so on, and pretty much the same amount of fun. Also with Clifton James, Bernard Lee, Lois Maxwell, David Hedison, and Geoffrey Holder. **Director**—Guy Hamilton. (PG) *121 minutes*

LOGAN'S RUN (1976)
★

Michael York
Richard Jordan
Jenny Agutter

A science-fiction adventure set in the 23rd century, when people reside in an elaborate, dome-enclosed city and aren't allowed to live past their 30th birthday. Those who try to avoid "renewal" and escape to the outside are chased and killed by special police-men. The elaborate production seems typical of many sci-fi films, with artifi-cial sets that look as if they were bor-rowed from Disneyland. There is equally artificial action; York gives an unmoving performance as a turncoat policeman who does make it to the outside. Also with Roscoe Lee Browne, Farrah Fawcett-Majors, and Peter Ustinov. **Director**—Michael Anderson. (PG) *120 minutes*

LOLITA (1962)
★★★

James Mason
Shelley Winters
Sue Lyon

This screen version of Vladimir Nabo-kov's sensational novel is watered
(Continued)

L
- The Loneliness of the Long Distance Runner
- Lonely Are the Brave
- Long Day's Journey Into Night
- The Longest Day
- The Longest Yard

(Continued)

down, but it's still effective. Mason performs well as the professor who's infatuated with a 14-year-old temptress, played by Lyon. To be near her, he marries her mother, played by Winters. The film offers notable moments of satire and drama, and it's as bizarre

FAYE DUNAWAY

Faye Dunaway was born in Bascom, Florida, in 1941. After she graduated from the University of Florida, where she majored in drama, she attended the Boston University School of Fine and Applied Arts. Her work there resulted in an audition for New York's Lincoln Center Repertory, and she was cast in Elia Kazan's production of Arthur Miller's After the Fall.

Later Dunaway was signed by producer Sam Speigel to make her movie debut in The Happening *(1967). She then appeared in Otto Preminger's* Hurry Sundown *(1967). Perhaps her most famous screen role came next in her third movie, the role of Bonnie Parker in the classic crime drama* Bonnie and Clyde *(1967). For this performance, she received her first Academy Award nomination as best actress.*

Dunaway's subsequent films have included The Thomas Crown Affair *(1968),* The Extraordinary Seaman *(1969),* A Place for Lovers *(1969),* The Arrangement *(1969),* Little Big Man *(1970),* Oklahoma Crude *(1973),* Chinatown *(1974), for which she received her second best actress nomination, and* Network *(1976), for which she won an Oscar.*

Some of her recent movies are The Eyes of Laura Mars *(1978),* The Champ *(1979),* The First Deadly Sin *(1980), and* Mommie Dearest *(1981).*

---

as the book. First-class performances from Winters and Peter Sellers. Also with Marianne Stone and Diana Decker. **Director**—Stanley Kubrick.
152 minutes b&w

THE LONELINESS OF THE LONG DISTANCE RUNNER (1962)
★★★★

Tom Courtenay
Michael Redgrave

An exceptional story of a delinquent youth in a reform school who attains recognition by competing in track contests. Courtenay is the rebellious youth, and Redgrave plays the school headmaster. Magnificent direction by Tony Richardson and all-around excellent performances maintain interest from start to finish. The film, which is brilliantly photographed and exquisitely produced, ends with a rousing big race sequence. Also with James Bolam, Avis Bunnage, and Alec McCowen.
103 minutes b&w

LONELY ARE THE BRAVE (1962)
★★★

Kirk Douglas

An unusual western about a middle-aged cowboy who gets himself thrown into jail to rescue a friend. The friend refuses to leave, so Douglas breaks out and runs for Mexico; he escapes the posse that pursues him, but not the modern world. It's an excellent juxtaposition of old and new life-styles, with a strong, sardonic ending. Douglas is in top form as the fugitive cowhand. The supporting cast includes Walter Matthau, Gena Rowlands, Michael Kane, Carroll O'Connor, and George Kennedy. **Director**—David Miller.
107 minutes b&w

LONG DAY'S JOURNEY INTO NIGHT (1962)
★★★★

Ralph Richardson
Katharine Hepburn
Jason Robards, Jr.

Eugene O'Neill's brilliant autobiographical play is transposed to the screen with considerable richness, and

---

it's superbly highlighted with fine acting. The stagey but compelling production is about a Connecticut family in the early 1900s, beset with emotional problems. Hepburn is fantastic as a drug-addicted wife, and Richardson is outstanding as her overbearing actor-spouse. Robards repeats his fine stage performance as the alcoholic eldest son. Sidney Lumet directs the film with care, and the result is astonishing impact. Also with Dean Stockwell and Jeanne Barr. **Academy Award Nomination**—Hepburn, best actress.
136 minutes b&w

THE LONGEST DAY (1962)
★★★

John Wayne
Robert Mitchum
Henry Fonda
Robert Ryan
Rod Steiger

Sprawling, ambitious war saga about the Allied invasion in Normandy during World War II, starring an army of well-known actors. The film is impressive for its grand details of the various events of the D-Day landings, but the huge cast is spread around rather thinly, thereby thwarting proper characterizations. Yet the spectacular account offers relentless fascination. Also among the huge cast are Robert Wagner, Stuart Whitman, Steve Forrest, Richard Todd, Richard Burton, Sean Connery, and Peter Lawford. **Directors**—Andrew Marton, Ken Annakin, and Bernhard Wicki. **Academy Award**—Jean Bourgoin, Henri Persin, Walter Wottitz, cinematography (black and white). **Nomination**—best picture. *180 minutes b&w*

THE LONGEST YARD (1975)
★★

Burt Reynolds
Eddie Albert

The movie is about life in prison, where the good guys are the cons and the bad guys are the guards. Reynolds plays a former professional football star who is sent to prison. Albert is the warden who sponsors a semi-pro team composed of the prison's guards. The cons put together a team, quarterbacked by Reynolds, and fight it out

- The Long Gray Line
- The Long Hot Summer
- Long John Silver
- The Long Riders
- Look Back in Anger
- Looker

L

In The Longest Yard, *Burt Reynolds is a former pro football star who's sent to prison.*

with the guards in a ferocious gridiron battle. Some fun, but hardly believable. Also with Ed Lanter, Michael Conrad, and James Hampton. **Director**—Robert Aldrich. (R)

123 minutes

THE LONG GRAY LINE (1955)
★★★

Tyrone Power
Maureen O'Hara

Tyrone Power and Maureen O'Hara in The Long Gray Line, *a warmhearted drama.*

Warmhearted drama about the long career of an athletic trainer at West Point. Power stars as an Irish immigrant who came to the military academy under humble circumstances and stayed on as a trainer for many years. O'Hara plays his wife. Director

John Ford contributes a special sentimental touch. Also with Donald Crisp, Ward Bond, Betsy Plamer, Robert Francis, Phil Carey, and Patrick Wayne. *138 minutes*

THE LONG HOT SUMMER
(1958)
★★★

Orson Welles
Paul Newman
Joanne Woodward

Moody, Deep South family drama expertly adapted from William Faulkner's short stories. Welles plays a strong-willed father with a determined daughter, played by Woodward. Sparks fly when Newman, a handyman, comes to town and wants to marry her. Director Martin Ritt lays on the atmosphere and brings out the characterizations, but the ending could have been better. The excellent cast also includes Anthony Franciosa, Lee Remick, and Angela Lansbury.

118 minutes

LONG JOHN SILVER (1953)
★★★

Robert Newton

Fairly entertaining continuation of the *Treasure Island* adventure, with Newton in the title role giving a hammy but lusty portrayal of the gruff buccaneer. In this film, Long John Silver and young Jim Hawkins return to the mysterious island with new clues for another attempt to recover pirate's treasure. Filmed in Australia. Also stars Kit Taylor, Connie Gilchrist, Rod Taylor, and Grant Taylor. **Director**—Byron Haskin. *109 minutes*

THE LONG RIDERS (1980)
★★

James Keach
Stacy Keach
David Carradine
Keith Carradine
Robert Carradine
Dennis Quaid
Randy Quaid

This rehash of the Jesse James legend adds little to what Hollywood has already told about it. The James

The James gang prepares to rob a bank in Minnesota in The Long Riders.

brothers, played by brothers James and Stacy Keach, are still portrayed as Robin Hood-type heros. But curiously, in this version, it's the other outlaws who ride with the James gang (the Miller boys, the Younger brothers) that seem more interesting. Allusions to the noble suffering of the post-Civil War homesteaders are supposed to provide social insight, but it's all rather vague. Also with Christopher and Nicholas Guest, Pamela Reed, and Amy Stryker. **Director**—Walter Hill. (R) *100 minutes*

LOOK BACK IN ANGER (1958)
★★★

Richard Burton
Claire Bloom
Mary Ure

Burton gives a powerful performance as a rebellious young man who displays anger at the government and at his marriage. This engrossing screen adaptation of John Osborne's stylish play features some smart dialogue and memorable scenes reflecting on the atmosphere of contemporary British life. Also with Edith Evans, Gary Raymond, and Donald Pleasence. **Director**—Tony Richardson.

99 minutes b&w

LOOKER (1981)
★

Albert Finney
James Coburn
Susan Dey

This slick mystery-drama about computers, advertising, and murder begins with promise, but quickly deteriorates into farfetched nonsense.

(Continued)

L
- Looking for Mr. Goodbar
- The Looney Looney Looney Bugs Bunny Movie
- Lord Jim
- Lord of the Flies
- Lord of the Rings
- The Lords of Flatbush
- Lost and Found

In Looker, Albert Finney and Susan Dey get caught up in intrigue and murder.

(Continued)
Finney stars as a Beverly Hills plastic surgeon who traces the murders of some of his women patients to a large corporation using strange advertising methods. Writer-director Michael Crichton tosses in numerous sci-fi gimmicks that are merely absurd and silly, and he never explains the reasons for the murders. (R)   *94 minutes*

LOOKING FOR MR. GOODBAR (1977)
★★★★

Diane Keaton
Richard Gere

Keaton gives an extraordinary, provocative performance in this powerful film version of Judith Rossner's best-selling novel. Keaton, as the girl who teaches deaf children by day and cruises singles bars at night, is sad, funny, vulnerable, sweet, and sexy. Writer-director Richard Brooks captures the sordidness and compassion throughout, as the film builds to its shattering climax. Great acting jobs, too, from Gere, Tuesday Weld, and Alan Feinstein. Also with William Atherton, Tom Berenger, Richard Kiley, and LaVar Burton. A devastating movie that will send you away with your mind churning. (R) **Academy Award Nominations**—Weld, best supporting actress; William A. Fraker, cinematography.   *135 minutes*

THE LOONEY LOONEY LOONEY BUGS BUNNY MOVIE (1981)
★★★

Animation maestro Friz Freleng presents a wonderful compilation of his best work, which represents some 50 years of cartooning. That "cwazy wab-bit" and many of his sidekicks—Yosemite Sam, Daffy Duck, Porky Pig, and so on—are up to their usual high jinks, and the result is nonstop hilarity. About 20 minutes of new material is mixed in with the older stuff, for an enjoyable romp with these lovable and indelible characters. (G)   *80 minutes*

LORD JIM (1965)
★★★

Peter O'Toole

Colorful screen version of Joseph Conrad's famous novel about the adventures of a British merchant seaman in the Far East during the late 1800s. The exotic tale, about a man's efforts to atone for an act of cowardice, is helped along with lavish location photography in the Orient and some decent acting. The film doesn't achieve the flavor and dramatic power of the book. Also with James Mason, Eli Wallach, Paul Lukas, Jack Hawkins, Daliah Lavi, Akim Tamiroff, and Curt Jurgens. **Director**—Richard Brooks.
154 minutes

LORD OF THE FLIES (1963)
★★★

James Aubrey
Tom Chapin

Unusual account of a group of English schoolboys stranded on a lonely island after a plane crash. Eventually, they revert to savagery. The compelling film, adapted from William Golding's allegorical novel, has many tense moments, but it isn't as engrossing as the book. The cast of youngsters also includes Hugh Edwards, Roger Elwin, and Tom Gaman. **Director**—Peter Brook.   *90 minutes b&w*

LORD OF THE RINGS (1978)
★★

Ralph Bakshi, an innovator of X-rated cartoons, applies his animating skills to the work of J.R.R. Tolkien. The two-hour film is technically impressive, but if you aren't skilled in the ways of Hobbits and Middle Earth, you'll most likely be overwhelmed by the flood of information. Bakshi only offers half a ring from the cult fantasy; the movie

Frodo Baggins at the Great Council in Rivendell in Lord of the Rings.

ends abruptly without reaching the conclusion of Tolkien's trilogy. The door is left open for a sequel to the saga. (PG)   *133 minutes*

THE LORDS OF FLATBUSH (1974)
★★★

Martin Davidson
Perry King
Sylvester Stallone
Henry Winkler

A frisky comedy about tough high school youths in Brooklyn in the late 1950s. The film is perhaps best remembered for the budding talents of Stallone and Winkler, who play colorful members of a Flatbush gang. Set much in the style of *The Blackboard Jungle*, but hardly as serious. A few scenes are real standouts. Also with Paul Mace, Susan Blakely, and Renée Paris. **Director**—Stephen F. Verona. (PG)   *88 minutes*

LOST AND FOUND (1979)
★★

George Segal
Glenda Jackson

George Segal and Glenda Jackson go for an ambulance ride in Lost and Found.

- Lost Honor of Katharina Blum
- Lost Horizon
- Lost in a Harem
- The Lost Weekend
- Love and Bullets
- Love and Death
- Love at First Bite

L

Jackson and Segal are reunited in this film for the first time since their successful 1973 film *A Touch of Class*. But in this lackluster romantic comedy, they lose their touch. Segal is a tweedy professor in a small-town university, and Jackson is his quarrelsome wife. Both strain at the slapstick routines, and the picture ends up a lost cause. Also with Maureen Stapleton, Hollis McLaven, and Paul Sorvino. **Director**—Melvin Frank. (PG)

112 minutes

LOST HONOR OF KATHARINA BLUM (1976)
★★★

Angela Winker
Dieter Laser

An emotional and compelling German film, which focuses on the excesses of a modern democracy and views the world in terms of good and evil. A young and reserved waitress takes home a young man suspected of radical political activities. For several days, she's harassed and humiliated by the police and a ruthless reporter because of the brief association. There are realistic performances by Winker as Katharina the waitress and Laser as the unscrupulous newsman. Adapted from a novel by Nobel Prize-winner Heinrich Boll. Written and directed by Volker Schlondorff and his wife, Margarethe von Trotta. In German with English titles. (R) *102 minutes*

LOST HORIZON (1973)
★

Peter Finch
Liv Ullmann

Foolhardy remake of the 1937 classic film based on James Hilton's romantic story of paradise found. The beginning adheres to the original movie's style about a small group of people who are kidnapped and find themselves in a strange but serene Tibetan mountain civilization. However, the film collapses into nonsense when Shangri-La is reached and some out-of-place song-and-dance numbers are injected. The rather good cast just can't pull it off. Also with Sally Kellerman, Bobby Van, George Kennedy, Michael York, Olivia Hussey, John

Gielgud, and Charles Boyer. **Director**—Charles Jarrott. (G)

143 minutes

LOST IN A HAREM (1944)
★★★

Bud Abbott
Lou Costello

Energetic Abbott and Costello high jinks, with Bud and Lou as magicians on tour in the Middle East and involved with a cunning sultan and a beautiful harem girl, played by Marilyn Maxwell. This feature, with the usual doses of slapstick and sight gags, is among the best of their films. Douglass Dumbrille is good as the sultan. Also with John Conte and Jimmy Dorsey and his orchestra. **Director**—Charles Riesner. *98 minutes b&w*

THE LOST WEEKEND (1945)
★★★★

Ray Milland
Jane Wyman

In The Lost Weekend, Ray Milland is a struggling writer who becomes an alcoholic.

Stark, powerful drama about a struggling writer, played by Milland, who becomes an alcoholic. Milland gives a striking performance, which effectively and sympathetically illuminates his desperate character. Billy Wilder's script and direction are relentless in providing the details of personal pain, dejection, and terror. Howard da Silva is exceptional in a supporting role as a bartender. There are other good performances, too, from Wyman, Philip Terry, Doris Dowling, and Frank Faylen. **Academy Awards**—best picture; Wilder, best director; Milland, best actor; Charles Brackett and Wilder, best writing (screenplay). **Nomination**—John F. Seitz, cinematography (black and white). *101 minutes b&w*

LOVE AND BULLETS (1979)
★

Charles Bronson
Rod Steiger
Jill Ireland

Bronson plays a craggy-faced cop on special assignment for the FBI in this limp and predictable adventure yarn. He flies off to Switzerland to retrieve a mobster's girl friend, played by Ireland, who hopefully will supply incriminating evidence. Steiger, of course, plays the gangster. Bronson and Ireland spend considerable time observing picturesque Swiss scenery, which is okay if you happen to like travelogues. But if you're looking for fast action and suspense, forget it. Also with Strother Martin, Bradford Dillman, and Henry Silva. **Director**—Stuart Rosenberg. (R) *103 minutes*

LOVE AND DEATH (1975)
★★

Woody Allen
Diane Keaton

Allen wrote, directed, and starred in this film of a militant coward in the land of *War and Peace*. He plays a Russian trying to avoid the draft during the Napoleonic War. There are enough laughs and wit, but it's often hard to grasp, especially the corny philosophizing about God, love, patriotism, and so on. Keaton plays his cousin Sonja, the girl he worships. Also with Georges Adel, Harold Gould, Frank Adu, and Alfred Lutter. (PG) *82 minutes*

LOVE AT FIRST BITE (1979)
★★★

George Hamilton
Susan Saint James

Alas, Count Dracula is evicted from his Transylvania castle. So he goes to New York City, where he raids the blood bank and falls in love with a fashion model, played by Saint James. This B-movie romantic comedy, starring Hamilton as a funny and engaging vampire, works most of the time. There are enough clever gags and high

(Continued)

L
- Love Bug
- The Loved One
- Love Is a Many-Splendored Thing
- Lovely To Look At
- Love Me or Leave Me
- Love on the Run

George Hamilton is a modern-day neck-nibbler in Love at First Bite.

(Continued)

spirits to even win a smile from Bela Lugosi. The excellent supporting cast, headed by Saint James, Richard Benjamin, Dick Shawn, Isabel Sanford, and Arte Johnson, hams it up with delight. **Director**—Stan Dragoti. (PG)

96 minutes

THE LOVE BUG (1968)
★★★

**Dean Jones
Michele Lee**

A fun-filled Disney romp about a Volkswagen Beetle automobile with a distinct personality and its own ideas of where it wants to go. This heart-warming family comedy is aimed at the kids, yet it offers a bit of unusual sophistication. The film contains ample slapstick and clever stunts, mostly set in the streets of San Francisco. Several *Love Bug* sequels followed. Also with David Tomlinson, Buddy Hackett, and Joe Flynn. **Director**—Robert Stevenson. (G)

107 minutes

THE LOVED ONE (1965)
★★★

**Robert Morse
John Gielgud
Ron Steiger**

An effective satire, based on Evelyn Waugh's novel about the funeral industry in the United States, that consistently hits the target with a combination of style and offensiveness. Morse stars as a young Britisher who attends his uncle's funeral in Los Angeles and gets stuck with an outrageous bill for the burial services. The black comedy is handled in a grand manner by a large pro cast that also includes Liberace, Jonathan Winters, Robert Morley, Dana Andrews, and Milton Berle. **Director**—Tony Richardson.

116 minutes b&w

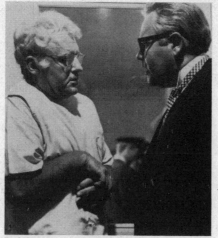

Rod Steiger and Jonathan Winters in The Loved One, *a satire.*

LOVE IS A MANY-SPLENDORED THING (1955)
★★

**Jennifer Jones
William Holden**

A tear-drenched soap-opera romance about a Eurasian woman doctor who falls in love with an American correspondent in Hong Kong at the time of the Korean Conflict. Jones is the Eurasian, and Holden is the journalist. The plot is routine, but the film is fairly well acted and produced. The movie is based on the autobiographical book by Han Suyin. The popular theme song gave the film added recognition. Also with Torin Thatcher, Isobel Elsom, Murray Matheson, and Richard Loo. **Director**—Henry King. **Academy Award**—Sammy Fain and Paul Francis Webster, best song ("Love Is a Many-Splendored Thing"). **Nominations**—best picture; Jones, best actress; Leon Shamroy, cinematography (color).

102 minutes

LOVELY TO LOOK AT (1952)
★★

**Howard Keel
Kathryn Grayson**

A tepid remake of the musical *Roberta*, set against the background of Paris fashion houses. The storyline is flimsy, but the great Jerome Kern songs, like "Smoke Gets In Your Eyes," and the lavish settings contribute some entertainment value. Grayson and Keel handle the singing with adequacy, and Marge and Gower Champion display their dancing talents. Ann Miller and Red Skelton round out the cast. **Director**—Mervyn Le Roy.

102 minutes

LOVE ME OR LEAVE ME (1955)
★★★

**Doris Day
James Cagney**

On-the-mark show-biz film biography about '20s singer Ruth Etting. Day, in the lead role, shows her talent to best advantage. Cagney, however, steals many a scene as her gangster boyfriend who propels her career, but also contributes to her drinking problem. Doris belts out some fine songs of the period, including "Ten Cents a Dance" and the title tune. Also with Cameron Mitchell, Robert Keith, Tom Tully, and Richard Gaines. **Director**—Charles Vidor. **Academy Award**—Daniel Fuchs, writing (motion picture story). **Nomination**—Cagney, best actor.

122 minutes

LOVE ON THE RUN (1979)
★

Jean-Pierre Leaud

French director François Truffaut carries on the adventures of Antoine Doinel in a fifth film. The story originated with the classic *The 400 Blows* in 1959. This time, Antoine, played by Leaud, is getting a divorce and shows no indication of maturing. By now, the series has grown stale, and this chapter is devoid of any fresh ideas. But Truffaut reminds us of his past successes by lacing in excerpts from his earlier Doinel films. Also with

- Lovers and Liars
- Lovers and Other Strangers
- Love Story
- Love With the Proper Stranger
- Loving Couples
- The L-Shaped Room

L

Marie-France Pisier and Claude Jade. In French with English titles. (No MPAA rating) *94 minutes*

LOVERS AND LIARS (1981)
★

Goldie Hawn
Giancarlo Giannini

Hawn teams up with Italy's popular Giannini for this mixed-bag comedy, but the film turns out half-baked. She's on vacation in Rome, and he's the liar who's married and looking for a fast fling. They're off to Pisa for a few days of romance, but it's an ill match from the start. A shabby script and awkward direction hamper Goldie's attempts at her familiar dizzy humor; she should have vacationed in the Bahamas. **Director**—Mario Monicelli. (R) *96 minutes*

LOVERS AND OTHER STRANGERS (1970)
★★★★

Gig Young
Anne Jackson

A rib-tickling, sophisticated comedy about two young people who decide to marry and their families who get hilariously wound up in the wedding plans. Bonnie Bedelia and Michael Brandon play the engaged couple. The witty farce abounds in priceless funny scenes, with many good players having a field day with some good lines. Young is memorable as the stalwart father of the bride; Jackson plays a cast-off mistress, and Richard Castellano is good as the father of the bridegroom. Also with Beatrice Arthur,

Anne Meara and Harry Guardino in the comedy Lovers and Other Strangers.

Robert Dishy, Harry Guardino, Cloris Leachman, Anne Meara, and Marion Hailey. **Director**—Cy Howard. (PG) **Academy Award Nominations**—Castellano, best supporting actor; Renée Taylor, Joseph Bologna, and David Zelag Goodman, best screenplay (based on material from another medium). *104 minutes*

LOVE STORY (1970)
★★★

Ali MacGraw
Ryan O'Neal

Ali MacGraw and Ryan O'Neal fall in love and marry in Love Story.

Effective film treatment of Erich Segal's sad tale of two college students. They fall in love and marry, and just when things are looking up, she dies. MacGraw and O'Neal play the star-crossed lovers. Ordinarily, this cliché-strewn film would be just another piece of sentimental Hollywood fluff. But the movie is made with above-average care and offers some good acting along with the flood of tears. Ray Milland and John Marley have supporting roles. **Director**—Arthur Hiller. (PG) **Academy Award Nominations**—best picture; Hiller, best director; O'Neal, best actor; MacGraw, best actress; Marley, best supporting actor; Segal, best story and screenplay (based on factual material or material not previously published). *100 minutes*

LOVE WITH THE PROPER STRANGER (1963)
★★★

Steve McQueen
Natalie Wood

Finely tuned romantic comedy-drama about an easygoing musician, played by McQueen, who falls in love with a store clerk, played by Wood. A combination of classy acting and impressive New York East Side setting makes this film above the ordinary. Edie Adams is good in a supporting role, and there are also excellent assists from Tom Bosley and Herschel Bernardi. **Director**—Robert Mulligan. **Academy Award Nominations**—Wood, best actress; Arnold Schulman, best story and screenplay (written directly for the screen); Milton Krasner, cinematography (black and white). *100 minutes b&w*

LOVING COUPLES (1980)
★★

Shirley MacLaine
James Coburn

An overly cute and predictable romantic comedy with MacLaine and Coburn as husband and wife doctors, who take a brief fling at mate-swapping. This theme had appeal in the '60s when Doris Day made bedroom eyes at Rock Hudson. But in regard to current moral standards, such escapades seem rather uneventful. Craggy-faced Coburn flashes a lot of teeth, while MacLaine strains to appear 10 years younger than she is. The film offers a few mild chuckles; the rest is just banal conversation. **Director**—Jack Smight. (PG) *97 minutes*

Stephen Collins, Shirley MacLaine, and James Coburn in Loving Couples.

THE L-SHAPED ROOM (1963)
★★★★

Leslie Caron

Top adult romantic drama with Caron in an outstanding role as a poor and pregnant French girl, living in a sleazy *(Continued)*

L·M

- Lucky Lady
- Luna
- Lust For Life
- MacArthur
- The Mackintosh Man
- The Macomber Affair

(Continued)
London rooming house. There, she encounters all sorts of interesting characters, including a determined young writer who offers her love and hope. Caron is perfectly cast, and she's backed up with superb supporting performances by Tom Bell, Brock Peters, Cicely Courtneidge, Avid Bunnage, and Emlyn Williams. Writer-director Bryan Forbes gets it all together with style. **Academy Award Nomination**—Caron, best actress.

125 minutes b&w

LUCKY LADY (1975)
★

Liza Minnelli
Gene Hackman
Burt Reynolds

The film cost about $13 million. The script is by Willard Huyck and Gloria Katz, who helped write *American Graffiti*. And it stars such heavies as Minnelli, Hackman, and Reynolds. With all that, this action comedy still turns out as a ridiculous, incoherent, and tasteless mess that's hardly funny. The stars are miscast together, and all seem to strain too hard. The three play small-time bootleggers who battle rival mobsters and the U.S. Coast Guard while transporting booze from Mexico to California. Also with Michael Hordern and Geoffrey Lewis. **Director**—Stanley Donen. (PG)

118 minutes

LUNA (1979)
★★

Jill Clayburgh
Matthew Barry

Clayburgh is miscast as an American opera star, a widow, who lives in Rome with her disturbed and drug-addicted teenage son, played by Barry. As she tries to console him and relieve his addiction, they develop a morbidly erotic relationship that involves a good deal of emotional and physical mayhem. Director Bernardo Bertolucci, who made *Last Tango in Paris*, directs with eloquence, but this long melodrama is unbelievable and absurd. Also with Veronica Lazar, Renato Salvatori, and Fred Gwynne. (R)

137 minutes

LUST FOR LIFE (1956)
★★★

Kirk Douglas
Anthony Quinn

Vivid and colorful screen treatment of Irving Stone's biography about the stormy life of famous artist Vincent Van Gogh. Douglas provides an absorbing portrayal of the master, who encountered much anguish along with his great artistic talent. Quinn excels as Van Gogh's close friend and mentor, artist Paul Gaugin. Many superb Van Gogh masterpieces are displayed. Also stars James Donald, Pamela Brown, Everett Sloane, and Lionel Jeffries. **Director**—Vincente Minnelli. **Academy Award**—Quinn, best supporting actor. **Nominations**—Douglas, best actor; Normin Corwin, writing (best screenplay—adapted).

122 minutes

M

MacARTHUR (1977)
★★★

Gregory Peck
Ed Flanders

Gregory Peck (center) plays the title role in the biographical film MacArthur.

Don't expect the snap and spirit of *Patton* here, but this biographical feature is an earnest and interesting account of the egocentric general's career from the beginning of World War II to his dismissal during the Korean Conflict. Peck's portrayal of the Great Commander is imposing and hauntingly convincing. Most of the supporting characters seem lost in the background, but Flanders sparkles as President Harry S Truman. A straightforward directing job by Joseph Sargent. Also with Dan O'Herlihy, Sandy Kenyon, Dick O'Neill, and Art Fleming. (PG)

144 minutes

THE MACKINTOSH MAN (1973)
★★

Paul Newman
James Mason

Busy, fast-paced spy caper about a British agent, played by Newman, who is assigned to expose a Communist infiltrator. The film offers ample excitement with the usual chases and narrow escapes, but the cold-war plot is déjà vu by now. The performances, however, are generally good, and the production is fairly well done. Mason stars as the double agent, and other supporting roles are played by Dominique Sanda, Nigel Patrick, Harry Andrews, and Ian Bannen. Filmed in England, Ireland, and Malta. **Director**—John Huston. (PG)

98 minutes

THE MACOMBER AFFAIR (1947)
★★★

Gregory Peck
Joan Bennett
Robert Preston

Taut, well-made safari adventure based on an Ernest Hemingway story, about the relationships among a husband, his wife, and their guide on a big-game hunting expedition. Peck turns in a superb performance as the guide, and there are fine acting jobs as well from Preston and Bennett as the couple with marital difficulties. An intelligent script contributes to the impact. Also stars Reginald Denny and Carl Harbord. **Director**—Zoltan Korda.

89 minutes b&w

- Madame Curie
- Madame Rosa
- Madam Kitty
- Mad Dog
- Madigan
- Mad Max
- Mado
- The Madwoman of Chaillot

M

MADAME CURIE (1943)
★★★

Greer Garson
Walter Pidgeon

A lofty, well-made film biography about the woman scientist who discovered radium. Rather slow-paced at times, but this intelligent production offers ample historical information and proceeds with showing the discovery of this vital element in an entertaining manner. Garson and Pidgeon shine as the Curies. There's notable support from Henry Travers, Albert Baserman, Robert Walker, C. Aubrey Smith, and Dame May Whitty. **Director**—Mervyn Le Roy. **Academy Award Nominations**—best picture; Pidgeon, best actor; Garson, best actress; Joseph Ruttenberg, cinematography (black and white).

124 minutes b&w

MADAME ROSA (1978)
★★

Simone Signoret

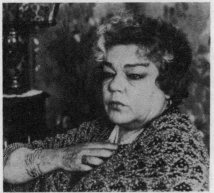

Simone Signoret, in Madame Rosa, *plays an aging former prostitute.*

Signoret plays an aging former prostitute with a big heart who cares for the children of streetwalkers. She summons a vivid characterization of a weary, proud woman grasping at the last threads of life. But aside from the dominant presence of Signoret, this overlong French drama is all downhill, with a muddled plot and excess sentimentality. Also with Claude Dauphin, Samy Ben Youb, and Gabriel Jabbour. **Director**—Mose Mizrahi. In French with English titles. (No MPAA rating) **Academy Award**—best foreign-language film (1977). *105 minutes*

MADAM KITTY (1977)
★★

Helmut Berger
Ingrid Thulin

A World War II Nazi brothel is the setting for this Italian-made soft-core porn epic, which earns its MPAA rating with a full catalog of sex and nudity. The international cast is headed by Berger and Thulin, but the real star is 21-year-old Therese Ann Savoy, a British actress who was the sex baby in *Bambina*. She gives her naked all as a nonprofessional whore in Madam Kitty's elegant house. **Director**—Tinto Brass. (X)

110 minutes

MAD DOG (1976)
★★

Dennis Hopper

Hopper stars in the title role of "Mad Dog" Daniel Morgan, a 19th-century Australian outlaw who terrorized the kangaroo territory and antagonized colonial officials. The film is rife with gore and brutality, such as a man choking to death on his own blood after his throat is slit. It depicts the so-called civilized people who hunt down the pitiful and mentally disturbed Morgan as no more moral than their quarry. Directed and written by Philippe Mora, whose efforts at social commentary fall flat. (R)

102 minutes

MADIGAN (1968)
★★★

Richard Widmark
Henry Fonda

A tough-talking, action-packed police yarn realistically set in New York City. Widmark is nicely cast as a determined detective who brings in his man at all costs. Other excellent characterizations are featured, especially Fonda as a hard-nosed police commissioner and Harry Guardino as Widmark's partner. The film offers some clear details of the workings of a big-city police department. Also stars James Whitmore, Inger Stevens, Michael Dunn, and Susan Clark. **Director**—Donald Siegal. *100 minutes*

MAD MAX (1980)
(no stars)

Mel Gibson

Trashy, brutal motorcycle film from Australia that lays on the gore and violence and steers clear of logic. Gibson, in the title role, is a clean-cut policeman who goes on a rampage of bloody revenge after a motorcycle gang kills his young son and injures his wife. The feeble plot is dreadful enough, but the film is made even more incoherent by poor dubbing of "American" for the heavy Australian dialect. Also with Joanne Samuel, Tim Burns, and Hugh Keays-Byrne. **Director**—George Miller. (R) *90 minutes*

MADO (1978)
★★

Michel Piccoli
Ottavia Piccolo

Director Claude Sautet's film about a "respectable" bourgeois real-estate promoter is an interesting study of character, but it ends there. The mushy screenplay is complicated with too many subplots and interrelationships; there's little that commands attention. Piccoli, as the promoter, and Piccolo, as the young woman in the title role, are essentially wasted. Also with Romy Schneider and Charles Denner. In French with English titles. (No MPAA rating) *135 minutes*

THE MADWOMAN OF CHAILLOT (1969)
★★

Katharine Hepburn

(Continued)

Katharine Hepburn and Edith Evans in The Madwoman of Chaillot.

M • Magic
• The Magic Flute
• The Magician of Lublin
• The Magic of Lassie
• The Magnificent Ambersons
• The Magnificent Seven

(Continued)
Much money and talent are squandered on this foolhardy effort to film Jean Giradoux's small-scale play about an oddball Parisian woman and her kooky friends who want to do good. The opulent treatment just doesn't fit the material, and the all-star spectacle quickly lapses into tedium. Hepburn is wasted in the title role, and some other talented actors are equally at sea. However, there are a few minor patches of brightness. Also stars Yul Brynner, Danny Kaye, Edith Evans, Charles Boyer, Claude Dauphin, Paul Henreid, and Richard Chamberlain. **Director**—Bryan Forbes. (G)

132 minutes

MAGIC (1978)
★★

**Anthony Hopkins
Ann-Margret
Burgess Meredith**

William Goldman's horror-suspense tale of a ventriloquist controlled by his dummy is reminiscent of the classic 1946 British chiller *Dead of Night*. This screen version of the popular novel, however, never lives up to its expectations, despite high-powered performances by Hopkins, as the ventriloquist, and Meredith. Ann-Margret plays an old sweetheart of Hopkins's. Director Richard Attenborough comes up with a few interludes of eerie suspense, but he doesn't have the magic touch to maintain tension to the end. Also with Ed Lauter and Jerry Houser. (R)

106 minutes

Ann-Margret, the acid-tongue dummy Fats, and Anthony Hopkins in Magic.

THE MAGIC FLUTE (1975)
★★★★

**Ulrik Gold
Josef Kostlinger**

Filming an opera is difficult indeed. But the magic of Swedish director Ingmar Bergman has pervaded *The Magic Flute*, the Mozart opera, and the result is a sparkling, funny, and intelligent movie. The film was initially made for Swedish TV at a modest cost of $650,000. Yet superb casting, quality camera work, exceptional sound reproduction, and Bergman's extraordinary directional ability have wrought a triumphant cinema experience. In Swedish with English titles. (G)

134 minutes

THE MAGICIAN OF LUBLIN
(1979)
★

**Alan Arkin
Louise Fletcher**

Director Menachem Golan fails dismally to capture on film Isaac Bashevis Singer's folktale, about a wandering Jewish magician who is a notorious womanizer. The film, set in Poland at the turn of the century, looks stiff and coarse most of the time. Singer's concept of an earthy and mystical atmosphere is nowhere in sight. There's no help either from Arkin, who portrays the lusty title character without con-

viction. Also with Valerie Perrine and Shelley Winters. (R) *105 minutes*

THE MAGIC OF LASSIE (1978)
★

**James Stewart
Mickey Rooney
Alice Faye**

A contrived, sugary dog episode that flagrantly manipulates children's emotions. This lackluster effort has none of the imagination or style of the popular 1943 *Lassie Come Home* film, which starred young Elizabeth Taylor. In this bland movie, Lassie, actually a descendant of the original movie collie, runs through a series of tragic adventures leading up to the eventual happy ending. It's not magic; it's more of a cheap trick. Also with Pernell Roberts and Mike Mazurki. **Director**—Don Chaffey. (G) *100 minutes*

THE MAGNIFICENT AMBERSONS (1942)
★★★★

**Joseph Cotten
Dolores Costello
Agnes Moorehead
Tim Holt**

Excellent adaptation of the Booth Tarkington novel, directed by Orson Welles at the peak of his creative prowess. The rich period drama concerns the decline of a wealthy family and the emotional relationship between the mother and the youngest son. It's a fascinating cinema treat, fast-paced and very much in control of its material; it's magnificent indeed. Good performances are given by Cotten, Costello, Moorehead, Holt, Anne Baxter, and Ray Collins. **Academy Award Nominations**—best picture; Moorehead, best supporting actress; Stanley Cortez, cinematography (black and white). *88 minutes b&w*

THE MAGNIFICENT SEVEN
(1960)
★★★

**Yul Brynner
Steve McQueen**

A supercharged western which closely follows the theme of the Japanese film

The Seven Samurai. A Mexican village is harassed by bandits, led by a greedy Eli Wallach, and the people hire seven American gunslingers to protect them. There's plenty of shoot-'em-up activity by a good cast especially suited for such parts. Also with Robert Vaughn, James Coburn, Charles Bronson, and Horst Buchholz. **Director**—John Sturges. *126 minutes*

MAGNUM FORCE (1973)
★★

**Clint Eastwood
Hal Holbrook**

More unrestrained gunfire in this diluted sequel to *Dirty Harry.* Tight-lipped Eastwood again stars as Harry Callahan, the invincible homicide cop, but this time he's after some colleagues, led by Holbrook, who do most of the killing as self-appointed executioners of underworld thugs. It has the usual amount of violence and brutality, but with less style than the first film. Also with Mitchell Ryan, David Soul, and Felton Perry. **Director**—Ted Post. (R) *124 minutes*

MAHOGANY (1975)
★★

**Diana Ross
Billy Dee Williams
Anthony Perkins**

In *Mahogany,* Diana Ross portrays an international model and fashion designer.

The incomparable Ross is stunning as a poor Chicago secretary turned international model and fashion designer, but a silly and shoddy script wastes such talent. Perkins plays a homosexual photographer responsible for her success in the fashion world. Also with Jean-Pierre Aumont, Nina Foch, and Beah Richards. **Director**—Berry Gordy. (PG) *110 minutes*

MAIN EVENT (1979)
★★★

**Barbra Streisand
Ryan O'Neal**

Streisand plays a wealthy perfume manufacturer who becomes the victim

Barbra Streisand and Ryan O'Neal spar in the comedy Main Event.

of embezzlement. She loses everything except her tax-shelter contract of reluctant prizefighter O'Neal. The screwball romance runs a delightful course of riotous comedy. Ryan and Streisand are better than they were in *What's Up Doc?* Director Howard Zieff and script writer Gail Parent keep the film as witty as it is zany. Also with Paul Sand, Patti D'Arbanville, and Whitman Mayo. (PG) *112 minutes*

MALIBU BEACH (1978)
★★

**Kim Lankford
James Daughton**

Formula youth-at-the-beach movie reminiscent of those beach-blanket movies of the late '50s. The empty-headed plot, aimed at young audiences, is a series of episodes concerning casual sex, pot-smoking, car-racing, and fistfights. Some nudity enters in with the help of a dog trained to snatch the tops of girls' bathing suits. Lankford and Daughton head the cast of unknowns having fun in the sun. **Director**—Robert J. Rosenthal. (R) *93 minutes*

JILL CLAYBURGH

Born in New York City, in 1944, Jill Clayburgh attended the Brearly School and earned her degree in theater arts at Sarah Lawrence College before she began her acting career. After a year with Boston's Charles Playhouse, she returned to New York for appearances in off-Broadway productions.

Her Broadway debut in The Rothchilds, *the hit musical about the famed banking family, showcased her singing voice and led to a role in the long-running hit play* Pippin *in 1970.*

Clayburgh made her motion-picture debut as a Sabra in Philip Roth's Portnoy's Complaint *(1972), she played Ryan O'Neal's ex-wife in* The Thief Who Came to Dinner *(1973), and was a hooker murdered by George Segal in* The Terminal Man *(1974) before getting her first starring role in* Gable and Lombard *(1976). Clayburgh went on to star in such hits as* Silver Streak *(1976) with Gene Wilder and Richard Pryor and* Semi-Tough *(1977) with Burt Reynolds and Kris Kristofferson. It was her multifaceted portrayal of Erica, however, in Paul Mazursky's* An Unmarried Woman *(1978), which brought Clayburgh international acclaim, her first Academy Award nomination, and the best actress award at the 1978 Cannes Film Festival. In 1979, she starred in* Luna, *and her role as a nursery school teacher in love with Burt Reynolds in* Starting Over *(1979) brought her a second Oscar nomination.*

M

- The Maltese Falcon
- A Man, a Woman and a Bank
- A Man Called Horse
- The Manchurian Candidate
- Mandy
- A Man for All Seasons

THE MALTESE FALCON (1941)
★★★★

**Humphrey Bogart
Mary Astor
Sydney Greenstreet**

This is the king of the crime capers, smartly executed by director John Huston with zip, punch, and even a bit of sentiment. Bogart is sensational as private-eye Sam Spade, hot on the trail of a mysterious statuette in this remake of a 1931 film. And he's backed to the hilt with memorable supporting parts from his client Astor, Greenstreet as the Fat Man, Peter Lorre as Joel Cairo, and gunsel Elisha Cook, Jr. Also with Barton MacLane, Lee Patrick, and Gladys George. See it twice, three times—it never seems to lose its fascination. Based on the novel by Dashiell Hammett. **Academy Award Nominations**—best picture; Greenstreet, best supporting actor; Huston, writing (screenplay).
101 minutes b&w

Peter Lorre, Mary Astor, and Humphrey Bogart in The Maltese Falcon.

A MAN, A WOMAN AND A BANK (1979)
★

**Donald Sutherland
Brooke Adams
Paul Mazursky**

Sutherland and Mazursky play clever con men whose plans to rob a Vancouver bank include invading the sophisticated security system during construction stages of the bank building. This drawn-out caper seems to have everyone running in place. There are so many unexciting complications and dull romantic interludes along the

Mazursky, Sutherland, and Adams in A Man, a Woman and a Bank.

way, one wishes the crooks would get on with the job, which isn't that exciting when they finally pull it off. Also with Allen Magicovsky. **Director**—Noel Black. (PG)
100 minutes

A MAN CALLED HORSE (1970)
★★

Richard Harris

An unusual story about American Indians, which strives to capture the authenticity of their culture and rituals, but mostly comes across with excessive harshness and gore. Harris portrays a polished Englishman who is captured by the Sioux in 1825 in the Dakotas; after some brutal torture, he's converted and accepted by the tribe and becomes a leader. Also with Judith Anderson, Jean Gascon, Manu Tupou, and Corinna Tsopei. It spawned a sequel, *The Return of a Man Called Horse*. **Director**—Elliot Silverstein. (PG)
114 minutes

THE MANCHURIAN CANDIDATE (1962)
★★★★

**Frank Sinatra
Janet Leigh
Laurence Harvey**

An intelligent and brilliantly conceived spy thriller about a Korean war veteran, played by Sinatra, who's brainwashed by the Communists. Turned into a zombie, he returns to the United States and attempts to assassinate a liberal politician, played by Harvey. The film, based on Richard Condon's novel, is both eerie and satirical, and it's well done in all

departments. The film was shot in Korea and in the United States. Also in the excellent cast are Angela Lansbury, Henry Silva, and James Gregory. **Director**—John Frankenheimer. **Academy Award Nomination**—Lansbury, best supporting actress.
126 minutes b&w

MANDY (1952)
★★★

**Jack Hawkins
Terence Morgan**

An engrossing drama about a young girl who is deaf and mute, struggling to make the most of her life. The semidocumentary film is handled with much sympathy and played professionally by a good cast that also includes Phyllis Calvert and Godfrey Tearle. Little Mandy Miller is excellent in the title role. Based on the novel *This Day Is Ours* by Hilda Lewis. **Director**—Alexander Mackendrick. **Alternate Title**—*The Crash of Silence*.
93 minutes b&w

A MAN FOR ALL SEASONS (1966)
★★★★

**Paul Scofield
Wendy Hiller
Robert Shaw**

Impeccable screen version of Robert Bolt's intelligent play about the falling-out between Sir Thomas More and King Henry VIII. Scofield plays More, Hiller is Alice More, and Shaw is the monarch. Period detail is brought out with splendor by director Fred Zinnemann, but the film truly soars because of the intense attention to character development. Scofield, as the exceptional religious leader, provides a superbly rich portrayal, and he's backed all the way with great support from Hiller, Shaw, Orson Welles, Leo McKern, Susannah York, and Vanessa Redgrave. **Academy Awards**—best picture; Zinnemann, best director; Scofield, best actor; Robert Bolt, best screenplay (based on material from another medium); Ted Moore, cinematography (color). **Nominations**—Shaw, best supporting actor; Hiller, best supporting actress.
120 minutes

● Man Friday
● The Man From Laramie
● Manhattan
● The Man in the Gray Flannel Suit
● The Man in the White Suit
● The Manitou
● The Man of a Thousand Faces

M

MAN FRIDAY (1976)
★

Peter O'Toole
Richard Roundtree

The Robinson Crusoe adventure classic is reworked into a chaotic blend of drama and whimsy with a modern twist. This version has Crusoe, played by O'Toole, as a Bible-banging white supremist, and his manservant Friday, played by Roundtree, as a black revolutionary. The idea quickly turns to tedium, the acting is disappointing, and stuck in the inane dialogue are several song-and-dance numbers. Also with Peter Cellier and Christopher Cabot. **Director**—Jack Gold. (PG) *115 minutes*

THE MAN FROM LARAMIE (1955)
★★★

James Stewart

Stewart is excellent as a stalwart cattleman who relentlessly pursues the killers of his brother. The gripping western combines moments of brutal action with some interesting characterizations. The supporting cast is good, too, with Arthur Kennedy, Donald Crisp, Cathy O'Donnell, Alex Nicol, Wallace Ford, and Jack Elam. **Director**—Anthony Mann.
104 minutes

MANHATTAN (1979)
★★★★

Woody Allen
Diane Keaton

Director-actor Allen returns to the satiric style of *Annie Hall* with greater success in his portraits of sophisticated New Yorkers and their foibles, fancies, loves, and frustrations. Not only do he and Keaton once again reveal their special brilliance for hilarious comedy, but Woody has developed a much deeper and more serious romantic spirit. His witty observations stir feelings while drawing laughter. A truly touching comic valentine to the Big Apple. Also with Michael Murphy, Mariel Hemingway, Meryl Streep, and Anne Byrne. (R) **Academy Award**

Diane Keaton and Woody Allen pause for a serious discussion in Manhattan.

Nominations—Hemingway, best supporting actress; Allen and Marshall Brickman, best screenplay (written directly for the screen).
96 minutes b&w

THE MAN IN THE GRAY FLANNEL SUIT (1956)
★★★

Gregory Peck
Fredric March

First-class rendering of Sloan Wilson's poignant novel about a New York public relations executive caught in the dilemma of succeeding in his high-pressure job or maintaining his integrity. It's all very slick and melodramatic, but the story moves briskly and maintains consistent interest. Peck is right at home in the title role as the button-down Madison Avenue type. Also with Jennifer Jones, Ann Harding, Arthur O'Connell, Henry Daniell, Lee J. Cobb, Keenan Wynn, and Gene Lockhart. **Director**—Nunnally Johnson. *153 minutes*

THE MAN IN THE WHITE SUIT (1952)
★★★★

Alec Guinness
Joan Greenwood
Cecil Parker

A nonstop comedy with Guinness and a top supporting cast generating an avalanche of fun and humor. Guinness is in great form as a scientist who invents an amazing textile that apparently won't wear out and actually repels dirt. Britain's textile industry is thrown into turmoil, and clothing makers scramble to get their hands on the astonishing material. A fantastic

combination of wit and rollicking high spirits. Also with Vida Hope, Michael Gough, and Ernest Thesiger. **Director**—Alexander Mackendrick. **Academy Award Nomination**—Roger MacDougall, John Dighton, and Mackendrick, writing (screenplay).
81 minutes b&w

THE MANITOU (1978)
★

Tony Curtis
Susan Strasberg

Curtis and Strasberg star in yet another cheap take-off on *The Exorcist* and *Rosemary's Baby*. In this case, the little devil is a 400-year-old Indian medicine man, who is found growing as a fetus on Strasberg's back. By now, even this absurd twist fails to produce any shock value and only succeeds in turning stomachs. Mani-poo! Also with Michael Ansara, Stella Stevens, and Ann Sothern. **Director**—William Girdler. (PG) *104 minutes*

Tony Curtis, a mystic, confers with Burgess Meredith in this scene from The Manitou.

THE MAN OF A THOUSAND FACES (1957)
★★★★

James Cagney
Dorothy Malone

An engaging film biography of silent-screen great Lon Chaney, who devised many intriguing characters with his amazing makeup skills. In *The Hunchback of Notre Dame*, Chaney wore some 40 pounds of makeup. The plot follows Chaney's screen career and private life. There's impressive detail and atmosphere from this period of filmmaking, yet interest is sidetracked at times because of numerous subplots. Cagney, in the title role, gives
(Continued)

M
- Man of Iron
- Man of La Mancha
- The Man on the Eiffel Tower
- Man on the Roof

- Manpower
- The Man Who Came to Dinner

(Continued)

another of his fantastic performances; Malone plays Chaney's first wife. Also with Jane Greer, Marjorie Rambeau, and Jim Backus. **Director**—Joseph Pevney. **Academy Award Nomination**—Ralph Wheelright, R. Right Campbell, Ivan Goff, and Ben Roberts, best story and screenplay (written directly for the screen).

122 minutes b&w

MAN OF IRON (1981)
★★★

Jerzy Radziwilowicz
Krystyna Janda

Fact and fiction are excitingly interwoven in this fresh account of recent history—the workers' rebellion in Poland and the rise of the Solidarity labor movement. Polish director Andrzej Wajda made this film as a sequel to his *Man of Marble*. This continuation involves political activities during the shipyard strike in Gdansk and a worker's love affair with a woman filmmaker. Even Solidarity leader Lech Walesa and other union notables have theatrical parts and appear in newsreel inserts. In Polish with English titles. (No MPAA rating) *140 minutes*

MAN OF LA MANCHA (1972)
★

Peter O'Toole
Sophia Loren

The classic Cervantes fable of Don Quixote, produced with extraordinary power and beauty on the stage, is incomprehensible on the screen. The brilliant musical numbers come across with dreariness, and the entire endeavor plods lamely along. The settings are impressive, but it's an essentially disappointing experience. Also with James Coco, Harry Andress, and John Castle. **Director**—Arthur Hiller. (PG) *140 minutes*

THE MAN ON THE EIFFEL TOWER (1949)
★★★

Charles Laughton
Burgess Meredith

An intense and intriguing crime drama, impressively set against the backdrop of Paris. Police Inspector Maigret and a mad killer relentlessly match wits and nerves until the mystery is solved in a tense climax. The production, based on a Simenon novel, is enhanced by excellent acting. Also with Franchot Tone, Robert Hutton, Jean Wallace, and Wilfrid Hyde-White. **Director**—Meredith.

97 minutes

MAN ON THE ROOF (1977)
★★

Carl-Gustaf Lindstedt
Sven Wollfer
Hakan Serner

Swedish director Bo Widerberg's unusual drama examines the complex relationships among policemen and presents a realistic example of plodding detective work. The film, based on the Martin Beck detective series, involves the trackdown of a heavily armed killer who wages war on the Stockholm police. The story is intelligent, but choppy construction spoils any opportunity for sustained suspense and interrupts the momentum. And the bloody climax between the rooftop sniper and the cops is overworked by now. In Swedish with English titles. (No MPAA rating)

110 minutes

MANPOWER (1941)
★★★

Edward G. Robinson
George Raft
Marlene Dietrich

Powerful action-packed adventure about the men who work on high-voltage power lines. Robinson and Raft, two such workers, argue over nightclub hostess Dietrich. The upshot is a gripping man-to-man fistfight on a powerline tower during a stormy night; the sparks fly in all directions. Also with Alan Hale, Frank McHugh, Eve Arden, Barton MacLane, and Ward Bond. **Director**—Raoul Walsh.

103 minutes b&w

THE MAN WHO CAME TO DINNER (1941)
★★★★

Monty Woolley
Bette Davis

Woolley is riotously funny in this sidesplitting comedy, as a bombastic celebrity who's injured while on tour and must stay with a local family to recuperate. He drives his hosts up the wall with his wacky antics and with the assorted oddball characters who

Jimmy Durante and Monty Woolley have fun in The Man Who Came to Dinner.

- The Man Who Fell to Earth
- The Man Who Loved Cat Dancing
- The Man Who Loved Women
- The Man Who Shot Liberty Valance
- The Man Who Skied Down Everest
- The Man Who Would Be King
- The Man With the Golden Arm

M

come to visit him. Despite its stagey setting, the activity moves quickly and generates an avalanche of laughter. Davis is wasted, but there are good caricatures from Jimmy Durante, Reginald Gardiner, and Ann Sheridan. Also with Billie Burke, Richard Travis, and Grant Mitchell. **Director**—William Keighley.

112 minutes b&w

THE MAN WHO FELL TO EARTH (1976)
★★★★

David Bowie

In The Man Who Fell to Earth, *David Bowie portrays an extraterrestrial visitor.*

Nicolas Roeg's riveting and fascinating sci-fi tale is about an extraterrestrial traveller who comes to Earth to find water for his dying planet. He organizes a vast scientific conglomerate, à la Howard Hughes, and becomes entangled in lots of earthly corruption. Rock star Bowie plays the visitor from outer space with credibility. Rip Torn, Buck Henry, and Candy Clark also deliver appealing performances. The film says much about life on Earth through the eyes of a man from another world. (R) *125 minutes*

THE MAN WHO LOVED CAT DANCING (1973)
★

Sarah Miles
Burt Reynolds
Lee J. Cobb

A sluggish western adventure about a restless wife who is kidnapped by train robbers and falls in love with one of the outlaws. Miles is the unhappy wife, and Reynolds plays the main desperado. Cobb leads a posse after the bandits. A rather impressive cast can't make much of this movie based

on the novel by Marilyn Dunham. And it gave Reynolds a double hernia for doing his own stunts. Also with Jack Warden, George Hamilton, Bo Hopkins, and Jay Silverheels. **Director**—Richard C. Sarafian. (PG)

114 minutes

THE MAN WHO LOVED WOMEN (1977)
★★★

Charles Denner
Leslie Caron

Director François Truffaut's charming tale of a Frenchman who is obsessed by women is witty and sophisticated. The appealing cast is headed by Denner, whose gentle manner makes the title character shine with a mixture of comic delight and innocence. The film doesn't measure up to earlier Truffaut artistic achievements, but it's still fun to watch for its clever variations on a familiar theme. Also stars Brigitte Fossey and Nelly Borgeaud. In French with English titles. (No MPAA rating) *119 minutes*

THE MAN WHO SHOT LIBERTY VALANCE (1962)
★★★

James Stewart
John Wayne
Vera Miles

A young man, played by Stewart, takes the bows for killing a notorious outlaw. But did the tenderfoot really fire that fatal shot? Fairly entertaining John Ford western with a good cast doing their utmost, although the story is unnecessarily strung out. Wayne is firmly in the saddle again, competing with Stewart over Miles. And Lee Marvin plays the villain again. Others in the cast include Edmond O'Brien, Andy Devine, and Jeanette Nolan.

122 minutes b&w

THE MAN WHO SKIED DOWN EVEREST (1976)
★★★

Yuichiro Miura

A feature-length documentary of Japanese athlete Miura's fascinating experience on the slopes of the world's

highest mountain. The camera captures the majestic beauty of the Himalayas and Miura's courageous 2½-minute descent on skis from the 29,000-foot-high peak. Some 800 men lugged 27 tons of equipment up the treacherous mountainside to record the feat. The film cost six lives and $3 million. There's some pompous narration expressing Miura's philosophy of life. **Directors**—F. R. Crawley, James Hager, and Dale Hartleben. (G) **Academy Award**—best documentary (feature). *86 minutes*

THE MAN WHO WOULD BE KING (1975)
★★★

Sean Connery
Michael Caine
Christopher Plummer

Connery and Caine play two soldiers-turned-con men who set themselves up as rulers of Kafiristan, a remote and primitive country, so they can loot the royal treasury. The film, based on Rudyard Kipling's romantic short story, succeeds as an exotically charming old-fashioned adventure tale, laced with comradeship and courage. The duo's scheme falls apart when Danny Dravot, played by Connery, becomes attached to his responsibilities as god-king. Plummer gives a remarkable but brief performance as Kipling. Also with Saeed Jaffrey and Jack May. **Director**—John Huston. (PG) **Academy Award Nomination**—Huston and Gladys Hill, best screenplay (adapted from another medium).

127 minutes

THE MAN WITH THE GOLDEN ARM (1955)
★★★

Frank Sinatra
Kim Novak

Sinatra is surprisingly good in this stark drama, based on a Nelson Algren novel, as a drug addict who painfully kicks the habit. The film was sensational at the time of its release, and it retains much of its power. Otto Preminger's direction, however, is slow-paced and even-handed. Elmer Bernstein's jazzy score heightens the

(Continued)

M
- Marathon Man
- March or Die
- Marjorie Morningstar
- The Mark of Zorro
- Marlowe
- The Marquise of O . . .
- The Marriage of Maria Braun

Frank Sinatra and Kim Novak star in the stark drama The Man With the Golden Arm.

(Continued)
mood. Also with Eleanor Parker, Darren McGavin, Arnold Stang, and Robert Strauss. **Academy Award Nomination**—Sinatra, best actor.

119 minutes

MARATHON MAN (1976)
★★★

**Dustin Hoffman
Laurence Olivier**

In Marathon Man, *Dustin Hoffman lashes out at Laurence Olivier, who plays a Nazi.*

Director John Schlesinger's supercharged thriller is about a Columbia University graduate who, for reasons he cannot understand, is pursued and tormented by a surviving Nazi war criminal. Hoffman is the student, and Olivier is the long-dormant Nazi who is also a former dentist. The film is paradoxical. At times, it generates tension that is nearly unbearable, and there are moments of intense excitement. It's crammed with brutal killings, bone-chilling torture, and triple crosses. Yet it's all wrapped in a murky and confusing plot that hardly makes much sense. Hoffman, Olivier, and the rest of the cast are in fine form. The screenplay was written by William Goldman from his own novel. Also with Marthe Keller, Roy

Scheider, and William Devane. (R) **Academy Award Nomination**—Olivier, best supporting actor.

125 minutes

MARCH OR DIE (1977)
★★

**Gene Hackman
Catherine Deneuve
Terence Hill**

Stiff, listless French Foreign Legion adventure that's high on beautiful location photography, but short on acting. Hackman, Deneuve, and other cast members mope about the desert as if they are suffering from sunstroke. Hill is lively, but acts silly. The story, which concerns an expedition to steal Arab treasure buried in the Sahara, is complicated and pedestrian. Also with Max Von Sydow and Ian Holm. **Director**—Dick Richards. (PG)

104 minutes

MARJORIE MORNINGSTAR (1958)
★★

**Natalie Wood
Gene Kelly**

A young Jewish girl with stars in her eyes strives to make it to the big time in New York City, but winds up as an ordinary housewife. This screen adaptation of Herman Wouk's popular novel never takes off, although a few scenes are moving. Wood seems ill at ease in the title role and so do most of the supporting players. Also with Claire Trevor, Everett Sloane, Ed Wynn, Martin Milner, Carolyn Jones, and Martin Balsam. **Director**—Irving Rapper.

123 minutes

THE MARK OF ZORRO (1940)
★★★★

**Tyrone Power
Basil Rathbone**

A ripsnorting swashbuckling adventure starring Power as Diego de Vega, an aristocrat who dons a mask and routs the bad guys in California in the early 1800s. Well-staged and executed with much energy, the film offers some of the best dueling scenes around. It's great fun for boys of all

ages. Power is as dashing as ever, and the excellent cast also includes Linda Darnell, J. Edward Bromberg, Eugene Pallette, and Montagu Love. **Director**—Rouben Mamoulian.

94 minutes b&w

MARLOWE (1969)
★★★

**James Garner
Rita Moreno**

Garner tries his hand at playing Philip Marlowe, the Raymond Chandler private-eye character, and the results are fairly good. A girl loses track of her brother so she hires Marlowe to find him. Moreno plays a stripper. The thriller, based on Chandler's *The Little Sister*, moves along at a brisk pace and displays some of the squalid atmosphere associated with such capers. But don't expect this adventure to match the Humphrey Bogart versions. Garner gets first-class assistance from Gayle Hunnicutt, Sharon Farrell, Carroll O'Connor, and Bruce Lee. **Director**—Paul Bogart. (PG) *95 minutes*

THE MARQUISE OF O . . . (1976)
★★

**Edith Clever
Bruno Ganz**

Director Eric Rohmer's film is an almost word-for-word adaptation of Heinrich von Kleist's 1808 comedy of manners about an Austrian widow who finds herself mysteriously pregnant. It's an elegant movie executed with a light touch. Yet it's perhaps too formal and meditative to be truly engrossing. Clever is likable as the Marquise; Ganz plays the courtly count who's responsible for her condition. Also with Peter Luhr, Edda Seippel, and Otto Sander. In German with English titles. (No MPAA rating)

102 minutes

THE MARRIAGE OF MARIA BRAUN (1980)
★★

**Hanna Schygulla
Klaus Lowitsch**

Sultry and beautiful Schygulla plays

the title role in this film about survival in postwar Germany. As Maria, she achieves success through shrewdness and energy as Germany emerges into a period of miraculous prosperity. Rainer Werner Fassbinder directs in his usual straightforward style, but the film has as many dull interludes as it has fascinating scenes. Also with Ivan Desny and Gottried John. In German with English titles. (No MPAA rating)
120 minutes

THE MARRYING KIND (1952)
★★★

**Judy Holliday
Aldo Ray**

An intelligent tragicomedy played with style and sensitivity by Holliday and Ray, a couple with marital problems who straighten things out after analyzing their lives. Holliday does a fine job with the serious moments as well as the comic opportunities. Madge Kennedy and Mickey Shaughnessy also star. **Director**—George Cukor. *93 minutes b&w*

MARTY (1955)
★★★★

**Ernest Borgnine
Betsy Blair**

This is one of the most compassionate and touching films about the lives and problems of ordinary people ever produced. Borgnine is perfectly cast as the lonely middle-aged butcher resigned to an unmarried life, who finally falls in love with a girl in similar circumstances; Blair plays the lonely girl. Paddy Chayefsky's script was intitially written as a TV play, and it gains further impact and importance as a feature film. It's a movie masterpiece,

Ernest Borgnine is a lonely butcher in the touching film Marty.

filled with subtleties, irony, and truth. Borgnine's performance is magnificent, and there's excellent support from Blair, Esther Minciotti, Joe Mantell, and Jerry Paris. **Director**—Delbert Mann. **Academy Awards**—best picture; Mann, best director; Borgnine, best actor; Chayefsky, writing (screenplay). **Nominations**—Mantell, best supporting actor; Blair, best supporting actress; Joseph LaShelle, cinematography (black and white).
91 minutes b&w

MARY POPPINS (1964)
★★★★

**Julie Andrews
Dick Van Dyke**

Dick Van Dyke and Julie Andrews in the Walt Disney fantasy Mary Poppins.

This delightful fantasy from Disney is about two English children minded by a strict but wonderful nanny who has magical powers and takes them on exciting adventures. Andrews, in her film debut, is splendid in the title role, and the film proceeds with charm and energy. It's great entertainment for the kids, and adults won't find it boring or trite. There's also a serious message involved: Kids need love and attention, not just wealthy surroundings, to truly make them happy. Also with David Tomlinson, Glynis Johns, Ed Wynn, Elsa Lanchester, and Arthur Treacher. **Director**—Robert Stevenson. **Academy Award**—Andrews, best actress. **Nominations**—best picture; Stevenson, best director; Bill

Walsh and Don DaGradi, best screenplay (based on material from another medium); Edward Colman, cinematography (color). *139 minutes*

M*A*S*H (1970)
★★★★

**Donald Sutherland
Elliott Gould
Sally Kellerman**

Elliott Gould and Donald Sutherland relax on a golf outing in the black comedy M*A*S*H.

Director Robert Altman scores big with this smart black comedy about doctors at a Mobile Army Surgical Hospital (MASH), in Korea, who relieve the boredom, tension, and horror of their situation by pulling pranks and defying authority. A trend-setting film and a most unusual farce, splendidly acted by Sutherland, Gould, and Kellerman in the key roles. The extraordinary screenplay by Ring Lardner, Jr., touches all the bases, and it's hilarious from start to finish. A great film that spawned an excellent TV show. Also stars Tom Skerritt, Robert Duvall, John Schuck, Jo Ann Pflug, and Gary Burghof. (PG) **Academy Award**—Lardner, best screenplay (based on material from another medium). **Nominations**—best picture; Altman, best director; Kellerman, best supporting actress. *116 minutes*

THE MASK OF DIMITRIOS (1944)
★★★

**Peter Lorre
Sydney Greenstreet
Zachary Scott**

Lorre and Greenstreet are right at home in this stylish tale of intrigue, based on an Eric Ambler novel. Lorre
(Continued)

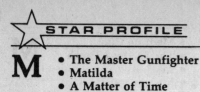

M • The Master Gunfighter
• Matilda
• A Matter of Time
• McCabe & Mrs. Miller

(Continued)

is a Dutch writer in the Middle East, seeking out a clever criminal, played by Scott. Plenty of good smoky atmosphere enhances the story and the characters. Also with Faye Emerson, Victor Francen, Steven Geray, and Florence Bates. **Director**—Jean Negulesco.   *113 minutes b&w*

THE MASTER GUNFIGHTER
(1975)
★

Tom Laughlin

Laughlin, who played the lead in the successful *Billy Jack* movies, fizzles in this plodding drama, set in early California. The plot deals with a struggle over a Spanish land grant. Our hero, who just hates to kill, slays a lot of people with a 12-shot revolver and a sword. Also stars Ron O'Neal, Lincoln Kilpatrick, Barbara Carrera, and Victor Campos. **Director**—Frank Laughlin. (PG)   *121 minutes*

MATILDA (1978)
★★

Elliott Gould
Robert Mitchum

A lightweight comedy about a boxing kangaroo who gets a shot at the world heavyweight title. The script occasionally produces a chuckle or two, but most of the time there's not enough punch to sustain prolonged interest. Gould is okay as a vaudeville promoter, while Mitchum sleepwalks through his role as a sportswriter. Matilda is actually a man in a kangaroo suit who looks like a youngster dressed up for Halloween. Also with Harry Guardino, Clive Revill, and Lionel Stander. **Director**—Daniel Mann. (G)   *103 minutes*

A MATTER OF TIME (1976)
★★

Liza Minnelli
Ingrid Bergman
Charles Boyer

Vincente Minnelli directs daughter Liza in this Cinderella story of a chambermaid who's transformed into a glamorous movie star. The film, set in Rome in 1949, is rich in lush scenery and glittery costumes, but the plot is tacky, and the dialogue is awkward. Bergman co-stars as an eccentric, down-and-out contessa who inspires the young peasant girl. Minnelli and Bergman perform spectacularly, but

BURT REYNOLDS

Born in Waycross, Georgia, in 1936, Burt Reynolds was reared in southern Florida, where his father was a police chief. He admits that he was a restless kid who at one point ran away from home and wound up in a South Carolina jail. The cell in which he spent a week now bears an engraved plaque that reads "Burt Reynolds Slept Here."

A high-school football star, Reynolds chose Florida State University over West Point because "the Academy didn't have any girls" and he was partial to FSU's football team. During his college grid career, he was named All-Florida and All-Conference halfback. He then enrolled at Palm Beach Junior College, where he credits the school's drama instructor with changing his life. A scholarship to New York's Hyde Park Playhouse led to his professional acting debut with Charlton Heston in a revival of *Mister Roberts.*

Moving to Los Angeles, Reynolds appeared in many television series, including Gunsmoke. *He also starred in three TV series—* Riverboat, Hawk, *and* Dan August.

Reynolds made his movie debut in Angel Baby *(1961), but it was his performance in* Deliverance *(1972) that made him a major star. His nude centerfold in* Cosmopolitan *magazine and the wry, self-depreciating humor he displayed on TV talk shows made him one of the most popular stars in the world. Some of his other movies include* The Longest Yard *(1974),* Hustle *(1976),* Gator *(1976),* Smokey and the Bandit *(1977),* Semi-Tough *(1977),* Hooper *(1978),* Starting Over *(1979),* Smokey and the Bandit II *(1980), and* Sharkey's Machine *(1981).*

Liza Minnelli and Ingrid Bergman star in A Matter of Time.

they're much too good for such mediocre material. Also with Tina Aumont and Spiros Andros. (PG)   *99 minutes*

McCABE & MRS. MILLER (1971)
★★★

Warren Beatty
Julie Christie

Director Robert Altman shows off his resourceful ability in this turn-of-the-century western, about a gambler who established a bordello in a remote Northwest community. Beatty's performance, as the gambler-braggart, is exceptionally moving and displays just the right amount of pathos and droll humor. He's matched all the way by Christie as his rather exceptional manager of operations. Based on the novel *McCabe* by Edmund Naughton. Supporting roles by René Auberjonois, Hugh Millais, Shelley Duvall, John Schuck, and Keith Carradine. (R) **Academy Award Nomination**— Christie, best actress.   *120 minutes*

● The McKenzie Break   ● Medium Cool
● McLintock!   ● The Medusa Touch
● Mean Streets   ● Meet Me in St. Louis
● Meatballs   ● Melvin and Howard

M

THE McKENZIE BREAK (1970)
★★★

**Brian Keith
Helmut Griem**

An intelligent and intense action drama about German prisoners during World War I who plot an escape from a POW camp in Scotland. There are convincing performances by Keith as an Irish prison commander and Griem as the leader of the prisoners. Suspense builds to a rousing climax. Also stars Ian Hendry, Jack Watson, and Patrick O'Connell. **Director**—Lamont Johnson. (PG)   *106 minutes*

McLINTOCK! (1963)
★★★

**John Wayne
Maureen O'Hara**

Big John demonstrates his ability as a laugh-getter in this wild and wooly western comedy. The Duke plays a formidable cattle baron who knows how to run his business and the community, but has trouble controlling his wife. Lots of high spirits and raucous slapstick maintain steady interest in this farce that parodies Shakespeare's *The Taming of the Shrew*. O'Hara is effective as Wayne's difficult wife, and there are other good performances by Yvonne de Carlo, Patrick Wayne, Stefanie Powers, Chill Wills, and Bruce Cabot. **Director**—Andrew V. McLaglen.   *127 minutes*

MEAN STREETS (1973)
★★★★

**Harvey Keitel
Robert De Niro**

A compelling and sharply detailed story about life in New York City's Little Italy, as seen through the experiences of a group of small-time hoods. Director Martin Scorsese captures the atmosphere of the area and expertly brings out the sense of competitiveness and family life of the inhabitants. Scorsese made a name for himself with this moody and brutal portrait. Also with David Proval, Amy Robinson, Cesare Danova, and Richard Romanus. (R)   *110 minutes*

MEATBALLS (1979)
★

**Bill Murray
Harvey Atkin
Kate Lynch**

This silly farce about life at summer camp is a concoction of *Animal House* crossbred with *M*A*S*H* and aimed at the under-16-year-old set. A lack of fresh comic invention will make anyone with an iota of sophisticated taste restless. What's left is predictable and infantile nonsense that might tickle the funnybones of kids just old enough to go to the movies by themselves. Also with Kristine DeBell, Russ Banham, and Sarah Torgov. **Director**—Ivan Reitman. (PG)   *92 minutes*

MEDIUM COOL (1969)
★★★

Robert Forster

A remarkable and revealing semi-documentary film about the effects of television on our life-styles and our perceptions of violence in contemporary society. Director Haskell Wexler sets his story in the arena of conflicts at the 1968 Democratic National Convention in Chicago, where he focuses on a TV news cameraman who mechanically goes about his duties in the midst of emotional events. Executed with style and intellience and wrapped up with a thoughtful ending. Forster plays the detached cameraman; he's supported by Verna Bloom, Peter Bonerz, and Marianna Hill. (R)   *110 minutes*

Harvey Keitel, in Mean Streets, *learns just what the film's title means.*

THE MEDUSA TOUCH (1978)
★

**Richard Burton
Lee Remick**

Burton plays a strange person with telekinetic power—the ability to move objects by will—in this pointless melodrama directed by Jack Gold. Remick is Burton's psychiatrist. The telekinesis gimmick is overdone when a jet plane crashes and Westminster Abbey crumbles under Burton's power. The big mystery, though, is why Burton and co-star Remick are involved in such an awful movie, which is bogged down by a dumb script, some awkward attempts at humor, and only a trace of suspense. Also with Lino Ventura, Harry Andrews, and Alan Badel. (PG)   *110 minutes*

MEET ME IN ST. LOUIS (1944)
★★★★

**Judy Garland
Margaret O'Brien**

A bright, charming musical in Hollywood's best tradition, about a family in St. Louis at the time of the 1903 World's Fair. Garland tops the cast, and she has a wonderful time with the sentimental songs, including "The Boy Next Door" and "Trolley Song." Leon Ames and Mary Astor are her parents; O'Brien is Judy's sister. It's all exceptionally romantic, nostalgic, and heartwarming. There's also fine support from June Lockhart, Harry Davenport, and Marjorie Main. **Director**—Vincente Minnelli. **Academy Award Nomination**—George Folsey, cinematography (color).   *113 minutes*

MELVIN AND HOWARD (1980)
★★★★

**Paul Le Mat
Jason Robards, Jr.
Mary Steenburgen**

A charming and often hilarious social satire taken from the much-publicized account of Melvin Dummar, the service station attendant who claims to be a beneficiary in Howard Hughes's
(Continued)

217

M
- The Memory of Justice
- The Men
- Men of the Fighting Lady
- Merrill's Marauders
- Merry Andrew
- Message From Space
- Meteor

Jason Robards and Paul Le Mat are Howard Hughes and Melvin Dummar in Melvin and Howard.

(Continued)

will. Le Mat plays Melvin with a likable freshness that colorfully illuminates this good-hearted character who is eluded by the American dream. Supporting players Robards, who plays Hughes, and Steenburgen contribute energy and a sense of reality to this stylish comedy. **Director—**Jonathan Demme. (R) **Academy Awards**—Steenburgen, best supporting actress; Bo Goldman, best screenplay (written directly for the screen). *95 minutes*

THE MEMORY OF JUSTICE (1976)
★★★★

An extraordinary documentary epic by director Marcel Ophuls, reexamining the principles of justice established at the 1946 Nuremberg Trials. This extremely long, intense film classic hammers the emotions with such questions as: Has one nation the right to judge another? How does Nuremberg justice apply to U.S. military actions in Vietnam, or to the conduct of French soldiers in Algeria? The production is mainly composed of old newsreel footage and filmed interviews of more than 40 persons. The experience is exhilarating. This is monumental filmmaking. (PG) *278 minutes*

THE MEN (1950)
★★★★

Marlon Brando
Teresa Wright

Brando debuts in this absorbing drama as a wounded war veteran struggling to overcome his disability, and his performance is impressive indeed. The entire production is excellent; there's fine acting and direction all around. The film is a realistic and penetrating treatment of a sensitive subject. Also with Everett Sloane, Jack Webb, and Howard St. John. **Director—**Fred Zinnemann. **Alternate Title—***Battle Stripe*. **Academy Award Nomination—**Carl Foreman, writing (story and screenplay). *85 minutes b&w*

MEN OF THE FIGHTING LADY (1954)
★★★

Van Johnson
Walter Pidgeon

Above-average saga of action aboard a U.S. aircraft carrier during the Korean Conflict. The characters are rather wooden, but the film moves briskly, with a semidocumentary flavor enhanced effectively by actual combat scenes worked in with the theatrics. Also with Keenan Wynn, Frank Lovejoy, Dewey Martin, Robert Horton, and Louis Calhern. **Director—**Andrew Marton. *80 minutes*

MERRILL'S MARAUDERS (1962)
★★★

Jeff Chandler
Ty Hardin

Rough, tough combat adventure with battle-hardened U.S. Army troops winning the hard way against enemy forces in Burma during World War II. Typical heroic stuff, with the emphasis on the limits of hardship under life-or-death conditions. Decently acted by Chandler—his final film—and supporting players, including Hardin, Andrew Duggan, Peter Brown, Will Hutchins, and Claude Akins. **Director—**Samuel Fuller. *98 minutes*

MERRY ANDREW (1958)
★★

Danny Kaye
Pier Angeli

A lesser Kaye musical comedy, but handled with adequate charm. It also features adequate music. Danny portrays a strict schoolteacher who loosens up when he joins a circus and falls for one of the performers, played brightly by Angeli. Enough songs and dancing come into play, but effective comedy—Kaye-style—is sorely lacking. The cast also features Baccaloni, Noel Purcell, and Robert Coote. **Director—**Michael Kidd. *103 minutes*

MESSAGE FROM SPACE (1978)
★★

Vic Morrow
Sonny Chiba

Squadrons of spaceships rocket among the planets. Heroes and villains duel with laser-beam swords. There's even a cute little robot. The message, obviously, is from *Star Wars*, and this imitation was made in Japan. The special effects have lots of zip, but the acting and plotting come through as warmed-over sukiyaki. Morrow, in a brief role, is the only familiar face in the crowd of unknown players, which includes many Japanese. **Director—**Kinji Fukasaku. (PG) *105 minutes*

METEOR (1979)
★★

Sean Connery
Natalie Wood
Karl Malden

This is one more disaster epic for fans who can't get enough of devastation by earthquakes, tidal waves, and so on. This time it's a gigantic meteor speeding toward earth, and the Americans and Russians combine nuclear technology to stop it. Connery, Wood, and other notables put in time at the movie factory to portray cardboard characters. Some of the special effects are interesting, such as Manhattan's

Sean Connery hugs Natalie Wood after their narrow escape in Meteor.

- Middle Age Crazy
- Middle of the Night
- The Middle of the World

- Midnight Cowboy
- Midnight Express
- Midway

M

destruction. Henry Fonda plays the President again. Also with Brian Keith, Martin Landau, Trevor Howard, and Richard Dysart. **Director—** Ronald Neame. (PG)   *103 minutes*

MIDDLE AGE CRAZY (1980)
★★

Bruce Dern
Ann-Margret

In Middle Age Crazy, *Ann-Margret and Bruce Dern are a couple with problems.*

Dern stars as a successful architect with a beautiful wife, played by Ann-Margret, who confronts a mid-life crisis. Dern gives the part ample warmth and appeal, but the tedious script is bogged down with clichés and sentimentality. The upshot is a disappointing film. This social problem has been explored time and again, and here the subject is overworked. The theme seems beset by its own mid-life crisis. **Director—**John Trent. (R)
89 minutes

MIDDLE OF THE NIGHT (1959)
★★★

Fredric March
Kim Novak

Satisfactory film rendition of Paddy Chayefsky's teleplay about a middle-aged widower in love with a much younger girl. March is convincing as the world-wise businessman seeking a new experience, but Novak isn't that persuasive as the youthful object of his affections. This isn't among the best of Chayefsky's efforts, but the story is moving nevertheless. Glenda Farrell, Jan Norris, Lee Grant, and Martin Balsam are adequate in supporting roles. **Director—**Delbert Mann.
118 minutes b&w

THE MIDDLE OF THE WORLD (1975)
★★★

Olimpia Carlisi
Philippe Leotard

An innovative film about a young actress from Italy with a deep sense of self-esteem. Carlisi portrays the sensitive heroine who refuses to accommodate a Swiss engineer, played by Leotard, who runs as a candidate for Parliament. It's simplistically funny at times and erotic with a complex intellectual underlay. Also with Juliet Berto. **Director—**Alain Tanner. In French with English titles. (No MPAA rating)   *115 minutes b&w*

MIDNIGHT COWBOY (1969)
★★★★

Jon Voight
Dustin Hoffman

Outstanding atmospheric drama about a naïve young man from Texas who comes to New York City to make it as a gigolo. He ends up being hustled, and he discovers it's just as dreary and lonesome in the big city as it was in the hick town he came from. The stark chain of events is played out against the squalid backdrop of New York's decaying 42nd Street area, and the film offers some memorable character studies of desperate souls. Voight is triumphant in the title role, and his excellent performance is matched beautifully by Hoffman as Ratso Rizzo, his disheveled friend. Sylvia Miles, John McGiver, and Brenda Vaccaro also star. **Director—**John Schlesinger. (R) **Academy Awards**—best picture; Schlesinger, best director; Waldo Salt, best screenplay (based on material from another medium). **Nominations**—Hoffman, Voight, best actor.   *113 minutes*

MIDNIGHT EXPRESS (1978)
★★★★

Brad Davis
John Hurt
Randy Quaid

Realistic, gut-wrenching portrayal of brutality, degradation, and frustration

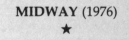
Brad Davis plays prisoner Billy Hayes in the gut-wrenching film Midnight Express.

suffered by a young American in a Turkish prison. The film is based on the true story of Billy Hayes, who was arrested in 1970 in Istanbul for trying to smuggle two kilos of hashish. Newcomer Davis, playing Billy, gives a remarkable performance; at times he resembles the late James Dean. Director Alan Parker expertly crafts the harrowing moods and sordid scenes of this latter-day version of Dante's *Inferno*. Also with Irene Miracle and Bo Hopkins. (R) **Academy Award—** Oliver Stone, best screenplay adaptation. **Nomination**—best picture; Parker, best director; Hurt, best supporting actor.   *121 minutes*

MIDWAY (1976)
★

Charlton Heston
Henry Fonda
Glenn Ford
James Coburn
Hal Holbrook

The sea-air Battle of Midway was a turning point in the Pacific during World War II, but this plodding and cliché-strewn film version is hardly a turning point in war movies. The lame script covers well-worn territory, and it's all wrapped in the Sensurround gimmick, which is more of an earache than an emotional effect. Veteran actors, including Robert Mitchum and Cliff Robertson, appear briefly to deliver a few stiff lines. Fonda has a
(Continued)

M
- Mighty Joe Young
- Mikey and Nicky
- Mildred Pierce
- The Miracle of Morgan's Creek
- The Miracle on 34th Street
- The Miracle Worker

Henry Fonda (center) portrays Admiral Chester Nimitz in Midway.

(Continued)
somewhat larger part as Admiral Nimitz. (PG)   *132 minutes*

MIGHTY JOE YOUNG (1949)
★★★

Terry Moore
Ben Johnson

A fairly competent retread of the *King Kong* fable, but not as stylish as the 1933 movie. A promoter brings back a gorilla from the African jungles and uses it in a nightclub routine. The animal breaks away and terrorizes the city. Just standard monkey business, with good special effects; Moore is in the Fay Wray role. Also with Robert Armstrong and Frank McHugh. **Director**—Ernest B. Schoedsack.
94 minutes b&w

MIKEY AND NICKY (1976)
★

Peter Falk
John Cassavetes

A painful and tedious melodrama by writer-director Elaine May, who took years to make it and shot three times as much footage as *Gone With the Wind*. It's a moody and jangling tale, about a love-hate relationship between two small-time hoods during a night of terror when a contract is out on one of them. Falk and Cassavetes give spellbinding performances as the hoods, but it's not enough to save this first dramatic attempt by May, who is superb with comedy. Also with Ned Beatty, Rose Arrick, and Joyce Van Patten. (R)   *119 minutes*

MILDRED PIERCE (1945)
★★★

Joan Crawford

First-class, glossy soap opera starring Crawford busily succeeding and suffering as a restaurateur, harassed mother, and lover. The mother-daughter relationship stands out, with Ann Blyth in top form as Crawford's unthankful offspring. There's also lots of romantic entanglement. Competent supporting roles by Jack Carson, Zachary Scott, Eve Arden, and Bruce Bennett. **Director**—Michael Curtiz. **Academy Award**—Crawford, best actress. **Nominations**—best picture; Arden, Blyth, best supporting actress; Ronald MacDougall, writing (screenplay); Ernest Haller, cinematography (black and white).   *113 minutes b&w*

THE MIRACLE OF MORGAN'S CREEK (1944)
★★★★

Betty Hutton
Eddie Bracken

A tip-top comic extravaganza by director Preston Sturges, about the misadventures of a girl made pregnant by a soldier at a party. But which soldier? This subject would have no problem today, but Hollywood faced persnickity censors in the '40s, and Sturges's treatment saved the film. It's an effective and fantastic assault on the funnybone dressed up smartly with good performances. Hutton is excellent as the hapless mother-to-be. William Demarest, Diana Lynn, and Brian Donlevy also star. **Academy Award Nomination**—Sturges, writing (original screenplay).   *99 minutes b&w*

THE MIRACLE ON 34TH STREET (1947)
★★★★

Edmund Gwenn
Maureen O'Hara
John Payne

An amazingly cheerful, heartwarming, and uplifting fable, about an elderly gentleman, hired as a department store Santa Claus, who claims to be the real St. Nick. It's a clever and charming blend of humor and pathos with a holiday message for young and old. This film seems as endurable as Christmas itself. Gwenn is delightful as "Kris Kringle." O'Hara, Payne, Natalie Wood, and Gene Lockhart are in fine supporting roles. **Director**—George Seaton. **Academy Awards**—Gwenn, best supporting actor; Valentine Davies, writing (original story); George Seaton, writing (screenplay). **Nomination**—best picture.   *94 minutes b&w*

THE MIRACLE WORKER (1962)
★★★★

Anne Bancroft
Patty Duke

An absorbing account of the early life of Helen Keller and her amazing strug-

John Payne, Maureen O'Hara, Natalie Wood, and Edmund Gwenn in The Miracle on 34th Street.

- Mirage
- The Mirror Crack'd
- The Misfits
- Miss Grant Takes Richmond
- The Missouri Breaks
- Mr. Billion

M

gle to overcome the multiple handicaps of being blind, deaf, and mute. The story is as much about her determined teacher, and the role is played brilliantly by Bancroft. Duke is excellent, too, as the young Keller who finally learns to communicate. A few scenes are exceptionally moving. Also with Victor Jory, Inga Swenson, Andrew Prine, and Beah Richards. **Director**—Arthur Penn. **Academy Awards**—Bancroft, best actress; Duke, best supporting actress. **Nominations**—Penn, best director; William Gibson, best screenplay (based on material from another medium).

107 minutes b&w

MIRAGE (1965)
★★★

Gregory Peck
Diane Baker
Walter Matthau

Expertly conceived thriller, presented much in the Hitchcock style, about a man with amnesia who becomes tangled in a murder mystery. Peck plays the amnesiac, Baker is a mysterious girl, and Matthau is a rumpled private detective. The suspense is effectively paced and developed, and the film is enhanced with striking photography of New York City locations. Peck does a fine acting job in the key role, and there's an interesting performance from Matthau. Also with Walter Abel, Kevin McCarthy, Jack Weston, Leif Erickson, and George Kennedy. **Director**—Edward Dmytryk.

109 minutes b&w

THE MIRROR CRACK'D (1980)
★★★

Angela Lansbury
Edward Fox

Stylish, tart Agatha Christie whodunit with an all-star cast, about murders on the set of an American movie being made in England. Elizabeth Taylor and Kim Novak, in their best roles in years, are delightful as rival fading movie stars. Lansbury is a convincing Miss Jane Marple who figures out who poisoned the drink at the cocktail party. Also with Rock Hudson, Tony Curtis, and Geraldine Chaplin. **Director**—Guy Hamilton. (PG) *105 minutes*

Angela Lansbury and Edward Fox try to solve some murders in The Mirror Crack'd.

THE MISFITS (1961)
★★★

Clark Gable
Marilyn Monroe
Montgomery Clift

Arthur Miller's pensive story about latter-day cowboys is alternately compelling and sullen. Monroe plays a confused divorcée involved with some western adventurers concerned with rounding up wild horses in the desert. Gable and Clift play the men in her life. The script only trots along, but some of the horse-chasing moves with energy. Monroe and Gable died shortly after the film's release. Also with Eli Wallach, Thelma Ritter, and Kevin McCarthy. **Director**—John Huston. *124 minutes b&w*

MISS GRANT TAKES RICHMOND (1949)
★★

Lucille Ball
William Holden

Ball plays a birdbrained secretary who helps put the lid on a bookie operation. Typical slapstick shenanigans, enjoyable if you love Lucy. Holden is an effective co-star. Also with Janis Carter, James Gleason, and Frank McHugh. **Director**—Lloyd Bacon.

83 minutes b&w

THE MISSOURI BREAKS (1976)
★★★

Marlon Brando
Jack Nicholson

Superstars Brando and Nicholson deliver delightful and dazzling performances in Arthur Penn's 1880 period western set in the majestic Montana hills. Brando plays an eccentric and sadistic hired gun commissioned by a wealthy cattle baron to wipe out a gang of horse thieves headed by Nicholson. But without these two magnificent talents, the film would be just another average horse opera. Screenwriter Thomas McGuane merely set the clock back on the plot that served his earlier film, *Rancho Deluxe*, and jazzed it up some with late 20th-century philosophizing. Newcomer Kathleen Lloyd demonstrates extraordinary potential in the role of the cattleman's liberated daughter, who falls in love with the likable Nicholson. Also with Randy Quaid and Frederic Forrest. **Director**—Arthur Penn. (PG) *126 minutes*

MR. BILLION (1977)
★

Terence Hill

In Mr. Billion, *Terence Hill is Guido, a mechanic who inherits a billion dollars.*

The threadbare plot of this inane comedy-adventure has been used in scores of films. It's about a poor Italian

(Continued)

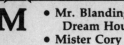

M
● Mr. Blandings Builds His
   Dream House
● Mister Cory

● Mr. Klein
● Mr. Lucky
● Mr. Mike's Mondo Video

(Continued)

mechanic who must reach San Francisco within 20 days to claim a $1-billion inheritance. En route, he's waylaid by numerous hustlers, and the outcome is predictable. Humor and suspense are sorely lacking, and the direction is sloppy. Hill, a popular European actor, has the lead. But here in his American film debut, he projects no talent or charisma. *Mr. Billion* isn't worth a dime. Also with Valerie Perrine, Jackie Gleason, Slim Pickens, and Chill Wills. **Director**—Jonathan Kaplan. (PG)   *93 minutes*

MR. BLANDINGS BUILDS HIS DREAM HOUSE (1948)
★★★★

**Cary Grant
Myrna Loy
Melvyn Douglas**

A rib-tickling middlebrow comedy about a New York advertising executive who decides to build a house in the suburbs and discovers the project is no piece of cake. There are loads of clever and funny moments in this slick production with the stars at their hilarious best. Grant is perfectly cast as the exasperated homeowner. Also with Reginald Denny, Louis Beavers, and Jason Robards. **Director**—H. C. Potter.   *84 minutes b&w*

MISTER CORY (1957)
★★★

**Tony Curtis
Martha Hyer**

Engaging, fast-paced account of a young man from a poor background who's taken in by high-society people and becomes wealthy. The smooth, no-frills script maintains consistent interest. Curtis is much at ease in the title role, which seems tailor-made for his style. Also with Charles Bickford and Kathryn Grant. **Director**—Blake Edwards.   *92 minutes*

MR. KLEIN (1977)
★★★

**Alain Delon
Jeanne Moreau**

Director Joseph Losey's stylish and bold thriller concerns a case of

JACK NICHOLSON

Jack Nicholson appeared in some 15 movies before his performance in Dennis Hopper's Easy Rider *(1969) and Bob Rafelson's* Five Easy Pieces *(1970) established him as an international film star.*

Nicholson was born in Neptune, New Jersey, in 1937. He first came to Hollywood in 1958, and was at MGM from 1959 to 1968, where he became part of a group of talented and ambitious iconoclasts who were trying to expand commercial cinema. During that time, Nicholson appeared in Monte Hellman's The Shooting *(1965) and* Ride the Whirlwind *(1965), which Nicholson co-scripted, as well as* Hell's Angels on Wheels *(1967) and* Psych-Out *(1968).*

In 1969, Nicholson replaced Rip Torn as the dipsomaniacal southern lawyer in Easy Rider, *and received an Academy Award nomination for his performance. He was also nominated for his work in* Five Easy Pieces, *and then appeared in Vincente Minnelli's* On a Clear Day You Can See Forever *(1970). He directed* Drive, He Said *(1970), appeared in Mike Nichol's* Carnal Knowledge *(1971) and Henry Jaglom's* A Safe Place *(1971), and then starred in Rafelson's* The King of Marvin Gardens *(1972). Nicholson also starred in Hal Ashby's* The Last Detail *(1974), for which he received another Oscar nomination.*

Nicholson's other films include Chinatown *(1974), for which he was again nominated for an Oscar, and* One Flew Over the Cuckoo's Nest *(1976), for which he won the Academy Award as best actor. He appeared in Michelangelo Antonioni's* The Passenger *(1974); Ken Russell's* Tommy *(1975); Elia Kazan's* The Last Tycoon *(1976); Goin' South *(1978), which he directed; Stanley Kubrick's* The Shining *(1980); and most recently in Rafelson's remake of* The Postman Always Rings Twice *(1981) and as Eugene O'Neill in* Reds *(1981).*

switched identities in Nazi-occupied Paris in 1942. The well-appointed film has Hitchcock-like tension and a conscience-stirring message about racism. Delon turns in a splendid performance in the role of a smug and foppish art dealer who profits from fleeing Jews by paying low prices for their personal treasures. Impact, however, is reduced somewhat by an elusive and complex plot. Also with Suzanne Flon. In French with English titles. (No MPAA rating)   *122 minutes*

MR. LUCKY (1943)
★★★

**Cary Grant
Laraine Day**

Grant is effectively charming and amusing as a gambling-ship owner who concocts a dubious scheme to raise cash. But love intervenes, and he goes straight. A smooth blend of comedy and drama, handled skillfully by a professional cast, which also includes Charles Bickford, Gladys Cooper, and Alan Carney. **Director**—H. C. Potter.   *98 minutes b&w*

MR. MIKE'S MONDO VIDEO (1979)
(no stars)

Director-producer Michael O'Donoghue apparently slapped this mess together for NBC, and then it was rejected as being inappropriate for television. The film seems to be a parody of the various *Mondo* movies of many years ago. Most of the gags flop, and many of the sketches are in bad taste or are merely absurd. For example, there's a piece about a swimming school for cats, and there's a clip of the late Sid Vicious wailing "My Way." (R)   *60 minutes*

● Mr. Peabody and the Mermaid ● Mr. Quilp ● Mister Roberts ● Mr. Smith Goes to Washington ● Mrs. Miniver ● Ms. 45 ● Mitchell ● Moby Dick

M

MR. PEABODY AND THE MERMAID (1948)
★★

William Powell
Ann Blyth

Mildly amusing whimsy about a middle-aged man who discovers a beautiful mermaid and takes a fresh look at his life. A few scenes work, but just as many are silly in this fantasy. Powell is suited for the title role. Also with Irene Hervey, Andrea King, and Clinton Sundberg. **Director**—Irving Pichel.
89 minutes b&w

MR. QUILP (1975)
★★

Anthony Newley

Charles Dickens's sentimental story *The Old Curiosity Shop* has been transformed into a sugary musical starring Newley, who also wrote the music and lyrics. There's no profound style at all to the movie, which resembles a recycled *Oliver*. Much of the book's dramatic excitement is lacking. Newley performs with energy, but most of Dickens's caricatures come across without distinction. Also with David Warner, Michael Hordern, David Hemmings, and Sarah-Jane Varley. Bland direction by Michael Tuchner. (G)
118 minutes

MISTER ROBERTS (1955)
★★★★

Henry Fonda
James Cagney
William Powell
Jack Lemmon

Boredom and pettiness are the targets of this winning comedy set aboard a supply ship in the Pacific during World War II. Fonda is great in the title role as a restless but likable Navy officer just itching to be transferred to a fighting ship. And there's rampant scene-stealing by Lemmon as a bumbling Ensign Pulver and Cagney as the neurotic skipper of the cargo vessel. Powell is the ship's doctor. A superb blend of hilarity and sentiment, based on the Broadway play by Joshua Logan and author Thomas Heggen.

Jack Lemmon, James Cagney, Henry Fonda, and William Powell in Mr. Roberts.

Also with Ward Bond, Betsy Palmer, and Phil Carey. **Directors**—John Ford and Mervyn Le Roy. **Academy Award**—Lemmon, best supporting actor. **Nomination**—best picture.
123 minutes

MR. SMITH GOES TO WASHINGTON (1939)
★★★★

James Stewart
Claude Rains
Jean Arthur

This is among the best of director Frank Capra's comedy-dramas. Stewart gives a stirring performance as a forthright freshman senator who encounters corruption in the nation's capital. It's a rather inspiring portrait of how elected officials ought to behave. The production is first-class in every department, and there are other brilliant performances from Rains, Arthur, Harry Carey, Thomas Mitchell, Edward Arnold, Guy Kibbee, and Beulah Bondi. **Academy Award**—Lewis R. Foster, writing (original story). **Nominations**—best picture; Capra, best director; Stewart, best actor; Carey, Rains, best supporting actor; Sidney Buchman, writing (screenplay). *130 minutes b&w*

MRS. MINIVER (1942)
★★★★

Greer Garson
Walter Pidgeon

A highly moving account of courageous British villagers struggling to cope with the hardships and dangers of World War II. The film is rather melodramatic, but it's extremely well made, and it served as an effective wartime morale booster. Fine performances throughout. Also with Teresa Wright, Henry Travers, Richard Ney, and Dame May Whitty. **Director**—William Wyler. **Academy Awards**—best picture; Wyler, best director; Garson, best actress; Wright, best supporting actress; George Froeschel, James Hilton, Claudine West, and Arthur Wimperis, writing (screenplay); Joseph Ruttenberg, cinematography (black and white). **Nominations**—Pidgeon, best actor; Travers, best supporting actor; Whitty, best supporting actress. *134 minutes b&w*

MS. 45 (1981)
(no stars)

Zoe Tamerlis

Gory, absurd movie, about an attractive young mute girl who embarks on a revengeful killing spree after being raped twice in one day. In one particular grisly sequence, she kills the second rapist, cuts the body into small pieces, and stows the parts in her refrigerator. Despite such horrendous scenes, Tamerlis displays impressive talent in the title role, and Abel Ferrara directs with noticeable style and pacing. Perhaps next time they'll find decent outlets for their skills. (R)
90 minutes

MITCHELL (1975)
★

Joe Don Baker

The film is about an honest Los Angeles detective on the trail of a big-time narcotics operation. There's plenty of violence and chasing around in automobiles within a dreary script, which lacks character development. Baker, who did well in *Walking Tall*, is miscast in the title role. Also with Martin Balsam, John Saxon, Linda Evans, and Merlin Olsen. **Director**—Andrew V. McLaglen. (R) *96 minutes*

MOBY DICK (1956)
★★★

Gregory Peck
Richard Basehart

Herman Melville's classic tale of a ship captain fiercely struggling to land a
(Continued)

M
- Modern Problems
- Modern Romance
- Mogambo
- Mohammad, Messenger of God
- The Molly Maguires
- Moment By Moment
- Mommie Dearest

(Continued)

great white whale is impressively produced for the screen, but the pace is somewhat patchy. Peck is ill at ease as Captain Ahab, the obsessed skipper, but there are some good moments here and there nevertheless. Basehart, Friedrich Ledebur, Leo Genn, Harry Andrews, and Orson Welles appear in supporting roles. **Director**—John Huston. *116 minutes*

MODERN PROBLEMS (1981)
★

Chevy Chase

A creaky clunker of a comedy with Chase playing a young blade who accidentally acquires telekinetic powers, which he uses to win back his former girl friend. The production is beset with problems—stale jokes, sloppy direction, shabby performances, and an unbearable script. Chevy mopes about with an amazing lack of energy and comic skill; the film is an unmitigated fiasco. Also stars Patti D'Arbanville, Mary Kay Place, Nell Carter, and Dabney Coleman. **Director**—Ken Shapiro. (PG) *92 minutes*

MODERN ROMANCE (1981)
★

Albert Brooks
Kathryn Harrold

In Modern Romance, *Kathryn Harrold and Albert Brooks talk about their relationship.*

Brooks, co-writer, director, and star, displays his limited talent in this tedious, low-key comedy about an on-again, off-again love affair. The lackadaisical script doesn't develop into anything significant. As a slice of life, it's cut rather thin. Brooks, who seems infatuated with his own performance, is on screen most of the time, engaged in slightly comic and irritating monologues. Beautiful Harrold plays the object of his confused affections. Also with Bruno Kirby. (R) *93 minutes*

MOGAMBO (1953)
★★★

Clark Gable
Ava Gardner
Grace Kelly

Romantic, adventuresome, darkest-Africa/white-hunter saga with plenty of colorful performances. Gable is tops as the pursuer of big game who becomes involved with two alluring women—Gardner and Kelly. A gorilla hunt highlights the jungle action. The film is a remake of *Red Dust*, with Gable repeating his role. Also with Donald Sinden, Laurence Naismith, and Philip Stainton. **Director**—John Ford. **Academy Award Nominations**—Gardner, best actress; Kelly, best supporting actress. *116 minutes*

MOHAMMAD, MESSENGER OF GOD (1977)
★

Anthony Quinn
Irene Papas

This well-intentioned attempt to detail the last 20 years of the Moslem prophet's life is uninspiring, mechanical, and innocuous. The sprawling epic, produced and directed by Moustapha Akkad, who appears to have studied at the Cecil B. DeMille school of religion, drones on for three hours. Yet it takes only 15 minutes to get the message. Quinn, in the key role, portrays Mohammad's uncle, who fights for the right of the prophet to practice his religion. Mohammad never appears on screen, in accordance with Islam. Also with Michael Ansara, Johnny Sekka, and Michael Forest. (PG) *180 minutes*

THE MOLLY MAGUIRES (1970)
★★

Richard Harris
Sean Connery

Partly engrossing account of a secret society of Pennsylvania coal miners in the 1870s using extreme measures to improve working conditions. A private detective infiltrates the group and reports on their violent activities. The serious, well-made film is based on true events. However, the story ends with a sense of vagueness. Connery is convincing as a leader of the society, and Harris performs well as the undercover Pinkerton man. Also stars Samantha Eggar, Frank Finlay, Anthony Zerbe, and Art Lund. **Director**—Martin Ritt. (PG) *123 minutes*

MOMENT BY MOMENT (1978)
★

Lily Tomlin
John Travolta

Lily Tomlin and John Travolta have an affair in Moment By Moment.

Tedious claptrap about a well-heeled middle-aged woman who has an affair with a young drifter. Tomlin and Travolta are the odd couple. Here we have two of Hollywood's brightest stars, but they don't click together. The main trouble seems to be with the humdrum script by writer-director Jane Wagner, who has worked with Tomlin for some time. With all the dumb dialogue, drippy clichés, and contrived situations, the film seems to drag on hour by hour. Also with Andra Akers and Bert Kramer. (R) *102 minutes*

MOMMIE DEAREST (1981)
★★★★

Faye Dunaway
Diana Scarwid

Dunaway plays screen idol Joan Crawford with extraordinary passion and

- Monkey Business
- The Monkey Hustle
- Mon Oncle D'Amerique
- Montenegro
- Monty Python and the Holy Grail
- The Moon Is Blue
- Moon Over Miami

M

Faye Dunaway stars as movie queen Joan Crawford in Mommie Dearest.

blazing energy in this film biography based on the book by Crawford's adopted daughter, Christina. The characterization is amazingly lifelike, with Dunaway committing body and soul to portray the hard-driving, ambitious, insecure, and occasionally raving-mad movie queen. Mara Hobel plays Christina as a child, and Scarwid plays her as an adult. Direction, editing, dialogue, and supporting parts are at top form in this good-looking period production. But it's Dunaway's all-out, showstopping performance that clinches this fantastic movie. Also with Steve Forrest and Henry da Silva. **Director**—Frank Perry. (PG)

129 minutes

MONKEY BUSINESS (1952)
★★★

Cary Grant
Ginger Rogers

A lot of good talent got together for this madcap comedy about a scientist who discovers an amazing elixir that restores youth. Grant plays the researcher, and Rogers plays his wife. A certain amount of corn is involved, but there's plenty to laugh about, with Cary performing at top speed. Charles Coburn plays Grant's boss, and Marilyn Monroe is a secretary. **Director**—Howard Hawks. *97 minutes b&w*

THE MONKEY HUSTLE (1977)
★

Yaphet Kotto
Rosalind Cash

This tasteless and wobbly movie is about individual moments among petty thieves and hustlers in a Chicago ghetto. It's loaded with confusing street talk, unnecessary brutality, and moral confusion. It's also shy on action. And it's the audience that will be hustled by this blatantly bad film.

Also with Rudy Moore and Kirk Calloway. **Director**—Arthur Marks. (PG) *90 minutes*

MON ONCLE D'AMERIQUE (1981)
★★

Gerard Depardieu
Nicole Garcia

Alain Resnais's dull comedy is a complex examination of human behavior. The film follows the lives of three ambitious but mixed-up characters. Resnais treats his subject with coyness, charm, and intelligence; but the various case histories aren't clearly connected, and this situation becomes an annoying distraction. Also with Roger-Pierre. In French with English titles. (No MPAA rating) **Academy Award Nomination**—Jean Gruault, best screenplay (written directly for the screen). *125 minutes*

MONTENEGRO (1981)
★★

Susan Anspach

Yugoslav director Dusan Makavejev presents a loosely constructed comedy that can be recognized for its intelligence, but fails to come across as worthwhile entertainment. The film, set in Sweden, centers on Anspach, the restless and rather loony American wife of a wealthy Swedish industrialist. She's kidnapped, almost willingly, by some freewheeling immigrants and held at a sleazy nightclub where she experiences a spiritual awakening. Makavejev makes an interesting social statement, but it's conveyed in a hodgepodge manner. Also stars Erland Josephson and Per Oscarsson. (No MPAA rating) *95 minutes*

MONTY PYTHON AND THE HOLY GRAIL (1975)
★★★★

Graham Chapman
John Cleese
Terry Gilliam
Eric Idle
Michael Palin

A cheerful, comic reworking of the legend of King Arthur and the search

Graham Chapman leads the comic quest in Monty Python and the Holy Grail.

for the Holy Grail. The quest leaves Camelot in a shambles of laughter. It's written and acted by the brilliant Monty Python troupe, who were first made famous on British TV. Plenty of laughs, chuckles, sight gags, sick jokes, and wit in this loony satire. **Directors**—Terry Gilliam and Terry Jones. (PG) *90 minutes*

THE MOON IS BLUE (1953)
★★

Maggie McNamara
David Niven
William Holden

This sex comedy raised eyebrows at the time of release because of the use of such then-shocking words as "virgin" and "mistress." Now the film is rather mild stuff, indeed, with most of the gags straining to evoke a smile or two. The story involves the escapades of an attractive lass, played by McNamara, who stirs the passions of several gentlemen. Also with Tom Tully and Dawn Adams. **Director**—Otto Preminger. **Academy Award Nomination**—McNamara, best actress. *96 minutes b&w*

MOON OVER MIAMI (1941)
★★★

Don Ameche
Betty Grable
Carole Landis

A pleasant musical, graced by a likable cast and based on the familiar theme of gorgeous girls on the prowl for rich husbands. Grable, Landis, and Charlotte Greenwood are the fortune-hunters who find romance and more in this colorful film. Musical numbers

(Continued)

M • Moonraker
• More American Graffiti
• The More the Merrier
• Moses
• Motel Hell
• Mother, Jugs & Speed

(Continued)
include the title song and "You Started Something." Also with Jack Haley and Robert Cummings. **Director**—Walter Lang. *92 minutes*

MOONRAKER (1979)
★★★★

Roger Moore
Lois Chiles
Richard Kiel

Roger Moore as 007 examines vials of deadly nerve gas in Moonraker.

Ageless, tireless James Bond saves the world from a cunning aerospace tycoon in this fantastic superspy thriller. It's the 11th film feature for Agent 007, played here by Moore, and the formula still works wonders. It's an irresistible entertainment feast, complete with spectacular sets, breathtaking stunts, oodles of secret-agent gadgets, and gorgeous women. Chiles is stunning as Bond's romantic interest, and Kiel reappears as the towering steel-toothed "Jaws." Also with Michael Lonsdale, Corinne Clery, Bernard Lee, and Lois Maxwell. **Director**—Lewis Gilbert. (PG) *126 minutes*

MORE AMERICAN GRAFFITI (1979)
★★

Candy Clark
Bo Hopkins
Ron Howard
Cindy Williams
Paul Le Mat

This clumsy sequel to the popular 1973 hit follows the lives of the characters

Ron Howard, Cindy Williams, Candy Clark, and Charles Smith in More American Graffiti.

through the turmoil of the mid '60s. The story is jumbled into four disjointed vignettes that range from the battlefields of Vietnam to the antiwar movement at home. Most of the original cast is back, and they're certainly appealing. But writer-director B.W.L. Norton overreaches, and he hasn't maintained the innocence and warmth that marked the original George Lucas version. Also with Charles Smith and Mackenzie Phillips. (PG) *111 minutes*

THE MORE THE MERRIER (1943)
★★★★

Jean Arthur
Joel McCrae
Charles Coburn

There's no shortage of effective comic situations in this funny tale of a girl who shares a small apartment with two men in Washington during a housing shortage during World War II. Arthur, McCrea, and Coburn keep the laughter and romance sailing along, with plenty of sparkling dialogue and excellent acting. It's thoroughly charming and exceptionally bright. Also with Richard Gaines and Bruce Bennett. **Director**—George Ste-

Rory Calhoun and Nancy Parson run the Motel Hello *in* Motel Hell.

vens. **Academy Award**—Coburn, best supporting actor. **Nominations**—best picture; Stevens, best director; Arthur, best actress; Frank Ross and Robert Russell, writing (original story); Richard Flournoy, Lewis R. Foster, Frank Ross, and Robert Russell, writing (screenplay). *104 minutes b&w*

MOSES (1976)
★

Burt Lancaster
Anthony Quayle
Ingrid Thulin

An overlong, noisy, talky, and boring biblical picture, first made as a six-hour TV feature. Lancaster stars as Moses, and his performance is disappointing and dispirited along with the entire production; Quayle plays Aaron. Even the parting of the Red Sea, through special effects, doesn't work. Gianfranco de Bosio takes the blame as director. Watching this film may make you appreciate Cecil B. DeMille. Also with Irene Papas. (PG) *141 minutes*

MOTEL HELL (1980)
(no stars)

Rory Calhoun

Kindly farmer Vincent, played by Calhoun, is also a motel keeper who runs a smoked-meat business on the side. His secret ingredient is human flesh blended in with the pork. A few laughs and a dash of suspense are mixed with the blood and gore, but there's not an iota of logic in this absurd horror film that aims for cult status. "Don't worry. I have a cast-iron stomach," chirps Nina Axelrod, as she innocently tours Vincent's meat preparation building. That's a warning for the audience, too! Also with Nancy Parsons. **Director**—Kevin Connor. (R) *106 minutes*

MOTHER, JUGS & SPEED (1976)
★★★

Bill Cosby
Raquel Welch
Harvey Keitel

Cosby, Welch, and Keitel star in a fast-

● Mother Kusters Goes to Heaven
● Mother's Day

● Mother Wore Tights
● Moulin Rouge
● Mountain Family Robinson
● The Mountain Men

M

paced black comedy about Los Angeles ambulance drivers. It's *M*A*S*H* in civilian clothes. There are some outrageous moments, but it does entertain with a contrasty blend of farce and serious drama. Welch, in a strong role as a fetching switchboard operator, complements her physical attractiveness with a competent performance. Cosby, Keitel, and the rest of the cast give their best. Director Peter *(Bullitt)* Yates lays on the freewheeling spirit. Also with Allen Garfield and Larry Hagman. (PG)

95 minutes

MOTHER KUSTERS GOES TO HEAVEN (1977)
★★★

Birgitta Mira

Rainer Werner Fassbinder, the prolific German filmmaker, comes a step closer to commercial success with this unique and provocative political comedy. Mira plays a naïve middle-aged woman who is thoroughly exploited by the press and political factions after her factory-worker husband murders one of his bosses and then commits suicide. Fassbinder's characters are endearingly human and fascinating. His film is cynical yet heartwarming. Also with Ingrid Caven and Armin Meier. In German with English titles. (No MPAA rating) *105 minutes*

MOTHER'S DAY (1980)
(no stars)

**Nancy Hendrickson
Deborah Luce
Tiana Pierce**

Director Charles Kaufman goes all out to exploit violence and terror in this bloodsoaked monstrosity. Three young women—Hendrickson, Luce, and Pierce—are abducted by two moronic brothers who relentlessly inflict torture as their sadistic mother cheers them on. You can witness such brutal scenes as a head being chopped off with a machete and an ax being hurled into someone's crotch, but there's nothing particularly suspenseful or chilling about all this gore. It's merely sickening. (R) *93 minutes*

MOTHER WORE TIGHTS (1947)
★★★

**Betty Grable
Dan Dailey**

Excellent showcase for the talents of Grable and Dailey as a vaudeville couple involved with their colorful career and raising a family. The production is colorful, and the film moves along smartly with charming song-and-dance numbers. Based on the book by Miriam Young. Also with Mona Freeman, Connie Marshall, Vanessa Brown, and Veda Ann Borg. **Director**—Walter Lang. **Academy Award Nomination**—Harry Jackson, cinematography (color). *107 minutes*

MOULIN ROUGE (1952)
★★★★

**José Ferrer
Zsa Zsa Gabor**

Brilliant film biography of French painter Henri Toulouse-Lautrec, who suffered from a tragic deformity. The dramatic and colorful account details the famous artist's sad outlook on the world and its despairing effect on his love affairs. Director John Huston presents a striking view of 19th-century Montmartre and its many flavorful characters. A magnificent can-can sequence is a real showstopper. Also with Suzanne Fion, Katherine Kath, Colette Marchand,

Eric Pohlman, and Christopher Lee. **Academy Award Nominations**—best picture; Huston, best director; Ferrer, best actor; Marchand, best supporting actress. *119 minutes*

MOUNTAIN FAMILY ROBINSON (1981)
★★

**Robert Logan
Heather Rattray
Ham Larsen**

This is the third film about the sentimental adventures of the rosy-cheeked family of four who escape traffic-snarled Los Angeles to reside in a mountain log cabin. But even in this wilderness paradise, they can't avoid government bureaucracy. A cranky forest ranger tries to evict them because they're on a government-controlled mining-claim area. Once again, the forest animals and the spectacular scenery upstage the human cast. **Director**—John Cotter. (G) *100 minutes*

THE MOUNTAIN MEN (1980)
★★

**Charlton Heston
Brian Keith**

Heston and Keith are grizzled Davy Crockett types who trap beavers and fight Indians in this routine outdoor
(Continued)

Colette Marchand and José Ferrer in Moulin Rouge, *a biography of Henri Toulouse-Lautrec.*

M

- Mourning Becomes Electra
- The Mouse That Roared
- Move Over, Darling
- Movie, Movie
- The Muppet Movie
- Murder By Death

(Continued)

adventure. Heston falls in love with a beautiful Indian girl, played by Victoria Racimo. She's also claimed by an Indian chief, and this conflict leads to some spectacular hand-to-hand combat. The film offers picturesque Wyoming settings and some snappy action scenes. But it's still familiar fare. **Director**—Richard Lang. (R) *102 minutes*

MOURNING BECOMES ELECTRA (1947)
★★

**Michael Redgrave
Rosalind Russell**

A good cast is bogged down in this heavy drama about tragedy striking a New England family during the Civil War. A wife murders her husband, and the children plot revenge. This film is based on the play by Eugene O'Neill. Also with Kirk Douglas, Katina Paxinou, and Raymond Massey. **Director**—Dudley Nichols. **Academy Award Nominations**—Redgrave, best actor; Russell, best actress.
170 minutes b&w

THE MOUSE THAT ROARED (1959)
★★★

**Peter Sellers
Jean Seberg**

A snappy topical satire about the Duchy of Grand Fenwick, a small bankrupt country that seeks to solve its financial problems by declaring war on the United States with the intention of losing the conflict and then receiving aid through the Marshall Plan. Sellers has a grand time playing three roles, including that of the Grand Duchess. There are many delightful moments that hit home. Also with David Kossoff, William Hartnell, Leo McKern, and Monty Landis. **Director**—Jack Arnold. *85 minutes*

MOVE OVER, DARLING (1963)
★★★

**Doris Day
James Garner
Polly Bergen**

Day, Garner, and Bergen have a fine time with this patchy remake of *My Favorite Wife*, although the original with Cary Grant and Irene Dunne was much better. A wife, presumed dead in a plane crash, returns home after five years and finds her husband on the threshold of remarrying. Some hilarious moments still work here, thanks to good jobs by the top cast. Also with Thelma Ritter, Chuck Conners, and Fred Clark. **Director**—Michael Gordon. *103 minutes*

MOVIE, MOVIE (1978)
★★★

**George C. Scott
Trish Van Devere
Eli Wallach
Red Buttons
Barbara Harris
Art Carney**

George C. Scott and Trish Van Devere in the clever parody Movie, Movie.

An affectionate, funny, and clever parody of '30s movies. The program, of course, is a double feature: first an up-from-the-slums boxing drama and then a corny backstage musical. Scott, Buttons, and Wallach have a great time twisting all those old movie clichés. Newcomers Harry Hamlin, Barry Bostwick, and Ann Reinking exude extraordinary youthful zeal. The film occasionally falls flat, but all in all it's a pleasant trip down Hollywood's memory lane. **Director**—Stanley Douen. (PG)
107 minutes color/b&w

THE MUPPET MOVIE (1979)
★★★

The Muppets

Jim Henson's lovable puppet characters star with style in their first feature film—an updated version of *The Wizard of Oz*. It's a bright, cheerful

Kermit the Frog strums his way to Hollywood in The Muppet Movie.

dandy of a musical comedy that will please children and adults. Kermit the Frog, who plans to become a star, sets off for Tinsel Town with Miss Piggy, the Great Gonzo, and other Muppeteers. Along the way they briefly encounter Mel Brooks, Steve Martin, Bob Hope, and other Hollywood notables. **Director**—James Frawley. (G)
94 minutes

MURDER BY DEATH (1976)
★★

**Peter Falk
Alec Guinness
Peter Sellers
Truman Capote
David Niven**

An all-star cast and stylish acting shore up Neil Simon's lightweight comedy spoof of detective fiction. Falk, Niven, Sellers, James Coco, and Elsa Lanchester play five famous fictional detectives invited to a spooky old mansion for dinner and a murder to be committed. The performances are superb, but the script makes little sense, and there aren't enough amusing lines to keep it moving briskly. Capote debuts as the host of honor—an eccentric amateur criminologist who believes he can outsmart the world's greatest sleuths. He's better off with his typewriter and the late-

Peter Sellers and Peter Falk are among the famous sleuths in Murder By Death.

- Murder By Decree
- Murderer's Row
- Murder, My Sweet
- Murder on the Orient Express
- Murders in the Rue Morgue
- The Music Man
- Mutiny on the Bounty (1935)

M

night talk shows. Also with Maggie Smith, Eileen Brennan, and Nancy Walker. **Director**—Robert Moore. (PG) *94 minutes*

MURDER BY DECREE (1979)
★★

**Christopher Plummer
James Mason**

In Murder By Decree, *Christopher Plummer and James Mason play Holmes and Watson.*

Plummer plays the intrepid Sherlock Holmes, and Mason is a delightful Dr. Watson. They attempt to solve the savage Jack the Ripper murders. The production design of 19th-century London is handsomely staged, with swirling fog, flickering gaslights, and rumbling carriages; but the plot is hardly elementary, my dear fellow—it's too complicated and unsuspenseful. This is the 134th movie to feature the famous English gumshoe; Holmes made his screen debut in a 1903 one-reeler. Also with Donald Sutherland, Geneviève Bujold, David Hemmings, John Gielgud, and Susan Clark. **Director**—Bob Clark. (PG) *121 minutes*

MURDERER'S ROW (1966)
★★

**Dean Martin
Ann-Margret**

Flimsy continuation of novelist Donald Hamilton's Matt Helm character, with Martin again playing the superspy role as a spoof. This time, Helm is after a sinister international operator, played by Karl Malden, who has kidnapped a scientist. Ann-

Margret is the scientist's daughter. Martin handles his part rather badly, and the sluggish material has little to offer. Set against the background of the Riviera. Also with Camilla Sparv, James Gregory, and Beverly Adams. **Director**—Henry Levin. *108 minutes*

MURDER, MY SWEET
See Farewell, My Lovely (1944)

MURDER ON THE ORIENT EXPRESS (1974)
★★★

**Albert Finney
Ingrid Bergman
Lauren Bacall
Wendy Hiller
Sean Connery
Vanessa Redgrave**

Lavish treatment of Agatha Christie's suspenseful whodunit, set in the 1930s aboard a train bound for Calais from Istanbul. On board is Belgian sleuth Hercule Poirot, played by Finney, who solves the murder of a passenger done in when the train hits a snowdrift. Many colorful characters are on board as suspects. There are many plodding moments along with the thrills, but mystery fans should have a good time all the same. Also among the all-star cast are Martin Balsam, Richard Widmark, Jacqueline Bisset, Rachel Roberts, John Gielgud, and Anthony Perkins. **Director**—Sidney Lumet. (PG) **Academy Award**—Bergman, best supporting actress. **Nominations**—Finney, best actor; Paul Dehn, best screenplay (adapted from other material); Geoffrey Unsworth, cinematography. *131 minutes*

MURDERS IN THE RUE MORGUE (1971)
★★

**Jason Robards, Jr.
Herbert Lom
Christine Kaufman**

So-so film version of Edgar Allen Poe's classic chiller, set in a Paris theater. The actors in a murder mystery become the real-life victims, and the police investigate. Lots of gory details. Also with Lilli Palmer, Adolfo Celi, and Michael Dunn. **Director**—Gordon Hessler. (PG) *86 minutes*

THE MUSIC MAN (1962)
★★★★

**Robert Preston
Shirley Jones**

A buoyant, thoroughly enjoyable romantic musical based on Meredith Wilson's hit Broadway production. Preston is fantastic as the city-slicker salesman who cons the citizens of a small Iowa town into organizing a high school band so he can sell them musical instruments. Jones also stands out as Marian the librarian, Preston's romantic interest. The film boasts colorful turn-of-the-century period detail and a strong statement about narrow-mindedness. Many of the musical numbers are real show-stoppers; they include " 'Til There Was You" and "76 Trombones." There's outstanding support from Hermione Gingold, Paul Ford, and Buddy Hackett. **Director**—Morton Da Costa. **Academy Award Nomination**—best picture. *151 minutes*

MUTINY ON THE BOUNTY (1935)
★★★★

**Charles Laughton
Clark Gable**

A classic movie adventure, indeed, based on Nordhoff and Hall's moving account of hardships aboard an 18th-
(Continued)

Clark Gable embraces Movita in the classic adventure Mutiny on the Bounty.

M
- Mutiny on the Bounty (1962)
- My Bloody Valentine
- My Bodyguard
- My Brilliant Career
- My Darling Clementine
- My Fair Lady
- My Favorite Blonde

(Continued)

century British man-of-war. Laughton is unforgettable as the heartless Captain Bligh, whose sadistic treatment of the crew provokes mutiny. The entire production is expertly handled, and its entertainment value is indelible. Gable also excels as first mate Fletcher Christian, and there are other good acting jobs from Franchot Tone, Herbert Mundin, Eddie Quillan, Dudley Digges, and Donald Crisp. **Director**—Frank Lloyd. **Academy Award**—best picture. **Nominations**—Lloyd, best director; Gable, Laughton, Tone, best actor; Jules Furthman, Talbot Jennings, and Carey Wilson, writing (screenplay). *135 minutes b&w*

MUTINY ON THE BOUNTY (1962)
★★★

Trevor Howard
Marlon Brando

Opulent, somewhat overblown remake of the 1935 film, competently done but not as effective despite the lavish production effort. Howard plays Captain Bligh, and Brando is Fletcher Christian; they're adequate, but not as good as Charles Laughton and Clark Gable in the earlier film. Brando's British accent also throws the movie slightly off course. Also stars Richard Harris, Hugh Griffith, Tarita, Richard Haydn, Percy Herbert, and Noel Purcell. **Director**—Lewis Milestone. **Academy Award Nominations**—best picture; Robert L. Surtees, cinematography (color). *185 minutes*

MY BLOODY VALENTINE (1981)
(no stars)

Paul Kelman
Lori Hallier

Revolting, gory horror story that stoops to the lowest levels for exploitation. Village folks stage a St. Valentine's Day dance that sets off some brutal murders. The ugly killings take place in a mine (the scene of an accident 20 years ago), where the murderer cuts out the hearts of his victims. Such grisly nonsense is made even shabbier by talentless acting and slipshod direction. **Director**—George Mihalka. (R) *91 minutes*

MY BODYGUARD (1980)
★★★

Chris Makepeace
Adam Baldwin
Ruth Gordon

A sensitive comedy-drama about high school students that depicts adolescent problems with realism and sympathy. Makepeace stars as a frail rich kid who is relentlessly harassed by bullies at school. He enlists a mysterious and strong classmate to protect him, and this relationship sparks a friendship that adds warmth and intelligence to the story. Tony Bill, making his directorial debut, brings out the best in the cast of young people. (PG) *99 minutes*

MY BRILLIANT CAREER (1980)
★★★

Judy Davis
Sam Neill
Wendy Hughes

This Australian film is a remarkable and spirited movie; it tells of the struggle of an impoverished and proud farm girl to become a writer. The movie is based on a 1901 semiautobiographical novel by Miles Franklin, who wrote convincingly on women's liberation when she was 16 years old. The story lapses at times, but the film is, nevertheless, skillfully directed by Gillian Armstrong. It features an energetic performance by Davis in the lead role. Let's hope we see more of her amazing talent. (No MPAA rating) *98 minutes*

MY DARLING CLEMENTINE (1946)
★★★★

Henry Fonda
Victor Mature
Walter Brennan

Among the best of director John Ford's westerns, all about Wyatt Earp, Doc Holliday, and the rest of that crowd; their activities in Tombstone, Arizona; and the famous shoot-out at the OK corral. Scene after scene is done with expert skill, and the acting is among the best for this sort of low-key production. Fonda shines as Earp, and Mature is credible as Holliday. Also with Linda Darnell, Cathy Downs, Tim Holt, Ward Bond, Alan Mowbray, and John Ireland. *98 minutes b&w*

MY FAIR LADY (1964)
★★★★

Rex Harrison
Audrey Hepburn
Stanley Holloway

Stanley Holloway and Audrey Hepburn in the delightful musical My Fair Lady.

Exuberant and highly entertaining screen version of the Broadway smash musical, based on George Bernard Shaw's *Pygmalion*. Harrison is delightful as Professor Henry Higgins, who sets out to make a lady of Eliza Doolittle, a cockney flower-seller, played by Hepburn. He succeeds, of course, and then falls in love with her. The Lerner and Loewe music is firmly intact and provides much charm. Scenery, photography, and costumes are enchanting, and most of the acting is tops. Also with Wilfrid Hyde-White, Theodore Bikel, and Gladys Cooper. **Director**—George Cukor. **Academy Awards**—best picture; Cukor, best director; Harrison, best actor; Harry Stradling, cinematography (color). **Nominations**—Holloway, best supporting actor; Cooper, best supporting actress; Alan Jay Lerner, best screenplay (based on material from another medium). *175 minutes*

MY FAVORITE BLONDE (1942)
★★★

Bob Hope
Madeleine Carroll

Top-notch Hope comedy caper. Bob plays a second-rate vaudeville performer who reluctantly gets mixed up in a spy adventure with beautiful British agent Carroll. The film is well put together, and the result is a laugh a minute. Also in the cast are Gale Sondergaard, George Zucco, and Victor Varconi. **Director**—Sidney Lanfield.

78 minutes b&w

MY FAVORITE BRUNETTE (1947)
★★★

Bob Hope
Dorothy Lamour

Laughs galore with Hope as a photographer masquerading as a private eye to help Lamour while he's being pursued by mobsters. Peter Lorre and Lon Chaney, Jr., are in the cast for a dash of realism in this romp, which parodies *Farewell, My Lovely*. Also with John Hoyt, Charles Dingle, and Reginald Denny. **Director**—Elliott Nugent.

87 minutes b&w

MY FAVORITE WIFE (1940)
★★★★

Cary Grant
Irene Dunne

Irene Dunne is one of Cary Grant's wives in the comedy My Favorite Wife.

Grant and Dunne have this clever comedy well in hand, and the result is a barrel of laughs. Dunne is an explorer, presumed lost in a shipwreck, who returns after five years to find her husband (Grant) remarried. It's a familiar situation, but the good talent gives it an expert and effective workout. Also with Gail Patrick, Randolph Scott, and Ann Shoemaker. **Director**—Garson Kanin. **Academy Award Nomination**—Leo McCarey, Bella Spewack, and Samuel Spewack, writing (original story).

88 minutes b&w

MY FRIEND FLICKA (1943)
★★★

Roddy McDowall
Preston Foster

Engaging and sentimental story about a boy who befriends a maverick horse. An expertly crafted animal film enhanced with magnificent scenery. McDowall does well as the winsome lad. Rita Johnson, James Bell, and Jeff Corey are also in the cast. A sequel, *Green Grass of Wyoming*, was made in 1945 with most of the same cast. **Director**—Harold Schuster. *89 minutes*

JAMES STEWART

James Stewart, who was born in 1908, left his hometown of Indiana, Pennsylvania, for the first time to enroll at Mercersburg Academy to get ready for his college choice, Princeton. As a Princeton freshman, he elected to major in electrical engineering, but later switched to architecture. He might have succeeded in either one had it not been for his love of acting.

Stewart graduated from Princeton with a degree in architecture, but promptly forgot it and joined a theatrical stock company led by Joshua Logan. When one of the company's efforts made it to New York, Stewart went with it and made his professional debut in Goodbye Again. *He also appeared in a series of New York plays before he won the role of Sergeant O'Hara in* Yellow Jack, *a part which put his name up in lights on Broadway for the first time. Soon afterward, Stewart signed a film contract and made his film debut in* The Murder Man *(1935).*

Within a few years, he had a string

of movie hits—Made for Each Other *(1938);* It's a Wonderful World *(1939);* Mr. Smith Goes to Washington *(1939), his first Oscar nomination;* Destry Rides Again *(1939);* The Shop Around the Corner *(1939); and* The Mortal Storm *(1940). He then won the Academy Award as best actor for* The Philadelphia Story *(1940).*

Stewart was among the first top screen stars to enter military service in World War II. He became a private in the Army Air Force before the attack on Pearl Harbor. Nine months later, because of his previous flying experience and education, Stewart was commissioned as a lieutenant. He served in the Air Force until 1945, when he was discharged from active duty with the rank of colonel. In 1959, he was promoted to brigadier general.

After the war, Stewart appeared in a number of successful movies. They include It's a Wonderful Life *(1946), for which he was nominated for an Oscar;* Call Northside 777 *(1947);* Rope *(1948), his first film for Alfred Hitchcock;* Winchester 73 *(1950);* Broken Arrow *(1950);* Harvey *(1950), which earned him his fourth Oscar nomination;* Rear Window *(1954);* The Man From Laramie *(1955);* Anatomy of a Murder *(1959), which got him his fifth Oscar nomination; and* Shenandoah *(1965).*

In recent years, Stewart has appeared in The Shootist *(1976) with John Wayne,* The Big Sleep *(1978), and* The Magic of Lassie *(1978).*

MY FRIEND IRMA (1949)
★★

Marie Wilson
John Lund

Wilson stars in the title role as a dumb blonde who becomes involved with a new singing sensation discovered at a refreshment stand. Comic-book-style humor abounds in this wacky comedy, based loosely on the radio series. Dean Martin and Jerry Lewis got their start in films in this movie. **Director**—George Marshall.

103 minutes b&w

231

M·N

- My Little Chickadee
- My Six Convicts
- The Mystery of Kasper Hauser
- Mystery Street
- The Naked and the Dead
- The Naked City
- Nashville
- Nasty Habits
- National Velvet

MY LITTLE CHICKADEE (1940)
★★★

Mae West
W. C. Fields

Memorable pairing of West and Fields in this dopey western comedy, which certainly would have faded into oblivion if not for the talent involved. Just watching the great Fields and the voluptuous West batting the corny dialogue back and forth is supreme joy; otherwise, the film never picks up steam. Joseph Calleia, Dick Foran, Margaret Hamilton, and Donald Meek also star. **Director**—Edward Cline.
83 minutes b&w

MY SIX CONVICTS (1952)
★★★

John Beal
Millard Mitchell
Gilbert Roland

An inventive comedy that takes place in a prison where a group of inmates strive to make the most out of a tough situation. They're helped by a sympathetic psychologist. The film is presented in semidocumentary fashion and offers some engagingly funny moments. Also stars Marshall Thompson and Regis Toomey. **Director**—Hugo Fregonese.   *104 minutes b&w*

THE MYSTERY OF KASPER HAUSER (1975)
★★

Bruno S.

A provocative film by director Werner Herzog about a mute 15-year-old boy who mysteriously appears in the Nuremberg main square in 1828, with apparently no prior contact with civilization. His educational development and innocence clash with his new environment. It's artistically portrayed, but it may be too ponderous for some. Stars Bruno S., believed to be an actual schizophrenic, as Hauser. Also with Walter Landengast and Brigitte Mira. In German with English titles. (No MPAA rating)
110 minutes b&w

MYSTERY STREET (1950)
★★★

Ricardo Montalban
Sally Forrest

Taut, well-made police caper set in Boston and accomplished with an authentic atmosphere. Detectives, with the help of pathologists, track down a killer by obtaining clues from the victim's body. Professional performances from Montalban, Forrest, Elsa Lanchester, Marshall Thompson, and Jan Sterling. **Director**—John Sturges. **Academy Award Nomination**—Leonard Spigelgass, writing (motion picture story).   *93 minutes b&w*

N

THE NAKED AND THE DEAD (1958)
★★

Aldo Ray
Cliff Robertson

This is a disappointing treatment of Norman Mailer's novel about a platoon of U.S. soldiers in combat in the Pacific during World War II. The story also touches on the tension between officers and the troops. There's a certain ordinariness about the production; there's second-rate direction, a so-so screenplay, and mediocre acting. Also with Raymond Massey, William Campbell, and Richard Jaeckel. **Director**—Raoul Walsh.   *131 minutes*

THE NAKED CITY (1948)
★★★★

Barry Fitzgerald
Don Taylor
Howard Duff

A captivating police drama—one of eight million stories in the naked city—filmed with realism in the streets of New York City. A girl is found brutally murdered, and cops launch a manhunt to find the killer. The documentary thriller offers considerable detail on police work and authentic scenes of city life. The good cast also includes Dorothy Hart, Ted de Corsia, and Adelaide Klein. **Director**—Jules

Dassin. **Academy Award**—William Daniels, cinematography (black and white); Marvin Wald, writing (motion picture story).   *96 minutes b&w*

NASHVILLE (1975)
★★★★

Ronee Blakley
Lily Tomlin

Nashville's country-and-western music scene is the setting for this panoramic reflection of America's joys, frustration, and complacency. Robert Altman, who directs the film with style, presents this mosaic of life as seen through more than 20 characters at a Nashville political rally. It's a masterful and free-flowing film with memorable performances and a shocking ending. Cast includes Karen Black, Keith Carradine, Geraldine Chaplin, Michael Murphy, Barbara Harris, Shelley Duvall, and Ned Beatty. (R) **Academy Award Nominations**—best picture; Altman, best director; Blakley, Tomlin, best supporting actress.
159 minutes

NASTY HABITS (1977)
★★

Glenda Jackson
Melina Mercouri
Geraldine Page
Sandy Dennis

This feeble lampoon of Nixon and the Watergate mess takes place in an imaginary Philadelphia convent, with some of the ambitious nuns engaging in assorted dirty tricks to win an election. It's a good comedy idea, but it could have been better executed. The vaguely written and choppy script lacks comic punch and generates only a few minor laughs. An aristocratic Glenda Jackson is the equivalent of Nixon, and a bespectacled Dennis plays a John Dean sort with blissful wit. **Director**— Michael Lindsay-Hogg. (PG)   *96 minutes*

NATIONAL VELVET (1945)
★★★

Mickey Rooney
Elizabeth Taylor

A captivating family drama about a

In National Velvet, *Elizabeth Taylor trains her horse for the Grand National race.*

plucky youngster who trains a horse to win the Grand National race. Enid Bagnold's novel is adapted for the screen with much of the heart-tugging sentiment in place. The film is most notable for the presence of Taylor as the young rider. Also with Anne Revere, Donald Crisp, Angela Lansbury, and Reginald Owen. **Director—** Clarence Brown. (G) **Academy Award** —Revere, best supporting actress. **Nominations**—Brown, best director; Leonard Smith, cinematography (color). *125 minutes*

NATURAL ENEMIES (1979)
★

Hal Holbrook
Louise Fletcher

Holbrook plays a successful magazine publisher who contemplates killing his wife, his children, and himself. Gloom and anguish relentlessly pervade this strange film. Almost every character is a grouch who rattles off lengthy lists of complaints, ranging from the national debt to potholes in the streets. Fletcher is the beautiful but depressed wife who checks in and out of psychiatric hospitals. Also with Peter Armstrong, José Ferrer, and Viveca Lindfors. **Director**—Jeff Kanew. (R)
100 minutes

NEA (1978)
★★

Samy Frey
Ann Zacharias

Director Nelly Kaplan's erotic fantasy dwells on feminist sexual liberation. What little charm there is slips away when the movie turns serious. The acting of Zacharias, who plays a rebellious 16-year-old in search of sensuality, is too self-conscious. She writes a pornographic novel, and Frey plays her editor. The rest of the cast fails to help the film, which is saddled with a trivial plot. Also with Kaplan and Micheline Presle. In French with English titles. (R) *95 minutes*

NEIGHBORS (1981)
★

John Belushi
Kathryn Walker
Cathy Moriarty
Dan Aykroyd

In Neighbors, *Cathy Moriarty is an extremely friendly neighbor to John Belushi.*

A weird couple moves next door to a peaceful suburbanite couple, played by Belushi and Walker, and sets out to drive Belushi up the wall with their peculiar antics. This fairly good comic idea soon turns sour and eventually falls apart at the seams. Many of the boisterous gags are tasteless and crude; they fizzle as rapidly as they're presented. Aykroyd and Moriarty overstrain as the strange new neighbors, and director John G. Avildsen is at sea with the absurd material. (R)
95 minutes

NEST OF VIPERS (1979)
★

Senta Berger
Onella Muti

A woman is seduced by her son's friend in this Italian film set in the '30s. Such a complicated romantic episode among the upper class is supposed to relate to the rise of fascism in Italy. Berger and Muti are stunning in the lead female roles, but the minimal excitement and intrigue are inadequate to sustain interest in this intense melodrama played among the elegant palazzi of Venice. **Director**—Tonino Cervi. (R) *105 minutes*

NETWORK (1976)
★★★★

Faye Dunaway
William Holden
Peter Finch

Television gets a working over in this provocative and outrageous satire about a network news department that will do anything to grab an audience. Paddy Chayefsky's original script is brilliant and audacious. There are excellent performances by Holden as a scrupulous news division chief, Dunaway as a cunning and predatory programming executive, and Finch as an anchorman who goes mad. The rest of the cast is also outstanding. Also with Robert Duvall, Beatrice Straight, Wesley Addy, and Ned Beatty. Sidney Lumet's superb direction helps to hammer the message home. (R) **Academy Awards**—Finch, best actor;
(Continued)

Peter Finch discusses his TV career with Faye Dunaway in the satire Network.

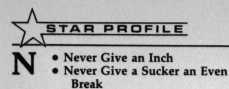
N
- Never Give an Inch
- Never Give a Sucker an Even Break
- Never on Sunday

- The New Centurions
- Newsfront
- New York Confidential

(Continued) Dunaway, best actress; Straight, best supporting actress; Chayefsky, best original screenplay. **Nominations**—best picture; Lumet, best director; Holden, best actor; Beatty, best supporting actor; Owen Roizman, cinematography. *120 minutes*

NEVER GIVE AN INCH
See Sometimes a Great Notion

NEVER GIVE A SUCKER AN EVEN BREAK (1941)
★★★★

W. C. Fields

The great Fields is the whole show in this wacky mishmash of a farce; it has virtually no plot, but plenty of hilarious scenes. Fields, three sheets to the wind, falls out of an airplane and lands in a strange country, where he meets an attractive girl who's never met a man. Much fun and frolic ensues, and it ends with an inventive chase sequence. Co-stars Margaret Dumont, Gloria Jean, Leon Errol, Franklin Pangborn, and Ann Miller. **Director**—Edward Cline.
70 minutes b&w

NEVER ON SUNDAY (1960)
★★★★

Melina Mercouri
Jules Dassin

Mercouri stands out in a memorable performance as a world-wise prostitute who resists being reformed by a stuffy tourist visiting Greece. Dassin, who directed, plays Homer, the frustrated tourist. The film is charmingly rendered, with the magnificent Melina shining all the way, and the title song helps set the mood. Also with Georges Foundas and Titos Vandis. **Academy Award Nominations**—Dassin, best director; Mercouri, best actress; Dassin, best story and screenplay (written directly for the screen).
91 minutes b&w

THE NEW CENTURIONS (1972)
★★★

George C. Scott
Stacy Keach

An unusual and insightful police drama, focusing on the personal and psychological pressures of being a cop. Scott contributes considerable dignity to the proceedings as the cynical veteran officer who shows his rookie partner the ropes; Keach plays the rookie cop. Competently based on Joseph Wambaugh's novel about men on the Los Angeles police force. Top performances all around. Also with Jane Alexander, Rosalind Cash, and Scott Wilson. **Director**—Richard Fleischer. (R) *103 minutes*

NEWSFRONT (1979)
★★★

Bill Hunter
Chris Haywood

An intriguing Australian film that vividly portrays the theatrical newsreel business during its waning years, just prior to the advent of television. This isn't a documentary, but actual clips of newsreel stories are woven into the fictional story, which romanticizes the personal lives of the characters behind the cameras. An excellent cast, headed by Hunter and Haywood, delivers polished portrayals of those almost-forgotten journalists. Also with Wendy Hughes, Gerard Kennedy, and Angela Punch. **Director**—Phillip Noyce. (No MPAA rating) *110 minutes color/b&w*

NEW YORK CONFIDENTIAL (1955)
★★

Broderick Crawford
Anne Bancroft

Rather undramatic yet authentic-looking account of organized crime in New York. A local syndicate boss is bumped off by one of his own henchmen. A good cast, headed by Crawford and Bancroft, heightens the otherwise routine proceedings, which depict racketeers as shrewd businessmen. Also with Richard Conte,

---

MARILYN MONROE

Marilyn Monroe was born Norma Jean Baker or Mortenson in Los Angeles in 1926. She lived in several foster homes and an orphanage, and during her childhood she was subjected to neglect, humiliation, and even rape.

At 16, she married a small-town policeman, but the marriage ended in divorce. During World War II, while working in a defense plant, she was discovered by a photographer who asked her to pose for pin-up pictures, which became popular among GIs. More modeling assignments followed,

and she was finally noticed by Hollywood studios who starred her in bit parts in poor movies in the late '40s and early '50s; she was usually cast as a dumb, bleached blonde.

In the mid '50s, Monroe's roles became more significant, and she became a top box-office attraction as a Hollywood sex queen. In 1954, Monroe married baseball star Joe DiMaggio, a relationship that lasted less than a year. In 1956, she married playwright Arthur Miller, and she divorced him five years later, just prior to the completion of her last film, The Misfits (1961).

About a month after the opening of The Misfits (the script was written by Arthur Miller), Monroe entered a mental hospital. In 1962, she died, apparently committing suicide with an overdose of drugs.

Some of Monroe's other major films include The Asphalt Jungle (1950), All About Eve (1950), Don't Bother To Knock (1952), Niagara (1952), Gentlemen Prefer Blondes (1953), How To Marry a Millionaire (1953), The Seven-Year Itch (1955), Bus Stop (1956), and Some Like It Hot (1959).

● New York, New York
● The Next Man
● Next Stop, Greenwich Village

● Niagara
● Nickelodeon
● Night and Day
● A Night at the Opera

N

Marilyn Maxwell, and J. Carrol Naish. **Director**—Russell Rouse.

87 minutes b&w

NEW YORK, NEW YORK (1977)
★★

**Liza Minnelli
Robert De Niro**

Liza Minnelli is a singer who becomes a star in New York, New York.

Director Martin Scorsese's big-band-era backstage romance begins with promise, but suddenly falls apart about a third of the way through and never recovers. The unbalanced film can't seem to keep pace with the extraordinary talents of De Niro, who portrays a jazz saxophonist, and Minnelli, who plays a Doris Day-type band singer. Scorsese seems to be trying hard to recapture the feel of those great Hollywood musicals of the '40s and '50s, but he can't quite make it. Also with Lionel Stander, Mary Kay Place, and Barry Primus. (PG)

137 minutes

THE NEXT MAN (1976)
★

**Sean Connery
Cornelia Sharpe**

Connery, who earned fame and fortune as James Bond, returns to the world of intrigue and adventure in this dull and confusing movie about power politics in the Middle East. He plays a Saudi Arabian diplomat who provokes violence when he tries to promote

peace with Israel. Sharpe co-stars as a spy who falls in love with the noble Arab, and her performance is awful; the rest of the cast is a mixed bag. Also with Albert Paulsen and Adolfo Celi. Richard C. Sarafian directs the film as if it were a travelogue with occasional murders. (R) *108 minutes*

NEXT STOP, GREENWICH VILLAGE (1976)
★★★

**Lenny Baker
Shelley Winters**

Director Paul Mazursky's warm and touching autobiographical film is about an aspiring young comedian's life in the Village in the 1950s. Lanky newcomer Baker, playing the awkward-looking Larry Lapinsky, heads an outstanding cast, which lends credibility and humanity to the story. Winters is convincing as an overbearing Jewish mother. The film is full of clear and nostalgic memories of this period. Also with Ellen Greene, Lou Jacobi, Christopher Walken, and Mike Kellin. (R) *109 minutes*

NIAGARA (1952)
★★★

**Joseph Cotten
Jean Peters
Marilyn Monroe**

Monroe plays Monroe to the hilt in this suspenseful tale about a faithless wife who schemes to kill her husband while on their honeymoon. Monroe is the bride, and Cotten plays the husband. Monroe is at her wiggling best, and the magnificent backdrop of Niagara Falls enhances the scenic interest. The Hitchcock-style plot packs a punch, although it leans toward the melodramatic at times. The cast also includes Don Wilson and Casey Adams. **Director**—Henry Hathaway.

89 minutes

NICKELODEON (1976)
★★★

**Ryan O'Neal
Burt Reynolds
Tatum O'Neal**

This movie is director Peter Bog-

Burt Reynolds listens to Ryan O'Neal in the slapstick drama Nickelodeon.

danovich's affectionate and entertaining tribute to the early pioneers of filmmaking. An excellent cast portrays the rollicking slapstick and madcap adventures of Hollywood before World War I, when America was charmed with its new plaything, the moving picture. It's uneven in places, but it's rich in feeling and educational as well. Also with Brian Keith, Stella Stevens, and John Ritter. (PG)

121 minutes

NIGHT AND DAY (1946)
★★★

**Cary Grant
Alexis Smith
Mary Martin**

The life of songwriter Cole Porter receives a Hollywood fictional treatment, and the events are presented in a creaky fashion. Yet Porter's wonderful music stands out, and an excellent cast puts on a worthy show. Grant is effective as the popular composer, and he sings "You're the Top." Another pleasant moment comes when Martin belts out "My Heart Belongs To Daddy." Also with Monty Woolley, Jane Wyman, Eve Arden, and Dorothy Malone. **Director**—Michael Curtiz.

132 minutes

A NIGHT AT THE OPERA (1935)
★★★★

Marx Brothers

A Marx Brothers comedy classic, with Groucho, Chico, and Harpo destroying and finally saving an opera production. The trio does many wacky deeds with the help of an effective musical score that perks up the hilarity to fever pitch. The magnificent lunacy

(Continued)

N
• The Night Caller
• Night Games
• The Night Has a Thousand Eyes
• Nighthawks
• A Night in Casablanca
• Nightmare
• Nightmare Alley

The Marx Brothers trigger most of the lunacy in A Night at the Opera.

(Continued)

is side-splitting and opera-splitting as well. Also with Margaret Dumont, Kitty Carlisle, Allan Jones, and Sig Rumann. **Director**—Sam Wood.

96 minutes b&w

THE NIGHT CALLER (1975)
★

Jean-Paul Belmondo

Belmondo stars as a French police detective who pursues a sex killer in Paris. The overworked *French Connection* chase scene is replayed when Belmondo hugs the roof of a speeding Metro train in an attempt to get the murderer, who's cornered in the car below. The rest of the action is hardly original or up to par. Also with Charles Denner and Adalberto-Maria Meril. In French with English titles. **Director**—Henri Verneuil. (R)

91 minutes

NIGHT GAMES (1980)
★

Cindy Pickett

French director Roger Vadim, who helped launch the careers of Brigitte Bardot and Jane Fonda, introduces Pickett in the role of a Beverly Hills woman who is haunted by sexual fantasies. The screenplay is so absurd that some of the most serious scenes generate laughter. Pickett displays meager acting talent. It's a silly, forgettable film, and Pickett will probably be forgotten as well. (R) *100 minutes*

THE NIGHT HAS A THOUSAND EYES (1948)
★★

Edward G. Robinson

Robinson stars as a vaudeville mentalist who discovers he actually has the ability to predict the future. The patchy drama is intriguing at times, but there are many dull moments. However, Edward G. is as watchable as ever. Co-stars Gail Russell, John Lund, Virginia Bruce, and William Demarest. **Director**—John Farrow.

80 minutes b&w

NIGHTHAWKS (1981)
★★★

Sylvester Stallone
Billy Dee Williams
Rutger Hauer

In Nighthawks, *Sylvester Stallone and Billy Dee Williams corner a killer.*

Stallone steps out of his *Rocky* role to play a tough New York City cop who, along with Williams, tracks down a diabolical international terrorist. This standard police story is uneven in spots, but it delivers excitement at a fast-paced clip. Stallone's cop is an enraged character, but he remains a hero with a conscience, and he eventually triumphs over evil. Dutch actor Hauer is quite impressive as the cold-blooded fiend who is brought to bay in a heart-pounding surprise finale. Also with Persis Khambatta. **Director**—Bruce Malmuth. (R) *99 minutes*

A NIGHT IN CASABLANCA (1946)
★★★

Marx Brothers

Groucho, Chico, and Harpo check into

a Casablanca hotel where they smoke out some Nazi spies. Not the best of the Marx Brothers, but there's enough sustained lunacy to please devotees. This film was perhaps the last big one for the zany trio. Co-stars Sig Rumann, Lisette Verea, Charles Drake, and Lois Collier. **Director**—Archie Mayo. *85 minutes b&w*

NIGHTMARE (1981)
(no stars)

Baird Stafford

A young man, played by Stafford, is released from a mental hospital and begins a brutal killing spree. Scant attention is paid to acting, script, and direction, but the filmmakers certainly lavish considerable care on violence and gore. There are beheadings and stabbings galore, with fresh corpses spurting rivers of blood all over the screen. The film lives up to its title and nothing more. Also with Sharon Smith and C. J. Cooke. **Director**—Romano Scavolini. (No MPAA rating)

97 minutes

NIGHTMARE ALLEY (1947)
★★★

Tyrone Power

Power skillfully portrays a carnival barker who succeeds for a while as a con man until his luck runs out. This is an odd, moody, and captivating drama, filled with strange intriguing characters; it's rather well done in all departments. Based on the novel by William Lindsay Gresham. Also with Colleen Gray, Joan Blondell, Helen Walker, Mike Mazurki, and Taylor Holmes. **Director**—Edmund Goulding. *111 minutes b&w*

Tyrone Power (right) portrays a con man in Nightmare Alley, *a captivating drama.*

- The Night of the Hunter
- The Night of the Iguana
- Night of the Juggler
- Night Passage
- The Night the Lights Went Out in Georgia
- The Night They Raided Minsky's
- A Night To Remember (1942)
- A Night To Remember (1958)

N

THE NIGHT OF THE HUNTER (1955)
★★★★

Robert Mitchum
Shelley Winters

A sinister, brooding tale about a religious zealot, played by Mitchum, relentlessly pursuing hidden money after he murders his wife. The film is ingeniously constructed and crackles with suspense and unexpected shocks. This was Charles Laughton's only film as director, and he handles the job expertly. Also with Lillian Gish, James Gleason, Evelyn Varden, and Peter Graves.   *93 minutes b&w*

THE NIGHT OF THE IGUANA (1964)
★★★

Richard Burton
Deborah Kerr
Ava Gardner

Intense, moody, and often amusing tale of a defrocked clergyman, played by Burton, struggling to reestablish his life in Mexico. There he becomes intimately involved with various women, including Kerr, a spinster, and Gardner, the sultry owner of a run-down tourist hotel. The screenplay faithfully adheres to Tennessee Williams's play and offers a vivid account of some interesting characters. There are competent performances, too, from Sue Lyon, Grayson Hall, and Cyril Delevanti. **Director**—John Huston. **Academy Award Nominations**—Hall, best supporting actress; Gabriel Figueroa, cinematography (black and white)   *125 minutes b&w*

NIGHT OF THE JUGGLER (1980)
★★

James Brolin

A nonstop chase thriller, with Brolin playing an ex-cop who relentlessly pursues his daughter's kidnapper through the crowded streets of New York City. The film has plenty of frantic action; apparently, dozens of cars were smashed up to achieve the breathless chase scenes. But the thin screenplay has credibility problems, and characters aren't developed in sufficient detail. Cliff Gorman, Richard Castellano, and Julie Carmen also star. **Director**—Robert Butler. (R)   *100 minutes*

NIGHT PASSAGE (1957)
★★★

James Stewart
Audie Murphy

A competently made western about a railroad man in charge of a train payroll, which an outlaw gang wants to steal. Further complications arise when it's learned that the railroad worker and the gang leader are brothers. Stewart plays the railroad man, and Murphy is the bandit leader. Sufficient action and excitement follow, and the film ends with a tense gunfight. Also with Dan Duryea, Brandon de Wilde, and Dianne Foster. **Director**—James Nielson.   *90 minutes*

THE NIGHT THE LIGHTS WENT OUT IN GEORGIA (1981)
★★

Dennis Quaid
Kristy McNichol

A listless story about the misadventures of a skirt-chasing country-western singer and his precocious teenage sister, who serves as his manager. The couple is played by Quaid and McNichol. While traveling to Nashville, the two are sidetracked at a hick town, where Quaid runs afoul of the law and falls for a local beauty. The script, padded with much idle chatter, resembles a few TV episodes strung together. Mark Hamill of *Star Wars* fame is hopelessly waxen as a friendly state trooper. **Director**—Ronald F. Maxwell. (PG)   *120 minutes*

Kristy McNichol and her dog in The Night the Lights Went Out in Georgia.

THE NIGHT THEY RAIDED MINSKY'S (1968)
★★★

Jason Robards Jr.
Britt Ekland

A colorful and captivating behind-the-scenes look at burlesque of yesteryear. The story revolves around the experiences of a shy country girl, played by Ekland, who comes to the big city and gets a job as a stripper in a burlesque show. She gets involved with Robards, a burlesque comic. The background detail is what really stands out, with nostalgic moments showing baggy-pants comics and the squalid atmosphere of the theater. Also with Norman Wisdom, Forrest Tucker, Joseph Wiseman, Bert Lahr, Harry Andrew, and Elliott Gould. **Director**—William Friedkin. (PG)   *99 minutes*

A NIGHT TO REMEMBER (1942)
★★★

Loretta Young
Brian Aherne

Aherne and Young play mystery writers living in Greenwich Village. After they discover a body in their apartment, the two set out to find the murderer. It's a clever and buoyant whodunit, with amusing moments and plenty of sparkling dialogue. Top performances bolster the production. Also with Jeff Donnell, William Wright, Sidney Toler, Gale Sondergaard, Donald MacBride, and Lee Patrick. **Director**—Richard Wallace.   *91 minutes b&w*

A NIGHT TO REMEMBER (1958)
★★★★

Kenneth More
Honor Blackman
David McCallum

An inspired semidocumentary about the sinking of the luxury liner *Titanic* in the North Atlantic in 1912. The account, based on Walter Lord's book, features much striking detail and scores of cameo roles to describe the heroism and drama of that fateful night when the vessel struck an   *(Continued)*

N
- Night Train
- Night Train to Munich
- Nightwing
- Nijinsky

- 1900
- 1941
- 1984

(Continued)
iceberg. Expert direction and superb performances combine for an admirable movie. Also with Michael Goodliffe, George Rose, Anthony Bushell, Jill Dixon, Alec McCowen, and Laurence Naismith. **Director**—Roy Baker.
123 minutes b&w

NIGHT TRAIN
See Night Train to Munich

NIGHT TRAIN TO MUNICH
(1940)
★★★★

Rex Harrison
Margaret Lockwood

Intrigue and comedy are cleverly blended in this excellent suspense film about the efforts of British agents to keep a secret formula from the clutches of the Nazis. Skillful use of meticulous detail enhances this movie, which is made much like an Alfred Hitchcock thriller. Also with Paul Henreid, Basil Radford, and Naunton Wayne. **Director**—Carol Reed. **Alternate Titles**—*Gestapo; Night Train.* **Academy Award Nomination**—Gordon Wellesley, writing (original screenplay). *93 minutes b&w*

NIGHTWING (1979)
★★

Nick Mancuso
David Warner
Kathryn Harrold

Thousands of plague-infested vampire bats invade an Indian reservation in yet another Hollywood version of Mother Nature on the rampage. It's supposed to scare the daylights out of you, but nothing doing: Up close, the bats reveal big teeth, but there's little bite in the predictable screenplay, and the special effects are unimaginative. Also with Stephen Macht, Strother Martin, and George Clutesi. **Director**—Arthur Hiller. (PG) *105 minutes*

NIJINSKY (1980)
★★

Alan Bates
George de la Pena

Director Herbert Ross (*The Turning*

Alan Bates is Diaghilev, and George de la Pena is Nijinsky in Nijinsky.

Point) tries another movie with a ballet theme, and this time it's based on the career of the legendary Vaslav Nijinsky, the great Russian dancer who ultimately descended into madness. The opulent but lethargic film basically dwells on Nijinsky's homosexual relationships. There really isn't enough dancing to satisfy ballet fans, and De la Pena, who plays the title role, never strikes any sparks as an actor or a great dancer. Bates plays impresario Sergei Diaghilev. Also with Leslie Browne. (R)
129 minutes

1900 (1977)
★★

Burt Lancaster
Robert De Niro

Director Bernardo Bertolucci's monumental chronicle of Italy's peasant-landowner struggle begins with grace and grandeur, but eventually withdraws into a bloated Marxist tract. A fine cast, including De Niro, Lancaster, Sterling Hayden, Donald Sutherland, and Dominique Sanda, creates moments of feeling. However, much of the acting and script are uninspired. The film contains some frontal nudity and disturbing violence. (R)
243 minutes

1941 (1979)
★★

Dan Aykroyd
John Belushi
Ned Beatty
Treat Williams

Steven Spielberg (*Jaws; Close Encounters of the Third Kind*) tries his hand at comedy and comes up with a film that's generous with style, but miserly with comic inspiration. This overblown, adolescent farce concerns a Japanese invasion of California on the heels of the Pearl Harbor attack. There's hysteria, brawling, silliness, destruction of buildings and vehicles, lots of noise, and minimal humor and wit. Belushi, Aykroyd, Williams, and Beatty are essentially wasted. Also with Robert Stack, Tim Matheson, Christopher Lee, and Toshiro Mifune. **Academy Award Nomination**—William A. Fraker, cinematography. (PG) *118 minutes*

John Belushi is an American pilot, and Toshiro Mifune commands a Japanese sub in 1941.

1984 (1955)
★★★

Michael Redgrave
Edmond O'Brien
Jan Sterling

A provocative screen version of George Orwell's prophetic tale of a sinister world, where people have limited freedom and live under the watchful eye of "Big Brother." O'Brien and Sterling play lovers who try to rebel. The film, like the novel, is convoluted and not completely satisfying, but there are many thoughtful points to ponder in this absorbing drama. Also with David Kossoff, Mervyn Johns, and Donald Pleasence. **Director**—Michael Anderson.
91 minutes b&w

- 9 to 5
- 92 in the Shade
- Nobody's Perfekt

- No Man Is an Island
- None But the Lonely Heart
- No Nukes
- Norman . . . Is That You?

N

9 to 5 (1980)
★★

Jane Fonda
Lily Tomlin
Dolly Parton

Jane Fonda, Lily Tomlin, and Dolly Parton make waves in the typing pool in 9 to 5.

Fonda, Tomlin, and Parton are secretaries who engineer an office revolt and wage war on their chauvinistic boss. With such a cast lineup and such a subject, the film should have been a ripsnorting comedy, but alas, its potential is only partially realized. The half-baked screenplay erratically hops from farce to satire to drumbeating about the feminist movement. The leading ladies put in their 35-hour work week, but it's not worth anybody's overtime. Also with Dabney Coleman, Sterling Hayden, Henry Jones, and Marian Mercer. **Director—** Colin Higgins. (PG)   *110 minutes*

92 IN THE SHADE (1976)
★★★

Peter Fonda

Thomas McGuane, who wrote *Rancho DeLuxe*, wrote and directed this cool film, and it has a genuine fascination. He again drives home his favorite theme of youth and the pursuit of false values. Fonda delivers a stylish performance; he plays a restless, spoiled, rich young man who breaks into the charter-fishing business in Key West. Warren Oates, Burgess Meredith, and Elizabeth Ashley play their parts with remarkable clarity. Also with Margot Kidder, Harry Dean Stanton, and Sylvia Miles. (R)   *93 minutes*

NOBODY'S PERFEKT (1981)
★

Gabe Kaplan
Alex Karras
Robert Klein

A ridiculous, lamebrained comedy about three dopey characters who decide to fight City Hall after their car is damaged hitting a pothole. The film lives up to its title, with jokes that fall flat and comic situations that are merely desperate. Kaplan, Karras, and Klein star as the bumbling trio. Their obvious lack of energy and style is enough to make The Three Stooges wince. Go back to TV, fellas; it's safer there. **Director—**Peter Bonerz. (PG)   *96 minutes*

NO MAN IS AN ISLAND (1962)
★★

Jeffrey Hunter

A Navy radioman, played by Hunter, is left behind on Guam after the Japanese attack, and fights the enemy as a guerrilla. This rather routine war adventure, based on a true story, is a bit adolescent in nature, but Hunter handles the acting well. The patchy production, however, isn't above the usual. Nicely photographed in the Philippines. Supporting roles by Marshall Thompson, Barbara Perez, and Ronald Remy. **Directors—**John Monks, Jr., and Richard Goldstone.   *114 minutes*

NONE BUT THE LONELY HEART (1944)
★★★

Cary Grant
Ethel Barrymore

An excellent drama that strikes the proper mood and profits from some good acting. Grant stars as a young Cockney roamer seeking self-satisfaction as World War II approaches; he's astonishingly good in this straight dramatic part. And there's top support from Barrymore, who plays his dying mother. An excellent script contributes to the film's quality. Also with June Duprez, Barry Fitzgerald, Jane Wyatt, George Coulouris, and Dan Duryea. **Director—** Clifford Odets. **Academy Award—** Barrymore, best supporting actress. **Nomination—**Grant, best actor.
113 minutes b&w

NO NUKES (1980)
★★

Jane Fonda
Ralph Nader

An earsplitting concert movie, based on a series of Madison Square Garden performances by well-known rock stars protesting the use of nuclear power. Scattered among the musical segments are some brief antinuclear documentary films and backstage conversations in which performers comment about the dangers of nuclear misuse; even Nader and Fonda pop in for a few remarks. The appeal is primarily for rock fans. Bruce Springsteen; the Doobie Brothers; Crosby, Stills & Nash; and others belt out the pounding musical numbers. **Director—**Julian Schlossberg, Danny Goldberg, and Anthony Potenza. (PG)
103 minutes

NORMAN . . . IS THAT YOU? (1976)
★

Redd Foxx
Pearl Bailey

Foxx and Bailey star in this tasteless and forced comedy about estranged parents who discover that their son, Norman, is a homosexual. The series of corny and poorly paced jokes resembles an elongated TV sitcom; it would have trouble finding a decent spot in prime time. As a stage play, *Norman*, closed on Broadway after only 12 performances. The film, which substitutes a black family for a Jewish one, isn't much better. Also with Dennis Dugan, Michael Warren, Tamara Dobson, and Jayne Meadows. Written and directed by George Schlatter. (PG)   *91 minutes*

239

N
- Norma Rae
- The Norseman
- The North Avenue Irregulars
- North By Northwest
- North Dallas Forty
- Northwest Mounted Police
- Northwest Passage

NORMA RAE (1979)
★★★★

**Sally Field
Ron Leibman**

Field stars in the title role of this refreshing, gritty, and intelligent film about textile factory workers in a Southern mill town. Under the superb direction of Martin Ritt, Field portrays a valiant young woman struggling with work, love, and family. And what a spirited performance it is. There are fine acting jobs by Leibman, as a union organizer, and Beau Bridges, as Norma Rae's husband. Also with Pat Hingle and Barbara Baxley. (PG) **Academy Award**—Field, best actress. **Nominations**—best picture; Irving Ravetch and Harriet Frank, best screenplay (adapted from another medium). *113 minutes*

THE NORSEMAN (1978)
★

Lee Majors

Majors, TV's *Six Million Dollar Man*, makes his film debut in what looks like a $600 B-movie. The story recounts the adventures of a band of Vikings that landed on North American shores about the 11th century. Majors and his buddies, all decked out like so many tin woodsmen of Oz, slosh around the Florida Everglades and fight the Injuns. Cornel Wilde and Mel Ferrer help out with the acting, which is mostly mediocre. Also with Jack Elam and Chris Connelly. **Director**—Charles B. Pierce. (PG) *90 minutes*

THE NORTH AVENUE IRREGULARS (1979)
★★★★

**Edward Herrmann
Barbara Harris
Susan Clark
Karen Valentine**

An eager-beaver minister and a posse of daffy housewives mop up local racketeers in this zany and frisky Walt Disney comedy. The plot is mostly Disney formula, but there are plenty of good characterizations and clever gags to keep mom and dad in stitches

Beau Bridges plays Sally Field's husband in the intelligent drama Norma Rae.

along with the kids. Herrmann makes a likable and amusing preacher, but the biggest scorer on the laugh meter is Harris, who pursues the crooks in a station wagon bulging with pets and youngsters. Also with Michael Constantine, Cloris Leachman, and Patsy Kelly. **Director**—Bruce Bilson. (G) *99 minutes*

NORTH BY NORTHWEST (1959)
★★★★

**Cary Grant
Eva Marie Saint
James Mason**

A lulu of a comedy-thriller from director Alfred Hitchcock, the master himself, who serves up a delightful smorgasbord of favorite tongue-in-cheek tricks. Suave Grant plays a businessman who's pursued by foreign agents; they believe he's a spy. The excitement never slackens, and some scenes are unforgettable—especially Grant being menaced in an open field by a crop-dusting plane. First-class support from Saint, Mason, Leo G. Carroll, Martin Landau, and Jessie Royce Landis. (PG) **Academy Award Nomination**—Ernest Lehman, best story and screenplay (written directly for the screen). *136 minutes*

NORTH DALLAS FORTY (1979)
★★★★

**Nick Nolte
Mac Davis**

This is a hard-hitting, realistic look at the win-at-all-cost business of pro football. Nolte gives a powerful performance as an over-the-hill wide receiver who rebels against any notion of team spirit. Lots of fine acting support from G. D. Spradlin as a goading

head coach and Davis and Bo Svenson as spirited teammates. It's a rough-and-tumble comedy that also effectively displays its anger and soul. Also with Charles Durning, Dayle Haddon, and Steve Forrest. **Director**—Ted Kotcheff. (R) *119 minutes*

Nick Nolte (#87) and Mac Davis (#16) star in North Dallas Forty, about pro football.

NORTHWEST MOUNTED POLICE (1940)
★★

**Gary Cooper
Paulette Goddard**

A lavish action adventure in the director's best style, yet the story is unmoving and rather forgettable. The plot involves the efforts of a Texas Ranger, played by Cooper, to locate a criminal hiding out in Canada. Goddard is a half-breed. The colorful outdoor scenes are obviously set-bound. Also with Preston Foster, Robert Preston, Lynne Overman, Madeleine Carroll, George Bancroft, and Akim Tamiroff. **Director**—Cecil B. DeMille. **Academy Award Nomination**—Victor Milner and W. Howard Greene, cinematography (color). *125 minutes*

NORTHWEST PASSAGE (1940)
★★★★

**Spencer Tracy
Robert Young
Walter Brennan**

Tracy is outstanding as frontier captain Robert Rogers of the Queen's Rangers in this rousing historical saga about adventurers seeking a route to the sea and braving hardships and Indian attacks along the way. Young and Brennan play two recruits under Tracy's command. The film is well made, with a sense of reality about it.

- Not As a Stranger
- Nothing Personal
- No Time for Breakfast
- No Time for Sergeants
- Notorious
- No Way To Treat a Lady
- Now, Voyager

N

Lots of excitement and suspense—especially likable for the kids. Also with Ruth Hussey, Nat Pendleton, and Donald MacBride. **Director**—King Vidor. **Academy Award Nomination**—Sidney Wagner and William V. Skall, cinematography (color).

126 minutes

NOT AS A STRANGER (1955)
★★★★

Robert Mitchum
Olivia de Havilland

Competent screen version of Morton Thompson's best-selling novel about a young physician who struggles with his career and his marriage. The story is part soap opera, but there are enough strong details about medical school and hospitals to offset such drawbacks. Mitchum does a credible job in the key part as a poor but bright medical student who becomes a country doctor. De Havilland is his wife, who supports him through medical school. Also with Broderick Crawford, Frank Sinatra, Charles Bickford, and Gloria Grahame. **Director**—Stanley Kramer. *125 minutes b&w*

NOTHING PERSONAL (1980)
★

Donald Sutherland
Suzanne Somers

A hopelessly romantic comedy that introduces Somers in her first major film feature. She plays a sexy lawyer who helps Sutherland, a professor, save baby seals from destruction. Somers is rather stiff in this acting assignment, and Sutherland looks as if he would rather be somewhere else than involved with such tedium. Direction, scripting, and editing are

Donald Sutherland and Suzanne Somers in Nothing Personal, *a romantic comedy.*

ragged and uninspired. Also with Dabney Coleman. **Director**—George Bloomfield. (PG) *96 minutes*

NO TIME FOR BREAKFAST (1978)
★★

Annie Girardot

Girardot stars in this French soap opera about a woman doctor caught between her gallant career and the demands of her family. She nobly encourages patients doomed by cancer, while she smokes too much and coughs a lot. Predictably, she gets cancer and reevaluates her past. This familiar scenario, which cannot be taken too seriously, borders on banality. Also with François Perier, Jean-Pierre Cassel, and Isabelle Huppert. **Director**—Jean-Louis Bertuccelli. In French with English titles. (No MPAA rating) *100 minutes*

NO TIME FOR SERGEANTS (1958)
★★★★

Andy Griffith

Griffith successfully repeats his Broadway role as the Georgia farm boy who joins the Army and cheerfully drives his superiors up the wall. It's obviously Griffith's best screen performance, and his hilarious antics are worth at least a laugh a minute. The supporting cast sparkles, too. Also with William Fawcett, Murray Hamilton, Myron McCormick, Nick Adams, and Don Knotts. **Director**—Mervyn Le Roy. *111 minutes b&w*

NOTORIOUS (1946)
★★★★

Cary Grant
Ingrid Bergman
Claude Rains

Another gem from director Alfred Hitchcock's collection of thrillers, smoothly played by a champagne cast. The setting is Rio de Janiero at the height of World War II. Bergman is involved in an espionage scheme to marry a Nazi spy, played by Rains, in the hope of helping an American agent, played by Grant. The atmo-

sphere is heavily charged with romance, tingling suspense, and high drama. Also with Louis Calhern, Leopoldine Konstantin, and Reinhold Schunzel. **Academy Award Nominations**—Rains, best supporting actor; Ben Hecht, writing (original screenplay). *101 minutes b&w*

NO WAY TO TREAT A LADY (1968)
★★★

Rod Steiger
George Segel

A smart mixture of mystery, suspense, and black farce, with Steiger doing a fabulous job as a psychotic killer of women. He traps his victims by the clever use of disguise. Segal is also outstanding as a detective tracking down the elusive mass murderer. Steiger shows off his acting skills by playing seven roles. The production is uneven in spots, but it succeeds overall. Also stars Lee Remick, Eileen Heckart, Murray Hamilton, and Michael Dunn. **Director**—Jack Smight. *108 minutes*

NOW, VOYAGER (1942)
★★★

Bette Davis
Claude Rains
Paul Henreid

A star-studded soap opera that works
(Continued)

In No Time for Sergeants, *Andy Griffith repeated his Broadway role.*

N·O

- The Nude Bomb
- The Nun's Story
- Nunzio
- The Nutty Professor
- Objective—Burma
- Obsession

(Continued)

to perfection because of the extraordinary skills of the performers; they seem to revel in the suffering of their emotional situations. Davis is outstanding as a lonely spinster who's helped by a psychiatrist, played by Rains. Then she becomes involved in a tragic romance with Henried. Slickly produced for the utmost in sentimental, yet effective, drama. Other supporting roles by Gladys Cooper, Ilka Chase, Bonita Granville, John Loder, and Franklin Pangborn. **Director**—Irving Rapper. **Academy Award Nominations**—Davis, best actress; Cooper, best supporting actress.

117 minutes b&w

THE NUDE BOMB (1980)
★★

Don Adams
Sylvia Kristal

Don Adams, playing Agent 86, answers a call on his boot phone in The Nude Bomb.

Aha! It's the old "let's-make-a-feature-movie-out-of-a-popular-TV-show" trick. Adams, as bumbling secret agent 86, saves the world from the sinister KAOS organization, which attempts to render mankind naked with clothes-destroying missiles. Adams is good enough to wring a few laughs from the plodding material based on the '60s *Get Smart* TV series. But would you believe this shtick was better on the tube? The biting satire, engaging dialogue, and such supporting-cast stalwarts as Barbara Feldon and Ed Platt are sorely missing. Also with Vittorio Gassman and Rhonda Fleming. **Director**—Clive Donner. (PG) *94 minutes*

THE NUN'S STORY (1959)
★★★★

Audrey Hepburn
Peter Finch

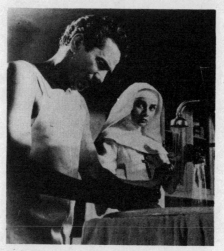

Peter Finch and Audrey Hepburn give excellent performances in The Nun's Story.

An exceptionally appealing story about a young nun, played by Hepburn, who serves under harsh conditions in the Belgian Congo and then quits the convent for an ordinary existence. The film, an intelligent rendition of Kathryn C. Hulme's book, is presented in a straightforward manner, with outstanding performances. Finch plays a physician, and Colleen Dewhurst is exceptional as a suicidal patient; Hepburn is convincing as the dedicated nun. Also with Edith Evans, Peggy Ashcroft, Dean Jagger, Mildred Dunnock, and Beatrice Straight. **Director**—Fred Zinnemann. **Academy Award Nominations**—best picture; Zinnemann, best director; Hepburn, best actress; Robert Anderson, best screenplay (based on material from another medium); Franz Planer, cinematography (color). *151 minutes*

NUNZIO (1978)
★★★

David Proval

Proval is convincing in his stalwart portrayal of a retarded Brooklyn grocery boy who's the object of ridicule, but at last becomes the neighborhood hero. The sentimental story has elements of *Rocky* and *Marty*, and is an earnest and endearing film that touches the heart despite too much reliance on melodramtics and emotional clichés. Also with James Andronica, Morgana King, Tovah Feldshuh, and Vincent Russo. **Director**—Paul Williams (R)

87 minutes

THE NUTTY PROFESSOR (1963)
★★★

Jerry Lewis
Stella Stevens

One of the best of Lewis's comedies, with a strong psychological message in its Dr. Jekyll and Mr. Hyde theme. Jerry portrays an awkward and shy professor who accidentally discovers a chemical potion that changes him into a brash, self-assured swinger. His handling of the two extreme personalities makes the picture most interesting and funny. Also with Howard Morris and Kathleen Freeman. **Director**—Lewis.

107 minutes

O

OBJECTIVE—BURMA (1945)
★★★

Errol Flynn
William Prince

A lively World War II adventure with Flynn leading American paratroopers against a Japanese radar station in Burma. It's somewhat drawn out, but there's plenty of exciting action and vivid combat scenes. Also with James Brown, George Tobias, Henry Hull, and Warner Anderson. **Director**—Raoul Walsh. **Academy Award Nomination**—Alvah Bessie, writing (original story). *142 minutes b&w*

OBSESSION (1976)
★★

Cliff Robertson
Geneviève Bujold

Director Brian De Palma's psychological mystery owes much to *Vertigo* in story and style, but it lacks the clarity and crispness of the Alfred Hitchcock classic. Screenwriter Paul Schrader leaves loose ends dangling everywhere. Yet there is adequate suspense

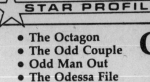

Geneviève Bujold and Cliff Robertson star in the mystery Obsession.

and ample atmosphere in this story of a young New Orleans businessman who agonizes over the kidnapping and then the deaths of his wife and daughter. Vivid performances by Robertson and Bujold, and an over-powering score by Bernard Herrmann. Also with John Lithgow, Sylvia Kuumba Williams, and Wanda Blackman. (PG)   98 minutes

THE OCTAGON (1980)
★★

Chuck Norris

Kung fu whiz Norris comes out of retirement to put down a cult of inter-national terrorists. Chop-socky fans won't be disappointed by the flashy finale when Norris dispatches a small army of bad guys in a blaze of martial-arts action. But for most of the movie, the audience will have to suffer through a complicated plot and boring dialogue that's akin to the Chinese water torture. This action exploitation film would have worked better with more chop-chop and less talk-talk. Director—Eric Karson. (R)
103 minutes

THE ODD COUPLE (1968)
★★★★

Jack Lemmon
Walter Matthau

The excellent pairing of Lemmon and Matthau in this Neil Simon comedy adds up to loads of laughter. The two play recently divorced characters— one meticulous and the other messy— who become roommates and quickly drive each other up the wall because of

their contrasting habits. Simon's screenplay, developed from his Broad-way play, offers plenty of reliable comic material for the duo to chew on. Also with John Fiedler, Herb Edel-man, Monica Evans, and Carole Shel-ley. **Director**—Gene Saks. (G) **Academy Award Nomination**—Simon, best screenplay (based on material from another medium).
105 minutes

ODD MAN OUT (1946)
★★★★

James Mason
Robert Newton

Searing drama about a wounded Irish rebel and his desperate struggle to avoid capture following a daring hold-up in Belfast. The amazingly sus-penseful story is assembled with expert skill and vivid detail; an unforgettable man-on-the-run movie. Excellent performances by Mason, Newton, Kathleen Ryan, and Dan O'Herlihy. **Director**—Carol Reed. **Alternate title**—*Gang War.*
115 minutes b&w

THE ODESSA FILE (1974)
★★

Jon Voight
Maria Schell
Maximilian Schell

Voight does a convincing job portray-ing an eager German journalist who tracks down a Nazi war criminal. The screenplay is heavy-going and cum-bersome, and the film eventually bogs down, although a few scenes stand out. It's a so-so screen adaptation of Frederick Forsyth's suspenseful novel. Maximilian Schell's portrayal as the sinister SS officer is interesting. Also with Mary Tamm, Derek Jacobi, and Noel Willman. **Director**—Ronald Neame. (PG)   129 minutes

DUSTIN HOFFMAN

Dustin Hoffman was born in Los Angeles in 1937 and grew up in Hollywood, where his father was, at one time, a set dresser. Named after the screen cowboy Dustin Farnum (Dustin's brother is named after Ronald Colman), Hoffman didn't consider acting as a career until his college days when he enrolled in the Pasadena Playhouse.

Hoffman made his acting debut in a college production of Gertrude Stein's Yes Is for a Very Young Man; *he appeared on Broadway for the first time with a walk-on part in* A Cook for Mr. General. *He joined the Theater Company of Boston for one season before returning to New York to work as director Ulu Grosbard's assistant on* A View From the Bridge.

Off-Broadway, Hoffman appeared in Harry, Noon and Night; Journey of the Fifth Horse, *for which he won an Obie award; and* Eh?, *for which he was honored with the Drama Desk, Vernon Rice, and Theater World awards as well as an invitation from Mike Nichols to test for the film* The Graduate *(1967). Hoffman got the title role and his performance earned him unanimous critical acclaim and his first Academy Award nomination.*

Hoffman then returned to New York to co-star with Jon Voight in Midnight Cowboy *(1969) for director John Schlesinger; he was nominated for his second Oscar. Hoffman got his third Academy Award nomination for* Lenny *(1974).*

On Broadway, Hoffman appeared in Jimmy Shine, *and he directed Murray Schisgal's farce,* All Over Town.

His other movies include John and Mary *(1969) opposite Mia Farrow,* Who is Harry Kellerman and Why Is He Saying Those Terrible Things About Me? *(1971),* Sam Peckinpah's Straw Dogs *(1972),* All the President's Men *(1976),* Marathon Man *(1976), and* Kramer vs. Kramer *(1979), for which he finally won an Oscar as best actor.*

ODE TO BILLY JOE (1976)
★★

Robby Benson
Glynis O'Connor

Bobbie Gentry's successful 1967 ballad has been transposed to a dreamy and romantic film drama. This story of puppy love and tragedy in Mississippi in 1953 fumbles and plods under the direction of Max Baer; there are just too many contradictions. Only a first-rate performance by O'Connor as a 15-year-old Juliet keeps the film above water. There are some appealing glimpses of Southern family life. Benson stars in the title role. Also with Joan Hotchkiss, Sandy McPeak, and James Best. (PG) *108 minutes*

OF HUMAN BONDAGE (1964)
★★

Laurence Harvey
Kim Novak

Harvey and Novak are unfortunately miscast in this third film version of the classic W. Somerset Maugham story of a doctor's tragic affair with a waitress. The overall production is a disappointment and doesn't do justice to Maugham's novel. The 1934 version, with Bette Davis and Leslie Howard, was better. Co-stars Nanette Newman, Roger Livesey, and Robert Morley. **Director**—Ken Hughes.

105 minutes b&w

OF MICE AND MEN (1939)
★★★★

Burgess Meredith
Lon Chaney, Jr.

Masterful filming of John Steinbeck's tragic tale of a migrant worker who protects his mentally retarded yet physically strong brother. Persuasively told and presented with much sensitivity. Chaney is excellent as Lenny, the feebleminded young man, and Meredith is outstanding as the dedicated brother. Also with Betty Field, Charles Bickford, and Noah Beery, Jr. **Director**—Lewis Milestone. **Academy Award Nomination**—best picture.

107 minutes b&w

OH, GOD! (1977)
★★★

George Burns
John Denver

A schmaltzy, entertaining, middlebrow comedy about a supermarket manager who is chosen by God to be a latter-day Moses. Denver, exuding his apple-pie good nature, debuts as the astonished storekeeper, and does justice to the part. Burns plays the Almighty, and—well—he's George Burns. Carl Reiner's direction has the proper control. Also with Teri Garr, Paul Sorvino, George Furth, and Ralph Bellamy. (PG) **Academy Award Nomination**—Larry Gelbart, best screenplay adaptation. *104 minutes*

OH GOD! BOOK II (1980)
★★

George Burns
Suzanne Pleshette
David Birney
Louanne

Burns returns as the Almighty in this movie sequel, spreading his gospel via one-liners. John Denver, who clicked smartly with Burns in the first film, is replaced by Louanne—a cute kid—to help deliver God's message. Although she and some of her playmates exude innocent charm, the script is stale, and most of the gags are rather familiar. Pleshette and Birney star as Louanne's estranged parents, who finally reconcile, thank God. **Director**—Gilbert Cates. (PG) *94 minutes*

Betty Field and Burgess Meredith in Of Mice and Men, *based on Steinbeck's tragic tale.*

OH HEAVENLY DOG (1980)
★

Chevy Chase
Jane Seymour

Chevy Chase, Jane Seymour, and Benji star in Oh Heavenly Dog.

Benji, the cute pooch and delight of children, tracks down a killer in London in his third feature film. But this time, director Joe Camp aims at an older audience by throwing in some sexual innuendoes and a bit of mild profanity. The flea-bitten plot, which leans on *Heaven Can Wait*, casts Chase as a gumshoe; Benji is his reincarnation. The result is scenes like Benji—with the mind of Chevy—jumping with glee into the bubble bath of an attractive magazine writer, played by Seymour. (PG) *103 minutes*

OH! WHAT A LOVELY WAR (1969)
★★★

Laurence Olivier
John Gielgud
Ralph Richardson
Michael Redgrave

Uneven yet inspired antiwar movie, set to music and presented as vignettes of events in World War I. Many of the musical sketches are impressive, but there are many slow moments as well. The satire of man's fascination with war has sufficient bite. The large all-star cast of British players also includes Jack Hawkins, John Mills, Kenneth More, Susannah York, Dirk Bogarde, and Venessa Redgrave. **Director**—Richard Attenborough. (G)

144 minutes

● Oklahoma!
● Oklahoma Crude
● Old Boyfriends
● Old Dracula
● The Old Man and the Sea
● Old Yeller

O

OKLAHOMA! (1955)
★★★

**Gordon MacRae
Shirley Jones
Rod Steiger**

Appealing family entertainment in the form of Rodgers and Hammerstein's fanciful musical about the love affair between a cowboy and a country girl. The memorable hit songs that captivated Broadway come across on the screen with gusto, and the colorful sets help maintain the pleasant mood. MacRae and Jones are ideally cast in the key roles, and they do justice to such numbers as "Oh, What a Beautiful Morning" and "People Will Say We're In Love." Also with Gloria Grahame, Charlotte Greenwood, James Whitmore, and Eddie Albert. **Director**—Fred Zinnemann.

143 minutes

OKLAHOMA CRUDE (1973)
★★★

**Faye Dunaway
George C. Scott**

This typical story about independent small-time operators up against big, impersonal business interests is quite entertaining. Dunaway portrays a gritty, hard-driving oil well owner in the early 1900s, desperately trying to hang on to her claim in the face of ruthless pressure from a giant petroleum company. Faye is impressive, and she gets good support from Scott, a drifter who comes to her aid. Jack Palance is convincing as the sinister company representative trying to drive Faye off her land. Also with John Mills and Woodrow Parfrey. **Director**—Stanley Kramer. (PG)

108 minutes

OLD BOYFRIENDS (1979)
★★

Talia Shire

Joan Tewkesbury, who wrote Robert Altman's *Nashville*, tries her hand at directing this ambitious film and achieves only middling results. It's about a young woman, played by Shire, who tracks down old boyfriends

Gloria Grahame and Eddie Albert watch a friendly couple in the musical Oklahoma!

in an effort to get her head together. Some appealing moments—especially Buck Henry as a private eye with a roving eye for his beautiful secretary. But most of the story is unclear because of a weak and wobbly script. Richard Jordan, Keith Carradine, John Belushi, and John Houseman also star. (R)

103 minutes

Talia Shire meets Keith Carradine in this scene from Old Boyfriends.

OLD DRACULA (1976)
★

**David Niven
Teresa Graves**

The charming Niven plays a modern Count Dracula who conducts tours through his horror castle and judges finalists in a *Playboy* magazine beauty contest. It's billed as a comedy, but there's no true focus on the humor; the film quickly becomes tedious and silly. Graves, of the TV series *Get Christy Love*, plays Dracula's wife,

Vampira. She's brought back to life after being on ice for the last 50 years because of an overdose of anemic blood. Also with Peter Bayliss and Linda Hayden. **Director**—Clive Donner. (PG)

89 minutes

THE OLD MAN AND THE SEA
(1958)
★★★

Spencer Tracy

Tracy, who gives this Ernest Hemingway tale his best, plays the aging fisherman braving rough seas in hope of catching a big fish. This one-character adventure isn't readily adaptable to the screen, but all hands try hard to sustain interest. Tracy's performance is really the main reason for seeing the film. Felipe Pazos and Harry Bellaver also star. **Director**—John Sturges. **Academy Award Nominations**—Tracy, best actor; James Wong Howe, cinematography (color).

89 minutes

OLD YELLER (1957)
★★★

**Dorothy McGuire
Fess Parker
Tommy Kirk**

Typical sentimental boy-and-his-dog movie from Walt Disney. Kirk plays a

(Continued)

O
- Oliver!
- Oliver's Story
- Oliver Twist
- The Omen
- On a Clear Day You Can See Forever
- Once in Paris

(Continued)

Texas farm boy in the mid-1800s who befriends a stalwart mongrel hound, and they become involved in numerous adventures. It's based on Fred Gipson's novel. Excellent family fare and almost a classic by now. McGuire and Parker play the hearty parents. Also with Kevin Corcoran and Chuck Connors. **Director**—Robert Stevenson. (G)   *83 minutes*

OLIVER! (1968)
★★★★

Ron Moody
Oliver Reed
Mark Lester

Mark Lester (Oliver) and Jack Wild in the successful musical Oliver!

A first-class musical based on Dickens's *Oliver Twist* and expertly adapted from the Broadway hit. The colorful production abounds with atmospheric setting, invigorating choreography, and memorable tunes by Lionel Bart. Child-star Lester is exceptionally good in the title role, as the young orphan who becomes involved with a group of thieves led by the unsavory Fagin, played by Moody. Songs include "Consider Yourself" and "As Long as He Needs Me." Top supporting work by Reed, Shani Wallis, and Jack Wild. **Director**—Reed. (G) **Academy Awards**—best picture; Reed, best director. **Nominations**—Wild, best supporting actor; Vernon Harris, best screenplay (based on material from another medium); Oswald Morris, cinematography.
                146 minutes

OLIVER'S STORY (1978)
★

Ryan O'Neal
Candice Bergen

Oliver, played by O'Neal, is numbed by the death of his young wife, and takes out his frustration by numbing the audience in this sequel to Eric Segal's *Love Story*. Oliver is now approaching middle age. He meets a rich girl, played by Bergen, but the romance soon falls apart. The movie is rather gloomy and far from the romantic mood of the first film. Also with Nicola Pagett, Edward Binns, and Ray Milland. **Director**—John Korty. (PG)   *92 minutes*

OLIVER TWIST (1948)
★★★★

Alec Guinness
Robert Newton
Francis L. Sullivan
Kay Walsh

This straight version of Charles Dickens's classic story is expertly done in all departments. Guinness perfectly portrays Fagin, the scoundrel who recruits the innocent orphan Oliver into a life of street crime. David Lean's direction is consistently on target, and he keeps the story moving along without a hitch. Excellent supporting performances all around. Also with John Howard Davies, Anthony Newley, Henry Stephenson, and Diana Dors.
                116 minutes b&w

THE OMEN (1976)
★★

Gregory Peck
Lee Remick

Peck and Remick unwittingly rear the son of Satan in this brutal and blood-obsessed horror film. The diabolical plot is implausible, but there are plenty of gory scare tactics to maintain tension and interest throughout. The entire effort, it seems, isn't to offer a meaningful story, but to bring on the shock effects—creepy graveyards, mysterious hangings, attacks by mad dogs, howling baboons. The cast performs well, and Richard Donner's direction is slick. Also with David Warner, Billie Whitelaw, and Leo McKern. (PG)   *111 minutes*

ON A CLEAR DAY YOU CAN SEE FOREVER (1970)
★★★

Barbra Streisand
Yves Montand

Yves Montand and Barbra Streisand in On a Clear Day You Can See Forever.

Streisand is outstanding in this vibrant musical; she plays a young woman who relives the past after undergoing hypnotic sessions from a psychiatrist, played by Montand. The production isn't as invigorating as the Broadway show, yet there are numerous good moments and outstanding settings that maintain consistent interest. The music by Alan Jay Lerner and Burton Lane is pretty much intact; memorable songs include "He Wasn't You" and "Come Back to Me." Vincente Minnelli's direction is among his best. There's fine support from Bob Newhart, Jack Nicholson, Larry Blyden, and Simon Oakland. (G)   *129 minutes*

ONCE IN PARIS (1978)
★★

Wayne Rogers
Gayle Hunnicutt
Jack Lenoir

A good-natured but sluggish little movie about an American screenwriter (Rogers) who goes to Paris on a short assignment. He becomes involved with a colorful French chauffeur (Lenoir) and an attractive English woman (Hunnicutt). Rogers, Hunnicutt, and Lenoir turn on the charm, but this romantic outing never really gets into high gear. Also with Clement Harari, Tanya Lopert, and Doris Roberts. Frank D. Gilroy wrote,

- Once Is Not Enough
- Once More, With Feeling
- The One and Only
- One-Eyed Jacks
- One Flew Over the Cuckoo's Nest
- One Foot in Heaven

O

directed, and produced. (No MPAA rating) *100 minutes*

ONCE IS NOT ENOUGH (1975)
★

Kirk Douglas
Alexis Smith

A movie based on Jacqueline Susann's sexual, psychological best-seller, about the Hollywood, New York, and Spain jet set. The performances are mediocre; the screenplay is ludicrous and boring. Also with David Janssen, Deborah Raffin, George Hamilton, Melina Mercouri, and Brenda Vaccaro. **Director**—Guy Green. (R) **Academy Award Nomination**—Vaccaro, best supporting actress. *121 minutes*

ONCE MORE, WITH FEELING (1960)
★★★

Yul Brynner
Kay Kendall

Brynner and Kendall battle one another as husband and wife in this scrappy upper-crust comedy of marital blitz. Brynner is commanding as a tyrannical symphony orchestra conductor who seems to have more control with his musicians than he does with his gorgeous wife, who wants out of the marriage. Kendall handles her part with skill and charm. Also with Geoffrey Toone, Maxwell Shaw, and Mervyn Johns. **Director**—Stanley Donen. *92 minutes*

THE ONE AND ONLY (1978)
★★★★

Henry Winkler
Kim Darby

Winkler is hilarious as a brassy show-off who fails to make it as a Broadway actor, but makes it big in the carnival world of professional wrestling. The story line of this fine film, directed by Carl Reiner, has a sweet upbeat flavor and a satisfying happy ending. Darby as Winkler's enduring wife, Herve Villechaize as a lascivious midget wrestler, and Gene Saks as a cynical promotor add warm and funny moments. Also with William Daniels and Polly Holiday. (PG) *98 minutes*

In One Flew Over the Cuckoo's Nest, *Jack Nicholson (center) fights the system.*

ONE-EYED JACKS (1961)
★★★

Marlon Brando
Karl Malden

Brando directed and stars in this tough western as an outlaw determined to settle a score with a buddy who was responsible for his imprisonment. Good character study and vivid detail, but Brando goes overboard with his acting and with the length of the film. Malden is convincing as the bandit's erstwhile friend turned sheriff. Also with Katy Jurado, Pina Pellicier, Slim Pickens, Ben Johnson, and Elisha Cook, Jr. **Academy Award Nomination**—Charles Lang, Jr., cinematography (color). *141 minutes*

ONE FLEW OVER THE CUCKOO'S NEST (1975)
★★★★

Jack Nicholson
Louise Fletcher

Ken Kesey's 1962 novel of rebellious insane asylum patients is faithfully reproduced in director Milos Forman's stylish and moving film. Nicholson was practically born to play the role of fast-talking R. P. McMurphy, the free-spirited fighter of the system. He's supported by excellent performances from Fletcher—a nurse—William Redfield, and Will Sampson. Dale Wasserman's off-Broadway version of this comedy-melodrama was popular among the young, mainly because of its antiestablishment theme. Also with Brad Dourif and Christopher Lloyd. (R) **Academy Awards**—best picture; Nicholson, best actor; Fletcher, best actress; Forman, best director. **Nominations**—Dourif, best supporting actor; Laurence Hauben and Bo Goldman, best screenplay (adapted from another medium); Haskell Wexler and Bill Butler, cinematography (color). *129 minutes*

ONE FOOT IN HEAVEN (1941)
★★★★

Fredric March
Martha Scott

A moving and charming story of a small-town minister and his wife trying to cope with fast-changing attitudes in America. Solid acting by March as the clergyman carries the film along despite an uncohesive plot. Scott is also good as his ever-faithful wife. A warmhearted, well-handled movie. Co-stars Beulah Bondi, Gene Lockhart, Elizabeth Fraser, and Harry Davenport. **Director**—Irving Rapper. **Academy Award Nomination**—best picture. *108 minutes b&w*

O

- One on One
- One Sings, the Other Doesn't
- One Touch of Venus
- One-Trick Pony
- One, Two, Three
- On Golden Pond
- On Her Majesty's Secret Service

ONE ON ONE (1977)
★★★

**Robby Benson
Annette O'Toole**

Robby Benson stars in One on One, *a movie about big-time college basketball.*

An engaging little movie about big-time college basketball, following the upbeat style of *Rocky*. Benson, who co-wrote the script with Jerry Segal, is fine as a naïve small-town basketball player who bucks a sadistic coach and finally triumphs on the college courts. The story is a strong statement against the over-commercialized world of college athletics. Effective performances, too, from G. D. Spradlin as the coach and O'Toole as Benson's romantic interest. Also with Gail Strickland and Melanie Griffith. **Director**—Lamont Johnson. (PG)   *98 minutes*

ONE SINGS, THE OTHER DOESN'T (1977)
★★

**Thérèse Liotard
Valerie Mairesse**

Director Agnes Varda's polemical movie is a cheery celebration of sisterhood. Some nice moments and appealing performances by Liotard and Mairesse, but the film is more of a simplistic social comment than entertainment. The drama recounts the lasting friendship of two young women as they seek to achieve personal liberation. In French with English titles. (No MPAA rating)   *120 minutes*

ONE TOUCH OF VENUS (1948)
★★★

**Ava Gardner
Robert Walker**

Pleasant and inventive romantic comedy about a statue of Venus that comes to life in a swank department store and becomes the love interest of a young employee. Gardner is exceptional as the beautiful Venus with arms, and she sings "Speak Low" with passion. Walker plays the employee. Based on the Broadway play by S. J. Perelman. Also stars Eve Arden, Dick Haymes, Olga San Juan, and Tom Conway. **Director**—William A. Seiter.   *82 minutes b&w*

ONE-TRICK PONY (1980)
★★

**Paul Simon
Blair Brown**

Simon, one of the singing sensations of the '60s, wrote and stars in this personal story of a popular musician beset by fading career and family problems. Simon is front and center throughout, and his music and lyrics continually accompany the film. In fact, the music is often more appealing than the laid-back dialogue or the colorless plot. Simon provides detailed glimpses of the music industry, but he doesn't allow for very much excitement. Also with Rip Torn. **Director**—Robert M. Young. (R)   *98 minutes*

ONE, TWO, THREE (1961)
★★★★

James Cagney

Smart, fast-paced Billy Wilder comedy set in West Berlin during the cold war. Cagney churns up a lot of laughs as a Coca-Cola executive trying to sell his product to the communists. The invigorating plot offers nonstop satire heavily laced with clever one-liners. André Previn's music adds to the sophisticated mood. Also stars Horst Buchholz, Arlene Francis, Pamela Tiffin, Red Buttons, and Lilo Pulver. **Academy Award Nomination**—Daniel L. Fapp, cinematography (black and white).   *115 minutes b&w*

ON GOLDEN POND (1981)
★★★

**Henry Fonda
Katharine Hepburn
Jane Fonda**

Henry Fonda and Katharine Hepburn are an elderly couple in On Golden Pond.

The main reason to see this sentimental drama is the magnificent casting of Henry Fonda and Katharine Hepburn as an elderly couple trying to enjoy perhaps their last summer together while embroiled as usual in family conflicts. Some shortcomings are a stagey atmosphere and a limited plot, yet Henry expertly breathes life into this intelligent story that combines pathos and the proper touch of humor. He's never been better in the role of the crotchety professor with obvious vulnerability. Jane Fonda is outstanding as the resentful daughter. **Director**—Mark Rydell. (PG)

109 minutes

ON HER MAJESTY'S SECRET SERVICE (1969)
★★★

**George Lazenby
Diana Rigg
Telly Savalas**

Lazenby substitutes for Sean Connery in this sixth James Bond adventure, and he's marginally competent. But don't despair; this movie is liberally salted with loads of exciting action, tongue-in-cheek humor, and gorgeous women to keep you comfortably in Bondage. As expected, Ian Fleming's hero saves mankind, this time from scoundrels threatening to unleash a deadly virus. Agent 007 travels to breathtaking Switzerland for his assignment and encounters the bad guys, led by Savalas, on the snowy

- The Onion Field
- Only Two Can Play
- Only When I Laugh
- On Moonlight Bay
- On the Beach
- On the Double
- On the Nickel

O

slopes, with thrilling chases on skis. Rigg plays a Spanish contessa. Also with Ilse Steppat, Gabriele Ferzetti, Bernard Lee, and Lois Maxwell. **Director**—Peter Hunt. (PG)   *140 minutes*

THE ONION FIELD (1979)
★★

John Savage
James Woods

This true story, about the abduction of two policeman and the murder of one of them by a couple of hoods, is based on a book by Joseph Wambaugh, who also wrote the screenplay. Decent acting and authentic atmosphere are the major virtues of a potentially absorbing portrayal of social, psychological, and moral development. But, unfortunately, the script is long and repetitious, and the direction is painfully slow. Also with Franklyn Seales, Ronny Cox, Ted Danson, and Diane Hull. **Director**—Harold Becker. (R)
122 minutes

John Savage is forced to give up his weapon in the dramatic film The Onion Field.

ONLY TWO CAN PLAY (1962)
★★★★

Peter Sellers
Mai Zetterling

Sellers is at his comic best in this lively adult comedy featuring several outstanding scenes. Sellers portrays an assistant librarian in a Welsh town, supposedly devoted to his wife. But he attempts an extramarital fling with a wealthy woman, and his bumbling efforts at love-making lead to many laughs. Zetterling is a riot as the desirable society woman. Also with Virginia Maskell, Richard Attenborough, Raymond Huntley, and Kenneth Grif-

fith. **Director**—Sidney Gilliat.
106 minutes b&w

ONLY WHEN I LAUGH (1981)
★★

Marsha Mason
Kristy McNichol

Neil Simon reworks his play *The Gingerbread Lady* as a screen comedy-drama; it's about a reformed alcoholic Broadway actress trying to reestablish her career and improve the relationship with her teenage daughter. Mason plays the actress, and McNichol is her daughter. Mason is excellent, but she's working with soap-opera material with some bittersweet comedy tossed in. It's sort of an insider show-biz story, and it lacks Simon's usual droll humor. James Coco and Joan Hackett do well in supporting roles. **Director**—Glenn Jordan. (R)   *120 minutes*

ON MOONLIGHT BAY (1951)
★★★

Doris Day
Gordon MacRae

A syrupy musical, competently made and ideally suited for the wholesome talents of Day and MacRae, who play sweethearts in Indiana. The nostalgic story, based on Booth Tarkington's novel, is set just before World War I. It's a lighthearted family tale, mixing drama, music, and comedy. Also stars Leon Ames, Rosemary De Camp, and Billy Gray. **Director**—Roy Del Ruth.
95 minutes

ON THE BEACH (1959)
★★★

Gregory Peck
Ava Gardner
Fred Astaire
Anthony Perkins

Intelligent, thought-provoking account of survivors of a nuclear attack awaiting their fate in Australia. The film is enhanced by top performances from Peck and Gardner, and convincing supporting roles by Astaire and Perkins. It's a grim subject, yet it presents a searing comment on atomic

In Only When I Laugh, Marsha Mason and Kristy McNichol *play mother and daughter.*

warfare and what could be the end of the world. Based faithfully on the novel by Nevil Shute. Also with Donna Anderson, John Tate, and Lola Brooks. **Director**—Stanley Kramer.
134 minutes b&w

ON THE DOUBLE (1961)
★★

Danny Kaye

Rather typical vehicle for Kaye, who plays a private impersonating a high-ranking British officer during World War II because of their resemblance to each other. The dowdy script limits some of Kaye's comedic opportunities, but he has a good time with several funny scenes. Others in the cast are Dana Wynter, Wilfrid Hyde-White, Margaret Rutherford, Diana Dors, and Jesse White. **Director**—Melville Shavelson.
92 minutes

ON THE NICKEL (1980)
★★

Donald Moffat

Ralph Waite (TV's Daddy Walton) wrote, directed, and acts in this sympathetic but rambling semidocumentary of life on skid row in Los Angeles. The slim story mainly concerns the special friendships among the wretched souls who congregate in this subculture by choice. The actors, mostly from New York's off-Broadway circuit, are fine—especially Moffat as an ex-drunk who returns to this sordid environment to save a dying friend. Also with Penelope Allen and James Gammon. (R)
96 minutes

ON THE RIGHT TRACK (1981)
★★

Gary Coleman

Gary Coleman portrays an orphan who lives in a train station in On the Right Track.

TV child-star Coleman makes his film debut in this innocuous comedy about a shoeshine boy whose home is a locker in Chicago's Union Station. Coleman is predictably adorable as a pint-sized con man who can predict the outcome of horse races. The script is adequately pleasing with its required romantic interludes, but this sort of stuff is familiar enough in countless TV sitcoms. Also with Michael Lembeck, Lisa Eilbacher, and Maureen Stapleton. **Director**—Lee Philips. (PG)   *97 minutes*

ON THE TOWN (1949)
★★★★

Gene Kelly
Frank Sinatra
Jules Munshin

Betty Garrett, Frank Sinatra, Ann Miller, Jules Munshin, Vera-Ellen, and Gene Kelly in the toe-tapping musical On the Town.

Energetic, toe-tapping musical that's among the best of its kind. Three sailors—Kelly, Sinatra, and Munshin—make the most of their 24-hour liberty in New York City. Kelly and Sinatra head the exuberant cast, dancing and singing all over town, with lively choreography designed by Kelly and tuneful songs from the hit Broadway show by Leonard Bernstein, Betty Comden, and Adolf Green. Effective moments of comedy enhance the proceedings. Excellent supporting work by Munshin, Vera-Ellen, Betty Garrett, Ann Miller, and Alice Pearce. **Directors**—Kelly and Stanley Donen.
98 minutes

ON THE WATERFRONT (1954)
★★★★

Marlon Brando
Eva Marie Saint
Lee J. Cobb

Marlon Brando and Eva Marie Saint in the powerful drama On the Waterfront.

Stark, powerful drama about corruption and despair among New York City longshoremen, brilliantly conceived and capped with a terrific performance by Brando. His portrayal of the young stevedore who bravely exposes the criminals who control the waterfront union is among the best of his distinguished career. Saint plays the girl he loves, and Cobb is Brando's waterfront boss. The pacing, the brooding atmosphere, and the intelligent dialogue are all consistently good. Excellent supporting performances by Rod Steiger, Karl Malden, Pat Henning, and Leif Erickson. **Director**—Elia Kazan. **Academy Awards**—best picture; Kazan, best director; Brando, best actor; Saint, best supporting actress; Budd Schulberg, writing (story and screenplay); Boris Kaufman, cinematography (black and white). **Nominations**—Cobb, Malden, Steiger, best supporting actor.
108 minutes b&w

ON THE YARD (1979)
★★

John Heard
Thomas Waites
Mike Kellin

Day-to-day prison life is rather routine and so is this film, directed by Raphael D. Silver. It's about a power struggle among inmates. Convict Heard makes a mistake when he runs afoul of inmate chieftain Waites. Silver avoids the usual clichés of familiar big-house movies, but he also neglects drama and emotion. It needs a little bit of Cagney, a dash of Bogart—or something. It's nicely acted, though, by Waites, Heard, and Kellin. The screenplay is based on a novel by Malcolm Braly, a former San Quentin inmate. Also with Joe Grifasi, Richard Bright, and Lane Smith. (R)
102 minutes

OPERATION PETTICOAT (1959)
★★★

Cary Grant
Tony Curtis

A better-than-average comedy made even better by the charming talent of Grant as skipper of a submarine in the South Pacific during World War II desperately trying to reactivate his damaged boat. Plenty of hilarious misadventures take place, and things really perk up when a group of nurses come aboard. Curtis shines as an officer with many outrageous schemes for getting the sub seaworthy. Also stars Joan O'Brien, Dina Merrill, Gene Evans, Richard Sargent, and Arthur O'Connell. **Director**—Blake Edwards. **Academy Award Nomination**—Paul King and Joseph Stone (story), Stanley Shapiro and Maurice Richlin (screenplay), best story and screen-

- Operation Thunderbolt
- Orca
- Orchestra Rehearsal
- Orchestra Wives
- Ordinary People
- Oscar Wilde
- Othello
- The Other Side of Midnight

O

play (written directly for the screen). *124 minutes*

OPERATION THUNDERBOLT (1978)
★★

**Klaus Kinski
Assaf Dayan
Yehoram Gaon**

This Israeli-made film retells the events of the lightning commando raid on Entebbe, when 104 hijacked passengers were rescued. There are occasional moments of suspense—especially the daring action sequences at the Ugandan airport. But mostly, the film smacks of official government propaganda. The characters are uninteresting cardboard stereotypes. Perhaps the real-life episode that dominated the headlines that July day in 1976 is too thrilling to rehash for the screen. Also with Gila Almagor and Shai K. Ophir. **Director**—Menahem Golan. (No MPAA rating)
125 minutes

ORCA (1977)
★

Richard Harris

Harris plays a shark-hunting boat skipper who is stalked by a super-intellegent killer whale. The whales are the real stars of this film, mainly because they don't participate in the ridiculous human dialogue. This production is a blatant attempt to cash in on the *Jaws* theme, but the entire mess just sinks to the bottom of the sea. Charlotte Rampling, Will Sampson, Keenan Wynn, and Bo Derek are also on board. **Director**—Michael Anderson. (PG) *92 minutes*

ORCHESTRA REHEARSAL (1979)
★★

**Balduin Baas
Clara Colosimo
Elisabeth Labi**

Italian movie maestro Federico Fellini uses a rebellious symphony orchestra as a metaphor for the decline of Western civilization. The musicians revolt against their conductor and quarrel with one another until the conductor restores order by turning into a ranting dictator. Clever moments, but rather tiresome overall. Fellini's parable is a somewhat simplistic and unconvincing description of a complex subject. In Italian with English titles. (No MPAA rating) *70 minutes*

ORCHESTRA WIVES (1942)
★★★

**Glenn Miller
Ann Rutherford
George Montgomery**

Miller and his orchestra take the spotlight in this backstage story about the private lives of the musicians and their spouses. The plot sustains adequate interest, but it's the wonderful swing music that keeps the film at a buoyant level. Miller and company belt out "I've Got a Gal in Kalamazoo," "Serenade in Blue," and more. Also with Lynn Bari, Jackie Gleason, Cesar Romero, and Carole Landis. **Director**—Archie Mayo. *97 minutes b&w*

ORDINARY PEOPLE (1980)
★★★

**Donald Sutherland
Mary Tyler Moore
Timothy Hutton**

Redford, first time out as director, fashions a moving, intelligent, but somber film about family conflict as seen through the eyes of a troubled teenage boy. Based on Judith Guest's best-selling novel, this powerful movie examines human behavior with extraordinary sensitivity. Yet the tone, at times, is soap opera, and Redford doesn't build much dramatic momentum. Moore, Sutherland, and Hutton are excellent as members of an ordi-

Mary Tyler Moore, Donald Sutherland, and Timothy Hutton in Ordinary People.

nary affluent family who have difficulty expressing love. Also with Judd Hirsh. (R) **Academy Awards**—best picture; Hutton, best supporting actor; Redford, best director; Alvin Sargent, best screenplay (adapted from another medium). **Nominations**—Hirsh, best supporting actor; Moore, best actress. *123 minutes*

OSCAR WILDE (1959)
★★★

Robert Morley

Adequate biography of the talented 19th-century playwright who was imprisoned on charges of being a sexual deviate. Morley, in the title role, repeats his stage portrayal and does a convincing job of conveying the complex personality. A similar account, *The Trials of Oscar Wilde*, was filmed about the same time, but this version is better. Also stars Ralph Richardson and John Neville. **Director**—Gregory Ratoff. *96 minutes b&w*

OTHELLO (1965)
★★★

Laurence Olivier

Magnificent screen version of Shakespeare's classic, with Olivier doing what comes naturally in repeating his brilliant stage portrayal. This production perhaps isn't as effective as other filmings of Shakespeare's dramas, but the performances are unexcelled. A worthwhile experience all the way in this virtually complete rendering of the great story of the Moor of Venice. Excellent supporting work from Frank Finlay, Joyce Redman, Maggie Smith, and Derek Jacobi. **Director**—Stuart Burge. **Academy Award Nominations**—Olivier, best actor; Finlay, best supporting actor; Redman, Smith, best supporting actress. *166 minutes*

THE OTHER SIDE OF MIDNIGHT (1977)
★★

**Marie-France Pisier
John Beck**

This slick adaptation of Sidney Sheldon's best-selling novel is a complex
(Continued)

O
- The Other Side of the Mountain
- The Other Side of the Mountain Part 2
- Our Hearts Were Young and Gay
- Our Man in Havana
- Our Town
- Our Winning Season
- Outland

John Beck and Marie-France Pisier await sentencing in The Other Side of Midnight.

(Continued)

soap opera dripping with just about every movie cliché. Pisier plays a poor French girl who finally becomes wealthy and famous and tries to get revenge on a dashing American cad, played by Beck, who abandoned her after a brief wartime romance. The corny plot spans some eight years and jumps between Europe and the United States. The title may have something to do with the film's length. Also with Susan Sarandon and Raf Vallone. **Director**—Charles Jarrott. (R)

165 minutes

THE OTHER SIDE OF THE MOUNTAIN (1975)
★★

Marilyn Hassett
Beau Bridges

Hassett and Bridges star in this so-so tearjerker about Jill Kinmont, a promising young skier who was critically injured in 1956 while competing for the U.S. Olympic team. There are a few genuinely touching moments, but most of it is formula movie-making, leaning on the *Love Story* theme. Bring plenty of handkerchiefs. Also with Belinda Montgomery, Nan Martin, and William Bryant. **Director**—Larry Peerce. (PG) *101 minutes*

THE OTHER SIDE OF THE MOUNTAIN PART 2 (1978)
★★

Marilyn Hassett
Timothy Bottoms

Part I told the tragic and true story of skier Jill Kinmont, who was crippled as the result of a downhill accident. Hassett is effective again as Jill in the second installment of this formula weepie, which has our heroine in love with a truck driver, played by Bottoms. The script, however, begs for interesting story angles. Director Larry Peerce manages to wring plenty of tears from moviegoers in the mood for a good cry. Also with Nan Martin, Belinda Montgomery, Gretchen Corbett, and William Bryant. (PG)

100 minutes

OUR HEARTS WERE YOUNG AND GAY (1944)
★★★

Gail Russell
Diana Lynn

An appealing piece of adolescent froth about two young women—Russell and Lynn—who, in 1923, travel to Paris where they have some romantic adventures. Not very deep, but a pleasant and scrubbed minor comedy, based on the book by Cornelia Otis Skinner. Also with Charles Ruggles, Dorothy Gish, Beulah Bondi, and James Brown. **Director**—Lewis Allen.

81 minutes b&w

OUR MAN IN HAVANA (1960)
★★★

Alec Guinness
Noel Coward

Guinness stars as the owner of a vacuum cleaner shop in pre-Castro Cuba. He's recruited by British intelligence agent Coward to spy for England. The blend of satire and drama works well, and the steamy setting of tropical Havana provides a good atmospheric mood. The script is based on Graham Greene's novel—not too faithfully, but it works well nonetheless. Ernie Kovacs is good as a skeptical Cuban police chief. Adequate performances, too, from Burl Ives, Maureen O'Hara, Ralph Richardson, and Jo Morrow. **Director**—Carol Reed. *107 minutes b&w*

OUR TOWN (1940)
★★★★

Frank Craven
William Holden
Martha Scott

Thorton Wilder's classic story of life and love in a small New England com-munity at the turn of the century is brought to the screen with its earnest, heartfelt attributes finely displayed. An excellent production in all departments, with outstanding performances by a top cast. Also with Thomas Mitchell, Beulah Bondi, Guy Kibbee, and Fay Bainter. **Director**—Sam Wood. **Academy Award Nominations**—best picture; Scott, best actress.

90 minutes b&w

OUR WINNING SEASON (1978)
★

Scott Jacoby

Jacoby and a supporting cast of unknowns star in this pale imitation of *One on One*. Familiar high school scenes are highlighted—necking at the drive-in, hanging out at the hamburger joint—while the story about a young athlete who finally makes good goes nowhere. There are occasional glimpses of good acting, but characters are not developed to the point of caring about them. A loser. Also with Deborah Benson, Dennis Quaid, and Randy Herman. **Director**—Joseph Ruben. (PG) *92 minutes*

OUTLAND (1981)
★★★★

Sean Connery
Peter Boyle

Connery plays a federal marshal with principle and determination; he tries to crack a drug-smuggling ring at a remote mining camp on Jupiter's third moon. Boyle is the manager of the mine colony. This rousing and stunning space opera is a close cousin to *High Noon* with a dash of James Bond thrown in. The drama and suspense are enchanced magnificently by some

Sean Connery, playing a lawman, trails drug smugglers in the sci-fi film Outland.

★ STAR PROFILE

● The Outlaw   ● The Outlaw Josey Wales
● Outlaw Blues   ● The Out of Towners   O
                 ● Outrageous!

great special effects and sci-fi settings that detail the bleak, synthetic outer-space environment and the rigors of working there. Also with Francis Sternhagen. **Director**—Peter Hyams. (R)   *109 minutes*

THE OUTLAW (1943)
★★★

Jack Beutel
Jane Russell

The main attraction in this tongue-in-cheek western seems to be the bosom of a young Russell, who frequently bulges forth in a low-cut blouse. But all this hoopla aside, the episodes involving Billy the Kid and Doc Holliday pack some punch, and there are decent performances by gunslingers Beutel and Walter Huston, who scrap over a half-breed beauty, played by Russell. Also with Thomas Mitchell and Joe Sawyer. **Director**—Howard Hughes.   *126 minutes b&w*

OUTLAW BLUES (1977)
★★★

Peter Fonda

In Outlaw Blues, *Peter Fonda is an ex-con who does some singing and picking.*

Fonda plays an ex-con who tries some picking and singing in this country musical-adventure; he does both rather well. The lighthearted plot moves along smartly, generating ample laughs and smiles; even a few standard chase scenes are appealing.

STEVE McQUEEN

During the '60s and '70s, Steve McQueen was a top box-office attraction and one of the highest-paid actors in Hollywood. He usually portrayed tough, intense, and independent characters with a touch of sex appeal.

McQueen was born in Slater, Missouri, in 1930. Abandoned by his parents, he found his childhood and early adult life difficult. He spent several years in a reform school and three years in the Marines, including about a month in the brig for being AWOL. Before and after his military service, he held a variety of jobs, among them lumberjack, carnival barker, and bartender.

In 1952, McQueen went to drama school in New York and gained some experience in summer stock. A break came when he was chosen to replace Ben Gazzara on Broadway in A Hatful of Rain, *and he was soon off to Hollywood for bit parts in minor movies. His first film was* Somebody Up There Likes Me *in 1956.*

In 1958, McQueen landed the lead role in a sci-fi potboiler, The Blob, *and soon was tapped for the lead in the TV series* Wanted: Dead or Alive. *In 1963, his movie popularity became established after an effective performance in* The Great Escape.

Some of McQueen's other movies include The Magnificent Seven *(1960),* Soldier in the Rain *(1963),* Baby the Rain Must Fall *(1965),* Nevada Smith *(1966),* The Sand Pebbles *(1966),* Bullitt *(1968),* Papillon *(1973), and* The Towering Inferno *(1974).*

McQueen died in 1981.

Most of the performances and Richard Heffron's direction are easy-going, making this not-too-serious but energetic film palatable fare for country-western fans. Also stars Susan Saint James, John Crawford, and James Callahan. (PG)   *100 minutes*

THE OUTLAW JOSEY WALES (1976)
★★★

Clint Eastwood

There's a new corpse just about every other minute in this post-Civil War drama about vengeance. Despite the excess violence, there's an intriguing and grimly suspenseful story supported by professional performances. Eastwood plays the lean, cool, tobacco-chewing Josey Wales, who embarks on a long trail of revenge and self-preservation after marauding Union soldiers kill his wife and son. Eastwood is also the director, and he capably handles the action scenes in a no-nonsense manner. Chief Dan George, Sondra Locke, Bill McKinney, and John Vernon also star. (PG)   *135 minutes*

THE OUT OF TOWNERS (1970)
★★★

Jack Lemmon
Sandy Dennis

New York City is seen as a nightmare of mishaps in this spry Neil Simon comedy about an executive who comes to the Big Apple for a job interview. The comedy is rather patchy, but there are some fine moments, with Lemmon, as the uptight visitor from Ohio, involved in some hair-raising episodes. Dennis plays his wife. Also with Sandy Baron, Anne Meara, Billy Dee Wiliams, and Carlos Montalban. **Director**—Arthur Hiller. (G)
98 minutes

OUTRAGEOUS! (1977)
★★★

Craig Russell
Hollis McLaren

Likable, energetic, but somewhat flawed Canadian film about an odd-couple relationship between a female
(Continued)

253

O·P

- Over the Edge
- The Owl and the Pussycat
- The Ox-Bow Incident
- A Pain in the A—

- Paint Your Wagon
- The Pajama Game
- The Paleface

(Continued)

impersonator and a beautiful schizophrenic girl. There's a winning, touching performance by McLaren as the troubled young woman. Some of the highlights, though, are the witty impersonations of famous women entertainers by Russell, who plays the transvestite. The film is more offbeat than it is outrageous. Written and directed by Richard Benner. (R)

100 minutes

OVER THE EDGE (1982)
★★

Michael Kramer
Pamela Ludwig
Matt Dillon

This vivid account of rebellious middle-class youths holds some fascination, but it is routinely acted. The kids in the movie turn to vandalism and drugs because of the boring sterileness of their environment and the benign neglect of their well-fixed parents. Their situations may be secure, but life offers little challenge. At times, the film seems as undramatic as the youths' banal existence. **Director—**Jonathan Kaplan. (PG)   *95 minutes*

THE OWL AND THE PUSSYCAT (1970)
★★★

Barbra Streisand
George Segal

Streisand and Segal work well together and cook up some funny situations in this risqué comedy. She's a dopey prostitute, and he's a stuffy bookstore clerk. They become roommates when she's ousted from her apartment. This odd-couple theme is déjà vu, but there are enough fresh antics to uphold interest. Funky dialogue and bawdy situations abound. Also with Robert Klein, Roz Kelly, and Allen Garfield. **Director—**Herbert Ross. (R)   *96 minutes*

THE OX-BOW INCIDENT (1943)
★★★★

Henry Fonda
Dana Andrews

Powerful, realistically told western

Henry Fonda holds the rope as a mob deals with accused murderers in The Ox-Bow Incident.

about a mob that lynches three men for murder despite the pleas of others who cry out for reason and justice. Fonda plays a cowboy with a conscience. The film is a strong statement against mob justice, expertly done. Also with Anthony Quinn, Henry Morgan, Mary Beth Hughes, William Blythe, and Jane Darwell. **Director—**William Wellman. **Academy Award Nomination—**best picture.

75 minutes b&w

P

A PAIN IN THE A— (1975)
★★★

Jacques Brel
Lino Ventura

A bumbling, suicidal shirt salesman comically thwarts an assassin in an adjoining hotel room in an attempt to murder a government official. Top performances by Brel in the title role and Ventura as the exasperated hit man. In French with English titles. **Director—**Edouard Molinaro. (PG)

90 minutes

PAINT YOUR WAGON (1969)
★★

Lee Marvin
Clint Eastwood
Jean Seberg

Lavish but humdrum screen version of the Lerner and Loewe Broadway musical about a couple of gold rush prospectors in the 1800s married to the same woman. Marvin and Eastwood are the prospectors, and Seberg is their wife. The dancing is minimal,

and some of the songs are forgettable; but there are a few bright moments in the long production. This wagon, unfortunately, is overloaded. "They Call the Wind Mariah" is among the songs. Also with Harve Presnell and Ray Walston. **Director—**Joshua Logan. (PG)   *166 minutes*

THE PAJAMA GAME (1957)
★★★

Doris Day
John Raitt

Doris Day and the chorus sing one of the numbers in The Pajama Game.

A labor-management dispute in a pajama factory is the theme of this lively movie musical, nicely adapted from the Broadway production. Day, well cast as the head of the grievance committee, winds up in love with the factory manager, played by Raitt. The film hums along, with some good songs, like "Hey There, You With the Stars in Your Eyes," and a good deal of effective humor. The main point of the labor dispute is a 7½¢ pay raise, but they all deserve more than that for such a good job of acting, singing, and dancing. Also with Eddie Foy, Jr., Carol Heney, Reta Shaw, and Bob Fosse. **Directors—**George Abbott and Stanley Donen.   *101 minutes*

THE PALEFACE (1948)
★★★

Bob Hope
Jane Russell

Highly entertaining spoof of western films, with Hope cast as a bumbling

- Pal Joey
- The Palm Beach Story
- The Panic in Needle Park
- Panic in the Streets
- The Paper Chase
- Paper Moon
- Paper Tiger
- Papillon

P

frontier dentist who helps pistol-packing Calamity Jane, played by Russell, take on some bad guys. There's nothing pale about the gags; they come across with plenty of zing. The Oscar-winning song "Buttons and Bows" is featured. Also stars Robert Armstrong, Iris Adrian, Robert Watson, and Jack Searle. This production led to a sequel, *Son of Paleface*, and a remake, *The Shakiest Gun in the West*. **Director**—Norman Z. McLeod.

91 minutes

PAL JOEY (1957)
★★★

Frank Sinatra
Rita Hayworth
Kim Novak

Sinatra is right at home in this slick musical as a nightclub operator who vacillates between being a heel and a good guy. There are plenty of good Rodgers and Hart tunes for Frank to sing, including "My Funny Valentine" and "The Lady Is a Tramp." And there are adequate romantic opportunities, with Hayworth and Novak vying for Sinatra's attention. The film isn't quite as vibrant as the Broadway production, but it's good fun all the same. Other cast members are Bobby Sherwood, Hank Henry, and Barbara Nichols. **Director**—George Sidney.

109 minutes

THE PALM BEACH STORY
(1942)
★★★★

Claudette Colbert
Joel McCrea
Rudy Vallee
Mary Astor

A smart screwball comedy, abounding with delightful zaniness, touching moments, and colorful characters. Colbert plays the ambitious wife of an engineer; she runs off to the posh Florida city where she engages in a romance with a snobby millionaire, played by Vallee. McCrea plays Colbert's husband, and Astor is Vallee's sister. An inventive, well-made production offering hilarity galore. Also with William Demarest, Sig Arno, and Jack Norton. **Director**—Preston Sturges.

88 minutes b&w

THE PANIC IN NEEDLE PARK
(1971)
★★★

Al Pacino
Kitty Winn

Hard-hitting account of a small-time thief and his girl friend who become involved with heroin and hit the skids. Pacino is the thief, and Winn is his hooked mistress. The squalid atmosphere of Manhattan's upper West Side ghetto is skillfully portrayed, and the production is made even more vivid by Pacino's astounding debut film performance. The movie is sort of an echo of *Days of Wine and Roses*. Also with Adam Vint and Richard Bright. **Director**—Jerry Schatzberg. (PG)

110 minutes

PANIC IN THE STREETS (1950)
★★★★

Richard Widmark
Jack Palance

Tense story of efforts to locate a gangster who's carrying the plague. Suspense mounts effectively in this semidocumentary film, set with considerable realism on the docks of New Orleans. Widmark and Palance have first-class support from Zero Mostel, Paul Douglas, and Barbara Bel Geddes. **Director**—Elia Kazan. **Academy Award**—Edna and Edward Anhalt, writing (motion picture story).

96 minutes b&w

THE PAPER CHASE (1973)
★★★

Timothy Bottoms
Lindsay Wagner
John Houseman

A captivating and intense story of the agony and frustration of a graduate student trying to make it through Harvard Law School. His problems are compounded when he falls in love with the divorced daughter of a demanding and cynical law professor. Bottoms is the student, and Wagner is the woman. Most of the performances are outstanding, and there are some realistic moments of classroom tension and humiliation. Houseman is excep-

tionally convincing as the tyrannical law professor. Well-done supporting roles by Wagner and James Naughton. Also with Graham Beckel and Edward Herrmann. **Director**—James Bridges. (PG) **Academy Award**—Houseman, best supporting actor; James Bridges, best screenplay (based on material from another medium). *111 minutes*

PAPER MOON (1973)
★★★★

Ryan O'Neal
Tatum O'Neal

An appealing offbeat comedy set in mid-America in the '30s. The story works to perfection, thanks in part to the nifty pairing of Ryan O'Neal and his real-life daughter, Tatum, as a couple of Bible-selling con artists. The precocious and beguiling Tatum steals many a scene, and the film shines with much glossy sentimentality. Based on the novel *Addie Pray* by Joe David Brown. Co-stars Madeline Kahn, John Hillerman, and P. J. Johnson. **Director**—Peter Bogdanovich. (PG) **Academy Award**—Tatum O'Neal, best supporting actress. **Nominations**—Kahn, best supporting actress; Alvin Sargent, best screenplay (based on material from another medium).

103 minutes b&w

PAPER TIGER (1976)
★★

David Niven

Niven stars as a kindly English schoolmaster who daydreams of becoming a hero. He finally gets his chance when he and his pupil, the son of the Japanese Ambassador, are kidnapped by terrorists. Ando plays the pupil, and Toshiro Mifune plays his distraught father. The story, awash in sentiment, may have emotional appeal for some. The direction by Ken Annakin lacks style. (PG) *99 minutes*

PAPILLON (1973)
★★★

Steve McQueen
Dustin Hoffman

A tense, gut-wrenching tale of horrible
(Continued)

P
• Paradise Alley
• The Parallax View
• Pardon Mon Affaire
• The Parent Trap
• The Passage
• Pat and Mike
• A Patch of Blue

(Continued)

conditions at the infamous Devil's Island prison colony, and of the daring escape of a man who claims he was falsely convicted of murder. McQueen plays the title role. There are lots of graphic scenes depicting the brutality of prison life—filthy living conditions, sadistic guards, and homosexuality among the inmates. They make the yearning for escape extremely compelling, and you'll be cheering for success. Based on the book by Henri "Papillon" Charrière. Also with Victor Jory, Don Gordon, Anthony Zerbe, and Robert Deman. **Director**—Franklin J. Schaffner. (R) *150 minutes*

PARADISE ALLEY (1978)
★★★★

Sylvester Stallone

Sylvester Stallone berates a monkey for not dancing in Paradise Alley.

Stallone, who triumphed with *Rocky*, has another winner with this uplifting, powerful film about three brothers who fight their way out of New York's Hell's Kitchen shortly after World War II. Stallone, who stars as one of the brothers, debuts as director; he skillfully draws winning performances from many promising new actors. The film is brimful of warm characters and the smoky atmosphere of New York City in the '40s. Also with Armand Assante and Lee Canalito. (PG)
109 minutes

THE PARALLAX VIEW (1974)
★★★

Warren Beatty
Paula Prentiss

Beatty stars as a determined reporter who relentlessly investigates the intri-gue surrounding the assassination of a U.S. Senator. The gripping political thriller is executed with much style and skill by director Alan Pakula, who keeps the suspense pot boiling to the end. Many subtle references to the Kennedys. Also with William Daniels, Hume Cronyn, and Walter McGinn. (R) *102 minutes*

PARDON MON AFFAIRE (1977)
★★

Jean Rochefort

French comedy about a plodding bureaucrat, played by Rochefort, who suddenly fancies himself as a gay blade. His complicated, coquettish misadventures may produce a few smiles, but nothing more. Daniele Delorme and Anny Duperey are also in the cast. Directed by Yves Robert, who made *The Tall Blond Man With One Black Shoe*. In French with English titles. (PG) *105 minutes*

THE PARENT TRAP (1961)
★★★

Hayley Mills
Maureen O'Hara
Brian Keith

Mildy amusing and often-clever adolescent romp from the Walt Disney studio, about twins who try to repair the broken marriage of their parents, played by O'Hara and Keith. Mills is likable in the roles of twin sisters who meet at a summer camp and discover they have the same mother and father. There are many bright scenes, but there's also some awkward slapstick. Also with Charles Ruggles, Leo G. Carroll, Una Merkel, and Joanna Barnes. **Director**—David Swift.
124 minutes

THE PASSAGE (1979)
★

Anthony Quinn
James Mason
Malcolm McDowell

Pedestrian direction, trite dialogue, and an excess of violence permeate this World War II action movie. Mason plays an American scientist trying to escape from a German SS officer,

In The Passage, *Anthony Quinn guides James Mason past a Nazi frontier post.*

played by McDowell. Mason acts as if he has a stomach ache, and McDowell resembles a grotesque cartoon character. Quinn plays a Basque shepherd who guides the professor and his family through the Pyrenees; he kills the enemy with emotionless abandon and does his familiar *paisan* folk dance. Also with Patricia Neal and Christopher Lee. **Director**—J. Lee Thompson. (R) *99 minutes*

PAT AND MIKE (1952)
★★★

Spencer Tracy
Katharine Hepburn

The delightful teaming of Tracy and Hepburn transcends any minor drawbacks in this frothy comedy about the world of professional sports. Kate plays a champion athlete, and Spence latches on as her manager; the partnership leads to romance. Sporting greats appear in cameo roles. Also with Aldo Ray, Jim Backus, and Sammy White. **Director**—George Cukor. **Academy Award Nomination**—Ruth Gordon and Garson Kanin, writing (story and screenplay).
95 minutes b&w

A PATCH OF BLUE (1965)
★★★

Sidney Poitier
Elizabeth Hartman

A touching story about a poor blind girl who falls in love with a kindhearted black and is unaware of his color. Hartman is the girl, and Poitier is the man. The film is a little too sentimental, but fine acting all around maintains interest. Shelley Winters is outstanding as the girl's mean-spirited mother. Also with Wallace Ford, Ivan Dixon, and John Qualen. **Director—**Guy Green. **Academy Award—**Winters, best supporting actress. **Nominations—**Hartman, best actress; Robert Burks, cinematography (black and white). *105 minutes b&w*

PATERNITY (1981)
★★

Burt Reynolds
Beverly D'Angelo

Burt Reynolds and Beverly D'Angelo, who agrees to be a surrogate mother, in Paternity.

Reynolds stars in this essentially flat romantic comedy as a slightly sappy man-about-town, looking for a woman to have his baby without the bother of marriage. The girl for the deal is a needy musician, played by D'Angelo. Now guess who's really in love and doesn't realize it? It's predictable and sentimental stuff, unevenly directed by stand-up comedian David Steinberg, with many contrived skits and one-liners and only a few truly funny situations. Reynolds's charm isn't enough to carry the film to full satisfaction. (PG) *94 minutes*

PATHS OF GLORY (1957)
★★★★

Kirk Douglas
Adolphe Menjou

A striking, powerful tale about incompetence in the French army's high command during World War I. Douglas is great as an officer who treats his troops with dignity; Menjou is among those in the high command. The sordid conditions in the trenches are vividly detailed. Director Stanley Kubrick brings out the best in a top cast; it's superb moviemaking. Also with George Macready, Wayne Morris, and Ralph Meeker. *86 minutes b&w*

PATTON (1970)
★★★★

George C. Scott
Karl Malden

Expertly crafted screen biography of Gen. George S. Patton, the brilliant and quick-tempered Army commander who led American forces in Europe and North Africa during World War II. Scott, in the title role, is cast as the bombastic general, and he gives the performance of his career in this magnificent, bigger-than-life portrayal. Malden is also outstanding in the role of Gen. Omar Bradley, displaying an impressive contrast as the tactful military strategist. Many of the battle scenes are realsitically staged. Also with Michael Bates, Stephen Young, Michael Strong, and Fran Latimore. **Director—**Franklin Schaffner. (PG) **Academy Awards—**best picture; Schaffner, best director; Scott, best

George C. Scott portrays Gen. George S. Patton in Patton.

actor (award declined); Frances Ford Coppola and Edmund H. North, best story and screenplay (based on factual material or material not previously published). **Nomination—**Fred Koenekamp, cinematography.

170 minutes

PATTY (1976)
(no stars)

Sarah Nicholson

If it weren't for the hullabaloo over Patty Hearst, this film might be just another dull patchwork of porno loops. Nicholson, a regular in the porno stable, plays the title role; she closely resembles the real Patty. Thrown in among the sex action are some absurd interviews with psychiatrists and actors playing Patty's parents. Directed and written by Bob Roberts. (X) *90 minutes*

THE PAWNBROKER (1965)
★★★★

Rod Steiger

Steiger is memorable in the title role of this compelling melodrama about a Harlem hock shop owner haunted by the lingering memories of his experiences in a Nazi concentration camp. Steiger keeps the complex character in perfect control, and the result is an honest study of a distrustful man who struggles to regain faith in mankind. Sidney Lumet's direction is nicely paced. Fine supporting work from Brock Peters, Geraldine Fitzgerald, Jaime Sanchez, and Thelma Oliver.

114 minutes b&w

PEKING EXPRESS (1951)
★★

Joseph Cotten
Corinne Calvet

Unimpressive rehash of *Shanghai Express* with various characters aboard a train traveling through Red China. Cotten stars as a doctor who becomes involved with an intriguing lady played by Calvet. It's a routine romantic adventure at best. Also with Edmund Gwenn, Marvin Miller, and Benson Fong. **Director—**William Dieterle. *90 minutes b&w*

P
- Penitentiary
- Pennies From Heaven
- The People That Time Forgot
- Peppermint Soda
- A Perfect Couple
- The Perils of Pauline

PENITENTIARY (1980)
★★

Leon Isaac Kennedy

A rough, tough prison drama, reminiscent of the black exploitation films of years ago. Kennedy is a young convict who avoids sexual abuse in prison by becoming a competent boxer. There's plenty of raw street language and a lot of brutal encounters among the inmates, but not much credibility about prison life. Also with Thommy Pollard, Hazel Spears, and Badja Djola. **Director**—Jamaa Fanaka. (R) *99 minutes*

PENNIES FROM HEAVEN (1981)
★★

Steve Martin
Bernadette Peters

A strange combination of comedy and drama set to music in a feeble attempt to show the contrast of upbeat Hollywood musicals with the grim realities of the period. Martin stars as a sheet-music peddler who fantasizes the lyrics of his songs even though his life is filled with doom and gloom. Many of the lavish musical numbers are inspired, but more often the film suffers from an awkward script and annoying dialogue. Martin, Peters, Christopher Walken, and Jessica Harper display amazing skill in the song and dance routines. **Director**—Herbert Ross. (R) *107 minutes*

THE PEOPLE THAT TIME FORGOT (1977)
★

Patrick Wayne
Doug McClure

In 1919, a band of hardy adventurers go on a mission to rescue McClure, marooned several years earlier, in the midst of prehistoric monsters and unfriendly natives on an imaginary Antarctic island. This comic-book movie, based on an Edgar Rice Burroughs fantasy, is a sequel to *The Land That Time Forgot*. The limited script and direction lack imagination, and the prehistoric trappings are as artificial as the acting. All in all, it's a film you're bound to forget quickly. Also with Dana Gillespie, Sarah Douglas, and Thorley Walters. **Director**—Kevin Connor. (PG) *90 minutes*

PEPPERMINT SODA (1979)
★★★

Elenore Klarwein
Odile Michel

French director Diane Kurys made this understated yet effective film about the traumas of adolescence as seen through the eyes of two teenage sisters, played by Klarwein and Michel. It's a sensitive chronicle that hits home because of a concentration on vivid and engaging details. Klarwein stands out as the younger sister, encountering the familiar crises of growing up. Also with Anouk Ferjac. In French with English titles. (PG) *97 minutes*

A PERFECT COUPLE (1979)
★★★

Paul Dooley
Marta Heflin

Marta Heflin and Paul Dooley portray A Perfect Couple in this social parody.

There's something uncanny and intelligent in this film from director Robert Altman, about a man and a woman from contrasting backgrounds who meet via a computer dating service. The story occasionally lapses, but there are so many warm and funny moments that the experience is unforgettable. Dooley and Heflin are convincing as the unlikely lovers. It's not the best of Altman, but it's rousing social parody from an extraordinary filmmaker. Also with Henry Gibson, Belita Moreno, and Titos Vandis. (PG) *110 minutes*

THE PERILS OF PAULINE (1947)
★★★

Betty Hutton
John Lund

The screen escapades of silent-film star Pearl White are fondly remembered in this energetic musical comedy, nicely adorned with Frank Loesser tunes. Hutton plunges into the title role with gusto as the frantic heroine who becomes involved in cliff-hanging predicaments. Lots of colorful slapstick scenes hark back to the days of Hollywood silents; but too much sentimentality finally creeps into the film. Others in the cast include Billy De Wolfe, William Demarest, and Constance Collier. **Director**—George Marshall. *96 minutes*

In Pennies From Heaven, *Steve Martin and dancers cavort through a bank lobby.*

- Pete Kelly's Blues
- Pete 'n' Tillie
- Peter Pan
- Pete's Dragon
- Peyton Place
- Phantasm

P

PETE KELLY'S BLUES (1955)
★★

Jack Webb
Edmond O'Brien
Janet Leigh

The jazz world of the '20s is recreated in this unmoving film. But it's improperly handled by Webb, who directs and plays the lead. The music is really of interest here, and that department is filled nicely with the talents of Peggy Lee and Ella Fitzgerald. Lee has a rare dramatic role, and she displays some extraordinary acting skills. Also with Andy Devine, Lee Marvin, and Martin Milner. **Academy Award Nomination**—Lee, best supporting actress. *95 minutes*

PETE 'N' TILLIE (1972)
★★

Walter Matthau
Carol Burnett

Matthau and Burnett are nicely paired as middle-aged oddball characters who marry. The film begins as wry comedy and then lapses into sentimental soap opera when the couple's son dies. The stars make the most of some absorbing moments, but there's not too much going on in between. It's merely an adequate time-passer. Also with Geraldine Page, René Auberjonois, Barry Nelson, and Henry Jones. **Director**—Martin Ritt. (PG) **Academy Award Nominations**—Page, best supporting actress; Julius J. Epstein, best screenplay (based on material from another medium). *100 minutes*

PETER PAN (1952)
★★★

Lively and colorful animated story from the Walt Disney studio, about the amazing boy who takes a trio of English children on an adventure to a magical land. They have a number of adventures involving Captain Hook, Tiger Lily, and Tinker Bell. Disney's fantastic skills are obviously in evidence. It's an exhilarating fantasy, based on Sir J. M. Barrie's book, for

In Peter Pan, *an amazing boy takes a trio of children on a magical adventure.*

the small fry—and for adults, too. (G) **Directors**—Wilfred Jackson, Clyde Geronomi, and Hamilton Luske. *76 minutes*

PETE'S DRAGON (1977)
★★★

Helen Reddy
Jim Dale
Mickey Rooney
Red Buttons

Shelley Winters threatens Charles Tyner in this scene from Walt Disney's Pete's Dragon.

What child could resist a jolly, cuddly green dragon—especially one with a potbelly and tiny pink wings? Elliot, the cartoon dragon in this Walt Disney romantic fantasy, is especially appealing as the companion and protector of Pete, a runaway orphan played by Sean Marshall. The music is bright, the action is vigorous, and the performances by the veteran cast are pleasant. The Disney folks, famous for this kind of children's treat, have done it again. Also with Shelley Winters and Jane Kean. **Director**—Don Chaffey. (G) *134 minutes*

PEYTON PLACE (1957)
★★★★

Lana Turner
Arthur Kennedy
Hope Lange

Russ Tamblyn and Diane Varsi are among the people who live in Peyton Place.

What could have been standard soap opera is handled with style and impressive dramatic skill. Grace Metalious's sensational novel about scandalous activity in a small New Hampshire community is expertly adapted, with talented performances and top production. Turner heads the fine cast of Peyton Place residents, which also includes Diane Varsi, Lee Philips, Lloyd Nolan, Russ Tamblyn, Terry Moore, and Betty Field. The film is an engrossing account of plain folks doing what is unexpected of them. **Director**—Mark Robson. **Academy Award Nominations**—best picture; Robson, best director; Turner, best actress; Kennedy, best supporting actor; Lange, Varsi, best supporting actress; John Michael Hayes, best screenplay (based on material from another medium); William Mellor, cinematography (color). *157 minutes*

PHANTASM (1979)
★

Michael Baldwin
Bill Thornbury

Cheap scare tactics and overblown gore dominate this shabby horror story about strange happenings in a suburban mortuary. The illogical plot lacks imagination or honest suspense. The most grisly scenes are unimpressive; the blood—both red and yellow—looks like spilled nail polish.

(Continued)

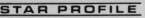
P
- The Phantom of the Opera
- Phantom of the Rue Morgue
- Phffft!
- The Philadelphia Story

(Continued)
Director-writer Don Coscarelli seems to be reaching for spookiness and sinister characters, but he merely serves up a lot of confusion. Also with Reggie Bannister, Kathy Lester, and Angus Scrimm. (R)   *87 minutes*

THE PHANTOM OF THE OPERA (1943)
★★★

Claude Rains
Nelson Eddy
Susanna Foster

A worthy remake of the impressive 1925 silent melodrama that starred Lon Chaney. There are some colorful scenes in this well-produced rendition, with Rains in the title role as the mad and disfigured composer who hides in the sewers under the Paris Opera House and plots revenge. Many moments are devoted to Eddy and Foster singing. Also stars Edgar Barrier, Leo Carrillo, and Hume Cronyn. **Director**—Arthur Lubin. **Academy Award**—Hal Mohr and W. Howard Greene, cinematography (color).   *92 minutes*

PHANTOM OF THE RUE MORGUE (1954)
★

Karl Malden

A rather limp rehash of the Edgar Allan Poe chiller "Murders in the Rue Morgue," which isn't scary at all. The setting is Paris, where a mad killer of pretty girls is on the loose. Malden gives a hammy and lackluster performance in a key role, and other characters do as well. Claude Dauphin, Patricia Medina, Steve Forrest, and Merv Griffin are also in the cast. Originally a 3-D film. **Director**—Roy Del Ruth.   *84 minutes*

PHFFFT! (1954)
★★★

Jack Lemmon
Judy Holliday

Lemmon and Holliday sparkle in this buoyant adult comedy, as a couple who separate and then discover that they were happier married. The situation is somewhat shopworn, but Lemmon and Holliday pull it off with style. Also with Kim Novak, Jack Carson, Donald Randolph, and Luella Gear. **Director**—Mark Robson.
91 minutes b&w

THE PHILADELPHIA STORY (1940)
★★★★

Katharine Hepburn
Cary Grant
James Stewart

A top cast, expert direction, and a smooth script combine to make this wise and witty romantic comedy, set among the upper crust of Philadelphia, worth viewing. The story, based on Philip Barry's play, involves a wealthy woman, played by Hepburn, who longs for the simple life as she's about to be married for the second time. Grant plays her ex-husband, and Stewart is a reporter who falls in love with her. All three shine in the choice roles. Also stars Ruth Hussey, Roland Young, John Howard, John Halliday, and Mary Nash. **Director**—George Cukor. **Academy Awards**—Stewart, best actor; Donald Ogden Stewart, writing (screenplay). **Nominations**—best picture; Cukor, best director; Hepburn, best actress; Hussey, best supporting actress.   *112 minutes b&w*

GARY COOPER

Gary Cooper was known to millions of movie-goers as a tall, silent man of action and few words. He starred in romantic, comedy, and adventure films, but perhaps he's best known for his work in westerns.

Cooper was born Frank J. Cooper in Helena, Montana, in 1901, the son of a state supreme court justice. He attended elementary school in England and later went to Wesleyan College in Montana and Grinnell College in Iowa.

After college, Cooper worked for a while as a guide at Yellowstone National Park and in 1924 went to California with the ambition of becoming a newspaper cartoonist.

However, he took jobs as a salesman for a photographer and as an advertising salesman for a theater.

In 1925, Cooper met some Hollywood casting directors and was given minor cowboy parts in westerns. The following year he got a break when he was chosen at the last moment to replace the second lead in The Winning of Barbara Worth, *starring Ronald Colman. The film was a hit, and it led to bigger acting opportunities for Cooper.*

In 1942, Cooper won the Academy Award for the title role in Sergeant York. *He won the Oscar again in 1952 for* High Noon.

Cooper died in 1961 at the age of 60.

Cooper's other films include Wings *(1927),* Lilac Time *(1928),* A Farewell To Arms *(1932),* City Streets *(1932),* The Lives of a Bengal Lancer *(1935),* Mr. Deeds Goes to Town *(1936),* The Plainsman *(1937),* Beau Geste *(1939),* Meet John Doe *(1941),* For Whom the Bell Tolls *(1943),* Vera Cruz *(1954),* The Court Martial of Billy Mitchell *(1955),* Friendly Persuasion *(1956),* Ten North Frederick *(1958), and* The Naked Edge *(1961).*

James Stewart, Katharine Hepburn, John Howard, and Mary Nash in The Philadelphia Story.

- Pickup on South Street
- Picnic
- The Picture of Dorian Gray
- A Piece of the Action
- Pillow Talk
- The Pink Panther
- The Pink Panther Strikes Again

P

PICKUP ON SOUTH STREET (1953)
★★★

Richard Widmark
Jean Peters

A well-crafted spy thriller about a pickpocket who steals a woman's wallet containing secret information; this small crime leads to his involvement with communist agents. Widmark is the light-fingered thief in this tough melodrama, which combines fast action and some violence. Excellent performances by a capable cast, which also includes Thelma Ritter and Richard Kiley. **Director**—Samuel Fuller. **Academy Award Nomination**—Ritter, best supporting actress.
80 minutes b&w

PICNIC (1955)
★★★★

William Holden
Kim Novak
Rosalind Russell

William Holden and Kim Novak in Picnic, a drama based on William Inge's play.

A memorable movie about a drifter, played by Holden, who comes to a Kansas farming community and has a profound impact on the local residents. This smart psychological drama, based on William Inge's play, combines wit and romance in a way that goes far beyond stereotyped characters in small-town America. It's well-acted throughout by a cast that also includes Susan Strasberg, Arthur O'Connell, Cliff Robertson, Betty Field, Verna Felton, and Nick Adams. **Director**—Joshua Logan. **Academy Award Nominations**—best picture; Logan, best director; O'Connell, best supporting actor. *113 minutes*

THE PICTURE OF DORIAN GRAY (1945)
★★★★

George Sanders
Hurd Hatfield

A clever and elegant Oscar Wilde tale about a man who remains forever young-looking while his portrait reveals his true age and evil nature. A stylish and sophisticated twist on the Jekyll and Hyde story, all well acted and effectively mounted. Hatfield, is Dorian, and Sanders plays the Devil. The cast also includes Angela Lansbury, Peter Lawford, and Donna Reed. **Director**—Albert Lewin. **Academy Award**—Harry Stradling, cinematography (black and white). **Nomination**—Lansbury, best supporting actress. *110 minutes b&w*

A PIECE OF THE ACTION (1977)
★★

Sidney Poitier
Bill Cosby

Poitier and Cosby team up again in this comedy-adventure, which recycles some of the plot from Poitier's *To Sir, With Love*. The two play likable and successful con men who are blackmailed into helping delinquent youths. The social comment seems too long, the comedy is too shallow, and the pacing is out of step. Also stars James Earl Jones, Denise Nicholas, and Hope Clark. **Director**—Poitier. (PG) *135 minutes*

PILLOW TALK (1959)
★★★

Doris Day
Rock Hudson
Tony Randall

Hudson and Day are perfectly matched in this fluffy romantic comedy as two people who can't stand each other, but fall in love on a telephone party line. Randall interferes with their romance. The lightweight story is handled with skill and style, and witty dialogue keeps the fun moving along. Doris is typically virginal, and Rock handles his part rather skillfully. Their successful pairing here led to similar movies. Also with Thelma Ritter, Nick Adams, Julia Meade, and Lee Patrick. **Director**—Michael Gordon. **Academy Award**—Russell Rouse, Clarence Greene (story); Stanley Shapiro and Maurice Richlin (screenplay), best story and screenplay (written directly for the screen). **Nominations**—Day, best actress; Ritter, best supporting actress.
105 minutes

THE PINK PANTHER (1964)
★★★★

David Niven
Peter Sellers

The incomparable Sellers is a riot as bumbling French Inspector Jacques Clouseau, who pursues a jewel thief in the Swiss Alps and, in the process, drives everyone around him up the wall. Niven plays the sophisticated thief, and Capucine is the inspector's wife. The film is a masterpiece of clever sight gags, pratfalls, and characterization. Smartly directed by Blake Edwards, who went on to do several more *Panther* movies with Sellers. You'll be tickled pink. Also with Claudia Cardinale and Robert Wagner. *113 minutes*

THE PINK PANTHER STRIKES AGAIN (1976)
★★★

Peter Sellers
Herbert Lom

French Inspector Jacques Clouseau,
(Continued)

Peter Sellers is Jacques Clouseau in disguise in The Pink Panther Strikes Again.

(Continued)
played with faithful perfection by Sellers, bumbles through a fourth chapter of comic misadventures. This time the zany Clouseau has driven his former superior—ex-Chief Inspector Dreyfus, played by Lom—insane. Lom then gains control of a doomsday device. The thin plot has many slow stretches, but the humor is solidly present as several honest belly laughs and lots of smiles. Also with Colin Blakely, Leonard Rossiter, Burt Kwouk, and Lesley-Anne Down. **Director**—Blake Edwards. (PG)
103 minutes

THE PINK TELEPHONE (1977)
★

Michael Lonsdale
Mireille Darc

This musty French soap opera is about a provincial factory owner who falls for an expensive call girl surreptitiously hired by a big American company to sweeten takeover negotiations. Darc, very blonde and super-chic, is properly seductive as the call girl; Lonsdale is often amusing as the American firm's president. The overloaded plot is shallow and unconvincing as a comedy that tries to get serious with sociological subjects. *Pink Telephone* is a bad connection. **Director**—Edouard Molinaro. (R) *95 minutes*

PINKY (1949)
★★★

Jeanne Crain

Powerful drama about a light-skinned black girl, played by Crain, who passes for white and encounters assorted problems. The subject, which was rather daring at the time of the film's release, seems dated now. But the story still packs a punch, and it's quite well done. Top performances from a good cast, which also includes Ethel Barrymore, Ethel Waters, William Lundigan, and Nina Mae McKinney. **Director**—Elia Kazan. **Academy Award Nominations**—Crain, best actress; Barrymore, Waters, best supporting actress.
102 minutes b&w

PINOCCHIO (1940)
★★★★

This children's classic from Walt Disney is certainly among the studio's great achievements. A poor lonely woodcutter builds a puppet, which comes to life only to fall in with bad company. When the puppet mends its ways, it becomes a real boy. The animation is colorful and lively, and the story brims with energy and charming characters; the fascination never ceases. **Supervisors**—Ben Sharpsteen and Hamilton Luske. (G) **Academy Awards**—Leigh Harlin and Ned Washington, best song ("When You Wish Upon a Star"); Harlin, Paul J. Smith, and Washington, original score. *77 minutes*

PIPE DREAMS (1976)
★★

Gladys Knight

Knight, a fine pop singer, falters as an actress in this movie about life in Alaska during the construction of the oil pipeline. At times the story, based on a screenplay by director Stephen Verona, attempts to be a morality tale of what happens when men and women seek their fortunes, but this theme never totally emerges. The result is a mishmash of events wrapped around a weak plot. However, there are some pleasant moments—including songs by Knight and the Pips—that keep the film from becoming a nightmare. Also with Barry Hankerson, Bruce French, and Sherry Bain. (PG) *89 minutes*

PIRANHA (1978)
★

Bradford Dillman
Heather Menzies

Schools of deadly piranha are no match for one shark as another movie tries to cash in on the success of *Jaws*. In this movie, we find the toothy little critters escaping from a military experimental station into a nearby lake, where they put the bite on summer campers and school kids taking

Swimmers have fun before schools of toothy critters show up in Piranha.

refreshing dips. The acting is routine, and the familiar scare tactics are hardly convincing. Also with Kevin McCarthy, Keenan Wynn, Dick Miller, and Barbara Steele. **Director**—Joe Dante. (R) *92 minutes*

THE PIT AND THE PENDULUM (1961)
★★★

Vincent Price

Price is at his sinister best in this creepy horror tale, loosely based on the Edgar Allan Poe story. The setting is just after the Spanish Inquisition, and the film is well stocked with all sorts of spooky goodies to make your skin crawl—musty torture chambers, misty castles, thunder and lightning, entombed bodies, and so on. The first half drags some, but then Price gets going and swings a mean pendulum. Also with Barbara Steele and John Kerr. **Director**—Roger Corman.
80 minutes

PIXOTE (1982)
★★

Fernando Ramos da Silva
Marília Pera

This Brazilian film is a grim account of poor Sao Paulo children who graduate from a squalid juvenile institution to a life of serious crime. Ten-year-old Da Silva is convincing in the title role. He plays an innocent-looking lad who engages in purse snatching, dope dealing, and finally murder; it's sort of a latter-day version of *Oliver Twist*, realistically told, but heavy going. Pera plays a prostitute who befriends Da Silva. Also with Jorge Juliao and Gilberto Moura. In Portuguese with English titles. **Director**—Hector Babenco. (R) *115 minutes*

● A Place in the Sun
● Planet of the Apes
● Players
● Play It Again, Sam
● Play Misty for Me
● Plaza Suite
● Please Don't Eat the Daisies

P

A PLACE IN THE SUN (1951)
★★★

Montgomery Clift
Elizabeth Taylor

A striking sociological/psychological film based on Theodore Dreiser's novel *An American Tragedy.* Clift is outstanding as a blue-collar worker who shuns a poor working girl for the love a wealthy girl, played by Taylor. The dramatically brilliant film emphasizes the contrasts between the wealthy and the lower classes. Also stars Shelley Winters, Raymond Burr, Ann Revere, Keefe Brasselle, and Fred Clark. **Director**—George Stevens. **Academy Awards**—Stevens, best director; Michael Wilson and Harry Brown, writing, (screenplay); William Mellor, cinematography (black and white). **Nominations**—best picture; Clift, best actor; Winters, best actress.

122 minutes b&w

PLANET OF THE APES (1968)
★★★★

Charlton Heston
Roddy McDowall
Kim Hunter

Innovative and thought-provoking science-fiction thriller about astronauts who land on an Earth-like planet where the apes have taken over and humans are subservient to them. The script, based on Pierre Boulle's novel *Monkey Planet,* is consistently engrossing. Special applause for the guys who did the magnificent ape makeup. Also with Maurice Evans, James Whitmore, James Daly, and Linda Harrison. A slew of sequels and a TV series followed. **Director**—Franklin Schaffner. (G)

119 minutes

PLAYERS (1979)
★

Ali MacGraw
Dean-Paul Martin

The world of professional tennis is the backdrop to this tedious film, that's continually marred by a love story so embarrassingly trite it gets unintentional giggles at every other line. Martin is convincing as the young man

Dean-Paul Martin and Ali MacGraw in Players, *a film set in the world of pro tennis.*

with tennis in his blood, but McGraw looks rather shopworn as a rich older woman torn between a rich older man, played by Maximilian Schell, and our hero. Also with Pancho Gonzalez and Steve Guttenberg. **Director**—Anthony Harvey. (PG)   *120 minutes*

PLAY IT AGAIN, SAM (1972)
★★★

Woody Allen
Diane Keaton

Allen mines some lively humor from the Bogart legend. He's an avid film fan who wants to revitalize his love life after his wife, played by Susan Anspach, abandons him. Keaton plays the wife of Woody's best friend. Woody uses the Bogey and Bergman encounters from *Casablanca* to best advantage, and there's plenty of Allen's skill at work to delight his fans. Also with Tony Roberts and Jerry Lacy. **Director**—Herbert Ross. (PG)

86 minutes

PLAY MISTY FOR ME (1971)
★★★

Clint Eastwood
Jessica Walter

An effective psychological shocker about a radio disc jockey, played by Eastwood, whose involvement with one of his female listeners leads to murder. This is Eastwood's first effort as director, and he does an impressive job of maintaining suspense and heightened drama. Walter also does a fine job as the unhinged woman who repeatedly asks him to *Play Misty for Me.* Also with Donna Mills and John Larch. (R)   *102 minutes*

PLAZA SUITE (1971)
★★★

Walter Matthau
Maureen Stapleton
Barbara Harris
Lee Grant

This Neil Simon comedy is among the best of the playwright's efforts to be adapted for the screen. The film is composed of three vignettes about different people who stay at a particular room in the posh New York hotel. Matthau is in all three segments in three different roles, and he scores in each situation. He's helped nicely with the talents of Stapleton, Harris, and Grant. Lots of laughs and lots of good scenes, all expertly Simonized. **Director**—Arthur Hiller. (PG)   *115 minutes*

PLEASE DON'T EAT THE DAISIES (1960)
★★★

Doris Day
David Niven

In Please Don't Eat the Daisies, *David Niven and Doris Day play a country couple.*

Buoyant situation comedy, based on Jean Kerr's play, about a drama critic who faces numerous problems with his job and his family when they move to the country. Cleverly executed with bright performances by the entire cast, which also includes Janis Paige, Spring Byington, Richard Haydn, and Patsy Kelly. Doris sings the title song. **Director**—Charles Walters.

111 minutes

P
- Pocketful of Miracles
- Polyester
- Pony Express
- Popeye
- Popi
- Porgy and Bess
- Pork Chop Hill

POCKETFUL OF MIRACLES
(1961)
★★★

**Bette Davis
Glenn Ford**

Director Frank Capra retreads his 1933 *Lady for a Day* as a slicker production for the wide screen. This version of the Damon Runyon tale isn't as bright as the earlier one, but it retains much of its charm and sentimentality. Davis plays the apple-seller who, with the help of gangsters, poses as a rich lady to impress her visiting daughter. There are some bumpy moments, but there are plenty of good scenes as well. A talented cast handles the Runyonesque character parts competently. Also with Hope Lange, Arthur O'Connell, Peter Falk, Jack Elam, Sheldon Leonard, Thomas Mitchell, and—in her first film—Ann-Margret. **Academy Award Nomination**—Falk, best supporting actor. *136 minutes*

POLYESTER (1981)
★★

**Divine
Tab Hunter**

Writer-director John Waters (*Pink Flamingoes*) made this fractured, soap-opera burlesque about the middle class, which is somewhat tamer than his previous outrageous fare. Divine—actually a transvestite—plays an overweight housewife who cares for a family of degenerates, and the strain is driving her insane. At last she's rescued by debonair Hunter, the man of her dreams. There's a steady stream of tacky humor, but the campy farce soon begins to wear, and the garishness becomes annoying. (R)
86 minutes

PONY EXPRESS (1953)
★★★

**Charlton Heston
Forrest Tucker**

Better-than-average western story, set in the 1860s, about the introduction of express mail service via a relay system of riders on horseback. The legendary Buffalo Bill Cody and Wild Bill Hickok take a hand in establishing the mail service routes in this film. Adequate action scenes and some decent acting enhance the production. Also with Rhonda Fleming and Jan Sterling. **Director**—Jerry Hopper.
101 minutes

POPEYE (1980)
★

**Robin Williams
Shelley Duvall**

Shelley Duvall says "Phooey" to Robin Williams, who plays the title role in Popeye.

What was charming and often rollicking in the comic strip fails to come to life in this overblown and overlong musical. Williams of TV's *Mork and Mindy* is in the title role, decked out with enormous forearms. Duvall is a perfect Olive Oyl. But for them and the rest of the cast, it's a losing battle. The humor, mostly slapstick, is only slightly more sophisticated than The Three Stooges. Toward the end, Popeye downs the spinach, and the film perks up, but it's too late. Also with Paul L. Smith (Bluto), Paul Dooley (Wimpy), and Wesley Ivan Hurt (Sweet Pea). **Director**—Robert Altman. (PG) *114 minutes*

POPI (1969)
★★★★

Alan Arkin

A heartwarming and moving story about the struggles of a Puerto Rican widower in Spanish Harlem trying to secure a better life for his young sons. Arkin is extremely convincing in the title role, as a determined man who works at multiple jobs and confronts the problems of ghetto life. The charming screenplay features an appropriate mixture of comedy and sentimentality. It's well done in all departments. Rita Moreno, Miguel Alejandro, and Ruben Figueroa perform in supporting roles. **Director**—Arthur Hiller. (G) *115 minutes*

PORGY AND BESS (1959)
★★★

**Sidney Poitier
Dorothy Dandridge**

George Gershwin's moving romantic opera could have been adapted for the screen with more skill, but the memorable music shines through with brilliance and keeps the film afloat. Poitier plays the crippled denizen of Catfish Row who falls in love with a beautiful but vulnerable girl, played by Dandridge. Sammy Davis, Jr., stands out in the role of Sportin' Life. The unforgettable songs include "Summertime" and "It Ain't Necessarily So." Pearl Bailey, Brock Peters, and Diahann Carroll are in supporting roles. **Director**—Otto Preminger. **Academy Award Nomination**—Leon Shamroy, cinematography (color). *138 minutes*

PORK CHOP HILL (1959)
★★★

**Gregory Peck
Harry Guardino**

The film is among the best war movies based on the Korean Conflict. Lots of gripping, rugged moments, as American troops try to gain a foothold on a strategic position as negotiators seek a truce at Panmunjom. There are plenty of authentic-looking fighting scenes embellished with rugged dialogue. Peck leads the fine cast, which also includes Rip Torn, George Peppard,

Gregory Peck (left) is an officer in Korea facing tough decisions in Pork Chop Hill.

- Portnoy's Complaint
- Portrait of Jennie
- The Poseidon Adventure
- Posse
- Possessed
- The Postman Always Rings Twice (1946)
- The Postman Always Rings Twice (1981)
- Practice Makes Perfect

P

George Shibata, and Woody Strode. **Director**—Lewis Milestone.

97 minutes b&w

PORTNOY'S COMPLAINT (1972)
★

Richard Benjamin

Director Ernest Lehman mangles Philip Roth's sensational novel about a young Jewish man overwhelmed with hangups. Benjamin plays the role of the neurotic Portnoy. Most of the performances are undermined by poor handling of the production and an absurd screenplay. The satirical spirit of the novel is left on the shelf. Portnoy isn't the only one who should complain. Also with Karen Black, Lee Grant, Jack Somack, and Jill Clayburgh. (R) *101 minutes*

PORTRAIT OF JENNIE (1948)
★★★★

Jennifer Jones
Joseph Cotten

Cotten stars as a poor artist who comes in contact with an unusual young woman, played by Jones. She becomes the subject of his paintings, they fall in love, and he wonders if she's the ghost of someone who died long ago. An unusual, haunting tale, obviously preposterous, but smoothly executed with style and intrigue; the acting is tops. It's a superb example of Hollywood fantasy in the best tradition. Also with Ethel Barrymore, David Wayne, and Lillian Gish. **Director**—William Dieterle. **Academy Award Nomination**—Joseph August, cinematography (black and white). *86 minutes b&w*

THE POSEIDON ADVENTURE (1972)
★★★

Gene Hackman
Ernest Borgnine
Shelley Winters
Red Buttons

Typical Hollywood disaster extravaganza about trapped passengers in a capsized luxury liner who gallantly struggle to escape a watery tomb. A somewhat absurd script and numerous flimsy characters are displayed, but the film has some heroic moments that offer sufficient thrills. Special effects seem to be the most entertaining attraction. It's escapist fare, indeed. Also with Carol Lynley, Leslie Nielson, Arthur O'Connell, Roddy McDowall, and Stella Stevens. **Director**—Ronald Neame. (PG) **Academy Award Nomination**—Winters, best supporting actress; Harold E. Stine, cinematography. *117 minutes*

POSSE (1975)
★★★

Kirk Douglas
Bruce Dern

An ambitious Texas marshal, played by Douglas, stakes his campaign for the U.S. Senate on the capture of a notorious outlaw, played by Dern, who's been robbing trains. A provocative and clever script and excellent performances by Douglas and Dern. Also with Bo Hopkins, James Stacy, and Luke Askey. **Director**—Douglas. (R) *94 minutes*

POSSESSED (1947)
★★★

Joan Crawford
Raymond Massey
Van Heflin

Crawford pours on the melodramatics in this highly charged romantic story about an unhinged woman involved in several love affairs. Massey and Heflin are two men in her life. The script is rather heavy going, but Crawford handles the material with unusual flair. An excellent piece of work for Crawford fans. Also with Geraldine Brooks. **Director**—Curtis Bernhardt. **Academy Award Nomination**—Crawford, best actress. *108 minutes b&w*

THE POSTMAN ALWAYS RINGS TWICE (1946)
★★★★

Lana Turner
John Garfield

Stylish, moody drama about a young woman who conspires with her lover to kill her husband. Turner and Garfield, who play the lovers, are perfectly matched in this efficient rendition of the James M. Cain novel. There are plenty of gripping and seductive scenes as the murderers execute what they believe to be the perfect crime. Also with Cecil Kellaway, Hume Cronyn, Leon Ames, and Audrey Totter. **Director**—Tay Garnett. *113 minutes b&w*

THE POSTMAN ALWAYS RINGS TWICE (1981)
★★★

Jack Nicholson
Jessica Lange

In The Postman Always Rings Twice, *Jack Nicholson drifts into the life of Jessica Lange.*

The second Hollywood version of James M. Cain's 1941 novel of passion, greed, and murder stars Nicholson and Lange as the brooding, adulterous lovers. The film is well acted and beautifully photographed, with explicit detail of the Depression era. Nicholson is at his best as the obsessive drifter who comes upon a dingy diner and lusts after the owner's wife. But keep your eye on the beautiful Lange as the sultry wife with murder on her mind; she makes the sparks fly. Also with John Colicos, Michael Lerner, and Angelica Huston. **Director**—Bob Rafelson. (R) *122 minutes*

PRACTICE MAKES PERFECT (1980)
★★

Jean Rochefort

Edouard Choiseul, played by Rochefort, is a celebrated concert pianist and—so it seems—France's greatest

(Continued)

P
- Pressure Point
- Pretty Baby
- Pride and Prejudice
- The Pride of St. Louis
- Pride of the Marines
- The Pride of the Yankees
- Priest of Love

(Continued)

lover. He's a perpetual adolescent who pursues almost simultaneously his latest girl friend, his ex-wife, his current wife, and the granddaughter of an old flame. It's a breezy farce that's spoiled, at last, by an unwelcome dissertation on morality. Director Philippe de Broca, who scored so well with *King of Hearts*, seems out of practice. Also with Nicole Garcia, Annie Girardot, Danielle Darrieux, and Lila Kedrova. In French with English titles. (No MPAA rating)
104 minutes

PRESSURE POINT (1962)
★★★

Sidney Poitier
Bobby Darin

Captivating high drama about a black prison psychiatrist, played by Poitier, struggling to deal with a violent inmate who's an American Nazi. The unusual story is quite engrossing, and it efficiently conveys the tense feelings surrounding a touchy subject. Darin is surprisingly good as the hate-filled prisoner, and Poitier's professional and cool demeanor offers an effective contrast. Supporting roles by Peter Falk and Carl Benton Reid. **Director—**Hubert Cornfield. *120 minutes b&w*

PRETTY BABY (1978)
★★

Brooke Shields
Keith Carradine

French director Louis Malle's first American film is about a 12-year-old prostitute, played by Shields, in New Orleans' legendary tenderloin district of the early 1900s. Carradine plays her photographer husband. The settings are pretty and lush, but the movie is

Brooke Shields distracts photographer Keith Carradine in Pretty Baby.

tedious and shallow and filled with hopelessly undefined characters. Too bad, because this intriguing subject could have been developed with drama and compassion. The title role is played with subtleness by 12-year-old Shields. Also with Susan Sarandon, Francis Faye, and Antonio Fargas. (R) *109 minutes*

PRIDE AND PREJUDICE (1940)
★★★★

Laurence Olivier
Greer Garson

Delectable comedy of manners set in 19th-century England, about five sisters who want to get married. The film, based faithfully on the Jane Austen novel, sparkles with wit and strikes the right mood of the period. Best of all, it features a splendid cast with everyone handling their parts with perfection. Also with Edmund Gwenn, Mary Boland, Melville Cooper, Edna May Oliver, Ann Rutherford, and Maureen O'Sullivan. **Director—**Robert Z. Leonard.
116 minutes b&w

THE PRIDE OF ST. LOUIS (1952)
★★

Dan Dailey
Joanne Dru

Standard film biography of baseball great Dizzy Dean, with Dailey in the role of the extraordinary pitcher who later became a baseball announcer. The production has its limits, but all involved seem to make an earnest effort. Also with Richard Haydn, Richard Crenna, and Hugh Sanders. **Director—**Harmon Jones. **Academy Award Nomination**—Guy Trosper, writing (motion picture story).
93 minutes b&w

PRIDE OF THE MARINES (1945)
★★★

John Garfield
Eleanor Parker
Dave Clark

Sentimental yet thoughtful account of a Marine who was blinded while fighting the Japanese during World War II. Garfield is convincing as brave fight-

ing man Al Schmid, who struggles to adjust to his disability. Clark plays his buddy. An excellent production enhanced by fine performances. Also with John Ridgely, Rosemary De Camp, and Tom D'Andrea. **Director—**Delmer Daves. **Academy Award Nomination**—Albert Maltz, writing (screenplay). *119 minutes b&w*

THE PRIDE OF THE YANKEES (1942)
★★★★

Gary Cooper
Teresa Wright

An exceptional film biography of Yankee baseball star Lou Gehrig. Cooper is just right in the role of the sports hero who died of leukemia at the peak of his astounding career; Wright plays Gehrig's wife. The sentimentality is predictable, yet it's handled with taste. The film ends with Gehrig's emotional farewell in Yankee Stadium. Also with Babe Ruth, Walter Brennan, and Dan Duryea. **Director—**Sam Wood. **Academy Award Nominations**—best picture; Cooper, best actor; Wright, best actress; Paul Gallico, writing (original story); Herman J. Mankiewicz and Joe Swerling, writing (screenplay); Rudolph Maté, cinematography (black and white).
127 minutes b&w

PRIEST OF LOVE (1981)
★★

Ian McKellen
Janet Suzman

A rather hollow film biography of controversial writer D. H. Lawrence, the author of *Lady Chatterley's Lover* and other much-censored novels. The story meanders from country to country as Lawrence, played adequately by McKellen, raves against the authorities and deals with a fatal case of tuberculosis. Most important, perhaps, is the role of his wife Frieda, played by Suzman, who was his inspiration and his protector. In any case, Lawrence's writings are far more engrossing than this story of his life. Also with Ava Gardner, Penelope Keith, Jorge River, and Sir John Gielgud. **Director—**Christopher Miles. (R)
125 minutes

- The Prime of Miss Jean Brodie
- The Prince and the Showgirl
- Prince of the City
- The Princess and the Pirate
- The Prisoner of Zenda
- Private Benjamin
- The Private Eyes

P

THE PRIME OF MISS JEAN BRODIE (1969)
★★★

Maggie Smith

Smith turns in an extraordinary tour-de-force performance as an eccentric schoolteacher at a swank Edinburgh girls' school during the 1930s. She invests much energy and skill in this unusual character, who finally reaches her downfall. Based on the novel by Muriel Spark. Also stars Robert Stephens, Pamela Franklin, and Celia Johnson. **Director**—Ronald Neame. (PG) **Academy Award**—Smith, best actress. *116 minutes*

Robert Stephens and Maggie Smith shock a pupil in The Prime of Miss Jean Brodie.

THE PRINCE AND THE SHOWGIRL (1957)
★★★

**Laurence Olivier
Marilyn Monroe**

Plush-looking period comedy with Olivier and Monroe perfectly matched in contrasting roles. He plays a European aristocrat, and she's an American showgirl. The setting is the 1911 coronation of George V in London. They meet, and together they find love and understanding. The film's pace is a little slow and stiff, but the performances are delightful. The movie, based on Terence Rattigan's play *The Sleeping Prince*, co-stars Sybil Thorndike, Richard Wattis, and Jeremy Spencer. **Director**—Olivier. *117 minutes*

PRINCE OF THE CITY (1981)
★★★

Treat Williams

Director Sidney Lumet's super-charged, relentless drama about a

In Prince of the City, *Treat Williams portrays a New York City detective.*

New York City undercover detective who investigates corruption. The film evokes mixed emotions. The story is powerful and fascinating in its treatment of conscience, loyalty, and human emotions; yet it's painfully complex and long. Williams stands out as the double-agent cop who exposes his colleagues. There are versatile supporting performances from novice actors Jerry Orbach, Richard Foronjy, and Don Billett. (R) *167 minutes*

THE PRINCESS AND THE PIRATE (1944)
★★★

**Bob Hope
Virginia Mayo**

In this film, Hope and Mayo try to elude a sinister pirate, played by Victor McLaglen. Walter Slezak plays a potentate. There's loads of wacky fun in this costume comedy to delight Hope fans. Other supporting roles are played by Walter Brennan, Marc Lawrence, and Hugo Maas. **Director**—David Butler. *94 minutes*

THE PRISONER OF ZENDA (1979)
★★

Peter Sellers

Sellers plays multiple roles in this remake of the masquerade story about the king of Ruritania. Sellers reliably delivers some pleasing comedy, and milks the listless material for more laughs than it's worth. But the film receives minimal help from director Richard Quine, who lacks the zip and flair to keep things humming along. Also with Lynne Frederick, Lionel Jeffries, Elke Sommer and Gregory Sierra. (PG) *108 minutes*

PRIVATE BENJAMIN (1980)
★★★

**Goldie Hawn
Eileen Brennan**

Hawn plays a pampered young woman who gets away from it all by joining the Army, where she wages comic warfare on the brass hats. Brennan plays her superior officer. The serviceable script is somewhat reminiscent of those "this is the Army" type comedies that were popular in the '40s and '50s. Goldie, as the Army's most unlikely soldier, updates this routine with her perky charm and comic style, and keeps the gags marching along at double time. After this, she deserves a promotion to corporal. **Director**—Howard Zieff. (R) **Academy Award Nominations**—Hawn, best actress; Brennan, best supporting actress; Nancy Meyers, Charles Shyer, and Harvey Miller, best screenplay (written directly for the screen). *110 minutes*

Goldie Hawn is a pampered young lady who joins the Army in Private Benjamin.

THE PRIVATE EYES (1981)
★

**Tim Conway
Don Knotts**

Conway and Knotts, who come off as a latter-day Abbott and Costello, investigate murders in the home of British aristocrats. The film begins as silly low comedy and just keeps sinking as the story progresses. It's an *(Continued)*

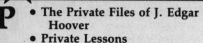

JANE FONDA

Born in New York City in 1937, Jane Fonda spent her early years in California. She made a hesitant acting debut with her father Henry Fonda in a summer stock production of The Country Girl *and appeared briefly with him in* The Male Animal *in Cape Cod. But her main interests were painting and languages, so, after studying at Vassar, Fonda left to study painting at Ecole de Chauviniere in Paris.*

Fonda returned to New York, and took up modeling; she appeared on the cover of Vogue *magazine twice. Then, in 1958, a meeting with Lee Strasberg led to studies at his Actors' Studio and to a sudden passion for acting.*

Fonda made her formal stage debut in The Moon Is Blue. *This led to her Broadway bow in 1960 in* There Was a Little Girl. *In the same year, she made her film debut in* Tall Story.

During her so-called "coltish ingenue" days, Fonda made a dozen more pictures including A Walk on the Wild Side *(1961),* The Chapman Report *(1962),* La Ronde *(1964), and* Cat Ballou *(1965), a western that changed the genre and established her as a superb commedienne.*

After French director Roger Vadim launched her as a sex-tigress in Barbarella *(1968), Fonda returned to California and made her dramatic film breakthrough as the embittered marathon dancer in* They Shoot Horses, Don't They? *(1969). For* Klute *(1971), her next film, she won her first Oscar. She won her second Academy Award for* Coming Home *(1978).*

Fonda has also starred in Steelyard Blues *(1972),* A Doll's House *(1974),* The China Syndrome *(1979),* The Electric Horseman *(1979),* 9 to 5 *(1981), and with her father in* On Golden Pond *(1982), a film that earned her an Oscar nomination as best supporting actress.*

(Continued)
obvious spoof of Sherlock Holmes, with Knotts bumbling about as Inspector Winship, and Conway cutting up as Dr. Tart. The routines seem to have been thrown together hastily. The boys have had better comic opportunities in television. **Director**—Michael Hui. (PG)   *100 minutes*

THE PRIVATE FILES OF J. EDGAR HOOVER (1980)
★★

Broderick Crawford

Director-writer Larry Cohen deglorifies the late top cop in this rather undramatic B-movie, which covers events from the killing of Dillinger to Watergate. Crawford plays the famous G-man with enough credibility, but the historical details are handled in a pedestrian style that produces few revelations about Hoover and his law-enforcement empire. Also with Dan

Dailey, José Ferrer, Rip Torn, Raymond St. Jacques, and Ronee Blakely. (PG)   *112 minutes*

PRIVATE LESSONS (1981)
★★

Eric Brown
Sylvia Kristel

This is a dubious comedy about a shy 15-year-old boy who's seduced by

Sylvia Kristel is a housekeeper who seduces a shy Eric Brown in Private Lessons.

the family's attractive housekeeper. Brown is the boy, and Kristel is the seducer. The low-budget film is done with obvious eagerness, and it primarily exploits soft-core sex with frequent nude scenes. The portrayal of an adolescent involved with an older woman adds a provocative dimension to the mostly awkward proceedings. Howard Hesseman and Ed Begley, Jr., also star. **Director**—Alan Myerson. (R)   *87 minutes*

THE PRIVATE LIFE OF HENRY VIII (1933)
★★★★

Charles Laughton
Elsa Lanchester

Classic movie about England's eccentric and much-married king. Laughton is sheer delight as the 16th-century ruler who beheaded two wives and acquired four others, and he captures the spirit of the part in fine style. Lanchester plays Anne of Cleves. Other rousing performances from Robert Donat, Miles Mander, Merle Oberon, and Binnie Barnes help make this historical film a gem. **Director**—Alexander Korda.   *97 minutes b&w*

PRIVATE'S PROGRESS (1956)
★★★

Ian Carmichael
Terry-Thomas

Delightful parody of the British army, with plenty of good gags and lively scenes. An awkward young man is called to serve his country and everything goes haywire. This British version of *No Time for Sergeants* and *Private Hargrove* works effectively, thanks to a good script and a top cast of British character actors. Also with Richard Attenborough, Dennis Price, Peter Jones, William Hartnett, and Ian Bannen. **Director**—John Boulting.   *97 minutes b&w*

THE PRIVATE WAR OF MAJOR BENSON (1955)
★★

Charlton Heston
Julie Adams

Heston stars as a tough Army officer

- The Prize
- The Producers
- The Professionals
- The Promise
- Promises in the Dark
- Prom Night
- Prophecy

P

who mellows a bit after taking charge of a military academy run by nuns. Heston handles the humor and the romantic stuff with ease. Adams plays the love interest in this rather syrupy comedy with some funny scenes, but mostly the film is farfetched and too sentimental. Also stars Tim Hovey, Sal Mineo, William Demarest, and Tim Considine. **Director**—Jerry Hopper. **Academy Award Nomination**—Joe Connelly and Bob Mosher, writing (motion picture story). *100 minutes*

THE PRIZE (1963)
★★★

Paul Newman
Elke Sommer
Edward G. Robinson

Slick, sleek spy thriller set against the backdrop of the Nobel Prize awards in Stockholm. An American writer, played by Newman, finds himself involved in a plot to abduct a famous scientist, played by Robinson. Sommer plays Robinson's daughter. The film, based on the Irving Wallace novel, takes on the style of a Hitchcock suspense movie and works with precision. The excellent cast also includes Diane Baker, Kevin McCarthy, and Leo G. Carroll. **Director**—Mark Robson. *135 minutes*

THE PRODUCERS (1968)
★★★

Zero Mostel
Gene Wilder

This film is an audacious mixture of hilarity, brilliance, and bad taste; it's about a Broadway producer who cooks up a wild scheme to raise money from investors by staging a flop musical. He sells much more than 100 percent of the show, but the plan backfires when the production becomes a hit. The script is patchy, but there are some inventive wild moments that keep the satire firmly afloat. The best portions involve the play, entitled *Springtime for Hitler*. Mostel is funny as the hustling theater producer; Wilder plays Mostel's meek accountant. Good support, too, from Kenneth Mars, Dick Shawn, Renée Taylor, and Estelle Winwood. **Director**—Mel Brooks. **Academy Award**—

Estelle Winwood, Zero Mostel, and Gene Wilder in the satire The Producers.

Brooks, best story and screenplay (written directly for the screen). **Nomination**—Wilder, best supporting actor. *98 minutes*

THE PROFESSIONALS (1966)
★★★★

Burt Lancaster
Lee Marvin

Rousing, spicy western adventure about a band of mercenaries sent to Mexico to rescue the wife of a wealthy rancher from the clutches of a vile bandit. Ralph Bellamy plays the rancher, and Claudia Cardinale is his abducted wife. Lancaster and Marvin lead the band of mercenaries, and Jack Palance is the chief villain. The expedition across the border pits rugged men against rugged men, and the film bristles with excitement and well-mounted suspense. A first-rate cast goes all out to provide gripping action. Also with Robert Ryan and Woody Strode. **Director**—Richard Brooks. **Academy Award Nominations**—Brooks, best director; Brooks, best screenplay (based on material from another medium); Conrad Hall, cinematography (color). *123 minutes*

THE PROMISE (1979)
★

Kathleen Quinlin
Stephen Collins
Beatrice Straight

Quinlan, Collins, and Straight star in this third-rate tearjerker that smacks of *Love Story* and a dozen other soap-opera movies. The talented actors try to play it straight, but they're tripped up by the absurd dialogue, which sometimes results in unintentional

hilarity. Promise yourself not to waste time on such junk. Also with Laurence Luckinbill and William Prince. **Director**—Gilbert Cates. (PG) *98 minutes*

PROMISES IN THE DARK (1979)
★★

Marsha Mason

The right-to-die issue is taken up in this gloomy movie about a bright-eyed 17-year-old girl, played by Kathleen Beller, who has terminal cancer. It's a difficult subject for a film, which could succeed if handled with sensitivity and pathos. But here, the story is a bland hype of tragic circumstances. The uninspired acting of Mason as the girl's gallant doctor doesn't help matters. Also with Ned Beatty, Susan Clark, Michael Brandon, and Paul Clemens. **Director**—Jerome Hellman. (PG) *115 minutes*

PROM NIGHT (1980)
★★

Jamie Lee Curtis
Leslie Nielsen

Scream queen Curtis and Nielsen star in this film in which a masked killer seeks revenge on teenagers attending a high school prom. This Canadian-made melodrama smacks of such chillers as *Carrie* and *Halloween*. The murder scenes are gruesome, but they always seem to stop short of producing the shock effects expected of this sort of movie. Director Paul Lynch set up a few tense moments, but most of the film is merely marking time while waiting for the killer to get into the act. Also with Eddie Benton. (R) *91 minutes*

PROPHECY (1979)
★★

Talia Shire
Robert Foxworth

Shire and Foxworth star in this silly minor-league monster movie that pretends to be spectacular. The villain is mercury poisoning from industrial pollution. Animals, including humans, are turned into horrible mutants that attack campers and forest *(Continued)*

Talia Shire and Robert Foxworth prepare to battle a deadly force in Prophecy.

(Continued)
rangers in the Maine woods. Director John Frankenheimer serves up plenty of gore and a lot of monster movie clichés. Also with Armand Assante, Richard Dysart, and Victoria Racimo. (PG)   *100 minutes*

PROVIDENCE (1977)
★

**Dirk Bogarde
John Gielgud
Ellen Burstyn**

French director Alain Resnais (*Last Year at Marienbad; Hiroshima; Mon Amour*) makes his first film in English with unfortunate results. The puzzling comedy, starring Bogarde, Gielgud, and Burstyn, is difficult to unravel. It's set inside the mind of a dying 78-year-old writer who drunkenly constructs a last novel about his family members. Most of the performances are feeble by way of miscasting or inadequate effort. The audience must work hard to fathom this film, which is actually a lot of fuss about nothing. Also with David Warner and Elains Stritch. (PG)
104 minutes

PSYCHIC KILLER (1976)
★★

**Jim Hutton
Julie Adams
Paul Burke**

This is an often-repulsive suspense shocker about a madman who seeks revenge on various people through parapsychology—a butcher is put through his own meat grinder; a nurse is scalded to death in a shower. It takes a friendly psychiatrist to finally figure out who has committed the

string of gruesome murders. The film, which moves along energetically, liberally imitates Hitchcock's *Psycho* but hardly touches its depth. Also with Aldo Ray, Neville Brand, and Whit Bissell. **Director**—Raymond Danton. (PG)   *90 minutes*

PSYCHO (1960)
★★★★

**Anthony Perkins
Vera Miles
John Gavin
Janet Leigh**

This classic horror story, based on the novel by Robert Bloch, is smartly served up by the great director Alfred Hitchcock, who goes right for the jugular and never lets go. Perkins plays the weird manager of a remote motel who isn't too accommodating to some of his guests; after a young woman and a private investigator hired to find her are killed, Perkins goes to great lengths to protect his mother. Watch out for that legendary shower scene—and mom. Also with John McIntire, Martin Balsam, and Simon Oakland. (PG) **Academy Award Nominations**—Hitchcock, best director; Leigh, best supporting actress; John L. Russell, cinematography (black and white).
109 minutes b&w

PT 109 (1963)
★★

Cliff Robertson

Mildly interesting account of the wartime exploits of John F. Kennedy, who skippered a PT boat in the Pacific during World War II as a Navy lieutenant. The famous personality makes the story somewhat intriguing, but the film is long and routinely done. Robertson does well in the role of Kennedy. Also with Ty Hardin, Robert Blake, and James Gregory. **Director**—Leslie H. Martinson.   *140 minutes*

THE PUBLIC ENEMY (1931)
★★★★

James Cagney

Powerful, stunning gangster film starring Cagney, who starts out as a small-

James Cagney and Jean Harlow in the powerful gangster film The Public Enemy.

time hood and graduates to the big leagues of gangsterdom. Cagney puts on quite a show as an Irish gangster, nails down his acting career, and establishes his reputation as a tough character in this film. The nerve-jangling story features some impressive and vivid scenes, including the notorious scene when Jimmy mashes a grapefruit into the face of Mae Clarke. Co-stars Edward Woods, Jean Harlow, Joan Blondell, and Donald Cook. **Director**—William Wellman. **Academy Award Nomination**—John Bright and Kubec Glasmon, writing (original story).   *90 minutes b&w*

PUMPING IRON (1977)
★★★

Arnold Schwarzenegger

This intelligent and lively documentary, all about the subculture of body-building, is based on the popular book by Charles Gaines and George Butler. It stars Schwarzenegger, that charming and spectacular champion of muscle-men who calls himself a sculptor of his own body. There's a good deal of suspense about who will win the titles of Mr. Universe and Mr. Olympia. The film makes it clear that the object of all the strenuous and painful weightlifting isn't strength, but appearance. Stylishly directed by Butler and Robert Fiore. (PG)   *85 minutes*

• The Pumpkin Eater
• The Pursuit of D. B. Cooper
• Quadrophenia
• The Quiet American
• The Quiet Man
• Quintet
• Quo Vadis

P·Q

THE PUMPKIN EATER (1964)
★★★

Anne Bancroft
Peter Finch

Solid acting by a fine cast enhances this soapy story about a thrice-married woman having husband trouble. Bancroft gives a superb performance as the bewildered and rather unstable mother of eight who finds yet another marriage falling apart. Finch is her unfaithful husband. The film is executed with considerable sensitivity and perception, and some of the scenes are memorable, indeed. Also with James Mason, Cedric Hardwicke, Maggie Smith, and Eric Porter. **Director**—Jack Clayton. **Academy Award Nomination**—Bancroft, best actress.
110 minutes b&w

THE PURSUIT OF D. B. COOPER (1981)
★★★

Treat Williams
Robert Duvall

In The Pursuit of D. B. Cooper, *Treat Williams plays the title role.*

A spirited bit of tongue-in-cheek fiction based on the daredevil skyjacker who jumped from a 727 jet with $200,000 ransom and was never found. Williams is sensational as the slippery extortionist who leads an insurance company detective, played by Duvall, and other pursuers on a merry chase. Duvall is also in top form in this lightweight high adventure. The film owes much of its success to some slick energetic stunts. Also with Kathryn Harrold, Ed Flanders, R. G. Armstrong, and Paul Gleason. **Director**—Robert Spottiswoode. (PG)
100 minutes

Q

QUADROPHENIA (1979)
★★★

Phil Daniels

This poignant British feature, with Daniels in the leading role, throbs with the music of The Who, but this isn't a rock concert film; it's an entertaining drama that effectively illuminates the frustrations and conflicts of British youth in the '60s. These are the disaffected young men and women who sought identity by joining such groups as the Mods or the Rockers. An excellent cast, which also includes Mark Wingett, Philip Davis, and Leslie Ash. **Director**—Franc Roddam. (R)
115 minutes

THE QUIET AMERICAN (1958)
★★

Michael Redgrave
Audie Murphy

A diluted film version of Graham Greene's complex novel about an American who goes to Vietnam with vague plans for ending the fighting. Murphy is only partially effective in the title role, but the film offers some notable performances by the rest of the cast. Redgrave plays the journalist who's deceived into betraying Murphy to the communists. Also with Claude Dauphin, Bruce Cabot, Giorgia Moll, and Richard Loo. **Director**—Joseph L. Mankiewicz.
122 minutes b&w

THE QUIET MAN (1952)
★★★★

John Wayne
Maureen O'Hara

Highly entertaining story about an ex-prizefighter who settles down in his native Ireland and woos a willful Irish lass. The film brims with energy and carries just the right amount of good-natured humor. The excellent production features sparkling scenes of the Irish countryside. Wayne does a good job in the title role, and O'Hara is per-

John Wayne is an ex-prizefighter who woos Maureen O'Hara in The Quiet Man.

fect as the woman he tames. There are other outstanding performances from Barry Fitzgerald, Victor McLaglen, and Ward Bond. Also with Mildred Natwick, Francis Ford, and Arthur Shields. **Director**—John Ford. **Academy Awards**—Ford, best director; Winton C. Hoch and Archie Stout, cinematography (color). **Nominations**—best picture; McLaglen, best supporting actor; Frank S. Nugent, writing (screenplay). *129 minutes*

QUINTET (1979)
★

Paul Newman

Director Robert Altman's 13th film is his fantasy of apocalypse. In a bleak, ice-crusted city, survivors play a deadly backgammon-like game where the winners murder the losers. It's a tedious movie about a relentlessly gloomy world. Newman heads the international cast, which also includes Vittorio Gassman, Fernando Rey, Bibi Andersson, and Nina Van Pallandt. They all seem bored and frozen to the bone. Even Altman devotees may have a hard time sitting through this one. (R) *110 minutes*

QUO VADIS (1951)
★★★

Robert Taylor
Deborah Kerr
Peter Ustinov

Lavish extravaganza about the plight of Christians under the heavy hand of Roman Emperor Nero. Rome burns, the lions eat some Christians, and Taylor plays a Roman soldier who romances Kerr. There's really too much to digest in this long movie, and boredom will eventually set in. But there
(Continued)

Q·R

- Rabbit Test
- Race for Your Life, Charlie Brown
- Race With the Devil
- Rachel, Rachel
- A Rage To Live
- Raggedy Ann and Andy
- Raggedy Man
- Raging Bull

(Continued)

are moments of impressive acting, and some spectacular scenes are outstanding. Also with Leo Genn, Patricia Laffan, Finlay Currie, and Buddy Baer. **Director**—Mervyn Le Roy. **Academy Award Nominations**—best picture; Genn, Ustinov, best supporting actor; Robert Surtees and William V. Skall, cinematography (color). *171 minutes*

R

RABBIT TEST (1978)
★

Joan Rivers
Billy Crystal

Comedienne Rivers directed this alleged comedy about the world's first pregnant man. She delivers a machine-gun barrage of silly one-liners that seldom click. The film's jokes hammer away at a variety of targets, including doctors and religion. A platoon of familiar performers march by for cameos—including George Gobel, Imogene Coca, and Paul Lynde. Maybe rabbits will think this one's funny. (PG) *86 minutes*

RACE FOR YOUR LIFE, CHARLIE BROWN (1977)
★★

The mere appearance of the lovable Peanuts gang should delight the kids, but this third animated screen feature of the famous comic strip is showing some wear. This time Charlie Brown and his pals are packed off to summer camp, where they give their neuroses the usual workout. The plot rambles, and the animation seems flat. Charles M. Schulz wrote the screenplay. **Director**—Bill Melendez. (G) *75 minutes*

RACE WITH THE DEVIL (1975)
★

Peter Fonda
Warren Oates

An adolescent, lamebrained horror film about four vacationers who are chased by a group of devil worshippers after stumbling upon a ritual killing in Texas. Fonda, Oates, Loretta Swit, and Lara Parker are the vacationers. Also with R. G. Armstrong. **Director**—Jack Starrett. (PG) *89 minutes*

RACHEL, RACHEL (1968)
★★★★

Joanne Woodward
Estelle Parsons

Joanne Woodward portrays a lonely schoolteacher in Rachel, Rachel.

Woodward is splendid as a schoolteacher in this deeply moving portrait of a middle-aged spinster facing a mid-life crisis. She's lonely, frustrated, and trapped in a small New England town. Parsons plays one of her colleagues. Under Paul Newman's direction, the film is a realistic slice of life and doesn't turn into a soap opera. Also with James Olson, Kate Harrington, Geraldine Fitzgerald, Donald Moffat, and Bernard Barrow. **Academy Award Nominations**—best picture; Woodward, best actress; Parsons, best supporting actress; Stewart Stern, best screenplay (based on material from another medium). *101 minutes*

A RAGE TO LIVE (1965)
★

Suzanne Pleshette
Bradford Dillman
Ben Gazzara

This screen version of John O'Hara's popular novel about a woman of easy virtue has been marred by heavy-handed Hollywood treatment. The film lacks the irony and characterization that make most of O'Hara's work famous. Pleshette does as well as can be expected as the near-nymphomaniac who discovers she needs more in life than just a husband. Also with James Gregory, Peter Graves, Bethel Leslie, and Ruth White. **Director**—Walter Grauman. *101 minutes b&w*

RAGGEDY ANN AND ANDY (1977)
★★

This animated cartoon, based on the famous Johnny Gruelle children's stories, is a technical achievement of sorts—but alas, the $4-million project fails to deliver enough satisfying entertainment for youngsters or adults. It's about two rag dolls who encounter a variety of unappealing creatures that screech and gurgle in a monotonous and ill-humored fashion. Songs by Joe Raposo of *Sesame Street* fame all seem to sound the same; they lack the lighthearted charm of the pleasant Disney cartoon features of years ago. **Director**—Richard Williams. (G) *85 minutes*

RAGGEDY MAN (1981)
★★

Sissy Spacek
Eric Roberts

Spacek is convincing as a lonely divorcée with two sons in a small Texas town in the mid '40s. She has a brief affair with a sailor, played by Roberts. The screenplay starts with such good intentions, as a charming, sensitive love story. But unfortunately, events turn sour as the sailor abruptly leaves, and Sissy is at the mercy of two redneck brutes. Finally the film emerges as merely another violent melodrama with an unsatisfying resolution. Also with Sam Shepard and R. G. Armstrong. **Director**—Jack Fisk. (PG) *94 minutes*

RAGING BULL (1980)
★★★★

Robert De Niro
Cathy Moriarty
Joe Pesci

Director Martin Scorsese's hard-hitting, high-voltage characterization

- Ragtime
- Raiders of the Lost Ark
- The Rainmaker
- Raintree County
- Raise the Titanic
- A Raisin in the Sun

R

Robert De Niro, as Jake La Motta, raises his arms in victory in Raging Bull.

of middleweight champ Jake La Motta is a brilliant study of brutality and torment in and out of the ring. De Niro, in the title role, stunningly portrays the Bronx Bull with grim, unsentimental reality. There's credible support from newcomers Pesci and Moriarty. The brief, supercharged boxing scenes are perhaps the best ever filmed. Superb direction and dazzling acting—a triumph for all involved. Also with Frank Vincent and Nicholas Colasanto. (R) **Academy Awards**—best picture; De Niro, best actor. **Nominations**—Scorsese, best director; Pesci, best supporting actor; Moriarty, best supporting actress. *119 minutes b&w*

RAGTIME (1981)
★★★

**James Cagney
Brad Dourif
Howard E. Rollins**

E. L. Doctorow's multifaceted historical novel of turn-of-the-century America is adapted for the screen with exquisite period detail, impeccable photography, and impressive acting by a large, first-rate cast. Yet much of the punch and style is frittered away because of an awkwardly handled multilayered plot that could take longer to figure out than the movie's running time. Old pro Cagney is spunky as ever as a crusty police commissioner, and newcomer Rollins

steals scenes as a young black piano player who resorts to extreme measures because of wounded pride. Also with Moses Gunn, Elizabeth McGovern, Kenneth McMillan, James Olson, Mandy Patinkin, and Mary Steenburgen. **Director**—Milos Forman. (PG) *156 minutes*

RAIDERS OF THE LOST ARK (1981)
★★★★

**Harrison Ford
Karen Allen**

George *(Star Wars)* Lucas and Steven *(Jaws)* Spielberg joined talents to make this ripsnorting, thrill-a-minute adventure. Ford plays Indiana Jones, a stubborn, rough-and-ready archaeologist who races the Nazis to find a lost ark supposedly containing remnants of the Ten Commandments. Allen is the leading lady who helps him in his efforts. The exotic, action-packed film harks back to those derring-do serials of the '30s and '40s, but this version is enhanced with magnificent technical sophistication for the ultimate in escapist entertainment. Also with Paul Freeman, Ronald Lacey, John Rhys-Davies, and Denholm Elliott. **Director**—Spielberg. (PG) *115 minutes*

In Raiders of the Lost Ark, *Harrison Ford is an adventuresome archaeologist.*

THE RAINMAKER (1956)
★★★

**Katharine Hepburn
Burt Lancaster**

Richard Nash's hit play about Starbuck, a phony rainmaker who's more successful at seducing a confirmed spinster, is too talky and doesn't make a good movie. But Hepburn performs well as the spinster in a Kansas town. She's romanced by the visiting con

man, played by Lancaster, who overacts in the title role. Also with Wendell Corey, Lloyd Bridges, Earl Holliman, and Wallace Ford. **Director**—Joseph Anthony. **Academy Award Nomination**—Hepburn, best actress. *121 minutes*

RAINTREE COUNTY (1958)
★★★

**Montgomery Clift
Elizabeth Taylor**

Taylor and Clift, with the help of an excellent supporting cast, keep this rambling Civil War story from becoming a dud. Taylor portrays a woman who stops at nothing to get what she wants. But when she gets her man, happiness still eludes her, and the war eventually tears her world apart. Clift plays her romantic interest. Also with Eva Marie Saint, Nigel Patrick, Lee Marvin, Rod Taylor, and Agnes Moorehead. **Director**—Edward Dmytryk. **Academy Award Nomination**—Taylor, best actress. *166 minutes*

RAISE THE TITANIC (1980)
★

**Jason Robards
Richard Jordan
Anne Archer**

There are some striking visual effects to simulate the resurrection of the famous ocean liner from the deep, but the script, acting, and direction should be relegated to Davy Jones's locker. This bloated film wastes considerable time with cardboard characters talking themselves into a stupor, and there's not much else in the screenplay to pep up the pace. The basic plot concerns the urgent recovery of a mysterious ore on board the vessel so the Russians can't grab it. **Director**—Jerry Jameson. (PG) *112 minutes*

A RAISIN IN THE SUN (1961)
★★★★

**Sidney Poitier
Ruby Dee
Claudia McNeil**

This is one of the first commercial films that makes an honest attempt to
(Continued)

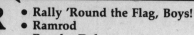

R
- **Rally 'Round the Flag, Boys!**
- **Ramrod**
- **Rancho Deluxe**
- **Random Harvest**

Sidney Poitier in A Raisin in the Sun, *a tale of a black family in a Chicago ghetto.*

(Continued)

deal with the black experience in a realistic and sensitive manner. This tale of a black family in Chicago, attempting to leave the ghetto to live in an all-white neighborhood, is enhanced by the fine acting of Poitier, Dee, and McNeil. The movie doesn't differ much from Lorraine Hansberry's Broadway play; the dialogue still bristles, and the story makes a sharp impact. Also with Diana Sands, Ivan Dixon, John Fielder, and Lou Gossett. **Director**—Daniel Petrie.

128 minutes b&w

RALLY 'ROUND THE FLAG, BOYS! (1958)
★★

Paul Newman
Joanne Woodward

Hollywood mishandles this film version of Max Shulman's witty novel, about Putnam's Landing, a small community upset over a proposed missile base. Newman and Woodward, a couple who get involved in the controversy, lack the comic acting touch needed to salvage this comedy, and they fail to bring the humor and charm of the book onto the screen. Jack Carson, Joan Collins, and Tuesday Weld also star. **Director**—Leo McCarey.

106 minutes

RAMROD (1947)
★★

Veronica Lake
Joel McCrae
Charles Ruggles

Lake plays a ruthless ranch owner in this western story about a territorial dispute. She hires a rough and vicious foreman to assist her in a confrontation with her father, played by Rug-

SPENCER TRACY

Spencer Tracy, born in Milwaukee, Wisconsin, in 1900, attended a Jesuit prep school with ambitions of becoming a priest, but interrupted his studies to join the Navy during World War I.

After the war, Tracy went to Northwestern Military Academy and Ripon College in Wisconsin, where he decided to make acting his profession. He also attended the American Academy of Dramatic Arts in New York City. After graduation, he supported himself by working as a janitor and bellhop while seeking theater work. Finally, after some

success on Broadway in the 1920s, director John Ford chose him for a major role in Up the River (1930), a gangster film. Quickly he became one of Hollywood's top actors, winning Oscars for Captains Courageous (1937) and Boys Town (1938).

Tracy married actress Louise Treadwell in 1923, but it was well known that Katharine Hepburn, his co-star in many films, was his true love. Tracy never divorced his wife although they lived apart for many years.

Tracy and Hepburn co-starred in his last film, Guess Who's Coming to Dinner in 1967. Tracy died soon after finishing the film.

Tracy's other major films include The Power and the Glory (1933), San Francisco (1936), Stanley and Livingstone (1939), Edison, the Man (1940), Tortilla Flat (1942), Cass Timberlane (1947), Adam's Rib (1949), Father of the Bride (1950), Pat and Mike (1953), The Old Man and the Sea (1958), The Last Hurrah (1958), Inherit the Wind (1960), and Judgment at Nuremberg (1961).

gles. There are several deaths and a stampede before the issues are resolved. Also with Preston Foster and Lloyd Bridges. **Director**—André de Toth.

94 minutes b&w

RANCHO DELUXE (1975)
★★★

Jeff Bridges
Sam Waterston

A kinky comedy of the tamed West, where modern buckaroos ride around in pickup trucks and fat-cat ranchers roam the range via helicopters. Bridges and Waterston star as aimless latter-day cattle rustlers, whose antics include sawing up steers with a chainsaw and holding a prize bull for ransom in a motel room. Screenwriter Thomas McGuane cleverly injects some off-beat dialogue, and director Frank Perry emphasizes the freewheeling spirit against the backdrop of wasted lives. Also with Elizabeth Ashley, Charlene Dallas, Clifton James, and Slim Pickens. (R)

93 minutes

RANDOM HARVEST (1942)
★★★

Ronald Coleman
Greer Garson

Coleman and Garson shine in this romance about an amnesia sufferer who forgets the woman he loves. Coleman plays a shell-shocked army officer who escapes from an asylum. Garson dutifully becomes his secretary as she attempts to rekindle the relationship he can't recall. Eventually, another shock years later restores Coleman's memory, and this Hollywood-style romance ends on a happy note. The superior acting of this splendid duo prevents an unbelievable plot, based on a James Hilton novel, from becoming mush. Also with Susan Peters, Philip Dorn, Reginald Owen, Edmund Gwenn, and Margaret Wycherly. **Director**—Mervyn Le Roy. **Academy Award Nominations**—best picture; Coleman, best supporting actor; Peters, best supporting actress; George Froeschel, Claudine West, and

● Ransom
● The Rat Race
● The Raven
● Rawhide

● The Razor's Edge
● Real Life
● Rear Window
● Rebecca

R

Greer Garson and Philip Dorn in Random Harvest, *about a man who forgets the woman he loves.*

Arthur Wimperis, writing (screenplay). *126 minutes b&w*

RANSOM (1955)
★★

Glenn Ford

Ford gives an uneven performance as an industrialist who debates whether to pay the ransom when his son is kidnapped. The story has been done better before and since, but there's enough suspense to keep the film interesting. Ford gets competent support from Donna Reed, Leslie Nielsen, and Robert Keith. **Director**—Alex Segal. *104 minutes b&w*

THE RAT RACE (1960)
★★

Tony Curtis
Debbie Reynolds

Curtis is a young jazz musician and Reynolds is a dancer in this comedy drama based on the Garson Kanin play. The story of show business people trying to make it in New York City has been told many times before, but the scenery of New York is pleasant, and some of the dialogue is top-notch. In addition, Jack Oakie, Kay Medford, and Don Rickles deliver interesting characterizations of typical New Yorkers. **Director**—Robert Mulligan. *105 minutes*

THE RAVEN (1963)
★★

Vincent Price
Peter Lorre
Boris Karloff

Price, Lorre, Karloff, and Jack Nicholson prevent this horror film from becoming a horrible bore. A climactic sorcerers' duel, in which two 15th-century conjurers battle each other in a deadly duel of magic, is the best part of the film. Alas, that part takes a long time to reach, and the earlier segments of the movie are less interesting. Also with Hazel Court. **Director**—Roger Corman. *86 minutes*

RAWHIDE (1950)
★★

Tyrone Power
Susan Hayward

A gang of four desperate outlaws terrorize Power and Hayward at a remote stagecoach stop in this suspenseful but slow-moving western. The shootout at the end highlights this film. Hugh Marlowe, Jack Elam, Dean Jagger, George Tobias, Edgar Buchanan, and Jeff Corey also star. **Director**—Henry Hathaway. **Alternate Title**—*Desperate Siege.* *86 minutes b&w*

THE RAZOR'S EDGE (1946)
★★★

Tyrone Power
Gene Tierney

Long and glossy version of W. Somerset Maugham's famous philosophical novel about a wealthy young man's search for faith. It becomes a rambling and tedious film, but some fine acting salvages this overly long movie. Power portrays the hero seeking goodness in life; Tierney is a social climber who rejects Power; Anne Baxter plays an alcoholic; Herbert Marshall plays the author; and Elsa Lanchester sparkles in a small role as a social secretary. Clifton Webb and John Payne also star. **Director**—Edmund Goulding. **Academy Award**—Baxter, best supporting actress. **Nominations**—best picture; Webb, best supporting actor. *146 minutes b&w*

REAL LIFE (1979)
★

Albert Brooks
Charles Grodin

Writer-director Brooks tries to parody the Public Broadcasting System TV series about the day-to-day events of a typical American family, but the film is an embarrassment to all involved. Brooks—who also stars—jabbers incoherently, acts silly, and fires off corny jokes that fall flat. Some of it is just bad taste—such as an attempt to film the wife's visit to her gynecologist. Also with Frances Lee McCain, J. A. Preston, and Matthew Tobin. (PG) *99 minutes*

REAR WINDOW (1954)
★★★★

James Stewart
Grace Kelly

Grace Kelly and James Stewart star in Alfred Hitchcock's Rear Window.

Director Alfred Hitchcock combines sophisticated comedy with superlative suspense scenes in this movie about a news photographer confined to his wheelchair who witnesses a murder. Stewart plays the photographer, and Kelly is charming as a society girl friend. The tension builds and becomes almost excruciating toward the end of the film as Hitchcock works his magic. Raymond Burr, Judith Evelyn, Wendell Corey, and Thelma Ritter perform well in supporting roles. **Academy Award Nominations**—Hitchcock, best director; John Michael Hayes, writing (screenplay); Robert Burks, cinematography (color). *112 minutes*

REBECCA (1940)
★★★★

Laurence Olivier
Joan Fontaine
George Sanders
Judith Anderson

Director Alfred Hitchcock adapted this award-winning story from Daphne du
(Continued)

R • Rebel Without a Cause
• The Red Badge of Courage
• Red Ball Express

• Red River
• Reds
• The Red Shoes

(Continued)

Maurier's novel about a naïve woman who marries a brooding British nobleman and finds that she must live in the shadow of Rebecca—his beautiful first wife. Hitchcock deftly combines romance, comedy, suspense, and mystery, with sets in Monte Carlo and Cornwall. Fontaine, Anderson, and Olivier perform superbly and receive excellent support from Sanders, Nigel Bruce, Gladys Cooper, Florence Bates, and Reginald Denny. Also with C. Aubrey Smith and Leo G. Carroll. **Academy Awards**—best picture; George Barnes, cinematography (black and white). **Nominations**—Hitchcock, best director; Olivier, best actor; Fontaine, best actress; Anderson, best supporting actress; Robert E. Sherwood and Joan Harrison, writing (screenplay). *130 minutes b&w*

REBEL WITHOUT A CAUSE
(1955)
★★★

James Dean
Natalie Wood

Dean became a star and a symbol to the nation after his role as a troubled teenager in this film. He plays a young man in conflict with the middle-class values of his parents, who finally finds some meaning in life when he befriends Wood and Sal Mineo, who perform well in supporting roles. But his friendship with the pair is shattered in an exciting and tragic end. Jim Backus, Ann Doran, Dennis Hopper, and Nick Adams also star. **Director**—Nicholas Ray. **Academy Award Nominations**—Mineo, best supporting actor; Wood, best supporting actress; Ray, writing (motion picture story). *111 minutes*

THE RED BADGE OF COURAGE
(1951)
★★★★

Audie Murphy

Stephen Crane's classic Civil War novel becomes one of the greatest war films under the brilliant writing and direction of John Huston. Murphy, Bill Mauldin, and John Dierkes give natural performances that further brighten this realistic drama of combat as seen through the eyes of a young recruit.

Audie Murphy in the film version of Stephen Crane's novel The Red Badge of Courage.

Before the young soldier becomes a brave soldier, he experiences fear, and the viewer gets a hint of the hell of war. Also with Douglas Dick, Royal Dano, Andy Devine, and Arthur Hunnicutt. *69 minutes b&w*

RED BALL EXPRESS (1952)
★★

Jeff Chandler

Chandler plays the gruff but human leader of an Army truck division—known as the Red Ball Express—that ferries war supplies from the beaches of Normandy to the outskirts of Paris during World War II. Sidney Poitier, Alex Nicol, Hugh O'Brien, Jack Kelly, and Jack Warden blend well in this conventional war story that has its share of action and adventure. **Director**—Budd Boetticher. *83 minutes b&w*

RED RIVER (1948)
★★★★

John Wayne
Montgomery Clift

Wayne and Clift star in this classic western story of a cattle baron and the dynasty he builds. Clift, in his movie debut, rebels against his foster father, played by Wayne, and the empire Wayne has developed. Joanne Dru, Walter Brennan, Colleen Gray, John Ireland, and Noah Berry, Jr., are also in top form in supporting roles. Besides the excellent acting and topflight action-packed story, the movie, under the direction of Howard Hawks, is beautifully filmed. **Academy Award Nomination**—Borden Chase, writing (motion picture story). *133 minutes b&w*

REDS (1981)
★★★★

Warren Beatty
Diane Keaton

A brilliant and passionately thick slice of history with Beatty splendidly playing radical journalist John Reed, who chronicled the Russian Revolution. The epic adventure also involves the stormy love affair between Reed and writer Louise Bryant, played exquisitely by Keaton. Although the remarkable story deals heavily in radical politics, it's amazingly lucid and invigorating. A triumph for Beatty, who also produced, wrote, and directed. He gets superb support from Jack Nicholson and Maureen Stapleton. Also with Edward Herrmann, Jerzy Kosinski, Paul Sorvino, and Gene Hackman. (PG) *200 minutes*

In the epic adventure Reds, *Warren Beatty portrays radical journalist John Reed.*

THE RED SHOES (1948)
★★★★

Anton Walbrook
Moira Shearer
Marius Goring

This sensitive and beautiful movie about a ballerina who gives up her romance with a composer to dedicate her life to ballet is enriched by superb dancing. The production, which stars Walbrook, Shearer, and Goring, offers an intimate and realistic slice-of-life view of the ballerina's world backstage. Also with Robert Helpmann, Albert Bassermann, Frederick Ashton, and Leonide Massine. **Director**—Michael Powell. **Academy Award Nominations**—best picture; Emeric Pressburger, writing (motion picture story). *136 minutes*

- Reflections in a Golden Eye
- The Reincarnation of Peter Proud
- The Reluctant Debutante
- The Reluctant Dragon
- The Remarkable Mr. Pennypacker
- Remember the Night
- Renaldo and Clara
- Replay
- Report to the Commissioner

R

REFLECTIONS IN A GOLDEN EYE (1967)
★

Marlon Brando
Elizabeth Taylor

A star-studded cast, which includes Brando, Taylor, Brian Keith, and Julie Harris, fails to salvage this cinema clunker about a homosexual Army officer stationed in Georgia. Most of the characters are insane, or at least eccentric, in this debased film version of Carson McCullers's perceptive novel. Some of the acting, however, is excellent. Brando, despite the faults of his method acting, still conveys, in a deeply moving way, the anguish of a homosexual Army officer. Robert Forster is the object of his affection, and Taylor plays Brando's wife. John Huston provides stylish direction, but fortunately his reputation has been secured by his other cinema efforts.
108 minutes

THE REINCARNATION OF PETER PROUD (1975)
★★★

Michael Sarrazin
Jennifer O'Neill
Margot Kidder

A California college professor, played by Sarrazin, believes he led an earlier life that ended in violence. He searches for his past in a suburban Massachusetts town and finds more than he bargained for. A suspenseful and moody drama, but there's no solid solution to the mystery. Good performances by Sarrazin, O'Neill, and Kidder. Also with Cornelia Sharpe and Paul Hecht. **Director**—J. Lee Thompson. (R) *104 minutes*

THE RELUCTANT DEBUTANTE (1958)
★★

Rex Harrison
Kay Kendall

Harrison and Kendall brighten this ho-hum British drawing-room comedy about an unorthodox British couple who choose to permit their daughter, educated in America, to make her soci-ety debut in England. Sandra Dee plays the daughter. Despite such a lean plot, there are some pleasant moments that make the movie mildly enjoyable. Also with John Saxon, Peter Myers, and Angela Lansbury. **Director**—Vincente Minnelli.
96 minutes

THE RELUCTANT DRAGON (1941)
★★

Robert Benchley

This studio tour of the fantastic and magical universe of Walt Disney gives young and old moviegoers an excellent chance to see how cartoons of the '30s and '40s were made. During this Disney studio tour, the enjoyable mixture of short subjects presented include *Baby Weems*, *How To Ride a Horse*, and the title story. The pleasant experience is enriched by the presence of Benchley, who's better known for his comic novels and humorous essays. **Director**—Alfred Werker. *72 minutes*

THE REMARKABLE MR. PENNYPACKER (1959)
★

Clifton Webb

Can a movie about bigamy be funny? Webb makes a valiant effort to be humorous in this story about a businessman who leads two lives and raises two families with a total of 17 children, but he doesn't succeed. Dorothy McGuire, Charles Coburn, Ray Stricklyn, Jill St. John, Ron Ely, and David Nelson also appear in this effort at sophisticated comedy, but fail to brighten it. **Director**—Henry Levin. *87 minutes*

REMEMBER THE NIGHT (1940)
★★★

Barbara Stanwyck
Fred MacMurray

MacMurray and Stanwyck shine in this delightful and sentimental story of an assistant district attorney who takes a shoplifter home with him when court recesses for the Christmas holidays. MacMurray plays the attorney who falls in love with Stanwyck, the shoplifter. Under Mitchell Leisen's direction, the film is typical of the special blend of comedy, romance, and drama that some of the finer films of this era achieved. Beulah Bondi, Elizabeth Patterson, Sterling Holloway, Paul Guilfoyle, and Willard Robertson do their share in supporting roles. *94 minutes b&w*

RENALDO AND CLARA (1978)
★

Bob Dylan

Only some Dylan devotees may find this film of interest; others will be frustrated by the nearly four-hour-long mishmash of musical interludes and an incoherent script. The movie mainly concerns a 1975 concert tour by Dylan, Joan Baez, and friends. Dylan was the writer, director, and musical supervisor. (R) *232 minutes*

REPLAY (1978)
★

Marie-José Nat
Victor Lanoux

French director Michel Drach reached for suspense on the order of Alfred Hitchcock in this film. Instead, we get a trivial domestic drama about a woman who suffers amnesia and then grows suspicious about her husband's activities. Nat and Lanoux play their roles to the hilt, but can't transcend the boring script. In French with English titles. (No MPAA rating)
96 minutes b&w

REPORT TO THE COMMISSIONER (1975)
★★

Michael Moriarty
Yaphet Kotto
Susan Blakely

A hippie undercover cop, played by Moriarty, is destroyed by his inept and aloof police department supervisors. Blakely plays an undercover cop. The film is more exploitation of the *French Connection* and *Serpico* themes, but the suspense hardly gets off the ground, and the plot bogs down in unlikely
(Continued)

R
- Reprieve
- Requiem for a Heavyweight
- The Rescuers

- Resurrection
- Retreat, Hell!
- Return From Witch Mountain

- The Return of a Man Called Horse
- The Return of Frank James
- The Return of the Pink Panther

(Continued) complications. Also with Hector Elizondo, Tony King, and Michael McGuire. **Director**—Milton Katselas. (PG)   *112 minutes*

REPRIEVE
See Convicts Four

REQUIEM FOR A HEAVYWEIGHT (1962)
★★★★

Anthony Quinn
Jackie Gleason
Mickey Rooney
Julie Harris

Quinn, Gleason, Rooney, and Harris contribute excellent performances in this tough, hard-hitting drama of a prizefighter in the twilight of his career. Quinn plays the washed-up boxer, Rooney is a pathetic friend, and Harris is a social worker. The movie, based on Rod Serling's play, has realistic and harsh fight scenes, which blend well with the superior acting. Also with Nancy Cushman, Madame Spivy, and Stan Adams. **Director**—Ralph Nelson.   *87 minutes b&w*

THE RESCUERS (1977)
★★★★

Imagination, expert craftsmanship, loving care, and plenty of expense have gone into this 22nd full-length animated feature by the Walt Disney studio. It's a lively and charming adventure about two brave mice who set out to rescue a kidnapped girl. The voices of Eva Gabor, Bob Newhart, Jim (Fibber McGee) Jordan, and Geraldine Page add delightful dimensions to the cartoon subjects. The Disney wizards have created magic again. **Directors** — Wolfgang Reitherman, John Lounsbery, and Art Stevens. (G)   *76 minutes*

RESURRECTION (1980)
★★

Ellen Burstyn

Burstyn dominates this unusual and uneven film with a glowing virtuoso performance. She plays an ordinary woman who discovers that after a serious accident, she can heal people with the laying on of hands. The flimsy story, however, never connects dramatically or emotionally; the treatment is neither an exposé of hokum nor a plug for divine faith. It is, more or less, a beautifully acted fable with vague perceptions of psychic healing. As for Burstyn's acting, she walks on water. Also with Eva Le Gallienne. **Director**—Daniel Petrie. (PG) **Academy Award Nominations**—Burstyn, best actress; Le Gallienne, best supporting actress.   *103 minutes*

RETREAT, HELL! (1952)
★

Frank Lovejoy
Richard Carlson

Action scenes and a few tense moments enliven this run-of-the-mill war story of a Marine unit fighting in Korea. Lovejoy and Carlson, in starring roles, provide the rough-and-tough characterization that's required in such movies. Also with Anita Louise and Russ Tamblyn. **Director**—Joseph H. Lewis.   *95 minutes b&w*

RETURN FROM WITCH MOUNTAIN (1978)
★★★

Bette Davis
Christopher Lee
Kim Richards
Ike Eisenmann

Richards and Eisenmann, two appealing kids from outer space, return in this Walt Disney-made sequel to *Escape From Witch Mountain* with their extraordinary powers. Lee and Davis play a pair of meanies who try to exploit the moppets for power and

As Anthony James and Bette Davis look on, Christopher Lee experiments on Ike Eisenmann in Return From Witch Mountain.

profit, but the two youngsters have dazzling Disney special effects on their side. The children will be enthralled; for adults, it's déjà vu. Also with Denver Pyle and Dick Bakalyan. **Director**—John Hough. (G)   *95 minutes*

THE RETURN OF A MAN CALLED HORSE (1976)
★★

Richard Harris

Harris stars in this mystical sequel to *A Man Called Horse*, in which he played the leading role. This time, he portrays an English nobleman who returns to South Dakota to rescue the Yellow Hand Sioux, his adopted tribe, from annihilation. Harris participates in yet another gruesome purification ritual in which his chest is pierced by small bones and then stretched; it's not for the squeamish. The film is mostly placid, but it's highlighted here and there with short periods of action. Also with Gale Sondergaard, Geoffrey Lewis, Bill Lucking, and Jorge Luke. **Director**—Irvin Kershner. (PG)   *129 minutes*

THE RETURN OF FRANK JAMES (1940)
★★★

Henry Fonda
Gene Tierney

Fonda plays Frank James, attempting to avenge brother Jesse's death, in this colorful and excellently photographed tale. The action is balanced by more characterization and humor than is found in most westerns of this era. Tierney makes her film debut in this sequel to *Jesse James*. Jackie Cooper, John Carradine, Henry Hull, J. Edward Bromberg, and Donald Meek also star. **Director**—Fritz Lang.   *92 minutes*

THE RETURN OF THE PINK PANTHER (1975)
★★★★

Peter Sellers
Christopher Plummer
Herbert Lom

Funnyman Sellers once again plays the accident-prone Inspector Jacques

- The Return of the Vampire
- Return to Macon County
- Return to Peyton Place
- The Revenge of Frankenstein
- Revenge of the Pink Panther
- The Revolt of Mamie Stover
- Rhapsody
- Rhapsody in Blue

R

In The Return of the Pink Panther, *Peter Sellers prepares to attack.*

Clouseau—hot on the trail of the fabled Pink Panther diamond, the national treasure of the State of Lugash, after it's stolen once more. Lom plays the Chief Inspector. It's slapstick carried to the most reckless degree, as the bumbling Clouseau drives those around him up the wall and gets himself into outrageous comic entanglements. Also with Catherine Schell, Bert Kwouk, Peter Arne, and Grégoire Aslan. **Director**—Blake Edwards. (PG) *113 minutes*

THE RETURN OF THE VAMPIRE (1943)

★★

Bela Lugosi

Lugosi returns in this spinoff of his previously successful performance as Dracula. One version of this monster would have been enough, and it seems unpatriotic to have Dracula reappear during the London Blitz. Despite these faults, this is an expertly plotted horror film with a fantastic final scene. Lugosi gives an excellent performance. Also with Nina Foch, Frieda Inescort, and Miles Mander. **Director**—Lew Landers.

69 minutes b&w

RETURN TO MACON COUNTY (1975)

★★

**Nick Nolte
Don Johnson
Robin Mattson**

In this sequel to *Macon County Line*, two young racing-car sports—Nolte and Johnson—head for California in a bright-yellow stock car, bent on becoming drag-racing champs. Along the way they latch on to a young girl—Mattson—who wants to be a movie star. The dull plot leans on the *American Graffiti* and *Bonnie and Clyde* themes, but it's merely another '50s nostalgia piece. Also with Robert Viharo and Eugene Daniels. Written and directed by Richard Compton. (PG) *90 minutes*

RETURN TO PEYTON PLACE (1961)

★

**Jeff Chandler
Carol Lynley
Eleanor Parker
Mary Astor**

This early 1960s version of a TV soap opera will appeal to the fans of such things. Parker, Astor, and Lynley perform competently, but the rest of the cast, including Chandler, Robert Sterling, Luciana Paluzzi, Brett Halsey, and Tuesday Weld, seem to be underachievers in this trite story. The action centers on the fallout after Allison Mackenzie, played by Lynley, writes a book about her notorious hometown and falls in love with her publisher. **Director**—José Ferrer. *122 minutes*

THE REVENGE OF FRANKENSTEIN (1958)

★★

Peter Cushing

In this well-made and well-acted sequel to *The Curse of Frankenstein*, Baron Von Frankenstein makes a new creation with the brain of a homicidal dwarf. Cushing is excellent as Dr. Frankenstein, and he gets able support from Michael Gwynn, Oscar Quitak, Lloyd Pack, Francis Matthews, Lionel Jeffries, John Welsh, and Eunice Gayson. The movie isn't without a message—especially in light of the advances in gene-splicing. **Director**—Terence Fisher. *89 minutes*

REVENGE OF THE PINK PANTHER (1978)

★★★

**Peter Sellers
Dyan Cannon**

Sellers as the bumbling French Inspector Jacques Clouseau is as durable a laugh-maker as W. C. Fields and Jack Benny. In this fifth *Pink Panther* film, the "world's greatest detective" breaks up the French Connection drug ring while the audience breaks up with laughter. Sellers is helped by Cannon, who's hilarious as the discarded mistress of the drug ring's boss. Robert Walker plays the drug kingpin. The film should tickle you pink. Also with Herbert Lom and Burt Kwouk. **Director**—Blake Edwards. (PG) *99 minutes*

THE REVOLT OF MAMIE STOVER (1956)

★

Jane Russell

Russell plays a woman who's forced to leave town and goes to Hawaii. As a saloon singer in the islands during World War II, she becomes wealthy. Jane does well in several enjoyable scenes, but can't overcome the weak plot, based on William Bradford Huie's novel. She's at her best when she sings "Keep Your Eyes on the Hands." Russell is joined by Agnes Moorehead and Richard Egan. **Director**—Raoul Walsh. *93 minutes*

RHAPSODY (1954)

★

**Elizabeth Taylor
Vittorio Gassman
John Ericson**

Taylor enlivens this romantic film about a three-cornered love story in which she can't decide between Gassman, a violinist, and Ericson, a pianist. Taylor's wardrobe resembles a fashion show for stylish 1954 clothing. The musical interludes are pleasing, but the movie still fails. Louis Calhern, Michael Chekhov, Barbara Bates, Celia Lovsky, and Richard Hageman also appear in supporting roles. **Director**—Charles Vidor. *116 minutes*

RHAPSODY IN BLUE (1945)

★★★

**Robert Alda
Joan Leslie**

This biography of George Gershwin, *(Continued)*

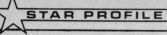
R • Rich and Famous
• Richard III
• Rich Kids
• Ride a Wild Pony

Joan Leslie and Robert Alda in Rhapsody in Blue, *a biography of George Gershwin.*

(Continued)

starring Alda and Leslie, captures the great composer's enthusiasm for his work and reveals some of the conflicts he faced, but as a biography it's thin and shallow. Fortunately, the movie is sprinkled with Gershwin's wonderful music. The cast also includes Alexis Smith, Charles Coburn, Julie Bishop, Albert Bassermann, Oscar Levant, Herbert Rudley, Al Jolson, Paul Whiteman, and Hazel Scott. **Director**—Irving Rapper. *139 minutes b&w*

SIDNEY POITIER

Sidney Poitier, a handsome black actor, shares some of the major credit for breaking down racial barriers in movies. His wide popularity and success in films from the '50s on helped other serious black actors to prosper in the movie industry.

Poitier was born in Miami in 1924, but spent his early years in the Bahamas. He left school at the age of 13, worked at several odd jobs, and

then served in the Army. After his discharge, he worked with the American Negro Theater and debuted on Broadway in the 1946 production of Lysistrata, *which featured an all-black cast.*

Poitier's first Hollywood film was No Way Out *in 1950. He quickly became a popular black star, working in numerous films through the '60s and '70s. He was nominated as best actor for his performance in* The Defiant Ones *(1958), and he won an Oscar for* Lilies of the Field *(1963). In the '70s, Poitier started directing his films. Most of these projects were dominated by black casts; he also played leading roles in them.*

Some of Poitier's other major movies include The Blackboard Jungle *(1955),* Porgy and Bess *(1959),* A Raisin in the Sun *(1961),* A Patch of Blue *(1965),* In the Heat of the Night *(1967),* Guess Who's Coming to Dinner? *(1967), and* Let's Do It Again *(1976).*

RICH AND FAMOUS (1981)
★

Jacqueline Bisset
Candice Bergen

Bisset and Bergen play friends from their Smith College days, who carry on a love-hate relationship over the years as they pursue separate literary careers. Veteran director George Cukor fashioned this so-called woman's film, which looks slick enough, but gradually deteriorates into a hysterical soap opera. Gerald Ayres's rather irritating screenplay is loosely based on the 1943 film *Old Acquaintances*, which starred Bette Davis and Miriam Hopkins. (R)   *117 minutes*

RICHARD III (1956)
★★★★

Laurence Olivier

Olivier, one of the greatest actors of the century, turns in a magnificent performance as both actor and director in this Shakespeare play about Richard Crookback, the evil king. The world's greatest playwright is difficult to transform to the screen, but Olivier has made the adaptation brilliantly in this story of Richard's seizure of the throne, his devious dealings in court, and his conquests on the battlefield. Superb performances are also delivered by Claire Bloom, Ralph Richardson, Cedric Hardwicke, John Gielgud, and Clive Morton. **Academy Award Nomination**—Olivier, best actor.

161 minutes

RICH KIDS (1979)
★★★★

Trini Alvarado
Jeremy Levy

Jeremy Levy and Trini Alvarado enjoy breakfast in bed in Rich Kids.

This is a warm, witty, and touching comedy about a disturbing and often sad situation—the effect of divorce on children. Alvarado and Levy are remarkable as bright New York adolescents who form a puppy-love relationship as shelter from their parents' messed-up marriages. Robert M. Young directs with style from an appealing script by Judith Ross. The adult roles are handled by rather unfamiliar players, who all perform splendidly. Also with John Lithgow, Kathryn Walker, and Terry Kiser. (PG)   *101 minutes*

RIDE A WILD PONY (1976)
★★

Robert Bettles
Eva Griffith

A poor boy and a wealthy handicapped girl struggle over the ownership of a pony in this middling melodrama from the Walt Disney organization. Youngsters Bettles and Griffith perform adequately in the pre-World War II Australian setting, but a

- Ride the High Country
- Ride, Vaquero
- Riffraff
- Rio Bravo
- Rio Grande
- Rio Lobo
- The Ritz

R

sluggish plot fails to develop the needed suspense. Also with Michael Craig, John Meillon, and Graham Rouse. **Director**—Don Chaffey. (G) *91 minutes*

RIDE THE HIGH COUNTRY (1962)
★★★★

Joel McCrea
Randolph Scott

Sam Peckinpah artfully directed this classic western about two aging lawmen—Scott and McCrea—who are reunited after 20 years to deliver a gold shipment but meet trouble along the way. Peckinpah, who has since become obsessed with violence, directed this fine yarn with sensitivity and subtlety. Scott and McCrea are excellent in their last performances as western heroes. The movie was shot on location at the beautiful Inyo National Forest in California. Also with Edgar Buchanan, Mariette Hartley, James Drury, and Warren Oates. *94 minutes*

RIDE, VAQUERO (1953)
★★

Robert Taylor
Ava Gardner

Sultry Gardner throws off enough sparks to make this western tale mildly interesting. The story, set on the Mexican border after the Civil War, is about a beautiful woman who causes the downfall of notorious outlaws. Also with Anthony Quinn and Howard Keel. **Director**—John Farrow. *90 minutes*

RIFFRAFF (1947)
★★★

Pat O'Brien

O'Brien defeats the bad guys in this well-done, fast-paced melodrama about shady characters attempting to take over oil fields in Panama. Besides some excellent scenes, there are above-average performances by O'Brien, Walter Slezak, Anne Jeffreys, Jason Robards, Percy Kilbride, and Jerome Cowan. **Director**—Ted Tetzlaff. *80 minutes b&w*

RIO BRAVO (1959)
★★★

John Wayne
Dean Martin
Ricky Nelson

In Rio Bravo, *John Wayne is a lawman trying to keep a killer in jail.*

Famed director Howard Hawks is in top form for this story about a sheriff trying to prevent the bad guys from helping a killer escape the town jail. Hawks has assembled a fine cast that includes Wayne, as the sheriff, Martin, as the town drunk, and Nelson, as the young cowhand ready to prove his manhood. Angie Dickinson is the love interest. Although the movie is long and, at first, seems to inch along, it's worthwhile to hang in there. Also with Walter Brennan, Ward Bond, Claude Akins, and Bob Steele. *141 minutes*

RIO GRANDE (1950)
★★★

John Wayne
Maureen O'Hara

Wayne is excellent as a tough cavalry commander on the Mexican border in the 1880s, conducting a vain campaign against Indians on the warpath. John Ford's classic directorial touch is aided by beautiful scenery, some good action scenes, and lots of human interest. The film is helped by the fine cast, which also includes Ben Johnson, Harry Carey, Jr., Chill Wills, J. Carrol Naish, and Victor McLaglen. *105 minutes b&w*

RIO LOBO (1970)
★

John Wayne
Jennifer O'Neill

The usually surefire western guarantee of Wayne and director Howard Hawks falls short in this rambling Civil War-era story. Wayne plays a Union colonel who recovers a gold shipment after it's stolen. The train robbery scenes at the beginning of the film are exciting, but after that the movie bogs down and becomes a slow-moving bore. O'Neill is beautiful, but a below-par actress here. The performances of Jorge Rivero, Jack Elam, and Chris Mitchum are average at best. (G) *114 minutes*

THE RITZ (1976)
★★★

Jack Weston
Rita Moreno

Jerry Stiller, Rita Moreno, and Jack Weston are among the stars in The Ritz.

Moreno steals the show in this riproaring film version of the brassy Broadway comedy about high jinks in a homosexual bathhouse. She was in the stage production, and she delivers the same energetic and madcap portrayal of Googie Gomez, the fiery Puerto Rican singer yearning for discovery by a gay Broadway producer. Weston plays a man fleeing from his brother-in-law. Richard Lester's direction is uneven and jumpy, but the fun and hilarity burst forth just the same. Also with Jerry Stiller, Kaye Ballard, Bessie Love, Treat Williams, and George Couloris. (R) *91 minutes*

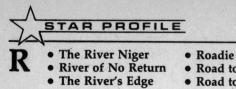

R
- The River Niger
- River of No Return
- The River's Edge
- Roadie
- Road to Morocco
- Road to Singapore

THE RIVER NIGER (1976)
★★

James Earl Jones
Cicely Tyson

The moving, award-winning Broadway play by Joseph A. Walker loses its punch on the screen. Much of the fault is uneven direction by Krishna Shah and a lot of unnecessary dialogue. The story is about a black family's struggle to survive in contemporary America. Jones stars as a house painter who writes poetry. Also with Glynn Turman, Lou Gossett, and Roger E. Mosley. (R) *105 minutes*

RIVER OF NO RETURN (1954)
★★

Robert Mitchum
Marilyn Monroe

The chemistry of Monroe and Mitchum under the direction of Otto Preminger and with some excellent location photography is stronger than the weak plot in which these two actors must function. Monroe, a saloon singer, hires Mitchum, a widower, to find the gambler husband who has deserted her and her 10-year-old son. The action takes place during the California gold rush. Tommy Rettig, Rory Calhoun, and Murvyn Vye also star. *91 minutes*

THE RIVER'S EDGE (1956)
★★★

Ray Milland
Anthony Quinn
Deborah Paget

Milland delivers an excellent portrayal as a fugitive bank robber who menaces his old girl friend, Paget, and threatens her husband, Quinn, in his attempt to escape over the mountains into Mexico with his fortune. Also with Byron Foulger. **Director**—Allan Dwan. *87 minutes*

ROADIE (1980)
★★★

Meat Loaf

An energetic, madcap parody of the rock 'n' roll scene, which stars popular rock star Meat Loaf in an effective nonsinging role. The screwball story features a number of hilarious slapstick escapades, and it zips along like a comic strip full of inventive chaos. There's a lot of nonstop, earsplitting rock music from a half-dozen performers, including Blondie and Alice Cooper. Also with Art Carney, Hank Williams, Jr., and Roy Orbison. **Director**—Alan Rudolph. (PG) *106 minutes*

Meat Loaf and Deborah Harry make some music on empty beer bottles in Roadie.

ROAD TO MOROCCO (1942)
★★★

Bob Hope
Bing Crosby
Dorothy Lamour

One of the best of the Hope and Crosby *Road* films. In this one, Bing sells Bob into slavery in exotic Morocco. Lamour is present for romantic high jinks, and Monte Blue, Yvonne de Carlo, Anthony Quinn, and Dona Drake join in the silliness. A few good songs, including "Moonlight Becomes You," and a talking camel add to the entertainment value of this fun-filled movie. **Director**—David Butler. **Academy Award Nomination**—Frank Butler and Don Hartman, writing (original screenplay). *83 minutes b&w*

ROAD TO SINGAPORE (1940)
★★★

Bob Hope
Bing Crosby
Dorothy Lamour

Hope and Crosby are rich playboys who swear off women, but then they meet a Singapore maiden, played by Lamour, and quarrel over her. As long as you don't take the flimsy plot too

ROBERT REDFORD

Robert Redford was born in 1937 in Santa Monica, California. As a child, he wanted to be an outlaw and an artist. Growing up near Hollywood where he could observe it at close quarters, he found it suspect and dropped out in Europe to "paint angry pictures."

Acting, however, tempted him, and he began acting in New York in 1959, going on to make a considerable splash in Neil Simon's Barefoot in the Park. Redford made his film debut—a small part—in War Hunt (1961). Later, during casting for an off-beat western, Paul Newman told the studio "No Redford, no Newman." Butch Cassidy and the Sundance Kid (1969) justified his stand.

Becoming fascinated with the Watergate affair when it was still a breaking news item, Redford was the moving spirit behind the film version of All the President's Men (1976), helping to make it "the thinking man's 'Jaws.'"

Redford's other major films include Inside Daisy Clover (1965), The Chase (1966), This Property Is Condemned (1966), Barefoot in the Park (1967), Tell Them Willie Boy Is Here (1969), Jeremiah Johnson (1972), The Candidate (1972), The Hot Rock (1972), The Way We Were (1973), The Sting (1973), A Bridge Too Far (1977), The Outlaw Trail (1978), and The Electric Horseman (1979).

In 1980, Redford received the Oscar as best director for Ordinary People.

seriously, this first of the duo's *Road* films is enjoyable. Also with Charles Coburn, Judith Barrett, Anthony Quinn, and Jerry Colonna. **Director**—Victor Schertzinger. *84 minutes b&w*

- Road to Zanzibar
- The Roaring Twenties
- The Robe
- Robert et Robert
- Robin and Marian
- Robin and the Seven Hoods
- Rock 'n' Roll High School
- Rocky

R

ROAD TO ZANZIBAR (1941)
★★★

Bob Hope
Bing Crosby
Dorothy Lamour

Anything goes in this satire of jungle pictures. Hope and Crosby play carnival hustlers on a safari in Africa. They are joined again by Lamour, and the trio searches for a diamond mine. The cast also includes Una Merkel, Eric Blore, Luis Alberni, and Douglass Dumbrille. **Director**—Victor Schertzinger.

92 minutes b&w

THE ROARING TWENTIES (1939)
★★★★

James Cagney
Humphrey Bogart

After World War I, Army pals Cagney, Bogart, and Jeffrey Lynn run into each other again. But now, Cagney is a gangster. This film version of the Mark Hellinger story, about a World War I veteran who becomes involved in crime during Prohibition, has a familiar plot, but Cagney is fantastic as the New York bootlegger who finds success in the underworld before dying in a gang war. Also with Priscilla Lane, Gladys George, and Frank McHugh. **Director**—Raoul Walsh.

106 minutes b&w

THE ROBE (1953)
★★★

Richard Burton
Jean Simmons
Michael Rennie
Victor Mature

This Bible epic features Burton as Gallio, a Roman tribune put in charge of the execution of Jesus Christ. Burton later converts to Christianity when he dons Christ's robe. Burton is joined by a large cast, which also includes Richard Boone, Dawn Addams, and Dean Jagger. The movie, the first film made in the Cinemascope process, is impressively produced, but the plot is mediocre. **Director**—Henry Koster. **Academy Award Nominations**—best picture; Burton, best actor; Leon Shamroy, cinematography (color).

135 minutes

ROBERT ET ROBERT (1980)
★★

Charles Denner
Jacques Villeret

A thin, slow-moving comedy about two lonely men—Denner and Villeret—who become pals while seeking the women of their dreams at a computer dating agency. Director-writer Claude Lelouch has concocted a cross between *Marty* and a Laurel and Hardy movie. There are some funny moments here and there, but Lelouch drags out his theme to the point of irritation. In French with English titles. (No MPAA rating) *105 minutes*

ROBIN AND MARIAN (1976)
★★

Sean Connery
Audrey Hepburn
Robert Shaw

The legend of Robin Hood is revised in this film. A middle-aged and battle-scarred Robin, played by Connery, returns to Sherwood Forest after fighting in the Crusades for 20 years. He looks up his old girl friend, Maid Marian, played by Hepburn, now an abbess. The Sheriff of Nottingham—Shaw—still controls the neighborhood. Robin takes him on, but appears to be suffering from a bad back and tired blood. The acting and photography are impressive, but screenwriter James Goldman has turned the colorful myth of Robin Hood and his merry men into a state of confusion. Also with Richard Harris, Nicol Williamson, and Ian Holm. **Director**—Richard Lester. (PG) *112 minutes*

ROBIN AND THE SEVEN HOODS (1964)
★★★

Frank Sinatra
Dean Martin
Bing Crosby
Sammy Davis, Jr.
Peter Falk

Sinatra, Martin, Crosby, Davis, and Falk star in this musical spoof set during Prohibition in Chicago. Sinatra and his friends—known as the Rat Pack by gossip columnists—seem to enjoy themselves and are well suited to their roles of small-time hoodlums who work as Chicago-style Robin Hoods; they steal from the rich and give to the poor. "My Kind of Town" and "Style" highlight the music. The cast also includes Barbara Rush, Edward G. Robinson, Victor Buono, Jack La Rue, and Hans Conried. **Director**—Gordon Douglas. *123 minutes*

ROCK 'N' ROLL HIGH SCHOOL (1979)
★★

P. J. Soles
Vincent Van Patten
Clint Howard

Silliness and exuberance are the mainstay of this youth fantasy, which seems to be inspired by such movies as *Grease* and *Animal House*. The kids engage in assorted escapades and provoke the displeasure of the school's stern principal; all this is carried out against a booming sound track of rock music. The young, unknown players go through their paces with plenty of gusto and minimal professional style. Also with The Ramones, Paul Bartel, and Alix Elias. **Director**—Allan Arkush. (PG)

93 minutes

ROCKY (1976)
★★★★

Sylvester Stallone
Talia Shire

This gritty Cinderella story of a luckless Philadelphia boxer who gets a chance at the world heavyweight championship is uplifting to the human spirit. Stallone, who wrote the film script, plays the aging prizefighter with feeling and power. Nice work, too, from the rest of the cast, especially Shire as the boxer's shy girl friend. The schmaltzy plot owes much to *Marty* and *On the Waterfront*, yet the cliché takes on new life with energy and atmosphere. Also with Burt Young, Carl Weathers, Burgess Meredith, and Thayer David. Crisply directed by John G. Avildsen. (PG)

(Continued)

R
- Rocky II
- Rogues of Sherwood Forest
- Rollerball
- Roller Boogie
- Rollercoaster
- Rolling Thunder
- Rollover

(Continued)
Academy Awards—best picture; Avildsen, best director. **Nominations**—Stallone, best actor; Shire, best actress; Meredith, Young, best supporting actor; Stallone, best original screenplay. *119 minutes*

ROCKY II (1979)
★★★★

Sylvester Stallone
Talia Shire

Sylvester Stallone trains for his fight in Rocky II *while Burgess Meredith (left) watches.*

Sequels seldom live up to the original, but this second chapter in the life of underdog boxer Rocky Balboa is an exception, indeed. The plot drags in spots, but that fantastic uplifting spirit is there again as Rocky, played by Stallone, prepares for the big bout with Apollo Creed, played by Carl Weathers. The same top-notch supporting cast is back in fine form. It all leads to an exciting and realistic fight finale that will have you cheering with gusto. Also with Burgess Meredith and Burt Young. **Director**—Stallone. (PG) *119 minutes*

ROGUES OF SHERWOOD FOREST (1950)
★★

John Derek

This time, the son of Robin Hood, played by Derek, helps the barons force the signing of the Magna Carta. The film's theme is tiresome and familiar, but the production is well done, and the sets and costumes are splendid. The competent cast also includes Diana Lynn, George Macready, Alan Hale, and Billy House. **Director**—Gordon Douglas. *80 minutes*

ROLLERBALL (1975)
(no stars)

James Caan

This sci-fi film, based on William Harrison's story, concerns a new sport that combines hockey, Roller Derby, motorcycle racing, and gladiatorial combat. Supposedly, it works off aggressions and keeps billions of people glued to their TV sets because other forms of violence have been outlawed. The planet has come under the control of the "major corporate conglomerates," but one man—Caan—attempts to regain individual freedom in this brave new world. The script drags the film down with an air of imitation Stanley Kubrick. Also with John Houseman, Ralph Richardson, Maud Adams, and Moses Gunn. **Director**—Norman Jewison. (R) *128 minutes*

ROLLER BOOGIE (1979)
(no stars)

Linda Blair

This dopey film stars Blair as a poor little rich girl who finds happiness disco-dancing on roller skates along the boardwalk in Venice, California. It's an obvious exploitation of the disco roller-skating craze, and it fails at all levels to maintain professional standards. Even a skating enthusiast will want more than this mindless junk to enjoy music and fancy skating. It makes those *Beach Blanket* films of another decade look like accomplished film art. Also with Jim Bray, Beverly Garland, Roger Perry, and Mark Goddard. **Director**—Mark L. Lester. (PG) *103 minutes*

ROLLERCOASTER (1977)
★★★

George Segal
Richard Widmark
Timothy Bottoms

There's plenty of suspense, ample excitement, and just the right touch of humor in this straightforward drama. It's about a clever mad bomber, played by Bottoms, who sabotages rollercoasters to blackmail amusement park

Thrill-seekers ride the Rebel Yell at King's Dominion in Rollercoaster.

owners. Segal is amusing and relaxed as a safety inspector who pursues the wily terrorist from coast to coast. The plot is uncluttered, and the violence isn't excessive. Widmark, Bottoms, and Henry Fonda contribute their talents. Also with Harry Guardino and Susan Strasberg. **Director**—James Goldstone (PG) *119 minutes*

ROLLING THUNDER (1977)
★★★

William Devane

A finely crafted film about a Vietnam veteran, played by Devane, who hunts down the killers of his wife and son. Scriptwriter Paul Schrader, who wrote *Taxi Driver*, uses his familiar explosive and complicated character again. The acting is excellent, and there's a convincing portrayal of small-town middle America. There's a considerable amount of blood and gore, which may be too heavy for some. Also with Tommy Lee Jones, Linda Haynes, James Best, and Dabney Coleman. **Director**—John Flynn. (R) *99 minutes*

ROLLOVER (1981)
★★

Jane Fonda
Kris Kristofferson

Fonda and Kristofferson star in this meandering message movie about the vulnerability of the world monetary system. The romantic thriller, set against the backdrop of banking and multinational corporations, is overburdened with technical economic jargon.

- Roman Holiday
- Romanoff and Juliet
- The Romantic Englishwoman
- Room at the Top
- Rooster Cogburn
- Rope
- The Rose

R

Fonda, dressed to the nines, plays a widow who takes over a petrochemical company after her husband's murder and tries to save the business from financial ruin. The film and Fonda look elegant, but the bottom line is confusion. Also stars Hume Cronyn, Josef Sommer, and Bob Gunton. **Director**—Alan J. Pakula. (R)

118 minutes

ROMAN HOLIDAY (1953)
★★★★

Gregory Peck
Audrey Hepburn

Peck and Hepburn are delightful in this story of a lonely princess who runs away from her official duties, meets a newspaperman, and falls in love with him. Hepburn is the princess, and Peck is the reporter. This captivating comedy—filmed in Rome—has enough drama under director William Wyler's skillful hand to make it a memorable film from start to finish. It also stars Eddie Albert, Hartley Power, and Harcourt Williams. **Academy Awards**—Hepburn, best actress; Ian McLellan Hunter, writing (motion picture story). **Nominations**—best picture; Wyler, best director; Albert, best supporting actor; Hunter and John Dighton, writing (screenplay); Frank Planer and Henry Alekan, cinematography (black and white). *118 minutes b&w*

ROMANOFF AND JULIET (1961)
★★★

Peter Ustinov
Sandra Dee
John Gavin

Ustinov is a triple-threat—he wrote, directed, and acted—in this satire, set in Concordia, a mythical land, where the daughter of the U.S. ambassador falls in love with the Russian ambassador's son. Dee and Gavin are the loving couple. Some of the comic-strip action falls flat, and at times, it seems Ustinov took too much upon himself; but his wit and the inspired premise make this movie worthwhile. Ustinov gets solid supporting help from Dee, Gavin, Akim Tamiroff, Tamara Shayne, and Peter Jones.

103 minutes

THE ROMANTIC ENGLISHWOMAN (1975)
★★

Glenda Jackson
Michael Caine

Joseph Losey directed this sophisticated yet complicated love story, about a successful paperback novelist whose money and intense love fail to fulfill his wife, who runs away with a gigolo poet. Jackson plays the would-be liberated housewife; Caine is her novelist-husband. There's lavish scenery and some witty dialogue, but the confusing love-triangle plot and poor casting override the assets. Also with Helmut Berger, Marcus Richardson, and Kate Nelligan. (R) *115 minutes*

ROOM AT THE TOP (1959)
★★★★

Laurence Harvey
Simone Signoret

Despite Harvey's wooden performance, this drama is a vivid and realistic look at British industrial life. He plays an egotistical, selfish clerk in a factory who jilts the woman who loves him to marry the daughter of the factory owner. Signoret plays Harvey's jilted mistress. Heather Sears, Donald Wolfit, Raymond Huntley, Donald Houston, Mary Peach, and Hermione Baddeley also star in this skillful screen adaptation of John Braine's novel. **Director**—Jack Clayton. **Academy Awards**—Signoret, best actress; Neil Paterson, best screenplay (based on material from another medium). **Nominations**—best picture; Clayton, best director; Harvey, best actor; Baddeley, best supporting actress.

117 minutes b&w

ROOSTER COGBURN (1975)
★★

John Wayne
Katharine Hepburn

Wayne—a one-eyed, booze-guzzling U.S. marshal—is on the trail of outlaws. Hepburn—the pastor's daughter—is at his side. The movie is a patchwork affair taken from *True Grit* and *The African Queen*. Watching such

Katharine Hepburn and John Wayne in the western Rooster Cogburn.

filmdom institutions as Wayne and Hepburn acting together may be entertaining for some, but the movie itself is nothing to get excited about. Also with Anthony Zerbe, Richard Jordan, John McIntyre, and Strother Martin. **Director**—Stuart Millar. (PG)

107 minutes

ROPE (1948)
★★★

James Stewart

Director Alfred Hitchcock is less than masterful in this film about two young men who kill a college friend as part of a thrill-seeking experiment. As the movie unfolds, the men ghoulishly reveal clues to the crime. The below-par effort was obviously inspired by the Loeb-Leopold murder case. It was also Hitchcock's first color film, and he unsuccessfully experimented with 10-minute takes in an effort to perfect the flow of the movie. Although he didn't perfect anything, the movie has its virtues. The performances of Stewart, John Dall, Farley Granger, Cedric Hardwicke, Joan Chandler, and Douglas Dick are above average.

80 minutes

THE ROSE (1979)
★★

Bette Midler
Alan Bates
Frederic Forrest

Midler, in her screen debut, plays a rock 'n' roll queen who self-destructs on alcohol, drugs, and the stresses of stardom. Forrest is good as the lover who wants her to quit. The screenplay is obviously based on the career of the late Janis Joplin. The film's hysterical, *(Continued)*

Bette Midler belts out a song in The Rose, *her motion-picture debut.*

(Continued)

hair-pulling pitch helps compensate for a shallow script—everything to be said comes in the first 10 minutes. If anything saves the film, it's Bette belting out the songs with all-out gusto. Also with Harry Dean Stanton, Barry Primus, and David Keith. **Director—**Mark Rydell. (R) **Academy Award Nominations—**Midler, best actress; Forrest, best supporting actor.

125 minutes

ROSELAND (1977)
★★

**Lou Jacobi
Teresa Wright**

This study of loneliness, set in New York City's famous Roseland dance hall, is divided into three interlocking vignettes and has a made-for-TV quality. There's pathos here, but it barely transcends the soft script. First-rate performances carry the film—especially a touching segment with Jacobi and Wright. Also with Christopher Walken, Helen Gallagher, Geraldine Chaplin, and Lilia Skala. **Director—**James Ivory. (No MPAA rating) *103 minutes*

ROSEMARY'S BABY (1968)
★★★★

**Mia Farrow
John Cassavetes**

An excellent cast combined with the provocative idea of witchcraft yields a top-notch thriller under director Roman Polanski's deft handling. Farrow and her overly ambitious husband, played by Cassavetes, naïvely become involved with diabolical neighbors—Ruth Gordon and Sidney Blackmer—resulting in devilish conse-

quences. The top-flight cast also includes Ralph Bellamy, Patsy Kelly, Maurice Evans, Charles Grodin, and Elisha Cook, Jr. Based on the novel by Ira Levin. **Academy Award—**Gordon, best supporting actress. **Nomination—**Polanski, best screenplay (based on material from another medium). *117 minutes*

In Rosemary's Baby, *Mia Farrow's husband gets involved in a witches' coven.*

THE ROSE TATTOO (1955)
★★★★

**Anna Magnani
Burt Lancaster**

Magnani gives a robust and earthy performance as a troubled widow who finds love again when she meets a rough-and-tumble truck driver, played by Lancaster. At times she seems larger than life and appears to be too powerful for the screen. This movie version of the Tennessee Williams play is ably directed by Daniel Mann and well photographed, with excellent supporting efforts from Virginia Grey, Jo Van Fleet, Ben Cooper, and Marisa Pavan. Williams productions often have too many eccentrics, but this time there are more real people, and this addition makes it a better film. **Academy Awards—**Magnani, best actress; James Wong Howe, cinematography (black and white). **Nominations—**best picture; Pavan, best supporting actress.

117 minutes b&w

ROUGH CUT (1980)
★★

**Burt Reynolds
Lesley-Anne Down**

Reynolds plays a smooth-talking American jewel thief who stages a diamond heist in Europe and seduces the beautiful woman sent to lure him into the crime. Down plays the alluring woman. Reynolds displays his reliable charm, but he's saddled with a hopeless script and wooden dialogue that merely mark time for most of the film. The story springs to action in the final quarter, but it's too late—interest has flagged by that time. Also with David Niven, Patrick Magee, and Timothy West. **Director—**Don Siegel. (PG) *112 minutes*

THE ROUNDERS (1965)
★★

**Henry Fonda
Glenn Ford**

Fonda and Ford are congenial modern cowboys in this comedy. The two are foiled by a stubborn horse that refuses to be trained. The horse gives them plenty of trouble and supplies many of the gags. Although the story is insubstantial and never seems to get going, this film, written and directed by Burt Kennedy, is pleasant fare for the entire family. Also with Sue Anne Langdon,

Anna Magnani portrays a troubled widow who finds love again in The Rose Tattoo.

- Royal Flash
- Royal Wedding
- Ruby
- The Runner Stumbles
- Running
- Run Silent, Run Deep
- Russian Roulette
- The Russians Are Coming, the Russians Are Coming!

R

Edgar Buchanan, Chill Wills, and Denver Pyle. *85 minutes*

ROYAL FLASH (1975)
★★

Malcolm McDowell

This film about the misadventures of Captain Harry Paget Flashman is a spoof at Victorian England, but it comes off as low-grade slapstick. Leading man McDowell tries hard, but director Richard Lester has exploited this swashbuckling theme before in *The Three Musketeers* and *The Four Musketeers*. The outcome this time is overkill; it's more of a flush. With Alan Bates, Britt Ekland, Oliver Reed, and Florinda Bolkan. (PG) *98 minutes*

ROYAL WEDDING (1951)
★★

Fred Astaire
Jane Powell

Astaire's brilliant dancing and Powell's delightful singing overcome a pedestrian plot in which he and Powell—who plays his sister—perform in London at the time of Queen Elizabeth II's marriage to Prince Philip. Alan Jay Lerner, of *My Fair Lady* fame, and Burton Lane wrote the songs. True to form in such films, brother and sister each eventually find true love. Watch for Fred to dance on the ceiling. Sarah Churchill, Peter Lawford, and Keeenan Wynn also star. **Director**—Stanley Donen. *93 minutes*

RUBY (1977)
★

Piper Laurie

Laurie, who has seen better days, plays Ruby, a former gun moll, in this unthrilling thriller about the supernatural. It seems Ruby's gangster boyfriend has come back from the dead in the body of their mute daughter to settle some old scores. Swimming around in this farfetched concoction are a few borrowed scenes from *The Exorcist*, plenty of blood and gore, and a measure of phony scientific mumbo jumbo. It's definitely no gem. Janet Baldwin, Stuart Whitman,

and Fred Kohler, Jr., also star. **Director**—Curtis Harrington. (R) *84 minutes*

THE RUNNER STUMBLES (1979)
★★

Dick Van Dyke
Kathleen Quinlan

Director Stanley Kramer, known for tackling touchy subjects, presents this film about a priest's romantic interest in a young, vivacious nun. Van Dyke plays the distraught priest with self-consciousness; Quinlan plays the perky nun. But celibacy is perhaps a bit too touchy even for Kramer, who seems overly cautious about treating the issue with depth or passion. The movie merely drifts along, and the story never comes into focus. Also with Maureen Stapleton, Ray Bolger, Tammy Grimes, and Beau Bridges. (PG) *99 minutes*

RUNNING (1979)
★★

Michael Douglas
Susan Anspach

Douglas plays a chronic loser who seeks redemption by competing for the United States Olympic running team. This is yet another athletic situation film that tries to parallel *Rocky*, but can't match the spirit of the Italian Stallion. Douglas is far above the meager material, which merely runs its course with minimal suspense and drama; Anspach is wasted as Douglas's ex-wife. Also with Larry Dane and Eugene Levy. **Director**—Steven Hilliard Stern. (PG) *103 minutes*

RUN SILENT, RUN DEEP (1958)
★★★

Clark Gable
Burt Lancaster

Gable, as the commander of a U.S. submarine, and Lancaster, as his lieutenant, provide competent, realistic portrayals in this suspenseful World War II drama. Besides the larger conflict with the Japanese Navy in Tokyo Bay, there's feuding between the two naval officers. There are also excellent sea-fighting sequences—an

Clark Gable and Jack Warden in Run Silent, Run Deep, *a realistic war movie.*

improvement over most submarine movies. Also with Jack Warden, Brad Dexter, Nick Cravat, Joe Maross, and Don Rickles. **Director**—Robert Wise. *93 minutes b&w*

RUSSIAN ROULETTE (1975)
★★

George Segal

Soviet Premier Alexei Kosygin comes to Canada to sign an arms ban treaty, and is marked for assassination by—of all people—Russian KGB agents. The elaborate plot, of course, is foiled by none other than an ex-Canadian Mountie, played by Segal. There's some suspense and fun scattered about the heavy atmosphere of Vancouver, but the story is farfetched and confusing. The film is another attempt to exploit the political assassination syndrome. With Denholm Elliott, Gordon Jackson, Christina Raines, and Richard Romanus. **Director**—Lou Lombardo. (PG) *93 minutes*

THE RUSSIANS ARE COMING, THE RUSSIANS ARE COMING! (1966)
★★

Carl Reiner
Eva Marie Saint
Alan Arkin

There are enough star performers in this cold-war farce about the forced landing of a Russian submarine off the shore of Nantucket to keep the plot from sinking into oblivion. Arkin, Reiner, and Jonathan Winters provide excellent comic acting, and are helped by the competent performances of Saint, John Philip Law, *(Continued)*

R·S

- Ryan's Daughter
- Sabrina
- The Sad Sack
- Safari
- Sahara
- Sailor Beware
- The Sailor Who Fell From Grace With the Sea

(Continued)

Paul Ford, Tessie O'Shea, Brian Keith, Theodore Bikel, and Ben Blue. If you don't expect too much and are willing to laugh at the Russians, this is a mildly enjoyable movie. The perceptive viewer will also notice that the movie was not photographed off of Nantucket and that the scenes are those of northern California. **Director**—Norman Jewison. **Academy Award Nominations**—best picture; Arkin, best actor; William Rose, best screenplay (based on material from another medium). *126 minutes*

RYAN'S DAUGHTER (1970)
★★★

**Sarah Miles
Robert Mitchum
Chris Jones**

The beautiful Irish scenery, superbly photographed, makes this simple love story seem more majestic than it really is. The story, about a schoolteacher's wife who falls in love with a British officer in 1916, in Ireland, is too long and fails to attain the greatness sought by director David Lean. His filmmaking technique is excellent, however, and the acting is above average. Miles plays the romantic adulteress, Mitchum is the moody schoolteacher, and Jones plays the soldier. John Mills, Trevor Howard, and Leo McKern also star. **Academy Awards**—Mills, best supporting actor; Freddie Young, cinematography. **Nomination**—Miles, best actress. (R) *206 minutes*

S

SABRINA (1954)
★★★

**Humphrey Bogart
William Holden
Audrey Hepburn**

Hepburn is exquisitely delightful in this excellent comedy about a chauffeur's daughter. She's romanced by Bogart, who plays a middle-aged tycoon, and by Holden, who's a playboy. There are many enjoyable scenes in this well-staged comedy, although Hepburn, Bogart, and Holden have been shown to better advantage in other films. Also appearing are Walter Hampden, John Williams, Martha Hyer, Joan Vohs, Francis X. Bushman, and Marcel Dalio. **Director**—Billy Wilder. **Academy Award Nominations**—Wilder, best director; Hepburn, best actress; Wilder, Samuel Taylor, and Ernest Lehman, best writing (screenplay); Charles Lang, Jr., cinematography (black and white). *113 minutes b&w*

THE SAD SACK (1957)
★★

Jerry Lewis

The French believe that Lewis is a comic genius; Americans know better—far too often he's just plain silly. In this uneven comic effort, inspired by the George Baker comic strip, Lewis plays a woebegone soldier who gets involved with spies and Arabian intrigues. Aside from Peter Lorre, who appears as an Arab in the latter part of the film, the rest of the cast is either 4F or below average. Also with David Wayne, Phyllis Kirk, and Joe Mantell. **Director**—George Marshall. *98 minutes b&w*

SAFARI (1956)
★★

**Victor Mature
Janet Leigh**

Mature gives an above-average performance in this suspenseful and action-packed adventure film. He plays the brave white hunter who heads a safari that encounters the vengeful Mau Maus. The savages kill Mature's boss, which works out because Mature has fallen in love with Leigh, the wife of his boss; widows don't spend too much time grieving in such films. Also with Roland Culver, John Justin, Earl Cameron, Liam Redmond, and Orland Martins. **Director**—Terence Young. *91 minutes*

SAHARA (1943)
★★★

Humphrey Bogart

Bogart stars in this action-packed war story, with fine supporting perfor-

Humphrey Bogart (second from the left) in Sahara, an action-packed war story.

mances by J. Carrol Naish and Rex Ingram. Bogey heads a British-American tank unit stranded in the Sahara Desert; they not only manage to survive, but outwit the Nazis. Other strong characterizations in this realistic drama are provided by Bruce Bennett, Lloyd Bridges, Dan Duryea, and Kurt Kreuger. **Director**—Zoltan Korda. **Academy Award Nomination**—Naish, best supporting actor; Rudolph Maté, cinematography (black and white). *97 minutes b&w*

SAILOR BEWARE (1952)
★★

**Dean Martin
Jerry Lewis**

Kids will probably find the adventures of Martin and Lewis in the U.S. Navy hilarious; adults will find them less amusing. This is one of the funnier movies the two made before going their separate ways. As unlikely as it sounds, in this film Lewis gets a reputation as a suave man among the ladies. The boxing and Army induction scenes are the highlights in this comedy, which also includes Robert Strauss, Leif Erickson, Marion Marshall, and Corinne Calvet. **Director**—Hal Walker. *103 minutes b&w*

THE SAILOR WHO FELL FROM GRACE WITH THE SEA (1976)
★

**Sarah Miles
Kris Kristofferson**

Miles and Kristofferson star in this film adaptation of an erotic novel by the Japanese writer Yukio Mishima. The setting is disastrously transplanted from Yokohama to Dart-

- St. Ives
- Saint Jack
- Saint Joan
- The St. Valentine's Day Massacre
- Salome
- Same Time, Next Year
- Sam Marlow, Private Eye
- Samson and Delilah

S

mouth, England, and Mishima's chilling story, which is reminiscent of *Lord of the Flies*, becomes merely grotesque as a movie. It's about a sailor who gives up the sea for domestic tranquility—an affair with a widow—and is gruesomely killed by a band of teenage boys, who determine he has violated the "perfect order of things." Miles is the widow and Kristofferson is the sailor. Also with Jonathan Kahn, Margo Cunningham, and Earl Rhodes. **Director**—Lewis John Carlino. (R)   *104 minutes*

ST. IVES (1976)
★★★

Charles Bronson

In St. Ives, *Charles Bronson lands a solid punch on an assailant.*

Bronson the unflappable plays an ex-crime reporter who suddenly finds himself involved as a go-between for an eccentric millionaire seeking the return of his stolen and incriminating journals. It's a change of pace for Bronson, who lays low on the violence. This witty and action-filled film manages to entertain despite an excessively complicated plot that finally unravels toward the end. It's reminiscent of those Bogart capers of the '40s and '50s. Also with John Houseman, Jacqueline Bisset, Maximilian Schell, and Elisha Cook, Jr. **Director**—J. Lee Thompson. (PG)   *93 minutes*

SAINT JACK (1979)
★★

**Ben Gazzara
Denholm Elliott**

Director Peter Bogdanovich's low-key melodrama is set in Singapore in the early '70s. It's rife with atmosphere, but the weak story never develops momentum. Jack Flowers, played by

Gazzara, is a pimp with a heart of gold and a sense of honor, who's determined to run the best brothel in town. There are masterful performances by Gazzara and Elliott, who plays a woebegone Englishman; their acting seems to tower over the sparse material. Also with James Villiers and Rodney Bewes. (R)   *112 minutes*

SAINT JOAN (1957)
★★

Jean Seberg

Although novelist Graham Greene wrote the screenplay for this George Bernard Shaw play, most of the high-quality actors are wasted, and the brilliant play is a clunker on the screen. Seberg is especially miscast as the Maid of Orleans. John Gielgud, however, is excellent, and Anton Walbrook, Richard Todd, Harry Andrews, Richard Widmark, and Felix Aylmer are worth watching. **Director**—Otto Preminger.   *110 minutes b&w*

THE ST. VALENTINE'S DAY MASSACRE (1967)
★

**Jason Robards, Jr.
George Segal**

As gangsters, Robards and Segal fail to measure up to the acting standards of James Cagney and Edward G. Robinson. Robards plays the role of Al Capone. When the famous massacre finally occurs in this uneven story, about Chicago racketeers of the 1920s, only diehard fans of this kind of adventure film will care. The performances of Ralph Meeker, Jean Hale, Bruce Dern, Clint Ritchie, and Reed Hadley help prevent this from being a total disappointment. **Director**—Roger Corman.   *99 minutes*

SALOME (1953)
★

Rita Hayworth

Even a superior actor like Charles Laughton looks below-average in this tedious biblical drama about a dancer, played by Hayworth, who offers to sacrifice her own life to save John the Baptist. Others who get mangled in

the unwieldly script include Stewart Granger, Judith Anderson, Cedric Hardwicke, Basil Sydney, Arnold Moss, and Rex Reason. Even the dance of the seven veils is scant justification for viewing this movie. **Director**—William Dieterle.   *103 minutes*

SAME TIME, NEXT YEAR (1978)
★★★

**Ellen Burstyn
Alan Alda**

This movie version of Bernard Slade's two-character Broadway hit looks somewhat stagebound, but this is a minor drawback—the warmth, humor, and appeal of the original play remain intact on the screen. Burstyn—repeating her stage role—and Alda give engaging performances as adulterers who meet for one weekend a year for 26 years. The finely crafted screenplay is rich with touching characterizations and intriguing surprises. **Director**—Robert Mulligan. (PG) **Academy Award Nominations**—Burstyn, best actress; Slade, best screenplay adaptation.   *117 minutes*

SAM MARLOW, PRIVATE EYE (1980)
★★

Robert Sacchi

A mystery comedy spoofing Humphrey Bogart and private-eye films of the '40s. Sacchi plays a man who undergoes plastic surgery so he resembles Bogart. He then becomes involved in a caper on the order of *The Maltese Falcon*. Sacchi does a convincing Bogey imitation, and there's a delightful takeoff by Misty Rowe as the dumb blonde secretary. But the film has problems with a complex script, which turns serious too often to sustain parody. Also with Michelle Phillips and Franco Nero. **Director**—Robert Day. (PG)   *111 minutes*

SAMSON AND DELILAH (1949)
★★

**Hedy Lamarr
Victor Mature**

Fans of epic films produced on a grand
(Continued)

S
- The Sand Pebbles
- The Sandpiper
- Sands of Iwo Jima
- Sandstone
- The San Francisco Story
- Sante Fe Trail
- Saratoga Trunk
- Sasquatch

(Continued)

scale should enjoy this biblical story about Samson, whose strength is sapped after devious Delilah cuts his curls. Mature and Lamarr play the title roles. Despite the epic theme, grand photography, and spectacular special effects—including the destruction of the temple and Samson's fight with a lion—the movie often drags and, at times, even seems silly. The cast also includes Angela Lansbury, George Sanders, Fay Holden, Russ Tamblyn, and Olive Deering. **Director**—Cecil B. DeMille. **Academy Award Nomination**—George Barnes, cinematography (color). *128 minutes*

THE SAND PEBBLES (1966)
★★★★

Steve McQueen
Richard Crenna

McQueen is superb as a sailor aboard a river gunboat who quarrels with his superiors and tries to warn them of the potential diplomatic pitfalls in dealing with Chinese warlords. Crenna plays the captain of the vessel. The well-paced movie, based on Richard McKenna's best-selling novel, is set on the Yangtze River during the 1920s. There are many inspired scenes, filled with suspense and excitement. Also with Candice Bergen, Richard Attenborough, Marayat Andriane, Mako, Simon Oakland, and Larry Gates. **Director**—Robert Wise. **Academy Award Nominations**—best picture; McQueen, best actor; Mako, best supporting actor; Joseph MacDonald, cinematography (color). *193 minutes*

THE SANDPIPER (1965)
★

Elizabeth Taylor
Richard Burton
Eva Marie Saint

Hollywood concocted this superficial tale to capitalize on the real-life romance of Taylor and Burton. The lovely scenery of the Big Sur and the exquisite beach scenes have more redeeming quality than the trite plot, which involves Taylor, playing a liberated artist with an illegitimate son, and Burton, who's an errant minister. Saint plays Bur-

ton's wife. Also with Charles Bronson, Robert Webber, and Torin Thatcher. **Director**—Vincente Minnelli.
116 minutes

SANDS OF IWO JIMA (1949)
★★★

John Wayne
John Agar

Wayne shines as a tough and capable Marine sergeant who must train young recruits and turn them into disciplined combat troops during World War II. Although some of the characterizations in this terse drama are obvious two-dimensional portraits and standard war-picture fare, the battle scenes are among the best ever filmed. The cast also includes Forrest Tucker, Arthur Franz, Adele Mara, Richard Jaeckel, and Julie Bishop. **Director**—Allan Dwan. **Academy Award Nominations**—Wayne, best actor; Harry Brown, writing (motion picture story). *109 minutes b&w*

SANDSTONE (1977)
★

A documentary about a southern California retreat where couples engage in open marriage and free love—but it's more like a commercial for this unusual sexually oriented resort. There are tedious interviews with the participants and boring scenes of nudity and mass sex. Directed by Jonathan and Bunny Peters Dana. (X) *75 minutes*

THE SAN FRANCISCO STORY
(1952)
★★

Joel McCrea
Yvonne de Carlo

McCrea and De Carlo star in this well-paced action film set in California during the gold rush era. The story focuses on the efforts of a miner and a newspaper editor in ridding San Francisco of vice and sweeping out the city's criminals. Sidney Blackmer and Florence Bates also star. **Director**—Robert Parrish. *90 minutes b&w*

SANTE FE TRAIL (1940)
★★

Errol Flynn
Olivia de Havilland
Raymond Massey

Flynn and De Havilland top the cast of this formula western, but the weak plot, indecisive direction, and slow pace spoil a potentially good tale. Flynn plays cavalry officer Jeb Stuart, and the action focuses on his efforts to capture John Brown, played by Massey. The supporting cast also includes Alan Hale, Gene Reynolds, Van Heflin, Henry O'Neill, and, oh yes—Ronald Reagan. **Director**—Michael Curtiz. *93 minutes b&w*

SARATOGA TRUNK (1946)
★★

Ingrid Bergman
Gary Cooper

This curious vehicle mounted for star performers is mishandled from beginning to end, and never seems to get unstuck from its mediocre plot. The movie is based on the novel by Pulitzer Prize-winning author Edna Ferber. Bergman plays a notorious woman who returns to New Orleans. She falls in love with Cooper, who portrays a handsome cowboy involved in a squabble among railroad owners. Supporting actors include Florence Bates, Flora Robson, and John Warburton. **Director**—Sam Wood. **Academy Award Nomination**—Robson, best supporting actress. *135 minutes b&w*

SASQUATCH (1978)
★

George Lauris

Seven men go tramping around the wilds of British Columbia to find the legendary Bigfoot. The semidocumentary film merely suggests that such a creature exists, and most moviegoers won't be impressed, convinced, or entertained by all the fuss. Some of the sequences dwell on the scenic beauty and natural wildlife of the area. At least this part is credible. Also with Steve Boergadine and Jim Bradford. **Director**—Ed Ragozzino. (G) *102 minutes*

- Saturday Night and Sunday Morning
- Saturday Night Fever
- Saturday the 14th
- Saturn 3
- Save the Tiger
- Sayonara
- Scanners

S

SATURDAY NIGHT AND SUNDAY MORNING (1960)
★★★★

Albert Finney
Rachel Roberts
Shirley Anne Field

Finney rose to stardom in this stark rendition of working-class life-styles in an English industrial community. Finney plays an impish, devious nonconformist who's unhappy as a factory worker. He also has an affair with a married woman, until he eventually settles for a more conventional existence. Roberts, as the married woman, and Field, as Finney's girl friend, give solid supporting efforts in this finely crafted drama. Other supporting actors include Hylda Baker, Bryan Pringle, and Norman Rossington. **Director**—Karel Reisz. *89 minutes b&w*

SATURDAY NIGHT FEVER (1977)
★★★

John Travolta

Travolta stars as a young disco stud in this energetic film about tough dead-end Brooklyn teenagers. He brings credibility to the role, and he stops the show several times with some impressive dancing; it's a stunning film debut. The pulsing music of the Bee Gees adds to the mood. The erratic script is loaded with clichés, yet it conveys a convincing statement about some aspects of our youth culture. Also with Karen Lynn Gorney, Barry Miller, Joseph Cali, Paul Pape, and Donna Pescow. **Director**—John Badham. (R) **Academy Award Nomination**—Travolta, best actor.

119 minutes

SATURDAY THE 14TH (1982)
★

Richard Benjamin
Paula Prentiss

Benjamin and Prentiss waste their time and talent in this tiresome parody of horror films. They play a married couple who inherit a spooky house and must contend with vampires, gruesome monsters, and even some-thing that resembles the creature from the Black Lagoon. It isn't funny, and it isn't scary. But it's an obvious display of weak inspiration and slack imagination. Severn Darden and Jeffrey Tambor also star. **Director**—Howard R. Cohen. (PG)   *79 minutes*

SATURN 3 (1980)
★

Kirk Douglas
Farrah Fawcett

In Saturn 3, Kirk Douglas and Farrah Fawcett are two scientists in outer space.

Two research scientists—Douglas and Fawcett—are busy growing food in outer space when along comes a bad spaceman, played by Harvey Keitel, who spoils their fun in this far-out Garden of Eden. That's the extent of the flimsy plot in this rather unappealing movie, which suffers from the blahs from beginning to end. The outer-space setting is peculiarly vast and gaudy and, at times, seems out of place in contrast to the routine action. Also with Douglas Lambert. **Director**—Stanley Donen. (R)   *88 minutes*

SAVE THE TIGER (1973)
★★★

Jack Lemmon
Jack Gilford

This honest effort—by Hollywood standards—to examine contemporary ethics in the United States is interesting, but less than satisfying as a course in ethics or as a film. Lemmon is excellent as a troubled businessman at the breaking point because of financial difficulties; it makes him decide to torch his warehouse so he can collect the insurance money. Gilford plays his partner. Lemmon's performance is ably supported by Gilford, Laurie Heineman, Thayer David, and Norman Burton. **Director**—John G. Avildsen. (PG) **Academy Award**—Lemmon, best actor. **Nominations**—Gilford, best supporting actor; Steve Shagan, best story and screenplay (based on factual material or material not previously published).

100 minutes

SAYONARA (1957)
★★★

Marlon Brando
Miyoshi Umeki
Red Buttons
Miiko Taka

This is another case in which the acting genius of Brando makes an average movie worthwhile. He plays an Air Force pilot who falls in love with Taka, who plays a Japanese entertainer, after the Korean Conflict. In this movie based on the James Michener novel, Brando gets quality support from Umeki and Buttons. The movie is also enhanced by Irving Berlin's theme song. Without Brando, this production would be a travel feature about life in the Far East. Also with Ricardo Montalban, James Garner, Patricia Owens, Kent Smith, and Martha Scott. **Director**—Joshua Logan. **Academy Awards**—Buttons, best supporting actor; Umeki, best supporting actress. **Nominations**—best picture; Logan, best director; Brando, best actor; Paul Osborn, best screenplay (based on material from another medium); Ellsworth Fredericks, cinematography.   *147 minutes*

Marlon Brando and Miyoshi Umeki in Sayonara, *based on James Michener's novel.*

SCANNERS (1981)
★★

Jennifer O'Neill
Patrick McGoohan

A sci-fi horror film with some grisly shock effects and a routine, cliché-

(Continued)

S • Scaramouche • Scent of a Woman
• Scared Stiff • School for Scoundrels
• Scavenger Hunt

(Continued) filled script, which is only moderately suspenseful. Scanners are seemingly normal people with telepathic superpowers who can physically manipulate and even kill other humans. In one gory scene, a man's head literally explodes. McGoohan plays a pompous scientist, and lovely O'Neill is cast as a "good guy" scanner. But the real stars are the makeup artists responsible for some mind-blowing scenes. **Director**—David Cronenberg. (R)

103 minutes

SCARAMOUCHE (1952)
★★★

Stewart Granger
Eleanor Parker
Janet Leigh

The near-perfect casting of Granger as a swashbuckler determined to avenge the death of his brother sets the tone and pace of this exciting adventure story based on Rafael Sabatini's novel set in 18th-century France. Granger is ably joined by two beauties—Parker and Leigh—who vie for his love. Mel Ferrer, Nina Foch, Henry Wilcoxon, Robert Coote, and Lewis Stone also star. **Director**—George Sidney.

115 minutes

SCARED STIFF (1953)
★★

Dean Martin
Jerry Lewis

In this comedy, Martin, a singer, and Lewis, his bus-boy sidekick, land on a mysterious island after fleeing from the police. Once settled, they get involved with Carmen Miranda. The combination of escape, escapades, romance, and a spooky castle spawns enough laughs to please fans of this zany duo. Also with Lizabeth Scott, George Dolenz, Dorothy Malone, Jack Lambert, and William Ching. This is a remake of *The Ghost Breakers* with Bob Hope. **Director**—George Marshall.

108 minutes b&w

JAMES CAGNEY

James Cagney, one of Hollywood's most famous stars of the '30s and '40s, was born in 1899. His father ran a saloon on New York's Lower East Side. At 14 he was an office boy at the New York Sun, *at 17 a bellhop in the Friars Club, and in between, a bundle wrapper at Wanamaker's, a ticket-seller for the Hudson River Day Line, a waiter, and a page. His first serious brush with show business was in a vaudeville show called* Every Sailor. *In 1920, he appeared in* Pitter Patter, *another musical, and managed to find time to court another member of the chorus, Frances Willard Vernon, whom he married in 1922.*

The year 1929 was a turning point for Cagney. After winning praise in George Kelly's Maggie the Magnificent, *he was hired for a role opposite Joan Blondell in* Penny Arcade, *which only lasted three weeks on Broadway, but finally got him to California.*

Cagney made his film debut in 1930 in Sinner's Holiday, *but made his first great impact on audiences and critics in* The Public Enemy *(1931), one of the first gangster films; he's remembered for smacking Mae Clark in the face with a grapefruit.*

Cagney quickly became a major star. Although primarily cast as a gangster, he also performed in comedies and musicals.

Some of Cagney's other memorable films include Lady Killers *(1933),* G-Men *(1935),* Angels With Dirty Faces *(1938),* The Roaring Twenties *(1939),* Yankee Doodle Dandy *(1942),* White Heat *(1949),* Mister Roberts *(1955),* Man of a Thousand Faces *(1957), and* One, Two, Three *(1961). He won an Oscar for his portrayal of George M. Cohan in* Yankee Doodle Dandy.

After a 20-year retirement, Cagney—at the age of 81—returned to the screen in Ragtime *(1981).*

SCAVENGER HUNT (1980)
(no stars)

Richard Benjamin
James Coco
Tony Randall
Cloris Leachman

A noisy and absurd comedy that features a large cast of familiar names in brief and embarrassing roles. Benjamin, Leachman, Coco, Randall, and others greedily scramble for strange objects, after Vincent Price, who plays an eccentric game manufacturer, wills $200 million to the winner of a scavenger hunt. The callous humor delights in degrading people with physical impairments. Also with Scatman Crothers, Ruth Gordon, Roddy McDowall, and Cleavon Little. Director Michael Schultz seems to have gone to the limit of bad taste. (PG)

117 minutes

SCENT OF A WOMAN (1976)
★★

Vittorio Gassman
Alessandro Momo

This comedy-drama is the story of a blind, retired Italian captain who hungers for life while fighting his affliction. On a train trip to Naples, he searches for a prostitute, claiming he can smell women. Gassman shores up the film with his polished performance of the brooding and arrogant captain. Momo is appealing as the young soldier who assists the captain on his trip and in his search for female companionship. There's a standard Hollywood-type sentimental ending when the captain softens his bitter attitude. Also with Agostina Belli. **Director**—Dino Risi. (R) **Academy Award Nomination**—best foreign-language film.

103 minutes

SCHOOL FOR SCOUNDRELS (1960)
★★★

Ian Carmichael
Alastair Sim
Terry-Thomas

Capable performers headed by Carmichael, Sim, and Terry-Thomas make this a school worth attending. The film

● Scorchy ● Scrooge (1951) ● The Sea Gypsies
● Scorpio ● Scrooge (1970) ● The Sea Hawk
● Scotland Yard ● The Sea Chase ● Search and Destroy

S

is based on Stephen Potter's books. In this movie, the training school teaches one-upmanship so that graduates can always come out on top in the game of life. Janette Scott, Dennis Price, Peter Jones, John Le Mesurier, and Edward Chapman also star in this amusing and enjoyable romp at a unique school. **Director**—Robert Hamer.

94 minutes b&w

SCORCHY (1976)
★

Connie Stevens

A dumb and poorly acted imitation of the *Police Woman* TV series, starring Stevens as a sexy narcotics agent. The scenes are mostly crime-film clichés stolen from *Bullitt, The French Connection*, and similar movies. Everyone chases around the city of Seattle in cars, motorboats, and other assorted vehicles for the sake of a $1-million heroin stash. Also with Cesare Danova, William Smith, Marlene Schmidt, and Normann Burton. (R) Written, produced, and directed by Hikmet Avedis. *99 minutes*

SCORPIO (1972)
★★

Burt Lancaster
Alain Delon
Paul Scofield

The top-level cast in this unbelievably complicated spy thriller has an international flavor, but the viewer is left in the cold trying to figure out what's happening at times. Lancaster is just right as the serious, intense CIA agent ticketed for extinction by fellow-agent Scorpio, played by French actor Delon. British actor Scofield plays a Russian agent. Also with John Colicos, Gayle Hunnicutt, and J. D. Cannon. **Director**—Michael Winner. (R)

114 minutes

SCOTLAND YARD (1941)
★

Nancy Kelly
Edmund Gwenn

If the viewer doesn't permit the almost unbelievable plot of this spy story to bother him, then this melodrama is

mildly interesting. The tale concerns the kidnapping of a London banker by the Nazis during World War II, and their use of his double to trick the Allies into turning funds over to their evil cause. The competent cast also includes Henry Wilcoxon, Norman Varden, Melville Cooper, and Gilbert Emery. **Director**—Norman Foster.

68 minutes b&w

SCROOGE (1951)
★★★★

Alastair Sim

This classic Charles Dickens tale, about a Victorian miser who meets the ghost of Christmas past and then reforms his ways, gets expert handling in this British film. Sim plays the title role. The superb cast also includes Mervyn Johns, Kathleen Harrison, Jack Warner, Michael Hordern, George Cole, Miles Malleson, and Hermione Baddeley. Director Desmond Hurst has taken the superior cast and directed them with just the right emphasis so the film never seems superficial. *86 minutes b&w*

SCROOGE (1970)
★

Albert Finney

Perhaps some future film historian will be able to figure out why anyone would want to make a musical out of Dickens's classic story of an old miser who is reformed by the ghost of Christmas past. At times, partly due to the skills of Finney and competent supporting actors, this version seems almost bearable, but then the characters burst into song, and the spirit of tolerance dissipates. Also with Michael Medwin, Alec Guinness, Kay Walsh, David Collings, Laurence Naismith, Edith Evans, and Kenneth More. **Director**—Ronald Neame. (G)

113 minutes

THE SEA CHASE (1955)
★★

John Wayne
Lana Turner

Wayne is competent as the German captain of a fugitive freighter trying to

reach the fatherland from Australia, but it seems downright un-American to have him toiling for the other side in this World War II adventure. Other aspects of the melodrama are standard and not as farfetched, including Turner as the romantic interest in Wayne's life. The assorted crew of supporting actors includes David Farrar, Tab Hunter, Dick Davalos, Lyle Bettger, and James Arness. **Director**—John Farrow. *117 minutes*

THE SEA GYPSIES (1978)
★★★

Robert Logan
Heather Rattray
Mikki Jamison-Olsen

Beautiful scenery, effective acting, and a lively plot enhance this engaging family adventure film. It's about a man, his two daughters, and a photographer, who are marooned on the Alaskan coast and learn to survive among the wild bear, moose, caribou, and sea lions. The story is predictable, but there's lots of excitement to delight the youngsters and involve the adults. Also with Shannon Saylor. **Director**—Stewart Raffill. (G) *101 minutes*

THE SEA HAWK (1940)
★★★

Errol Flynn
Flora Robson

Flynn is at his swashbuckling best, dueling and fighting on the high seas in this dynamic sea adventure set at the time of Elizabeth I and England's encounters against the Spanish. Robson plays the Queen. The photography and pace are excellent under Michael Curtiz's direction, and the costumes are beautiful. The cast also includes Brenda Marshall, Claude Rains, Donald Crisp, Henry Daniell, Alan Hale, Una O'Connor, and William Lundigan. *122 minutes b&w*

SEARCH AND DESTROY (1981)
★

Perry King

An ill-conceived, grim drama about a Vietnamese soldier who comes to the
(Continued)

(Continued)
United States seeking revenge on some Americans who abandoned him in the South Vietnam jungles. The far-fetched script has the disgruntled soldier and a veteran GI, played by King, shooting it out on the streets of Niagara Falls. Some picturesque views of the falls are the only interesting aspects of this otherwise desperate movie. Tisa Farrow and George Kennedy co-star. **Director**—William Fruet. (PG)   *93 minutes*

THE SEARCHERS (1956)
★★★

**John Wayne
Jeffrey Hunter
Natalie Wood**

Wayne and Hunter search for a girl, played by Wood, who was kidnapped by Indians. This attractive western, set after the Civil War, is buoyed by excel-lent photography, beautiful scenery, and John Ford's direction. The acting of Wayne, Hunter, and Wood, and solid supporting performances by Vera Miles, Antonio Moreno, Ward Bond, John Qualen, and Henry Brandon also help the film.   *119 minutes*

THE SEA WOLF (1941)
★★★

Edward G. Robinson

A great cast keeps this fast-paced adventure at sea afloat. This movie version of Jack London's novel about a sadistic sea captain is overly involved with what makes the captain, played by Robinson, tick. The story deals with how the captain brutally treats the survivors he has rescued from a ferry boat collision in San Francisco Bay. Among the survivors and the rest of the cast are such excellent support-ing actors as Alexander Knox, Ida Lupino, John Garfield, Gene Lockhart, Barry Fitzgerald, Howard da Silva, and David Bruce. **Director**—Michael Curtiz.   *90 minutes b&w*

THE SEA WOLVES (1981)
★★★

**Roger Moore
Gregory Peck
David Niven
Trevor Howard**

Potbellied, polo-playing, British busi-nessmen form a commando team and destroy a secret Nazi radio transmitter somewhere in the Indian Ocean. This daring charge of the geriatric brigade is a likable World War II adventure with plenty of stiff-upper-lip atmo-sphere. Stars of yesteryear—Peck, Niven, Howard—keep the suspense and action moving, but the film really belongs to Moore who, as a young British officer, contributes a proper amount of dash and romance. **Direc-tor**—Andrew V. McLaglen. (PG)
          120 minutes

A SECOND CHANCE (1981)
★

Catherine Deneuve

Beautiful Deneuve gives a seemingly unenthusiastic performance as a mur-deress who bears a son while in jail and then is reunited with him after her release. This confusing and preposter-ous drama, awkwardly directed by Claude Lelouch, becomes even more muddled by the use of numerous dis-connected flashbacks. Lelouch, who's known for decent work, seems out of sorts with this project, and such con-duct apparently has infected the spirit of the cast as well. In French with English titles. (R)   *99 minutes*

SECOND HAND HEARTS (1981)
★

**Robert Blake
Barbara Harris**

Blake and Harris star as a couple of lost souls on their way to California, trying to make the most of a rickety marriage. The performances are exceptionally bad, but it's only in keeping with the dialogue, which

RICHARD BURTON

Richard Burton, the brooding Welsh actor, is as competent on the stage as he is on the screen. He's known for his commanding presence and his fine speaking voice, but he's perhaps as well known for his tumultuous love affairs and two marriages to actress Elizabeth Taylor.

He was born Richard Jenkins in South Wales in 1925, the son of a coal miner. He took the name Burton from his schoolmaster, who was partly responsible for Burton receiving a scholarship to Oxford.

Burton made his stage debut in Druid's Rest, in 1943. From 1944 to 1947, he served as a navigator in the Royal Air Force. After his discharge in 1948, he resumed his stage career and also starred in his first film, The Last Days of Dolwyn. *By the mid-'50s, he was recognized as one of Britain's best young actors.*

In 1952, Burton came to Hollywood to star in My Cousin Rachel, *and then played in a series of costume dramas, such as* The Robe *(1953),* Prince of Players *(1954), and* Alexander the Great *(1956).*

During the filming of Cleopatra *(1962), his much publicized romance with Elizabeth Taylor, his co-star, began, and his reputation as a serious actor declined while his popularity as a movie idol rose. Burton still found opportunities to star in various legitimate productions including Shakespearean dramas.*

Burton starred in a variety of film roles during the late '60s and throughout the '70s, but many of the assignments made few demands on his acting talent. He has received six Academy Award nominations, but has never won an Oscar.

Some of Burton's other movies include Look Back in Anger *(1959),* The V.I.P.s *(1963),* Becket *(1964),* The Night of the Iguana *(1964),* Who's Afraid of Virginia Woolf? *(1966),* The Taming of the Shrew *(1967),* Anne of the Thousand Days *(1970),* Exorcist II *(1977), and* Equus *(1977).*

- The Secret Life of an American Wife
- The Secret Life of Walter Mitty
- The Secret of Santa Vittoria
- The Seduction
- The Seduction of Joe Tynan
- See Here, Private Hargrove
- Seems Like Old Times

S

wavers from silly to absurd. The two travel in a beat-up station wagon, run out of gas, lose their way, and suffer mechanical breakdowns. Clutter and confusion are everywhere. **Director**—Hal Ashby. (PG) *98 minutes*

THE SECRET LIFE OF AN AMERICAN WIFE (1968)

★

Walter Matthau
Anne Jackson

Jackson portrays a bored suburban housewife who decides to seduce a movie star sex idol in this insipid and unsatisfying comedy, which has a message lurking somewhere on suburban life-styles of the 1960s. Matthau plays the cinema sex idol. Both stars have done much better work in other films and seem miscast in this production. Patrick O'Neal, Edy Williams, Richard Bull, and Paul Napier appear in supporting roles. **Director**—George Axelrod. *92 minutes*

THE SECRET LIFE OF WALTER MITTY (1947)

★★★★

Danny Kaye

Kaye is charming in this entertaining story about a man who lives in a fantasy world where he leads an exciting life. In the real world, he's mild-mannered and cowardly. Viewers expecting a faithful film version of James Thurber's story will be disappointed, but excellent songs—including Kaye's rendition of his famed "Anatole of Paris"—and enjoyable comedy sequences makes this a movie the whole family will enjoy. Also with Virginia Mayo, Boris Karloff, Reginald Denny, Florence Bates, Ann Rutherford, and Fay Bainter. **Director**—Norman Z. McLeod. *110 minutes*

THE SECRET OF SANTA VITTORIA (1969)

★★★

Anthony Quinn
Anna Magnani

The entertaining tale takes place in an Italian village during the last months of World War II and depicts the efforts of the villagers in saving their precious hoard—one million bottles of wine—from German soldiers during the occupation. The story, based on Robert Crichton's novel, is interesting at times, but the film is too long and needlessly meanders. The stars, Quinn and Magnani, are adequate, and Hardy Kruger is excellent as a German officer. Also with Virni Lisi, Sergio Franchi, and Renato Rascel. **Director**—Stanley Kramer. (PG) *140 minutes*

THE SEDUCTION (1982)

(no stars)

Morgan Fairchild
Andrew Stevens

This amateurishly made turkey stars Fairchild of TV fame. She plays a glamorous news reporter who's pursued by a peeping-tom photographer, played by Stevens. Fairchild displays plenty of flesh, but her "Barbie Doll" beauty is as plastic as her acting. Writer-director David Schmoeller's idea of suspense is cheap fright tactics embellished with purring telephone conversations. It's a trite, aimless effort, which hardly lives up to its title. Michael Sarrazin and Vince Edwards also star. (R) *104 minutes*

THE SEDUCTION OF JOE TYNAN (1979)

★★

Alan Alda
Barbara Harris
Meryl Streep

Meryl Streep and Alan Alda are two of the stars in The Seduction of Joe Tynan.

Alda is in the title role, playing a liberal, charming New York senator ambitiously pursuing his career and struggling with his domestic life. Harris plays the senator's attractive wife, and Streep is a Southern labor lawyer who has an affair with the senator. Alda, Harris, and Streep deliver some remarkable performances, but the flat yet literate script, written by Alda, fails to offer badly needed excitement and drama. Also with Rip Torn, Charles Kimbrough, and Melvyn Douglas. **Director**—Jerry Schatzberg. (R) *107 minutes*

SEE HERE, PRIVATE HARGROVE (1944)

★★★

Robert Walker
Donna Reed
Keenan Wynn

If you've served in the military, you should appreciate the humor in this story about a raw recruit going through his paces in the U.S. Army. Walker, Reed, and Wynn star in this film adaptation of Marion Hargrove's best-selling novel. Also with Robert Benchley, Bob Crosby, Chill Wills, Ray Collins, and Grant Mitchell. **Director**—Wesley Ruggles.

102 minutes b&w

SEEMS LIKE OLD TIMES (1980)

★★

Goldie Hawn
Chevy Chase
Charles Grodin

Hawn plays an affluent liberal lawyer with a soft spot for stray dogs, her down-and-out clients, and her ex-husband, played by Chase, who's on the lam after two criminals force him to help them rob a bank. Grodin plays her current husband, a district attorney. Hawn, making the most of this broad comedy, is as bright-eyed and zany as ever, and she works well with Chase. But Neil Simon's uneven screenplay never catches hold; the familiar one-liners are mostly uninspired, and the laughs come at infrequent intervals. **Director**—Jay Sandrich. (PG) *102 minutes*

S
- The Sellout
- Semi-Tough
- The Sensual Man
- The Sentinel
- Separate Tables
- September Affair

THE SELLOUT (1951)
★★

Walter Pidgeon
John Hodiak
Audrey Totter

Pidgeon, Hodiak, and Totter star in this melodrama about political corruption. Pidgeon portrays a small-town crusading newspaper editor at odds with corrupt police and city officials. Thomas Gomez, who plays a sheriff on the take, is joined in supporting roles by Karl Malden, Cameron Mitchell, Everett Sloane, and Paula Raymond. **Director**—Gerald Mayer.
82 minutes b&w

SEMI-TOUGH (1977)
★★★

Burt Reynolds
Kris Kristofferson
Jill Clayburgh

A lively, whacky, romantic satire that demolishes professional football and self-improvement fads. Reynolds, Kristofferson, and Clayburgh work well together as a platonic *ménage-à-trois*. Director Michael Ritchie (*Smile*; *Bad News Bears*) is at home with this material, which tosses barbs at various hypocrisies. Walter Bernstein's script contains a lot of locker-room language.

Also with Robert Preston, Bert Convy, and Lotte Lenya. (R) *108 minutes*

THE SENSUAL MAN (1977)
★

Giancarlo Giannini

Italian comedy starring Giannini as a man who tries to find some sensual pleasure while he grows older. The déjà vu story of the male in constant pursuit contains a few minor touches of humor, but there really isn't that much of interest. Marco Vicario's limp direction dwells on dark, over-decorated settings. In Italian with English titles. (R) *108 minutes*

THE SENTINEL (1977)
★★★

Christina Raines
Ava Gardner
Chris Sarandon
Burgess Meredith

There's enough creepy goings-on in this bone-chilling horror film to give you nightmares for weeks. It's about an innocent and attractive fashion model, played by Raines, who rents a room in an old Brooklyn brownstone building that's actually a gateway to Hell. Director Michael Winner assembles a horrifying assortment of gro-

Christina Raines, who plays a model in The Sentinel, *is interviewed at an ad agency.*

tesque characters and nerve-jangling effects—mysteriously swaying chandeliers, strange footsteps in the night. And there's a final scene so gruesome that you may you lose your appetite, so view it after dinner. Effective performances from Raines, Meredith, and Sarandon. Also with Sylvia Miles, José Ferrer, Arthur Kennedy, and John Carradine. (R) *93 minutes*

SEPARATE TABLES (1958)
★★★★

Burt Lancaster
Rita Hayworth
David Niven
Deborah Kerr

Brilliant acting and excellent direction smooth the transition of Terence Rattigan's play from the stage to the screen. Under Delbert Mann's direction, the characterizations are sensitive, and the emotional conflicts are deftly portrayed in this story about the guests at a British seaside resort. Among the stars are Kerr, who plays a spinster; Niven, a troubled ex-colonel; and Wendy Hiller, the owner of the resort and Lancaster's mistress. Hayworth is surprisingly good as Lancaster's ex-wife who begs him for another chance. Also with Gladys Cooper, Cathleen Nesbitt, Felix Aylmer, Rod Taylor, May Hallat, and Audrey Dalton. **Academy Awards**—Niven, best actor; Hiller, best supporting actress; **Nominations**—best picture; Kerr, best actress; Rattigan and John Gay, best screenplay (based on material from another medium); Charles Lang, Jr., cinematography (black and white).
98 minutes b&w

SEPTEMBER AFFAIR (1950)
★★

Joseph Cotten
Joan Fontaine

Cotten and Fontaine star in this romantic melodrama. It's about two lovers married to other people who suddenly have a chance to start life anew together when they discover they are erroneously reported as missing in an airplane crash. The treatment is standard and competent considering the farfetched plot. Françoise Rosay, Jessica Tandy, Robert Arthur,

● September 30, 1955
● Sgt. Pepper's Lonely Hearts
Club Band

● Sergeants Three
● Sergeant York
● Serial
● The Serpent's Egg

S

and Jimmy Lydon appear in supporting roles. **Director**—William Dieterle.
104 minutes b&w

SEPTEMBER 30, 1955 (1978)
★

Richard Thomas

The title, in case you're wondering, has to do with the day actor James Dean died in a car crash. This tedious '50s youth film tells how Arkansas college student Jimmy J. goes bananas over the news of Dean's death. It's rather difficult to identify with such a peculiar and naïve adolescent character. Thomas, who played John-Boy on TV's *The Waltons*, gives an unconvincing and bland performance as Jimmy J. And James Bridges directs with an eye on *American Graffiti*; he doesn't come close. Also with Susan Tyrell, Deborah Benson, and Lisa Blount. (PG)
101 minutes

SGT. PEPPER'S LONELY HEARTS CLUB BAND (1978)
★★

Peter Frampton
The Bee Gees

This loosely constructed film is based on the music of the Beatles—more than 25 songs are featured—and stars Peter Frampton, the Bee Gees, and dozens of other rock performers. A few scenes are outstanding, but the outcome is a garish mishmash. The silly plot—what there is of it—is merely a vehicle for introducing the musical numbers. Most of the musicians aren't particularly good actors. Also with George Burns, Frankie Howard, Donald Pleasence, and Steve Martin. **Director**—Michael Schultz. (PG)
111 minutes

SERGEANTS THREE (1962)
★★

Frank Sinatra
Dean Martin
Peter Lawford
Sammy Davis, Jr.
Joey Bishop

Sinatra and some of his cronies—Martin, Davis, Lawford, and Bishop—star in this adventure yarn that resembles a western parody of *Gunga Din*. In this movie, Davis turns heroic in Gunga Din fashion. The story is set just after the Civil War, when three cavalry sergeants—Sinatra, Martin, and Lawford—with the assistance of Davis, dispose of hostile Indians. There's more than enough spirited action and fun for fans of this quintet, but the plot is trite, and much of the story is boring. Ruta Lee and Henry Silva also appear. **Director**—John Sturges.
112 minutes

SERGEANT YORK (1941)
★★★★

Gary Cooper

Cooper is perfectly cast as the backwoods farm boy—a pacifist—drafted into the Army who becomes the greatest U.S. hero of World War I. Under Howard Hawks's intelligent direction, the portrait of York is sensitive and compassionate, yet Hawks keeps the film moving along nicely without making it just another action-packed war movie. Besides Cooper, the excellent cast includes Joan Leslie, Walter Brennan, George Tobias, David Bruce, Ward Bond, Margaret Wycherly, and Dickie Moore. **Academy Award**—Cooper, best actor. **Nominations**—best picture; Hawks, best director; Brennan, best supporting actor; Wycherly, best supporting actress; Harry Chandlee, Abem Finkel, John Huston, and Howard Koch, writing (original screenplay); Sol Polito, cine-

In Sergeant York, Gary Cooper portrays a pacifist who's drafted in World War I.

matography (black and white).
134 minutes b&w

SERIAL (1980)
★★

Martin Mull
Tuesday Weld

Martin Mull gives orders to one of the cyclists he's recruited in Serial.

Mull and Weld star as a me-generation couple in this silly satire of trendy lifestyles in affluent Marin County, California. The rapid-fire dialogue seems as if it were gleaned from *Psychology Today* magazine. The soap-opera screenplay delves into hot tubs, open marriages, cult religions, consciousness-raising, and organic foods. There are some amusing moments amid the smorgasbord of pop jargon, but a lot of it is just dead air. Also with Sally Kellerman, Bill Macy, Peter Bonerz, Christopher Lee, and Tom Smothers. **Director**—Bill Persky. (R)
91 minutes

THE SERPENT'S EGG (1978)
★★

Liv Ullmann
David Carradine

This film is set in Berlin during the early '20s, when poverty, fear, and despair haunted the populace on the eve of Hitler's rise to power. In this English-language film, director
(Continued)

S
• Serpico
• Servant and Mistress
• Seven Beauties

• Seven Brides for Seven Brothers
• Seven Days in May

• The Seven Little Foys
• The Seven-Per-Cent Solution

(Continued)

Ingmar Bergman captures the grim and depressing mood in his usual intelligent fashion, but the point of the story is unclear. Bergman, who wrote the screenplay, leaves unanswered questions dangling everywhere. Carradine plays an out-of-work American circus performer floundering among the demoralized Germans, and Ullmann is a cabaret performer—both roles lack depth. Also with Gert Frobe, Glynn Turman, and James Whitmore. (R) *120 minutes*

SERPICO (1973)
★★★

Al Pacino

Pacino is brilliant as Frank Serpico, a dedicated New York City cop, who's appalled by police corruption and decides to expose the sleazy practices. The story, based on a book by Peter Maas, is about the problems and adventures of this honest nonconformist, but there's enough hard-hitting action for fans of cops-and-robbers movies. On-location filming gives the production a realistic tone under the excellent direction of Sidney Lumet. Also with John Randolph, Jack Kehoe, Biff McGuire, Barbara Eda-Young, Cornelia Sharpe, and Tony Roberts. (R) **Academy Award Nominations**—Pacino, best actor; Waldo Salt and Norman Wexler, best screenplay (based on material from another medium). *130 minutes*

SERVANT AND MISTRESS (1978)
★★★

Victor Lanoux
Andrea Ferreol

A debonair diplomat, played by Lanoux, returns home thinking he'll inherit a fortune from his departed uncle. But he's surprised to learn that the maid, played by Ferreol, gets everything. Thus begins an engrossing tale of role-reversal, with the nephew assuming the humiliating duties of servant to the new lady of the manor. Lanoux and Ferreol act with conviction in this intriguing study of callousness. **Director**—Bruno Gantillon. In French with English titles. (No MPAA rating) *90 minutes*

SEVEN BEAUTIES (1976)
★★★★

Giancarlo Giannini
Shirley Stoler

Director Lina Wertmuller's fifth movie is a masterpiece; it's rich with irony, paradox, and humor, and deals with the fundamental theme of survival. Giannini, in one of his best performances, plays a small-time hood from Naples, nicknamed "Seven Beauties," who deserts the Italian army and is sent to a concentration camp by the Germans. To survive, he desperately attempts to seduce the camp's hefty and ferocious female commandant, played effectively by Stoler. The movie is Wertmuller's best effort to date, as she reaffirms her political and philosophical beliefs. Also with Fernando Rey, Elena Fiore, and Enzo Vitale. In Italian with English titles. (R) **Academy Award Nominations**—best foreign-language film; Wertmuller, best director; Giannini, best actor; Wertmuller, best original screenplay. *115 minutes*

SEVEN BRIDES FOR SEVEN BROTHERS (1954)
★★★★

Howard Keel
Jane Powell

Powell and Keel star in this delightful western musical. After Keel decides to marry Powell, his six rowdy brothers resolve to find wives for themselves. There comic antics, skillful dance numbers, and pleasant musical selections, all focusing on the manner in which the brothers get their brides. The fun in this robust film is topped by the barn-raising scenes. Stanley Donen's direction is excellent, but Michael Kidd's choreography makes the movie something special. The production, inspired by a Stephen Vincent Benét story, also stars Jeff Richards, Russ Tamblyn, Matt Mattox, Tommy Rall, Howard Petrie, and Jacques d'Amboise. **Academy Award Nominations**—best picture; Albert Hackett, Frances Goodrich, and Dorothy Kingsley, writing (screenplay); George Folsey, cinematography (color). *104 minutes*

SEVEN DAYS IN MAY (1964)
★★★

Kirk Douglas
Burt Lancaster
Fredric March

This tense and exciting political drama about a plot by the military to overthrow the United States government is enhanced by a fine cast, solid direction, and a first-rate script. Lancaster and Douglas play military leaders, and March is outstanding as the President who must confront the plotters. Rod Serling wrote the taut, intelligent screenplay, which, under John Frankenheimer's direction, moves right along to a suspenseful climax. Also with Ava Gardner, John Houseman, Edmond O'Brien, George Macready, and Martin Balsam. **Academy Award Nomination**—O'Brien, best supporting actor. *120 minutes b&w*

THE SEVEN LITTLE FOYS (1955)
★★★

Bob Hope

Hope stars in this spirited musical biography of vaudevillian Eddie Foy and his family of performers. Hope is surprisingly skilled in his role, displaying admirable footwork and even some acting talent. He's aided by above-average production numbers and James Cagney's guest appearance as George M. Cohan. Milly Vitale, George Tobias, Herbert Heyes, and Angela Clark also star. **Director**—Melville Shavelson. **Academy Award Nomination**—Shavelson and Jack Rose, writing (story and screenplay). *95 minutes*

THE SEVEN-PER-CENT SOLUTION (1976)
★★

Nicol Williamson
Alan Arkin
Robert Duvall

Nicholas Meyer wrote the screenplay for this film, based on his own bestseller about the imaginary collaboration between Sherlock Holmes and Sigmund Freud on a criminal investigation. A star-studded cast adds class,

● 1776
● The Seventh Veil
● The Seven Year Itch

● Sex and the Single Girl
● Sextette
● Shadow of a Doubt

S

Alan Arkin and Nicol Williamson in The Seven-Per-Cent Solution.

but a confusing and colorless storyline detracts from the production. Williamson plays Holmes, Arkin is Dr. Freud, and Duvall is Dr. Watson. But alas, the spirit and intrigue associated with stories of the master sleuth are nowhere to be found. Someone owes an apology to Sir Arthur Conan Doyle. Also with Vanessa Redgrave, Laurence Olivier, Joel Grey, and Samantha Eggar. **Director**—Herbert Ross. (PG) **Academy Award Nomination**—Meyer, best screenplay adaptation.

113 minutes

1776 (1972)
★★★

William Daniels
Howard da Silva

Peter Stone's Pulitzer Prize-winning musical about the heroes involved in America's struggle for independence is competently adapted to the screen. The film is entertaining; fortunately, it doesn't seem like a dry history lesson, although a few awkward moments mar the movie. Almost all of the original Broadway cast members appear, with Daniels as John Adams and Da Silva as Ben Franklin. Donald Madden, David Ford, Ron Holgate, Virginia Vestoff, Blythe Danner, and Ken Howard star in supporting roles. **Director**—Peter H. Hunt. (G) **Academy Award Nomination**—Harry Stradling, Jr., cinematography.

141 minutes

THE SEVENTH VEIL (1946)
★★★

James Mason
Ann Todd

Mason and Todd star in this modern romantic drama about a woman who leaves her family to become a concert pianist. she's romantically torn among her psychiatrist, her guardian, and two other men. Mason plays the role of her guardian. At times, this excellent movie borders on soap opera, but it's technically well done and tastefully produced in light of the subject matter. The performances of Mason and Todd are masterful. Also with Herbert Lom, Yvonne Owen, Manning Whiley, David Horne, Albert Lieven, and Hugh McDermott. **Director**—Compton Bennett. **Academy Award**—Muriel and Sydney Box, writing (original screenplay). *94 minutes b&w*

THE SEVEN YEAR ITCH (1955)
★★★★

Tom Ewell
Marilyn Monroe

Ewell and Monroe are a delightful combination in this comedy about a married man who becomes infatuated with a model. She moves into his apartment building while his wife is away on a long summer vacation. Monroe plays the sexy model; Ewell is the married man. He has a fine comic touch, which energizes the film just when it seems ready to falter. Robert Strauss, Marguerite Chapman, Evelyn Keyes, Sonny Tufts, Victor Moore, Carolyn Hones, and Oscar Homolka appear in supporting roles. **Director**—Billy Wilder. *105 minutes*

SEX AND THE SINGLE GIRL (1964)
★★

Natalie Wood
Tony Curtis
Lauren Bacall
Henry Fonda

This splashy comedy has major stars, but it's never as witty or funny as it intends to be and never realizes its potential. Curtis is a writer for a smut magazine, who woos Wood, a psychologist. Everyone is supposed to be surprised when we learn what makes her tick. Bacall and Fonda play an embattled married couple. Otto Kruger, Mel Ferrer, Edward Everett Horton, and Fran Jeffries also appear in this sexcapade based on the successful book by Helen Gurley Brown. **Director**—Richard Quine. *114 minutes*

SEXTETTE (1979)
(no stars)

Mae West

West thumbs her nose at sexual taboos in this awkward and dreadful musical comedy, based on a play she wrote more than 50 years ago. Mae plays a much-wed movie star who attempts to consummate her sixth marriage amid interruptions from the press, spies, friends, and former husbands. She flubs the musical numbers, and her attempt to appear sexy is a terrible embarrassment. The cast also includes George Hamilton, Dom DeLuise, Tony Curtis, Ringo Starr, and Timothy Dalton. **Director**—Ken Hughes. (PG) *91 minutes*

SHADOW OF A DOUBT (1943)
★★★★

Joseph Cotten
Teresa Wright

Director Alfred Hitchcock is in top form in this story about a psychopathic killer known as the Merry Widow murderer. The killer, played by Cotten, visits relatives in a small California town, in a desperate effort to escape the police. Wright is a niece who suspects her uncle is the murderer. The memorable suspense yarn about a killer on the run is contrasted with noble values and virtues of small-town America. Cotten is marvelous as the glib and devious killer, posing as a congenial relative. He gets excellent support from Wright, Hume Cronyn, Henry Travers, Wallace Ford, Patricia Collinge, and Macdonald Carey. The script was well-written by
(Continued)

In Shadow of a Doubt, *Joseph Cotten, who plays a killer, shakes a little girl's hand.*

S
- Shadow of the Hawk
- Shaft
- The Shaggy D.A.
- The Shaggy Dog
- Shake Hands With the Devil
- Shampoo
- Shamus
- Shane

(Continued)
Thornton Wilder, Sally Benson, and Alma Reville. **Academy Award Nomination**—Gordon McDonell, writing (original story). *108 minutes b&w*

SHADOW OF THE HAWK (1976)
★

**Jan-Michael Vincent
Chief Dan George**

A tedious story about Indians in the Pacific Northwest. George wants his grandson, a computer executive played by Vincent, to assume his duties as the tribal medicine man and rid the neighborhood of destructive spirits. As expected, the spirits are exorcised, but not before they burn buildings, make ugly faces, and try to kill the grandson. Also with Marilyn Hassett. **Director**—George McCowan (PG) *92 minutes*

SHAFT (1971)
★★★

Richard Roundtree

Roundtree plays John Shaft, a tough but cool black private eye, in this action-packed thriller; it seemed more relevant in the 1970s when civil rights and equal opportunity were very intense issues. It remains an interesting action movie, although there are heavy doses of sex and violence. Gwenn Mitchell, Moses Gunn, Charles Cioffi, and Christopher St. John appear in supporting roles. The film inspired some sequels—*Shaft's Big Score* and *Shaft in Africa*. **Director**—Gordon Parks. (R) *100 minutes*

THE SHAGGY D.A. (1977)
★

Dean Jones

The Walt Disney studio trots out their faithful pooch in this sequel to their successful 1959 moneymaker *The Shaggy Dog*. Jones plays a man who is miraculously transformed into the canine while running for district attorney against a corrupt incumbent. All the familiar slapstick tricks—pie-throwing, auto chases, shoot-outs, and so on—are there en masse; such

stuff is boring by now. Suzanne Pleshette, Tim Conway, Keenan Wynn, and Jo Ann Worley also star. **Director**—Robert Stevenson. (G) *91 minutes*

THE SHAGGY DOG (1959)
★★

Fred MacMurray

This enjoyable Walt Disney fantasy about a boy who changes into a shaggy Old English sheepdog by means of a magical device is pleasant film fare for the kids. The switch from boy to dog is made so some thugs can be caught and brought to justice. There are enough funny moments, despite the sluggish script, to keep parents and kids amused. The cast also includes Jean Hagen, Annette Funicello, Jack Albertson, Tim Considine, Alexander Scourby, and Tommy Kirk. **Director**—Charles Barton. *101 minutes b&w*

SHAKE HANDS WITH THE DEVIL (1959)
★★★

James Cagney

Cagney gives a solid performance in this action-packed drama about Ireland during the rebellion of the 1920s. Cagney, who plays a rebel leader, gets excellent supporting help from Don Murray, Dana Wynter, Glynis Johns, Michael Redgrave, Richard Harris, Noel Purcell, Cryil Cusack, and Sybil Thorndike. Despite the fine acting and vivid on-location photography, the weak script detracts from the film's effectiveness. **Director**—Michael Anderson. *110 minutes b&w*

SHAMPOO (1975)
★★★

**Warren Beatty
Julie Christie**

Beatty plays a hedonistic Beverly Hills hairdresser whose clients like to get into his bed as well as under his drier. It's witty, funny, and sometimes disturbing cynical mayhem, set against the backdrop of Nixon's 1968 election victory. Also with Lee Grant, Goldie Hawn, Jack Warden, Tony Bill, and

Julie Christie (center) and Warren Beatty (right) star in the witty and funny Shampoo.

Carrie Fisher. **Director**—Hal Ashby. (R) **Academy Award**—Grant, best supporting actress. **Nominations**—Warden, best supporting actor; Robert Towne and Beatty, best original screenplay. *110 minutes*

SHAMUS (1972)
★★

**Burt Reynolds
Dyan Cannon**

Reynolds stars in this simple-minded, confusing, and violent remake of a "typical" 1940s private-eye film. Reynolds is hired to recover stolen jewels and find a killer. In the process, he performs numerous heroic feats and tries to recover from a number of beatings. Cannon plays one of his girlfriends. John Ryan, Joe Santos, Giorgio Tozzi, and Ron Weyland are also in the cast, but everyone is overshadowed by Reynolds. **Director**—Buzz Kulik. (PG) *98 minutes*

SHANE (1953)
★★★★

**Alan Ladd
Jean Arthur
Van Heflin**

This story about a mysterious ex-gunfighter who helps a family of homesteaders is one of the finest westerns ever made. Under the skilled direction of George Stevens, the film unfolds slowly with just the proper amount of dramatic tension. Ladd is the stranger, and Heflin, Arthur, and Brandon De Wilde are members of the homesteading family he aids. The excellent story and cast are enhanced by superb prizewinning photogra-

- Sharks' Treasure
- Sharky's Machine
- She
- Shenandoah
- The Sheriff of Fractured Jaw
- Sherlock Holmes' Smarter Brother
- She Wore a Yellow Ribbon
- Shine on Harvest Moon

S

phy. Also with Jack Palance, Ben Johnson, Edgar Buchanan, and Elisha Cook, Jr. **Academy Award**—Loyal Griggs, cinematography (color). **Nominations**—best picture; Stevens, best director; De Wilde, Palance, best supporting actor; A. B. Guthrie, Jr., writing (screenplay). *118 minutes*

SHARKS' TREASURE (1975)
★

Cornel Wilde

Wilde wrote, directed, and stars in this drama about a group of adventurers who battle sharks and escaped convicts while trying to recover sunken treasure in the Caribbean. This time the sharks are real, but they don't perform as well as the huge mechanical shark in *Jaws*. In fact, neither does anyone else in this amateurish production. Also with Yaphet Kotto, John Neilson, Dave Canary, and Cliff Osmond. (PG) *95 minutes*

SHARKY'S MACHINE (1981)
★★★

Burt Reynolds

Reynolds is director and star of this gripping, action-packed police thriller, and he handles the assignments with extraordinary flair and energy. He plays a wiley undercover cop, who cracks a high-flying prostitution and drug operation while encountering an overwhelming amount of blood, gore, and brutality in the process. In fact, Sharky bears a likeness to Clint Eastwood's *Dirty Harry* character, but Reynolds accomplishes the feat with more style and glamour. Also with Vittorio Gassman, Brian Keith, Charles Durning, Earl Holliman, Bernie Casey, Henry Silva, and Rachel Ward. (R) *122 minutes*

SHE (1965)
★★

Ursula Andress
John Richardson

Andress and Richardson spark enough energy in this story about the search for the Flame of Eternal Life to please fans of African adventure films. Andress plays Ayesha, the queen who never grows old. Richardson leads the quest for the Flame. The production, based on the H. Rider Haggard novel, takes itself too seriously, however, and would have been more effective as a fantasy. Peter Cushing, Christopher Lee, Bernard Cribbins, Rosenda Monteros, and André Morell appear in supporting roles. **Director**—Robert Day. *105 minutes*

SHENANDOAH (1965)
★★★

James Stewart

James Stewart (kneeling) is the head of a Virginia family in Shenandoah.

Stewart portrays the head of a Virginia household disrupted by the Civil War in this well-acted and competently directed western. The film is loaded with crisis upon crisis and, at times, borders on a western soap opera. But the fine performance of Stewart and quality supporting efforts of Rosemary Forsyth, Doug McClure, Katherine Ross, George Kennedy, Patrick Wayne, Glenn Corbett, and Philip Alford keep the production on track. **Director**—Andrew V. McLaglen. *105 minutes*

THE SHERIFF OF FRACTURED JAW (1959)
★

Kenneth More
Jane Mansfield

This British comedy western is about an English gunsmith who becomes the sheriff of a troubled town. More makes a solid effort as the gunsmith-turned-lawman, and Mansfield, who plays a saloon hostess, is pleasing to look at, but the film falls flat. Also with Robert Morley, Eynon Evans, Bruce Cabot, William Campbell, David Horne, Henry Hull, and Ronald Squire. **Director**—Raoul Walsh. *103 minutes*

SHERLOCK HOLMES' SMARTER BROTHER (1975)
★★

Gene Wilder

Maybe this title should have been *Sherlock Holmes' Silly Brother*. Wilder, who apprenticed at the Mel Brooks comedy school, wrote, directed, and stars in this spoof about the famous fictional sleuth. However, the film isn't the clever, zany romp expected from a member of the Brooks family. It is, rather, adolescent foolishness with only a smattering of true comic situations. Marty Feldman, Madeline Kahn, and Dom DeLuise—all of the Brooks company—are on board for this slapstick workout, which is merely elementary. (PG) *91 minutes*

SHE WORE A YELLOW RIBBON (1949)
★★★

John Wayne

Wayne is excellent as a rugged cavalry officer about to retire. But before he can leave the range for a retirement home, he faces a last encounter with some rampaging Indians. The film has all of director John Ford's vintage ingredients: quality acting, beautiful photography, and a good story. Joanne Dru, John Agar, Ben Johnson, Harry Carey, Jr., Mildred Natwick, Arthur Shields, Victor McLaglen, and George O'Brien also star. **Academy Award**—Winton Hock, cinematography (color). *103 minutes*

SHINE ON HARVEST MOON (1944)
★★

Ann Sheridan
Dennis Morgan

Some enjoyable tunes make this lightweight musical about the lives of vaudevillians Nora Bayes and Jack Norworth worthwhile. Sheridan and Morgan play the two entertainers. If you want to learn the real story about
(Continued)

S
- The Shining
- Shining Star
- Ship of Fools
- Shock Treatment
- The Shoes of the Fisherman
- Shogun Assassin
- Shoot

(Continued)

these famous entertainers, you won't find it in this film. But the performances of Sheridan and Morgan are pleasant enough, and they receive competent support from S. Z. Sakall, Marie Wilson, the Step Brothers, Robert Shayne, Jack Carson, and Irene Manning. **Director**—David Butler.

112 minutes b&w/color

THE SHINING (1980)
★★★

**Jack Nicholson
Shelley Duvall**

A maniacal Jack Nicholson says "Here's Johnny!" in a scene from The Shining.

Director Stanley Kubrick's haunted-hotel film, based on Stephen King's best-selling novel, is a fascinating thriller about horror, rage, and frustration. Yet as sumptuous and spellbinding as it is, many horror scenes wind up in puzzling dead ends; Kubrick seems to be trying too hard to be diabolical. Nicholson gives a smashing performance as a congenial father who is gradually transformed into a snarling demon bent on killing his family with an ax. Duvall plays his wife, and Danny Lloyd is his son. Also with Scatman Crothers and Anne Francis. (R) *146 minutes*

SHINING STAR (1977)
★

Harvey Keitel

A thin, awkward exposé of grubby and corrupt business practices in the pop music scene. Keitel is convincing as an influential but frustrated record producer. However, there's not enough going on to overcome Sig Shore's choppy direction; the monotone music by the rock group Earth, Wind, and Fire; and lackluster performances by the rest of the cast. The screenplay is by newspaper columnist Robert Lipsyte. Also with Ed Nelson, Cynthia Bostick, Bert Parks, and Jimmy Boyd. (PG) *100 minutes*

SHIP OF FOOLS (1965)
★★★

**Vivien Leigh
Simone Signoret
Oskar Werner
Heinz Ruhmann**

Director Stanley Kramer tries hard to be faithful to the best-selling novel by Katherine Anne Porter, but far too often he fails to do the book justice. Fortunately, the superior performances of Leigh, Signoret, Werner, and Ruhmann keep the ship from sinking. The movie is about a voyage in 1933 from Vera Cruz to Bremerhaven and the eccentricities of its various passengers. Leigh plays a divorcée, and Signoret and Werner are lovers. Also with Michael Dunn, Lee Marvin, José Ferrer, Elizabeth Ashley, Lilia Skala, José Greco, George Segal, and Karen Verne. **Academy Award**—Ernest Laszlo, cinematography (black and white). **Nominations**—best picture; Werner, best actor; Signoret, best actress; Dunn, best supporting actor; Abby Mann, best screenplay (based on material from another medium).

150 minutes b&w

SHOCK TREATMENT (1982)
★

**Cliff DeYoung
Richard O'Brien**

This film is a failed effort to capture the magic of *The Rocky Horror Picture Show* by the same folks who conceived the earlier cult classic. This musical follow-up tries to lampoon TV game shows and soap operas; the result is a dull, witless, and confusing production, which isn't worth viewing. The attempt at camp is all too obvious and strained. **Director**—Jim Sharman. (PG) *94 minutes*

THE SHOES OF THE FISHERMAN (1968)
★★

**Anthony Quinn
David Janssen
Laurence Olivier**

A fine cast can't salvage this confusing, boring, and long saga of a Russian cardinal who becomes the Pope. Quinn plays the Pontiff, Janssen is a journalist, and Olivier is the Russian premier. The story is supposedly based on Morris L. West's best-selling novel; but the book was a thoughtful and sensitive effort to explore complex life and death issues; the movie is superficial and fails to be of interest to either Christians or non-Christians. Also with Vittorio de Sica, Clive Revill, Paul Rogers, Barbara Jefford, and Leo McKern. **Director**—Michael Anderson. *157 minutes*

SHOGUN ASSASSIN (1980)
★

Tomisaburo Wakayama

This is an exceedingly gory film set in medieval Japan. A samurai warrior, played by Wakayama, has been exiled, so he's forced to wander around the countryside, pushing his small son in a cart. Every few minutes it seems, they're attacked by bands of Ninja. Heads, hands, and feet are whacked off with abandon and blood gushes freely—all to the tune of disco music. The samurai manages to leave plenty of bodies in his wake, while his son tries to keep an accurate body count. It appears that at least two Japanese films were spliced together and redubbed to create *Shogun Assassin*. The dialogue is ridiculous, and the acting is second-rate; but the result is a grisly parody of such movies that's often hilarious. **Director**—Robert Houston. (R) *86 minutes*

SHOOT (1977)
★

**Cliff Robertson
Ernest Borgnine**

Robertson and Borgnine star in this farfetched movie about two groups of weekend hunters who engage in a mil-

- The Shootist
- Shoot the Moon
- Short Eyes
- A Shot in the Dark
- The Shout
- Shout at the Devil

S

itary-type shoot-out. The film is supposed to be a statement favoring gun control, but it's too simplistic and unbelievable to be taken seriously. The performances are dreary, and the direction is lackluster. *Shoot* is way off target. Also with Larry Reynolds, Henry Silva, and James Blendick. **Director**—Harvey Hart. (R)

98 minutes

THE SHOOTIST (1976)
★★

John Wayne
Lauren Bacall
James Stewart

John Wayne plays a legendary gunfighter facing death in The Shootist.

A moving, last film performance by Wayne as an aging frontier gunfighter who's dying of cancer. He wants to die in peace, but his reputation won't let him. He meets death his own way in a *High Noon* shoot-out with local adversaries. Bacall plays the owner of a rooming house, and Stewart is a doctor friend of Wayne's. The film, which might have been one of the Duke's greatest, is unfortunately bogged down with too much useless dialogue and a lot of pompous philosophizing. There's no significant action until the end, and it's rather pat. Also with Ron Howard, Richard Boone, Hugh O'Brien, Harry Morgan, John Carradine, and Scatman Crothers. **Director**—Don Siegel. (PG)   *99 minutes*

SHOOT THE MOON (1982)
★★

Albert Finney
Diane Keaton

Albert Finney and Diane Keaton are a newly separated couple in Shoot the Moon.

An honest drama about the breakup of a 15-year marriage and the devastating effect on family members. Finney and Keaton are exceptionally good as the estranged couple, and some scenes are moving, indeed. But alas, such virtues don't connect to form an appealing movie. Director Alan Parker (*Fame*) relentlessly lingers on the pain until the film becomes labored and irritating. Also with Karen Allen and Peter Weller. (R)   *124 minutes*

SHORT EYES (1977)
★★★

Bruce Davison
José Perez
Joe Carberry

Davison, Perez, and Carberry star in this tough-talking, semidocumentary based on Miguel Pinero's award-winning play about prison life. It has a rawboned sort of entertaining quality that steers clear of the usual prison movie sentimentality. The cast—a mixture of ex-cons, street people, and professional actors—performs well. Filmed entirely in The Tombs, New York City's Men's House of Detention. Also with Don Blakely and Nathan George. **Director**—Robert M. Young. (R)   *104 minutes*

A SHOT IN THE DARK (1964)
★★★

Peter Sellers
Elke Sommer
George Sanders

Sellers is at his best in this comic adventure as he once again plays the inept French police inspector Jacques Clouseau. Sommer, a refreshing partner in this comic romp through Paris, is a murder suspect in a crime at the home of Sanders. Pacing is a main ingredient in such a film, and under the direction of Blake Edwards, everything flows so perfectly you don't have time to question some of the more preposterous sequences. The scene at a nudist colony is hilarious. Also with Herbert Lom, Tracy Reed, and Graham Stark.   *101 minutes*

THE SHOUT (1979)
★★

Alan Bates
Susannah York
John Hurt

An eerie and thoroughly muddled movie about a strange madman who can kill someone with a loud yell. Bates delivers a keen performance as a mental patient who acquired his terrifying knack from Australian Aboriginies. Hurt plays a composer, and York is his wife. The film's material is unfathomable, and the sound track, as if to emphasize the point of the film, is turned up extra loud. Also with Tim Curry and Robert Stephens. **Director**—Jerzy Skolimowski. (R)

87 minutes

SHOUT AT THE DEVIL (1976)
★★★

Lee Marvin
Roger Moore

Action fans should like this old-fashioned African adventure; there are sea battles, run-ins with hungry crocodiles, narrow escapes, aerial derring-do, and hand-to-hand combat. It's based on a novel by Wilbur Smith. Marvin plays a gin-soaked ivory poacher who feuds with the local German commissioner on the eve of World War I. And there's Moore as Marvin's veddy British partner. The film is perhaps too long, and the plot sags in places; otherwise, it's acceptable escapist entertainment. Also with Barbara Parkins, René Kolldehoff, Karl Michael Vogler, Ian Holm, and George Coulouris. **Director**—Peter Hunt. (PG)   *126 minutes*

S ● Show Boat ● The Silencers
● Sidewinder 1 ● Silent Movie
● Silence of the North

KATHARINE HEPBURN

Katharine Hepburn's long and distinguished film career has earned her 12 Academy Award nominations and three Oscars. Despite her remarkable talent, however, she was once regarded as an outsider by the Hollywood establishment and for a while had a reputation as box-office poison.

Hepburn was born in Hartford, Connecticut, in 1907, one of six children of an upper-class family. She began acting while at Bryn Mawr college.

Shortly after graduation, she made her professional stage debut in Baltimore. She then left for Broadway, where she gained a reputation for temperamental and independent behavior; she was often fired by the director or producer before a play opened.

Her first film, A Bill of Divorcement (1932), was an immediate success and this led to a succession of film roles. Her third movie, Morning Glory (1933), brought her first Academy Award. In the late '30s, she co-starred with Cary Grant in some of her finest movies.

Hepburn was turned down for the part of Scarlett O'Hara in Gone With the Wind, *so she returned to Broadway to play the lead in* The Philadelphia Story, *for which she obtained the film rights. The story was later brought to MGM for a movie. This 1940 film, which also starred Cary Grant and James Stewart, became a box-office success. In 1942, Hepburn made* The Woman of the Year, *her first film with Spencer Tracy. This experience lead to their legendary 27-year romance and eight more delightful screwball comedies together. Their last film together was* Guess Who's Coming to Dinner? *(1967). She won her second Oscar for her performance, and Tracy died shortly after the film was released.*

Hepburn starred with John Wayne in Rooster Cogburn *(1975) and acted in the TV version of* The Corn Is Green *(1979). She was splendid opposite Henry Fonda in the sentimental film* On Golden Pond *(1981), for which she received her latest Oscar nomination.*

Other notable films include Bringing Up Baby *(1938),* Adam's Rib *(1949),* The African Queen *(1951),* Pat and Mike *(1952),* Long Day's Journey Into Night *(1962), and* The Lion in Winter *(1968), the movie that earned her a third Academy Award.*

SHOW BOAT (1951)
★★★

Kathryn Grayson
Howard Keel

Some excellent Jerome Kern songs and energetic dancing make this a worthwhile film for musical fans. The movie, based on Edna Ferber's novel about life on the Mississippi River in the 1900s, is enriched by the performances of Grayson, Keel, and Joe E. Brown. Marge and Gower Champion, Ava Gardner, William Warfield, Agnes Moorehead, and Robert Sterling appear in supporting roles. Songs include "My Bill," "Can't Help Loving That Man," and "Old Man River." **Director**—George Sidney. **Academy Award Nomination**—Charles Rosher, cinematography (color). *108 minutes*

SIDEWINDER 1 (1977)
★★

Michael Parks

Lackluster acting and a weak plot make up this formula movie about motocross racing, another name for racing motorcycles across rough terrain. At first some of the racing action perks things up, but even this finally becomes monotonous. Parks, who resembles a poor imitation of Steve McQueen, stars as the hero of the race course. Also with Marjoe Gortner, Susan Howard, and Alex Cord. **Director**—Earl Bellamy. (PG) *97 minutes*

SILENCE OF THE NORTH (1982)
★★

Ellen Burstyn

Burstyn portrays a plucky young woman who survives harrowing experiences and brutal conditions in the northern Canadian territory in the early 1900s. The story, based on the life of Olive Fredrickson, is presented as an undramatic series of episodes. The film seems to work best as a travelogue, with breath-taking wilderness scenery upstaging everything else. Co-stars Tom Skerritt and Gordon Pinsent. **Director**—Allan Winton King. (PG) *94 minutes*

THE SILENCERS (1966)
★★

Dean Martin
Stella Stevens

Martin plays secret agent Matt Helm in this effort to capitalize on the success of James Bond films. But this movie lacks all of the charm of the Bond productions. Stevens, however, perks up the movie slightly. There are other sexual attractions and action scenes galore, but most of the footage falls flat. Nevertheless, there were several sequels. Arthur O'Connell, Cyd Charisse, Robert Webber, James Gregory, Victor Buono, and Daliah Lavi appear in supporting roles. **Director**—Phil Karlson. *103 minutes*

SILENT MOVIE (1976)
★★★★

Mel Brooks
Marty Feldman
Dom DeLuise

Comedy king Brooks proves that silence is golden by taking a chance and making an actual silent movie. The result is a procession of hilarious sight gags (what else?), somewhat on the order of The Marx Brothers and The Three Stooges. The film also conveys warmth as well as humor, but don't expect the outrageous side-

- The Silent Partner
- Silent Running
- Silent Scream
- Silk Stockings
- Silver Bears
- Silver Streak
- Simon

S

splitting antics of Brooks's *Blazing Saddles*. In the movie, Brooks plays a director named Mel Funn who tries to save a film studio from a takeover by a New York-based conglomerate. DeLuise and Feldman are his lunatic sidekicks. Splendid cameo appearances by Paul Newman, Burt Reynolds, and Liza Minnelli, and an uproarious nightclub tango routine with Anne Bancroft and the three leads. With English titles. (PG)

86 minutes

Dom DeLuise, Marty Feldman, and Mel Brooks try to save a studio in Silent Movie.

THE SILENT PARTNER (1979)
★★★

Elliott Gould
Christopher Plummer

A drab bank teller and a vicious, psychotic bank robber engage in a battle of wits in this nifty suspense film from Canada. Gould is the teller, and Plummer is the robber. The story moves briskly along with intriguing twists and turns while cleverly depicting the monotonous lives of the central characters. Performances throughout are superior; Gould is especially convincing as a man constantly teetering on the brink of disaster or victory. Also with Susannah York, Celina Lopez, Michael Kirby, and John Candy. **Director**—Daryl Duke. (R)

103 minutes

SILENT RUNNING (1971)
★★★

Bruce Dern

A fairly well-made sci-fi adventure about a 21st-century space station crew trying to keep the last of Earth's vegetation from being destroyed. Dern is outstanding as the head of the space scientists aboard the verdant

In Silent Running, *Bruce Dern attempts to save the last of Earth's vegetation.*

space ark, and there's a nice touch from two charming robots. The big star of this movie is the magnificent special effects handled skillfully by director Douglas Trumbull who contributed so much to *2001: A Space Odyssey*. Also with Cliff Potts, Ron Rifkin, and Jesse Vint. (PG) *90 minutes*

SILENT SCREAM (1980)
★

Yvonne De Carlo
Cameron Mitchell

A maniac murders some college students who move into a spooky old house. This is a predictable, cheaply made fright film that grows more ludicrous by the minute. The shabby-looking production stars De Carlo and Mitchell in rather unappealing roles. This formula haunted-house number has been done to death, yet haunted houses continue to haunt Hollywood. Also stars Rebecca Balding and Barbara Steele. **Director**—Denny Harris. (R)

86 minutes

SILK STOCKINGS (1957)
★★★

Fred Astaire
Cyd Charisse

Astaire and Charisse star in this musical version of the famous *Ninotchka*, which starred Greta Garbo. Charisse plays a Russian agent trying to bring a Russian composer living in Paris back to Moscow. Astaire is a dapper Hollywood producer who sidetracks Charisse from her mission. The Garbo film was better, but the personable team of Astaire and Charisse and the Cole Porter music make this a highly acceptable substitute. Janis Paige, Peter Lorre, George Tobias, Jules

Munshin, and Joseph Buloff also star. **Director**—Rouben Mamoulian.

116 minutes

SILVER BEARS (1978)
★

Michael Caine
Martin Balsam

A crude, cynical comedy adapted from Paul Erdman's best-selling 1974 novel about the world silver market. Caine is sent on a mission to Switzerland to buy a bank for syndicate head Balsam. A talented group of performers is wasted straining to produce laughs that never come. Ivan Passer directed this disaster, which also stars Cybill Shepherd, Louis Jourdan, and Tom Smothers. (PG) *113 minutes*

SILVER STREAK (1976)
★

Gene Wilder
Richard Pryor

An exasperating and witless comedy-adventure set mostly aboard a Los Angeles-to-Chicago train. Wilder plays an editor who becomes involved in a murder. There's really nothing much to laugh about until Pryor comes along about an hour into the film. He teams up with Wilder for a few hilarious scenes, but these moments quickly cut to a heavy-handed tangle of action and a phony train crash special effect. Colin Higgins's tacky screenplay just keeps getting sidetracked and director Arthur Hiller is little help at the throttle. Also with Jill Clayburgh, Patrick McGoohan, Ned Beatty, Ray Walston, and Scatman Crothers. (PG) *113 minutes*

SIMON (1980)
★★

Alan Arkin

Writer-director Marshall Brickman, who collaborated with Woody Allen on several hit films, solos with this droll half-baked comedy. It's about some zany think-tank geniuses who, out of boredom, brainwash a psychology professor into believing he's an alien from outer space. The professor

(Continued)

S

- Sinbad and the Eye of the Tiger
- Sinbad the Sailor
- Sincerely Yours
- Since You Went Away
- Singin' in the Rain
- Sink the Bismarck!
- Sirocco

(Continued)

is played by Arkin, who relentlessly hams it up. The Brickman script needles some absurdities of contemporary civilization, but after awhile, the needle becomes dull. Allen may be able to go it alone, but Brickman seems to need Allen's magic. Also with Madeline Kahn, Austin Pendleton, Fred Gwynne, William Finley, and Judy Graubart. (PG) *97 minutes*

SINBAD AND THE EYE OF THE TIGER (1977)
★★★

**Patrick Wayne
Jane Seymour**

Dazzling special effects are the mainstay of this third Arabian Nights film adventure aimed at preteen audiences. Sinbad, played by Wayne, and Princess Farah, played by Seymour, go on a dangerous journey to rescue her brother who has been changed into a baboon. They battle supernatural creatures and prehistoric monsters along the way, so parents may find it a bit silly. Also with Taryn Power and Margaret Whiting. **Director**—Sam Wanamaker. (G) *113 minutes*

SINBAD THE SAILOR (1947)
★★★

**Douglas Fairbanks, Jr.
Maureen O'Hara**

With Fairbanks as the swashbuckling hero, this high-seas adventure is great fun for fans of seafaring thrillers. Fairbanks has just the right touch for this kind of film fare, as he seeks the lost treasure of Alexander. The movie also has a lovely princess, played by O'Hara, which, of course, is another necessary ingredient in such stories. Walter Slezak, Jane Greer, Anthony Quinn, Sheldon Leonard, George Tobias, and Mike Mazurki appear in supporting roles. **Director**—Richard Wallace. *117 minutes*

SINCERELY YOURS (1955)
★

Liberace

Liberace, the skilled but peculiar piano player, is the centerpiece in this story about a pianist who has gone deaf. After deciding to help the downtrodden, he eventually finds the courage to have an operation to restore his hearing. Dorothy Malone, Joanne Dru, William Demarest, and Alex Nicol also appear in this off-key remake of *The Man Who Played God.* **Director**—Gordon Douglas.
115 minutes

SINCE YOU WENT AWAY (1944)
★★★

**Claudette Colbert
Joseph Cotten
Jennifer Jones
Shirley Temple**

This star-studded tearjerker deals with how a typical family copes with the tragedies of World War II as well as its daily ordeals. Colbert, Cotten, Jones, and Temple are used to good advantage; Colbert is especially radiant in this well-made movie. It's so refreshing to see such an unabashedly pro-American film, that its faults and excess flag-waving are easily forgiven. Also with Lionel Barrymore, Guy Madison, Agnes Moorehead, Monty Woolley, Robert Walker, Hattie McDaniel, Albert Basserman, Keenan Wynn, and Craig Stevens. **Director**—John Cromwell. **Academy Award Nominations**—best picture; Colbert, best actress; Woolley, best supporting actor; Jones, best supporting actress; Stanley Cortez and Lee Garmes, cinematography (black and white).
172 minutes b&w

SINGIN' IN THE RAIN (1952)
★★★★

**Gene Kelly
Donald O'Connor
Debbie Reynolds
Jean Hagen**

Kelly, O'Connor, Reynolds, and Hagen sparkle in this marvelous musical spoof about Hollywood during the period when talkies first replaced silent films. Among the hit songs are "Make 'em Laugh," "My Lucky Star," "Broadway Melody," "Good Morning," and the title tune. Rita Moreno, Cyd Charisse, Douglas Fowley, and Millard Mitchell also star in what many critics consider the greatest Hollywood musical of all time. **Direc-**

Gene Kelly acts out the title of Singin' in the Rain, *one of Hollywood's greatest musicals.*

tors—Kelly and Stanley Donen. **Academy Award Nomination**—Hagen, best supporting actress.
102 minutes

SINK THE BISMARCK! (1960)
★★★

**Kenneth More
Dana Wynter**

Exciting sea battles and good acting make this semidocumentary about the British hunt for the famed German battleship during World War II worthwhile viewing. Besides the search and eventual sinking of the German man-of-war, the personal dramas of the British sailors heighten the film's realism. More and Wynter star, with Karel Stepanek, Geoffrey Keen, Esmond Knight, Michael Hordern, Maurice Denham, Laurence Naismith, and Carl Mohner in supporting roles. **Director**—Lewis Gilbert.
97 minutes b&w

SIROCCO (1951)
★★

**Humphrey Bogart
Marta Toren
Lee J. Cobb**

Bogart manages to make this melodrama about gunrunning in the 1920s mildly interesting. Toren and Cobb also give artful performances, but the slow-moving story, set in Damascus,

- Sitting Ducks
- Sitting Pretty
- Six Bridges To Cross
- Skatetown, U.S.A.
- Skirts Ahoy!
- Sky Riders
- The Slap
- Slap Shot

S

lacks firepower. Zero Mostel also makes an appearance in a supporting role, but he doesn't make any difference to the outcome. Also with Gerald Mohr, Onslow Stevens, and Everett Sloane. *Casablanca* it ain't. **Director**—Curtis Bernhardt. *98 minutes b&w*

SITTING DUCKS (1980)
★

Michael Emil
Zack Norman

Emil and Norman star in this amateurishly made comedy about two odd con men who steal $700,000 from a gambling syndicate and hightail it to Miami. Everyone talks at once, babbling and bickering about sex, health, and money. Director Henry Jaglom's improvised style is hard to fathom. Even a duck would have difficulty sitting through all this gibberish. Also with Patrice Townsend. (R)
90 minutes

SITTING PRETTY (1948)
★★★

Clifton Webb
Robert Young
Maureen O'Hara

Clifton Webb is an effective but stern babysitter in the comedy Sitting Pretty.

Webb is delightful in this comedy. He plays Mr. Belvedere, an eccentric genius who works as a babysitter for Young and O'Hara. When he writes a successful novel about his experiences, he throws gossipy neighbors into a tizzy. Webb became famous in this role, and two other Mr. Belvedere films followed. Also with Richard Haydn, Larry Olsen, Louise Allbritton, Ed Begley, and Randy Stuart. **Director**—Walter Lang. **Academy**

Award Nomination—Webb, best actor. *84 minutes b&w*

SIX BRIDGES TO CROSS (1955)
★★

Tony Curtis

Apparently inspired by the Boston Brink's robbery, this well-made film depicts the life and hard times of a Boston gangster in the 1930s. Curtis is at his best as the hoodlum who gets involved with crime and can't abide by the law no matter how hard he tries to go straight. He finally masterminds a robbery involving more than 2½ million dollars. George Nader, Sal Mineo, Jan Merlin, Julie Adams, and Jay C. Flippen appear in supporting roles. **Director**—Joseph Pevney.
96 minutes b&w

SKATETOWN, U.S.A. (1979)
★

Scott Baio
Flip Wilson
Ron Palillo

Baio, Wilson, and Palillo head the cast of this empty-headed juvenile film, aimed at capitalizing on the roller-disco fad. There's plenty disco-skating action, but nothing in the way of a meaningful story. It's about a young lad who tries to win the roller-disco contest by overcoming the bad guys in black leather jackets. A lot of silly jokes and many cardboard characters get tangled in the wheels. Also with Ruth Buzzi, Dave Mason, and Billy Barty. **Director**—William A. Levey. (PG) *98 minutes*

SKIRTS AHOY! (1952)
★

Esther Williams
Vivian Blaine
Joan Evans

Williams, Blaine, and Evans star in this typical 1950s musical. Although they perform with energy and vitality, they're sunk by the silly plot's triteness. The trio joins the Navy as Waves and find romance with Dean Miller, Barry Sullivan, and Keefe Brasselle—a switch of the usual procedure in such films. Even the music of Billy

Eckstine and the DeMarco Sisters fails to keep this production afloat. Also with Debbie Reynolds and Bobby Van. **Director**—Sidney Lanfield.
105 minutes

SKY RIDERS (1976)
★★★

James Coburn
Susannah York
Robert Culp

Daredevil hang-gliding stunts jazz up this well-photographed action drama filmed in Greece. The familiar and unbelievable plot, however, hardly gets off the ground. A wife and two children of a wealthy industrialist, played by Culp, are kidnapped by political terrorists and are held at a remote mountain fortress. The wife's ex-husband, played by Coburn, tracks down the hideaway and hires a group of hang-gliding commandos for the thrilling rescue. Douglas Hickox does a fair job of directing. Bob and Chris Wills and their hang-glider team fly away with the movie. Also with Charles Aznavour, Werner Pochath, and Harry Andrews. (PG)
93 minutes

THE SLAP (1976)
★

Isabelle Adjani
Lino Ventura
Annie Girardot

A French comedy of sorts, featuring such big-name stars as Adjani, Ventura, and Girardot. But the story is lightweight fare; it resembles a 1960s TV sitcom. The plodding film is about a conflict between a 51-year-old professor and his rebellious 18-year-old daughter who contemplates moving in with her boyfriend. Limp direction by Claude Pinoteau. In French with English titles. (No MPAA rating)
98 minutes

SLAP SHOT (1977)
★★★

Paul Newman

An exhilarating and freewheeling comedy that probes the violence of professional ice hockey. Newman
(Continued)

S
- Slaughterhouse Five
- Slaughter on Tenth Avenue
- Sleeper
- The Sleeping Beauty
- The Slipper and the Rose
- Slither
- Slow Dancing in the Big City

Paul Newman (left) and his teammates brawl on the ice in Slap Shot.

(Continued)
stars as a broken-down player-coach of a fourth-rate minor-league team, which suddenly becomes popular by playing dirty. The zestful screenplay by Nancy Dowd presents some lively and believable characters, although several soap opera-like subplots get in the way. The film is well salted with locker-room humor and plenty of expletives. Newman handles his part well, and the lesser roles are all excellent. Also with Michael Ontkean, Lindsay Crouse, Melinda Dillon, Jennifer Warren, and Strother Martin. Directed with gusto by George Roy Hill. (R)   *122 minutes*

SLAUGHTERHOUSE FIVE (1972)
★★

Michael Sacks
Ron Leibman
Sharon Gans

The very bizarre—almost mystical—antiwar novel by Kurt Vonnegut, Jr., is difficult to transfer to the screen. But there are still many good moments in this complex film about a New York optometrist who has fantasies about a strange futuristic planet and nightmares about Nazi prisoner-of-war camps. Many of the images are brilliant, but the movie is hard to follow at times, even for those who read the book. Sacks, Leibman, and Gans star, with Eugene Roche, Valerie Perrine, John Dehner, and Sorrell Booke in supporting roles. **Director**—George Roy Hill. (R)   *104 minutes*

SLAUGHTER ON TENTH AVENUE (1957)
★★★

Richard Egan
Jan Sterling
Dan Duryea
Walter Matthau

Another drama about murder and corruption on the New York City waterfront. Egan, Sterling, Duryea, and Matthau star in this well-constructed production about an assistant district attorney struggling to convict gangsters who control the waterfront. The movie *On the Waterfront* was better, but this is a respectable movie in the genre. The fine cast also includes Julie Adams, Charles McGraw, Sam Levene, and Harry Bellaver. **Director**—Arnold Laven.   *103 minutes b&w*

SLEEPER (1973)
★★★★

Woody Allen
Diane Keaton

Allen is in top form as writer, actor, and director in this story. It's about a health food store owner who's frozen after an operation and awakens 200 years later in 2173 to find himself in a weird police state. Keaton is charming as his love interest of the future. There are good sight gags and enough one-liners to keep the story rolling at a brisk pace. John Beck, Mary Gregory, Don Keefer, and John McLiam are competent in supporting roles, and the Preservation Hall Jazz Band gives the enterprise an extra lift. (PG)   *88 minutes*

THE SLEEPING BEAUTY (1958)
★★★

This classic fairy tale gets conscientious and sensitive handling from the gang at Walt Disney. By and large, they have followed the original story faithfully and with great detail. Kids will enjoy this cartoon feature, and parents might also find themselves watching it with more than routine interest. **Director**—Clyde Geronomi.   *75 minutes*

THE SLIPPER AND THE ROSE (1976)
★★

Richard Chamberlain
Gemma Craven

This musical adaptation of the Cinderella story is too long for most children, and the sluggish screenplay is no help either. Chamberlain plays the Prince, and Craven is Cinderella. The production was designed to make room for a lot of pedestrian songs from the Sherman Brothers, who did well with their numbers for *Mary Poppins*. Occasional flashes of charm are contributed by Michael Hordern and Edith Evans. Also with Kenneth More, Margaret Lockwood, and Christopher Gable. **Director**—Bryan Forbes. (G)   *128 minutes*

SLITHER (1972)
★★★

James Caan
Sally Kellerman
Peter Boyle
Louise Lasser

Caan, Kellerman, Boyle, and Lasser star in this zany romp about a search—by means of trailers and campers—for a hidden cache of money in California. At times the movie appears shrill, and it isn't always easy to tolerate the glib blend of violence and comedy. However, the film is engaging and well made. Allen Garfield and Richard B. Shull appear in supporting roles. **Director**—Howard Zieff. (PG)   *96 minutes*

SLOW DANCING IN THE BIG CITY (1978)
★★

Paul Sorvino
Anne Ditchburn

A cliché-strewn boy-meets-girl story set in New York City. It's directed by John G. Avildsen who brought us *Rocky*. Again, Avildsen goes all out for sentimentality and the uplifting spirit, but the approach is so overdone the film lapses into triteness. Sorvino is excellent as a gruff newspaper columnist who falls for a struggling but ail-

● Small Change   ● A Small Town in Texas   **S**
● A Small Circle of Friends   ● Smile
● Small Town Girl   ● Smokey and the Bandit
● Smokey and the Bandit II

ing young ballerina, played by Ditchburn. It's sort of *Rocky* in leotards. Also with Nicolas Coster, Anita Dangler, and Hector Jaime Mercado. (PG)   *101 minutes*

SMALL CHANGE (1976)
★★★★

Eva Truffaut
Geory Desmouceaux
Philippe Goldman
Tania Torrens

French children who star in François Truffaut's entertaining film Small Change.

Director François Truffaut's 15th feature film is an endearing and entertaining celebration of childhood. The film consists of a series of vignettes about a group of French children in a small village who manage to survive in an adult world with or without love. Truffaut lovingly treats his children as human beings—not as gimmicks for entertainment or exploitation. *Small Change* is for everyone, except perhaps those who don't like children. Also with Jean-François Stevenin, Claudio Deluca, and Frank Deluca. In French with English titles. (PG)   *104 minutes*

A SMALL CIRCLE OF FRIENDS
(1980)
★★

Brad Davis
Karen Allen
Jameson Parker

A glossed-over look at student life in the late '60s, when Vietnam war protests, drugs, and the sexual revolution made news. The story follows the college careers of three students, played enthusiastically by Davis, Allen, and Parker. But Rob Cohen directs at such a frantic pace that the story loses its perspective and burns out in the final segments. It seems as if the principals

in this venture were too close to this period to effectively reflect on the times. (R)   *113 minutes*

SMALL TOWN GIRL (1953)
★★

Jane Powell
Farley Granger
Ann Miller
Bobby Van

Powell, Granger, Miller, and Van star in this pleasant musical about a small-town girl. In this case, Powell falls in love with Granger, a handsome playboy who gets arrested in her Connecticut hometown for speeding. This musical version of a 1936 film lacks the dynamic pace and tempo of the better musicals, but it's still enjoyable. Miller almost steals the show with "I've Gotta Hear That Beat," staged by Busby Berkeley. S. Z. Sakall, Billie Burke, Robert Keith, Nat King Cole, and Fay Wray also appear. **Director—**Leslie Kardos.   *93 minutes*

A SMALL TOWN IN TEXAS
(1976)
★★

Timothy Bottoms
Susan George
Bo Hopkins

A young man comes home after serving time in prison on a pot rap and seeks revenge on the sheriff who busted him. It's pretty much B-picture melodrama, with plot sections stolen from *The Last Picture Show* and *Dirty Mary, Crazy Larry*. There's plenty of car-chase action and stunt crashes apparently aimed at the youth audience. Hopkins performs rather well as the mean sheriff, and he upstages Timothy Bottoms who plays the lead. George helps Bottoms against the cops. **Director—**Jack Starrett. (PG)   *95 minutes*

SMILE (1975)
★★★

Barbara Feldon
Bruce Dern

This satirical film, directed by Michael Ritchie, dissects the callousness and competitiveness of beauty contests,

while also taking a hard look at small-town life in America. The somewhat documentary story, starring Feldon and Dern, is alternately amusing and tragic. Dern plays the pageant's sponsor—a used-car salesman—and Feldon is the woman who shepherds the contestants. Also with Michael Kidd, Geoffrey Lewis, Nicholas Pryor, Colleen Camp, and Melanie Griffith. (PG)   *113 minutes*

SMOKEY AND THE BANDIT
(1977)
★★

Burt Reynolds
Sally Field
Jackie Gleason
Jerry Reed

Fast cars and an 18-wheel trailer truck are the stars of this comedy about a couple of good ol' boys who try to bootleg 400 cases of beer from Georgia to Texas under the noses of the cops. The film evolves into a drawn-out car chase, punctuated with predictable crash stunts and laced with CB jargon. Grinning Reynolds and singing Reed are so-so as the happy-go-lucky bootleggers. Gleason overacts as the frustrated Texas sheriff in hot pursuit. Field, a damsel in distress, gives the only commendable performance. Also with Mike Henry, Paul Williams, and Pat McCormick. **Director—**Hal Needham. (PG)   *96 minutes*

SMOKEY AND THE BANDIT II
(1980)
★★★

Burt Reynolds
Sally Field
Jackie Gleason
Dom DeLuise

Once again the frustrated Sheriff Buford T. Justice, played by Gleason, is in long, hot pursuit of the Bandit (Reynolds), the Frog (Field), and their pals, who are transporting a pregnant elephant to Dallas to earn $400,000. Reynolds and company have spiced up their act to make this mindless, cartoonlike comedy more entertaining than the 1977 *Smokey* film. There are plenty of laughs and plenty of spectacular stunts, and the cast carries on in good-natured harmony. It's adoles-
(Continued)

S
- The Snake Pit
- The Snows of Kilimanjaro
- Snow White and the Seven Dwarfs
- S.O.B.
- So Dear To My Heart
- Sodom and Gomorrah

Burt Reynolds and Sally Field shepherd an elephant in Smokey and the Bandit II.

cent humor at best, but it works. Also with Paul Williams. **Director**—Hal Needham. (PG)   *95 minutes*

THE SNAKE PIT (1948)
★★★★

Olivia de Havilland

Olivia de Havilland and Mark Stevens in The Snake Pit, about life in a mental hospital.

This drama about life in a crowded mental hospital is a fine example of what Hollywood can do to improve society when it latches onto a worthwhile cause and makes a plea. In this case, there's a pitch for improved care of the mentally ill. De Havilland is excellent as a woman trying to overcome mental illness and has horrifying experiences in a mental institution. Leo Genn, Mark Stevens, Celeste Holm, Lee Patrick, Natalie Schaefer, Glenn Langan, Beulah Bondi, and Leif Erickson give good performances in supporting roles. **Director**—Anatole Litvak. **Academy Award Nominations**—best picture; Litvak, best director; De Havilland, best actress; Frank Partos and Millen Brand, writing (screenplay).   *108 minutes b&w*

THE SNOWS OF KILIMANJARO
(1952)
★★

Gregory Peck
Susan Hayward
Ava Gardner

Hollywood gives the star treatment to this Ernest Hemingway short story about a wounded white hunter contemplating his life as he awaits death. Unfortunately, most of the performers are less than stirring, although Peck is competent as the wounded man. Hayward and Gardner are less than satisfactory, and a weak film script doesn't help them overcome their limitations. Also with Leo G. Carroll, Marcel Dalio, Torin Thatcher, and Hildegard Neff. **Director**—Henry King. **Academy Award Nomination**—Leon Shamroy, cinematography (color).
117 minutes

SNOW WHITE AND THE SEVEN DWARFS (1937)
★★★★

This classic cartoon—Disney's first full-length feature—is as fresh and delightful now as when it was made. Besides the excellence of the production, the superb filming, and wonderful songs, there's the first-rate dramatic tension of Ms. White and her little friends confronting villains. Eight Disney writers worked on the Brothers Grimm fairy tale, with Larry Morey and Frank Churchill writing the songs.   *82 minutes*

S.O.B. (1981)
★★

Julie Andrews
Richard Mulligan

Director Blake Edwards (*The Pink Panther* series; *10*) fries the Hollywood establishment in a cauldron of bitter comedy that often backfires and peters out midway. The hysterical broadside comes off mostly as an inside joke. Mulligan plays a producer who makes a $30-million flop musical, which he salvages by turning it into a soft-core porn extravaganza. Squeaky-clean

Julie Andrews is the star of S.O.B., *a bitter movie-within-a-movie comedy.*

Andrews, the star of the movie-within-the-movie, goes topless to salvage the project. The event is a cheap shot. (R)   *121 minutes*

SO DEAR TO MY HEART (1948)
★★

Burl Ives
Beulah Bondi

Adults will find this Walt Disney story about a boy's determination to tame a black sheep and enter it in the competition at the state fair too nostalgic and sentimental, but it should appeal to most young children. The film, which includes some animated sequences, manages to capture the mood and charm of an American farm in the early 1900s. The cast also includes Harry Carey, Bobby Driscoll, and Luana Patten. **Director**—Harold Schuster.   *84 minutes*

SODOM AND GOMORRAH
(1962)
★

Stewart Granger
Stanley Baker
Pier Angeli
Anouk Aimée

This made-in-Italy biblical extravaganza about the Helamite plot to take over the wicked cities of Sodom and Gomorrah stars Granger, Baker, Angeli, and Aimée. Fortunately, the acting has merit, because the overly long story becomes boring despite the vice and gore. Such violence, however, doesn't pass for action. Part of

● So Fine
● Soldier in the Rain
● Soldier of Fortune
● The Solid Gold Cadillac

● Solomon and Sheba
● So Long at the Fair
● Somebody Killed Her Husband

S

the problem in this production is caused by the inability of the French and Italian producers to work well together. Also with Rossana Podesta. **Director**—Robert Aldrich.

154 minutes

SO FINE (1981)
★★

Ryan O'Neal
Jack Warden

O'Neal seems out of place in this uneven comedy involving New York City's garment industry. He plays a tweedy college professor who improves his father's faltering clothing business by accidentally introducing designer jeans with see-through bottoms. The improbable story wavers between sophisticated humor and Marx Brothers-type slapstick, with too few laughs coming across. Only Warden registers well, as the unrefined, huffing and puffing dress factory owner. Mariangela Melato and Richard Kiel also star. **Director**—Andrew Bergman. (R)   *89 minutes*

SOLDIER IN THE RAIN (1963)
★★

Steve McQueen
Jackie Gleason

McQueen and Gleason star in this tragi-comedy about the friendship between two Army sergeants. As expected, Gleason brings humor and mirth to the film, but his attempts at meaningful drama falter; he never seems to accomplish much on a serious level. However, there are enough comic moments to make the film worthwhile—especially for Gleason or McQueen fans. Tuesday Weld, Tom Poston, John Hubbard, Tony Bill, and Ed Nelson also star. **Director**—Ralph Nelson.   *87 minutes b&w*

SOLDIER OF FORTUNE (1955)
★★

Clark Gable
Susan Hayward

Gable and Hayward are slightly better than average in this adventure film set in Hong Kong. Gable, a smuggler, is hired to find Hayward's photog-

rapher husband, played by Gene Barry, who's missing in Red China. The plot and script are slightly less than adequate, although the excellent photography and adventure sequences should make viewing worthwhile if you're a Gable fan. Also with Anna Sten, Michael Rennie, Leo Gordon, Russell Collins, Tom Tully, and Alex D'Arcy. **Director**—Edward Dmytryk.   *96 minutes*

THE SOLID GOLD CADILLAC (1956)
★★★

Judy Holliday
Paul Douglas

Paul Douglas and Judy Holliday in the comedy The Solid Gold Cadillac.

The comic genius of Holliday merges expertly with the brilliant acting skills of Douglas in this enjoyable comedy. She plays a minor stockholder in a big company who tries to fire a corrupt board of directors. The movie is based on the play of George S. Kaufman and Howard Teichman, with the screen version written by Abe Burrows. John Williams, Fred Clark, Neva Patterson, Ray Collins, and Arthur O'Connell also star; George Burns narrates. Originally, the final scene was in color. **Director**—Richard Quine.

99 minutes b&w/color

SOLOMON AND SHEBA (1959)
★★

Yul Brynner
Gina Lollobrigida

This well-filmed biblical spectacle,

photographed in Spain, takes a light-hearted try at telling what happened when David's older son plotted revenge after learning that David had named a younger brother heir. Mostly, this is just a splashy action film, with Lollabrigida as the alluring Queen of Sheba and Brynner as King Solomon. The large cast includes George Sanders, David Farrar, Marisa Pavan, Harry Andrews, and Alejandro Rey. **Director**—King Vidor.

139 minutes

SO LONG AT THE FAIR (1950)
★★★

Jean Simmons
Dirk Bogarde

Simmons and Bogarde star in this mystery, set during the 1889 Paris Exposition. It's about a woman searching for her brother, who has mysteriously vanished during their visit to the exposition without a trace. The theme of torment and terror of vainly seeking help to find a missing person has been done better by Alfred Hitchcock and others, but this rendition is well made and worth viewing. David Tomlinson, Marcel Poncin, Cathleen Nesbitt, Felix Aylmer, André Morell, and Honor Blackman star in supporting roles. **Director**—Terence Fisher.   *86 minutes b&w*

SOMEBODY KILLED HER HUSBAND (1978)
★★

Farrah Fawcett-Majors
Jeff Bridges

Fawcett-Majors proves her worth as an adroit screen actress in this glossy mystery-comedy set in New York City. Farrah and friend, played by Bridges, set out to solve the murder of her estranged husband. But director Lamont Johnson fails to keep the tension working, and the film peters out in the final frames. Farrah's winning performance and her famous smile survive the rough treatment. Also with John Wood, Tammy Grimes, Patricia Elliott, and John Glover. (PG)

97 minutes

S • Somebody Up There Likes Me
• Some Came Running
• Some Like It Hot
• Something Short of Paradise
• Sometimes a Great Notion
• Somewhere in Time

SOMEBODY UP THERE LIKES ME (1956)
★★★

Paul Newman
Pier Angeli

Paul Newman (left) portrays Rocky Graziano in Somebody Up There Likes Me.

Boxer Rocky Graziano rose from the slums of New York City and reform school to become the middleweight boxing champion of the world. Newman does an excellent job of portraying Rocky in this film biography, and Angeli is splendid as his wife. Joseph Buloff plays an earthy, streetwise philosopher. Eileen Heckart is Rocky's mom, and Everett Sloane is a fight promoter. The production is well done, although at times there's an excess of sentiment and violence. Sal Mineo, Robert Loggia, and Steve McQueen appear in supporting roles. **Director**—Robert Wise. **Academy Award**—Joseph Ruttenberg, cinematography (black and white).
112 minutes b&w

SOME CAME RUNNING (1958)
★★

Frank Sinatra
Dean Martin
Shirley MacLaine

Some viewers will be disappointed by the hatchet job that was done on the novel by James Jones. This melancholy story about a moody writer trying to adjust to his small hometown in the South after returning from the Army after World War II becomes an aimless melodrama on screen. However, excellent performances by Sinatra, MacLaine, and Martha Hyer make the movie worthwhile. Dean Martin, Nancy Gates, Leora Dana, and Arthur Kennedy appear in supporting roles. **Director**—Vincente Minnelli. **Academy Award Nominations**—MacLaine, best actress; Kennedy, best supporting actor; Hyer, best supporting actress.
127 minutes

SOME LIKE IT HOT (1959)
★★★★

Jack Lemmon
Tony Curtis
Marilyn Monroe

Lemmon, Curtis, and Monroe form a fine comic trio in this free-flowing comedy about two unemployed musicians—Lemmon and Curtis—on the run from mobsters after they witness a gangland slaying. Disguised as women, they join an all-girl orchestra. At times, the laughs seem to gush forth in this uninhibited farce—and one of Hollywood's funniest movies ever. The trio gets fine supporting performances from George Raft, Joe E. Brown, Joan Shawlee, Pat O'Brien, Nehemiah Persoff, and George E. Stone. For extra measure, Monroe sings "Running Wild," and wide-mouthed Brown delivers the film's classic closing line. **Director**—Billy Wilder. **Academy Award Nominations**—Wilder, best director; Lemmon, best actor; Wilder and I.A.L. Diamond, best screenplay (based on material from another medium); Charles Lang, Jr., cinematography (black and white). *122 minutes b&w*

SOMETHING SHORT OF PARADISE (1979)
★★

Susan Sarandon
David Steinberg

This contemporary romantic comedy is about an on-again, off-again affair between a klutzy art house proprietor and a magazine writer. Sarandon is the writer, and Steinberg is the proprietor. The movie often appears to parallel the Woody Allen/Diane Keaton style of film with a few variations: Steinberg is less of a sad sack than Allen, while Sarandon is less zany than Keaton. There are some funny moments, although the humor is generally low-key. Marilyn Sokol is excellent as a cunning member of the singles jungle. Also with Robert Hitt, Jean-Pierre Aumont, and Joe Grifasi. **Director**—David Helpern, Jr. (PG)
91 minutes

SOMETIMES A GREAT NOTION (1971)
★★★

Paul Newman
Henry Fonda
Michael Sarrazin
Richard Jaeckel

Newman directed and stars in this beautifully filmed story about a logging family in Oregon. The members of the family believe in individuality so they defy a local strike by staying on the job. The father is played by Fonda, and Newman, Sarrazin, and Jaeckel are his sons. The movie isn't particularly faithful to Ken Kessey's novel nor even to its own good intentions, but the acting is excellent. The star-studded cast also includes Lee Remick, Cliff Potts, and Linda Lawson. (PG) **Alternate Title**—*Never Give an Inch.* **Academy Award Nomination**—Jaeckel, best supporting actor.
114 minutes

SOMEWHERE IN TIME (1980)
★

Christopher Reeve
Jane Seymour

A schmaltzy, sentimental love story with Reeve as a young playwright

Jane Seymour and Christopher Reeve get together at last in Somewhere in Time.

● A Song Is Born
● The Song of Bernadette
● Song of Norway
● Song of the South
● The Song Remains the Same
● Son of Dracula
● Son of Frankenstein

S

who crosses the time barrier to find his true love, played by Seymour. After falling in love with an old photograph, Reeve wills himself back in time to meet the woman. This sort of mystical romance was done well in the '40s. Remember *Portrait of Jennie*? But Reeve is no Joseph Cotten, and this silly film misfires for lack of inspiration and imagination. Seymour looks beautiful, but she's all surface and bogged down with trite dialogue. Also with Teresa Wright. **Director**—Jeannot Szwarc. (PG) *103 minutes*

A SONG IS BORN (1948)
★★

Danny Kaye
Virginia Mayo

Kaye and Mayo get great support from jazz greats Benny Goodman, Charlie Barnet, Louis Armstrong, Lionel Hampton, and Tommy Dorsey, but the weak script sinks the whole show in this musical remake of *Ball of Fire*, a comedy starring Gary Cooper. Hugh Herbert, Jr., Edward Bromberg, Mary Field, Steve Cochran, Felix Bressart, and Mel Powell appear in supporting roles. **Director**—Howard Hawks.
113 minutes

THE SONG OF BERNADETTE (1943)
★★★★

Jennifer Jones

In Song of Bernadette, *Jennifer Jones plays the role of a pious French girl.*

Jones became a star after her portrayal of Bernadette, a pious French girl who has a vision of the Virgin Mary at Lourdes, a site that became a shrine. Although the movie is long and the handling of a sensitive religious subject is at times heavy-handed, the film's virtues outweigh its faults. Also with Vincent Price, William Eythe, Charles Bickford, Lee J. Cobb, Sig Rumann, Gladys Cooper, and Anne Revere. **Director**—Henry King. **Academy Awards**—Jones, best actress; Arthur Miller, cinematography (black and white). **Nominations**—best picture; King, best director; Bickford, best supporting actor; Cooper, Revere, best supporting actress; George Seaton, writing (screenplay). *156 minutes b&w*

SONG OF NORWAY (1970)
★

Florence Henderson
Toralv Maurstad

This biographical mishmash about the life of Edvard Grieg is pleasant to watch—especially with its splendid landscapes. However, it's poorly made and almost totally lacking in substance; the music is also substandard. The cast also includes Edward G. Robinson, Harry Secombe, Oscar Homolka, Robert Morley, Christina Schollin, and Frank Porretta, but none is able to salvage this dud. **Director**—Andrew L. Stone. (G) *141 minutes*

SONG OF THE SOUTH (1947)
★★★

Ruth Warrick
Bobby Driscoll

This charming children's story about Uncle Remus and Brer Rabbit is interspersed with cartoon segments. Most adults find only the cartoons charming and the rest of the Disney enterprise weak. But many kids will probably enjoy the whole show, as small boys on a southern plantation listen to Uncle Remus, an old black servant tell Brer Rabbit stories. The cast also includes James Baskett, Lucile Watson, Hattie McDaniel, and Luana Patten. **Director**—Harve Foster.
94 minutes

THE SONG REMAINS THE SAME (1976)
(no stars)

This long, ear-shattering feature covers the Led Zeppelin's 1973 Madison Square Garden appearance. Going to this movie is supposed to be the equivalent of attending such a concert by the British rock group, but it doesn't work. Gone is the sense of physical presence and the ability of an audience to communicate excitement to the performers. What's left is an unbearable sound assault, which may leave you with a headache. **Directors**—Peter Clifton and Joe Massot. (PG) *136 minutes*

SON OF DRACULA (1943)
★★

Lon Chaney, Jr.
Louise Albritton

The cast in this horror film has all the standard operatives for such tales—Albritton, Chaney, Frank Craven, J. Edward Bromberg, Evelyn Ankers, Samuel S. Hinds, and Robert Paige. If horror fare is your pleasure, then this story of Count Alucard—Dracula spelled backwards—who visits a southern plantation and terrorizes much of the neighborhood might even be enjoyable. **Director**—Robert Siodmak. *80 minutes b&w*

SON OF FRANKENSTEIN (1939)
★★★

Basil Rathbone
Boris Karloff
Bela Lugosi
Lionel Atwill

Classic horror film characters, including Rathbone, Karloff, Lugosi, Atwill, and Edgar Norton, make this a top-rated entry of the genre. There are numerous tense, spine-tingling moments as the son of Frankenstein tries to capture an old monster created by his father. The production is well staged, although at times there's too much dialogue. Lawrence Grant, Donnie Dunagan, Josephine Hutchinson, and Emma Dunn appear in supporting roles. **Director**—Rowland V. Lee.
99 minutes b&w

S • Son of Paleface
  • Sons and Lovers
  • The Sons of Katie Elder
  • So Proudly We Hail

SON OF PALEFACE (1952)
★★★

Bob Hope
Roy Rogers
Jane Russell

Hope stars in this whacky comedy about a bumbling fellow who goes West to collect his inheritance. Some of the bids at humor are a bit strained and pale by comparison, but there's enough fun to make viewing worthwhile. Shapely Russell is a pleasant addition and inspiration for Hope. Rogers and his famous horse Trigger also make an appearance. Bill Williams, Harry Von Zell, Douglass Dumbrille, and Lloyd Corrigan appear in supporting roles. **Director**—Frank Tashlin.   *95 minutes*

SONS AND LOVERS (1960)
★★★★

Dean Stockwell
Trevor Howard
Wendy Hiller

D. H. Lawrence's autobiographical novel about a sensitive youth pushed by his mother to make a life for himself away from the Nottingham coal mines is faithfully brought to the screen by director Jack Cardiff; it's also well-adapted by the screenplay of Gavin Lambert and T.E.B. Clarke. Stockwell plays the youth, Hiller is his mother. The movie is enhanced by the star performances of Howard as the boy's gruff father and Mary Ure as the woman in the life of the would-be artist. The photography does an excellent job of conveying the mood probably intended by Lawrence. Heather Sears, Donald Pleasence, Ernest Thesiger,

GOLDIE HAWN

In the late '60s, the television series Laugh-In introduced Goldie Hawn, whose irrepressible giggle, delightful malapropisms, and radiant physical presence captured the hearts of the public. However, with her first film, Cactus Flower (1969), Hawn showed that she possessed more than most of the other blonde favorites of the past; she walked off with an Academy Award as best supporting actress. In subsequent films, such as The Sugarland Express (1973), The Girl From Petrovka (1974), and Shampoo (1975), she extended her range beyond comedy.

Born Jeanne Hawn in Washington, D.C., in 1945, Goldie is the daughter of Laura and Edward Rutledge Hawn, a descendent of Edward Rutledge of South Carolina, who was one of the signers of the Declaration of Independence. At the age of three, she began studying ballet and later took up tap-dancing and modern jazz.

At the Texas Pavilion at New York World's Fair in 1964-65, she made her professional dancing debut in Can-Can. She continued working in musical comedies in New York, as a dancer in Puerto Rico, as a choreographer in California, and as a dancer in a Las Vegas revue.

After her Las Vegas stint, she returned to Los Angeles and danced on an Andy Griffith television special. She then received attention for a continuing role in a short-lived but critically well received TV series entitled, Good Morning, World. Her flair for comedy was evident to audiences, and she was then signed as a regular on Rowan and Martin's Laugh-In series.

After her successful debut in Cactus Flower, she appeared in There's a Girl in My Soup (1970) opposite Peter Sellers; $ (1971) with Warren Beatty; and Butterflies are Free (1972). After several dramatic roles, she returned to comedy in The Duchess and the Dirtwater Fox (1976) opposite George Segal. Her more recent movies include Foul Play (1978), Seems Like Old Times (1980), and Private Benjamin (1980).

and William Lucas also star. **Academy Award**—Freddie Francis, cinematography (black and white). **Nominations**—best picture; Cardiff, best director; Howard, best actor; Ure, best supporting actress; Lambert, best screenplay (based on material from another medium).   *103 minutes b&w*

THE SONS OF KATIE ELDER (1965)
★★

John Wayne
Dean Martin
Michael Anderson, Jr.
Earl Holliman

Wayne, Martin, Anderson, Holliman—the sons of frontier woman Katie Elder—set out to avenge their mother's death, but town thugs and other villains give them trouble. Much of the action is predictable, but the stars make the film worthwhile and entertaining for western fans. George Kennedy, Martha Hyer, James Gregory, Paul Fix, and Jeremy Slate appear in supporting roles. **Director**—Henry Hathaway.   *112 minutes*

SO PROUDLY WE HAIL (1943)
★★

Claudette Colbert
Paulette Goddard
Veronica Lake

This patriotic film about Army nurses serving bravely on Bataan during World War II is conscientiously done and makes a valiant bid to give another view of the hell of war. It seems dated now and too melodramatic, but the performances of Colbert, Goddard, and Lake were well

Heather Sears, Dean Stockwell, and Wendy Hiller in Sons and Lovers.

- Sorcerer
- Sorrowful Jones
- Sorry, Wrong Number
- The Sound and the Fury
- Sounder
- Sounder, Part 2
- The Sound of Music

S

received at the time the movie was released. The cast also includes George Reeves, Barbara Britton, Walter Abel, Sonny Tufts, and John Litel. **Director**—Mark Sandrich. **Academy Award Nomination**—Goddard, best supporting actress; Allan Scott, writing (original screenplay); Charles Lang, cinematography (black and white).   *125 minutes b&w*

SORCERER (1977)
★★★

Roy Scheider

Director William Friedkin has done a masterful job at building suspense and capturing the gritty details of despair in this intense thriller, which is a remake of H. G. Clouzot's *The Wages of Fear*. The film is about four desperate men, stuck in a squalid South American country, who drive two truckloads of nitroglycerin on bumpy roads through 200 miles of steaming jungle. Scheider stands out as one of the antiheroes; it's a role Humphrey Bogart would have found to his liking. (PG)   *122 minutes*

SORROWFUL JONES (1949)
★★

Bob Hope
Lucille Ball

Hope and Ball star in this overly sentimental Damon Runyon comedy about a bookie, deeply involved with mobsters, who unofficially adopts an orphan. Hope, of course, plays the title role of the bookie. There are some pleasant moments and occasional laughs, but the earlier film, *Little Miss Marker* with Shirley Temple, was superior. Also with William Demarest, Thomas Gomez, Houseley Stevenson, Bruce Cabot, Mary Jane Saunders, and Tom Pedi. **Director**—Sidney Lanfield.   *88 minutes b&w*

SORRY, WRONG NUMBER (1948)
★★★

Barbara Stanwyck
Burt Lancaster

This tense thriller, with Stanwyck as a bedridden neurotic who overhears a plot to murder her, tries a bit too hard to be a classic instead of just a good film. But at times, Stanwyck's performance is near perfection, and Lancaster, who plays her murderous husband, helps to make the production an effective suspense movie. Wendell Corey, Ed Begley, Leif Erickson, William Conrad, Harold Vermilyea, and Ann Richards also star. **Director**—Anatole Litvak. **Academy Award Nomination**—Stanwyck, best actress.   *89 minutes b&w*

THE SOUND AND THE FURY (1959)
★★

Yul Brynner
Joanne Woodward

There's too much misspent fury and not enough sound filmmaking in this strange production based on William Faulkner's novel. Hollywood tries to convey the decadence of the South in this story of a young lady seeking independence from her strict family, but they end up showing a misconception of the Faulkner novel. Brynner, Woodward, Margaret Leighton, Stuart Whitman, Ethel Waters, Jack Warden, and Françoise Rosay are good enough to create some fine moments amid the rubble. **Director**—Martin Ritt.   *117 minutes*

SOUNDER (1972)
★★★★

Paul Winfield
Cicely Tyson

Brilliant performances by Winfield and Tyson help to make this story about a family of sharecroppers in Louisiana during the Depression one of the finest movies about blacks ever filmed in this country. The excellent direction of Martin Ritt and splendid supporting performances by Kevin Hooks, Carmen Mathews, James Best, and Taj Mahal make the experiences of the family devastatingly real and compelling. Although this is a realistic view of problems faced by blacks, it's still a warm and compassionate movie for the whole family. (G) **Academy Award Nominations**—best picture; Winfield, best actor; Tyson, best actress; Lonne

Cicely Tyson looks at Paul Winfield (left) in the warm, compassionate film Sounder.

Elder III, best screenplay (based on material from another medium).
105 minutes

SOUNDER, PART 2 (1976)
★★

Harold Sylvester
Ebony Wright

This sequel about the struggles of poor black sharecroppers in Louisiana during the '30s isn't in the same league with the popular and moving 1972 film. This episode has the Morgan family involved with building a schoolhouse for the neighborhood. The idea is embarrassingly drowned in sentimentality and gloominess, and the film has nothing to do with the family's battered hound dog Sounder, who remains merely in the background. Also with Darryl Young, Annazette Chase, and Taj Mahal. **Director**—William Graham. (G)
98 minutes

THE SOUND OF MUSIC (1965)
★★★★

Julie Andrews

Andrews sings and acts and radiates with such vitality that her performance overshadows some of the sugary excesses in this film, and one even forgets that the movie is too long. The beautiful scenery and excellent music also make this film worthwhile. The movie is based on the life of the Von Trapp family. Andrews plays Maria Von Trapp, who escapes the Nazis in Austria with her children to Switzerland. Other stars in this Rodgers and Hammerstein musical include Peggy Wood, Christopher Plummer, Richard
(Continued)

Julie Andrews portrays Maria Von Trapp in the musical The Sound of Music.

(Continued)

Haydn, Anna Lee, Eleanor Parker, and Marnie Nixon. **Director**—Robert Wise. **Academy Awards**—best picture; Wise, best director. **Nominations**—Andrews, best actress; Wood, best supporting actress; Ted McCord, cinematography (color). *172 minutes*

SOUTHERN COMFORT (1981)
★★

Keith Carradine
Powers Boothe

Nine weekend warriors in the National Guard become lost in the Louisiana bayous and wind up in a mini-war with local Cajun hunters. The uneven story is unconvincing, mean-spirited, and unnecessarily violent. The pretentious plot apes *Deliverance*, but this film hardly delivers any worthwhile entertainment. Carradine and Boothe have key roles as the only intelligent soldiers in the military unit. **Director**—Walter Hill. (R) *101 minutes*

SOUTH PACIFIC (1958)
★★

Mitzi Gaynor
Rossano Brazzi

This musical version about life in the South Pacific during World War II and the love story of an American Navy nurse and a middle-aged French planter lacks the superstars needed to

make it a production with clout. The location photography is beautiful, and the Rodgers and Hammerstein music is delightful; numbers include "Some Enchanted Evening," "Younger Than Springtime," "There Is Nothing Like a Dame," "Bali Ha'i," and "You've Got To Be Taught." Gaynor is pleasant but not dynamic enough as the nurse, and Brazzi is lackluster as the planter. Other performers in this long musical are France Nuyen, John Kerr, Ray Walston, and Juanita Hall. **Director**—Joshua Logan. **Academy Award Nomination**—Leon Shamroy, cinematography (color). *170 minutes*

THE SPANISH MAIN (1945)
★★★

Paul Henreid
Maureen O'Hara
Walter Slezak

In this pirate movie, a swashbuckling adventurer (Henreid) confronts the bad guy (Slezak) and eventually wins the hand of the beautiful maiden (O'Hara). There's plenty of fun and adventure for fans of this genre, and the actors give the story the right emphasis. Supporting actors include Jack LaRue, Victor Kilian, Binnie Barnes, Barton MacLane, Fritz Leiber, Nancy Gates, Mike Mazurki, and J. M. Kerrigan. **Director**—Frank Borzage. **Academy Award Nomination**—George Barnes, cinematography (color). *101 minutes*

SPARKLE (1976)
★★

Lonette McKee
Irene Cara
Philip M. Thomas

A familiar melodrama about three Harlem sisters who become pop singers in the '50s. Aside from scattered bright moments, the story and acting are routine and shallow, following well-worn paths of violence, drug addiction, and family crisis. The music of Curtis Mayfield helps out at times, and there are some well-composed scenes of murky nightclubs. Also with Dwan Smith, Mary Alice, Tony King, and Dorian Harewood. **Director**—Sam O'Steen. (PG) *100 minutes*

SPARTACUS (1960)
★★★

Kirk Douglas
Laurence Olivier
Peter Ustinov

Between the gaudy scenes and the trite moments, there are some thoughtful sequences and excellent characterizations in this long and, at times, thrilling historical epic about slaves in revolt in ancient Rome. Douglas, Olivier, and Ustinov are superb in major parts; Kirk plays the title role. The script by Dalton Trumbo is another plus. The large cast also includes Charles Laughton, John Gavin, Nina Foch, Joan Simmons, Tony Curtis, Woody Strode, Herbert Lom, and John Ireland. **Director**—Stanley Kubrick. **Academy Awards**—Ustinov, best actor; Russell Metty, cinematography (color). *196 minutes*

A SPECIAL DAY (1977)
★★

Sophia Loren
Marcello Mastroianni

Loren plays a bedraggled Italian housewife who finds a brief moment of passion with an intellectual homosexual neighbor, played by Mastroianni. As always, the two stars work well together. But the syrupy, two-character drama is as shabby and trite as the downtrodden apartment setting, which it never leaves. This brief encounter—Italian style—takes place in 1938 on a day when all Rome turned out to rally for Hitler. Also with John Vernon, Nicole Magny, and Françoise Berd. **Director**—Ettore Scola. In Italian with English titles. (No MPAA rating) **Academy Award Nominations**—best foreign-language film; Mastroianni, best actor.

106 minutes

SPECIAL DELIVERY (1977)
★★

Bo Svenson
Cybill Shepherd

Shepherd, looking like a scrubbed campus queen, plays a divorcée who cuts herself in on a bank heist pulled

off by an ex-Marine, played by Svenson. The comic melodrama maintains a degree of suspense as other bystanders try to horn in on the loot. It's a better-than-average B-movie, with some interesting performances and a touch of good humor. The adventure ends with a screeching car chase that's rather overused in such films. Also with Tom Atkins, Vic Tayback, Michael Gwynne, and Sorrell Booke. **Director**—Paul Wendkos. (PG)
99 minutes

SPECIAL SECTION (1975)
★★

Louis Seigner
Michel Lonsdale

A political drama about the Vichy government in France, which set up special courts (special sections) to try and sentence Frenchmen to appease the Nazis. The film is directed by Costa-Gavras, the maker of *Z* and *State of Siege*. But *Special Section* lacks the drive and emotional impact of his previous works. Characters come and go rather mechanically, and the cast consists mostly of unfamiliar actors. The story is based on an actual event—the killing of a German officer by young Marxists in a Paris subway. Also with Ivo Garrani, Bruno Cremer, Pierre Dux, and Henri Serre. In French with English titles. (PG) *110 minutes*

SPELLBOUND (1945)
★★★

Ingrid Bergman
Gregory Peck

Bergman portrays a psychiatrist who hides a patient accused of murder from the police until she's able to solve his emotional problems in this less-than-perfect Alfred Hitchcock suspense film. There are many fascinating aspects to this psychological mystery, including fine acting and Salvador Dali dream sequences, but the plot is occasionally farfetched and too tricky to be believable. Michael Chekhov, Rhonda Fleming, Leo G. Carroll, Steve Geray, Wallace Ford, and Norman Lloyd also star. **Academy Award Nominations**—best picture; Hitchcock, best director; Chekhov, best supporting actor;

Lesley-Anne Down, a young Egyptologist, gets involved with criminals in Sphinx.

George Barnes, cinematography (black and white). *111 minutes b&w*

SPENCER'S MOUNTAIN (1963)
★★

Henry Fonda
Maureen O'Hara
James MacArthur
Wally Cox

Fonda, O'Hara, MacArthur, and Cox are saddled with an inferior script in this soap opera about a Wyoming landowner who keeps promising to build another house for his family of nine. Despite its faults, this sentimental entry, set in the '30s, evolved into the TV series *The Waltons*. Also with Donald Crisp, Mimsy Farmer, and Lilian Bronson. **Director**—Delmer Daves. *121 minutes*

In Spellbound, *Ingrid Bergman (left) hides a patient from the law.*

SPHINX (1981)
★

Lesley-Anne Down
Frank Langella

Egyptologist Erica Baron, played by Down, goes to the land of the pharaohs, where she witnesses a murder, dodges bullets, fends off a rape attack, gets thrown into a dungeon, and—get this—falls through the floor of a men's room into a tomb filled with ancient treasures. She's out of breath by the second reel, and so is the audience. Langella, playing an Egyptian diplomat, pops up now and then; it's his worst film performance. Franklin Schaffner lamely directed this idiotic gibberish. *Sphinx* stinks. (PG)
119 minutes

THE SPIRAL STAIRCASE (1946)
★★★★

Dorothy McGuire

There isn't a wasted action or word in this taut and well-directed suspense film about a killer who terrorizes deformed girls. McGuire is brilliant as the mute servant girl in an eerie house trying to avoid the killer's evil clutches. At times, it seems—with the vivid and dreary New England setting—that Alfred Hitchcock's hand is
(Continued)

S
- The Spirit of St. Louis
- Splendor in the Grass
- Springfield Rifle
- The Spy Who Came In From the Cold
- The Spy Who Loved Me
- Squeeze Play
- Squirm

(Continued)

present, but the credit goes to director Robert Siodmak for this masterful mystery. George Brent, Kent Smith, James Bell, Sara Allgood, Gordon Oliver, Ethel Barrymore, and Rhonda Fleming appear in supporting roles. **Academy Award Nomination**—Barrymore, best supporting actress.

83 minutes b&w

THE SPIRIT OF ST. LOUIS (1957)
★★

James Stewart

Stewart is fine as Charles Lindbergh and makes a spirited effort to create a passable movie, but there are too many trite and dull scenes. The production seems long because there are many scenes that show Lindy flying solo, especially on his 3,600-mile, 33½-hour New York-to-Paris flight in 1927, and it isn't possible to have much interesting action in such situations. Marc Connelly, Patricia Smith, and Murray Hamilton are competent in supporting roles. **Director**—Billy Wilder. *135 minutes*

SPLENDOR IN THE GRASS (1961)
★★

Natalie Wood
Warren Beatty

Elia Kazan skillfully directed this William Inge story about two young people falling in love. Kazan has captured the feel of a small Kansas town in the 1920s superbly, but the characterizations and story ring false at times. Beatty—in his film debut—and Wood are splendid as the young lovers. Also with Pat Hingle, Audrey Christie, Sean Garrison, Phyllis Diller, Sandy Dennis, Zohra Lampert, and Barbara Loden. **Academy Award**—Inge, best story and screenplay (written directly for the screen). **Nomination**—Wood, best actress.

124 minutes

SPRINGFIELD RIFLE (1952)
★★

Gary Cooper

Cooper gives a conventional performance in this standard Civil War-era western. He plays an ex-Union officer who joins the Confederates as a spy to find a traitor who is stealing government rifles. Also with Phyllis Thaxter, Guinn Williams, Paul Kelly, David Brian, and Lon Chaney, Jr. **Director**—André de Toth. *93 minutes*

THE SPY WHO CAME IN FROM THE COLD (1965)
★★★

Richard Burton
Claire Bloom
Oskar Werner

The mood, tempo, and tension are adequately conveyed in this film based on the best-selling John Le Carré spy novel, but the plot becomes needlessly tangled and complex. Burton is well-cast as the bitter agent who goes undercover in a bid to infiltrate the communists. Bloom and Werner are in top form, and the skilled photography of Oswald Morris contributes the vivid realism needed for this kind of story. At the time of release, James Bond movies were much in vogue and glorified the spying in a superficial manner; this movie put the grisly trade of espionage into its proper perspective. Rupert Davies, Peter Van Eyck, Sam Wanamaker, Cyril Cusack, Beatrix Ichmann, Bernard Lee, and George Voskovec appear in supporting roles. **Director**—Martin Ritt. **Academy Award Nomination**—Burton, best actor. *112 minutes b&w*

THE SPY WHO LOVED ME (1977)
★★★

Roger Moore
Curt Jurgens

British superspy James Bond is back for his 10th action-packed screen adventure, and this one is lavish and sleek, indeed. Debonair Moore is enjoyable as agent 007, who has one hour to overcome Karl Stromberg, a villain deluxe, who wants to rule the world by gaining control of the seas. Jurgens is the heavy in this thriller. As usual, the special gadgets are fascinating, the locales are exotically stunning, and the women are fetching. Also

Roger Moore as 007 delivers a disabling kick to Milton Reid during a fight on a rooftop in The Spy Who Loved Me.

with Barbara Bach, Richard Kiel, Caroline Munro, and Bernard Lee. Classy direction by Lewis Gilbert. (PG) *125 minutes*

SQUEEZE PLAY (1981)
★★

Jim Harris
Jenni Hetrick

The guys are forever playing softball, so the gals fight back by forming their own team, in this goofy but lively low-level comedy. There are plenty of harmless pranks, slapstick happenings, and sexual shenanigans, which manage to provoke a few laughs. The players—mostly unknowns—frolic through their routines with ample energy. It all ends with a predictable softball game between the sexes. **Director**—Samuel Well. (R)

92 minutes

SQUIRM (1976)
(no stars)

Don Scardino
Patricia Pearcy

Millions of worms writhe on the screen while stomachs turn in the audience. The wiggler warfare takes place in a Georgia hamlet after a downed power line jolts hordes of the slithering creatures out of the ground and to the attack. The whole movie is preposterous and revolting. A relatively unknown cast squirms through mediocre performances within an inane plot. Also with R. A. Dow, Peter MacLean, Jean Sullivan, and Fran Higgins. Written and directed by Jeff Lieberman. (R) *92 minutes*

- Stagecoach (1939)
- Stagecoach (1966)
- Stalag 17
- Stardust
- Stardust Memories
- A Star Is Born (1954)
- A Star Is Born (1977)

S

STAGECOACH (1939)
★★★★

**John Wayne
Claire Trevor
Thomas Mitchell
George Bancroft**

This classic by director John Ford about the relationship among passengers on a stagecoach under the stress of an Indian attack is a model for all subsequent serious westerns. The brilliant acting of Wayne, Trevor, Mitchell, Bancroft, Berton Churchill, John Carradine, and Donald Meek is enhanced by the splendid photography of Bert Glennon. This production shows that westerns can be serious with well-written scripts, yet still have lots of action. Andy Devine, Louise Platt, Tim Holt, and Chris-Pin Martin also star. **Academy Award**—Mitchell, best supporting actor. **Nominations**—best picture; Ford, best director; Glennon, cinematography (black and white). *99 minutes b&w*

STAGECOACH (1966)
★★

**Ann-Margret
Alex Cord
Bing Crosby
Van Heflin**

This remake might more appropriately be called *Son of Stagecoach* or *Stagecoach Returns*. Although there's still plenty of action and some vivid scenery, it's at best half as good as the 1939 John Ford classic. This time around, Cord has the John Wayne role. Cord, Ann-Margret, Crosby, Heflin, and Red Buttons do a conscientious job, but the characterizations are much weaker than those in the earlier film. Also with Slim Pickens, Robert Cummings, Michael Connors, Stefanie Powers, and Keenan Wynn. **Director**—Gordon Douglas. *114 minutes*

STALAG 17 (1953)
★★★★

**William Holden
Don Taylor
Otto Preminger**

This is one of the most popular and well-liked American movies of all time. The story of U.S. prisoners in a Nazi POW camp has all the necessary ingredients for a quality viewing experience—good acting, fine plot, tension, a message, good guys and villains, expert characterization, a well-written script, a mixture of humor and drama, and action. Holden heads the list of stars, but Taylor, Preminger, Robert Strauss, Sig Rumann, and Harvey Lembeck are almost as good. If you find the viewing tame, maybe it means you've seen this film too often. **Director**—Billy Wilder. **Academy Award**—Holden, best actor. **Nominations**—Wilder, best director; Strauss, best supporting actor. *120 minutes b&w*

STARDUST (1975)
★★

**David Essex
Adam Faith**

Essex and Faith star in this story about a young, working-class British rock star who finally makes it to the big time and becomes a victim of his own success. The story seems to accurately parallel the world of Richie Havens or Janis Joplin—a dazzling display of money, screaming groupies, unscrupulous promoters, internal squabbles, and finally death from a drug overdose. Yet, instead of probing deeply, the movie skips from one situation to another, and it's as commercial as rock itself. Also, it's difficult to understand much of the Cockney dialect. Also with Larry Hagman and Dave Edmund. **Director**—Michael Apted. (R) *97 minutes*

STARDUST MEMORIES (1980)
★★

**Woody Allen
Charlotte Rampling**

This overcrowded and jumbled film is Allen's version of Fellini's *8½*. Allen plays a harassed celebrity filmmaker who discovers there's meager satisfaction in such adoration. The movie is filled with numerous harried crowd scenes, which produce a desperate and overheated tone, although Woody's caustic wit occasionally shines through. Also with Jessica Harper and Marie-Christine Barrault. (PG) *89 minutes b&w*

A STAR IS BORN (1954)
★★★

**Judy Garland
James Mason**

Judy Garland (center) performs in the musical version of A Star Is Born.

This musical version of the 1937 David O. Selznick movie is still good entertainment, but it loses some of its dramatic force in the shift to music. Garland is in top form and makes the movie as good as it is, as she belts out such songs as "Born in a Trunk" and "The Man That Got Away." Mason's performance is just a notch below Judy's. Also with Charles Bickford, Jack Carson, Tommy Noonan, Lucy Marlow, and Amanda Blake. **Director**—George Cukor. **Academy Award Nominations**—Mason, best actor; Garland, best actress. *154 minutes*

A STAR IS BORN (1977)
★★

**Barbra Streisand
Kris Kristofferson**

Streisand dominates this third rehash of the show-biz soap opera so much that it comes off as her own ego trip. In this rock version about an unknown singer's rise to fame, Streisand is billed as the star, executive producer, co-songwriter, and wardrobe consultant; it's obvious she usurped the direction from Frank Pierson, and she had a hand in the editing. The result is a lukewarm movie hardly the caliber of the 1954 Judy Garland-James Mason production. Kristofferson has a major part, but he too, is unnecessarily upstaged. Also with Gary Busey, Paul Mazursky, and Oliver Clark. (R) *140 minutes*

S
• Stars and Stripes Forever
• Starship Invasions
• The Star Spangled Girl
• Star Spangled Rhythm
• Starting Over
• Star Trek—The Motion Picture

STARS AND STRIPES FOREVER
(1952)
★★

Clifton Webb

Clifton Webb (left) portrays march king John Philip Sousa in Stars and Stripes Forever.

Webb does a fine job as march king John Philip Sousa, a musician who wanted to write ballads, but eventually found success as a bandmaster and writer of rousing marches. Some of the march music gets a bit tedious and jarring after a while, but the band plays on, and its music is expertly spliced into the plot. Debra Paget, Robert Wagner, Lester Matthews, Finlay Currie, and Ruth Hussey appear in supporting roles. **Director**—Henry Koster. *89 minutes*

STARSHIP INVASIONS (1978)
★

**Robert Vaughn
Christopher Lee**

This low-budget film from Canada is bent on capitalizing from the success of science-fiction hits. However, this junky film has neither the charm of those old Flash Gordon episodes or the special-effects razzle-dazzle of blockbusters like *Star Wars*. The plot is old hat, and the shoddy sets are unimpressive. Vaughn plays one of the good guys. Lee plays the villainous alien. Also with Helen Shaver. **Director**—Ed Hunt. (PG) *89 minutes*

THE STAR SPANGLED GIRL
(1971)
★

Sandy Duncan

There are no big stars in this movie about a nice girl from Texas who hooks up with two student radicals. This story is one of the few times that playwright Neil Simon has struck out on stage and on the silver screen. The film script of his play, written by Arnold Margolin, is so mediocre that the performances of Duncan, Tony Roberts, Todd Susman, and Elizabeth Allen are dwarfed. **Director**—Jerry Paris. (G) *92 minutes*

STAR SPANGLED RHYTHM
(1942)
★★★

**Bing Crosby
Betty Hutton
Victor Moore
Walter Abel**

This is the kind of movie that must be taken on its own terms. If you expect a plot or any degree of meaningful characterization, you'll be disappointed. However, if you accept the fact that it's a star-studded variety show, you'll find a great deal of enjoyment in this World War II song-and-dance fest. Tunes include "Time To Hit the Road to Dreamland" and "That Old Black Magic." Some of those within this galaxy of stars are Preston Sturges, Eddie Bracken, Bob Hope, Paulette Goddard, Veronica Lake, Dorothy Lamour, Ray Milland, William Bendix, Arthur Treacher, Rochester, Alan Ladd, and Susan Hayward. **Director**—George Marshall.

99 minutes b&w

STARTING OVER (1979)
★★★★

**Burt Reynolds
Jill Clayburgh
Candice Bergen**

Reynolds casts aside his good ol' boy macho routine for a superb sympathetic role in this thoroughly enjoyable romantic comedy, which views the man's side of divorce. There's a witty script, crisp direction by Alan J.

In Starting Over, *Jill Clayburgh and Burt Reynolds begin a romance.*

Pakula of *Klute* fame, and a richness of satire. Other first-rate performances are turned in by Clayburgh and Bergen. Clayburgh plays a nursery school teacher who establishes a romance with our hero. Bergen is the ex-wife. Also with Charles Durning, Frances Sternhagen, Paul Sorvino, Mary Kay Place, and Austin Pendleton. **Academy Award Nominations**—Clayburgh, best actress; Bergen, best supporting actress. (R) *106 minutes*

STAR TREK—THE MOTION PICTURE (1979)
★★

**William Shatner
Leonard Nimoy**

The producers lavished millions of dollars on hardware and special effects for this epic, based on the popular television series. But they seemed to have run out of funds when it came to character and script development. The spaceship U.S.S. *Enterprise* is back in action with Captain Kirk (Shatner), Mr. Spock (Nimoy), and other familiar crew members combatting a menacing force in space. The super gadgetry blasts away while the story—reminiscent of an old TV episode—plods. Strictly for Trekkies. Also with

Leonard Nimoy and William Shatner discuss Persis Khambatta in Star Trek—The Motion Picture.

- Star Wars
- State Fair
- State of the Union
- Stay As You Are
- Stay Hungry
- Steel
- The Steel Trap
- Steelyard Blues

S

Stephen Collins, Persis Khambatta, DeForest Kelly, George Takei, and Michelle Nichols. **Director**—Robert Wise. (G)   *132 minutes*

STAR WARS (1977)
★★★★

**Mark Hamill
Harrison Ford
Alec Guinness
Carrie Fisher**

R2-D2 and C-3PO watch rebel troops defend the Rebel Blockade Runner in Star Wars.

A magnificent intergalactic adventure for the kid in everyone. The movie is part *Flash Gordon*, part *Wizard of Oz*. Dazzling special effects, a booming sound track, and a simple good-guys bad-guys plot bring back old-time fun. A marvelous achievement for writer-director George Lucas. R2-D2 and C-3P0, a pair of robots, steal the show. Also with Anthony Daniels, Kenny Baker, Peter Cushing, and David Prowse. (PG) **Academy Award Nominations**—best picture; Lucas, best director; Guinness, best supporting actor; Lucas, best original screenplay.   *121 minutes*

STATE FAIR (1945)
★★★

**Charles Winninger
Jeanne Crain
Dana Andrews**

The fine songs of Rodgers and Hammerstein flourish in this entertaining musical about a family's experiences at the Iowa State Fair. The script and plot lack substance, but that's not very important in this kind of musical show. Tunes include "Grand Night for Singing" and "It Might As Well Be Spring." Fay Bainter, Frank McHugh,

Vivian Blaine, Donald Meek, and Dick Haymes also star. **Director**—Walter Lang. **Alternate Title**—*It Happened One Summer.*   *100 minutes*

STATE OF THE UNION (1948)
★★★★

**Spencer Tracy
Katharine Hepburn**

Tracy and Hepburn click in this political comedy about a man who runs for President and has problems with his wife. Tracy and Hepburn are the couple. Angela Lansbury plays a millionairess who bankrolls the campaign, and Van Johnson is appealing as the campaign manager. This film version of the Howard Lindsay-Russel Crouss play is expertly directed by Frank Capra. It has the rare quality of being intelligent and enlightening about political campaigns while being entertaining. Lewis Stone, Howard Smith, Charles Dingle, Raymond Walburn, and Adolphe Menjou appear in supporting roles.   *124 minutes b&w*

STAY AS YOU ARE (1980)
★★

**Marcello Mastroianni
Nastassia Kinski**

Mastroianni is smitten by a coquettish beauty, played by Kinski, who's young enough to be his daughter. In fact, she is his daughter! This dilemma of incest is the centerpiece of this comedy-romance, which gives Mastroianni ample opportunity to display his talent and charm. But it really goes no further than this. The comedy is strained and mired in sentimentality. **Director**—Alberto Lattuada. In Italian with English titles. (No MPAA rating)   *118 minutes*

STAY HUNGRY (1976)
★★

**Jeff Bridges
Sally Fields**

Essentially this is a story about a wealthy young man of the New South who becomes involved with the freaky world of body builders by investing in a gym. The rich heir is played by Bridges, who, as usual, does a fine

job. Field helps out with a professional performance. Muscle-man Arnold Schwarzenegger plays a muscle man. The film is a mulligan stew of plots, subplots, characters, and themes, that become tangled up to the point of utter confusion. Bob Rafelson's ramshackle direction lacks appeal and impact. Also with Joe Santo, Scatman Crothers, Roger Mosley, and R. G. Armstrong. (PG)   *103 minutes*

STEEL (1980)
★★★

**Lee Majors
Jennifer O'Neill**

High drama on the high-rise building, as tough, gritty steelworkers rush to complete a skyscraper before the bank forecloses. The uncomplicated script is reminiscent of those '30s formula melodramas from Warner Brothers. Majors, O'Neill, Art Carney, and George Kennedy turn in good performances, along with several supporting players who portray the redoubtable construction men. The film is innocent, predictable, and hokey—but some fun nevertheless. **Director**—Steven Carver. (PG)   *99 minutes*

THE STEEL TRAP (1952)
★★★

**Joseph Cotten
Teresa Wright**

Cotten is ideally cast as a banker manager who steals a half-million dollars from his bank on Friday, but decides to return it by Monday because his conscience troubles him. This twist on the common crime caper is pleasant viewing and well done, with plenty of suspense and an element of doubt until the conclusion. Also stars Jonathan Hale and Walter Sande. **Director**—Andrew L. Stone.
            85 minutes b&w

STEELYARD BLUES (1973)
★★

**Donald Sutherland
Jane Fonda
Peter Boyle**

With three stars like Sutherland,
(Continued)

S
- The Stepford Wives
- The Sterile Cuckoo
- Stevie
- The Sting
- Stir Crazy
- The Stork Club
- Stormy Weather
- Story of Adele H

(Continued)

Fonda, and Boyle in the same film, you might expect more than what is produced here. Still, despite the trio's failure to deliver as expected in this antiestablishment yarn, there are some funny moments as they try a bizarre plan to get an abandoned airplane working again. John Savage, Garry Goodrow, and Howard Hesseman appear in supporting roles. **Director**—Alan Myerson. (PG) **Alternate Title**—*The Final Crash. 92 minutes*

THE STEPFORD WIVES (1975)
★★★

Katharine Ross
Paula Prentiss

Men who feel threatened by the women's liberation movement may take mild delight in this suspense film about suburban Connecticut housewives who are always pleasant; they're never shrill or overly strident. Women may want to watch to see the vile deeds of men who oppose equality of the sexes. Some viewers will say that the wives in Stepford become docile because they read mediocre Connecticut newspapers too often, but the answer—based upon Ira Levin's best-selling novel—is a bit more complex than that. Toward the end of the film, the story weakens, but the performances of Ross, Prentiss, and Tina Louise, sustain the movie. Peter Masterson, Nanette Newman, and Patrick O'Neal appear in supporting roles. **Director**—Bryan Forbes. (PG) *110 minutes*

THE STERILE CUCKOO (1969)
★★★★

Liza Minnelli
Wendell Burton

Minnelli steals the show in this story about Pookie Adams, a neurotic college student who plays at love and then finds it on campus with Burton. It's fortunate that Minnelli is so fine in this portrayal, because the script and plot are sometimes trite and cumbersome. But the movie is a sensitive look at young love. Also with Tim McIntire, Austin Green, and Sandra Faison. **Director**—Alan J. Pakula. (PG) **Academy Award Nomination**—Minnelli, best actress. *107 minutes*

STEVIE (1981)
★★★

Glenda Jackson

Jackson, in the title role, delivers a spellbinding performance straight from the heart in this screen adaptation of Hugh Whitemore's play about the late British poet, Stevie Smith. The film is rather stage-bound, but the extraordinary acting and characterizations more than make up for such drawbacks. Jackson's acute portrayal of the gentle woman's life is enhanced with expert reading of her verses. Mona Washbourne is remarkable as Stevie's stalwart spinster aunt. Also with Trevor Howard and Alec McCowen. **Director**—Robert Enders. (No MPAA rating) *102 minutes*

THE STING (1973)
★★★★

Paul Newman
Robert Redford
Robert Shaw

This story of two small-time Chicago con men who revenge the death of a friend by tricking, or stinging, a big-time mobster sparkles with vibrant action. Newman and Redford play the con men, and Shaw is the subject of the sting. The plot is complex, but that doesn't really spoil the overall enjoyment of the film. More important, the key scenes at the end, when the swindle of the mobster takes place, are easily comprehensible. Eileen Brennan, Ray Walston, Harold Gould, and Charles Durning also star. Scott Joplin's ragtime music is another plus. **Director**—George Roy Hill. (PG) **Academy Awards**—best picture; Hill, best director; David S. Ward, best story and screenplay (based on factual material or material not previously published). **Nominations**—Redford, best actor; Robert Surtees, cinematography. *129 minutes*

STIR CRAZY (1980)
★

Gene Wilder
Richard Pryor

Wilder and Pryor mug and bumble through this lamebrained comedy about two buddies who land in the slammer because they're mistaken for bank robbers. Practically all the gags fizzle, and many comic setups run into dead ends. Part of the problem seems to be Bruce J. Friedman's uninspired script. Wilder and Pryor strain under this witless material, as they try to outmaneuver prison officials and fellow inmates, but they merely look silly, and the audience gets a bum rap. Also with George Stanford Brown. **Director**—Sidney Poitier. (R) *111 minutes*

THE STORK CLUB (1945)
★★

Betty Hutton
Barry Fitzgerald

A very ordinary story about a poor nightclub hatcheck girl, played by Hutton. She meets Fitzgerald, a wealthy man, but she thinks he's broke. The lightweight comedy is saved by above-average acting. Hutton sings "Doctor, Lawyer, Indian Chief." Also with Mary Young, Bill Goodwin, Don Defore, Andy Russell, Iris Adrian, Robert Benchley, and Mikhail Rasumny. Ironically, the Stork Club in New York City has closed down, but the film survives. **Director**—Hal Walker. *98 minutes b&w*

STORMY WEATHER (1943)
★★★

Bill Robinson
Lena Horne

Many musicals have silly plots, and this all-black talent show based on the life of Bill Robinson is no exception. But the delightful performers far overshadow the triteness in this movie. The stars also include Fats Waller, Ada Brown, Eddie Anderson, Flournoy Miller, Dooley Wilson, Cab Calloway, and Katherine Dunham. Horne sings the title song, and Waller does "Ain't Misbehavin'." **Director**—Andrew L. Stone. *77 minutes b&w*

STORY OF ADELE H (1976)
★★★★

Isabelle Adjani

Director François Truffaut has created a passionate and intelligent movie

★ STAR PROFILE

● Story of GI Joe ● The Story of Seabiscuit
● The Story of O ● The Story of Will Rogers
● Straight Time

S

about a woman obsessed with love itself. It's the true story of the youngest daughter of French writer Victor Hugo. When she's rejected by a young British officer, her love becomes more intense and devastating. Adjani plays the lead role with impact and grace, and the film is beautifully photographed. Also with Bruce Robinson, Sylvia Marriott, Joseph Blatchley, and Reubin Dorey. In French with English titles. (PG) **Academy Award Nomination**—Adjani, best actress. *97 minutes*

STORY OF GI JOE (1945)
★★★

**Burgess Meredith
Robert Mitchum**

Meredith gives a stirring performance

as Ernie Pyle, the famed war correspondent, in this drama set during the Italian campaign of World War II. Pyle earned a reputation as a friend of the typical infantry soldier and lived with them in the foxholes and on the front lines. The movie offers thoughtful characterization and the usual combat action seen in such films. Mitchum stars as a soldier, with Freddie Steele, Wally Cassell, Jimmy Lloyd, and Jack Reilly in supporting roles. **Director**—William Wellman. *108 minutes b&w*

THE STORY OF O (1975)
(no stars)

Corinne Clery

A sadomasochism story based on Pauline Reage's classic novel. This is really just another trashy soft-core

movie. "O" is passed from man to man for numerous sexual torments and humiliations, including whippings and a branding; much of the action is heard and not seen. The monotony of this film is likely to induce as much suffering on the audience as "O" supposedly faces from her lashings. Clery plays the title role. **Director**—Just Jaeckin. In French with English titles. (X) *97 minutes*

THE STORY OF SEABISCUIT
(1949)
★★

**Shirley Temple
Barry Fitzgerald**

Fitzgerald is very believable as a crusty trainer of race horses, but this movie about the famous racehorse runs out of the money. This below-average racing picture does star Temple and has several excellently photographed racing scenes, but even they aren't enough to make it a winner. Donald McBride, Lon McCallister, Pierre Watkin, and Rosemary DeCamp appear in supporting roles. **Director**—David Butler. *98 minutes*

THE STORY OF WILL ROGERS
(1950)
★★

**Will Rogers, Jr.
Jane Wyman**

Rogers gives a faithful and conscientious portrait of his folk-philosopher father, one of the nation's best-loved public figures who was killed in a 1935 plane crash. Unfortunately, the movie's pace is too slow, and it's a tall order for the son to follow in his father's footsteps, even in a film. Will, Jr., does a good job, but he doesn't have his father's charm and wit. Wyman plays Will's wife. Also with James Gleason, Eddie Cantor, Mary Wickes, and Carl Benton Reid. **Director**—Michael Curtiz. *109 minutes*

STRAIGHT TIME (1978)
★★★

Dustin Hoffman

Hoffman portrays Max Dumbo, an ex-

MERYL STREEP

Born in Bernardsville, New Jersey, in 1949, of a non-theatrical family, Meryl Streep has become a popular actress among playgoers and movie audiences. Growing up in a middle-class New Jersey suburb, she developed a promising coloratura voice and became a protégé of Estelle Liebling, the celebrated teacher of Beverly Sills. It was at Vassar College, however, that Streep discovered her true vocation.

At her first college audition, she won the lead in August Strindberg's Miss Julie *and caused an immediate stir with her performance. Streep went on to the Yale School of Drama.*

A summer with the O'Neill Playwrights Conference in Connecticut led to her debut in New York in Joseph Papp's Lincoln Center production of Trelawny of the Wells. *Her next performance as the slovenly Flora in Tennessee Williams's*

27 Wagons Full of Cotton brought her the Outer Circle Critics' and Theater World awards—and a Tony nomination.

A season with the New York Shakespeare Festival led to such productions as the Broadway musical Happy End, Taming of the Shrew, *and the musical* Alice, *but it was Streep's Emmy-winning performance as a Catholic married to a Jew in the TV mini-series* Holocaust *that brought her to the notice of a larger audience.*

Streep made her screen debut in Julia *(1977), where she played Jane Fonda's society friend in a brief scene. Next came her performance as the steel-town girl friend in* The Deer Hunter *(1978), for which she received an Oscar nomination and the New York Film Critics Award, followed by the part of Woody Allen's lesbian ex-wife in* Manhattan *(1979). In* The Seduction of Joe Tynan *(1979), Streep played opposite Alan Alda as the tough-minded attorney having an affair with a married senator who is running for President. Next came her Academy Award-winning performance in* Kramer vs. Kramer *(1979), for which she also won a Golden Globe Award as best supporting actress. Most recently, Streep was nominated for her dual role in* The French Lieutenant's Woman *(1981).*

(Continued)

S • Strange Behavior   • The Stranger (1967)   • A Stranger Is Watching
    • Strange Cargo   • The Stranger and the   • Strangers on a Train
    • The Strange Door   Gunfighter
    • The Stranger (1946)

(Continued)

con who's his own worst enemy and is following a course of self-destruction. Hoffman's performance is stylish and cleanly executed; genuine interest in the character develops with clarity. The film is based on a novel by ex-convict Edward Bunker. Harry Dean Stanton, M. Emmet Walsh, and Gary Busey are excellent in supporting roles. Also with Theresa Russell and Rita Taggart. **Director**—Ulu Grosbard (R)   *114 minutes*

STRANGE BEHAVIOR (1981)
★★

Michael Murphy
Louise Fletcher
Fiona Lewis

A slightly addled, offbeat horror drama about a series of teenage murders in a small Midwestern college town. The film, which smacks of a '50s-style thriller, offers some impressive special effects and a bit of campy horror, but the plot often goes awry, and the usual predictable gruesome killings are much in evidence. Michael Laughlin debuts as director in this film, and he shows promise of better work to come. (R)   *99 minutes*

STRANGE CARGO (1940)
★★

Clark Gable
Joan Crawford

If you take this film too seriously, you'll find it strange, indeed. But as an adventure or as a chance to see Gable and Crawford in action, it's worthwhile viewing. The story is about a group of convicts who escape from Devil's Island. They are forced to

Clark Gable romances Joan Crawford in Frank Borzage's Strange Cargo.

choose between good in the form of Ian Hunter or evil in the form of Paul Lukas. Peter Lorre, J. Edward Bromberg, Eduardo Ciannelli, and Albert Dekker also brighten the cast of characters. **Director**—Frank Borzage.
105 minutes b&w

THE STRANGE DOOR (1951)
★

Charles Laughton
Boris Karloff

Laughton and Karloff star in this horror story. Laughton plays a deranged tyrant who traps a nobleman in a castle. The movie is based on the Robert Louis Stevenson chiller, but instead of chills, there's unintentional comedy as Karloff and Laughton overact in a futile bid to salvage this horrid horror film. Also with Alan Napier, Sally Forrest, Michael Pate, and Richard Stapley. **Director**—Joseph Pevney.
81 minutes b&w

THE STRANGER (1946)
★★★

Edward G. Robinson
Orson Welles
Loretta Young

Robinson is well cast as a government agent with a keen mind who's tracking down a Nazi, played by Welles. The trail ends in a small Connecticut town, where the Nazi poses as a respectable professor. Young plays the woman in the life of the Nazi—unaware of his real convictions. The skilled direction of Welles and the vivid photography sweeten this melodrama, which seems slightly dated now. Richard Long and Philip Merivale also star. **Academy Award Nomination**—Victor Trivas, writing (original story).
95 minutes b&w

THE STRANGER (1967)
★★★

Marcello Mastroianni

Mastroianni is superb as the antihero estranged from society in this film version of Albert Camus's existential tale *L'Stranger*. Although the French author and existentialism were more popular at the time of the filming, the

story under Luchino Visconti's direction is still meaningful and relevant to our times. Also with Anna Karina, Bernard Blier, Bruno Cremer, and Georges Wilson.   *105 minutes*

THE STRANGER AND THE GUNFIGHTER (1976)
★

Lee Van Cleef
Lo Lieh

A gunfighter of the Old West and a karate-chopping Chinese man of the new East join forces to hunt for a fortune, which once belonged to a Chinese warlord. Clues to the treasure are tattooed on the backsides of four women. The kung fu and gunfighting scenes are unbelievable; the humor is adolescent. The scenery is spectacular; the film is not. Filmed in Hong Kong and Spain. Also with Patty Shepard, Julian Ugarte, Karen Yeh, and George Rigaud. **Director**—Anthony Dawson. (PG)   *107 minutes*

A STRANGER IS WATCHING (1982)
★★

Rip Torn
Kate Mulgrew

Director Sean Cunningham, best known for his low-budget *Friday the 13th* bloodbath, tones down the gore in this shocker, but it's still a routine movie at best. The complex plot involves a brutal criminal who holds a child and a woman TV reporter hostage in the murky bowels of Grand Central Station. Torn is convincing as the nasty kidnapper, but other cast members perform rather woodenly. Mulgrew plays the reporter. Also with James Naughton and Shawn Von Schreiber. (R)   *92 minutes*

STRANGERS ON A TRAIN (1951)
★★★★

Farley Granger
Robert Walker

This super Alfred Hitchcock suspense film is based on the outrageous premise that two strangers who meet on a train can agree to swap murders to

● Strange Shadows in an Empty Room
● Strategic Air Command
● The Strawberry Blonde
● The Strawberry Statement
● Straw Dogs
● A Streetcar Named Desire

S

make it difficult for the authorities to catch each killer. In a world in which most strangers barely grunt hello to one another, it's a testimonial to Hitchcock's genius that he not only makes this film work, but that it's believable and extremely suspenseful. Another reason for the success of the movie is Walker's brilliant acting, as the psychotic who promptly acts on his part of the murder deal. Granger plays a tennis star who's reluctant to uphold his end of the murderous bargain; he's also convincing. Also with Ruth Roman, Marion Lorne, Laura Elliott, Leo G. Carroll, and Howard St. John. **Academy Award Nomination**—Robert Burks, cinematography (black and white). *101 minutes b&w*

STRANGE SHADOWS IN AN EMPTY ROOM (1977)
★★

Stuart Whitman

Plenty of well-worn action tricks—car chases, fisticuffs, gunfights—override an absurd plot in this standard crime melodrama filmed in Montreal. Whitman plays a police detective out to solve the murder of his lovely sister. He charges all over the Canadian countryside, leaving a trail of smashed cars and broken bones to the delight of action fans. Also with John Saxon, Martin Landau, Gayle Hunnicutt, Carole Laure, and Tisa Farrow. **Director**—Martin Herbert. (R) *99 minutes*

STRATEGIC AIR COMMAND (1955)
★★

James Stewart
June Allyson
Frank Lovejoy

Stewart, Allyson, and Lovejoy are vibrant and wholesome in this story about a baseball star who interrupts his career to return to the U.S. Air Force and the Strategic Air Command. Stewart plays the baseball player, and Allyson plays his wife. Hollywood doesn't make such unabashed pro-American movies anymore, but it's still nice to see them occasionally. This movie is ordinary at best; the flying sequences and patriotism are all that make the movie worth viewing. Also

Farley Granger and Robert Walker make an unusual pact in Strangers on a Train.

with Jay C. Flippen, Alex Nicol, Barry Sullivan, and Bruce Bennett. **Director**—Anthony Mann. **Academy Award Nomination**—Beirne Lay, Jr., writing (motion picture story). *114 minutes*

THE STRAWBERRY BLONDE (1941)
★★★

James Cagney
Olivia de Havilland
Rita Hayworth

Cagney is at his best in this 1890s love story about a Brooklyn dentist. Hayworth and De Havilland are competent as the women in his life, but without Cagney this comedy enterprise would be worthless. Jack Carson, Alan Hale, George Reeves, and Una O'Connor also star. **Director**—Raoul Walsh. *97 minutes b&w*

THE STRAWBERRY STATEMENT (1970)
★★

Bruce Davison
Kim Darby

Students occupy a college campus building in this film adaptation of James Simon Kunen's novel, but after that the movie limps along with nothing better to do than offer watered-down radical philosophy from the late '60s. Some of the intellectual posturings seem dated, but the performances of Darby and Davison are still vivid reminders of that historical and hysterical period. Murray MacLeod, Bud Cort, Jeannie Berlin, James Kunen, and Bob Balaban are also in the cast. **Director**—Stuart Hagman. (R) *109 minutes*

STRAW DOGS (1971)
★★

Dustin Hoffman
Susan George

Senseless violence reigns in this tasteless film in which director Sam Peckinpah pushes his gruesome themes to their outer limits. Hoffman plays a pacifist American professor living in England who's provoked into violence by the men of a remote Cornish village. George plays his wife, and her rape by villagers is the trigger to the violent excess. Despite its faults, the movie is well-conceived and deftly executed; Hoffman and George give good performances. Also with T. P. McKenna, Colin Welland, Peter Vaughan, and David Warner. (R) *118 minutes*

A STREETCAR NAMED DESIRE (1951)
★★★★

Marlon Brando
Vivian Leigh

Brando is masterful in this Tennessee Williams story about a brute who's in conflict with his wife's neurotic sister, played by Leigh. The story often creaks, as Williams attempts to contrast the new cultural values (Brando) with the decaying values of the Old South (Leigh), but the acting is among

(Continued)

Marlon Brando and Vivian Leigh in the powerful A Streetcar Named Desire.

S
- Street People
- Streets of Laredo
- Strike Up the Band
- Stripes
- Student Bodies
- The Student Prince
- The Stunt Man

(Continued)

the best in American cinema history. The on-location New Orleans photography of Harry Stradling blends vividly with the mood created by the actors. Kim Hunter and Karl Malden star in supporting roles. **Director**—Elia Kazan. **Academy Awards**—Leigh, best actress; Malden, best supporting actor; Hunter, best supporting actress. **Nominations**—best picture; Kazan, best director; Brando, best actor; Williams, writing (screenplay); Harry Stradling, cinematography (black and white).

122 minutes b&w

STREET PEOPLE (1976)
★★

Roger Moore
Stacy Keach

Moore and Keach perform with gusto in this action-filled Mafia story about narcotics smuggling. The confusing plot, which is mostly warmed-over and reworked portions of *The Godfather*, fails to develop characters properly. There's an amusing car-smash sequence, which adds some comic relief to the mystery of who smuggled $3 million worth of narcotics into San Francisco inside a crucifix imported from Sicily. Also with Fausto Tozzi, Ivo Garrani, and Ettore Manni. **Director**—Maurice Lucidi. (R)   *92 minutes*

STREETS OF LAREDO (1949)
★★★

William Holden
Macdonald Carey
William Bendix

Holden, Carey, and Bendix star in this nicely plotted western. Two ex-outlaws who become law-abiding citizens and join the Texas Rangers confront an old friend who has remained an outlaw. Mona Freeman appears in a supporting role. **Director**—Leslie Fenton.   *92 minutes*

STRIKE UP THE BAND (1940)
★★★

Judy Garland
Mickey Rooney

Garland and Rooney energize what would otherwise be a dated and trite musical. Even with this talented duo, the production still seems slightly out of step. Rooney leads a high school band competing in Paul Whiteman's nationwide radio contest, and Garland shines when she sings "Our Love Affair," "Nell of New Rochelle," and "Do the Conga." William Tracy, Larry Nunn, and June Preisser are also in this well-plotted venture by director Busby Berkeley.   *120 minutes b&w*

STRIPES (1981)
★★

Bill Murray

In Stripes, Bill Murray stars as the modern Army's unlikeliest hero.

Murray stars in this typical Army comedy, which pits reluctant privates against sergeants and officers. The film is composed of inconsistent episodes strung together with Murray's wise-guy humor. After bungling their way through basic training, Murray and his fellow misfits hightail it to Europe, where they inadvertently create havoc in Czechoslovakia. As far as lampooning the military, Goldie Hawn did it better in *Private Benjamin*, and Beetle Bailey does it better in the comics. **Director**—Ivan Reitman. (R)   *106 minutes*

STUDENT BODIES (1981)
★

Kristen Riter
Matthew Goldsby
Richard Brando

Writer-director Mickey Rose attempts to parody those heavy-breathing teenage horror films like *Friday the 13th*, but he doesn't earn a passing grade. Rose, who collaborated with Woody Allen on many successes, just can't muster enough good gags to sustain comic momentum here. The silly high jinks in this attempt involve a high school class where numerous young people are murdered as they are about to engage in sex. Much strained humor is substituted for the usual graphic violence and gore. (R)

86 minutes

THE STUDENT PRINCE (1954)
★★

Edmund Purdom
Ann Blyth

The music of Sigmund Romberg and the singing of Mario Lanza brighten this otherwise dull operetta about a young prince who falls in love with a beautiful barmaid in old Heidelberg. Purdom plays the prince, and Blyth is the barmaid. The voice of Lanza is dubbed on the soundtrack because he became too fat to play the leading role. Also with John Williams, Evelyn Varden, Louis Calhern, Betta St. John, Edmund Gwenn, and S. Z. Sakall. **Director**—Richard Thorpe.

107 minutes

THE STUNT MAN (1980)
★★★

Peter O'Toole
Steve Railsback

A rowdy, off-beat movie-within-a-movie about a fugitive, played by Railsback, who stumbles on a movie in the making and becomes a stunt man. The busy script is cluttered with riddles and tricky illusions, but such drawbacks are often overcome by the film's amazing energy and subtle humor. O'Toole, playing the omnipotent and fey director, gives a virtuoso comic performance—his best in years.

- The Subject Was Roses
- Suddenly Last Summer
- The Sugarland Express
- Sullivan's Travels
- Summerdog
- Summer of '42
- A Summer Place

S

The film offers plenty of hair-raising stunts. Also with Barbara Hershey. **Director**—Richard Rush. (R) **Academy Award Nominations**—Rush, best director; O'Toole, best actor; Rush, best screenplay (adapted from another medium). *129 minutes*

THE SUBJECT WAS ROSES
(1968)
★★★

Patricia Neal
Jack Albertson
Martin Sheen

Patricia Neal and Martin Sheen dance in the living room in The Subject Was Roses.

Frank D. Gilroy's Pulitzer Prize-winning play is weakened when it is transferred to the big screen, but the story of a young World War II veteran trying to cope with his quarreling parents is still vivid and compelling. Neal and Albertson play Sheen's parents. Neal's appearance was her first movie after a near-fatal stroke. Elaine Williams, Don Saxon, and Grant Gordon star in supporting roles. **Director**—Ulu Grosbard. (G) **Academy Award**—Albertson, best supporting actor. **Nomination**—Neal, best actress. *107 minutes*

SUDDENLY LAST SUMMER
(1959)
★★★

Katharine Hepburn
Elizabeth Taylor
Montgomery Clift

The great acting of Hepburn and Clift salvage this mediocre Tennessee Williams play and make Gore Vidal's incompetent film script even seem coherent at times. Future film historians will probably wonder if the screenwriter, or anyone else involved in the production, knew what it was about.

Clift plays a neurosurgeon thrust into the position of acting as a psychiatrist so he can determine what caused Hepburn's niece, played by Taylor, to have a nervous breakdown. Also with Gary Raymond, Albert Dekker, and Mercedes McCambridge. **Director**—Joseph L. Mankiewicz. **Academy Award Nominations**—Hepburn, Taylor, best actress. *114 minutes b&w*

THE SUGARLAND EXPRESS
(1974)
★★★

Goldie Hawn
William Atherton

Hawn and Atherton star in this overly involved comic adventure of fugitive parents trying to reclaim their baby from foster parents. Much of the film, based on a true 1969 incident, centers on the pursuit of the couple by Texas state police. The production is deftly handled, but the chase gets tedious at times and wears thin by the end of the movie. Hawn and Atherton are superb, with fine support from Ben Johnson and Michael Sacks. **Director**—Steven Spielberg. (PG) *110 minutes*

SULLIVAN'S TRAVELS (1941)
★★★★

Joel McCrae
Veronica Lake

McCrea is splendid in this charming satirical story about a disgruntled film director who goes out into the real world to learn about the life-styles of real people. The comic sequences prevail under the excellent screenwriting and directing by Preston Sturges, but the movie isn't without a message, and the lessons remain with you after the mirth fades away. Robert Warwick, Jimmy Conlin, Franklin Pangborn, Eric Blore, Margaret Hayes, and Porter Hall also star. *90 minutes b&w*

SUMMERDOG (1977)
★★

James Congdon
Elizabeth Eisenman

Just another run-of-the-mill shaggy-dog movie, which may be of interest to small fry, but will obviously put grownups to sleep. The predictable plot is about a playful mutt named Hobo, who's adopted by a family vacationing in the country. The acting is exaggerated, and the dialogue is corny. **Director**—John Clayton. (G) *90 minutes b&w*

SUMMER OF '42 (1971)
★★

Jennifer O'Neill
Gary Grimes

This story of young love is expertly produced and photographed, but the nostalgia approaches nausea at times. Herman Raucher's autobiographical screenplay also makes the mistake of putting the sexual attitudes and the emphasis on permissiveness of the late 1960s and 1970s into the 1940s. Grimes plays a teenager of 15 who's infatuated with a 22-year-old war bride, played by O'Neill; both are superior to their material. When the subject isn't sex, the mood and tempo of the early '40s is superbly evoked. Jerry Houser, Oliver Conant, Christopher Norris, Katherine Allentuck, and Lou Frizell appear in supporting roles. **Director**—Robert Mulligan. (PG) **Academy Award Nomination**—Raucher, best story and screenplay (based on factual material or material not previously published); Robert Surtees, cinematography. *103 minutes*

A SUMMER PLACE (1959)
★★

Richard Egan
Dorothy McGuire
Sandra Dee
Troy Donahue

Novelist Sloan Wilson has an unerring instinct when it comes to portrayals of middle-class people and their value systems. This film version of his novel captures that aspect expertly, but the script and plot don't measure up to the characterizations. Egan, McGuire, Dee, and Donahue appear to follow director Delmer Daves's directions exactly, in this story about adultery and young love at a summer resort in Maine. Arthur Kennedy, Beulah Bondi, and Constance Ford also star. *130 minutes*

S
- Summer Wishes, Winter Dreams
- The Sun Also Rises
- Sunburn
- Sunday, Bloody Sunday
- Sunday Lovers
- The Sunday Woman
- The Sundowners

SUMMER WISHES, WINTER DREAMS (1973)
★★★

**Joanne Woodward
Martin Balsam
Sylvia Sidney**

Woodward is captivating as a troubled housewife who's disturbed by the death of her mother, played by Sidney. Despite the kindness of Balsam, her understanding husband, Woodward lives in the past. But she finds new meaning in life when she accompanies her husband to sites where he served during World War II. The movie has its weaknesses, but the superior acting of this trio makes it a worthwhile viewing experience. Also with Dori Brenner, Win Forman, and Ron Rickards. **Director**—Gilbert Cates. (PG) **Academy Award Nominations**—Woodward, best actress; Sidney, best supporting actress.
93 minutes

THE SUN ALSO RISES (1957)
★★

**Tyrone Power
Ava Gardner
Errol Flynn**

On screen, Ernest Hemingway's novel of the Lost Generation loses much of its punch; the characters seem to flutter, and the plot sputters. Some of the scenery—filmed in Mexico—is attractive, although the book dealt with adventures in Spain and Paris of the 1920s. Flynn is good and almost steals the show from the weaker acting efforts of Power and Gardner. Gregory Ratoff, Henry Daniell, Eddie Albert, Juliette Greco, Mel Ferrer, and Robert Evans are also in the cast. **Director**—Henry King.
129 minutes

SUNBURN (1979)
★

**Farrah Fawcett-Majors
Charles Grodin
Art Carney**

Fawcett-Majors is lovely to look at and so is the lush Acapulco scenery, but that's all this silly comic mystery has going for it. Grodin and Carney work hard as oddball insurance inves-

In Sunburn, Farrah Fawcett-Majors is a model turned amateur sleuth.

tigators who crack a blackmail caper. Yet the film is mostly a setup for Farrah, who plays a model posing as Grodin's wife. All in all, it smacks of a limp TV pilot, with Farrah flashing her famous smile and repeating her *Charlie's Angels* bit. Also with Joan Collins, Alejandro Rey, and William Daniels. **Director**—Richard C. Sarafian. (PG)
94 minutes

SUNDAY, BLOODY SUNDAY (1971)
★★★

**Glenda Jackson
Peter Finch
Murray Head**

Jackson, Finch, and Head star in this story about a bisexual triangle, in which Finch and Jackson are both in love with Head. The prudish will object to the casual way the risqué subject is handled, but most of the movie is tastefully and superbly crafted. The acting of Jackson and Finch is excellent. Also with Tony Britton, Peggy Ashcroft, Maurice Denham, Harold Goldblatt, and Vivian Pickles. **Director**—John Schlesinger. (R) **Academy Award Nominations**—Schlesinger, best director; Finch, best actor; Jackson, best actress; Penelope Gilliatt, best story and screenplay (based on factual material or material not previously published).
110 minutes

SUNDAY LOVERS (1981)
(no stars)

**Roger Moore
Gene Wilder**

The amorous escapades of four middle-aged men are presented as four short films, produced in four separate countries, with four sets of stars. Moore, in the British segment, is miscast as a chauffeur who chases airline stewardesses. But the worst of the lot involves Wilder in America. He plays a mental patient who tries to solve his sexual problems with the help of Kathleen Quinlan. After four disappointing innings, there are no laughs, no decent acting, and lots of errors. **Director**—Edouard Molinara. (No MPAA rating)
125 minutes

THE SUNDAY WOMAN (1976)
★★

**Marcello Mastroianni
Jacqueline Bisset**

A murder mystery set among the rich and bored of Turin, Italy. Mastroianni plays a police inspector on the trail of the killer of a vulgar architect. There are plenty of interesting suspects among the smart set, including the beautiful Bisset who plays the wife of a big-shot industrialist. The plot rambles on and provides no real excitement. Also with Jean-Louis Trintignant, Aldo Reggiani, and Pino Caruso. **Director**—Luigi Comencini. (R)
110 minutes

THE SUNDOWNERS (1960)
★★★

**Robert Mitchum
Deborah Kerr
Glynis Johns
Peter Ustinov**

A splendid cast and excellent on-location photography in Australia brighten this tale of a 1920s sheepherding family. At times, the movie drags along and the production seems longer than it actually is, but the characterizations are superb, with especially good acting by Mitchum, Kerr, Johns, Ustinov, and Wylie Watson. Dina Merrill, Chips Rafferty, and

- Sunnyside
- Sunrise at Campobello
- Sunset Boulevard
- The Sunshine Boys
- Superfly
- Superman
- Superman II

S

Deborah Kerr, Robert Mitchum, and Peter Ustinov in The Sundowners.

Michael Anderson, Jr., perform well in supporting roles. Despite some faults, it's a film the entire family will enjoy. **Director**—Fred Zinnemann. **Academy Award Nomination**—best picture; Zinnemann, best director; Kerr, best actress; Johns, best supporting actress; Isobel Lennart, best screenplay (based on material from another medium).

133 minutes

SUNNYSIDE (1979)
★

Joey Travolta

Joey—John's older brother—stars in this minor-league film about a young man's effort to move away from his tough New York neighborhood. The movie blatantly tries to capitalize on the resemblance and popularity of brother John. There's all sorts of obvious similarities, including some to *Saturday Night Fever*. Joey does a respectable job in his tough-kid role despite the shabby material and the stale direction. Also with Stacey Pickren, Andrew Rubin, John Lansing, Talia Balsam, Michael Tucci, and Joan Darling. **Director**—Timothy Galfas. (R) *100 minutes*

SUNRISE AT CAMPOBELLO (1960)
★★★

Ralph Bellamy
Greer Garson

Bellamy and Garson give very convincing performances as Mr. and Mrs. Franklin Delano Roosevelt in this biography about the early years of FDR's adult life, as he enters politics and confronts polio. This moving drama, however, was better as a Broadway play. Too much of the movie is static because of the less-than-successful transfer to the screen. Also with Hume Cronyn, Jean Hagen, Lyle Talbot, Tim Considine, and Ann Shoemaker. **Director**—Vincent J. Donehue. **Academy Award Nomination**—Garson, best actress. *143 minutes*

SUNSET BOULEVARD (1950)
★★★★

Gloria Swanson
William Holden

An impoverished screenwriter, played by Holden, becomes the kept man of an aging movie queen, played by Swanson, in this memorable drama. The story is farfetched and has numerous flaws, but the acting is splendid. Just the cynical and acid commentary about Hollywood life-styles and morality would make the movie worthwhile. But there's much more, including superb photography and Billy Wilder's excellent direction. Erich Von Stroheim, Fred Clark, Nancy Olson, Buster Keaton, Hedda Hopper, Jack Webb, Nancy Olson, and Cecil B. De Mille star in supporting roles. **Academy Award**—Charles Brackett, Wilder, and D. M. Marsham, Jr., writing (story and screenplay). **Nominations**—best picture; Wilder, best director; Holden, best actor; Swanson, best actress; Von Stroheim, best supporting actor; Olson, best supporting actress; John F. Seitz, cinematography (black and white). *110 minutes b&w*

THE SUNSHINE BOYS (1975)
★★★

Walter Matthau
George Burns

Matthau and Burns play two aging and feuding vaudeville partners who are reunited for a TV special after an 11-year separation. The lightweight comedy by Neil Simon is based on his Broadway play. Matthau and Burns are an effective comic combination, exuding warmth and charm as they bat their one-liners back and forth. It's an amusing and entertaining movie, yet the Simon touch lacks heft, and at times, it's like watching a TV sitcom. Also with Richard Benjamin and Carol Arthur. **Director**—Herbert Ross. (PG) **Academy Award**—Burns, best supporting actor. **Nominations**—Matthau, best actor; Simon, best screenplay (adapted from another medium). *111 minutes*

SUPERFLY (1972)
★★

Ron O'Neal
Carl Lee

O'Neal and Lee star in this vulgar tale glorifying Harlem drug traffic. It's about a drug dealer who vows to make one last big score before retiring. Admittedly, there's a lot of action in this well-made film, and there are comic moments, but there is excessive violence. Also with Julius W. Harris. **Director**—Gordon Parks, Jr. (R) *98 minutes*

SUPERMAN (1978)
★★★

Christopher Reeve
Margot Kidder
Marlon Brando
Gene Hackman

That durable comic-book hero comes to the screen in this elaborate, $35-million production; it's great juvenile fun, and the special effects are super. Yet, the movie seems too extravagant for such mindless material. Reeve does yeoman's work as the Man of Steel who busily fights crime, saves airplanes, and courts Lois Lane (Kidder). Brando gets top billing—and top dollar—as Superman's father, but it seems he's on and off the screen faster than a speeding bullet. Also with Ned Beatty, Jackie Cooper, Glenn Ford, and Valerie Perrine. **Director**—Richard Donner. (PG) *143 minutes*

SUPERMAN II (1981)
★★★★

Christopher Reeve
Margot Kidder
Gene Hackman

The Man of Steel, played by Reeve, is
(Continued)

S • Supervixens
• Support Your Local Gunfighter
• Support Your Local Sheriff
• Suppose They Gave a War and Nobody Came?
• Susan Slept Here
• Suspiria
• The Swan

Christopher Reeve plays Superman at his Fortress of Solitude in Superman II.

(Continued)

a super lover who takes Lois Lane to bed tastefully in this thrilling sequel that outshines the 1978 film. Lois is once again played by Kidder. The film brims with exquisite special effects, heroic splendor, and some surprising humanizing touches. This time, Earth is threatened by three power-crazed villains from the planet Krypton. But our hero triumphs over evil in a glorious, slam-bang battle amid Manhattan's skyscrapers. Also with Jackie Cooper, Valerie Perrine, and Susannah York. **Director**—Richard Lester. (PG)   *127 minutes*

SUPERVIXENS (1975)
(no stars)

Director Russ Meyer once again comes up with a mixture of nudity, brutality, simulated sex, and cheap jokes. The film is sophomoric and idiotic through and through. (X)   *106 minutes*

SUPPORT YOUR LOCAL GUNFIGHTER (1971)
★★

James Garner

Garner fans might enjoy this weak and silly movie about a gambler who flees from a woman who wants to marry him. Many of the attempts at laughs are keyed to Garner's subsequent plight when he's mistaken for a professional gunfighter. The supporting cast includes Harry Morgan, Suzanne Pleshette, Joan Blondell, Jack Elam, and Chuck Connors, and they are all in step with the spirit of this enterprise. **Director**—Burt Kennedy. (G)   *92 minutes*

SUPPORT YOUR LOCAL SHERIFF (1969)
★★★

James Garner
Joan Hackett

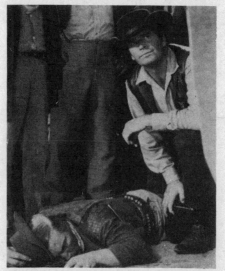

In Support Your Local Sheriff, *James Garner kneels over the loser of a gunfight.*

In this amusing movie, spoofing many conventional westerns, Garner becomes sheriff of a town. He outwits the bad guys and romances Hackett. Garner has just the right comic touch for such a farce. And the performances of Hackett and Walter Brennan, as the chieftain of the bad guys, enhance the production. Jack Elam, Bruce Dern, Henry Jones, and Harry Morgan appear in supporting roles. **Director**—Burt Kennedy. (G)   *92 minutes*

SUPPOSE THEY GAVE A WAR AND NOBODY CAME? (1970)
★

Tony Curtis
Brian Keith
Ernest Borgnine
Ivan Dixon

This lackluster comedy revolves around the conflicts caused in a Southern town by the presence of an Army base. Curtis, Keith, Borgnine, and Dixon have all been better in other movies. Even a potentially good scene—when the soldiers arrive at a dance in a tank—falls flat. The supporting cast includes Tom Ewell, Don Ameche, Arthur O'Connell, and Suzanne Pleshette. **Director**—Hy Averback. (PG) **Alternate Title**—*War Games*.   *114 minutes*

SUSAN SLEPT HERE (1954)
★★

Dick Powell
Debbie Reynolds

Powell and Reynolds star in this comedy about a Hollywood scriptwriter who's doing a movie about juvenile delinquency. He's given custody of a problem child, and that development is supposed to be the foundation for a lot of laughs. Instead the production crumbles. Powell is the scriptwriter, and Reynolds is the delinquent. Also with Anne Francis, Horace MacMahon, Alvy Moore, and Glenda Farrell. **Director**—Frank Tashlin.   *98 minutes*

SUSPIRIA (1977)
(no stars)

Jessica Harper

A forced, grisly shocker about murders in a German ballet academy. Writer-director Dario Argento drips blood and guts all over the screen to the accompaniment of loud, nerve-jangling music. Bad acting and an uneven script don't help matters. Your stomach or patience may not make it to the end. Also with Alida Valli, Stefania Casini, Joan Bennett, and Flavio Bucci. (R)   *97 minutes*

THE SWAN (1956)
★★

Grace Kelly
Alec Guinness
Louis Jourdan

This movie is famous because it was Kelly's last Hollywood film, but it lacks any other mark of distinction—despite the presence of Guinness and Jourdan. The story is about the search by a prince for a wife and is based on the play by Ferenc Molnar. Guinness

- The Swarm
- Swashbuckler
- Sweet Bird of Youth
- Sweet Movie
- Sweet Rosie O'Grady
- Sweet Smell of Success
- Swept Away . . . By an Unusual Destiny in the Blue Sea of August

S

plays the prince. Guess who married a prince after this movie? Also with Agnes Moorehead, Estelle Winwood, Robert Coote, Leo G. Carroll, and Jessica Royce Landis. **Director**—Charles Vidor. *112 minutes*

THE SWARM (1978)
★

Michael Caine
Katharine Ross

Zillions of African killer bees are on the rampage in this movie by director Irwin (*The Towering Inferno*) Allen. The enraged insects attack an Air Force ICBM base and a nearby town, but they can't measure up in scariness to man-eating sharks or overgrown gorillas. The movie plods on with a lot of dull dialogue, questionable credibility, and not much sting. An all-star cast, which seems to number as many players as there are bees on screen, also includes Richard Widmark, Henry Fonda, Olivia de Havilland, Fred Mac-Murray, Richard Chamberlain, Lee Grant, Ben Johnson, and José Ferrer. (PG) *116 minutes*

SWASHBUCKLER (1976)
★

Robert Shaw
James Earl Jones

A lavish yet tacky pirate adventure

Robert Shaw and crewmates get safely aboard their ship in Swashbuckler.

photographed mostly around Puerto Vallarta, Mexico. Shaw and Jones are a pair of daring pirates bent on ridding Jamaica of a corrupt governor, played by Peter Boyle. The uneven film can't make up its mind whether it's straight action melodrama or burlesque; it's mostly tedious and hardly in the spirit of those colorful pirate adventures of 20 years ago. Now Errol Flynn—there was a swashbuckler! Also with Geneviève Bujold, Beau Bridges, and Geoffrey Holder. **Director**—James Goldstone. (PG) *101 minutes*

SWEET BIRD OF YOUTH (1962)
★★★

Paul Newman
Geraldine Page
Ed Begley

Newman, Page, and Begley sparkle in this film version of Tennessee Williams's play about a Hollywood actor who returns to his hometown with an aging and neurotic film star. Newman is the actor, and Page is the aging glamor queen. Newman confronts the boss of the corrupt Southern town, and they renew an old feud. It's fortunate that this trio shines so brightly because much of the original Williams play has been emasculated for its screen appearance. Nonetheless, there are vivid characterizations, crisp dialogue, and memorable scenes. Also with Rip Torn, Madeleine Sherwood, and Shirley Knight. **Director**—Richard Brooks. **Academy Award**—Begley, best supporting actor. **Nominations**—Page, best actress; Knight, best supporting actress. *120 minutes*

SWEET MOVIE (1975)
★

Yugoslav director Dusan Makavejev presents a mishmash political satire, which depicts capitalist exploitation and communist brutalization. There are scenes showing urination and love-making in a bed filled with sugar. There's also a barge named *Survival*, which carries a gigantic papier-mâché head of Karl Marx on its prow. It's a creative film, it's also distasteful and hardly stimulating. (No MPAA rating) *95 minutes*

SWEET ROSIE O'GRADY (1943)
★★

Betty Grable
Adolphe Menjou

Menjou is suave, debonair, and charming in this enjoyable musical about a former burlesque star and a reporter's efforts to dig into her past. Grable, the burlesque star, is attractive and lovely to look at—no wonder she was the favorite sex symbol of thousands of GIs. Unfortunately, most of the movie's songs are second-rate, but that doesn't jar the pleasant tone of this enterprise. Robert Young, Alan Dinehart, Reginald Gardiner, Virginia Grey, and Phil Regan appear in supporting roles. **Director**—Irving Cummings. *79 minutes*

SWEET SMELL OF SUCCESS (1957)
★★★

Burt Lancaster
Tony Curtis

The characterizations are stunning in this startling drama of the rough and tumble world of a New York-based newspaper columnist and his dealings with a vile press agent. Curtis is superb as the scheming PR man, while Lancaster is competent but less convincing as the vicious columnist. The splendid photography of James Wong Howe adds to the realistic quality of the movie. Also with Barbara Nichols, Emily Meyer, Martin Milner, Susan Harrison, and Sam Levene. **Director**—Alexander Mackendrick.

96 minutes b&w

SWEPT AWAY. . . BY AN UNUSUAL DESTINY IN THE BLUE SEA OF AUGUST (1975)
★★★

Giancarlo Giannini
Mariangela Melato

Melato plays a spoiled, arrogant, and wealthy capitalist. Giannini is a communist deckhand on the yacht she has chartered. They become shipwrecked on an island, and the tables are turned as he dominates her in this gripping, political film by director Lina Wert-
(Continued)

S·T
- The Swiss Family Robinson
- Take a Hard Ride
- Take Care of My Little Girl
- Take Me Out to the Ball Game

(Continued)
muller about the battle of the classes and sexes. In Italian with English titles. (R)   *116 minutes*

THE SWISS FAMILY ROBINSON (1960)
★★★

John Mills
Dorothy McGuire
James MacArthur

John Mills and Dorothy McGuire in The Swiss Family Robinson, *a children's classic.*

This Walt Disney version of the famed Johann Wyss children's classic is an almost total escape into a fantasy world—no small accomplishment when you think about the harsh realities of the real world. The movie shows how a family—shipwrecked en route to New Guinea—adjusts superbly to life on a desert island, as they build a paradise of their own and dispatch pirate invaders. Also with Sessue Hayakawa, Janet Munro, Tommy Kirk, Cecil Parker, and Kevin Corcoran. **Director**—Ken Annakin.
          126 minutes

T

TAKE A HARD RIDE (1975)
★★

Jim Brown
Jim Kelly
Lee Van Cleef
Fred Williamson

A familiar western period drama where the good guys, like Brown, are blacks, and the villains like Van Cleef, are white. The story involves the transporting of $86,000 hundreds of

---

MICKEY ROONEY

Mickey Rooney, a diminutive, energetic, and versatile actor of movies and stage, was enormously popular as a child star, and from the age of seven to the present he has rarely been out of work.

He was born Joe Yule, Jr., in Brooklyn, New York, in 1920. His parents were vaudeville performers, and he joined the family act when less than two years old. His first film role was at the age of six, when he played a midget in Not To Be Trusted, and he went on to star in some 50 short comedies in the Mickey McGuire series.

His career took off when he portrayed the stalwart American youth in the ever-popular Andy Hardy series for MGM. He also was successfully cast opposite Judy Garland in a series of breathless

miles from Texas to a family in Mexico. All sorts of plotters, ready to grab the loot, pop out of the brush along the way. Also with Catherine Spaak, Dana Andrews, Barry Sullivan, and Harry Carey, Jr. **Director**—Anthony M. Dawson (PG)   *109 minutes*

TAKE CARE OF MY LITTLE GIRL (1951)
★★

Jeanne Crain
Mitzi Gaynor
Dale Robertson

Crain, Gaynor, and Robertson star in this melodrama about university life and the dynamics and demerits of belonging to a campus sorority. Even viewers who recall their school days

---

musicals and, by 1939, he was Hollywood's top box-office attraction.

Rooney entered military service during World War II, but after his discharge his career faltered, and he was beset with financial difficulties. Eventually, he was able to demonstrate that his talent as a child star was just as formidable as an adult. He excelled during the '50s in The Bold and the Brave (1956) and Baby Face Nelson (1958).

He had more financial woes in the '60s, and alimony payments—he was married and divorced eight times—ate into his earnings. But the determined and plucky Rooney, exuding teenage friskiness even into middle age, bounced back in the '70s in numerous film and stage roles.

In 1938, Rooney received a special Academy Award. Since then, he's been nominated four times for an Oscar.

Most recently, Rooney has been as exuberant as ever opposite Anne Miller in the Broadway production of Sugar Babies.

Some of his notable feature films include A Midsummer Night's Dream (1935), A Family Affair (1937), Boys Town (1938), Babes in Arms (1939), The Human Comedy (1943), National Velvet (1944), The Bridges at Toko-Ri (1954), The Last Mile (1959), and The Black Stallion (1979).

with fondness will probably find this movie basically routine. Other cast members include George Nader, Jean Peters, Jeffrey Hunter, and Helen Westcott. **Director**—Jean Negulesco.
          93 minutes

TAKE ME OUT TO THE BALL GAME (1949)
★★★

Gene Kelly
Frank Sinatra
Esther Williams
Betty Garrett

Kelly, Sinatra, Williams, and Garrett star in this unpretentious, turn-of-the-century musical about a woman who owns a baseball team. The plot is weak and most of the songs are forgettable,

- Take the Money and Run
- Take This Job and Shove It
- The Taking of Pelham One Two Three
- A Tale of Two Cities
- The Talk of the Town
- Tall in the Saddle
- The Tall Men

T

but the stars put enough of their energy into the show to make it highly pleasing for those who don't approach it with great expectations. "The Hat My Father Wore on St. Patrick's Day" and "O'Brien to Ryan to Goldberg" are two of the better-known songs. Also with Richard Lane, Tom Dugan, Edward Arnold, and Jules Munshin. **Director**—Busby Berkeley.

93 minutes

TAKE THE MONEY AND RUN (1969)
★★★

Woody Allen

Allen is in top form as writer, director, and actor in this comedy about the life of an inept thief. Some of the jokes fail and not all of the sight gags work, but the uninhibited spoof of gangster films is exhilarating at times because the laughs comes at such a rapid rate. Janet Margolin, Marcel Hillaire, Jacquelyn Hyde, Louise Lasser, Lonny Chapman, and Mark Gordon also appear, with Jackson Beck as the narrator in the documentary-style sequences. (PG)   *85 minutes*

TAKE THIS JOB AND SHOVE IT (1981)
★★

Robert Hays

Hays of *Airplane* fame stars as a young man on the way up the corporate ladder who joins brewery workers protesting the takeover of their local brewery. The title is interesting, but the film doesn't live up to its potential of effectively revealing the tensions between labor and management. The up-the-conglomerate-and-down-with-computers theme is occasionally

Two employees try to get Robert Hays (center) drunk in Take This Job and Shove It.

amusing, but there's too much triteness in the uneven script, which seems to have been written by a clock watcher. **Director**—Gus Trikonis. (PG)   *100 minutes*

THE TAKING OF PELHAM ONE TWO THREE (1974)
★★

Walter Matthau
Robert Shaw

A great idea doesn't necessarily make a great or even a good movie. This story about four gangsters who hold the passengers of a New York City subway car hostage falters because the script is needlessly confusing and too much of the acting is uninspired. Yet there is enough suspense to keep viewers interested. Matthau, who plays a transit detective, and Shaw, as a ruthless gang leader, have their moments. Martin Balsam, James Broderick, Hector Elizondo, Tony Roberts, and Earl Hindman appear in supporting roles. **Director**—Joseph Sargent. (PG)   *104 minutes*

A TALE OF TWO CITIES (1935)
★★★★

Ronald Colman

A tremendous cast fortifies this film version of the classic Charles Dickens tale of the French Revolution. Although the production has a lavish Hollywood aura, it's a faithful reproduction of Dickens's masterpiece. Colman stars as the British lawyer who aids victims of the Reign of Terror and sacrifices his life to save another man from the guillotine. Also with Edna May Oliver, Elizabeth Allan, Fritz Leiber, Basil Rathbone, Claude Gillingwater, H. B. Warner, and Donald Woods. **Director**—Jack Conway.

121 minutes b&w

THE TALK OF THE TOWN (1942)
★★★★

Ronald Colman
Cary Grant
Jean Arthur

Coleman, Grant, and Arthur star in

this compelling tale of a woman in love with a suspected murderer and the attorney who defends him. This charming and intelligent comedy about civil liberties is a fine example of Hollywood at its best. Today, such a theme would be presented with a heavy dose of profanity and loads of violence. Other stars in the cast include Charles Dingle, Rex Ingram, Glenda Farrell, Edgar Buchanan, and Emma Dunn. **Director**—George Stevens. **Academy Award Nominations**—best picture; Sidney Harmon, writing (original story); Sidney Buchman and Irwin Shaw, writing (screenplay); Ted Tetzlaff, cinematography (black and white).   *118 minutes b&w*

TALL IN THE SADDLE (1944)
★★★

John Wayne
Ella Raines

Wayne plays a cowpoke who hates women. But then—true to form in such western adventures—a spinster and her young niece take over the ownership of the ranch where the Duke is foreman. Raines is the ranch owner. Despite these predictable twists and turns in the plot, this is an enjoyable film. Also with Ward Bond, Gabby Hayes, Elisabeth Risdon, Raymond Hatton, Russell Wade, Paul Fix, and Audrey Long. **Director**—Edwin L. Marin.   *87 minutes b&w*

THE TALL MEN (1955)
★★

Clark Gable
Jane Russell
Robert Ryan

Gable, Russell, and Ryan bolster the appeal of this standard western yarn, but it doesn't really have much to offer beyond some action scenes and Russell's profile. Gable and Ryan play two Texans who head to Montana after the Civil War in search of their fortunes and meet many hazards along the way—including Indians, of course. Also with Cameron Mitchell, Emile Meyer, Juan Garcia, Mae Marsh, and Harry Shannon. **Director**—Raoul Walsh.   *122 minutes*

T
- The Tamarind Seed
- The Taming of the Shrew
- Tammy and the Bachelor
- Taps
- Taras Bulba
- Tarzan, the Ape Man
- Task Force
- Tattoo

THE TAMARIND SEED (1974)
★★

Julie Andrews
Omar Sharif

Andrews and Sharif star in this romance with an international backdrop—London, Paris, and Barbados—and an espionage theme. Andrews plays a British widow who falls in love with a Russian agent, played by Sharif. The plot substitutes confusion for suspense, but the stars shine often enough to keep the story interesting. The cast includes Anthony Quayle, Oscar Homolka, Daniel O'Herlihy, and Sylvia Sims. **Director**—Blake Edwards. (PG)   *123 minutes*

THE TAMING OF THE SHREW (1967)
★★★

Richard Burton
Elizabeth Taylor

At times, William Shakespeare seems to take a back seat in this movie, but there are enough remnants of the Bard's brilliance to tame the most critical of viewers. In addition, Burton is superb as Petruchio, Taylor is good as Kate, the supporting cast is first-rate, and the color photography is exquisite. The supporting actors include Michael York, Cyril Cusack, Victor Spinetti, Michael Hordern, Vernon Dobtcheff, Natasha Pyne, and Alan Webb. **Director**—Franco Zeffirelli.   *126 minutes*

TAMMY AND THE BACHELOR (1957)
★★

Debbie Reynolds
Leslie Nielsen

Reynolds, in the title role, nurses an injured pilot, played by Nielsen, back to health in this lightweight comedy-romance. She falls in love with him, of course, and the rest is sweetness and corn and everything nice. The performance of Reynolds is spirited, energetic, and contagious enough so that the whole cast gets into step and makes the best of average material. Also with Walter Brennan, Fay Wray,

Mala Powers, Louise Beavers, Sidney Blackmer, and Mildred Natwick. **Director**—Joseph Pevney.   *89 minutes*

TAPS (1981)
★★

George C. Scott
Timothy Hutton

An ambiguous and rather farfetched drama about military school cadets who take up arms to defend their academy and prevent it from being converted to a condominium development. Essentially, the film is a sentimental analogy of the attitude that led to involvement in Vietnam. The ponderous and predictable story stars Hutton as a gung ho and misguided cadet leader; Scott is delightful as the school's superintendent, but he fades away before the film is half over. Also with Ronny Cox, Tom Cruise, and Sean Penn. **Director**—Harold Becker. (PG)   *130 minutes*

TARAS BULBA (1962)
★★

Yul Brynner
Tony Curtis

Action, violence, and superior photography prevail in this Nicolai Gogol tale of a 16th-century revolt in Poland. Brynner portrays Taras Bulba, the famed Cossack leader, and Curtis plays one of the Cossack's sons. They merely give the conventional performances such films require. Also with Sam Wanamaker, Guy Rolfe, Abraham Sofaer, Christine Kaufmann, and Vladimir Sokoloff. **Director**—J. Lee Thompson.   *122 minutes*

TARZAN, THE APE MAN (1981)
★

Bo Derek
Miles O'Keeffe

The lord of the jungle is dethroned and relegated to the role of a mere silent sex symbol in this labored and shabby remake, which looks more like a pinup calendar layout than a movie. Practically all the attention is on Jane, played by beautiful Bo who's frequently photographed in various stages of undress. Jane loses her way

Cheta the chimp, Miles O'Keeffe, and Bo Derek in Tarzan, the Ape Man.

in the jungle, where she finds the magnificent ape man played by O'Keeffe, and the two monkey around together. Tarzan doesn't say a word, which is probably wise because everyone else is saddled with silly dialogue. **Director**—John Derek. (R)   *111 minutes*

TASK FORCE (1949)
★★

Gary Cooper
Walter Brennan
Jane Wyatt

Cooper, Brennan, and Wyatt star in this story about the growth of naval aviation and the development of aircraft carriers. At times, the plot seems to be lost at sea, and when the film does roll along, there's too much emphasis on Navy propaganda. But the acting is good, and there are some fine action sequences. Julie London, Jack Holt, Wayne Morris, Stanley Ridges, and Bruce Bennett appear in supporting roles. **Director**—Delmer Daves.   *116 minutes b&w/color*

TATTOO (1981)
★

Bruce Dern
Maud Adams

Dern once again portrays a weird character; this time he's a tormented tattoo artist who kidnaps a glamorous model, played by Adams, and plies

● Taxi Driver
● Tea and Sympathy
● Teacher's Pet
● Tea for Two
● The Teahouse of the August Moon
● Telefon

T

In Tattoo, Maud Adams becomes a living canvas for an obsessed Bruce Dern.

his needlework all over her beautiful body. The story, which borrows heavily from *The Collector*, starts with some promise, but turns sour and predictable about midway and eventually falls apart at the seams. With Adams in a state of undress so often as Dern's human canvas, the film eventually resembles a sleazy soft-core skin flick. **Director**—Bob Brooks. (R)

102 minutes

TAXI DRIVER (1976)
★★

Robert De Niro
Jodie Foster

Director Martin Scorsese's brutally disturbing film about a lonely and psychotic New York cabbie parallels the lives of such latter-day psychopaths as Arthur Bremer and Charles Whitman. The experience evokes mixed emotions; it's depressing, violent, and cyn-

Cybill Shepherd and Robert De Niro in Martin Scorsese's brutal Taxi Driver.

ical. The script is inconsistent. Yet there's a dazzling performance by De Niro, as the quiet and unhinged Travis Bickle who stalks a presidential candidate, but instead turns his sudden fury on the pimp of a young prostitute. There are other impressive performances, including those by Harvey Keitel as the pimp and Foster as a 12-year-old hustler. The sleazy underside of city life is clearly illustrated by Scorsese through the eyes of Travis. The film is haunting and unforgettable, but only barely entertaining. Also with Cybill Shepherd, Peter Boyle, and Leonard Harris. (R) **Academy Award Nomination**—best picture; De Niro, best actor; Foster, best supporting actress.   *113 minutes*

TEA AND SYMPATHY (1956)
★★★

Deborah Kerr
John Kerr

Deborah Kerr and John Kerr—they're not related—both give extremely sensitive performances in this movie about a troubled schoolboy's affair with a teacher's wife. This film version of Robert Anderson's successful Broadway play drags at times, but the superior acting and characterizations more than justify the pace of the production. Leif Erickson, Edward Andrews, Norma Crane, Dean Jones, and Darryl Hickman also star. **Director**—Vincente Minnelli.   *122 minutes*

TEACHER'S PET (1958)
★★★

Clark Gable
Doris Day
Gig Young

Gable, Day, and Young are in fine form and give this unpretentious and enjoyable comedy just the right emphasis. Gable plays a tough newspaper editor who enrolls in Day's journalism course. He tries to romance her, but must also deal with the intellectual and eccentric Young. The supporting cast includes Nick Adams, Mamie Van Doren, and Charles Lane. **Director**—George Seaton. **Academy Award Nominations**—Young, best supporting actor; Fay and Michael Kanin, best story and screenplay (writ-

ten directly for the screen).
120 minutes b&w

TEA FOR TWO (1950)
★★

Doris Day
Gordon MacRae

A congenial cast including Day, MacRae, Eve Arden, and Billy De Wolfe keep this musical, inspired by the play *No, No, Nanette*, perking right along. Although amusing and enjoyable, the whole production is lacking in substance; most of the activity centers on Day's decision to become interested in show business. Gene Nelson, Patrice Wymore, Bill Goodwin, and S. Z. Sakall, round out the cast. **Director**—David Butler.   *97 minutes*

THE TEAHOUSE OF THE AUGUST MOON (1956)
★★★

Marlon Brando
Glenn Ford

Brando is miscast as a cunning native interpreter in this pleasing film version of John Patrick's successful Broadway play. Fortunately, Ford, who plays a U.S. Army captain in charge of the rehabilitation of an Okinawan village in 1944, has a keen comic touch and carries the film to its enjoyable conclusion. Also with Machiko Kyo, Paul Ford, Henry Morgan, and Eddie Albert. **Director**—Daniel Mann.   *123 minutes*

TELEFON (1977)
★★

Charles Bronson
Lee Remick

Bronson and Remick play two Russian spies who pursue a Russian saboteur in the United States who's trying to trigger World War III. The plot, which is hard to take seriously, owes much to *The Manchurian Candidate*; it's based on Walter Wager's novel. Bronson maintains his usual stone face amid the numerous action sequences that fade away moments after they start. Locations range all over the globe—Moscow, Canada, and several cities in
(Continued)

T
- Tell Me a Riddle
- Tell Me That You Love Me, Junie Moon
- Tell Them Willie Boy Is Here
- 10
- The Tenant
- The Ten Commandments
- The Tender Trap

(Continued)
the United States. Also with Donald Pleasence, Tyne Daly, Patrick Magee, and Alan Badel. **Director**—Don Siegel. (PG)   *102 minutes*

TELL ME A RIDDLE (1981)
★★★

**Melvyn Douglas
Lila Kedrova**

Douglas and Kedrova star in this dignified, low-key film about an elderly couple who reconcile their long, quarrelsome marriage. Douglas and Kedrova create heartwarming, memorable characterizations. The film is often lacking in dramatic momentum, but there are many moments of beauty and sensitivity. Based on Tillie Olsen's acclaimed 1961 novella. Lee Grant, in her first time out as director, handles the job in a straightforward manner. (PG)   *90 minutes*

TELL ME THAT YOU LOVE ME, JUNIE MOON (1969)
★★★

**Liza Minnelli
Ken Howard
Robert Moore**

There are some superb and moving moments in this strange tragi-comedy about three handicapped people who decide to live together. The excellent acting of Minnelli (facially scarred), Howard (an epileptic), and Moore (a homosexual paraplegic) helps to carry the film over its rough spots. There are many flaws in this movie, but this is a rare case in which Hollywood must be commended for having the courage to tackle a difficult subject. The supporting cast includes James Coco, Fred Williamson, Kay Thompson, and Leonard Frey. **Director**—Otto Preminger. (PG)   *113 minutes*

TELL THEM WILLIE BOY IS HERE (1969)
★★★

**Robert Redford
Robert Blake**

Redford and Blake star in this tale about an Indian who flees after killing a man in self-defense. Unlike most western adventures, this movie, under the excellent writing and direction of Abraham Polonsky, also explores the cruel treatment of the American Indian by the white man. Redford is good as the sheriff who hunts down the killer. Blake, who plays the fugitive Indian, is close to perfect. Also with Susan Clark, Barry Sullivan, Katharine Ross, John Vernon, Charles McGraw, and Charles Aidman. (PG)   *96 minutes*

10 (1979)
★★★

**Dudley Moore
Julie Andrews
Bo Derek**

Moore stars as a middle-aged Hollywood songwriter in this romantic comedy about the frustrating pursuit of happiness. Director Blake Edwards skillfully sets up a number of funny situations for Moore, who stumbles and bumbles after a vision of beauty and youth, played by Derek. There are some slow spots, but Moore manages to keep the comic momentum rolling along. Andrews, in a brief throwaway role, is Moore's long-standing girl friend. Also with Robert Webber, Sam Jones, Dee Wallace, Max Showalter, and Brian Dennehy. (R)   *122 minutes*

THE TENANT (1976)
★★★

**Roman Polanski
Isabelle Adjani
Melvyn Douglas
Shelley Winters**

Polanski directs and stars in this horror tale about a mild-mannered young Pole who rents a Paris apartment and believes he's being persecuted by his neighboring tenants. Polanski delivers striking shock effects and an intense performance of a man creating his own torture. However, the film doesn't reach the same degree of suspense or polish as Polanski's *Rosemary's Baby* or *Chinatown*. Excellent support from Winters, Adjani, and Douglas. Also with Jo Van Fleet, Bernard Fresson, and Claude Dauphin. Poor English dubbing of French-speaking cast members. (R)
125 minutes

In 10, Bo Derek is the object of Dudley Moore's bumbling affections.

THE TEN COMMANDMENTS (1956)
★★★

**Charlton Heston
Yul Brynner**

This biblical extravaganza about the life of Moses and leading the Jews out of Egypt to the Promised Land has all the good and bad points of such pictures. On the plus side, there's a star-studded cast, lush photography, and brilliant dramatic moments. However, the movie occasionally is monotonous because of a heavy-handed plot and trite dialogue. Heston, who plays Moses, and Brynner head the huge cast, with Anne Baxter, Edward G. Robinson, Yvonne De Carlo, Martha Scott, Vincent Price, John Carradine, Cedric Hardwicke, John Derek, and Nina Foch among the many supporting actors. **Director**—Cecil B. DeMille. (G) **Academy Award Nominations**—best picture; Loyal Griggs, cinematography (color).   *219 minutes*

THE TENDER TRAP (1955)
★★★

**Frank Sinatra
Debbie Reynolds
David Wayne
Celeste Holm**

Delightful acting performances by Sinatra, Reynolds, Wayne, and Holm

- Ten North Frederick
- Terror Train
- Tess
- Thank God, It's Friday
- That Certain Feeling
- That Darn Cat!
- That Forsyte Woman

T

vitalize this ordinary comedy and make it worth viewing. Sinatra plays a New York agent who has a way with gals until he eventually falls for the trap of marriage set by Reynolds. Lola Albright, Tom Helmore, and Carolyn Jones are fine in supporting roles. **Director**—Charles Walters.

111 minutes

TEN NORTH FREDERICK (1958)
★★

Gary Cooper
Geraldine Fitzgerald

Cooper plays a wealthy man pushed by his domineering wife into involvement with national politics. His bid for a shot at the vice presidential nomination of his party never gets off the ground because of his family problems. Fitzgerald plays his wife. The movie doesn't reach its full potential either, although the acting and characterizations are interesting. Based on John O'Hara's novel. Also with Diane Varsi, Suzy Parker, Tom Tully, Stuart Whitman, and Ray Stricklyn. **Director**—Philip Dunne. *102 minutes b&w*

TERROR TRAIN (1980)
★★

Jamie Lee Curtis
Ben Johnson

This is another bloody, formula horror film that trips in the tracks of such shockers as *Halloween* and *The Fog*. The setting is an excursion train, filled with partying college students chugging through Canada. On board is a revenge-seeking psychotic, who assumes various disguises as he murders some of the students and the train crew. Curtis, a regular in this sort of film, plays the heroine in routine fashion. Also with Hart Bocher. **Director**—Roger Spottiswoode. (R)

97 minutes

TESS (1980)
★★

Nastassia Kinski
Peter Firth
Leigh Lawson

Director Roman Polanski's screen adaptation of the classic Victorian

Nastassia Kinski plays the title role in Tess, based on Thomas Hardy's novel.

novel by Thomas Hardy is physically beautiful, but slow-paced and exceedingly long. Lovely Kinski plays the exploited peasant girl who resorts to murder. Unfortunately, she doesn't have the maturity the role demands. Polanski, however, remains faithful to the novel and the historic period, and there are lush settings and striking costumes. Firth and Lawson co-star. Also with John Colin. (R) **Academy Award Nominations**—best picture; Polanski, best director. *180 minutes*

THANK GOD, IT'S FRIDAY (1978)
★★

Donna Summer
Valerie Landsburg
Terri Nunn

Like the title, there's little originality in this adolescent film about an evening at a Los Angeles discotheque. The style smacks of *Saturday Night Fever*; the climax is built around a dance contest. There's no plot to speak of—just a series of breathless vignettes acted out by a cast of newcomers. More than 30 ultraloud pop songs, including "Last Dance," are featured for the delight of teenagers. Also with Chick Vennera, Ray Vitte, and Jeff Goldblum. (PG) **Director**—Robert Klane.

90 minutes

Donna Summer and Ray Vitte in Thank God, It's Friday, *a contemporary comedy.*

THAT CERTAIN FEELING (1956)
★

Bob Hope

Hope is able to deliver some funny lines, and there are some delightful moments in this story about a syndicated comic-strip artist who hires a "ghost" to do his work, but most of the movie is dismal. When Hope must act—he portrays a troubled cartoonist—he falters, and the rest of the cast, which includes George Sanders, Pearl Bailey, Eva Marie Saint, and Al Capp, fails to come to his rescue. **Directors**—Norman Panama and Melvin Frank.

102 minutes

THAT DARN CAT! (1965)
★★

Hayley Mills
Dean Jones

Most Walt Disney animal films are pretty much the same—only the animals seem to change. Fortunately, kids and adults can take comfort in this movie about a talented cat who leads an FBI agent, played by Jones, to the lair of the gangsters to rescue a kidnapped woman. The film maintains the standards of wholesomeness that parents have come to expect of Disney productions. The talented cast also includes Roddy McDowall, Ed Wynn, Dorothy Provine, and Elsa Lanchester. **Director**—Robert Stevenson. *116 minutes*

THAT FORSYTE WOMAN (1949)
★★

Greer Garson
Errol Flynn
Robert Young

Garson, Flynn, and Young make a valiant bid to bring the film version of John Galsworthy's novel *A Man of Property* to the screen with style and vitality. Although they succeed, Galsworthy on film is a fairly dull achievement. Garson is excellent as a faithless woman who falls in love with the man her niece plans to marry. Flynn and Young are good, too, with competent supporting performances from Walter

(Continued)

(Continued)
Pidgeon, Janet Leigh, Aubrey Mather, and Harry Davenport. **Director**—Compton Bennett.   *114 minutes*

THAT HAMILTON WOMAN (1941)
★★★

Laurence Olivier
Vivien Leigh

Olivier and Leigh sparkle in this costume drama, detailing the tragic romance of British naval hero Lord Nelson and Lady Emma Hamilton. The movie is too long, but many attractive scenes and excellent acting make the movie worthwhile. The cast also includes Gladys Cooper, Alan Mowbray, Sara Allgood, Henry Wilcoxon, Halliwell Hobbes, and Heather Angel. **Director**—Alexander Korda. **Academy Award Nomination**—Rudolph Maté, cinematography (black and white).   *128 minutes b&w*

THAT'S ENTERTAINMENT, PART 2 (1976)
★★★★

Fred Astaire
Gene Kelly

This is another delightful stroll down Hollywood's memory lane, with more snippets from MGM's classic movies. The experience is like a visit with friends you haven't seen in 20 years. The well-constructed compilation of scenes are taken from more than 70 musicals, dramas, and comedy treasures from the MGM library. Some 100 top performers are featured. Old pros Kelly and Astaire narrate to bridge the footage. It's as good, if not better, than the 1974 *That's Entertainment*. It was, and still is, great entertainment. **Director**—Kelly. (G)   *133 minutes*

THAT'S MY BOY (1951)
★★

Dean Martin
Jerry Lewis

This early Martin and Lewis comedy has too much serious subject matter to ever be very funny. It's about a clumsy son pushed by his father into becoming a football player just like the old man. Lewis is the teenage son, and Eddie Mayehoff is his father. Martin is hired to coach Lewis. Fans of Martin and Lewis might find something of merit, but otherwise it has little value. Also with Marion Marshall, Polly Bergen, and John McIntire. **Director**—Hal Walker.   *98 minutes b&w*

THAT TOUCH OF MINK (1962)
★★★

Cary Grant
Doris Day

Grant is so suave and debonnair in this fluffy story about a wealthy businessman who romances an unemployed secretary that it doesn't matter that the plot is silly and the script is flimsy. Day plays the secretary. Grant is tops, and Day, Gig Young, John Astin, Audrey Meadows, and Dick Sargent are adequate for the task at hand. **Director**—Delbert Mann. **Academy Award Nomination**—Stanley Shapiro and Nate Monaster, best story and screenplay (written directly for the screen).   *99 minutes*

THEATRE OF BLOOD (1973)
★★★

Vincent Price
Diana Rigg

Price portrays a Shakespearean actor who gets even with eight critics who have panned his performances by killing them. Rigg plays his daughter. Wise and careful critics won't have any conscience pangs judging this one: Price is fine as the demented thespian, but there are too many violent scenes, and the idea wears thin by the end, despite Price's acting skills and the fine supporting cast of Rigg, Robert Morley, Ian Hendry, Harry Andrews, Robert Coote, Jack Hawkins, Diana Dors, Milo O'Shea, Denis Price, Eric Sykes, and Joan Hickson. We don't blame Vincent; we blame the director and scriptwriter. **Director**—Douglas Hickox. (R)   *104 minutes*

JACK LEMMON

Jack Lemmon, who was born in Boston in 1925, was educated at Harvard, where he was active in dramatics. After graduating in 1946, Lemmon served in the U.S. Navy as an officer aboard an aircraft carrier.

After military service, Lemmon worked in New York at odd jobs, such as a food checker in a restaurant, while waiting for a show-business opening. He finally got one as master of ceremonies at the Old Knick Music Hall, a converted movie house. Lemmon also worked in radio; he had running parts in several soap operas, including The Brighter Day *and* Road to Life. *He soon found himself working steadily in television, and gave about 500 television performances, almost all of them live, on such shows as* Studio One, Robert Montgomery Presents, Suspense, *and* Playhouse 90.

In 1953, Lemmon made his Broadway debut in Room Service. *He started his screen career soon afterward in a pair of Judy Holliday movies,* It Should Happen to You *(1953) and* Phfft *(1954). After making only five movies, Lemmon won an Academy award, receiving an Oscar for best supporting actor for his portrayal of Ensign Pulver in John Ford's* Mr. Roberts *(1955). He won another Oscar, as best actor, for* Save the Tiger *(1973).*

Lemmon has also received five other nominations—all for best actor—during his career.

Some of Lemmon's other movies include Some Like It Hot *(1959),* The Apartment *(1960),* Irma La Douce *(1963),* The Great Race *(1965),* The Odd Couple *(1968),* The Entertainer *(1975),* The China Syndrome *(1979),* Tribute *(1980), and* Buddy Buddy *(1981).*

- Them!
- There's a Girl in My Soup
- There's No Business Like Show Business
- They All Laughed
- They Died With Their Boots On
- They Drive by Night
- They Shoot Horses, Don't They?
- Thief

T

THEM! (1954)
★★★

Edmund Gwenn
James Whitmore

The giant ants are so vivid in this science-fiction film you might want to avoid picnics for a while. The mutated ants, in the giant economy size thanks to A-bomb radiation, run amok in the southwestern part of the United States. The movie is well done, and some of the scenes are truly startling—especially the tense climax in the sewers of Los Angeles. Joan Weldon, Fess Parker, James Arness, and Onslow Stevens do their share in supporting roles with quality acting. **Director—**Gordon Douglas.

94 minutes b&w

THERE'S A GIRL IN MY SOUP (1970)
★★

Peter Sellers
Goldie Hawn
Tony Britton

Sellers, Hawn, and Britton shine in this well-paced movie version of a successful play by Terence Frisby, but the plot and laugh rate are as blah as cold broth. Sellers plays a television gourmet in search of fun, and Hawn becomes the disruptive force in his life. Diana Dors, Judy Campbell, Nicky Henson, and John Comer appear in supporting roles. **Director—**Roy Boulting. (R) *96 minutes*

THERE'S NO BUSINESS LIKE SHOW BUSINESS (1954)
★★

Ethel Merman
Dan Dailey
Marilyn Monroe
Donald O'Connor

Vibrant Irving Berlin music props up this weak musical about a family of vaudevillians and its struggles on and off stage. Merman and Dailey play the parents; Monroe and O'Connor are among their children. The rest of the cast includes Mitzi Gaynor, Hugh O'Brian, Frank McHugh, and Johnny Ray. Merman sings the title song with gusto, and other tunes include "Play a Simple Melody" and "Heat Wave." **Director—**Walter Lang. **Academy Award Nomination—**Lamar Trotti, writing (motion picture story).

117 minutes

THEY ALL LAUGHED (1981)
★

Audrey Hepburn
Ben Gazzara

Director-writer Peter Bogdanovich misfires with this meandering comedy starring Hepburn and Gazzara. Essentially, it's about some inept private detectives in New York City who are assigned to trail various good-looking women married to jealous husbands. Yet nothing of great interest happens in this overstuffed sex farce; it has a hodgepodge of forgettable characters chasing around Manhattan. The film does feature some beauties like the late *Playboy* bunny Dorothy Stratten. (PG) *116 minutes*

THEY DIED WITH THEIR BOOTS ON (1941)
★★★

Errol Flynn

Hollywood gives General George Armstrong Custer's fight at the Little Big Horn the lavish treatment with loads of stars, but little attention to historical accuracy. Flynn is dashing and fine as the defeated general, with Olivia de Havilland, Arthur Kennedy, Anthony Quinn, Gene Lockhart, Sydney Greenstreet, Charles Grapewin, Hattie McDaniel, Stanley Ridges, and Walter Hampden in supporting roles. **Director—**Raoul Walsh.

139 minutes b&w

THEY DRIVE BY NIGHT (1940)
★★★

George Raft
Humphrey Bogart
Ann Sheridan
Ida Lupino

The fine acting of Raft, Bogart, Sheridan, and Lupino and sparkling dialogue fuel this melodrama about honest drivers battling against corruption in the trucking industry. The story lags at times, but there's enough excitement to please fans of action films, and the quality performances will satisfy everyone else. Also with Alan Hale, Gale Page, George Tobias, and John Litel. **Director—**Raoul Walsh. *92 minutes b&w*

THEY SHOOT HORSES, DON'T THEY? (1969)
★★★

Gig Young
Jane Fonda
Michael Sarrazin
Susannah York

This movie about a six-day marathon dance exquisitely captures the impoverished mood during the Great Depression. The production is well conceived and expertly staged, with good acting. Unfortunately, a superficial quality prevails at the serious moments, and the strange ending is unjustified by the events in the film. Young, Fonda, Sarrazin, York, and Red Buttons are superb and make the movie seem better than it really is. Also with Bruce Dern, Bonnie Bedelia, and Allyn Ann McLerie. **Director—**Sydney Pollack. (PG) **Academy Award—**Young, best supporting actor. **Nominations—**Pollack, best director; Fonda, best actress; York, best supporting actress; James Poe and Robert E. Thompson, best screenplay (based on material from another medium). *123 minutes*

THIEF (1981)
★★★★

James Caan
Tuesday Weld

Caan stars as a free-lance safecracker
(Continued)

In Thief, James Caan confronts a crime boss who tried to rip him off.

T
- The Thief of Baghdad
- The Third Man
- The Thirty-Nine Steps
- Thirty Seconds Over Tokyo
- This Gun for Hire
- This Is Elvis

(Continued)
who pursues the American dream with passion and daring. He's in top form with this gripping character study, which involves stark, streetwise realism yet manages to evoke sympathy. Director-writer Michael Mann is off to an impressive start with his first theatrical production; he demonstrates a talented style of suspense, technical detail, and sleek drama. (R) *126 minutes*

THE THIEF OF BAGHDAD (1940)
★★★

Conrad Veidt
Sabu

This enchanting fairy tale is about a young thief, played by Sabu, who prevails over the forces of evil. Veidt plays an evil magician. The tale remains fresh for those who don't take the story too seriously. The excellent photography and the good acting of Sabu, Veidt, and Rex Ingram capture the quality of *Arabian Nights* on film. The cast also includes John Justin, June Duprez, Mary Morris, and Miles Malleson. **Directors**—Michael Powell, Ludwig Berger, and Tim Whelan. **Academy Award**—George Perinal, cinematography (color). *107 minutes*

THE THIRD MAN (1950)
★★★★

Joseph Cotten
Trevor Howard
Orson Welles
Alida Valli

This is one of the best thrillers in the history of cinema. Graham Greene's story about vile black market operations in Vienna after World War II is still fresh because of Carol Reed's direction, excellent acting, and Anton Karas's haunting zither music. Cotten portrays an American who writes westerns. He's in search of Harry Lime, a mystery man of dubious morals played by Welles—and therein lies the fascinating tale. Howard and Valli are excellent in supporting roles. Also with Wilfrid Hyde-White, Bernard Lee, Paul Hoerbiger, and Siegfried Breuer. **Academy Award**—Robert Krasker, cinematography (black and

Alida Valli and Joseph Cotten in The Third Man, *one of cinema's best thrillers.*

white). **Nomination**—Reed, best director. *104 minutes b&w*

THE THIRTY-NINE STEPS (1935)
★★★★

Robert Donat
Madeleine Carroll

This memorable story is the model for many subsequent spy yarns and one of the best movies director Alfred Hitchcock ever made. Donat stars as an innocent man who becomes involved in espionage. He must flee from England to Scotland before he is able to find the real villains and clear his name. Carroll plays a woman who believes Donat is the criminal. Godfrey Tearle, Wylie Watson, and Peggy Ashcroft also star in this comedy-thriller classic. *81 minutes b&w*

THIRTY SECONDS OVER TOKYO (1944)
★★★

Van Johnson
Spencer Tracy

Johnson and Tracy star in this exciting World War II film about the first attack on the Japanese mainland by the U.S. Army Air Force. Tracy plays Col. James Doolittle. Screenwriter Dalton Trumbo has done a fine job of providing lots of action in an enterprise that, at times, becomes a semidocumentary. Robert Walker, Phyllis Thaxter, Robert Mitchum, Louis Jean Heydt, Paul Langton, Stephen McNally, and Scott McKay appear in supporting roles. **Director**—

Mervyn Le Roy. **Academy Award Nomination**—Robert Surtees and Harold Rosson, cinematography (black and white). *132 minutes b&w*

THIS GUN FOR HIRE (1942)
★★★

Alan Ladd
Veronica Lake

Ladd and Lake rose to stardom in this film version of the Graham Greene novel *A Gun for Sale*, about a hired killer who seeks revenge after being double-crossed. Ladd plays the professional killer. Laird Cregar, Robert Preston, and Tully Marshall also star in this well-made production and contribute to the stark realism the movie evokes. **Director**—Frank Tuttle. *81 minutes b&w*

THIS IS ELVIS (1981)
★★

A blend of old newsreels, videotapes, and even home movies provides an absorbing sociological portrait of the rock 'n' roll hero and the era of this popular music. The fascinating documentary segments are effective in charting Elvis Presley's rise and fall. Unfortunately, the film is flawed with false and poorly recreated scenes using actors for Presley at various stages of his life. Still, the faithful can savor the real Elvis, including some candid, unforgettable material and 38 songs. **Directors**—Malcolm Leo and Andrew Solt. (PG) *88 minutes*

Paul Boensch III, portraying young Elvis gets a guitar lesson in This Is Elvis.

- This Is the Army
- This Thing Called Love
- The Thomas Crown Affair
- Thoroughly Modern Millie
- Those Lips, Those Eyes
- Those Magnificent Men in Their Flying Machines, or

How I Flew From London to Paris in 25 Hours and 11 Minutes
- A Thousand Clowns

T

THIS IS THE ARMY (1943)
★★

George Murphy

Song-and-dance man Murphy gets top billing in this wartime musical about soldiers during World War II who stage a show with the songs of Irving Berlin. Some of the material is dated now, and even at the time of its production much of it was mediocre, but there are still some entertaining moments. Among the many other performers are Ronald Reagan, Joan Leslie, Alan Hale, Irving Berlin, Joe Louis, Kate Smith, George Tobias, Una Merkel, and Rosemary de Camp. **Director**—Michael Curtiz. *121 minutes*

THIS THING CALLED LOVE (1941)
★★★

Rosalind Russell
Melvyn Douglas

Russell and Douglas star in this slightly saucy adult comedy about newlyweds who agree to test their marriage by not sleeping together for the first three months. Although the movie seems tame now and just mildly delightful, it was banned by the Legion of Decency on its release. Binnie Barnes and Lee J. Cobb also star, with Allyn Joslyn, Gloria Dickson, Don Bedoe, and Gloria Holden in supporting roles. **Director**—Alexander Hall. *98 minutes b&w*

THE THOMAS CROWN AFFAIR (1968)
★★

Steve McQueen
Faye Dunaway

McQueen stars as a debonair millionaire who engineers a bank robbery because he's bored. Dunaway plays a glamorous investigator for an insurance company who stalks the suave robber. Unfortunately, you'll soon get bored with this overly slick production, which lacks any substance aside from Dunaway's pursuit of McQueen. Jack Weston, Biff McGuire, and Paul Burke also appear. **Director**—Norman Jewison. *102 minutes*

THOROUGHLY MODERN MILLIE (1967)
★★

Julie Andrews

Andrews shines in this musical spoof about a young lady who comes to New York City in the 1920s, falls in love with her boss, and becomes modern in the process. But even her immense talent can't sustain the production beyond the first hour. Despite its faults, there are some fine songs and dancing, plus quality supporting performances by Carol Channing, Beatrice Lillie, and James Fox. The cast also includes Mary Tyler Moore, John Saxon, Anthony Dexter, and Jack Soo. **Director**—George Roy Hill. (G) **Academy Award Nomination**—Channing, best supporting actress. *138 minutes*

THOSE LIPS, THOSE EYES (1980)
★★★

Frank Langella

In *Those Lips, Those Eyes, Frank Langella leads the chorus in a performance.*

Langella stars as a charming second-rate actor who dreams of making it big on Broadway in this '50s backstage romance. But there's nothing second-rate about Langella's performance here as he exudes poise, confidence, and pathos. It's his presence that makes the picture really click. Although somewhat limited in scope, this film is a shining tribute to those striving and hopeful thespians performing in summer stock and other byways of the theater. Also with Glynnis O'Connor and Thomas Hulce. **Director**—Michael Pressman. (R) *106 minutes*

THOSE MAGNIFICENT MEN IN THEIR FLYING MACHINES, OR HOW I FLEW FROM LONDON TO PARIS IN 25 HOURS AND 11 MINUTES (1965)
★★★

Stuart Whitman
Robert Morley
Sarah Miles
Terry-Thomas

This long, lavish production with its superb photography and many stars starts well, but instead of soaring until the end it sputters a bit and becomes a little boring. Yet a comedy-adventure about a 1910 airplane race from London to Paris, with some cunning characters vying for the prize, should not have such a problem. Whitman plays an American cowboy turned pilot, and Terry-Thomas portrays a devious rogue out to win at any cost. Red Skelton does a pleasant prologue to the film; he details the early history of aviation—one reason the movie starts so well. The large cast also includes Eric Sykes, Alberto Sordi, Gert Frobe, James Fox, Benny Hill, and Sam Wanamaker. **Director**—Ken Annakin. (G) **Academy Award Nomination**—Jack Davies and Annakin, best story and screenplay (written directly for the screen). *132 minutes*

A THOUSAND CLOWNS (1965)
★★★

Jason Robards, Jr.
Martin Balsam
Barry Gordon
Barbara Harris

The splendid acting of Robards and Balsam sustains this strange comedy about a nonconformist New Yorker (Robards) who has dropped out of society's rat race for a life of philosophical introspection. The plot gets tangled when a social worker, played by Harris, pressures him to conform again for the sake of Gordon, who plays his teenage nephew. Balsam plays a wealthy and successful brother of Robards. Also with William Daniels and Gene Saks. **Director**—Fred Coe. **Academy Award**—Balsam, best supporting actor. **Nominations**—best pic-
(Continued)

T
- Thousands Cheer
- Three Coins in the Fountain
- Three Days of the Condor
- The Three Faces of Eve
- Three Little Words
- The Three Musketeers
- Three Women

(Continued)
ture; Herb Gardner, best screenplay (based on material from another medium). *118 minutes b&w*

THOUSANDS CHEER (1943)
★★★

Kathryn Grayson
Gene Kelly

Grayson and Kelly head an all-star cast in this World War II musical about an army base that stages a variety show. Although the plot is pretty flimsy, the entertainment is tops. The large cast of stars includes Red Skelton, Lena Horne, Mary Astor, Margaret O'Brien, Judy Garland, June Allyson, Mickey Rooney, Eleanor Powell, and Lionel Barrymore. **Director**—George Sidney. **Academy Award Nomination**—George Folsey, cinematography (color).
126 minutes

THREE COINS IN THE FOUNTAIN (1954)
★★★

Clifton Webb
Dorothy McGuire
Louis Jourdan
Jean Peters

This comedy-romance, set in Rome, is about the search for love by three American secretaries—McGuire, Peters, and Maggie McNamara. It's a pleasant film, which never makes the mistake of taking itself too seriously. The superior acting of Webb and Jourdan adds to the production's competence; the splendid on-location photography in Rome is another plus. Also with Rossano Brazzi, Howard St. John, and Cathleen Nesbitt. **Director**—Jean Negulesco. **Academy Awards**—Milton Krasner, cinematography (color); Jule Style and Sammy Cahn, best song ("Three Coins in the Fountain"). **Nomination**—best picture. *102 minutes*

THREE DAYS OF THE CONDOR (1975)
★★

Robert Redford
Faye Dunaway

Redford plays a tweedy bookworm

researcher working for a CIA department. One day he finds all his co-workers mysteriously murdered. He flees for his life, pursued by several factions within the spy agency. Dunaway is the girl who hides him. The movie is both slick and confusing in an attempt to exploit the post-Watergate syndrome. Based on James Grady's novel *Six Days of the Condor*. Also with Cliff Robertson, Max Von Sydow, John Houseman, and Walter McGinn. **Director**—Sydney Pollack. (R)
117 minutes

THE THREE FACES OF EVE (1957)
★★★

Joanne Woodward
Lee J. Cobb

Woodward stars as a troubled woman with three different personalities in this well-made drama about schizophrenia. Cobb is excellent as a psychiatrist who tries to cure her so she can lead a normal life, but Alistair Cooke almost spoils the movie with his typically pompous narration. David Wayne, Edwin Jerome, Nancy Kulp, and Vince Edwards appear in supporting roles. **Director**—Nunnally Johnson. **Academy Award**—Woodward, best actress. *91 minutes b&w*

THREE LITTLE WORDS (1950)
★★★

Fred Astaire
Red Skelton

This musical about famed songwriters Bert Kalmar and Harry Ruby is nourished by lots of good dancing, snappy

Sissy Spacek and Shelley Duvall in Robert Altman's daring drama Three Women.

songs, and pretty girls. Astaire and Skelton play the tunesmiths with charm and vitality, but the thin plot doesn't help them. In addition, the lack of dance numbers for Astaire weakens the show. The pretty girls include Vera-Ellen, Arlene Dahl, Gale Robbins, Debbie Reynolds, and Gloria DeHaven. Also with Keenan Wynn and Phil Regan. **Director**—Richard Thorpe. *102 minutes*

THE THREE MUSKETEERS (1939)
★★★

Don Ameche
The Ritz Brothers
Binnie Barnes

There are at least four versions of Alexandre Dumas's classic adventure tale and some cinema historians claim there might be as many as 10. This film with Ameche, the Ritz Brothers, Barnes, and Joseph Schildkraut in the key roles is certainly not the worst, and you might rate it tops if you can accept the idea of the Ritz Brothers as musketeers. The movie has vibrant music, and the original story remains intact with the proper dose of romance and chivalric tradition. Also with Lionel Atwill, Miles Mander, and John Carradine. **Director**—Allan Dwan.
73 minutes b&w

THREE WOMEN (1977)
★★★★

Sissy Spacek
Shelley Duvall
Janice Rule
Robert Fortier

Director Robert Altman's daring and absorbing psychological excursion of soul and character will send you away with your imagination spinning. Duvall's memorable and striking performance as the lonely and ostracized thoroughly modern Millie Lammoreaux is the cornerstone of this examination of the quality of American life. Brilliant acting and characterizations from Spacek and Fortier add to the emotion and poetry. It's one of Altman's best films, and Duvall emerges as a major actress. Also with Ruth Nelson and John Cromwell. (PG)
125 minutes

- The Thrill of It All
- Thunderball
- Thunder Bay
- A Thunder of Drums
- Thunder Road
- Ticket to Heaven
- The Tiger Makes Out
- Tight Little Island

T

THE THRILL OF IT ALL (1963)
★★★

**Doris Day
James Garner**

Day brightens this farce about a doctor's wife who becomes a star in television commercials. And Garner is able as her doctor-husband. Carl Reiner wrote the script, and anyone who has ever been angered or just mildly annoyed by the junk on TV and by the idiocy of most commercials will appreciate the brilliance of Reiner's counterattack against the tube. Also with Arlene Francis, Zasu Pitts, Edward Andrews, Elliot Reid, and Reginald Owen. **Director**—Norman Jewison.
108 minutes

THUNDERBALL (1965)
★★★

**Sean Connery
Adolfo Celi**

Connery is in top form as James Bond, and Celi is equally good as the arch-villain who almost matches secret agent 007 step for step in this fourth Bond yarn, about a SPECTRE plot to destroy the city of Miami if a huge ransom isn't paid. The plot is somewhat weak, but there are many slick gimmicks and the usual bevy of beautiful girls. The cast also includes Claudine Auger, Lois Maxwell, Luciana Paluzzi, and Bernard Lee, **Director**—Terence Young. *132 minutes*

THUNDER BAY (1953)
★★★

**James Stewart
Joanne Dru**

Off-shore drilling for oil is taken for granted now, but it wasn't always a fact of life. In this action-packed film, Stewart stars as an engineer who's convinced oil can be pumped from the sea off the coast of Louisiana. The conflicts between oil prospectors and shrimp fisherman provide the tension and action in the movie. Marcia Henderson, Dan Duryea, Gilbert Roland, Jay C. Flippen, and Anthony Moreno also appear in supporting roles. **Director**—Anthony Mann. *102 minutes*

A THUNDER OF DRUMS (1961)
★★

**Richard Boone
George Hamilton**

This western tale about a young new officer striving for acceptance from his superiors and fellow soldiers has been told many times before. And the story of the Apaches fighting the U.S. Cavalry is even more familiar. Fortunately, above-average performances by Boone, Hamilton, Charles Bronson, Slim Pickens, Richard Chamberlain, and Luana Patten keep the movie from being totally ordinary. **Director**—Joseph M. Newman. *97 minutes*

THUNDER ROAD (1958)
★★★

**Robert Mitchum
Keely Smith**

Mitchum and Smith star in this exciting story about bootleggers in Kentucky. Mitchum is close to brilliant at times, as he wisely understates his performance to accommodate the plot. Smith is good as a country girl who likes her natural man, played by Mitchum. The splendid car chases over winding back roads with a bluegrass music background are exciting. Gene Barry and Jacques Aubuchon also star. **Director**—Arthur Ripley.
92 minutes b&w

TICKET TO HEAVEN (1981)
★★★

Nick Mancuso

Nick Mancuso in Ticket to Heaven, *a docu-drama about religious cults.*

A hard-hitting docu-drama about religious cults as experienced by a young Toronto schoolteacher, played by Mancuso. He joins such a group in California and is at last rescued by friends and family. The film vividly details the young man's transformation into a near-robot through powerful indoctrination methods, and it concludes with a gut-wrenching deprogramming session. Some scenes are rather heavy-going, and the young man's background is never fully understood. Yet the story is consistently engrossing. Also stars Saul Rubinek, Meg Foster, and R. H. Thompson. **Director**—R. L. Thomas. (PG) *109 minutes*

THE TIGER MAKES OUT (1967)
★★

**Eli Wallach
Anne Jackson**

Wallach is excellent as a frustrated postman-turned-kidnapper, and Jackson is good as the suburban housewife Wallach holds captive; in fact, she seems to enjoy the experience. Charles Nelson Reilly, Elizabeth Wilson, Bob Dishy, Ruth White, and John Harkins give solid supporting performances, but quality acting can't rescue this weird endeavor. Dustin Hoffman made his film debut in this wacky and uneven comedy. Fortunately, he has appeared in much better movies since. **Director**—Arthur Hiller. *94 minutes*

TIGHT LITTLE ISLAND (1948)
★★★★

**Basil Radford
Joan Greenwood**

Fine actors keep the laughs coming in this droll British comedy about a ship with a cargo of whiskey that is wrecked off a Scottish island during World War II. The thirsty natives covet the cargo, of course, and humorous problems and situations are created as they confront the local customs agent. Radford and Greenwood star in this fast-paced delight, with Jean Cadell, Catherine Lacey, Bruce Seton, Wylie Watson, Gordon Jackson, A. E. Matthews, and Compton Mackenzie starring in supporting roles. **Director**—Alexander Mackendrick.
82 minutes b&w

T
- Till the Clouds Roll By
- Till the End of Time
- Till We Meet Again
- Time After Time
- Time Bandits
- The Time of Their Lives
- The Time of Your Life

TILL THE CLOUDS ROLL BY (1946)
★★

Robert Walker

The entertaining songs of Jerome Kern make this star-studded movie about the life of the composer bearable. Walker does a passable job playing Kern. June Allyson, Judy Garland, Van Johnson, Lena Horne, Tony Martin, Lucille Bremer, Kathryn Grayson, Frank Sinatra, Virginia O'Brien, Dinah Shore, Van Helfin, and Mary Nash are delightful in guest appearances, but too much of the movie is overly sentimental drivel. **Director**—Richard Whorf. *137 minutes*

Mary Steenburgen and Malcolm McDowell travel through time in Time After Time.

TILL THE END OF TIME (1946)
★★★

Dorothy McGuire
Guy Madison
Robert Mitchum
Bill Williams

This powerful drama about the romances and adjustment problems of three GIs returning to their hometown after service in World War II seems slightly dated now. Despite this, the excellent acting of McGuire, Madison, Williams, and Mitchum keeps the story fresh for contemporary viewers. Also with William Gargan, Jean Porter, and Tom Tully. **Director**—Edward Dmytryk. *105 minutes b&w*

TILL WE MEET AGAIN (1944)
★★

Ray Milland
Barbara Britton

Britton plays a French nun who helps Milland, an American pilot, elude the Nazis and return to the Allies in this World War II drama. The good intentions surpass the weak plot, and the acting is rather good. Also with Mona Freeman, Walter Slezak, Vladimir Sokoloff, Lucile Watson, and Konstantin Shayne. **Director**—Frank Borzage. *88 minutes b&w*

TIME AFTER TIME (1979)
★★

Malcolm McDowell
David Warner

H. G. Wells and Jack the Ripper travel via time machine to contemporary San Francisco, where the Ripper resumes his favorite pastime of carving up prostitutes. Wells's vision of a future Utopia is dashed when he realizes the Ripper's bloodthirsty behavior is small potatoes compared with violence wrought by modern technology. A clever idea, but writer-director Nicholas Meyer's execution is clumsy, and the plot has a few loopholes. McDowell, as Wells, can't seem to muster enough spirit to make the part enjoyable. Warner plays the Ripper. Also with Mary Steenburgen, Charles Cioffi, and Kent Williams. (PG) *112 minutes*

TIME BANDITS (1981)
★★★

John Cleese
Sean Connery
Shelley Duvall
Ian Holm

A lively fantasy, done in imaginative Monty Python comedy style. It mocks science-fiction history, and good-vs.-evil conflicts. An 11-year-old English lad, played by Craig Warnock, joins a band of dwarfs in a rollicking romp through time holes in space, where they meet such historical figures as Napoleon (Holm), Greek warrior Agamemnon (Connery), and Robin Hood (Cleese). The film has appeal to children of all ages, and it boasts a playful script, tasteful direction, and splendid special effects. Also with Katherine Helmond, Michael Palin, Ralph Richardson, Peter Vaughn, and David Warner. **Director**—Terry Gilliam. (PG) *116 minutes*

THE TIME OF THEIR LIVES (1946)
★★★

Bud Abbott
Lou Costello
Marjorie Reynolds

This imaginative comedy about ghosts haunting a country estate is one of the best Abbott and Costello films. Costello and Reynolds play ghosts from Revolutionary times. They complicate life for Abbott and his friends. In this movie, Bud and Lou don't play as a team. Fine supporting performances by Binnie Barnes, Jess Barker, Jess Shelton, and Gale Sondergaard help to make this a pleasant viewing experience. **Director**—Charles Barton. *82 minutes b&w*

THE TIME OF YOUR LIFE (1948)
★★★★

James Cagney
William Bendix

Super acting by Cagney and Bendix spark this film version of the prizewinning play by William Saroyan. Broderick Crawford, James Barton, Wayne Morris, Paul Draper, and Ward Bond also star in this whimsical story about a group of off-beat characters who discuss their lives and the nature of things as they sit and drink in a small saloon in San Francisco. Although there's little action, everything is well handled. **Director**—H. C. Potter. *109 minutes b&w*

Sean Connery, as King Agamemnon, gives Craig Warnock a ride in Time Bandits.

- Times Square
- A Time To Love and a Time To Die
- The Tin Drum
- Tin Pan Alley
- Titanic
- Tobacco Road
- To Be or Not To Be
- Tobruk

T

TIMES SQUARE (1980)
★★

Trini Alvarado
Robin Johnson
Tim Curry

Alvarado plays a runaway teenager whose land of Oz is the glittering sleaze of New York City's 42nd Street. She teams up with a streetwise urchin, played by Johnson, and together they perform in a strip joint—without stripping—put on a punk rock concert, and engage in various pranks. Curry plays a disc jockey. The film, aimed at teenagers, has ample energy, but the story is hardly convincing. The production seems mostly a promotion for the soundtrack, which contains some 20 New Wave musical numbers. **Director**—Alan Moyle. (R)

111 minutes

A TIME TO LOVE AND A TIME TO DIE (1958)
★★★

John Gavin
Lilo Pulver

At the time of this movie's release, it was unique because it portrayed soldiers in Nazi Germany during World War II in a human light. Gavin stars as a German officer who falls in love with a woman during a furlough. She's played by Pulver. The acting in this film version of Erich Maria Remarque's novel is above average, and there are some good scenes in the early part of the movie before the plot and script weaken. The cast also includes Remarque, Keenan Wynn, and Jock Mahoney. **Director**—Douglas Sirk. *132 minutes*

THE TIN DRUM (1980)
★★★

Angela Winkler
Mario Adorf
Daniel Olbrychski
David Bennent

Artistic, stirring, yet complex allegory based on the epic German novel by Günter Grass. Bennent, who was 12 when filming began, is extraordinary as a dwarf who refused—from the age of three—to grow anymore as a protest against the absurdities and obscenities of the adult world. Director Volker Schlondorff captures much of the anguish of the Nazi period with haunting pictorial splendor. Yet the film is as puzzling as it is moving. In German with English titles. (R) **Academy Award**—best foreign-language film. *142 minutes*

TIN PAN ALLEY (1940)
★★★

Alice Faye
Betty Grable
John Payne
Jack Oakie

There isn't an original thought in this typical musical about two struggling songwriters during and after World War I, but the music and dancing are so delightful it doesn't matter that the story is trite. Inspired performances by Faye, Grable, Payne, and Oakie are the main reason the production sparkles. The cast also includes Elisha Cook, Jr.; Esther Ralston; Allen Jenkins; Billy Gilbert; and John Loder. **Director**—Walter Lang.

95 minutes b&w

TITANIC (1953)
★★

Clifton Webb
Barbara Stanwyck
Robert Wagner

Good acting by Webb, Stanwyck, Wagner, Thelma Ritter, and Richard Basehart keep this production from sinking to the level of a mediocre documentary about the destruction of the famous ship in 1912. There are some good scenes involving personal dramas before the vessel's collision with the iceberg, but the movie should have been much better considering the ingredients. Also with Audrey Dalton, Brian Aherne, and Allyn Joslyn. **Director**—Jean Negulesco. **Academy Award**—Charles Brackett, Walter Reisch, and Richard Breen, writing (story and screenplay).

98 minutes b&w

TOBACCO ROAD (1941)
★★★

Charley Grapewin
Elizabeth Patterson

This film version of Erskine Caldwell's famed novel and play loses some of its punch in its translation to the screen, but some vivid scenes remain in this tragi-comedy about poor whites in Georgia being pushed off their land. Grapewin and Patterson star, with Dana Andrews, Marjorie Rambeau, Gene Tierney, William Tracy, Russell Simpson, and Grant Mitchell in supporting roles. **Director**—John Ford.

84 minutes b&w

TO BE OR NOT TO BE (1942)
★★★★

Jack Benny
Carole Lombard

This brilliant black comedy is about a group of actors in Poland who get involved in a plot to outwit the invading Nazis. At times, it seems to take on a life of its own under the skillful direction of Ernst Lubitsch. He gets considerable help from the excellent acting of Benny, Lombard, Lionel Atwill, Sig Rumann, Tom Dugan, Robert Stack, Stanley Ridges, and Felix Bressart. At the time of its release, some critics thought this propaganda movie was in bad taste, but now it's obvious a difficult subject was handled in a superb manner. It was Lombard's last movie. *99 minutes b&w*

TOBRUK (1967)
★★

Rock Hudson
George Peppard

Hudson and Peppard are well cast in this adventure tale about a small band of soldiers assigned to destroy German Field Marshal Erwin Rommel's fuel supply at Tobruk in North Africa during World War II. Nigel Green, Jack Watson, Liam Redmond, Guy Stockwell, Percy Herbert, and Leo Gordon appear in supporting roles. The acting is passable, and the production is well done, but there's noth-

(Continued)

T • To Catch a Thief
• To Have and Have Not
• To Hell and Back
• To Kill a Mockingbird

• Tokyo Joe
• Tom Horn
• Tom Jones

(Continued)
ing about this movie to distinguish it from dozens of others. **Director**—Arthur Hiller.   *110 minutes*

TO CATCH A THIEF (1955)
★★

Cary Grant
Grace Kelly

This story is about a jewel thief—retired on the French Riviera—who's suspected of returning to his trade. The movie has a lot of charm, but little substance and none of the verve associated with an Alfred Hitchcock production. Grant, who plays the reformed thief, and Kelly, as the woman in his life, account for much of the film's enchanting quality. The beautiful scenery is another small plus. Jessie Royce Landis, Charles Vanel, Brigitte Auber, and John Williams star in supporting roles. **Academy Award**—Robert Burks, cinematography (color).   *97 minutes*

TO HAVE AND HAVE NOT (1945)
★★★★

Humphrey Bogart
Lauren Bacall

Bogart and Bacall are marvelous in this story about a fishing boat captain who reluctantly gets involved in fighting the Nazis. Some of the brilliant dialogue has become muted because the movie has been seen so often and become an object of adoration by the Bogart cult. The movie is very loosely based on one of Ernest Hemingway's worst novels. In this case, Hollywood helped—rather than hindered—the great novelist. Walter Brennan heads

Humphrey Bogart and Lauren Bacall foil the Nazis in To Have and Have Not.

the supporting cast, which also includes Marcel Dalio, Sheldon Leonard, Dan Seymour, Dolores Moran, and Hoagy Carmichael. It was Bacall's film debut. **Director**—Howard Hawks.   *100 minutes b&w*

TO HELL AND BACK (1955)
★★

Audie Murphy

Murphy stars in this story based on his military career in World War II; he was the nation's most decorated soldier. Murphy is surprisingly good and doesn't overdo the heroics, although the temptation is always there. The battle sequences are superior to the weak story line. The above-average supporting performances of Susan Kohner, Marshall Thompson, Charles Drake, Paul Picerni, Jack Kelly, and David Janssen also fortify the film. **Director**—Jesse Hibbs.   *106 minutes*

TO KILL A MOCKINGBIRD (1962)
★★★

Gregory Peck

This movie is one of Hollywood's better efforts at filming a story dealing with racial problems in the United States. Peck stars as a lawyer in a small Southern town who successfully defends a black man accused of rape. Peck gets top-notch acting support from Mary Badham, Philip Alford, John Megna, and Brock Peters. Screenwriter Horton Foote did an excellent job of translating Harper Lee's novel to the screen, and much of the atmosphere of the time and place remains intact. **Director**—Robert Mulligan. **Academy Awards**—Peck, best actor; Foote, best screenplay (based on material from another medium). **Nominations**—best picture; Mulligan, best director; Badham, best supporting actress; Russell Harlan, cinematography (black and white).
129 minutes b&w

TOKYO JOE (1949)
★

Humphrey Bogart

Bogart stars in this dull, slow melo-

drama about an ex-nightclub owner who returns to Tokyo after World War II and becomes involved in smuggling and blackmail to protect his ex-wife and child. There are occasional moments that are reminiscent of better Bogart films, but they are few and far between. Also with Sessue Hayakawa, Florence Marly, Alexander Knox, Jerome Courtland, and Lora Lee Michel. **Director**—Stuart Heisler.
88 minutes b&w

TOM HORN (1980)
★

Steve McQueen

In Tom Horn, *Steve McQueen is hired to rid an area of cattle rustlers.*

In this film, McQueen comes off as a second-rate actor in what appears to be a second-rate horse opera. He plays a cowpoke with a license to kill. He's hired to eliminate cattle rustlers, and he does such a thorough job that his alarmed bosses frame him for murder. Just about everything is off base with the film—sloppy editing, uninspired direction, routine acting, and a lack of energy. Also with Richard Farnsworth and Linda Evans. **Director**—William Wiard. (R)   *98 minutes*

TOM JONES (1963)
★★★★

Albert Finney

Finney is splendid as the impish, free-spirited hero of this 18th-century story, based on Henry Fielding's

● Tommy ● Topaz
● Tom Sawyer ● Top Hat
● Tony Rome ● Topkapi
● Tora! Tora! Tora!

T

novel. At times, there's too much emphasis on the bawdy humor, as if the production was geared for *Playboy* keyholders. But there's so much exuberance, the joy of the story prevails, and the sexual high jinks and culinary exploits of Tom Jones are enjoyed. Finney gets royal acting support from Susannah York, Edith Evans, Diane Cilento, Joan Greenwood, Joyce Redman, Rachel Kempson, Wildfrid Lawson, and Hugh Griffith. **Director**—Tony Richardson. **Academy Awards**—best picture; Richardson, best director; John Osborne, best screenplay (based on material from another medium). **Nominations**—Finney, best actor; Griffith, best supporting actor; Cilento, Evans, Redman, best supporting actress.

131 minutes

TOMMY (1975)
★★★

Ann-Margret
Oliver Reed
Roger Daltrey

This celebrated rock opera sung by The Who is a clamorous, energetic film about a child who becomes deaf, mute, and blind, after seeing his father killed. He grows up to become pinball champion of the world and a messiah. The colorful cast also includes Elton John, Jack Nicholson, Eric Clapton, Keith Moon, and Tina Turner. **Director**—Ken Russell. (PG) **Academy Award Nomination**—Ann-Margret, best actress. *111 minutes*

TOM SAWYER (1973)
★★

Johnnie Whitaker
Jeff East
Jodie Foster

This musical version of the Mark Twain classic is too squeaky clean to have much appeal for adults, but kids might still find it enjoyable. Whitaker and East play Tom Sawyer and Huck Finn, respectively. Although they haven't captured the magic of the characters, Foster plays Becky Thatcher with the gusto Twain seems to have had in mind. Celeste Holm (Aunt Polly) and Warren Oates (Muff Potter) appear in supporting roles.

Filmed on location in Missouri. **Director**—Don Taylor. (G) *102 minutes*

TONY ROME (1967)
★★★

Frank Sinatra

This detective tale is about Tony Rome, a Miami private eye who tries to solve a jewel robbery and the murder of a beautiful woman. In some ways, it's reminiscent of the better 1940s films of the genre, but Sinatra lacks the grace of the Bogey-type detective. Nonetheless, there's some appeal to the tough dialogue, and there's enough sex and action to please most fans. The cast also includes Simon Oakland, Sue Lyon, Jill St. John, Richard Conte, Lloyd Gough, Lloyd Bochner, Jeffrey Lynn, and Gena Rowlands. **Director**—Gordon Douglas. *110 minutes*

TOPAZ (1969)
★★

Frederick Stafford
John Forsythe

This espionage adventure about a French intelligence agent who works with an American agent because of Russian involvement in Cuba lacks any sparkling performances and seldom seems like a film directed by Alfred Hitchcock. Stafford plays the French spy, and Forsythe is the U.S. agent. John Vernon, Michel Piccoli, Philippe Noiret, Karin Dor, Roscoe Lee Browne, and Dany Robin give competent supporting performances in this rather routine enterprise, based on the Leon Uris novel. (PG)

124 minutes

TOP HAT (1935)
★★★★

Fred Astaire
Ginger Rogers

Astaire and Rogers are magnificent in this musical, and the superficial aspects of the mistaken-identity plot don't hamper the brilliance of the production one bit, as Fred pursues the love of his life from England to Italy. The performances of Edward Everett Horton, Erik Rhodes, Helen Brod-

erick, and Eric Blore add to this film's charm and vibrancy. Irving Berlin songs include "Top Hat, White Tie and Tails" and "Cheek to Cheek." It's top-notch. **Director**—Mark Sandrich. **Academy Award Nomination**—best picture. *107 minutes b&w*

TOPKAPI (1964)
★★★

Melina Mecouri
Maximilian Schell
Peter Ustinov
Robert Morley

At moments when this jewel theft caper starts to take itself too seriously, the comic skills of Ustinov and Morley come to the rescue. The movie, based on Eric Ambler's novel *The Light of Day*, is about an international gang after jewels in the Topkapi Museum in Istanbul. Some of the richness of the story can be traced to Ambler. For the rest, credit excellent acting by Ustinov, Morley, Mercouri, Schell, and Akim Tamiroff. **Director**—Jules Dassin. **Academy Award**—Ustinov, best supporting actor. *119 minutes*

TORA! TORA! TORA! (1970)
★★★

Martin Balsam
Jason Robards, Jr.
Joseph Cotten

At the time of its release, some jokesters quipped that this movie about the attack on Pearl Harbor cost more than the actual military operation; the cost of the movie was estimated at about $25 million. Aside from the expense, this is an above-average war movie, but many cheaper ones have been much better. The film is at its best when it documents—from both sides—historical events, such as mistakes by those in charge, and reproduces the horrors of the infamous attack. Also with James Whitmore, E. G. Marshall, Soh Yamamura, Edward Andrews, Leon Ames, and Takahiro Tamura. **Directors**—Richard Fleischer, Ray Kellogg, Toshio Masuda, and Kinji Fukasaku. (G) **Academy Award Nomination**—Charles F. Wheeler, Osami Furuya, Sinsaku Himeda, and Masamichi Satoh, cinematography. *144 minutes*

T
- Torn Curtain
- Torpedo Run
- Torrid Zone
- Tortilla Flat
- To Sir, With Love
- Touched By Love
- A Touch of Class
- The Towering Inferno

TORN CURTAIN (1966)
★★

Paul Newman
Julie Andrews

This was director Alfred Hitchcock's 50th film, but the story of an American science professor who becomes involved with espionage and missions in East Germany falls flat and isn't worthy of the master of suspense. Newman, who plays the professor, is competent in his role, and Andrews sparkles as his secretary and lover. Also with Lila Kedrova, Ludwig Donath, Wolfgang Kieling, Tamara Toumanova, and David Opatoshu.

128 minutes

TORPEDO RUN (1958)
★★★

Glenn Ford
Ernest Borgnine

Ford and Borgnine star in this well-made submarine adventure. Ford plays a sub commander who sinks a ship carrying members of his own family and must live with the knowledge. The action sequences are better than the story, but there's enough of interest to make it worthwhile viewing for fans of such movies. Dean Jones and Diane Brewster appear in supporting roles. **Director**—Joseph Pevney. *98 minutes*

TORRID ZONE (1940)
★★★

James Cagney
Pat O'Brien
Ann Sheridan

Cagney, O'Brien, and Sheridan are at their ripsnorting best in this period piece about action and romance on a banana plantation in Central America. Cagney and O'Brien are rivals for Sheridan's affections. Sharp dialogue hides some of the holes in the plot and helps the trio brighten the movie. Also with George Tobias, George Reeves, Helen Vinson, Jerome Cowan, and Andy Devine. **Director**—William Keighley. *88 minutes b&w*

TORTILLA FLAT (1942)
★★★

Spencer Tracy
Hedy Lamarr
John Garfield
Frank Morgan

Dog-lover Frank Morgan in Tortilla Flat, *a film based on John Steinbeck's novel.*

This uneven film version of John Steinbeck's novel is too philosophical and slow-moving to be a great film, but outstanding performances by Tracy, Garfield, and Morgan make the movie worth viewing. The story concerns the joys and sorrows of a group of poor Mexicans in a California fishing community. The three stars get excellent support from Lamarr, Akim Tamiroff, Connie Gilchrist, Henry O'Neill, Sheldon Leonard, John Qualen, and Donald Meek. **Director**—Victor Fleming. **Academy Award Nomination**—Morgan, best supporting actor. *106 minutes b&w*

TO SIR, WITH LOVE (1967)
★★★

Sidney Poitier

Poitier is charming as a West Indian schoolteacher who's assigned to instruct tough white pupils in London's rough East End. The story borders on mush at times, as Poitier copes with his students, but his acting and good performances by Judy Geeson, Suzy Kendall, Christian Roberts, Patricia Routledge, and Faith Brook prevent the movie from becoming sentimental trash. **Director**—James Clavell. *105 minutes*

TOUCHED BY LOVE (1980)
★★

Diane Lane
Deborah Raffin

A warm, sympathetic but bland account of a young cerebral palsy victim, played by Lane, who's helped by a compassionate nurse, played by Raffin. Part of the rehabilitation involves some remarkable pen-pal correspondence between the youngster and Elvis Presley. The production is enhanced with breathtaking scenes at the residence school near Calgary, Alberta, and some enthusiastic performances from the children there. But despite good intentions, the film is rather undramatic. **Director**—Gus Trikonis. (PG) *95 minutes*

A TOUCH OF CLASS (1973)
★★★

Glenda Jackson
George Segal

Without the classy performances of Jackson and Segal, this production would seem more like a touch of trash. The story is about an American insurance broker, played by Segal, who has an affair with Jackson, a British dress designer. There isn't much more to this romantic comedy than that, and even with the keen acting of the twosome, the tale falters at times. Paul Sorvino and Hildegard Neil also sparkle in supporting roles. **Director**—Melvin Frank. (PG) **Academy Award**—Jackson, best actress. **Nominations**—best picture; Frank and Jack Rose, best story and screenplay (based on factual material not previously published). *105 minutes*

THE TOWERING INFERNO
(1974)
★★

Paul Newman
Steve McQueen
William Holden

This tasteless production about a raging fire at the world's tallest building could be defended as a fire-prevention movie if it weren't so well done. The special effects are brilliant, and the all-

- Tower of London (1939)
- Tower of London (1962)
- Toys in the Attic
- The Train
- The Train Robbers
- Trapeze
- Treasure Island

T

star cast performs professionally. But alas, the point of the film seems to be about gruesome ways of dying in a fire. The all-star cast also includes Fred Astaire, Susan Blakely, O. J. Simpson, Robert Wagner, Richard Chamberlain, Robert Vaughn, and Jennifer Jones. **Directors**—John Guillermin and Irwin Allen. (PG) **Academy Award**—Fred Koenekamp and Joseph Biroc, cinematography. **Nomination**—best picture; Astaire, best supporting actor.

165 minutes

TOWER OF LONDON (1939)
★★

**Basil Rathbone
Boris Karloff**

Rathbone and Karloff—those horror movie regulars—are present and in fine form in this movie, which distorts British history to give this view to the return to the throne of an exiled king—apparently Richard III. Some of the scenes are quite good for those who care about such things, and the acting is fine. Also with Nan Grey, Barbara O'Neill, Ian Hunter, Vincent Price, and Leo G. Carroll. **Director**—Rowland V. Lee. *92 minutes b&w*

TOWER OF LONDON (1962)
★

Vincent Price

There are no towering performances in this flat remake of the 1939 movie, about a wicked king trying to return to power. Price, who played the Duke of Clarence in the earlier film, does a nice job of portraying Richard III in this effort. But aside from Price and the vivid addition of ghostly visions, there's little to warrant the price of admission. The cast also includes Joan Freeman, Robert Brown, Michael Pate, Bruce Gordon, Sara Salby, and Justice Eatson. **Director**—Roger Corman. *79 minutes b&w*

TOYS IN THE ATTIC (1963)
★

**Geraldine Page
Wendy Hiller
Dean Martin**

Lillian Hellman's stimulating and provocative play becomes as uninteresting as a dull soap opera in this film treatment. Page and Hiller star as two spinster sisters who must deal with their roguish brother when he brings home his childlike bride. Martin is miscast as the brother, but Gene Tierney, Larry Gates, Yvette Mimieux, and Nan Martin are superior to the material they have to work with. **Director**—George Roy Hill.

90 minutes b&w

THE TRAIN (1965)
★★★★

**Burt Lancaster
Paul Scofield
Michel Simon**

This story about the efforts of the French Resistance to prevent the Nazis from removing French art treasures by train in 1944 is basically a simple story. Under John Frankenheimer's deft direction, there isn't a wasted moment, as he creates supreme tension up to the conclusion in a railroad yard. Lancaster plays a railroad boss, Scofield is a German officer, and Simon is a train engineer. Also with Albert Remy, Wolfgang Preiss, Jeanne Moreau, and Suzanne Flon. **Academy Award Nomination**—Franklin Coen and Frank Davis, best story and screenplay (written directly for the screen). *113 minutes b&w*

THE TRAIN ROBBERS (1973)
★

**John Wayne
Ann-Margret**

Wayne and Ann-Margret head the cast of this dismal western in which the Duke is enlisted to help a widow recover gold stolen by her late husband. Ann-Margret plays the widow. They should have gotten on the train and ridden off the set rather than tarnish their acting reputations with this worthless enterprise. There's some action, but not enough to interest fans of blazing guns and ambushes. Rod Taylor, Ben Johnson, Christopher George, Ricardo Montalban, and Bobby Vinton appear in supporting roles. **Director**—Burt Kennedy. (PG) *92 minutes*

TRAPEZE (1956)
★★★

**Burt Lancaster
Tony Curtis
Gina Lollobrigida**

Burt Lancaster and Tony Curtis in Trapeze, *a movie about circus life.*

Lancaster, Curtis, and Lollobrigida star in this thoughtful, well-made circus movie that's long on atmosphere, but short on plot. Lancaster and Curtis portray old and young aerialists, respectively, while Lollobrigida supplies some charm and lots of curves. The cast also includes Katy Jurado, Sidney James, Albert Evans, Thomas Gomez, and John Puleo. **Director**—Carol Reed. *105 minutes*

TREASURE ISLAND (1950)
★★★

**Robert Newton
Bobby Driscoll**

Newton is splendid as Long John Silver, and Driscoll is competent as Jim Hawkins, in this Walt Disney version of the Robert Louis Stevenson tale, about the discovery of a pirate map that leads to a search for buried treasure. There's nothing really wrong with this movie, and kids are sure to enjoy it; but it could have been much better if there was more attention to the detail of the original story and fewer glossy theatrics. Basil Sydney, Denis O'Dea, Ralph Truman, Walter Fitzgerald, Finlay Currie, and Geoffrey Wilkinson appear in supporting roles. **Director**—Byron Haskin. (G) *96 minutes*

T • Treasure of Matecumbe
• The Treasure of the Sierra Madre
• A Tree Grows in Brooklyn
• The Trials of Oscar Wilde
• Tribute
• The Trouble With Angels
• True Confessions

TREASURE OF MATECUMBE
(1976)
★★★

Robert Foxworth
Joan Hackett
Peter Ustinov

A formula Walt Disney action adventure: Two appealing youngsters search for a buried chest and outsmart a lot of unpleasant grownups along the way. Johnny Doran and Billy Attmore play the spunky lads. The film is a cut above some recent children-oriented movies, thanks to a sturdy plot and an excellent cast. There are sparkling performances by Hackett as a runaway bride-to-be and by Ustinov as a rotund medicine man. The film is a bit long, but it packs plenty of fun. **Director**—Vincent McEveety. (G)   *117 minutes*

THE TREASURE OF THE SIERRA MADRE (1948)
★★★★

Humphrey Bogart
Walter Huston
Tim Holt

This is one of those rare Hollywood movies that tells a vivid story and provides a message. The objective is reached because of the excellent direction and screenwriting of John Huston, the vitality of the original novel by the mysterious B. Traven, the intense and realistic mood created by the superb photography of Ted McCord, and the stunning acting. Bogart, Walter Huston, and Holt star as three prospectors who find gold and are then done in by greed. Barton MacLane, Bruce Bennett, and Alfonso Bedoya star in supporting roles. **Academy Awards**—John Huston, best director; Walter Huston, best supporting actor; John Huston, writing (screenplay). **Nomination**—best picture.   *126 minutes b&w*

A TREE GROWS IN BROOKLYN
(1945)
★★★★

Peggy Ann Garner
James Dunn

Garner and Dunn star in this sensitive story about a troubled Irish family in Brooklyn tenements at the turn of the century. Dunn plays an alcoholic father, and Garner portrays a young lady trying to mature despite her dismal surroundings. Joan Blondell, Lloyd Nolan, Dorothy McGuire, James Gleason, Charles Halton, Ted Donaldson, Ruth Nelson, and John Alexander provide fine supporting performances in this excellently directed film. **Director**—Elia Kazan. **Academy Award**—Dunn, best supporting actor. **Special Academy Award**—Garner, outstanding child actress. **Nomination**—Frank Davis and Tess Slesinger, writing (screenplay).   *128 minutes b&w*

THE TRIALS OF OSCAR WILDE
(1960)
★★

Peter Finch
James Mason
Nigel Patrick
John Fraser

Excellent acting performances by Finch, Mason, Patrick, and Fraser sustain this flat account of the eccentric playwright's libel trial and subsequent prosecution for sodomy. Finch's portrayal of Wilde is a full and vivid characterization, although some might claim it puts him in too favorable a light. Yvonne Mitchell, Lionel Jeffries, James Booth, Maxine Audley, and Emrys Jones appear in supporting roles. **Director**—Ken Hughes.
123 minutes

TRIBUTE (1980)
★★

Jack Lemmon
Robby Benson

Bernard Slade's play, about a strained relationship between father and son, doesn't transfer to the screen. This emotionally unrewarding film provides a tour-de-force role for Lemmon, who mugs away as the clownish father dying of cancer. But what is supposed to be drama is merely a string of self-pitying temper tantrums. Benson, as the priggish and obnoxious son, performs mechanically and unevenly. Also with Lee Remick. **Director**—Bob Clark. (PG) **Academy Award Nomination**—Lemmon, best actor.
123 minutes

In Tribute, Robby Benson (left) plays the son of Jack Lemmon, who's dying.

THE TROUBLE WITH ANGELS
(1966)
★★

Rosalind Russell
Hayley Mills
June Harding

Mills and Harding give enthusiastic performances in this mild comedy about the fun and pranks that occur at a convent school where Russell is the Mother Superior in charge. This is an inoffensive movie, but it's also almost totally unappealing. Mary Wickes, Margalo Gillmore, Binnie Barnes, Gypsy Rose Lee, and Marge Redmond appear in supporting roles. **Director**—Ida Lupino.   *112 minutes*

TRUE CONFESSIONS (1981)
★★★★

Robert De Niro
Robert Duvall

De Niro and Duvall brilliantly play two brothers—De Niro as a priest, Duvall as a police detective—brought into conflict over a prostitute's murder. The grisly crime leads to the core of this engrossing film, based on John

Robert De Niro hears Robert Duvall's confession in True Confessions.

- True Grit
- The Tunnel of Love
- The Turning Point
- Twelve Angry Men
- Twelve O'Clock High
- 20,000 Leagues Under the Sea
- Twilight's Last Gleaming

T

Gregory Dunne's novel; it explores hyprocrisy among high church officials. Acting at all levels is superb, and the 1940s settings are rich with atmosphere. It's a tough, intriguing film, masterfully directed by Ula Grosbard. Also with Charles Durning, Ed Flanders, and Burgess Meredith. (R)

110 minutes

TRUE GRIT (1969)
★★★★

John Wayne
Kim Darby

Although Wayne turned in many top-drawer performances, this movie was a turning point in his career because he got wider recognition than praise from fans of westerns and war movies by winning an Academy Award. Wayne plays Rooster Cogburn, a one-eyed, tough old marshal, who responds to the plea of a young girl, played by Darby, who wants to avenge the slaying of her father. Dennis Hopper, Robert Duvall, Jeff Corey, Strother Martin, and Jeremy Slate provide polished supporting performances. The use of pop singer Glen Campbell is the movie's only major distraction. **Director**—Henry Hathaway. (G) **Academy Award**—Wayne, best actor. *128 minutes*

THE TUNNEL OF LOVE (1958)
★★

Richard Widmark
Doris Day

Widmark and Day provide winsome performances in this somewhat vulgar movie that lacks much winning material. They portray a couple coping with insensitive bureaucrats as they endeavor to adopt a baby. Some bright dialogue and solid performances by Gig Young, Gia Scala, Elizabeth Wilson, and Elizabeth Fraser enhance the movie. **Director**—Gene Kelly.

98 minutes b&w

THE TURNING POINT (1977)
★★

Anne Bancroft
Shirley MacLaine

Bancroft and MacLaine play old rivals

Shirley MacLaine and Anne Bancroft portray old rivals in The Turning Point.

who are reunited in this backstage ballet drama, and their roles seem extracted from daytime TV soap operas. In addition, the script is rather mechanical; only the dance scenes perk up portions of the film. The young Russian-born dancer Mikhail Baryshnikov steals a few scenes with his acting as well as his ballet performance. Also with Tom Skerritt, Martha Scott, and Leslie Browne, **Director**—Herbert Ross. (PG) **Academy Award Nomination**—best picture; Ross, best director; Bancroft, MacLaine, best actress; Baryshnikov, best supporting actor; Browne, best supporting actress; Arthur Laurents, best original screenplay. *119 minutes*

TWELVE ANGRY MEN (1957)
★★★★

Henry Fonda
Lee J. Cobb
E. G. Marshall
Jack Warden

A better title might have been *One Angry Man* because Fonda plays a conscientious and moral juror at the trial of a teenager accused of killing his father, and he prevails on eleven other jurors not to rush to judgment. The premise of the movie that a lawyer would be careless in the defense of a client borders on the preposterous, but it does set the stage for a superb drama in which Fonda defends the youth. The sensational cast also includes Ed Begley, Martin Balsam, Jack Klugman, Edward Binns, Joseph Sweeney, Robert Webber, George Voskovec, and John Fiedler. **Director**—Sidney Lumet. **Academy Award Nominations**—best picture; Lumet, best director; Reginald Rose, best screenplay (based on material from another medium). *95 minutes b&w*

TWELVE O'CLOCK HIGH (1949)
★★★★

Gregory Peck
Dean Jagger

Peck and Jagger are at the top of their acting skills in this story about the stress of leading U.S. fliers into combat during World War II. Peck plays the commander of a bomber unit based in England. All of the characterizations are excellent and far superior to the two-dimensional portraits seen in most war films. Hugh Marlowe, Gary Merrill, Millard Mitchell, John Kellogg, Paul Stewart, and Robert Arthur are among the fine supporting actors. **Director**—Henry King. **Academy Award**—Jagger, best supporting actor. **Nominations**—best picture; Peck, best actor. *132 minutes b&w*

20,000 LEAGUES UNDER THE SEA (1954)
★★★

Kirk Douglas
James Mason
Paul Lukas

The universe of novelist Jules Verne springs to life in this exciting Walt Disney production of life aboard a futuristic submarine. Douglas, Peter Lorre, and Paul Lukas get aboard Captain Nemo's sub for scintillating adventures. Nemo is played by Mason. All involved perform admirably as befits this cosmic tale. Carleton Young, Ted De Corsia, and Robert J. Wilke appear in supporting roles. **Director**—Richard Fleischer. (G)

122 minutes

TWILIGHT'S LAST GLEAMING (1977)
★★★

Burt Lancaster
Richard Widmark
Charles Durning

This political suspense-thriller stars Lancaster as a disgruntled U.S Air Force general who blackmails the government by threatening to unleash nuclear missiles on Russia. Director Robert Aldrich forcefully fashions *(Continued)*

(Continued)

ample suspense and taut confrontations through his use of split-screen sequences. Lancaster and other Hollywood elder statesmen, such as Melvyn Douglas, Joseph Cotten, and Widmark, move the action along energetically. Durning plays the President. The compelling screenplay stirs the conscience about the Vietnam War era, but there are many lapses of credibility. Also with Paul Winfield, Richard Jaeckel, Burt Young, and Roscoe Lee Browne. (R)   *146 minutes*

Paul Winfield and Burt Lancaster in the suspense-thriller Twilight's Last Gleaming.

TWO-MINUTE WARNING
(1976)
★★

Charlton Heston
John Cassavetes

A sniper, perched above the scoreboard of the Los Angeles Coliseum, opens fire on fans watching a championship football game. This gory action sequence takes place during the last 15 minutes of the movie. The rest is filled with tedious slice-of-life vignettes about selected spectators, who are eventually killed or injured. It's much in the familiar disaster genre of *The Towering Inferno*, *The Hindenburg*, and so on. It also resembles a patchwork affair of TV dramas. The large cast also includes Martin Balsam, Beau Bridges, David Janssen, Jack Klugman, and Gena Rowlands. **Director**—Larry Peerce. (R)

115 minutes

2001: A SPACE ODYSSEY (1968)
★★★

Keir Dullea
William Sylvester
Gary Lockwood

Much of this production about a jour-

GLENDA JACKSON

Glenda Jackson was born in Cheshire, England, in 1936, the daughter of a construction worker. At 16, she quit high school to become an actress, and with considerable determination, she supported herself as a waitress and receptionist between jobs in the theater.

Jackson studied at the Royal Academy of Dramatic Art and found work with the Royal Shakespeare Company in 1963. She gained significant attention with her stage role of Charlotte Corday in Marat/Sade, *a part she was to repeat on film.*

In 1963, a minor part in This Sporting Life *launched her movie career. She went on to perform in leading roles in two Ken Russell films,* Women in Love *(1969) and* The Music Lovers *(1970). She won the Oscar for her performance in* Women in Love.

Although Jackson initially was cast as an abrasive and uptight woman, her mannerisms didn't prevent her from broadening her range, and she excelled in her first comedy, A Touch of Class (1973), for which she received her second Academy Award.

Jackson's other movies include Sunday, Bloody Sunday *(1971),* Mary, Queen of Scots *(1971),* House Calls *(1978),* Lost and Found *(1979), and* Hopscotch *(1980).*

ney into another realm of thought and time is masterful. There are so many special effects and visual tricks that, at times, it seems that actors aren't necessary, but Dullea and Lockwood are fine as two astronauts traveling to Jupiter with a computer called HAL. Despite the many fascinating scenes, there are many faults like obscure symbolism. The movie and director Stanley Kubrick might have made it into outer space, but somewhere along the way the production lost some of its coherence and meaning. Also with Daniel Richter. (G) **Academy Award Nominations**—Kubrick, best director; Kubrick and Arthur C. Clarke, best story and screenplay (written directly for the screen).   *140 minutes*

In 2001: A Space Odyssey, Keir Dullea is an astronaut who takes an unusual journey.

TWO WEEKS IN ANOTHER TOWN (1962)
★★

Kirk Douglas

Douglas stars in this solid melodrama as a former alcoholic trying to make a comeback in the film industry. The movie is based on Irwin Shaw's best-selling novel. Douglas does his best to capture the better aspects of the book, but he's only successful some of the time. Also with Edward G. Robinson, Cyd Charisse, Claire Trevor, George Hamilton, Constance Ford, Dalia Lavi, George Macready, and Rosanna Schiaffino. **Director**—Vincente Minnelli.   *107 minutes*

TWO YEARS BEFORE THE MAST (1946)
★★

Alan Ladd
Brian Donlevy

When Richard Henry Dana's book *Two Years Before the Mast* was published, it caused a stir because it exposed the many sordid conditions under which

• Typhoon
• The Ugly American
• Unchained
• The Undefeated
• Undercovers Hero
• Undercurrent
• Under Ten Flags
• Under the Rainbow

T·U

sailors were forced to work during the 19th century. The film, however, doesn't attempt to be an exposé, and regrettably it fails to capture much of the book's excitement. Donlevy plays Dana, Ladd is a sailor, and Howard da Silva plays the role of an oppressive captain. Also with William Bendix and Barry Fitzgerald. **Director**—John Farrow. *98 minutes b&w*

TYPHOON (1940)
★★

Dorothy Lamour

Beautiful Lamour does her thing with a sarong—although that wasn't the way such things were said at the time of the film's release—in this romantic tale. In the film, sailors discover her on an island and learn that she has been there since childhood; the story builds from there. Lynne Overman, J. Carrol Naish, Robert Preston, Frank Reicher, and Jack Carson handle the supporting roles. **Director**—Louis King. *70 minutes*

U

THE UGLY AMERICAN (1963)
★★

Marlon Brando

By Hollywood standards, this movie was a sincere effort to deal with America's confrontation with communism in Southeast Asia. Unfortunately, the story bogs down. Brando never shines as the U.S Ambassador who fumbles his assignment and causes new problems in an Asian country despite his good intentions. Eiji Okada, Arthur Hill, Sandra Church, Jocelyn Brando, and Pat Hingle appear in supporting roles. **Director**—George H. Englund. *120 minutes*

UNCHAINED (1955)
★★

Chester Morris
Elroy Hirsch

Life on a prison farm in California is presented in vivid, realistic terms in this very untypical film. Morris and Hirsch star in this movie, based on a true story about a warden administrator who runs a prison without bars. Also with Barbara Hale, Jerry Paris, Peggy Knudsen, and Johnny Johnston. **Director**—Hall Bartlett. *75 minutes b&w*

THE UNDEFEATED (1969)
★★

John Wayne
Rock Hudson

In The Undefeated, *Rock Hudson and John Wayne are former Civil War enemies who join forces against Mexican marauders.*

Wayne plays an ex-Union colonel in the horse-trading business who confronts Hudson, a former Confederate colonel. They mend their past differences just in time to fight together against Mexican marauders in this mediocre Civil War-era western. Tony Aguilar, Lee Meriwether, Bruce Cabot, Roman Gabriel, Merlin Olsen, and Ben Johnson are ordinary in supporting roles. **Director**—Andrew V. McLaglen. (G) *119 minutes*

UNDERCOVERS HERO (1975)
★★

Peter Sellers

Sellers, who often played multiple roles, has six parts in this British sex farce, set in a Paris bordello during the Nazi occupation in World War II. The talented Sellers—who impersonates Hitler, a French general, a British intelligence agent, and so on—is amusing indeed. However, the story itself is lamebrained and incoherent. With Lila Kedrova, Curt Jurgens, and Beatrice Romand. **Director**—Roy Boulting. (R) *95 minutes*

UNDERCURRENT (1946)
★★

Katharine Hepburn
Robert Taylor
Robert Mitchum

Hepburn, Taylor, and Mitchum give solid performances in this movie about a woman who gradually discovers that her husband is an evil man. The story drags, however, and isn't very well told. Modern viewers might give it more of a feminist interpretation, although it won't make this seem a better movie. Also with Edmund Gwenn, Marjorie Main, Dan Tobin, and Jayne Meadows. **Director**—Vincente Minnelli. *116 minutes b&w*

UNDER TEN FLAGS (1960)
★★

Van Heflin

This story about a kindly captain of a German attack ship during World War II who keeps escaping the British is one of those rare war movies told from the enemy point of view. Despite the different perspective, it's still just an average war story. Heflin plays the German raider captain. Charles Laughton, Mylene Demongeot, and John Ericson appear in supporting roles. **Director**—Duilio Coletti and Silvio Narizzano. *92 minutes b&w*

UNDER THE RAINBOW (1981)
★

Chevy Chase
Carrie Fisher

Chase and Fisher star in this meandering, unworkable comedy, which
(Continued)

Carrie Fisher and Chevy Chase are up to their hips in Munchkins in Under the Rainbow.

U
- Under the Yum Yum Tree
- Unfinished Business
- The Unforgiven
- Unholy Partners
- The Uninvited
- Union Station
- An Unmaried Woman

(Continued)

mainly deals with the problems caused by the scores of midgets hired as Munchkins for the 1939 *Wizard of Oz* movie. Involved with the various cornball incidents are Japanese and German spies, touring Japanese photographers, and a duke and duchess threatened with assassination. There seems to be a lot going on, but there's nothing here that produces any solid laughs. **Director**—Steve Rash. (PG)

98 minutes

UNDER THE YUM YUM TREE
(1963)
★

Jack Lemmon
Carol Lynley
Dean Jones

The comic talents of Lemmon are wasted in this tasteless tale about a lecherous landlord who has designs on a cute coed tenant, played by Lynley. She, in turn, is involved with her fiancé, played by Jones. If you get involved in this silly, tedious story, don't say you haven't been warned. Paul Lynde, Robert Lansing, Imogene Coca, and Edie Adams appear in supporting roles. **Director**—David Swift.

110 minutes

UNFINISHED BUSINESS (1941)
★★

Irene Dunne
Robert Montgomery

Dunne and Montgomery star in this romantic comedy about a small-town girl's search for love and adventure in the big city. This silly story has been told many times before, and this version lacks energy and forcefulness. Eugene Pallette, Preston Foster, Esther Dale, Dick Foran, Samuel S. Hinds, and June Clyde star in supporting roles. **Director**—Gregory La Cava.

95 minutes b&w

THE UNFORGIVEN (1960)
★★

Burt Lancaster
Audrey Hepburn

Lancaster and Hepburn star in this uneven western drama with loads of conflicting elements. Charles Bickford, Lillian Gish, Lancaster, and Hepburn are all fine actors, but only Bickford and Gish seem at home in a western setting; the other two seem miscast. John Huston is a fine director, and there are some vivid scenes, including the Indian attack climax. At other points in the film, it seems that Huston was absent and that a committee of directors took over for him. And so it goes in this story of racism. It's about a woman living with whites, who's suspected of being an Indian. Hepburn is the woman. You'll have to decide if the good parts are worth savoring.

125 minutes

UNHOLY PARTNERS (1941)
★★

Edward G. Robinson
Edward Arnold

Robinson and Arnold sparkle in this story about the editor of a scandal sheet who accepts financial aid from a gangster. Robinson plays the newspaperman, and Arnold is the gangster. This unlikely premise mars the movie, but does provide action and conflict when the editor decides to expose the hoodlum and his rackets. Laraine Day and Marsha Hunt also star, with Don Beddoe, Marcel Dalio, Walter Kingsford, William T. Orr, and Charles Dingle in supporting performances. **Director**—Mervyn Le Roy.

94 minutes b&w

THE UNINVITED (1944)
★★★

Ray Milland
Ruth Hussey
Gail Russell

If you don't like to be scared out of your wits, you might find this movie ghastly. But fans of chillers will find it one of the best in cinema history. Milland, Hussey, and Russell play their parts superbly, in this story about a haunted house and evil spirits. Also with Donald Crisp, Alan Napier, Cornelia Otis Skinner, Dorothy Stickney, and Barbara Everest. **Director**—Lewis Allen. **Academy Award Nomination**—Charles Lang, cinematography (black and white).

98 minutes b&w

UNION STATION (1950)
★★★

William Holden
Barry Fitzgerald

Real locations and loads of action enliven this suspense film starring Holden and Fitzgerald. It's about the kidnapping of a blind girl, played by Allene Roberts. The title refers to the crowded train station that the kidnappers decide to use as the ransom collection point. Also with Lyle Bettger, Nancy Olson, Robert Preston, and Jan Sterling. **Director**—Rudolph Maté.

80 minutes b&w

AN UNMARRIED WOMAN
(1978)
★★★★

Jill Clayburgh

Jill Clayburgh and Alan Bates in the bittersweet satire An Unmarried Woman.

This bittersweet satire, concerning a woman's struggle to piece her life together after her husband walks out, has a lot going for it—sophistication, wit, sensitivity, polished dialogue, superb acting, and Clayburgh in the title role. Clayburgh gives a triumphant performance. Writer-director Paul Mazursky skillfully explores America's rootless affluent society in this uncompromising film. Also stars Alan Bates, Michael Murphy, Lisa Lucas, Cliff Gorman, Pat Quinn, and Kelly Bishop. (R) **Academy Award Nominations**—best picture; Clayburgh, best actress; Mazursky, best original screenplay.

124 minutes

- The Unsinkable Molly Brown
- Untamed
- Up in Arms
- Up in Smoke
- Up the Academy
- Up the Down Staircase
- Uptown Saturday Night
- Urban Cowboy

U

THE UNSINKABLE MOLLY BROWN (1964)
★★★

**Debbie Reynolds
Harve Presnell**

Reynolds is delightful in this lively comedy-musical about a country girl who rises to social prominence and wealth in Denver. She plays the title role and gets able support from Presnell, who portrays her gold-prospecting husband. The production is well-staged, and the music of Meredith Wilson is above average although unsensational. Ed Begley, Martita Hunt, Jack Kruschen, and Hermione Baddeley also star. **Director**—Charles Walters. **Academy Award Nominations**—Reynolds, best actress; Daniel L. Fapp, cinematography (color). *128 minutes*

UNTAMED (1955)
★★

**Tyrone Power
Susan Hayward**

Power woos Hayward in this romantic adventure about a Boer journey through the hostile South African countryside and close encounters with Zulu warriors. The plot gets tedious at times and the romance too complicated, but solid acting will eventually tame the restless viewer. Richard Egan, John Justin, Albert Evans, Rita Moreno, Agnes Moorehead, and Henry O'Neill are among the supporting actors. **Director**—Henry King. *110 minutes*

UP IN ARMS (1944)
★★

Danny Kaye

This musical about a neurotic Army recruit in World War II and his misadventures made Kaye a film star. As an actor, he has done much better since, but the movie is enjoyable, and the performances of Dinah Shore, Dana Andrews, Lyle Talbot, Constance Dowling, Virginia Mayo, Elisha Cook, Jr., and Margaret Dumont enrich the production. **Director**—Elliott Nugent. *106 minutes*

UP IN SMOKE (1978)
★★

**Cheech Marin
Tommy Chong**

Cheech and Chong make their debut in this uneven comedy based on the rock and marijuana scene. The story is no more than a concoction of the boys' familiar routines of bathroom humor and slapstick sketches, and just about everyone on screen gets high on grass. For many in the audience, it could be a low. Also with Stacy Keach, Tom Skerritt, Edie Adams, and Strother Martin. **Director**—Lou Adler. (R) *86 minutes*

UP THE ACADEMY (1980)
★★

**Ron Leibman
Wendell Brown**

This uneven comedy, presented by *Mad* magazine, lampoons the military, blacks, women, Arabs, and other vulnerable targets. The so-so screenplay concerns the misadventures of four students at the unlikely Sheldon R. Weinberg Military Academy. The students tangle with Major Liceman, the school's scowling disciplinarian played with relish by Leibman. When he's on the screen, the film perks up nicely; otherwise, it stumbles along with a "What, me worry?" attitude. **Director**—Robert Downey. (R) *96 minutes*

UP THE DOWN STAIRCASE (1967)
★★★

Sandy Dennis

Dennis is sensational as a beleaguered schoolteacher in the New York City school system who tries to overcome the negativism of administrators while solving the problems of her high school students. Although there are weak parts in which there is a shrill emphasis on comedy, it's still one of the best motion pictures about teaching. Also with Ellen O'Mara, Jean Stapleton, Patrick Bedford, Eileen Heckart, Ruth White, Roy Poole, and Sorrel Booke. **Director**—Robert Mulligan. *124 minutes*

UPTOWN SATURDAY NIGHT (1974)
★★★

**Sidney Poitier
Bill Cosby**

Poitier and Cosby star in this uninhibited comedy about their efforts to recover stolen money and a winning lottery ticket before their wives discover that the items are missing. The good-natured performances of this pair get pleasant support from Harry Belafonte, who does an imitation of Marlon Brando's *Godfather* role. The movie also stars Richard Pryor, Flip Wilson, Roscoe Lee Browne, Paula Kelly, and Rosalind Cash. The film, under Poitier's direction and Richard Wesley's script, never makes the mistake of taking itself too seriously. (PG) *104 minutes*

URBAN COWBOY (1980)
★★

John Travolta

Travolta plays a refinery worker who spends his nights at a huge honky-tonk on the outskirts of Houston, where he acts out his macho cowboy fantasies. Travolta has grown from tough teenager to young man, and he still exhibits some special screen magnetism. But this low-key and rather routine melodramatic/love story is no

(Continued)

John Travolta relaxes on a mechanical bull in the melodrama/love story Urban Cowboy.

U·V
- Used Cars
- The Valachi Papers
- The Valley of Decision
- Valley of the Dolls
- Vanishing Point
- The Velvet Touch
- Vera Cruz
- The Verdict
- Vertigo

(Continued)

equal to the flashy and energetic *Saturday Night Fever* or *Grease*, which starred Travolta at his best. Debra Winger and Scott Glenn give first-rate supporting performances. Also with Bonnie Raitt and the Charlie Daniels Band. **Director**—James Bridges. (PG) *135 minutes*

USED CARS (1980)
★

Kurt Russell
Jack Warden

The idea is intriguing: a comedy about unscrupulous competition between neighboring used-car dealers. But in the hands of writer-director Robert Zemeckis, the film falls apart amid stale jokes, uneven direction, and crude dialogue. The film is mean-spirited, too; the sort that finds humor in someone dying from a heart attack. It's a rusty clunker of a movie that should be relegated to the junk heap. Also with Gerrit Graham. (R)
113 minutes

THE VALACHI PAPERS (1972)
★

Charles Bronson

Instead of drawing on the available factual information from the life of Mafia informer Joseph Valachi, director Terence Young mistakenly decided to make just another cliché-ridden gangster film. Bronson is competent as Valachi, the gangster who talked about his career in the mob, and Lino Ventura is good in the role of Vito Genovese, but the other performances are as mediocre as the rest of this violent movie. Also with Fred Valleca, Gerald S. O'Loughlin, Joseph Wiseman, and Walter Chiari. (R)
127 minutes

THE VALLEY OF DECISION
(1945)
★★

Greer Garson
Gregory Peck

Garson portrays a young woman who becomes a servant in the home of an industrialist and later marries his son, played by Peck. Garson and Peck are fine in this rags-to-riches tale set in Pittsburgh, and there are excellent supporting performances by Donald Crisp, Lionel Barrymore, Preston Foster, Gladys Cooper, and Marsha Hunt. The movie, however, never delivers much excitement. **Director**—Tay Garnett. **Academy Award Nomination**—Garson, best actress. *115 minutes b&w*

VALLEY OF THE DOLLS (1967)
★

Barbara Parkins
Patty Duke
Sharon Tate

Three young women—Parkins, Duke, and Tate—decide on a career in show business in this trashy film version of Jacqueline Susann's pulp novel. They are lovely to behold, but their acting is terrible, and no one else in this sorry affair does much better. The old adage that there's no business like show business is pushed to its outer limits in this production; intelligent viewers have no business watching it. Also with Susan Hayward, Paul Burke, Martin Milner, Charles Drake, and Lee Grant. **Director**—Mark Robson. (PG)
123 minutes

VANISHING POINT (1971)
★

Barry Newman
Cleavon Little

There are enough serious moments in this silly story about a long car chase from Colorado to California to make one wonder what director Richard C. Sarafian had in mind. Newman stars as the driver of the car, and Little plays a blind, black disc jockey who helps him avoid the police. Victoria Medlin, Dean Jagger, Bob Donner, and Paul Koslo appear in supporting roles. Fans of rock will appreciate the music. (PG)
107 minutes

THE VELVET TOUCH (1948)
★★

Rosalind Russell

Russell stars in this murder mystery as a stage actress who kills her producer. Her conscience prevails at about the same time the detective assigned to the case solves the crime. The cast also includes Leo Genn, Sydney Greenstreet, Frank McHugh, Claire Trevor, and Leon Ames. The theater scenes add to the film's appeal. **Director**—John Gage. *97 minutes b&w*

VERA CRUZ (1954)
★★★

Gary Cooper
Burt Lancaster

Cooper and Lancaster provide the energy and pace that keeps this western from being ordinary. They play adventurers who become involved in the plot to unseat Emperor Maximilian from power in Mexico. Cesar Romero, George Macready, Ernest Borgnine, Denise Darcel, Charles Bronson, and Sarita Montiel appear in supporting roles and don't detract from the enjoyment of the film. **Director**—Robert Aldrich. *94 minutes*

THE VERDICT (1946)
★★

Sydney Greenstreet
Peter Lorre

There are so many tricky twists and turns in this murder mystery that, at times, it seems that Greenstreet and Lorre don't even know what comes next. These veterans are excellent in this film about an ex-Scotland Yard inspector, played by Greenstreet, who continues to work on a strange case despite his forced retirement. Good acting, however, can't salvage an overly contrived detective yarn. The cast also includes Joan Lorring, Arthur Shields, George Coulouris, Paul Cavanagh, Rosalind Ivan, and Holmes Herbert. **Director**—Don Siegel.
86 minutes b&w

VERTIGO (1958)
★★★★

James Stewart
Kim Novak

When each sequence in this Alfred Hitchcock thriller about a detective who's drawn into a complex plot because he fears heights is analyzed, it

- Vice Squad
- Victory
- The View From Pompey's Head
- The Vikings
- Village of the Damned
- The Villain
- Vincent, François, Paul and the Others
- The Violent Men

V

makes sense. The sum of all of its parts, however, is less than an understandable film. It is testimony to Hitchcock's genius that he makes this movie work brilliantly despite its flaws. Excellent acting by Stewart, who plays the detective. And Novak, Barbara Bel Geddes, Henry Jones, and Tom Helmore help to make this a superb cinema experience.

120 minutes

VICE SQUAD (1982)
★★

Season Hubley
Gary Swanson

This gripping police drama, set against the seedy underworld of nighttime Los Angeles, is typical sensational fare designed to exploit mindless brutality. But there are some remarkable virtues among the grim torture and killing—an imaginative, fast-paced script and decent acting by a rather unknown cast. Hubley performs ably as a "good girl" prostitute who's threatened by a sadistic pimp, played by Wings Hauser. Swanson is convincing as a cynical vice squad cop. **Director—**Gary A. Sherman. (R)   *94 minutes*

Sylvester Stallone, Pele, and Michael Caine during soccer practice in Victory.

VICTORY (1981)
★★

Michael Caine
Sylvester Stallone

Allied POWs and a professional German soccer team vie for athletic victory in a jam-packed Paris stadium in this World War II escape drama. The banal screenplay smacks of *Hogan's Heroes*, and the sentimental attitudes about winning the game strain credibility. However, the film, directed by John Huston, comes to life when the players take the field with legendary soccer great Pele going through his extraordinary maneuvers. (PG)   *110 minutes*

THE VIEW FROM POMPEY'S HEAD (1955)
★★★

Richard Egan
Dana Wynter

Where does soap opera end and the fabric of great drama begin? This movie about a New York City-based lawyer who returns to his small southern hometown on business and falls in love again with an old girl friend touches on the eternal issues of love and a death quite artfully, although it does get slightly soapy at times. Egan plays the lawyer, and Wynter is his sweetheart. Sidney Blackmer, Marjorie Rambeau, and Cameron Mitchell are fine in supporting performances. **Director—**Philip Dunne.   *97 minutes*

THE VIKINGS (1958)
★★

Kirk Douglas
Tony Curtis
Janet Leigh

If you've seen one Viking adventure, you've probably seen them all. This one, however, has a strong cast with Douglas, Curtis, and Leigh in starring roles and vivid on-location photograpy in Norway. Action fans should enjoy the battle sequences and the invasion of England by the Vikings. Also with Ernest Borgnine, Maxine Audley, and Frank Thring. **Director—**Richard Fleischer.   *115 minutes*

VILLAGE OF THE DAMNED (1960)
★★★

George Sanders
Barbara Shelley

Barbara Shelley and George Sanders kiss in Village of the Damned.

This low-budget, well-made chiller proves beyond a doubt that good movies need not be costly. There isn't a wasted motion in this story about an English village terrorized by strange children. Sanders and Shelley star in the movie, based on John Wyndham's novel *The Midwich Cuckoos*. Also with Martin Stephens, Michael Gwynn, Laurence Naismith, John Phillips, and Richard Vernon. This one may rivet you to your seat. **Director—**Wolf Rilla.

78 minutes b&w

THE VILLAIN (1979)
(no stars)

Kirk Douglas
Ann-Margret

Western movies are worked over in this crude and unfunny burlesque. Numerous comic cartoon stunts are reused with live-action situations. Douglas is in the title role, playing a bad-guy gunslinger who's often upstaged by his horse. The tedious and absurd material is mostly an embarrassment to the cast, which also includes Arnold Schwarzenegger, Paul Lynde, Foster Brooks, Ruth Buzzi, and Jack Elam. **Director—**Hal Needham. (PG)   *89 minutes*

VINCENT, FRANÇOIS, PAUL AND THE OTHERS (1976)
★★

Yves Montand

Director Claude Sautet's film is about three middle-aged, middle-class friends who undergo a change of life and count on one another for support. There's a worthy performance by Montand as Vincent, a small-factory owner whose business is failing. The plot, however, plods along in tiresome fashion. Also stars Michel Piccoli and Serge Reggiani. In French with English titles. (No MPAA rating)

118 minutes

THE VIOLENT MEN (1955)
★★

Edward G. Robinson
Barbara Stanwyck

Robinson portrays a corrupt, crippled
(Continued)

V
- The V.I.P.s
- Virginia City
- Virility
- Visit to a Small Planet
- Viva Italia
- Viva Knievel!
- Viva Zapata!

(Continued)
cattle baron in this western saga that shows some promise before falling flat. Stanwyck plays his wife. Robinson, Stanwyck, and Ford provide good performances, and Brian Keith, Basil Ruysdael, Dianne Foster, Richard Jaeckel, and May Wynn are fine in supporting roles. The action sequences highlight the movie. **Director**—Rudolph Maté.   *96 minutes*

THE V.I.P.s (1963)
★★★

Richard Burton
Elizabeth Taylor
Maggie Smith
Rod Taylor

Louis Jourdan, Richard Burton, and Elizabeth Taylor in a scene from the V.I.P.s.

Quality acting and an excellent script by famed British writer Terence Rattigan makes this story about passengers stranded at a London airport because of fog excellent entertainment. Under less-competent direction it would be a soap opera, but the characters and their adventures prove to be very believable. Margaret Rutherford is the star among stars, but Burton, Elizabeth Taylor, Smith, Rod Taylor, Louis Jourdan, Orson Welles, and Elsa Martinelli also shine. Many other famous actors make an appearance. **Director**—Anthony Asquith. **Academy Award**—Rutherford, best supporting actress.   *119 minutes*

VIRGINIA CITY (1940)
★★

Errol Flynn
Randolph Scott
Miriam Hopkins
Humphrey Bogart

Flynn, Scott, Hopkins, and Bogart star in this Civil War western about a plot to steal a gold shipment for the Confederate cause. There's an uneven quality to the movie, as if there were five or six directors instead of just Michael Curtiz. The movie was intended as a serious western, but the action sequences are the best part of the film—so much for creating movies by committee. Also with Frank McHugh, Alan Hale, Douglass Dumbrille, and Guinn Williams.
          121 minutes b&w

VIRILITY (1976)
★★

Turi Ferro
Agostina Belli
Marc Porel

This is an occasionally charming sex farce produced by Carlo Ponti. A doting Sicilian father must disprove gossip that his London-educated son is a homosexual. The film gets off to a fairly good start, but begins to drift after awhile and never regains its legs. **Director**—Paolo Cavara. (R)
          87 minutes b&w

VISIT TO A SMALL PLANET (1960)
★

Jerry Lewis

Believe it or not this silly Lewis film is based on an urbane, satirical Gore Vidal play, in which a being from outer space visits Earth to get an insight into our strange habits. Lewis is the alien creature, and he plays the part for heavy-handed laughs as slapstick prevails. Joan Blackman, Earl Holliman, Fred Clark, Lee Patrick, Gale Gordon, John Williams, and Jerome Cowan appear in supporting roles and don't prevail. Even Vidal deserves better treatment than this. **Director**—Norman Taurog.
          87 minutes b&w

VIVA ITALIA (1978)
★★

Alberto Sordi
Vittorio Gassman

Some of Italy's top directors try their hands at humor in a series of nine vignettes, but there's little to laugh about. The morbid satire doesn't sit well. In one sketch, a terrorist makes love to an attractive airline hostess and then plants a bomb in her suitcase. Reliable actors Sordi and Gassman provide a few nice moments, but the film doesn't measure up to its exultant title. **Directors**—Mario Monicelli, Dino Risi, and Ettore Scola. In Italian with English titles. (No MPAA rating)   *90 minutes*

VIVA KNIEVEL! (1977)
★

Evil Knievel

This tacky, self-congratulatory film speaks no evil about daredevil cyclist Knievel; he plays himself in this silly story about crooks who want to use his van to smuggle drugs into the United States. But the film, more or less, seems designed to promote Knievel's image as pal and good-guy hero to kids. Gene Kelly has an embarrassing role as an alchoholic living off Knievel's kindness. You can jump right over this one. Lauren Hutton, Red Buttons, Leslie Nielsen, and Frank Gifford also star. **Director**—Gordon Douglas. (PG)   *106 minutes*

VIVA ZAPATA! (1952)
★★★★

Marlon Brando
Jean Peters
Anthony Quinn

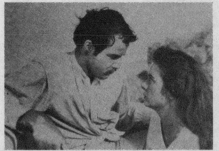

Marlon Brando and Jean Peters in the provocative classic Viva Zapata!

Brando, Peters, and Quinn are splendid in this classic about a Mexican peasant who becomes the president of his country during the Mexican Revolution. Brando plays Emiliano Zapata, and Quinn plays his brother. John Steinbeck's script is provocative without being preachy, and under Elia

- Voices
- Volcano
- Von Ryan's Express

- Voyage of the Damned
- Voyage to the Bottom of the Sea
- Wabash Avenue

- The Wackiest Ship in the Army
- Wait 'Til the Sun Shines, Nellie

V·W

Kazan's superb direction the agony as well as the glory of the revolution is clearly presented. Joseph Wiseman, Arnold Moss, Frank Silvera, Margo, and Mildred Dunnock are fine in supporting roles. **Academy Award**—Quinn, best supporting actor. **Nominations**—Brando, best actor; Steinbeck, writing (story and screenplay). *113 minutes b&w*

VOICES (1979)
★★

Michael Ontkean
Amy Irving

A lackluster boy-meets-girl story about a young musician who falls in love with an overprotected deaf woman. The film is cluttered with contrived subplots. Ontkean, as the struggling rock singer, seems stifled in his role. The only appeal is from Irving as the girl who realizes her dream to become a ballerina despite her handicap. It all takes place in Hoboken, New Jersey. Also with Alex Rocco, Barry Miller, and Viveca Lindfors. **Director**—Robert Markowitz. (PG) *107 minutes*

VOLCANO (1977)
★★

An interesting but unsatisfying documentary about the life and tragic death of Malcolm Lowry, the British writer who produced only a single major novel, *Under the Volcano*. Donald Brittain, who wrote and directed the film with sympathy, unfortunately neglected a firm point of view about his subject and dwells too much on unnecessary objectivity. Some of Lowry's actual words are spoken with eloquence by Richard Burton. (No MPAA rating) *100 minutes*

VON RYAN'S EXPRESS (1965)
★★★★

Frank Sinatra
Trevor Howard

This action yarn about a group of prisoners who escape from an Italian POW camp is made memorable when they take over a German freight train in their bid for freedom. Sinatra is

Frank Sinatra and Trevor Howard ponder their escape in Von Ryan's Express.

splendidly cast as an American colonel, leading English prisoners in their escape. Howard plays an English officer outranked by Sinatra. There are fine performances, too, from Sergio Fantoni, Edward Mulhare, Raffaella Carra, and Brad Dexter. **Director**—Mark Robson. *117 minutes*

VOYAGE OF THE DAMNED (1976)
★★★

Faye Dunaway
Oscar Werner
Max Von Sydow
Orson Welles

This compelling melodrama deals with a tragic World War II episode, when a shipload of Jews sailed from Germany to Cuba only to be returned to face death. The film plods through a parade of soap opera-like vignettes, yet the historical subject matter is so vital and absorbing that the ponderous form can be forgiven. A huge all-star cast portrays the doomed passengers and the onshore characters. Such luminaries as Welles and José Ferrer are there for fleeting moments. Dunaway and Von Sydow are outstanding in more significant roles. Also with Malcolm McDowell, James Mason, and Lee Grant. **Director**—Stuart Rosenberg. (PG) **Academy Award Nomination**—Grant, best supporting actress; Steve Shagan and David Butler, best screenplay adaptation. *134 minutes*

VOYAGE TO THE BOTTOM OF THE SEA (1961)
★★

Walter Pidgeon
Robert Sterling
Joan Fontaine

Excellent trick photography and entertaining action sequences make this sci-ence-fiction tale worthwhile for fans of such movies. The adventures of the atomic submarine assigned to destroy a radiation belt that threatens the planet are superficial by and large, but the acting of Pidgeon, Sterling, Fontaine, Peter Lorre, Frankie Avalon, and Barbara Eden make the sub's mission seem more important than it really is. **Director**—Irwin Allen. *105 minutes*

W

WABASH AVENUE (1950)
★★★

Betty Grable
Victor Mature
Phil Harris

Mature and Harris have designs on Grable in this musical set during the 1892 Chicago World's Fair. Grable sparkles as she sings, dances, and tries to decide which man she'll have in her life in this colorful production. The cast also includes Reginald Gardiner, Margaret Hamilton, James Barton, and Barry Kelley. **Director**—Henry Koster. *92 minutes*

THE WACKIEST SHIP IN THE ARMY (1960)
★★

Jack Lemmon
Ricky Nelson

This entertaining movie, starring Lemmon and Nelson, treads a thin line between comedy and serious drama. It involves a reconditioned sailing ship that an inexperienced crew plans to use to land an agent behind Japanese lines in the South Pacific during World War II. Also with John Lund, Chips Rafferty, Joby Baker, and Tom Tully. **Director**—Richard Murphy. *99 minutes*

WAIT 'TIL THE SUN SHINES, NELLIE (1952)
★★★

David Wayne
Jean Peters

Wayne and Peters star in this wholesome story about a small-town barber, *(Continued)*

W
- Wake Me When It's Over
- Wake of the Red Witch
- Walk a Crooked Mile
- Walk, Don't Run
- Walking My Baby Back Home
- Walking Tall
- Walking Tall—Part 2

(Continued)

played by Wayne, in the early 1900s. The characterizations of all the cast members are on the mark, and Wayne is superb in his portrayal of a typical American's life. Hugh Marlowe, Warren Stevens, Albert Dekker, Helene Stanley, and Alan Hale, Jr., are among the supporting actors. **Director**—Henry King. *108 minutes*

WAKE ME WHEN IT'S OVER (1960)
★★

**Ernie Kovacs
Dick Shawn**

Kovacs and Shawn try a bit too hard to be funny in this comedy about soldiers who establish a luxury hotel on a Pacific island, using U.S. Army supplies. The cast also includes Jack Warden, Margo Moore, Robert Emhardt, Nobu McCarthy, and Don Knotts. **Director**—Mervyn Le Roy. *126 minutes*

WAKE OF THE RED WITCH (1948)
★★★

**John Wayne
Luther Adler**

Gig Young (left) and John Wayne (right) check out the area in Wake of the Red Witch.

Missing pearls, combative treasure-seekers, and an alluring woman yield a standard adventure film and some action scenes. Wayne and Adler play two treasure seekers. The story gets confusing at times, as the men seek their fortune in the East Indies, but there are enough good sequences to make the viewing worthwhile. Gail Russell, Gig Young, Dennis Hoey, Henry Daniell, and Paul Fix also appear in supporting roles. **Director**—Edward Ludwig. *106 minutes b&w*

WALK A CROOKED MILE (1948)
★★

**Louis Hayward
Dennis O'Keefe**

Hayward and O'Keefe star in this conventional semidocumentary melodrama. British and FBI agents search for a spy who's giving U.S. atomic secrets to the Russians. The story, which has been told many times before and since, is rather routine. It seems as if standard sets are kept handy just for such movies. Also with Louise Allbritton, Onslow Stevens, and Raymond Burr. **Director**—Gordon Douglas. *91 minutes b&w*

WALK, DON'T RUN (1966)
★★

**Cary Grant
Samantha Eggar
Jim Hutton**

Only the charm and comic acting skills of Grant salvages this witless farce about two men and a young woman who share an apartment in Tokyo during the 1964 Olympics. Instead of winning the girl, this time Grant is a matchmaker and helps Eggar and Hutton find love; the viewer will find boredom. After this film, Grant retired from movies. John Standing, Ted Hartley, and Miiko Taka appear in supporting roles. **Director**—Charles Walters. *114 minutes*

WALKING MY BABY BACK HOME (1953)
★★

**Donald O'Connor
Janet Leigh
Buddy Hackett**

O'Connor, Leigh, and Hackett brighten this lightweight musical, but they can't restore the tarnished plot. The dancing of O'Connor and Leigh is pleasant to see, and the music is fairly entertaining although often second-rate. Hackett's brand of comedy is funny more often than not. Also with Lori Nelson, Scatman Crothers, John Hubbard, and Kathleen Lockhart. **Director**—Lloyd Bacon. *95 minutes*

WALKING TALL (1973)
★★★

**Joe Don Baker
Elizabeth Hartman**

Joe Don Baker comforts Elizabeth Hartman, who plays his wife, in Walking Tall.

This highly successful but too violent movie vividly depicts the courageous stand of Tennessee sheriff Buford Pusser against mobsters. The movie might have been even better without the emphasis on blood and gore. The story of a hero, however, remains. Baker is believable in the role of Pusser, and Hartman portrays his wife, who's murdered by the local mob. Noah Berry, Gene Evans, and Felton Perry appear in supporting roles. **Director**—Phil Karlson. (R) *125 minutes*

WALKING TALL—PART 2 (1975)
★★

Bo Svenson

A continuation of the legend of Buford Pusser, the big-stick-wielding Tennessee sheriff who was determined to rid his community of the bad guys. Svenson takes over for Joe Don Baker in the lead role of this watered-down expansion of the popular and financially successful original film. Shot on location in Tennessee. Also with Luke Askew, Richard Jaeckel, Noah Berry, Jr., and Robert DoQui. **Director**—Earl Bellamy. (PG) *109 minutes*

● A Walk in the Sun
● Walk on the Wild Side
● Walk Proud
● Walk the Proud Land
● The Waltz of the Toreadors
● The Wanderers
● War and Peace

W

A WALK IN THE SUN (1946)
★★★★

Dana Andrews
Richard Conte
Sterling Holloway
John Ireland

In A Walk in the Sun, Dana Andrews comes to the aid of a frightened Lloyd Bridges.

Honest characterizations by fine actors amid realistic settings make this one of the finest war films in cinema history. Andrews, Conte, Holloway, and Ireland star in the story of an Army platoon of infantrymen in Italy who must attack a German-held farmhouse. The production avoids the superficiality of so many war movies by stressing the human element over battlefield action. Also with George Tyne, Herbert Rudley, Richard Benedict, Norman Lloyd, Lloyd Bridges, and Huntz Hall. **Director**—Lewis Milestone.

117 minutes b&w

WALK ON THE WILD SIDE (1962)
★

Jane Fonda
Capucine
Barbara Stanwyck
Laurence Harvey

This self-conscious piece of trash misrepresents perversion for characterization. Stanwyck plays a lesbian madam of a brothel, Fonda and Capucine portray prostitutes, and Harvey is a troubled man in search of his lost love. None of them lifts this production beyond the potboiler level. The movie is based on one of Nelson Algren's better novels; unfortunately, the story was left behind, and just the seamy elements were brought to the screen. Also with Anne Baxter and Richard

Rust. **Director**—Edward Dmytryk.
114 minutes b&w

WALK PROUD (1979)
★★

Robby Benson
Sarah Holcomb

Soft-spoken, clean-cut Benson plays a tough Chicano youth in this gang movie that leans heavily on *West Side Story*. Despite heavy makeup and an all-too-obvious accent, Benson is unconvincing in this portrayal, which is far removed from his typical wholesome kid characters. The déjà vu plot focuses on Benson's conflict between his love of an Anglo girl, played by Holcomb, and his loyalty to his gang friends. Also with Henry Darrow, Domingo Ambriz, and Pepe Serna. **Director**—Robert Collins. (PG)
102 minutes

WALK THE PROUD LAND (1956)
★★

Audie Murphy

Murphy is in fine form in this sensitive western as an Indian agent attempting to bring peace between the Apaches and white settlers. Some of the dialogue is riddled with clichés, but there are enough good scenes to keep most viewers interested. Also with Anne Bancroft, Pat Crowley, Robert Warwick, Charles Drake, Tommy Rall, and Jay Silverheels. **Director**—Jesse Hibbs.
88 minutes

THE WALTZ OF THE TOREADORS (1962)
★★

Peter Sellers

The translation of Jean Anouilh's saucy comedy from stage to the screen is mishandled. However, Sellers, playing a lecherous retired general, does a fine job as he tries to keep his young mistress away from his son. The movie is interesting, although the vibrance of the play is missing. Also with Margaret Leighton, Dany Robin, John Fraser, Prunella Scales, and Cyril Cusack. **Director**—John Guillermin.
105 minutes

THE WANDERERS (1979)
★★

Ken Wahl
John Friedrich
Karen Allen

Ken Wahl (left) and fellow gang members harass a girl in The Wanderers.

A disoriented gang movie about growing up absurd in the Bronx in the '60s. The film, based on the novel by Richard Price, is a chop-suey affair of blaring vignettes. The Wanderers are Italian youths who try to survive in the city jungle among the fearsome Irish Ducky Boys, the grotesque Fordham Baldies, and other adversaries. Although the movie is overbearing, the young novice cast is rather appealing. Also with Alan Rosenberg, Linda Manz, and Toni Kalem. **Director**—Philip Kaufman. (R)
113 minutes

WAR AND PEACE (1956)
★★

Audrey Hepburn
Henry Fonda
Mel Ferrer
Herbert Lom
John Mills

This film version of Leo Tolstoy's great novel about Russia during the time of Napoleon's invasion is presented like a Cecil B. De Mille Bible epic—there's too much emphasis on sweeping battle scenes and other spectacles. Because of this misplaced focus, Tolstoy's brilliant characterizations are lost despite an excellent cast of actors that also includes Barry Jones, Oscar Homolka, Wilfrid Lawson, Vittorio Gassman, Anita Ekberg, Helmut Dantine, and Mai Britt. **Directors**—King
(Continued)

⭐ STAR PROFILE

W
- War Games
- Warlock
- Warlords of Atlantis
- The Warriors
- The War Wagon
- The Watcher in the Woods

SEAN CONNERY

Sean Connery was born Thomas Connery in Edinburgh, Scotland, in 1930. At 16, he joined the Royal Navy for a 12-year hitch, but three years later he was mustered out with ulcers, caused, he believes, by submission to discipline imposed by others. He returned to Edinburgh and worked briefly as a coalman, a mixer of cement, ditch-digger, truck driver, bricklayer, steel bender, printer's assistant, and lifeguard.

After modeling at the Edinburgh School of Art, he was chosen to represent Scotland in the 1950 Mr. Universe contest in London, where he auditioned for and won a role in South Pacific.

In 1956, when Jack Palance pulled out of a tough role in a TV version of Requiem for a Heavyweight, Connery got the role—and then a succession of minor film parts. In 1962, Harry Saltzman and Cubby Broccoli chose Connery to star as James Bond in Doctor No. He went on to star in more Bond thrillers, including From Russia With Love (1963), Goldfinger (1964), Thunderball (1965), You Only Live Twice (1967), and Diamonds Are Forever (1971).

Connery's other movies include Murder on the Orient Express (1974), The Man Who Would Be King (1976), Robin and Marion (1976), A Bridge Too Far (1977), Meteor (1979), Cuba (1979), Outland (1981), and Time Bandits (1981).

(Continued)
Vidor and Mario Soldati. **Academy Award Nominations**—Vidor, best director; Jack Cardiff, cinematography (color). *208 minutes*

WAR GAMES
See Suppose They Gave a War and Nobody Came

WARLOCK (1959)
★★★

**Henry Fonda
Richard Widmark
Anthony Quinn**

Fonda, Widmark, and Quinn star in this story that has more characterization than the typical western. Fonda plays a gunfighter hired to bring law and order to a small western town. The movie focuses on his rise when he succeeds in removing the bad guys and his fall when his friend, played by Quinn, betrays him. Some might object to the overuse of symbolism and excessive number of subplots. Also with Dorothy Malone, Richard Arlen, and Regis Toomey. **Director**—Edward Dmytryk. *123 minutes*

WARLORDS OF ATLANTIS (1978)
★

**Doug McClure
Cyd Charisse**

A group of explorers visit the lost continent of Atlantis, where they encounter all sorts of makeshift monster creatures that look like they were borrowed from Macy's Thanksgiving Day parade. The dialogue is just as shabby. This is merely another B-movie with little inspiration, as demonstrated by one predictable scene that has a giant octopus attacking the explorers' ship. Also with Pete Gilmore, Daniel Massey, and Shane Rimmer. **Director**—Kevin Connor (PG) *96 minutes*

THE WARRIORS (1979)
★★

**Michael Beck
James Remar
Thomas Waites**

Youth gangs roam New York City's streets and subways in this glossy film that looks like a contemporary *A Clockwork Orange*. The story focuses on one gang, which is falsely accused of murder. They spend the movie making a dash for their home turf in Coney Island while being chased by rival gangs and the cops. There's lots of head-bashing along the way, but not much good acting by the cast of unknowns. Walter Hill's direction, however, is slick and spectacular. Also with Dorsey Wright, Brian Tyler, and Deborah Van Valkenburgh. (R) *90 minutes*

THE WAR WAGON (1967)
★★★

**John Wayne
Kirk Douglas**

Wayne and Douglas are at their best in this western about an ex-con, played by Wayne, bent on revenge. Wayne teams up with Douglas to rob an armored wagon filled with gold; he believes it rightfully belongs to him. The plot is weak, but the action and solid performances will keep your interest. The excellent cast also includes Howard Keel, Robert Walker, Keenan Wynn, Bruce Dern, Gene Evans, Bruce Cabot, and Joanna Barnes. **Director**—Burt Kennedy. *99 minutes*

THE WATCHER IN THE WOODS (1980)
★★

**Bette Davis
Carroll Baker**

Davis and Baker star in this flimsy and silly suspense movie from the Walt Disney studio. It's about an American family that rents an old house in England and becomes involved with a supernatural mystery. The film maintains tension, but it's chock full of contrived scare effects that strain credibility. Davis has a minor role as the crusty landlady of the strange house where her daughter mysteriously vanished 30 years ago. She's terrific despite the nonsensical material. Also with Lynn-Holly Johnson, Kyle Richards, and David McCallum. **Director**—John Hough. (PG) *100 minutes*

WATCH ON THE RHINE (1943)
★★★

Paul Lukas
Bette Davis

Bette Davis and Paul Lukas in Watch on the Rhine, *set during World War II.*

Parts of this film seem superficial now, and propaganda gets in the way of some dramatic situations, but the brilliant performances of Lukas and Davis still brighten the movie. Lukas portrays a German underground leader confronted by Nazis wherever he goes—even Washington, D.C. Davis plays his wife. The movie is based on Lillian Hellman's play, and the film script was written by Dashiell Hammett, her good friend of many years. The excellent cast also includes Lucile Watson, George Coulouris, Henry Daniell, Donald Woods, and Geraldine Fitzgerald. **Director**—Herman Shumlin. **Academy Award**—Lukas, best actor. **Nominations**—best picture; Watson, best supporting actress; Hammett, writing (screenplay).
114 minutes b&w

WATERLOO (1970)
★

Rod Steiger
Christopher Plummer

The title, of course, refers to one of the most famous military encounters in history. Unfortunately, the movie treats this piece of history as just another historical-action flick, and the mediocre performances reflect the dreary plot. Plummer is competent as the victorious Wellington who defeats Napoleon, but Steiger, as the famed French leader, delivers a losing performance. Other good actors lost in the enterprise include Jack Hawkins, Virginia McKenna, Orson Welles, Ian Ogilvy, Michael Wilding, and Dan O'Herlihy. **Director**—Sergei Bondarchuk. (G) *123 minutes*

WATERMELON MAN (1970)
★★

Godfrey Cambridge

Cambridge stars in this comedy about a bigoted white insurance salesman who wakes up one morning to discover he's suddenly black. Once the impact of the funny and preposterous premise subsides, the movie drags, and some of the inherent social satire is weakened. Also with Estelle Parsons, Howard Caine, Mantan Moreland, Kay Kimberly, and D'Urville Martin. **Director**—Melvin Van Peebles. (R) *100 minutes*

WATERSHIP DOWN (1978)
★★

This is an animated fantasy about rabbits based on Richard Adams's best-selling novel. No, it doesn't star Bugs Bunny. This is a serious story, with the cottontails fleeing their burrow because of man's encroachment. In their painful search for a new home, the rabbits are attacked by dogs, snared, ravaged by hawks, and set upon by other rabbits. It's perhaps too gruesome and unrelenting for children and somewhat unsophisticated for most adults. Sir Ralph Richardson and Zero Mostel provide some of the voices. **Director**—Martin Rosen. (PG) *92 minutes*

THE WAY WE WERE (1973)
★★★

Barbara Streisand
Robert Redford

The splendid performances of Strei-sand and Redford sustain this nostalgic journey from the 1930s to the 1950s, including the McCarthy era. Parts of the film are worthwhile, such as when Streisand and Redford fall in love. But some of the nostalgia turns to mush, and the movie isn't a particularly accurate portrayal of the period. Bradford Dillman, Lois Chiles, Murray Hamilton, Patrick O'Neal, and Viveca Lindfors are fine in supporting roles. **Director**—Sydney Pollack. (PG) **Academy Award Nominations**—Streisand, best actress; Harry Stradling, Jr., cinematography. *118 minutes*

W.C. FIELDS AND ME (1976)
★★

Rod Steiger
Valerie Perrine

Steiger manages to give a moving interpretation of the enigmatic comic with the help of expert make-up and a close resemblance to Fields's voice. The dreary script, however, sabotages Steiger's hard work. Bob Merrill's misleading screenplay disregards many important facts about the life of Fields and fails to provide any emotional dimension. Perrine plays Carlotta Monti, the comic's mistress. There are no real big laughs; only a half-funny scene where Fields spikes a child performer's orange juice, and the kid staggers out of the comic's trailer dressing room. Also with Jack Cassidy and Bernadette Peters. **Director**—Arthur Hill. (PG) *111 minutes*

A WEDDING (1978)
★★★

Carol Burnett
Desi Arnaz, Jr.
Amy Stryker

Innovative director Robert Altman reveals a host of family emotions and crises during an extraordinary wedding day. The tart, energetic comedy is rich with Altman's gems of insight and satire about marriage, religion, and middle-class values. A first-rate cast includes many newcomers with the veterans; they all do a great job. Altman fans won't be disappointed. Also with Vittorio Gassman, Geraldine Chaplin, Mia Farrow, Paul
(Continued)

Desi Arnaz, Jr., and Amy Stryker are the newlyweds in the comedy A Wedding.

(Continued)

Dooley, Lillian Gish, and Howard Duff. (PG)   125 minutes

WEEKEND AT THE WALDORF (1945)
★★

**Ginger Rogers
Walter Pidgeon
Van Johnson
Lana Turner**

This pleasant entertainment is a weak sister of the famous *Grand Hotel*, with less-competent actors in a New York setting. If you don't expect too much, the characters at New York's largest hotel are interesting enough. The cast also includes Keenan Wynn, Robert Benchley, Edward Arnold, and Phyllis Thaxter. **Director**—Robert Z. Leonard.   130 minutes b&w

WE'RE NO ANGELS (1955)
★★★

**Humphrey Bogart
Peter Ustinov
Aldo Ray**

Bogart, Ustinov, and Ray are delightful in this lighthearted story about three escapees from Devil's Island who help a beleaguered shopkeeper prosper and outwit his foes. The production would have been better, however, if the Albert Husson play wasn't adapted to the screen so literally. Joan Bennett, Basil Rathbone, John Smith, and Leo G. Carroll star in supporting

roles. **Director**—Michael Curtiz.
          106 minutes

WE'RE NOT MARRIED (1952)
★★★

**Ginger Rogers
Fred Allen
Victor Moore
Paul Douglas**

The ingenious premise of this film—five married couples are advised that their marriages are not legal—provides the fodder for a fine comedy with a provocative message. Married viewers will find themselves asking: How would I react if I got such a notice? The film, written by famed screenwriter Nunnally Johnson, is presented in five sequences, with the Allen and Rogers scene surpassing the others. The all-star cast also includes Eddie Bracken, James Gleason, Jane Darwell, Eve Arden, Marilyn Monroe, David Wayne, Louis Calhern, Mitzi Gaynor, and Zsa Zsa Gabor. **Director**—Edmund Goulding.
          85 minutes b&w

THE WESTERNER (1940)
★★★

**Gary Cooper
Walter Brennan**

Cooper and Brennan star in this tale about land disputes and the problems they caused in the Old West. And Brennan shines in the role of Judge Roy Bean. Also with Fred Stone, Dana Andrews, Chill Wills, Doris Davenport, Forrest Tucker, Tom Tyler, Charles Halton, and Lillian Bond. **Director**—William Wyler. **Academy Award**—Brennan, best supporting actor. **Nomination**—Stuart N. Lake, writing (original story). *98 minutes b&w*

Humphrey Bogart, Peter Ustinov, and Aldo Ray in We're No Angels.

WESTERN UNION (1941)
★★★

**Randolph Scott
Robert Young
Dean Jagger**

This intelligent western, based on the Zane Grey novel, pinpoints the problems involved in constructing the first coast-to-coast Western Union wire in 1861. Scott, Young, and Jagger give polished performances, with Virginia Gilmore, Barton MacLane, John Carradine, and Chill Wills in supporting roles. **Director**— Fritz Lang.
          94 minutes

WEST SIDE STORY (1961)
★★★★

**Natalie Wood
Richard Beymer
Russ Tamblyn
Rita Moreno
George Chakiris**

This dynamite musical remains fresh and vibrant many years after its release. Wood and Beymer seem slightly miscast at times in this story about rival gangs in a New York ghetto, but Moreno, Chakiris, and Tamblyn are superb. The excellent on-location photography enhances the Romeo and Juliet theme, and the Leonard Bernstein-Stephen Sondheim music is icing on the cake. **Directors**—Robert Wise and Jerome Robbins. **Academy Awards**—best picture; Wise and Robbins, best director; Chakiris, best supporting actor; Moreno, best supporting actress; Daniel L. Fapp, cinematography (color). **Nomination**—Ernest Lehman, best screenplay (based on material from another medium).   155 minutes

WESTWORLD (1973)
★★★

**Yul Brynner
Richard Benjamin
James Brolin**

Brynner portrays a robot who runs amok at a futuristic vacation resort that offers fantasies in this engaging science-fiction film. Brynner is as competent as an actor can be playing a

- What Did You Do in the War, Daddy?
- What Ever Happened To Baby Jane?
- What Price Glory?
- What's New, Pussycat?
- What's Up Doc?
- The Wheeler Dealers
- When a Stranger Calls

Yul Brynner, who plays a robot in Westworld, *studies a duplicate.*

robot. Benjamin and Brolin are fine as 21st-century men whose fantasy about the Wild West becomes real when the robot starts to stalk them. Victoria Shaw, Norman Bartold, and Alan Oppenheimer appear in supporting roles. **Director**—Michael Crichton. (PG)   *90 minutes*

WHAT DID YOU DO IN THE WAR, DADDY? (1966)
★★

**James Coburn
Dick Shawn**

A competent cast is unable to brighten this inane comedy about a group of American soldiers who must convince the eccentric residents of an Italian town during World War II that it's time to give up. The weak comedy that does emerge is keyed to the terms of surrender that the Italians seek. Also with Harry Morgan, Aldo Ray, Sergio Fantoni, Giovanna Ralli, Leon Askin, and Carroll O'Connor. **Director**—Blake Edwards.   *119 minutes*

WHAT EVER HAPPENED TO BABY JANE? (1962)
★★★

**Bette Davis
Joan Crawford
Victor Buono**

This grim and chilling black comedy about an ex-child movie star who tor-

tures her crippled sister and eventually kills her is made interesting by the excellent acting of Davis, Crawford, and Buono. If the plot had been better constructed and if the movie was cut by about 30 minutes—with improved editing—it could have been a gem. Also with Anna Lee and Marjorie Bennett. **Director**—Robert Aldrich. **Academy Award Nominations**—Davis, best actress; Buono, best supporting actor; Ernest Hall, cinematography (black and white).   *132 minutes b&w*

WHAT PRICE GLORY? (1952)
★★

**James Cagney
Dan Dailey
Corinne Calvet**

Energetic performances by Cagney and Dailey brighten this remake of the silent film classic about two tough Marines in love with the same woman in France during World War I. Calvet is the woman they love. The original film was better because it made a brilliant antiwar statement, but this version has some good moments, too. The cast also includes James Gleason, William Demarest, Robert Wagner, and Marisa Pavan. **Director**—John Ford.   *111 minutes*

WHAT'S NEW, PUSSYCAT? (1965)
★

**Peter Sellers
Peter O'Toole
Woody Allen**

At some future time, film historians may point to this tasteless production as an example of what was considered comedy in the new morality days of the 1960s, although Woody Allen wrote the script. Even at the time of its release, this story about an eccentric psychiatrist (Sellers) and a troubled fashion editor (O'Toole) who's obsessed with women, seemed weak. The cast includes Ursula Andress, Capucine, Romy Schneider, Louise Lasser, and Paula Prentiss, who are exploited here for their good looks. Allen was learning his craft at this point, but that's no reason why you should suffer. **Director**—Clive Donner.   *108 minutes*

WHAT'S UP DOC? (1972)
★★★

**Barbara Streisand
Ryan O'Neal**

In What's Up, Doc?, *Barbra Streisand gives Ryan O'Neal a ride during a climactic chase.*

Director Peter Bogdanovich fails to successfully capture the uninhibited quality of the better 1930s comedies, but he came close enough to make viewing this movie worthwhile. A vibrant performance by Streisand as a wacky coed who manages to disrupt the life-styles of a square musicologist (O'Neal) and his fiancée (Madeline Kahn) makes the director seem better than he really is. Kenneth Mars, Austin Pendleton, Sorrell Booke, Michael Murphy, and Mabel Albertson appear in supporting roles. (G)   *94 minutes*

THE WHEELER DEALERS (1963)
★★

**James Garner
Lee Remick**

Garner and Remick star in this comedy about a Texas oil millionaire who decides to have some fun on Wall Street with the stock market. There's nothing about the plot or the production that justify such solid performances by Remick, Jim Backus, Phil Harris, and Louis Nye so you should be grateful for unexpected pleasures. The cast also includes John Astin, Shelley Berman, and Chill Wills. **Director**—Arthur Hiller.   *106 minutes*

WHEN A STRANGER CALLS (1979)
★★

**Carol Kane
Charles Durning**

This suspense thriller gets off to a pro-
(Continued)

W
- When Time Ran Out
- When Worlds Collide
- When You Comin' Back, Red Ryder?
- Where Angels Go, Trouble Follows
- Where Eagles Dare
- Where's Charley?
- Where the Boys Are

(Continued)

mising start—a babysitter, played by Kane, is alone in a dark house and receives threatening phone calls. But the film soon goes rapidly downhill. Even a psychopathic killer, played by Tony Beckley, needs some kind of psychology to give the story meaning. Instead, everything happens with little more than scary effects in mind. Durning plays a pursuing detective; it's a skimpy role in a meatless script. Also with Colleen Dewhurst, Rachel Roberts, and Ron O'Neal. **Director**—Fred Walton. (R)   *97 minutes*

WHEN TIME RAN OUT (1980)
★

Paul Newman
Jacqueline Bisset

Irwin Allen, who brought us *The Towering Inferno* and other disaster movies, takes one more crack at his favorite subject. This time, he unleashes an erupting volcano on a Hawaiian resort hotel in rather routine fashion. Newman and other well-known stars slog through a dull script. Most of the cast is killed off by the force of nature while a few make it to safety. Allen seems to have run out of fresh ideas. Also with William Holden, Red Buttons, Ernest Borgnine, and James Franciscus. **Director**—James Goldstone. (PG)
121 minutes

WHEN WORLDS COLLIDE (1951)
★★

Richard Derr
Barbara Rush

Vivid and spectacular effects make this science-fiction tale about the rush to build a spaceship worthwhile. The reason for the haste is that Earth is going to be destroyed by another planet, so every second counts. The plot is weak, and the dialogue is trite. Aside from the splendid photography, the movie is ordinary. Derr and Rush star, with Peter Hanson, John Hoyt, and Larry Keating in supporting roles. **Director**—Rudolph Maté. **Academy Award Nomination**—John F. Seitz and W. Howard Greene, cinematography (color).   *80 minutes*

WHEN YOU COMIN' BACK, RED RYDER? (1979)
★★

Marjoe Gortner

In When You Comin' Back, Red Ryder?, *Marjoe Gortner attempts to humiliate Lee Grant as her husband (Hal Linden) watches.*

Gortner stars as an enraged Vietnam veteran who terrorizes some nice folks in a sleepy New Mexico diner. There are some decent performances by Gortner, Peter Firth, and Stephanie Faracy. However, the story, which was taken from the 1973 stage production, loses much of its sizzle by dwelling too long on the various characters before the action in the diner begins. The finale has its taut moments, but the outcome leaves a bad aftertaste. Also with Hal Linden, Lee Grant, Candy Clark, and Pat Hingle. **Director**—Milton Katselas. (R)
118 minutes

WHERE ANGELS GO, TROUBLE FOLLOWS (1968)
★★

Rosalind Russell
Stella Stevens

This overly cute and simplistic story of nuns in conflict and their pupils threatening to get out of control holds little interest. Russell plays a Mother Superior who's challenged by Stevens, a younger and more progressive nun in this sequel to *The Trouble With Angels*. The supporting cast of Binnie Barnes, Susan St. James, Milton Berle, Arthur Godfrey, William Lundigan, Van Johnson, Robert Taylor, Mary Wickes, and Barbara Hunter brighten the production, but only slightly. **Director**—James Neilson.   *95 minutes*

WHERE EAGLES DARE (1969)
★★★

Richard Burton
Clint Eastwood

This good old-fashioned adventure story about a dangerous mission to rescue an American officer from an escape-proof German prison has lots of action and many tense moments. Burton and Eastwood star as the leaders of the rescue expedition, with Patrick Wymark, Michael Hordern, Robert Beatty, Mary Ure, Donald Houston, and Peter Barkworth in supporting roles. Director Brian G. Hutton has the good sense not to take the movie too seriously. Based on the novel by Alistair MacLean. (PG)
156 minutes

WHERE'S CHARLEY? (1952)
★★★

Ray Bolger

Bolger sparkles in this musical version of *Charley's Aunt*, the story of an Oxford student who impersonates his best friend's rich aunt to solve problems only to end up causing new complications. Bolger is at his best singing "Once in Love With Amy," but the other Frank Loesser songs are good, too. The cast also includes Robert Shackleton, Allyn McLerie, Horace Cooper, Mary Germaine, and Margaretta Scott. **Director**—David Butler.
95 minutes

WHERE THE BOYS ARE (1960)
★★

George Hamilton
Dolores Hart
Paula Prentiss
Jim Hutton

Hamilton, Hart, Prentiss, and Hutton star in this silly musical about college boys and girls on vacation in Fort Lauderdale, Florida. The movie never pretends to be anything other than what it is—a teenage beach movie. The cast also includes Yvette Mimieux, Connie Francis, Barbara Nichols, Chill Wills, and Frank Gorshin. **Director**—Henry Levin.   *99 minutes*

- Where the Buffalo Roam
- Where the Red Fern Grows
- Where There's Smoke
- Which Way Is Up?

- Whispering Smith
- White Cargo
- White Christmas
- The White Cliffs of Dover

W

WHERE THE BUFFALO ROAM (1980)
★★

Bill Murray

Low comedy about the high jinks of outrageous gonzo journalist Hunter Thompson, who ruffled the establishment's feathers in the late '60s. Murray, playing the role of Thompson, generates a few laughs as he covers a marijuana trial, the Super Bowl, and the Presidential election. But it's mostly preposterous slapstick that wears thin as the movie wears on. **Director**—Art Linson. (R)

98 minutes

WHERE THE RED FERN GROWS (1976)
★★

James Whitmore
Stewart Peterson

This children's movie, set in the Ozarks during the '30s, concentrates on family virtue. It's about a backwoods lad who struggles so he can eventually enter the big coon hunt competition. The coon chases are interesting, but poorly photographed. Whitmore plays the grandfather, and Peterson plays the boy. Also with Beverly Garland, Jack Ging, and Lonny Chapman. **Director**—Norman Tokar. (G) *90 minutes*

WHERE THERE'S SMOKE (1975)
★★

Bernard Fresson
Annie Girardot

An honest doctor takes on the corrupt politicians in a wealthy Paris suburb. Fresson is the young, doctor-mayoral candidate; Girardot plays his loyal wife. The villainous incumbents resort to blackmail and murder, and adhering to French realism, win in the end. The film produces emotional impact in arousing indignation at the triumph of evil, but the pedestrian plot is overdone, and the direction is uninspired. **Director**—André Cayatte. In French with English titles. (No MPAA rating) *112 minutes*

WHICH WAY IS UP? (1977)
★

Richard Pryor

Comic Pryor, generally successful in screen endeavors, takes a step backward in this crude adaptation of Lina Wertmuller's Italian comedy, *The Seduction of Mimi.* Pryor plays three roles, but primarily he portrays a poor fruit picker who becomes a farm labor union organizer. Most of the material is shallow, and much is ruined by unnecessary vulgar language. Also with Lonette McKee, Margaret Avery, and Dewayne Jessie. **Director**—Michael Schultz. (R) *94 minutes*

WHISPERING SMITH (1948)
★★★

Alan Ladd
Robert Preston
Brenda Marshall

Robert Preston (center) and Donald Crisp (seated at right) in Whispering Smith, *in which Alan Ladd plays the title role.*

Ladd, Preston, and Marshall star in this western, which combines a well-developed story with sufficient action. It deals with a government detective, played by Ladd, who discovers that a friend is involved in a series of robberies. The cast also includes Donald Crisp, William Demarest, Frank Faylen, Fay Holden, and Murvyn Vye. **Director**—Leslie Fenton. *88 minutes*

WHITE CARGO (1942)
★

Hedy Lamarr
Walter Pidgeon

Lamarr plays Tondelayo, a scheming native girl who entices British rubber planters, in this campy film that's so bad it's worth seeing just as a frame of reference so other inept movies can be judged. Pidgeon plays the planter who loves Lamarr most of all. Other actors who risked their reputations in this movie include Richard Carlson, Reginald Owen, Frank Morgan, Bramwell Fletcher, and Richard Ainley. Good for laughs. **Director**—Richard Thorpe. *90 minutes b&w*

WHITE CHRISTMAS (1954)
★★★

Bing Crosby
Danny Kaye
Dean Jagger

A star-studded cast brightens this musical package about two old Army friends—Crosby and Kaye—who aid Jagger, an ex-officer, at his winter resort. The limp plot is merely a device for Crosby, Kaye, Rosemary Clooney, Vera-Ellen, Grady Sutton, Sig Rumann, and Mary Wickes to perform. The Irving Berlin songs—including the title tune—enrich the production. **Director**—Michael Curtiz. *120 minutes*

THE WHITE CLIFFS OF DOVER (1944)
★★

Irene Dunne

This patriotic tearjerker, about an American woman in Britain who loses her husband during World War I and her son in World War II, has many vivid scenes although the production seems too melodramatic now. Dunne gives an intelligent, controlled performance as the wife and mother, and there are solid supporting appearances by Alan Marshal, C. Aubrey Smith, Frank Morgan, Roddy McDowall, Dame May Whitty, Van Johnson, and Peter Lawford. **Director**—Clarence Brown. **Academy Award** *(Continued)*

367

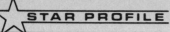

W
- White Heat
- White Line Fever
- Who Is Killing the Great Chefs of Europe?
- Who'll Stop the Rain?

(Continued)
Nomination—George Folsey, cinematography (black and white).

126 minutes b&w

WHITE HEAT (1949)
★★★★

**James Cagney
Edmond O'Brien**

Cagney is in top form in this realistic story of a psychopathic gangster. The movie vividly depicts his violent lifestyle and also gets top grades for excellent action sequences and lots of suspense. O'Brien plays the clever cop who infiltrates Cagney's gang and finally collars him. The excellent cast also includes Margaret Wycherly, Virginia Mayo, John Archer, and Steve

Cochran. **Director**—Raoul Walsh. **Academy Award Nomination**—Virginia Kellogg, writing (motion picture story).

114 minutes b&w

WHITE LINE FEVER (1975)
★★★

**Jan-Michael Vincent
Kay Lenz**

This action drama focuses on the long-haul trucking business. The story is about a young veteran who returns home, purchases a diesel truck, and battles the corruption of the bigger interests who want him to smuggle contraband across state lines. Although the plot is loaded down with clichés, the huge, barreling trucks are a show in themselves, and one smash-

em-up scene is said to have cost $130,000. Vincent and Lenz do a good job of revving up the action along with the big trucks. The title refers to the tiring, hypnotic effect of the highway's white center line on drivers during long trips. Also with Slim Pickens, L. Q. Jones, and Don Porter. **Director**—Jonathan Kaplan. (PG)   *89 minutes*

WHO IS KILLING THE GREAT CHEFS OF EUROPE? (1978)
★★★★

**George Segal
Jacqueline Bisset
Robert Morley**

By Jove, it's that rotund Englishman Morley—overflowing with bombast and eating his way to oblivion as publisher of a gourmet food magazine. Segal and Bisset get top billing in this mystery comedy, but the film belongs to Morley who provides most of the laughs with his caustic dialogue. The story is set mostly in famous European hotels and elegant restaurants, with scrumptious shots of marvelous dishes. It's entertaining, funny, suspenseful, and mouth-watering too. Also with Jean-Pierre Cassel, Philippe Noiret, Jean Rochefort, and Madge Ryan. **Director**—Ted Kotcheff. (PG)

112 minutes

WHO'LL STOP THE RAIN (1978)
★★★

**Nick Nolte
Tuesday Weld**

JUDY GARLAND

The fabulous career of Judy Garland was marked by exuberance and brilliance as well as disasters, nervous breakdowns, and various failed marriages. Judy was born Frances Gumm, the daughter of vaudeville parents, in Grand Rapids, Minnesota, in 1922. She made her stage debut at the age of three with her sisters as The Gumm Sisters singing act. When she was nine, the stage name was changed to Garland, and the act eventually broke up when one of the sisters married.

At 13, Garland was hired by MGM, where she gained success as a teenage star, often opposite Mickey Rooney. Her career soared when she captivated audiences with her portrayal of Dorothy in The Wizard of Oz (1939), a role initially slated

for Shirley Temple, and one which won Garland a special Oscar.

Several years later, Garland married musician David Rose, but divorced him four years later. In 1944, Judy starred in Meet Me in St. Louis, and a year later married Vincente Minnelli, the film's director.

Some of Garland's best movies were made during her association with Minnelli. Others of the period include The Clock (1945), Ziegfeld Follies (1945), and The Pirate (1947).

Garland made a comeback with personal performances in London and New York and an excellent screen performance in A Star is Born (1954).

In the late '50s, her career faltered again, and she was plagued with breakdowns, lawsuits, and chronic marital problems with Sid Luft, her third husband, whom she divorced in 1965.

After a brief marriage to actor Mark Herron, Garland went to London and married Mickey Deans, a nightclub manager, and starred in a disastrous cabaret act. In 1969, she died from an accidental drug overdose.

Some of Garland's other movies include Babes in Arms (1939), Strike Up the Band (1940), For Me and My Gal (1942), The Harvey Girls (1946), Easter Parade (1948), A Star Is Born (1954), Judgment at Nuremberg (1960), and I Could Go On Singing (1963).

Nick Nolte and Tuesday Weld share a rare light moment in Who'll Stop the Rain?

- Wholly Moses
- Who's Afraid of Virginia Woolf?
- Who's Been Sleeping in My Bed?
- Whose Life Is It Anyway?
- Who Was That Lady?
- Why Would I Lie?

W

This hard-hitting action drama about a couple on the lam is based on *Dog Soldiers*, Robert Stone's emotional novel involving the backwash of the Vietnam War. Nolte is terrific as an ex-Marine who smuggles heroin into the U.S., and then, in company with a friend's wife, is relentlessly pursued by three colorful but sadistic villains. The woman is played by Weld. The film, like the novel, maintains a sense of tension and reflects on the war's impact on America. Also with Michael Moriarty, Anthony Zerbe, Richard Masur, and Ray Sharkey. **Director—**Karel Reisz. (R)   *126 minutes*

WHOLLY MOSES (1980)

★★

Dudley Moore

Moore stars in this sporadically funny Bible tale that seems to be inspired by the *Life of Brian*, but is nowhere as outrageous. Moore plays a shepherd who's somehow two steps behind Moses when a famous incident occurs. Moore works in some mildly comic routines, but the film is in dire need of at least a few side-splitting laughs. Dom DeLuise, Madeline Kahn, John Houseman, and Richard Pryor contribute some nice cameo performances—especially Pryor as a formidable pharaoh. **Director—**Gary Weis. (PG)   *109 minutes*

WHO'S AFRAID OF VIRGINIA WOOLF? (1966)

★★★

Richard Burton
Elizabeth Taylor
George Segal
Sandy Dennis

Richard Burton, George Segal, Elizabeth Taylor, and Sandy Dennis in the highly emotional Who's Afraid of Virginia Woolf?

This famous but overrated Edward Albee play successfully makes the translation to the motion picture screen. And excellent performances by Burton, Taylor, Segal, and Dennis give the story, about a troubled middle-aged couple who impose on an innocent younger couple, a supercharged quality. In the final analysis, however, vulgarity and shouting don't pass for honest characterization and astute plot development. That's why many crude people who make a habit of abusive shouting at their mates mistake this ordinary play and movie for great art. It's merely a good show. **Director—**Mike Nichols. **Academy Awards—**Taylor, best actress; Dennis, best supporting actress; Haskell Wexler, cinematography (black and white). **Nominations—**best picture; Nichols, best director; Burton, best actor; Segal, best supporting actor; Ernest Lehman, best screenplay (based on material from another medium).
129 minutes b&w

WHO'S BEEN SLEEPING IN MY BED? (1963)

★★

Dean Martin
Elizabeth Montgomery

In this inoffensive comedy, Martin plays a TV star who's being pushed to the altar by his fiancée because she's worried by the competition. Montgomery plays his fiancée. Some bright dialogue sparks this very ordinary story, and some solid supporting efforts by Carol Burnett, Louis Nye, Elizabeth Fraser, Martin Balsam, Jill St. John, Yoko Tani, and Richard Conte also push it up from mediocrity. **Director—**Daniel Mann.   *103 minutes*

WHOSE LIFE IS IT ANYWAY? (1981)

★★★★

Richard Dreyfuss

It's a grim subject, indeed: A quadriplegic with no chance of recovery fights for his right to die with dignity. Yet this amazing film is handled with such warmth, wit, and humanity that it evolves into a captivating experience, ably transcending any morbidity. The performance by Dreyfuss as

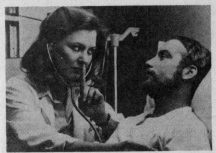

Christine Lahti and Richard Dreyfuss in the touching drama Whose Life Is It Anyway?

the gutsy paralyzed sculptor is spellbinding. And the touching drama moves with dynamic precision despite the confined hospital setting. There's masterful support from Janet Eilber, John Cassavetes, Christine Lahti, and Bob Balaban. **Director—**John Badham. (R)   *118 minutes*

WHO WAS THAT LADY? (1960)

★★

Tony Curtis
Dean Martin
Janet Leigh

Curtis and Martin star in this entertaining farce. They pretend to be FBI agents to fool Leigh, who plays Curtis's wife, but new problems arise when foreign spies become interested in their identities. Although the movie begins well, it weakens near the end. The cast also includes James Whitmore, Larry Keating, John McIntire, and Barbara Nichols. **Director—**George Sidney.   *115 minutes b&w*

WHY WOULD I LIE? (1980)

★

Treat Williams

Williams is a colorful liar in this romantic comedy that's too contrived in the romance department and weaker yet as a comedy. Williams plays an obscure character, who works as a social worker, adopts a young boy, and locates the boy's mother with whom he falls in love. All the sentimental complications are incredible, and the story is strictly corn—almost tastelessly so. Why would we lie? Also with Lisa Eichhorn, Jocelyn Brando, and Gabriel Swann. **Director—**Larry Peerce. (PG)   *105 minutes*

W
- The Wilby Conspiracy
- The Wild Blue Yonder
- The Wild Bunch
- The Wilderness Family—Part 2
- The Wild Geese
- The Wild McCullochs
- The Wild One

THE WILBY CONSPIRACY
(1975)
★★★

**Michael Caine
Sidney Poitier**

In The Wilby Conspiracy, *Sidney Poitier is a political activist who struggles to be free.*

Poitier plays a political activist on the lam from the police in Cape Town, South Africa. He's locked together with a white apolitical businessman, played by Caine, a situation reminiscent of *The Defiant Ones*. The film is amusing and suspenseful, set against the backdrop of South African racism. Filmed mostly in Kenya. Also with Nicol Williamson and Persis Khambatta. **Director**—Ralph Nelson. (PG)
101 minutes

THE WILD BLUE YONDER
(1952)
★★

**Wendell Corey
Vera Hruba Ralston
Forrest Tucker**

The real hero and star of this movie about World War II is the B-29 bomber, and there are some sterling scenes of this stalwart aircraft doing its thing in the Pacific. The plot also involves the friendships and rivalries of pilots Corey and Tucker and the woman in their life, played by Ralston. The cast of this ordinary flag-waving movie also includes Phil Harris, Ruth Donnelly, and Walter Brennan. **Director**—Allan Dwan.
98 minutes b&w

THE WILD BUNCH (1969)
★★★

**William Holden
Ernest Borgnine
Robert Ryan**

This so-called modern western has loads of explicit violence as a gang confronts the law as well as the Mexican Army in 1914 along the Texas-Mexico border. There are many symbolic flourishes and brilliantly filmed scenes, but only you can decide if the violence is justified in that larger cinematic context. Holden, Borgnine, and Ryan star, with Edmond O'Brien, Warren Oates, Ben Johnson, Jaime Sanchez, Strother Martin, and L. Q. Jones in supporting roles. **Director**—Sam Peckinpah. (R) **Academy Award Nomination**—Walon Green, Roy N. Sickner, and Peckinpah, best story and screenplay (based on material not previously published or produced).
145 minutes

THE WILDERNESS FAMILY—PART 2 (1979)
★★

**Robert Logan
Susan Damante Shaw
Heather Rattray**

More fun and adventures for this suburban family of four who roughs it in the snowy mountains. This second chapter doesn't add much to the 1975 film. The slow plot is interrupted occasionally by some action scenes, which include an avalanche and an attack by wolves. Once more, the animals and the scenery upstage the actors. Mom, dad, and the kids look like they can't wait for the cameras to stop rolling so they can return to their carpeted split-levels. **Director**—Frank Zuniga. (G)
105 minutes

THE WILD GEESE (1978)
★★★

**Richard Burton
Roger Moore
Richard Harris**

Burton, Moore, and Harris lead a mercenary army to Africa to rescue a

Richard Burton plays one of the mercenary leaders in the adventure The Wild Geese.

kidnapped African president. The story is somewhat routine, but it's filled with ripsnorting action and adventure for traditional escapist appeal. The high-calibre cast does an effective job of portraying some interesting characters and giving the audience a full dose of jungle fighting. Also with Hardy Kruger, Stewart Granger, Jack Watson, and Frank Finlay. **Director**—Andrew V. McLaglen. (R)
132 minutes

THE WILD McCULLOCHS (1975)
★

**Forrest Tucker
Max Baer
Julie Adams**

No, it's not about a bunch of unruly chainsaws; it's a mediocre and predictable 1950s-type melodrama about a wealthy, two-fisted Texas truck owner who wants his peace-loving son to fight and his daughter not to marry one of his truckers. Also with Janice Heiden, Dennis Renfield, William Demarest, and Don Grady. Directed and written by Baer. (PG)
93 minutes

THE WILD ONE (1954)
★★★★

**Marlon Brando
Lee Marvin**

Motorcycle technology has changed more than Brando's acting technique, but this realistic slice of life about a gang of cyclists raising hell in a small California town still packs a wallop. Brando plays the sleazy leader of the pack. Other fine performances by Marvin, Mary Murphy, Robert Keith,

- Willie & Phil
- Will Success Spoil Rock Hunter?
- Wilson

- Winchester '73
- The Wind and the Lion
- The Window
- Windows

W

In The Wild Ones, *Marlon Brando makes Terry Moore an offer she can't refuse.*

and Jay C. Flippen. **Director**—Laslo Benedek.   *79 minutes b&w*

WILLIE & PHIL (1980)
★★

**Michael Ontkean
Ray Sharkey
Margot Kidder**

Margot Kidder is a woman determined to become "somebody important" in Willie & Phil.

Ontkean, Sharkey, and Kidder are appealing Bohemian types who develop a deep friendship in this comic romance that satirizes life in the '70s. Paul Mazursky directs with the same skill he showed in *An Unmarried Woman*, but the weakness here is that neither the characters nor the story go beyond parody. Mazursky's people are charming stereotypes; the more serious their story becomes, the less believable they are. (R)   *116 minutes*

WILL SUCCESS SPOIL ROCK HUNTER? (1957)
★★

**Jane Mansfield
Tony Randall**

Mansfield and Randall star in this unsuccessful comedy that attempts to poke fun at TV commercials and the wimpy moral attitude of the 1950s. The plot, about a press agent who gets involved in touting the world's greatest lover, is disjointed, and the movie never seems to get organized. The performances of the stars don't salvage the effort. And the acting of supporting actors Betsy Drake, Mickey Hargitay, Joan Blondell, John Williams, Henry Jones, and Groucho Marx doesn't spoil the film. **Director**—Frank Tashlin.   *95 minutes*

WILSON (1944)
★★★

Alexander Knox

This honest and accurate biography of a great American president stars Knox in the title role. It's a rare biography by Hollywood standards because it doesn't compromise the story of the man to achieve short-term glory with a flashy motion picture. Wilson's noble philosophy as well as his faults are portrayed. The outstanding cast also includes Geraldine Fitzgerald, Charles Coburn, Cedric Hardwicke, Thomas Mitchell, Vincent Price, Francis X. Bushman, Mary Anderson, Ruth Nelson, Ruth Ford, and Eddie Foy, Jr. **Director**—Henry King. **Academy Awards**—Lamar Trotti, writing (original screenplay); Leon Shamroy, cinematography (color). **Nominations**—best picture; King, best director; Knox, best actor.   *154 minutes*

WINCHESTER '73 (1950)
★★★★

**James Stewart
Shelley Winters**

Stewart and Winters star in this marvelous western about Stewart's search for an old foe and a stolen rifle. Before Stewart finds his man and settles the score, there's plenty of action. The excellent cast also includes Dan Duryea, Rock Hudson, Tony Curtis, Steve Brodie, Stephen McNally, Millard Mitchell, and John McIntire. This movie was so well received after its release that it sparked a revival in western films. **Director**—Anthony Mann.   *92 minutes b&w*

THE WIND AND THE LION (1975)
★★

**Sean Connery
Candice Bergen**

Teddy Roosevelt sends the U.S. Marines to Morocco in 1904 to rescue an American widow and her children who are kidnapped by the last of the Barbary pirates. An elaborate but absurd adventure. Connery plays the head pirate, Bergen is the widow, and Brian Keith is Teddy. Also with John Huston, Geoffrey Lewis, and Steve Kanaly. **Director**—John Milius. (PG)   *119 minutes*

THE WINDOW (1949)
★★★

Bobby Driscoll

This compelling thriller about a slum kid who witnesses a murder, but can't convince his parents about what he saw is deftly executed and excrucitingly tense as the boy and murderer parry. Driscoll is excellent in the role of a boy who is often caught telling tales. And there are fine supporting performances by Arthur Kennedy, Ruth Roman, Barbara Hale, and Paul Stewart. The photography of William Steiner sets the mood and tempo of the story. **Director**—Ted Tetzlaff.   *73 minutes b&w*

WINDOWS (1980)
★

**Talia Shire
Elizabeth Ashley**

A gloomy, would-be thriller about a young woman, played by Shire, who's harassed by a psychotic lesbian, played by Ashley. The shoddy screenplay quickly deteriorates into a stale rip-off of *Klute*. Low-key and over-   *(Continued)*

W
- Windwalker
- Winged Victory
- The Winslow Boy
- Winter Kills

Elizabeth Ashley tries to assuage the fears of Talia Shire in Windows.

(Continued)

wrought performances misfire, resulting in unintentional humor. Gordon Willis, the noted cinematographer (*The Godfather; Manhattan*), debuts in this movie as director. He offers some stunning views of New York City, but everything else is ridiculous and irrevelant. Also with Joseph Cortese. (R)   *96 minutes*

WINDWALKER (1981)
★★

Trevor Howard

Howard plays a dying Cheyenne warrior who relates the tragic adventures of his life, much of it dealing with feuding between his tribe and the neighboring Crows. With the exception of Howard, who's unconvincing in the title role, cast members are Indians who perform adequately. The sentimental story, however, never develops with sufficient clarity or impact. Even the various battles involving revengeful Indians and wild animals become tiresome and exceedingly violent for this sort of wilderness film. Also with Nick Ramus and James Remar. **Director**—Keith Merrill. In Crow and Cheyenne with English titles. (PG)   *108 minutes*

WINGED VICTORY (1944)
★★★

Lon McCallister
Jeanne Crain
Edmond O'Brien

A star-studded cast bolsters this film version of Moss Hart's story about young men training as pilots prior to combat in World War II. The patriotic tone might now seem misplaced, but the film is well done and entertaining. The performances of McCallister, Crain, O'Brien, Jo-Carroll Dennison, Judy Holliday, Peter Lind Hayes, Red Buttons, Karl Malden, Lee J. Cobb, Barry Nelson, and Gary Merrill also make the movie worth viewing. **Director**—George Cukor. *130 minutes b&w*

THE WINSLOW BOY (1948)
★★★★

Robert Donat
Cedric Hardwicke
Margaret Leighton
Frank Lawton

The splendid acting of Donat, Hardwicke, Leighton, and Lawton make this real-life story a gem of a film. It's about an attorney, played by Donat, who defends a naval cadet falsely accused of stealing. Based on a play by Terence Rattigan, the production brilliantly conveys the mood of British society and that country's legal system. The excellent cast also includes Ernest Thesiger, Neil North, Jack Watling and Basil Radford. **Director**—Anthony Asquith.   *117 minutes b&w*

WINTER KILLS (1979)
★★

Jeff Bridges

Bridges plays the half-brother of an American President who was assassinated 19 years ago, and now he sets out to solve the crime at a breathless pace. Bridges chases after CIA operatives, organized crime figures, eccentric industrial tycoons, and a Jack Ruby character. The film, based on the Richard Condon novel, is only entertaining in spots. Mostly, it's confusing and makes little sense. John Huston, Anthony Perkins, Eli Wallach, and

FRED ASTAIRE

Born Frederick Austerlitz in Omaha, Nebraska, in 1899, Fred Astaire started his career at the age of five as part of a dancing team with his sister Adele. Their mother was so convinced there was a future in entertainment for her children she moved the family to New York, where Fred and Adele began training at Ned Wayburn's Dancing Academy.

Hailed as child prodigies, the pair toured the Orpheum vaudeville circuit, and as soon as they reached legal working age they made their Manhattan debut at Proctor's Fifth Avenue Theater. The Astaires danced their way through such successes as Gershwin's Lady Be Good *and* Funny Face, *and soon became the*

darlings of Broadway musicals. In 1932, The Bandwagon marked Fred's last appearance with his sister, who married and retired from the stage.

Soon afterward, Fred turned to motion pictures and made his film debut at the age of 34 in Dancing Lady *(1933). For his next movie,* Flying Down to Rio *(1933), he was teamed with Ginger Rogers. Astaire made eight more films with her, and they became the biggest money-making team in screen history. When they finally broke up, Astaire helped to sweep a succession of new film partners to new acclaim—Eleanor Powell, Paulette Goddard, Rita Hayworth, and others.*

Astaire's other memorable films with Ginger Rogers are Roberta *(1935),* Top Hat *(1935),* Follow the Fleet *(1936),* Swing Time *(1936),* Shall We Dance? *(1937),* Carefree *(1938),* The Story of Vernon and Irene Castle *(1939), and* The Barkleys of Broadway *(1948).*

In 1949, Astaire received a special Academy Award.

Some of Astaire's other movies include Easter Parade *(1948),* Daddy Long Legs *(1955),* Funny Face *(1957),* On the Beach *(1959),* Finian's Rainbow *(1968),* The Towering Inferno *(1975), and* Ghost Story *(1981).*

• Wise Blood
• With a Song in My Heart
• Without Warning

• With Six You Get Egg Roll
• Witness for the Prosecution
• The Wiz

Kneeling behind a slain cop, Jeff Bridges fights for his life in Winter Kills.

Sterling Hayden make the most of their supporting roles. Also with Richard Boone, Ralph Meeker, and Dorothy Malone. **Director**—William Richert. (R)　　　*96 minutes*

WISE BLOOD (1979)
★★

Brad Dourif

Director John Huston's 33rd feature film is a puzzling, offbeat story about Bible Belt evangelism that starts off as a parody, but then shifts into a gruesome nightmare. The film was shot in Georgia, but the setting seems to be the private world of some very eccentric characters. Dourif, who played the stutterer in *One Flew Over the Cuckoo's Nest*, turns in an intense performance as a preacher who's also an atheist. Huston's direction carries impact, but the film remains unclear. Also with Amy Wright and Harry Dean Stanton. (No MPAA rating)　*108 minutes*

WITH A SONG IN MY HEART
(1952)
★★

Susan Hayward

Hayward gives a vivid portrayal of Jane Froman, a singer who struggles to return to show business after being seriously injured in an airplane crash. Although Hayward is convincing as the crippled singer, the songs are actually sung by Froman. Those who find the story too much like soap opera will be able to take some consolation from the music. David Wayne, Rory Calhoun, Thelma Ritter, Helen Westcott, Una Merkel, and Robert Wagner appear in supporting roles. **Director**—Walter Lang. **Academy Award Nominations**—Hayward, best actress;

Ritter, best supporting actress.
　　　　　　　117 minutes

WITHOUT WARNING (1980)
(no stars)

Jack Palance
Martin Landau

Palance and Landau star and waste their talents in this shoddy rip-off of *Alien*. The movie features strange creatures who attack their victims with flying leechlike flapjacks. When someone tries to pry these horrible parasites loose, they merely get messier and more firmly embedded. The acting and direction are also a mess, and the absurd script is riddled with holes. Don't waste your time with such nonsense; you've been warned. **Director**—Greydon Clark. (R)　*89 minutes*

WITH SIX YOU GET EGG ROLL
(1968)
★★

Doris Day
Brian Keith

This pleasant production finds a widow with three children and a widower with one child creating a new family. Day is the widow, and Keith is the widower. Their merger causes problems, of course, and the search for harmony brings some laughs. The movie shows flashes of potential, but never really catches fire; at times, it's as boring as service in a second-rate restaurant. Also with Pat Carroll, Barbara Hershey, Alice Ghostley, and George Carlin. **Director**—Howard Morris. (G)　　　*99 minutes*

WITNESS FOR THE
PROSECUTION (1957)
★★★★

Charles Laughton
Tyrone Power
Marlene Dietrich

Clever dialogue, brilliant acting by Laughton, and some devious twists and turns in the plot make this ordinary production, based on an Agatha Christie play, seem extraordinary more often than not. Dietrich plays the wife of Power, an alleged killer. Laughton is hired to defend him.

Excellent acting by Power, Dietrich, Elsa Lanchester, Ian Wolfe, John Williams, and Henry Daniel enhance this suspenseful courtroom drama. Christie invariably pulls one trick too many, thus lessening any chance an intelligent viewer has to solve the crime, and this movie is no exception. **Director**—Billy Wilder. **Academy Award Nominations**—best picture; Wilder, best director; Laughton, best actor; Lanchester, best supporting actress.　　*114 minutes b&w*

THE WIZ (1978)
★★★★

Diana Ross
Michael Jackson
Nipsey Russell
Ted Ross
Richard Pryor

Diana Ross plays the role of Dorothy in The Wiz, *a black version of* The Wizard of Oz.

Somewhere over the Brooklyn Bridge, skies are blue. Here we find Dorothy (Diana Ross), the Scarecrow (Jackson), the Tin Man (Russell), and the Cowardly Lion (Ted Ross) following the Yellow Brick Road in search of miracles from the Wiz; he's played by Pryor and is ensconced in the World Trade Center. This extravagant film musical, a black version of *The Wizard of Oz* adapted from the smash Broadway production, offers dazzling beauty, rousing singing and dancing, and a touching contemporary recreation of the famous children's fantasy. It's a sure-fire hit, but it doesn't upstage the enduring Judy Garland

(Continued)

W ● The Wizard of Oz ● The Woman in the Window
● Wolfen ● The Woman Next Door
● The Wolf Man ● Woman of the Year

(Continued)
version. Also with Mabel King and Theresa Merritt. **Director**—Sidney Lumet. **Academy Award Nomination**—Oswald Morris, cinematography (G) *133 minutes*

THE WIZARD OF OZ (1939)
★★★★

**Judy Garland
Frank Morgan
Ray Bolger
Jack Haley
Bert Lahr**

This fantastic tale about a Kansas farm girl who's spirited off to the land of Oz still tingles with freshness. Garland as the girl is memorable, and such songs as "Over the Rainbow" are unforgettable. The charming cast of this classic also includes Margaret Hamilton, Clara Blandick, Charley Grapewin, and Billie Burke. For added measure, the superb songs of E. Y. Harburg and Harold Arlen blend beautifully with the photography of Harold Rosson. **Director**—Victor Fleming. (G) **Academy Awards**—Arlen and Harburg, best song ("Over the Rainbow"); Garland, special award for her performance as a screen juvenile. **Nomination**—best picture.
101 minutes b&w/color

Jack Haley, Ray Bolger, Frank Morgan, Judy Garland, and Bert Lahr in The Wizard of Oz.

WOLFEN (1981)
★★

Albert Finney

This is a stunning, nerve-jangling horror film with many attributes and, unfortunately, a muddled and preposterous conclusion that cancels out some of the thrills. Finney gives a classy performance as a shrewd New York City homicide detective, who connects some brutal murders to a marauding pack of superwolves. Director Michael Wadleigh creates an extraordinary eerie atmosphere, but the film becomes bogged down with unclear rationalization about man's callousness toward nature. (R)
114 minutes

THE WOLF MAN (1941)
★★★

**Lon Chaney, Jr.
Claude Rains**

Chaney, Rains, Bela Lugosi, and Maria Ouspenskaya appear in this grim, intelligent, and well-made horror classic about Larry Talbot, an ordinary man who turns peculiar whenever there's a full moon. Chaney, of course, is the troubled man; Rains plays his

father. The movie is eerie enough to make you think twice about going out for a walk at night. The outstanding cast of this engrossing film also includes Ralph Bellamy, Warren William, Patric Knowles, Evelyn Ankers, and Fay Helm. **Director**—George Waggner. *70 minutes b&w*

THE WOMAN IN THE WINDOW (1944)
★★★

**Edward G. Robinson
Joan Bennett**

Robinson and Bennett shine in this taut thriller about a professor, played by Robinson, who befriends a beautiful woman, played by Bennett, while his family is on vacation and then becomes involved in a murder case. The movie weakens slightly toward the end, but not enough to spoil a top-notch film. Raymond Massey, Dan Duryea, Arthur Loft, Bobby Blake, Edmund Breon, and Dorothy Peterson also star. **Director**—Fritz Lang.
99 minutes b&w

THE WOMAN NEXT DOOR (1981)
★★★

**Gerard Depardieu
Fanny Ardant**

Writer-director François Truffaut deftly guides this extraordinary film of passion and tragedy that brims with inventive surprises. Depardieu and Ardant play star-crossed lovers who had an affair eight years ago. After they broke up, they each married someone else. Coincidentally, they become neighbors, and the flame is rekindled, with the guilt and frustration causing havoc. Depardieu's performance is limited, but Ardant is especially appealing; she almost steals the movie. In French with English titles. (No MPAA rating) *106 minutes*

WOMAN OF THE YEAR (1942)
★★★

**Spencer Tracy
Katharine Hepburn**

Tracy and Hepburn are charming in this story about a sports writer and a

● The Women
● Women in Love
● The Wonderful Crook
● Wonder Man
● Won Ton Ton, the Dog Who Saved Hollywood
● The World of Henry Orient
● The World of Suzie Wong

W

famed political columnist, who seems to know about everything except sports. Tracy is the sports reporter, and Hepburn plays the political commentator. The acting and dialogue are tops, although the comedy falters at times, as the couple struggles to keep love free from the intrusion of world events. Fay Bainter, William Bendix, Reginald Owen, Roscoe Karns, Minor Watson, and Dan Tobin star in supporting roles. This was the first pairing of Tracy and Hepburn on the screen. **Director**—George Stevens. **Academy Award**—Michael Kanin and Ring Lardner, writing (original screenplay).

114 minutes b&w

THE WOMEN (1939)
★★★

Norma Shearer
Joan Crawford
Rosalind Russell

This comedy-drama is well-titled because it has a cast of more than 125 women. It seems tame now, but there are still enough sparks and barbs in the complex plot to please most viewers. The large cast also includes Paulette Goddard, Mary Boland, Margaret Dumont, Hedda Hopper, Ruth Hussey, and Marjorie Main. Anita Loos and Jane Murfin wrote the script for this film version of the Clare Boothe Luce play and had the wisdom to keep much of the original biting dialogue intact. The story—keyed to a socialite's divorce—gets muddled at times, however. **Director**—George Cukor.

132 minutes b&w

WOMEN IN LOVE (1970)
★★★

Glenda Jackson
Jennie Linden
Alan Bates

Jackson, Linden, and Bates star in this film version of D. H. Lawrence's celebrated novel. Whereas Lawrence attempted to be honest and realistic, the movie in director Ken Russell's inept hands is too self-conscious and even ostentatious. However, the period sets of the Midlands of England during the 1920s, the excellent acting, and a provocative nude wrestling scene make the film worthwhile.

Oliver Reed, Eleanor Bron, Alan Webb, and Michael Gough appear in supporting roles. (R) **Academy Award**—Jackson, best actress. **Nominations**—Russell, best director; Larry Kramer, best screenplay (based on material from another medium).

130 minutes

THE WONDERFUL CROOK (1977)
★★★

Gerard Depardieu
Marlene Jobert

Swiss filmmaker Claude Goretta weaves grace and charm throughout this neat little comedy. It's about a young furniture factory owner who robs banks to meet his company's payroll. The acting is extraordinary and delightful, especially when dealing with small and subtle events that concern the quality of life. Depardieu—in the title role—and Jobert are appealing with their complex and delicately humorous parts. In French with English titles. (No MPAA rating)

122 minutes

WONDER MAN (1945)
★★★

Danny Kaye

Kaye is sensational in this story of twins. Kaye, of course, plays both of them—one a quiet studious type, the other a brash nightclub entertainer. The action and comic pace pick up when the entertainer is killed, and the bookish twin must replace him. Virginia Mayo, Vera-Ellen, S. Z. Sakall, Donald Woods, Ed Brophy, and Steve Cochran also appear in this colorful and delightful production. **Director**—H. Bruce Humberstone. **Academy Award**—John Fulton and A. W. Johns, special effects. *96 minutes*

WON TON TON, THE DOG WHO SAVED HOLLYWOOD (1976)
★

Art Carney
Madeline Kahn
Bruce Dern

This movie is just a strained and disor-

ganized string of anemic gags in a thin plot. It's about a German shepherd who becomes a movie star in the 1920s. The film is about as funny and interesting as TV pet food commercials. More than 60 veteran film personalities appear in fleeting cameo roles with scant impact. Carney, Kahn, and Dern head the human cast as film-studio denizens. All are lackluster and are upstaged by Augustus Von Schumacher, the dog. *Won Ton Ton*, the movie, does little to save Hollywood. **Director**—Michael Winner. (PG)

92 minutes

THE WORLD OF HENRY ORIENT (1964)
★★★

Tippy Walker
Merri Spaeth
Peter Sellers

Walker and Spaeth play two rich New York teenagers who adore an eccentric pianist, played by Sellers, in this congenial yet sensitive comedy. The young duo just about steal the show from Sellers and the other veterans as they harass the pianist by following him around New York City. The teens idolize him because they believe love is missing in their own lives. The minor theme of misplaced love is touchingly portrayed. The cast also includes Paula Prentiss, Phyllis Thaxter, Angela Lansbury, and Tom Bosley. **Director**—George Roy Hill.

106 minutes

THE WORLD OF SUZIE WONG (1960)
★

William Holden
Nancy Kwan

The world in the title is that of a prostitute in Hong Kong, but in this insensitive Hollywood treatment everything is presented merely as offbeat. Holden gives a wooden performance as an artist who falls in love with Suzie, played competently by Kwan. The phony plot and the pace of the story also mar the movie. Sylvia Syms, Michael Wilding, Laurence Naismith, and Jackie Chan appear in supporting roles. **Director**—Richard Quine.

129 minutes

W·X·Y

- The World's Greatest Lover
- Written on the Wind
- The Wrong Arm of the Law
- Wrong Kind of Girl
- Wuthering Heights
- W.W. and the Dixie Dancekings
- Xala
- Xanadu
- Yankee Doodle Dandy

THE WORLD'S GREATEST LOVER (1978)
★

Gene Wilder

Wilder—director, star, writer—can't make the humor click in this frantic tale about a Milwaukee baker who longs to become a silent-screen star in the '20s. The silly gags produce too few laughs, and the pacing is choppy. Wilder, who studied at the Mel Brooks comedy school, doesn't come close to the level of the master. This movie is a far cry from the world's greatest comedy. Also with Dom DeLuise, Carol Kane, Fritz Feld, and Carl Ballentine. (PG)   *89 minutes*

WRITTEN ON THE WIND (1956)
★★★

Lauren Bacall
Robert Stack
Dorothy Malone

Bacall, Stack, and Malone star in this trite melodrama about the many problems within a wealthy oil family. The movie, however, is stabilized by some fine acting. In any case, the movie is so well-paced that many of the faults diminish. The cast also includes Rock Hudson, Robert Keith, and Grant Williams. **Director**—Douglas Sirk. **Academy Award**—Malone, best supporting actress. **Nomination**—Stack, best supporting actor.   *100 minutes*

THE WRONG ARM OF THE LAW (1963)
★★★

Peter Sellers

This British comedy about gangsters who impersonate cops and take loot from robbers they capture keeps the laughs coming at a fast pace. Sellers plays the brain behind the unusual London mob and seems at home with the role. He gets excellent support from Lionel Jeffries, Bernard Cribbins, Bill Kerr, and Davy Kaye. **Director**—Cliff Owen.   *92 minutes b&w*

WRONG KIND OF GIRL
See Bus Stop

WUTHERING HEIGHTS (1939)
★★★★

Laurence Olivier
Merle Oberon

A first-rate cast transforms the classic Victorian novel by Emily Brontë into a fine motion picture. Olivier plays the strange Heathcliff, and Oberson is Cathy, the woman who loves him. David Niven, Hugh Williams, Flora Robson, Geraldine Fitzgerald, Donald Crisp, Miles Mander, and Leo G. Carroll also star. Under William Wyler's excellent direction, with the well-written script by Ben Hecht and Charles MacArthur, this great love story never falters. **Academy Award**—Gregg Toland, best cinematography (black and white). **Nominations**—best picture; Wyler, best director; Olivier, best actor; Fitzgerald, best supporting actress; Ben Hecht and Charles MacArthur, writing (screenplay).
104 minutes b&w

W.W. AND THE DIXIE DANCEKINGS (1975)
★★

Burt Reynolds
Art Carney

A friendly hold-up man, played by Reynolds, gets involved with a third-rate country-and-western music group in the '50s and leads them on to Nashville for a crack at Grand Ol' Opry stardom. The movie has ample good humor and energy, but an empty script. Carney plays an amusing preacher-detective. Also with Conny Van Dyke, Jerry Reed, and Ned Beatty. **Director**—John Avildsen. (PG)   *106 minutes*

X

XALA (1975)
★★★

An intriguing African film about the clash of modern aspirations amid traditional customs and lingering superstitions in a nation emerging from colonialism. The story focuses on a bourgeois businessman who fails to consummate his third polygamous marriage. "Xala" means the curse of impotence. The film is sophisticated, glowing, and amusing, and a triumph for Senegalese writer-director Osmane Sembene. In French with English titles. (No MPAA rating) *116 minutes*

XANADU (1980)
★★

Olivia Newton-John
Michael Beck
Gene Kelly

Gene Kelly and Olivia Newton-John sing and tap dance in the musical Xanadu.

Newton-John plays a glowing, singing, rollerskating muse who inspires a young artist, played by Beck, to open a disco. So much for the absurd plot. The only thing worthwhile in this mediocre movie is some fine singing and dancing, primarily by Newton-John. The always-charming Kelly plays a former clarinetist who was once smitten by the same muse; he does a number or two—rather well—with Olivia. But why he came out of retirement for this gig is puzzling. **Director**—Robert Greenwald. (PG)
93 minutes

Y

YANKEE DOODLE DANDY (1942)
★★★★

James Cagney
Joan Leslie
Walter Huston

Cagney, Leslie, and Huston star in this stunning musical about the life

- Yanks
- The Yearling
- The Yellow Cab Man
- Yellow Sky
- You Can't Cheat an Honest Man
- You Light Up My Life
- You'll Never Get Rich

Y

James Cagney and Joan Leslie in Yankee Doodle Dandy, *about George M. Cohan.*

and times of George M. Cohan, the famed vaudevillian song-and-dance man. Cagney is superb as Cohan. Someone else might be able to make a good movie with the Cohan songs, but Cagney, almost on his own, has made this a great production. Even the slightly heavy dose of patriotism doesn't tarnish the effort. Also with Richard Whorf, George Tobias, Eddie Foy, Jr., and Frances Langford. **Director**—Michael Curtiz. **Academy Award**—Cagney, best actor. **Nominations**—best picture; Curtiz, best director; Huston, best supporting actor; Robert Buckner, writing (original story). *126 minutes b&w*

YANKS (1979)
★★

Richard Gere
Vanessa Redgrave
William Devane

This movie is a sentimental account about the effect American soldiers had on an English community during their brief stay during World War II. The film is rich in detail and beautifully photographed, but the script suffers from the blahs. The events are predictable and are rarely exciting. Gere, Redgrave, and Devane are the principal players involved in various romantic episodes among the GIs and the English girls. Also with Chick

Vannera, Rachel Roberts, and Wendy Morgan. **Director**—William Schlesinger. (R) *139 minutes*

THE YEARLING (1946)
★★★★

Gregory Peck
Jane Wyman
Claude Jarman, Jr.

This sensitive story of a young farm boy, who's devoted to a pet fawn that his father must destroy, is one of the finest family films of all time. The characterizations are vivid, and the emotions are honest in this rare motion picture. Peck, Wyman, and Jarman star, with Chill Wills, Clem Bevans, June Lockhart, Forrest Tucker, and Henry Travers in supporting roles. **Director**—Clarence Brown. **Academy Awards**—Charles Rosher, Leonard Smith, and Arthur Arling, cinematography (color). **Nominations**—best picture; Brown, best director; Peck, best actor; Wyman, best actress. *134 minutes*

THE YELLOW CAB MAN (1950)
★★

Red Skelton

Skelton is in top comic form in this tale about an off-beat cab driver who invents unbreakable glass, picks up pretty girls, and has trouble with gangsters and shady businessmen. The production has its rough spots, however, and at times it seems that Skelton tries too hard to get laughs. Walter Slezak and Gloria De Haven also star, with James Gleason, Jay C. Flippen, Edward Arnold, and Polly Moran in supporting roles. **Director**—Jack Donohue. *84 minutes b&w*

YELLOW SKY (1948)
★★★

Gregory Peck
Anne Baxter
Richard Widmark

Peck and Widmark face off in an Arizona ghost town in this exciting and well-mounted western. It involves a feud over stolen gold and a woman, played by Baxter. The excellent cast also includes Robert Arthur, Henry

Morgan, John Russell, and James Barton. **Director**—William Wellman. *98 minutes b&w*

YOU CAN'T CHEAT AN HONEST MAN (1939)
★★★

W. C. Fields
Edgar Bergen

If you had to spend the rest of your life in Philadelphia with just one Fields film, this wouldn't be the one to take. However, this slice of nonsense about beleaguered circus owner Larson E. Whipsnade, who must elude the law and deal with the likes of Bergen's pals Charlie McCarthy and Mortimer Snerd, is still a lot of fun. Fields, of course, plays the role of Whipsnade. The cast also includes Constance Moore, James Bush, Mary Forbes, Edward Brophy, Thurston Hall, and Charles Coleman. **Director**—George Marshall. *79 minutes b&w*

YOU LIGHT UP MY LIFE (1977)
★

Didi Conn
Joe Silver

This melodrama about a young girl's struggle to become a pop singer is supposed to be a warm and touching film, but it never comes off as intended. Former ad man Joseph Brooks, who produced, directed, and wrote the screenplay, overstuffed the plot with too much triteness and sentimentality. Conn in the lead role, however, manages to exude some appeal. And Silver, who plays the girl's father—a second-rate stand-up comedian—does rather well among a cast of mostly unknowns. Also with Michael Zaslow, Melanie Mayron, and Stephen Nathan. (PG) *90 minutes*

YOU'LL NEVER GET RICH (1941)
★★★

Fred Astaire
Rita Hayworth

Astaire and Hayworth sparkle in this comedy musical. It's about a showman who's still able to put on his show and

(Continued)

Y
- Young at Heart
- Youngblood
- Youngblood Hawke
- The Young Lions
- Young Man With a Horn

GEORGE C. SCOTT

George C. Scott, a distinguished actor who seems to dominate his movies, was the first actor to refuse an Academy Award. Born in 1926 in Wise, Virginia, and raised in Detroit, Scott served four years in the U.S. Marines before studying journalism at the University of Missouri. After he performed in five plays there, his interests shifted from journalism to acting. In the early 1950s, he worked in stock while supporting himself as a truck driver, formsetter on a road gang, roofer, and proof-machine operator. In 1956, he read for the New York Shakespeare Festival and landed the role of Richard III. He next appeared as Jacques in As You Like It, following this with an award-winning performance in Children of Darkness at the Circle-in-the-Square.

Scott made his Broadway debut with Judith Anderson in Comes a Day and then performed in The Andersonville Trial, which he later directed for the Public Broadcasting System on television. Scott starred on Broadway in Plaza Suite in 1968 and in Uncle Vanya in 1973. In 1975, he directed and starred in Arthur Miller's Death of a Salesman.

Scott made his film debut in The Hanging Tree (1959). This was followed by Anatomy of a Murder (1959), The Hustler (1962), The List of Adrian Messenger (1963), Dr. Strangelove (1963), The Yellow Rolls Royce (1964), The Bible . . . In the Beginning (1966), Not With My Wife You Don't (1966), The Flim Flam Man (1967), and Petulia (1969).

In 1970, Scott declined an Academy Award for his performance in Patton. His other movies include They Might Be Giants (1971); The Hospital (1972); The New Centurions (1972); The Day of the Dolphin (1973); Rage (1973), which he also directed; The Savage Is Loose (1974); Movie, Movie (1978); Hardcore (1979); and Taps (1981).

Formerly married to actress Colleen Dewhurst, Scott now makes his home in Connecticut with his actress wife Trish Van Devere.

(Continued)
land the girl of his dreams even though he's drafted into the Army. The plot and story line are as limp as those in most musicals, but the dancing is fine, and the Cole Porter music is great. John Hubbard, Robert Benchley, Osa Massen, Frieda Inescort, and Guinn Williams appear in supporting roles. **Director**—Sidney Lanfield.

88 minutes b&w

YOUNG AT HEART (1954)
★★★

Doris Day
Frank Sinatra

Sinatra romances Day in this polished musical version of *Four Daughters*, a story about the problems of a musical family in a small town. The singing and acting of the stars are at a high level, with fine supporting performances by Ethel Barrymore, Gig Young, Robert Keith, Alan Hale, Jr., and Dorothy Malone. **Director**—Gordon Douglas. *117 minutes*

YOUNGBLOOD (1978)
★★

Lawrence-Hilton Jacobs

Jacobs stars in this typical youth gang and drugs melodrama set in a Los Angeles ghetto. The story overplays the hard realism of street life and neglects drama and entertainment value. Tight direction keeps the action moving, but basically the film is familiar stuff with the inevitable neighborhood rumble, fatherless family situations, and so on. Also with Ren Woods and Bryan O'Dell. **Director**—Noel Nosseck. (R) *90 minutes*

YOUNGBLOOD HAWKE (1964)
★★

James Franciscus

Despite a trite plot and mediocre acting in some key roles, there's enough vitality derived from the Herman Wouk novel to make this movie about a Southerner who becomes a successful novelist entertaining at times. Franciscus is close to awful, but Mary Astor and Edward Andrews shine in supporting roles. Also with Genevieve Page, Suzanne Pleshette, and Eva Gabor. **Director**—Delmer Daves.

132 minutes b&w

THE YOUNG LIONS (1958)
★★★

Marlon Brando
Montgomery Clift
Dean Martin

Brando, Clift, and Martin star in this World War II tale that comes close to becoming a great film. It falls short of greatness because the plot is too complex, the story development is uneven, and the movie is too long. The story deals with the fate of two Americans—Clift and Martin—and a German officer, played by Brando. The cast also includes Hope Lange, Maximilian Schell, Mai Britt, Barbara Rush, and Lee Van Cleef. **Director**—Edward Dmytryk. **Academy Award Nomination**—Joe MacDonald, cinematography (black and white).

167 minutes b&w

YOUNG MAN WITH A HORN (1950)
★★★

Kirk Douglas
Lauren Bacall
Doris Day

Douglas shines as a troubled and compulsive trumpet player in this biography about the life of famed jazz musician Bix Beiderbecke. Bacall and Day portray the women in his life. Hoagy Carmichael, Juano Hernandez, Nestor Paiva, Mary Beth Hughes, and Jerome Cowan appear in supporting

- Young Mr. Lincoln
- The Young Philadelphians
- Young Tom Edison
- You Only Live Twice
- You're in the Army Now
- Yours, Mine and Ours
- Your Turn, My Turn
- You Were Never Lovelier

Y

roles. **Director**—Michael Curtiz.
112 minutes b&w

YOUNG MR. LINCOLN (1939)
★★★★

Henry Fonda
Alice Brady

Good movies about great people are infrequent, but Fonda succeeds admirably in the role of young Abraham Lincoln in this story about the early years of the 16th President of the United States. Under John Ford's excellent direction, the attention to period atmosphere, such as a log-splitting contest and a tug of war, enhance the quality of the movie. Brady gives Fonda good support. Donald Meek, Eddie Quillan, Spencer Charters, Marjorie Weaver, and Arleen Whelan also star in supporting roles. **Academy Award Nomination**—Lamar Trotti, writing (original story).
100 minutes b&w

THE YOUNG PHILADELPHIANS (1959)
★★

Paul Newman
Barbara Rush

Despite the "young" in the title, this story about a young but poor lawyer on the make in Philadelphia society has been told many times before—and much better at that. Newman plays the role of the lawyer; Rush is a society girl he's pursuing. Solid performances by Newman, Rush, Alexis Smith, Robert Vaughn, Otto Kruger, Brian Keith, and Diana Brewster buoy this conventional potboiler. **Director**—Vincent Sherman. **Academy Award Nominations**—Vaughn, best supporting actor; Harry Stradling, cinematography (black and white).
136 minutes b&w

YOUNG TOM EDISON (1940)
★★★

Mickey Rooney

Rooney in the title role of Tom Edison has the good sense to cool his usual exuberance and to play this modest biography conventionally. The movie traces the brilliant inventor's early

Fay Bainter and Mickey Rooney in a scene from Young Tom Edison.

experiments and details the problems he faced. Although the story is less than complete—some facts are out of focus—it's the kind of motion picture young people should find inspiring. Parents should appreciate the solid performances of Rooney, Fay Bainter, George Bancroft, Victor Kilian, and Virginia Weidler. **Director**—Norman Taurog.
82 minutes b&w

YOU ONLY LIVE TWICE (1967)
★★

Sean Connery

If it wasn't for the violence, the bizarre story developments, the extravagant sets, and the superb special effects, this fifth James Bond movie could be mistaken for a travel film—*Agent 007 in Japan* or some such title. The production will please Bond fans despite the weak plot that has Connery, as the dashing hero, facing the villians from SPECTRE. Those who are neutral—or unBonded—might find some solace in the excellent performance of Donald Pleasence as the head of the bad guys. The cast also includes Bernard Lee, Karin Dor, Charles Gray, Lois Maxwell, Tetsuro Tamba, Akiko Wakabayashi, and Mie Hama. **Director**—Lewis Gilbert.
117 minutes

YOU'RE IN THE ARMY NOW (1941)
★★

Jimmy Durante
Phil Silvers

Durante and Silvers portray two incompetent vacuum cleaner salesmen who join the Army by mistake in this enjoyable comedy. The veteran comics perform with the irresistible charm and congeniality they're famous for, but

the story line sometimes creaks, as if it wasn't plugged into the same circuit as these famed entertainers. Donald MacBride, Jane Wyman, and Regis Toomey appear in supporting roles. **Director**—Lewis Seiler.
79 minutes b&w

YOURS, MINE AND OURS (1968)
★★★

Lucille Ball
Henry Fonda

Ball and Fonda star in this well-made farce about a widow and widower—both with large families—who marry. The problems encountered when two large families live in the same house create the comic situations in this movie. At times, the problems are so obvious they fail to bring laughs, but there are enough good moments to make this film mildly entertaining. Van Johnson and Tom Bosley appear in supporting roles. **Director**—Melville Shavelson. *111 minutes*

YOUR TURN, MY TURN (1979)
★★★

Marlene Jobert
Philippe Leotard

François Leterrier's honest look at marriage and romance is set in modern Paris. This comedy-drama touchingly illustrates how a wife and mother, played by Jobert, is beset with obstacles posed by her child and by society in which men are allowed more freedom. There are likable performances from Jobert and Leotard, who plays her lover. In French with English titles. (PG) *101 minutes*

YOU WERE NEVER LOVELIER (1942)
★★★

Fred Astaire
Rita Hayworth

If the viewer can forgive the inept plot and silly dialogue, this musical with Jerome Kern-Johnny Mercer songs and Astaire's dancing will still be delightful entertainment. Adolphe Menjou plays a matchmaking father

(Continued)

Y·Z
- Zabriskie Point
- Ziegfeld Follies
- Ziegfeld Girl
- Zoot Suit
- Zorba the Greek
- Zorro, the Gay Blade

(Continued)

for his daughter, played by Hayworth. Astaire, of course, is the other part of the matchup. The rest of the cast includes Leslie Brooks, Larry Parks, Adele Mara, and Xavier Cugat and his orchestra. The songs include "I'm Old-Fashioned," "Dearly Beloved," and the title tune. **Director**—William A. Seiter. *97 minutes b&w*

Z

ZABRISKIE POINT (1970)
★★

Mark Frechette
Daria Halprin

It appears that director Michelangelo Antonioni tried to make this motion picture about decadence in the United States larger than life. Instead, he delivers a strange rambling movie that's often emotionally out of focus even when the camera zooms in on a vivid image. The photography of Alfio Contini is excellent, and that's the only thing to recommend about this production. The acting of Frechette, Halprin, Rod Taylor, Paul Fix, and Kathleen Cleaver is only a shade better than mediocre and certainly not good enough to bring this film out of the twilight zone. (R) *111 minutes*

ZIEGFELD FOLLIES (1946)
★★

Fred Astaire
Lucille Ball
William Powell

A better title for this all-star musical would have been *Heavenly Follies* or *Ziegfeld Follies in Heaven*. It's the kind of show you shouldn't take too seriously, as Powell, playing Ziegfeld, narrates the affair from Heaven. The movie has some splendid production numbers and some mediocre ones, and there are so many stars that you're bound to find someone you like. Besides Astaire, Ball, and Powell, the cast includes Jimmy Durante, Fannie Brice, Lena Horne, Gene Kelly, Hume Cronyn, Judy Garland, Red Skelton, Lucille Bremer, Victor Moore, and Edward Arnold. **Director**—Vincente Minnelli. *110 minutes*

ZIEGFELD GIRL (1941)
★★

James Stewart
Judy Garland
Hedy Lamarr
Lana Turner

Stewart, Garland, Lamarr, and Turner star in this musical about the problems and triumphs of a "typical" Ziegfeld girl. Musicals that don't attempt to tell a story with any degree of seriousness are usually tolerable, but this production starts to creak and groan—after a delightful beginning—when it delves too deeply into the lives of Ziegfeld girls. The rest of the cast includes Tony Martin, Jackie Cooper, Charles Winninger, Al Shean, Dan Dailey, Eve Arden, and Edward Everett Horton. The movie is noted for Garland's rendition of "Minnie from Trinidad" and "I'm Always Chasing Rainbows," but a Busby Berkeley number called "You Stepped Out of a Dream" is the best in the show. **Director**—Robert Z. Leonard. *131 minutes b&w*

ZOOT SUIT (1982)
★★★

Daniel Valdez
Edward James Olmos
Tyne Daly

This is a powerful and colorful musical drama that captures the Chicano spirit and presents a compelling social message about racial prejudice. This worthy screen version of Luis Valdez's play involves a group of Mexican-Americans in 1942 Los Angeles, who were sent to prison on trumped-up charges. Even though the drama falters some, the Chicano characters are memorable because of fine acting by a novice cast. **Director**—Valdez. (R) *103 minutes*

ZORBA THE GREEK (1964)
★★★

Anthony Quinn
Alan Bates
Lila Kedrova

The mood and atmosphere of Nikos Kazantzakis's great novel are captured in this visually beautiful production, but the soul of the book and the major

Alan Bates and Anthony Quinn discuss a plan to get logs down a hill in Zorba the Greek.

character remain elusive on screen. Quinn makes a commendable effort as the congenial Greek peasant, and Bates is excellent as the English writer who befriends him on Crete. Kedrova and Irene Papas also deliver solid performances in supporting roles. **Director**—Michael Cacoyannis. **Academy Awards**—Kedrova, best supporting actress; Walter Lassally, cinematography (black and white). **Nominations**—best picture; Cacoyannis, best director; Quinn, best actor; Cacoyannis, best screenplay (based on material from another medium). *142 minutes b&w*

ZORRO, THE GAY BLADE (1981)
★★

George Hamilton

George Hamilton as the foppish twin brother of Don Diego Vega in Zorro, the Gay Blade.

Hamilton knocks himself out in this wild spoof about the legendary masked-man adventures, made famous by Douglas Fairbanks, Sr., and Tyrone Power. Hamilton hams it up with a mock Spanish accent as he plays the role of Don Diego Vega, a champion of "the poor pipples" of Los Angeles. He also takes a turn playing foppish twin brother Bunny Wigglesworth, a swishbuckler indeed. But the jokes comes across with a dull edge. Ron Leibman and Brenda Vaccaro co-star. **Director**—Peter Medak. (PG) *93 minutes*

Front cover, top row (l to r): **Smokey and the Bandit II** © 1980 Universal City Studios, Inc.; **The Wizard of Oz** © 1939 Metro-Goldwyn-Mayer, Inc.; **Raiders of the Lost Ark** © 1981 Lucasfilm, Ltd.; **The Blue Lagoon** © 1980 Columbia Pictures Industries, Inc. Bottom row: **9 to 5** © 1980 20th Century-Fox Film Corp.; **Singin' in the Rain** © 1952 Metro-Goldwyn-Mayer, Inc.; **The French Lieutenant's Woman** © 1981 United Artists Corp.

Back cover, top row (l to r): **The Sound of Music** © 1965 20th Century-Fox Film Corp.; **Dogs of War** © 1979 United Artists Corp.; **Whose Life Is It Anyway?** © 1981 Metro-Goldwyn-Mayer, Inc.; **Butch Cassidy and the Sundance Kid** © 1969 20th Century-Fox Film Corp. Bottom row: **Popeye** © 1980 Paramount Pictures Corp. and Walt Disney Productions; **Raging Bull** © 1980 United Artists Corp.; **True Confessions** © 1981 United Artists Corp.

pgs. 4 & 5 top row (l to r): **Beloved Infidel** © 1959 20th Century-Fox Corp.; **Adam's Rib** © 1950 Metro-Goldwyn-Mayer, Inc.; **Angels With Dirty Faces** © 1938 United Artists Corp.; **A Connecticut Yankee at King Arthur's Court** © 1948 Paramount Pictures, Inc. Middle row: **Giant** © 1956 Warner Bros., Inc.; **Cheyenne Autumn** © 1964 Warner Bros., Inc.; **From Here to Eternity** © 1953 Columbia Pictures Corp.; **The Barkleys of Broadway** © 1974 Metro-Goldwyn-Mayer, Inc.; **Hans Christian Anderson** © 1954 RKO Radio Pictures, Inc.; **The Drowning Pool** © 1975 Warner Bros., Inc.; **All That Jazz** © 1979 20th Century-Fox Film Corp.; **The Bridge on the River Kwai** © 1974 Columbia Pictures Industries, Inc.; **Rich Kids** © 1979 United Artists Corp. Bottom row: **The Great Muppet Caper** © 1981 Henson Associates, Inc.; **Life of Brian** © 1979 Warner Bros., Inc.; **The Desert Fox** © 1951 Warner Bros.-Seven Arts, Inc.

pg.   6 © 1948 Universal-International Pictures Corp.
pg.   7 © 1950 Metro-Goldwyn-Mayer, Inc.
pg.   8 © 1951 IFD/Romulus-Horizon
pg.   9 © 1979 Warner Bros., Inc.
        © 1980 Paramount Pictures Corp.
        © 1979 Universal City Studios, Inc.
pg. 10 © 1960 United Artists
        © 1965 Sheldrake Films, Ltd.
pg. 11 © 1979 Columbia Pictures Industries, Inc.
        © 1979 20th Century-Fox Film Corp.
pg. 12 © 1979 20th Century-Fox Film Corp.
pg. 13 © 1950 Columbia Pictures Corp.
        © 1976 Warner Bros., Inc.
pg. 14 © 1981 Barclay's Mercantile Industrial Finance, Ltd.
        © 1979 Paramount Pictures Corp.
pg. 15 © 1980 Paramount Pictures Corp.
pg. 16 © 1973 Universal City Studios, Inc.
        © 1951 Metro-Goldwyn-Mayer, Inc.
        © 1981 Universal City Studios, Inc.
pg. 17 © 1976 United Artists Corp.
pg. 18 © 1956 20th Century-Fox Film Corp.

© 1979 Columbia Pictures Industries, Inc.
pg. 19 © 1938 United Artists Corp.
pg. 20 © 1977 United Artists Corp.
pg. 21 © 1980 Warner Bros., Inc.
        © 1960 United Artists Corp.
pg. 22 © 1979 United Artists Corp.
pg. 23 © 1956 United Artists Corp.
        © 1981 Orion Pictures Co.
pg. 24 © 1980 The Merchant Trust Co. in Trust
pg. 25 © 1958 Warner Bros., Inc.
        © 1979 United Artists Corp.
pg. 26 © 1980 Orion Pictures Co.
        © 1957 United Artists Corp.
pg. 27 © 1945 RKO Radio Pictures, Inc.
pg. 28 © 1955 Metro-Goldwyn-Mayer, Inc.
        © 1977 Paramount Pictures Corp.
pg. 29 © 1942 Walt Disney Productions
pg. 30 © 1940 Universal Pictures
        © 1974 Metro-Goldwyn-Mayer, Inc.
pg. 31 © 1980 Time-Life Productions
pg. 32 © 1979 Universal City Studios, Inc.
        © 1976 Universal Pictures
pg. 33 © 1964 Metro-Goldwyn-Mayer, Inc.
pg. 34 © 1951 Universal-International Picture Corp.
        © 1980 Master Mace, Ltd.
        © 1979 United Artists Corp.
pg. 35 © 1979 Avco Embassy Pictures
        © 1959 20th Century-Fox Film Corp.
pg. 37 © 1954 RKO Radio Pictures, Inc.
pg. 38 © 1955 Metro-Goldwyn-Mayer, Inc.
pg. 39 © 1956 Warner Bros., Inc.
        © 1980 Lorimar Productions, Inc.
pg. 40 © 1946 United Artists Corp.
        © 1981 Warner Bros., Inc.
pg. 41 © 1963 Universal Pictures Co., Inc.
pg. 42 © 1976 United Artists Corp.
pg. 43 © 1979 Walt Disney Productions
pg. 44 © 1979 United Artists Corp.
        © 1973 Warner Bros., Inc.
pg. 45 © 1981 Filmways Pictures, Inc.
        © 1966 Metro-Goldwyn-Mayer, Inc.
pg. 46 © 1978 Universal City Studios, Inc.
pg. 47 © 1980 Universal City Studios, Inc.
pg. 48 © 1981 The Ladd Co.
        © 1945 RKO Radio Pictures, Inc.
        © 1967 Warner Bros.-Seven Arts, Inc.
pg. 49 © 1979 Paramount Pictures, Inc.
pg. 50 © 1976 United Artists Corp.
pg. 51 © 1978 20th Century-Fox Film Corp.
pg. 52 © 1980 Associated Film Distribution
pg. 53 © 1979 20th Century-Fox Film Corp.
pg. 54 © 1941 United Artists Corp.
        © 1974 Columbia Pictures Industries, Inc.
pg. 55 © 1954 Metro-Goldwyn-Mayer, Inc.
        © 1980 Warner Bros., Inc.
pg. 56 © 1981 Universal City Studios, Inc.
pg. 57 © 1978 Columbia Pictures Industries, Inc.
pg. 58 © 1981 Universal City Studios, Inc.
pg. 59 © 1972 Columbia Pictures Industries, Inc.
        © 1977 Columbia Pictures, Industries, Inc.

pg. 60 © 1972 ABC Pictures/Allied Artists
pg. 61 © 1981 Columbia Pictures Industries, Inc.
pg. 62 © 1973 Warner Bros., Inc.
pg. 63 © 1981 Eurasia Investments, Ltd.
        © 1978 Warner Bros., Inc.
pg. 64 © 1975 Incorporated Television Co., Inc.
pg. 65 © 1981 Avco Embassy Pictures
        © 1976 United Artists Corp.
        © 1976 Universal Pictures
pg. 66 © 1943 United Artists Corp.
pg. 67 © 1978 Walt Disney Productions
pg. 68 © 1981 United Artists Corp.
pg. 69 © 1979 Columbia Pictures Industries, Inc.
        © 1981 Warner Bros., Inc., and The Ladd Co.
pg. 70 © 1981 Barclay's Mercantile Industrial Finance, Ltd.
        © 1950 20th Century-Fox Film Corp.
pg. 71 © 1964 Warner Bros., Inc.
pg. 72 © 1978 Columbia Pictures Industries, Inc.
pg. 73 © 1976 Gelderse Maatschappij N.V.
pg. 74 © 1981 Simon Film Productions, Inc.
        © 1941 RKO Radio Pictures, Inc.
pg. 75 © 1981 Titan Productions
        © 1977 Columbia Pictures Industries, Inc.
pg. 76 © 1980 Universal City Studios, Inc.
        © 1977 Metro-Goldwyn-Mayer, Inc.
pg. 77 © 1978 United Artists Corp.
pg. 78 © 1976 Gelderse Maatschappij N.V.
        © 1978 United Artists Corp.
pg. 80 © 1948 Paramount Pictures, Inc.
        © 1981 Universal City Studios, Inc.
pg. 81 © 1978 United Artists Corp.
        © 1967 Jalem/Warner
pg. 82 © 1976 Dino De Laurentiis Corp.
pg. 83 © 1973 American International Television, Inc.
        © 1975 Libra Films
pg. 84 © 1947 RKO Radio Pictures, Inc.
pg. 85 © 1980 Lorimar Productions, Inc.
        © Columbia Pictures Corp.
pg. 86 © 1979 United Artists Corp.
pg. 87 © 1954 Warner Bros.-Seven Arts, Inc.
        © 1958 Warner Bros., Inc.
pg. 89 © 1963 Continental Distributing, Inc.
        © 1981 Warner Bros., Inc.
pg. 90 © 1962 Warner Bros., Inc.
pg. 91 © 1981 Warner Bros., Inc.
pg. 92 © 1951 Columbia Pictures Corp.
        © 1978 EMI Films, Ltd.
pg. 93 © 1978 Universal City Studios, Inc.
pg. 94 © 1951 Warner Bros.-Seven Arts, Inc.
pg. 95 © 1943 Vitagraph, Inc.
pg. 96 © 1964 Universal Pictures Co., Inc.
pg. 97 © 1959 20th Century-Fox Film Corp.
        © 1971 Warner Bros., Inc.
pg. 98 © 1978 Universal City Studios, Inc.
pg. 99 © 1963 Columbia Pictures Corp.
        © 1975 Warner Bros., Inc.
pg. 100 © 1980 United Artists Corp.
pg. 101 © 1944 Paramount Pictures Corp.

PHOTO CREDITS

© 1979 Warner Bros.-Seven Arts, Inc.
pg. 208 © 1978 20th Century-Fox Film Corp.
pg. 209 © 1975 Jobete Film Corp.
© 1981 Paramount Pictures Corp.
© 1979 Warner Bros., Inc.
pg. 210 © 1941 United Artists Corp.
© 1979 Avco Embassy Pictures Corp.
pg. 211 © 1979 United Artists Corp.
© 1978 Avco Embassy Pictures Corp.
pg. 212 © 1941 Vitagraph, Inc.
pg. 213 © 1976 British Lion
pg. 214 © 1956 United Artists Corp.
© 1976 Gelderse Maatschappij N.V.
pg. 215 © 1955 United Artists Corp.
© 1964 Walt Disney Productions
© 1969 20th Century-Fox Film Corp.
pg. 216 © 1981 Paramount Pictures Corp.
© 1976 American International Pictures
pg. 217 © 1973 Warner Bros., Inc.
pg. 218 © 1980 Universal City Studios, Inc.
© 1979 American International Pictures
pg. 219 © 1980 20th Century-Fox Film Corp.
© 1978 Columbia Pictures Industries, Inc.
pg. 220 © 1976 Universal Pictures
© 1947 20th Century-Fox Film Corp.
pg. 221 © 1980 Associated Film Distribution
© 1977 20th Century-Fox Film Corp.
pg. 222 © 1981 Barclay's Mercantile Industrial Finance, Ltd.
pg. 223 © 1955 Warner Bros., Inc.
pg. 224 © 1981 Columbia Pictures Industries, Inc.
© 1978 Universal City Studios, Inc.
pg. 225 © 1981 Paramount Pictures Corp.
© 1975 EMI/Python Pictures
pg. 226 © 1979 Danjaq, S.A.
© 1979 Universal City Studios, Inc.
© 1980 United Artists Corp.
pg. 227 © 1952 United Artists Corp.
pg. 228 © 1978 Warner Bros., Inc.
© 1979 Henson Associates, Inc.
© 1976 Columbia Pictures Industries, Inc.
pg. 229 © 1979 Avco Embassy Pictures Release
© 1935 Metro-Goldwyn-Mayer, Inc.
pg. 230 © 1964 Warner Bros. Pictures Distributing Corp.
pg. 231 © 1940 RKO Radio Pictures, Inc.
© 1976 Dino De Laurentiis Corp.
pg. 233 © 1945 Metro-Goldwyn-Mayer, Inc.
© 1981 Columbia Pictures Industries, Inc.
© 1976 United Artists Corp.
pg. 234 © Paramount Pictures Corp.
pg. 235 © 1977 United Artists Corp.
© 1976 Columbia Pictures Industries, Inc.
pg. 236 © 1935 Metro-Goldwyn-Mayer, Inc.

© 1981 Universal City Studios, Inc.
© 1947 20th Century-Fox Film Corp.
pg. 237 © 1981 Avco Embassy Pictures
pg. 238 © 1980 Paramount Pictures Corp.
© 1979 Universal City Studios, Inc.
pg. 239 © 1980 20th Century-Fox Film Corp.
pg. 240 © 1979 20th Century-Fox Film Corp.
© 1979 Paramount Pictures Corp.
pg. 241 © 1980 American International Pictures
© 1958 Warner Bros., Inc.
pg. 242 © 1980 Universal City Studios, Inc.
© 1959 Warner Bros., Inc.
pg. 243 © 1976 Columbia Pictures Industries, Inc.
© 1979 Columbia Pictures Industries, Inc.
pg. 244 © 1939 Hal Roach
© 1980 20th Century-Fox Film Corp.
pg. 245 © 1956 20th Century-Fox Film Corp.
© 1979 Avco Embassy Pictures
pg. 246 © 1974 Columbia Pictures Industries, Inc.
© 1970 Paramount Pictures Corp.
pg. 247 © 1975 Fantasy Films and United Artists Corp.
pg. 248 © 1977 Warner Bros., Inc.
© 1981 Universal City Studios, Inc.
pg. 249 © 1979 Avco Embassy Pictures
© 1981 Columbia Pictures Industries, Inc.
© 1981 Zephyr Productions
pg. 250 © 1949 Metro-Goldwyn-Mayer, Inc.
© 1954 Columbia Pictures Industries, Inc.
pg. 251 © 1980 Paramount Pictures Corp.
pg. 252 © 1977 20th Century-Fox Film Corp.
© 1981 The Ladd Co.
pg. 253 © 1977 Warner Bros., Inc.
© 1980 Paramount Pictures Corp.
pg. 254 © 1943 20th Century-Fox Film Corp.
© 1957 Warner Bros., Inc.
pg. 256 © 1978 Universal City Studios, Inc.
© 1979 United Artists Corp.
pg. 257 © 1981 Paramount Pictures Corp.
© 1970 20th Century-Fox Film Corp.
pg. 258 © 1981 Metro-Goldwyn-Mayer Film Co.
© 1979 20th Century-Fox Film Corp.
pg. 259 © 1952 Walt Disney Productions
© 1977 Walt Disney Productions
© 1957 20th Century-Fox Film Corp.
pg. 260 © Paramount Pictures Corp.
© 1940 Metro-Goldwyn-Mayer, Inc.
pg. 261 © 1955 Columbia Pictures Industries, Inc.
© 1976 United Artists Corp.
pg. 262 © 1978 National Screen Service Corp.
pg. 263 © 1979 Paramount Pictures Corp.

© 1970 Metro-Goldwyn-Mayer, Inc.
pg. 264 © 1980 Paramount Pictures Corp. and Walt Disney Productions
© 1959 Warner Bros., Inc.
pg. 265 © 1981 Lorimar Film und Fernsehproduktion Gmblt.
pg. 266 © 1977 Paramount Pictures Corp.
pg. 267 © 1969 20th Century-Fox Film Corp.
© 1981 Orion Pictures Co.
© 1980 Warner Bros., Inc.
pg. 268 © 1981 Orion Pictures Co.
© 1981 National Screen Service Corp.
pg. 269 © 1968 Avco/Springtime/MGM/ Crossbow
pg. 270 © 1979 Paramount Pictures Corp.
© 1931 United Artists Corp.
pg. 271 © 1981 Universal City Studios, Inc.
© 1952 Republic Pictures Corp.
pg. 272 © 1968 Warner Bros., Inc.
pg. 273 © 1980 United Artists Corp.
© 1981 Lucasfilm, Ltd.
pg. 274 © 1961 Columbia Pictures Corp.
© Metro-Goldwyn-Mayer, Inc.
pg. 275 © 1942 Loew's, Inc.
© 1954 Warner Bros., Inc.
pg. 276 © 1951 Metro-Goldwyn-Mayer, Inc.
© 1981 Barclay's Mercantile Industrial Finance, Ltd.
pg. 278 © 1978 Walt Disney Productions
pg. 279 © 1975 United Artists Corp.
pg. 280 © 1945 Warner Bros., Inc.
© Columbia Pictures Industries, Inc.
© 1979 United Artists Corp.
pg. 281 © 1959 Warner Bros., Inc.
© 1976 Warner Bros., Inc.
pg. 282 © 1980 United Artists Corp.
© 1977 Joseph E. Levine Presents, Inc.
pg. 284 © 1979 United Artists Corp.
© 1977 Universal City Studios, Inc.
pg. 285 © 1981 Universal City Studios, Inc.
pg. 286 © 1979 20th Century-Fox Film Corp.
© 1967 Paramount Pictures Corp.
© 1955 Paramount Pictures Corp.
pg. 287 © 1958 United Artists Corp.
pg. 288 © 1943 Columbia Pictures Industries, Inc.
pg. 289 © 1976 Warner Bros., Inc.
pg. 291 © 1979 Associated Film Distribution
© 1957 Warner Bros., Inc.
pg. 292 © 1981 Dino De Laurentiis Corp.
pg. 294 © 1977 United Artists Corp.
pg. 295 © 1979 Universal City Studios, Inc.
pg. 296 © 1977 Universal Pictures
pg. 297 © 1941 Warner Bros., Inc.
© 1980 Paramount Pictures, Corp.
pg. 299 © 1976 Universal Pictures
© 1969 Screen Gems
pg. 300 © 1975 Columbia Pictures Industries, Inc.
pg. 301 © 1965 Universal-International Pictures Corp.
pg. 302 © 1980 Warner Bros., Inc.
pg. 303 © 1976 Dino De Laurentiis Corp.

PHOTO CREDITS